The Microsoft®
Data Warehouse
Toolkit

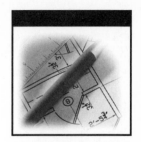

The Microsoft® Data Warehouse Toolkit

With SQL Server™ 2005 and the Microsoft® Business Intelligence Toolset

Joy Mundy and
Warren Thornthwaite
with Ralph Kimball

WILEY

Wiley Publishing, Inc.

The Microsoft® Data Warehouse Toolkit:
With SQL Server™ 2005 and the Microsoft® Business Intelligence Toolset
Published by
Wiley Publishing, Inc.
10475 Crosspoint Boulevard
Indianapolis, IN 46256
www.wiley.com

Copyright © 2006 by Wiley Publishing, Inc., Indianapolis, Indiana

Published simultaneously in Canada

ISBN-13: 978-0-471-26715-7
ISBN-10: 0-471-26715-5

Manufactured in the United States of America

10 9 8 7 6 5 4 3 2

1B/SW/QR/QW/IN

For general information on our other products and services or to obtain technical support, please contact our Customer Care Department within the U.S. at (800) 762-2974, outside the U.S. at (317) 572-3993 or fax (317) 572-4002.

Library of Congress Cataloging-in-Publication Data

Mundy, Joy, 1961–
  The Microsoft data warehouse toolkit : with SQL Server 2005 and the Microsoft Business Intelligence toolset / Joy Mundy and Warren Thornthwaite with Ralph Kimball.
    p. cm.
  Includes index.
  ISBN-13: 978-0-471-26715-7 (paper/website)
  ISBN-10: 0-471-26715-5 (paper/website)
  1. Data warehousing. 2. SQL server. I. Thornthwaite, Warren, 1957– II. Kimball, Ralph. III. Title.
  QA76.9.D37M95 2006
  005.74—dc22
                              2005032275

About the Authors

Joy Mundy, a member of the Kimball Group, has been developing, consulting on, and speaking and writing about business intelligence systems and technology since 1992. Joy began her career as a business analyst in banking and finance as one of the power users we talk about in business intelligence. In 1992 she joined the data warehouse team at Stanford University, an effort that was both educational and character building. She next co-founded InfoDynamics LLC, a data warehouse consulting firm, and then joined Microsoft WebTV to develop closed-loop analytic applications and a packaged business intelligence system.

From 2000 to 2004, Joy worked with the Microsoft SQL Server Business Intelligence product development team. She managed a team that developed the best practices for building business intelligence systems on the Microsoft platform. Joy graduated from Tufts University with a B.A. in Economics, and from Stanford with an M.S. in Engineering Economic Systems.

Warren Thornthwaite, a member of the Kimball Group, has been building decision support and data warehousing systems since 1980. Warren co-authored the best-selling *Data Warehouse Lifecycle Toolkit* (Wiley, 1998).

Warren worked at Metaphor Computer Systems for eight years starting in 1983, where he managed the consulting organization and implemented many major data warehouse systems. After Metaphor, Warren managed the enterprise-wide data warehouse development at Stanford University. He then co-founded InfoDynamics LLC, a data warehouse consulting firm. Warren joined up with WebTV to help build a world-class, multi-terabyte customer-focused data warehouse before returning to consulting.

In addition to designing data warehouses for a range of industries, Warren has extensive experience helping clients develop scalable, practical information access architectures. Warren holds an MBA in Decision Sciences from the University of Pennsylvania's Wharton School, and a BA in Communications Studies from the University of Michigan.

Ralph Kimball, Ph.D., founder of the Kimball Group, has been designing information systems and data warehouses since 1972.

Ralph wrote his Ph.D. dissertation in the Electrical Engineering department at Stanford University on the design of a man–machine system for tutoring mathematics students. In 1972 he joined the Xerox Palo Alto Research Center as a research scientist. Over the following ten years at Xerox, he became a development manager and the product marketing manager for the Xerox Star workstation, the first commercial product that used windows, icons, and the mouse. For this work at Xerox, he received the Alexander Williams Award from the IEEE Human Factors Society for user interface design.

Following his years at Xerox, Ralph was a vice president and member of the founding team at Metaphor Computer Systems, the first data warehousing company. Between 1982 and 1986, Metaphor installed many client-server data warehouse systems. In 1986 Ralph founded Red Brick Systems, which developed the first high-performance relational database for decision support. Since 1993, Ralph has designed data warehouse systems, written bestselling data warehouse books, and taught data warehousing skills to more than 10,000 IT professionals.

Credits

Executive Editor
Robert Elliott

Development Editor
Sara Shlaer

Copy Editor
Nancy Rapoport

Editorial Manager
Mary Beth Wakefield

Production Manager
Tim Tate

Vice President and Executive Group Publisher
Richard Swadley

Vice President and Executive Publisher
Joseph B. Wikert

Project Coordinator
Ryan Steffen

Graphics and Production Specialists
Denny Hager
Jennifer Heleine
Stephanie D. Jumper
Lynsey Osborn

Quality Control Technicians
Joe Niesen

Proofreading
TECHBOOKS Production Services

Indexing
Richard T. Evans

Contents

Foreword

I've known Joy Mundy and Warren Thornthwaite for a number of years. I won't speak for them, but I've reached the age where I don't want to remember how long I've known people!

My respect and admiration for Joy began from the day we met at WebTV. Microsoft had recently acquired WebTV, so the SQL Server BI team went to take a look at their data warehouse. We quickly learned how much we didn't know. I met Warren slightly later at WebTV, where he impressed us deeply as well. Both Joy and Warren were clearly fine practitioners in the art of data warehousing.

After several years, Joy became a principal member of the SQL Server BI Practices team. While he was working independently, Warren's ongoing feedback and commentary on our SQL Server 2005 product efforts frequently led to changes in our thinking or implementation. Both authors have affected the direction of our product. We deeply appreciate their contributions.

In time, Joy joined Warren at the Kimball Group. We miss her still. On the other hand, we have always enjoyed a great relationship with the Kimball Group. Ralph Kimball's pioneering work in data warehousing has fundamentally influenced the SQL Server BI toolset in numerous ways. There are many Kimball Group Toolkits on my team's bookshelves.

Now, let me discuss the book you have in your hands. I love this book. When you build software, the thing you hope for most is that customers will use it in some way to improve their business, as in our case, or maybe even their lives. Time will tell if we have met that bar. When authors write books about software, they hope that their work will play a role in the readers' quests. I think this book will help you get the most out of our software, SQL Server 2005.

The first ten chapters address designing and building a DW/BI system. The rest of the book discusses how to secure, deploy, and operate the system. The book is filled with prescriptive guidance and helpful hints. While the chapters are mostly independent of one another, I believe you should read them in order. Joy and Warren will teach you the Business Dimensional Lifecycle methodology from the ground up. Reading out of order or skipping chapters won't hurt you; I just think you get more than the sum of the parts by building your skills in life-cycle order. For example, in Chapter 2 the authors discuss data-driven models versus requirements-driven models. In following this discussion, you will be well served to have read Chapter 1 on gathering business requirements. Chapter 2 is a very strong tutorial on dimensional modeling. If you want to delve deeper, I suggest you take a Kimball University course, starring one or both of your authors.

Chapters 5 and 6 are important. They cover ETL (Extraction, Transformation, and Loading), a key to the success of any data warehouse or business intelligence project. Various estimates indicate that ETL work constitutes at least three-quarters of the effort of a successful data warehouse. Our goal with SQL Server Integration Services is to lower the ETL effort required. We built a highly productive environment for building ETL "packages," including interactive and visual debugging of data flows. But we can go only so far with software. Joy and Warren provide practical advice on top of what we provide in the bits. For example, they recommend building a source-system sandbox when you find that your source exploration is going too slowly because of system load or is in fact adding to the system load.

Chapter 10 addresses data mining. At Microsoft we believe deeply in the potential of data mining in BI applications. We've gone a long way, we think, toward making data mining far more accessible than ever before. Joy and Warren don't rehash the material you already have in Books Online. Instead, they teach you how to approach a data mining problem. Using case studies, they teach you how to think about and experiment with data.

I could list highlights from every chapter. But I suspect you're ready to get going on your own project! Let this book guide you along the way. Try to take Joy and Warren's advice; they have been building data warehouses and teaching data warehouses, successfully, for quite a while. We built SQL Server 2005 to help you succeed in your business. I could not be happier than to have Joy and Warren, and this book, help you get there.

Bill Baker (bill.baker@microsoft.com)
General Manager, SQL Server Business Intelligence, Microsoft
Redmond, WA

Preface

As engineers, we in the Kimball Group want to "build things that work." We are fascinated with the process of building a data warehouse as well as how the end users get value from a data warehouse and the resulting BI systems. At the same time, we are appalled by the difficulty of the design task. For more than twenty years, as we have been constructing data warehouses, we have looked for ways to simplify and compartmentalize the design process. When we have seen the same design pattern repeatedly, we have given the technique a name and tried to explain it in a clear way. This collection of "named" design techniques is called the Kimball Method. This book is a good introduction to these techniques.

The development of the Kimball Method has gathered significant momentum. In the past ten years, we have trained more than 10,000 data warehouse designers and sold more than 200,000 books, all explaining the Kimball Method. More recently, we have seen a significant adoption of the Kimball Method by the leading technology vendors in the data warehouse space. As you read this book, keep your radar active for Microsoft features in the SQL Server 2005 family of products with names like "the Slowly Changing Dimension wizard." The dimensional approach we espouse has become a dominant theme in the leading industry tool sets.

Even armed with the Kimball Method, the task of building a data warehouse and the dependent BI systems requires the thoughtful exercise of perspective and judgment. Although this book may superficially resemble a dozen or more similarly thick books on Microsoft SQL Server 2005, it is very different. This is a true "judgment book," not a how-to book. In writing this book, Joy and Warren have applied their unique perspectives both as very experienced data warehouse architects and as former Microsoft employees who helped bring SQL Server 2005 to the marketplace.

I hope you will appreciate the very measured and thoughtful approach Joy and Warren have taken. When a subject is just plain complicated, they pull no punches. In a few places, when Microsoft could have made a feature simpler, they say that in so many words. But mostly, the book tries very hard to visualize what you, the data warehouse designer, should be thinking about at each stage of using SQL Server 2005. I think Joy and Warren have succeeded in combining higher-level design judgment with a lot of useful comments about the tool details. I am proud to have played a role in contributing to the Kimball Method sections of this book.

Ralph Kimball

Acknowledgments

First, we want to thank the thousands of you who have read the Kimball Group's *Toolkit* books, attended our courses, and engaged us in consulting projects. We always learn from you, and you've had a profound impact on our thinking and the business intelligence industry.

This book would not have been written without the assistance of many people on the SQL Server product development team. Of special note is Donald Farmer, who gave generously of his time in clarifying ideas and reviewing the chapters related to Integration Services and metadata. Siva Harinath and Stephen Quinn contributed material for the real-time chapter. Stuart Ozer reviewed the entire book, at a point when his time was at a premium (which is almost always the case at Microsoft!). Others at Microsoft reviewed individual chapters and answered many questions. These reviewers, listed alphabetically, include Carolyn Chau, Grant Dickinson, Jamie MacLennan, John Miller, Ashvini Sharma, Dave Wickert, and Rob Zare.

We especially thank Bill Baker, the General Manager of SQL Server Business Intelligence at Microsoft, for his vision of "BI for the masses," for his leadership of the SQL BI product development team, and for his support for our project.

Our colleagues at the Kimball Group were invaluable. Their encouragement kept us going while we were writing the book, and their reviews helped us polish and prune material. Ralph Kimball, of course, had a huge impact on the book, not just from his writing and thinking in the business intelligence arena but more directly by helping us improve the book's overall structure and flow. Bob Becker and Margy Ross helped enormously.

Carl Rabeler of Solid Quality Learning provided an especially detailed review of the entire book. We're indebted to him. Sara Shlaer and Bob Elliott, our editors at Wiley, have been very helpful and encouraging. It's been a pleasure to work with them.

To our life partners, thanks for being there when we needed you, for giving us the time we needed, and for occasionally reminding us that it was time to take a break. Tony Navarrete and Elizabeth Wright, the book wouldn't exist without you.

Introduction

This book describes how to build a successful business intelligence system and its underlying data warehouse databases using the Microsoft SQL Server 2005 product set. The key word here is "successful."

The Data Warehouse and Business Intelligence System

Data warehousing and business intelligence are fundamentally about providing business people with the information and tools they need to make both operational and strategic business decisions. We'll break this down a bit so you can really understand the nature and magnitude of what you're about to take on.

First, your customers are the business people in the organization. But not all business people carry the same importance to you—you're especially concerned with those who make strategic business decisions. Why? Because this is where the big money is. One well-made business decision can translate to millions of dollars in many organizations. Your main customers are executives, managers, and analysts throughout the organization. Therefore, the data warehouse and business intelligence (DW/BI) system is high impact and high profile.

Strategic also means important. These are decisions that can make or break the organization. Therefore, the DW/BI system is a high-risk endeavor. When strategic decisions are made, someone often wins or loses. Therefore the DW/BI system is a highly political effort.

Increasingly, the DW/BI system supports operational decisions, especially where the decision maker needs to see historical data or integrated data from multiple sources. Many "analytic applications" have this operational focus.

Whether the decision making is strategic or operational, from a technical perspective, you need to provide the information necessary to make decisions. Any given decision will likely require a unique subset of information. You'll need to build an information infrastructure that pulls data from across the organization, and potentially from outside the organization, and then cleans, aligns, and restructures the data to make it as flexible and usable as possible. Whereas most transaction system modules work with one type of information, such as billings, orders, or accounts receivable, the DW/BI system must eventually integrate them all. Therefore, the DW/BI system requires technically sophisticated data gathering and management.

Finally, you need to provide the business decision makers with the tools they need to make use of the data. In this context, "tools" means much more than just software. It means everything the business users need to understand what information is available, find the subsets they need, and structure the data to illuminate the underlying business dynamics. Therefore, "tools" means training, documentation, and support, along with ad hoc query tools, reports, and analytic applications.

Let's review. The DW/BI system:

- Is high profile and high impact
- Is high risk
- Is highly political
- Requires technically sophisticated and complex data gathering and management
- Requires intensive user access, training, and support

Creating and managing the DW/BI system is an extremely challenging task. We want you to take on this task with full knowledge of what you're getting into. In our experience, it's easier to deal with all of the challenges if you're at least somewhat forewarned.

We don't mean this to discourage you, but rather to warn you before you jump in that the waters are swift and deep. In our experience, all the reasons that make the data warehouse challenging are also what make it a fun and exciting project.

The Kimball Group

While it's true that building and managing a successful DW/BI system is a challenge, it's also true that there are ways to approach it that will increase your likelihood of success. That's what the Kimball Group is all about. We've been working in the DW/BI area for more than 20 years. The authors of this book, who are members of the Kimball Group, have spent their careers working on data warehousing and business intelligence systems as vendors, consultants, implementers and users. Our motto is "Practical techniques—proven results." We share a common drive to figure out the best way to build and manage a successful DW/BI system. We are also teachers at heart, with a strong desire to help you succeed and avoid the mistakes we and others have made.

Why We Wrote This Book

Data warehousing and business intelligence have been around in much the same form since at least the 1970s, and continue to enjoy an incredibly long technology lifecycle. In 1995, when the primary authors formed our first consulting organization, one of us voiced the opinion that data warehousing was finished, that the wave had crested and we'd be lucky to get a few more projects before we had to go find real jobs again. Twelve years later, data warehousing and business intelligence are still going strong. In fact, it's been only in the last few years that we've seen signs of maturation in the industry.

One of the signs of a mature market is the emergence of single-source providers—a safe choice for risk-averse organizations. The data warehousing technology stack covers everything from esoteric source system knowledge to user interface design and best-practice BI applications. While many of the vendors scrambled to position themselves as end-to-end providers in recent years, it was clear to us that the database vendors are the only ones who can truly provide end-to-end solutions. In 2001, when we first discussed this book, we felt Microsoft was going to force the concept of a viable, single-source data warehouse system provider into reality, and at an attractive price.

Our belief in the move toward single-source providers means we must extend the Kimball Method techniques to the product-specific level, making them directly available to the market that will respond to the single-source provider. We chose the Microsoft toolset as our test case for two main reasons. First, the SQL Server 2005 is a strong BI platform. Microsoft has been investing heavily in extending and enhancing its business intelligence capabilities since the mid-1990s, when it invested in what has become the Analysis Services engine. The level of investment has since ramped up dramatically. With the start of development for SQL Server 2005, the SQL Server BI development team grew to over 200 people. Microsoft seems serious about bringing business intelligence to the mainstream market. Second, the two authors both worked at Microsoft from 1997 to 2002 or 2004. In particular, Joy was the manager of the SQL Server BI Best Practices group within the SQL Server Business Intelligence development team. This gave us a set of strong working relationships and access to key support resources. Who could pass that up?

Who Should Read This Book

This book covers the entire data warehouse lifecycle. As a result, it offers useful guidance to every member of the data warehouse team, from the project manager to the business analyst, data modeler, ETL developer, DBA, analytic application developer, and even to the business user. We believe the book will be valuable to anyone working on a Microsoft SQL Server 2005 data warehouse project.

The primary audience for this book is the new DW/BI team that's launching a project on the Microsoft SQL Server platform. We don't assume you already have experience in building a DW/BI system. We do assume you have a basic familiarity with the Microsoft world: operating systems, infrastructure components, and resources. We also assume a basic understanding of relational databases (tables, columns, simple SQL) and some familiarity with the SQL Server 2000 relational database, although that's not a requirement. Throughout the book we provide many references to other books and resources.

A second audience is the experienced Kimball Method DW/BI practitioner who's new to the Microsoft SQL Server 2005 toolset. This audience might need to do some reading to catch up on the infrastructure, especially if you've never worked on a Windows server before. We'll point out which sections and chapters will be review for anyone who's read our other *Toolkit* books and practiced our methodology. But we've found that it doesn't hurt to read this material one more time!

Whatever your background, you'll benefit most if you're just starting on a new project. While we do provide suggestions on working with existing data warehouses, in the ideal case you won't have to contend with any existing data warehouse or data marts—at least none that will remain in place after the new system is deployed.

The Business Dimensional Lifecycle

We've all felt the empty pit of panic in our stomach when, deep into a project, we realize the scope and scale of the effort before us will take much more work than we imagined at the outset. Many BI/DW projects begin with the notion that you'll just move some data to a new machine, clean it up a little, and develop some reports. Doesn't sound so bad—six weeks of effort, two months at the most. You wade into the river and are waist deep before realizing you should have built a bridge.

The best way to avoid this sense of panic—and the resulting disaster—is to figure out where you're going before you jump in. It helps to have a roadmap and directions to lead you safely through unfamiliar territory—one that will tell you the places you have to visit and point out the danger zones on the trip ahead. This book is that roadmap for the Microsoft SQL Server BI/DW system project. This book follows the basic flow of the Business Dimensional Lifecycle first described in the book *The Data Warehouse Lifecycle Toolkit* (Wiley, 1998). The steps, tasks, and dependencies of the Lifecycle were crafted based on our collective experience of what works. The Lifecycle is an iterative approach based on four primary principles:

- *Focus on the business:* Concentrate on identifying business requirements and their associated value. Use these efforts to develop solid relationships with the business side and sharpen your business sense and consultative skills.

- *Build an information infrastructure:* Design a single, integrated, easy-to-use, high-performing information foundation that will meet the broad range of business requirements you've identified across the enterprise.

- *Deliver in meaningful increments:* Build the data warehouse in increments that can be delivered in 6 to 12 month timeframes. Use clearly identified business value to determine the implementation order of the increments.

- *Deliver the entire solution:* Provide all the elements necessary to deliver value to the business users. This means a solid, well-designed, quality-tested, accessible data warehouse database is only the start. You must also deliver ad hoc query tools, reporting applications and advanced analytics, training, support, web site, and documentation.

This book helps you follow these four principles by using the Business Dimensional Lifecycle to build your DW/BI system. These four principles are woven into the fabric of the Lifecycle. The secret to understanding the Business Dimensional Lifecycle is cleverly hidden in its name: It is business-based, it takes a dimensional approach to designing data models for end-user presentation, and it is a true lifecycle.

Lifecycle Tracks and Task Areas

The BI/DW system is a complex entity, and the methodology to build that system must help simplify that complexity. Figure 1 outlines the Lifecycle. The 13 boxes show the major task areas involved in building a successful data warehouse and the primary dependencies among those tasks.

BETTER LATE THAN NEVER

Delivering the entire solution has always been one of our fundamental principles. We wouldn't even consider building a data warehouse without delivering what is now known as the Business Intelligence layer. The rest of the industry came to this understanding in the late 1990s after years of failed projects that focused on creating the data warehouse database. Their general approach was "build it and they will come." This almost never works.

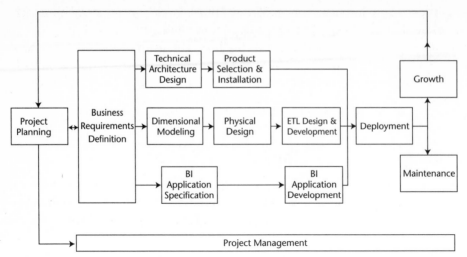

Figure 1: The Business Dimensional Lifecycle

There are several observations to make about the Lifecycle at this level. First, notice the central role of the Business Requirements Definition box. Business requirements provide the foundation for the three tracks that follow. They also influence the project plan, hence the arrow pointing back to the Project Planning box. You usually end up modifying the plan based on a more detailed understanding of the business requirements and priorities.

Second, the three tracks in the middle of the lifecycle concentrate on three separate areas:

- *The top track is about technology.* These tasks are primarily about planning which pieces of Microsoft technology you'll use, and how you'll install and configure them.

- *The middle track is about data.* In the data track you'll design and instantiate the dimensional model, and develop the Extract, Transformation, and Load (ETL) system to populate it. You could think of the data track as "building the data warehouse databases," although your data warehouse will not succeed unless you surround it with the rest of the Lifecycle tasks.

- *The bottom track is about business intelligence applications.* In these tasks you design and develop BI applications for the business users.

The tracks combine when it's time to deploy the system. This is a particularly delicate time because there's only one chance to make a good first impression. Maintaining the DW/BI system doesn't begin after deployment. You need to design your system with the ability and tools for maintaining it. The growth phase of the project links to the arrow heading back to the beginning.

This simple arrow has major implications. The Lifecycle's incremental approach is a fundamental element of delivering business value.

Underlying the entire Lifecycle is the Project Management box. The most important thing to remember here is that you need a leader, and that person needs access to senior management. The team leader is ideally one of those difficult-to-find people who can communicate effectively with both technologists and business people, including the most senior executives in the company.

Key Terminology and the Microsoft Toolset

The business intelligence industry is plagued with terminology that's used imprecisely, or in contradictory ways. Some of the most long-standing debates in the industry derive as much from misunderstandings about what others mean by a term, as from true differences in philosophy. Keeping that in mind, we'll try to be clear and consistent even if we don't settle all the historical debates. We highlight some of the key terms here.

As we define each term, we are highlighting the associated Microsoft technologies, most of which are components of SQL Server 2005.

- The *data warehouse* is the "platform for business intelligence." In the Kimball Method, the data warehouse includes everything from the original data extracts to the software and applications that users see. We disagree with other authors who insist that the data warehouse is merely a centralized and highly normalized store of data in the back room, far from the end users. To reduce confusion, in this book we consistently use the phrase "data warehouse/business intelligence system" (DW/BI system) to mean the entire end-to-end system. When we're talking specifically and exclusively about the atomic-level, user-queryable data store, we call it the *data warehouse database*.

- The *business process dimensional model* is a specific discipline for modeling data that is an alternative to normalized modeling. A dimensional model contains the same information as a normalized model but packages the data in a symmetrical format whose design goals are user understandability, business intelligence query performance, and resilience to change. Normalized models, sometimes called *third normal form* models, were designed to support the high-volume, single-row inserts and updates that define transaction systems, and generally fail at being understandable, fast, and resilient to change.

  We use the term "business process dimensional model" to refer both to the logical dimensional model that supports a business process and the corresponding physical tables in the database. In other words, dimensional models are both logical and physical.

- The *relational database* is a general-purpose technology for storing, managing, and querying data. The SQL Server 2005 database engine is Microsoft's relational database engine. The business process dimensional model can be stored in a relational database. Normalized data models that support transaction processing can also be stored in a relational database.

- The *online analytic processing (OLAP) database* is a technology for storing, managing, and querying data specifically designed to support business intelligence uses. SQL Server 2005 Analysis Services is Microsoft's OLAP database engine. The business process dimensional model can be stored in an OLAP database, but a transactional database cannot, unless it first undergoes transformation to cast it in an explicitly dimensional form.

- An *Extract, Transformation, and Load (ETL)* system is a set of processes that clean, transform, combine, de-duplicate, household, archive, conform, and structure data for use in the data warehouse. These terms are described in this book. Early ETL systems were built using a combination of SQL and other scripts. While this is still true for most smaller ETL systems, larger and more serious systems use a specialized ETL tool. Moving forward, almost every DW/BI system will use an ETL tool such as SQL Server 2005 Integration Services because the benefits are significant and the incremental dollar cost is low or zero.

- *Business intelligence (BI) applications* are predefined applications that query, analyze, and present information to support a business need. There is a spectrum of BI applications, ranging in complexity from a set of predefined static reports, all the way to an analytic application that directly affects transaction systems and the day-to-day operation of the organization. You can use SQL Server Reporting Services to build a reporting application, and a wide range of Microsoft and third-party technologies to build complex, analytic applications.

- A *data mining model* is a statistical model, often used to predict future behavior based on data about past behavior. Data mining is a term for a loose (and ever-changing) collection of statistical techniques or algorithms that serve different purposes. The major categories are clustering, decision trees, neural networks, and prediction. Analysis Services Data Mining is an example of a data mining tool.

- *Ad hoc queries* are formulated by the user on the spur of the moment. The dimensional modeling approach is widely recognized as the best technique to support ad hoc queries because the simple database structure is easy to understand. Microsoft Office, notably Excel pivot tables, is the most popular ad hoc query tool on the market. You can use Reporting Services Report Builder to perform ad hoc querying and simple report definition. Nonetheless, many systems supplement Excel and Report Builder with a third-party ad hoc query tool for their power users.

■ Once again, the *data warehouse/business intelligence (DW/BI) system* is the whole thing: source system extracts, ETL, dimensional database in both relational and OLAP, BI applications, and an ad hoc query tool. The DW/BI system also includes management tools and practices, user-oriented documentation and training, a security system, and all the other components that we discuss in this book.

Roles and Responsibilities

The DW/BI system requires a number of different roles and skills, from both the business and technical communities, during its lifecycle. In this section, we review the major roles involved in creating a DW/BI system. There is seldom a one-to-one relationship between roles and people. We've worked with teams as small as one person, and as large as forty (and heard of much larger teams). The vast majority of DW/BI teams fall between three and seven full-time members, with access to others as required.

It's common for a single DW/BI team to take on both development and operational duties. This is different from most technology project teams, and is related to the highly iterative nature of the DW/BI project development cycle. The following roles are associated with design and development activities:

■ The *DW/BI manager* is responsible for overall leadership and direction of the project. The DW/BI manager must be able to communicate effectively with both senior business and IT management. The manager must also be able to work with the team to formulate the overall architecture of the DW/BI system.

■ The *project manager* is responsible for day-to-day management of project tasks and activities during system development.

■ The *business project lead* is a member of the business community and works closely with the project manager.

■ The *business systems analyst* (or business analyst) is responsible for leading the business requirements definition activities, and often participates in the development of the business process dimensional model. The business systems analyst needs to be able to bridge the gap between business and technology.

■ The *data modeler* is responsible for performing detailed data analysis including data profiling, and developing the detailed dimensional model.

- The *system architect(s)* design the various components of the DW/BI system. These include the ETL system, security system, auditing system, and maintenance systems.

- The *development database administrator (DBA)* creates the relational data warehouse database(s) and is responsible for the overall physical design including disk layout, partitioning, and initial indexing plan.

- The *OLAP database designer* creates the OLAP databases.

- The *ETL system developer* creates Integration Services packages, scripts, and other elements to move data from the source databases into the data warehouse.

- The *DW/BI management tools developer* writes any custom tools that are necessary for the ongoing management of the DW/BI system. Examples of such tools include a simple UI for entering metadata, scripts or Integration Services packages to perform system backups and restores, and a simple UI for maintaining dimension hierarchies.

- The *BI application developer* is responsible for building the BI applications, including the standard reports and any advanced analytic applications required by the business. This role is also responsible for developing any custom components in the BI portal and integrating data mining models into business operations.

Most of the rest of the roles play a part in the latter stages of the DW/BI project development cycle, as the team moves toward deploying and operating the system. A few of the roles are strictly operational.

- The *data steward* is responsible for ensuring the data in the data warehouse is accurate.

- The *security manager* specifies new user access roles that the business users need, and adds users to existing roles. The security manager also determines the security procedures in the ETL "back room" of the DW/BI system.

- The *BI portal content manager* manages the BI portal. She determines the content that's on the portal and how it's laid out, and keeps it fresh.

- The *DW/BI educator* creates and delivers the training materials for the BI/DW system.

- The *relational database administrator (DBA)* is responsible for managing the performance and operations of the relational data warehouse database.

- The *OLAP DBA* is responsible for managing the performance and operations of the OLAP data warehouse database.

- The *compliance manager* is responsible for ensuring that the DW/BI policies and operations comply with corporate and regulatory directives such as privacy policies, HIPAA, and Sarbanes-Oxley. The compliance manager works closely with the security manager and Internal Audit.

- The *metadata manager* has the final word on what metadata is collected, where it is kept, and how it's published to the business community. As we discuss in Chapter 13, metadata tends not to be managed unless there's a person identified to lead the charge.

- The *data mining analyst* is deeply familiar with the business and usually has some background in statistics. The data mining analyst develops data mining models and works with the BI application developers to design operational applications that use the data mining models.

- *User support* personnel within the DW/BI team must be available to help business users, especially with ad hoc access. Corporate-wide help desks tend not to have the specialized expertise necessary to do more than assist with minor connectivity issues.

How This Book Is Organized

We've divided the book into five parts:

I. Requirements, Realities, and Architecture

II. Developing and Populating the Databases

III. Developing the BI Applications

IV. Deploying and Managing the DW/BI System

V. Extending the DW/BI System

Part I: Requirements, Realities, and Architecture

Part I sets the stage for the rest of the book. Most of you are eager to get your hands on the Microsoft toolset. That's fine while you're experimenting and learning about the technology, but it's the kiss of death for a project. Stop, back away from the keyboard, and think about what you're setting out to do.

Chapter 1: Defining Business Requirements

The book begins with a brief summary of the Business Dimensional Lifecycle. We drill down on the most important step, gathering the business requirements, and briefly present the business requirements for the Adventure Works

Cycles case study used throughout the book. Chapter 1 refers to the Business Requirements Definition box in Figure 1.

Readers who are very familiar with the Kimball Method can skip the first part of the chapter but should read the case study.

Chapter 2: Designing the Business Process Dimensional Model

We present a brief primer on how to develop a dimensional model. This chapter presents terminology and concepts used throughout the book, so it's vital that you understand this material. This chapter refers to the Dimensional Modeling box in Figure 1.

Readers who are very familiar with the Kimball Method can skim most of this material and review the Adventure Works case study at the end of the chapter.

Chapter 3: The Toolset

The Architecture and Product Selection tasks are straightforward for a Microsoft DW/BI system. In this short chapter we talk in more detail about how and where to use the various components of SQL Server 2005, other Microsoft products, and even where you're most likely to use third-party software in your system. This chapter provides a brief overview of the Technical Architecture Design and Product Selection & Installation boxes in Figure 1.

Even readers who are very familiar with SQL Server 2000 should review this chapter, as it contains information about the new features of SQL Server 2005, some of which are significantly different.

Part II: Developing and Populating the Databases

The second part of the book presents the steps required to effectively build and populate the data warehouse databases. Most Microsoft DW/BI systems will implement the dimensional data warehouse in both the relational database and the Analysis Services database.

Chapter 4: Setup and Physical Design

Chapter 4 describes how to install and configure the various components of SQL Server 2005. We talk about system sizing and configuration, and how—and why—you might choose to distribute your DW/BI system across multiple servers.

The physical data model in the relational database should be virtually identical to the dimensional model we discuss in Chapter 2. There are some physical design issues to consider, notably whether to partition the fact tables. You also need to develop the initial indexing plan for the relational database.

Chapter 4 is focused on the Product Selection & Installation and the Physical Design boxes of Figure 1, but it doesn't complete that discussion. The physical design issues for Analysis Services are postponed to Chapter 7.

Chapter 5: Designing the ETL System

The ETL portion of the DW/BI system is always a design challenge. In this chapter we introduce SQL Server's new ETL technology, Integration Services. Then we talk about how to write the design specification for your ETL system.

Chapters 5 and 6 cover most of the tasks in the ETL Design & Development box in Figure 1, although we return to these issues several times in the book.

Chapter 6: Developing the ETL System

Finally it's time to start moving data. This chapter talks about the basic design for your ETL system in Integration Services. We walk through the details of loading dimension tables, starting with a fairly detailed example for a simple table. The chapter isn't a tutorial, however, and soon we pick up speed and address the key dimension management issues such as surrogate key assignment and attribute change management.

Next, we explain how to load fact tables. We illustrate the surrogate key pipeline and discuss some advanced topics such as maintaining snapshot fact tables and handling late-arriving data.

Chapter 7: Designing the Analysis Services OLAP Database

We recommend that your Microsoft DW/BI system use Analysis Services as the main database for users to query. The more closely the relational database and ETL process are designed to meet your business requirements, the easier it is to design the Analysis Services database. Analysis Services includes lots of features for building an OLAP database on top of a poorly constructed database, but your results will be better if you've followed our instructions and have a clean and conformed relational data warehouse as your starting point for the OLAP database.

The Analysis Services wizards are easy to use, and with a small system, you don't need to worry very much about advanced settings. However, if you have large data volumes or a lot of users, you need to develop a deep understanding of the OLAP engine. Much of this chapter is focused on helping you learn enough to implement Analysis Services across your enterprise.

The Analysis Services chapter takes on the Physical Design and ETL boxes of Figure 1, this time from the perspective of the OLAP database engine.

Part III: Developing the BI Applications

The third part of the book presents the steps required to present the data to the business users. We start with a chapter that clearly defines what we mean by BI applications. Then we talk about how to use Reporting Services to deliver the initial set of predefined reports.

Data mining can deliver huge value to your business, by looking for hidden relationships and trends in the data. Chapter 10 talks about how to use Analysis Services to build data mining models.

Chapter 8: Business Intelligence Applications

Some people seem to think that the job of developing a data warehouse begins and ends in Part II, "Developing and Populating the Databases." But please remember our definition of the data warehouse: It is the *complete* system all the way to the user's screen. You are building a DW/BI system, not just a database. We've argued forcefully that if you skimp on the early phases in Part I of the Lifecycle, the databases you develop won't be very useful. Similarly, you need to deliver some applications in Part III, or the business users won't be able to use the system.

Most users of your DW/BI system are simply going to consume predefined reports. They won't create new reports, much less perform the kind of complex analysis that's possible with the system. Instead, they'll run and review reports, perhaps parameterized reports that use picklists. You need to provide a reasonably complete set of reports when the system goes live. Most often, these reports are delivered within a BI portal.

The other kind of BI application is an analytic application. An analytic application is centered on a specific business process and encapsulates a certain amount of domain expertise about how to analyze and interpret that business process. It may go so far as to include complex, code-based algorithms or data mining models that help identify underlying issues or opportunities.

Chapter 8 addresses the tasks in the BI Application Specification box in Figure 1.

Chapter 9: Building the BI Application in Reporting Services

In this chapter, we begin by describing the criteria for a report development and delivery system, and discuss how SQL Server Reporting Services meets those criteria. The online documentation does a good job of showing you how to create simple reports, so we focus our attention on harder problems. We walk you through an example of creating a moderately complex report from the relational database. We demonstrate how to source a similar report from Analysis Services.

Chapters 9 and 10 describe the tasks in the Lifecycle box called BI Application Development.

Chapter 10: Incorporating Data Mining

Data mining is perhaps the most powerful—and certainly the least understood—technology in the BI toolkit. This chapter defines data mining, and provides examples of how it can be used. We talk about Microsoft's data mining technology, including the algorithms that are included with SQL Server Analysis Services. We provide practical guidance on how to build a data mining model and how to incorporate the results of data mining into your systems. To make this theoretical discussion more concrete, we work through two case studies.

Part IV: Deploying and Managing the DW/BI System

The fourth section of the book includes information about how to deploy and operate your DW/BI system.

Chapter 11: Working with an Existing Data Warehouse

Although the primary audience for this book is a DW/BI project team that's working on a new system, we recognize that's not always going to be the case. This chapter describes how to work with an existing system, beginning with an evaluation of what's working—and not working—in your current systems.

We talk about how to upgrade a SQL Server 2000 DW/BI system to SQL Server 2005 and strongly recommend that most components be selectively rewritten rather than upgraded. SQL Server technologies are designed to work well in a heterogeneous environment. We discuss the components of the DW/BI system that you can implement in non-Microsoft technology, and highlight the (relatively few) features that don't work as well in a heterogeneous environment as they do in an all–SQL Server implementation.

Chapter 11 doesn't map exactly to one of the boxes in Figure 1, although it's closest to the technology track at the top.

Chapter 12: Security

We start our discussion of the DW/BI system's security by encouraging you to develop an open access policy for information. Sensitive data must of course be protected, but we think most contents of the data warehouse should be available to most authenticated users.

Authentication is an important concept: It's really important that only authenticated users have access to the system. And access control begins with the physical servers. There's no point in putting a complex security system in place if anyone can walk into the server closet and access the machine directly.

Recognizing that not everyone can implement an open security policy, we describe how to control access in the various components of SQL Server: Reporting Services, the relational database, and Analysis Services. We also discuss the separate issues of security in the back room development area of the data warehouse.

The discussion of security is most closely related to the Deployment and Maintenance boxes of Figure 1.

Chapter 13: Metadata Plan

Lots of people talk about metadata, but we've seen few examples of it being implemented thoroughly and successfully. We'd like to have seen an integrated metadata service in Microsoft SQL Server 2005, which we could simply describe to you, but that's not the case. Instead, we spend most of this chapter detailing the metadata that we think is most important, and describing the steps to maintain and publish that information.

Metadata is related to the Deployment and Maintenance boxes of Figure 1.

Chapter 14: Deployment

Deploying the DW/BI system consists of two major sets of tasks. First, you need to deploy the system. This effort consists primarily of testing: testing of data, processes, performance, and deployment scripts themselves. The deployment scripts should include a playbook, with step-by-step instructions for how to deploy the system changes.

The other major set of deployment activities is focused more on the business users than on the technology. You need to develop and deliver training and documentation materials. You need to pull together the BI portal that we describe in Chapters 8 and 9. And you need to develop a plan for supporting the business users, who will inevitably have questions.

Chapter 15: Operations and Maintenance

As business people begin to use the warehouse to answer their questions on a regular basis, they will come to rely on it. If users don't believe the warehouse is reliable, they will go back to their old ways of getting information. This reliance is a kind of trust, and you must do everything you can to build and keep that trust. You need to monitor usage and performance—both for data loads and user queries. Track system resources and make sure you don't run out of disk space. In short, maintain the warehouse as the production system it now is. You must be meticulous in your attention to the quality of the data that's loaded into the data warehouse. Once a business user loses trust in the accuracy of the data, that trust is nearly impossible to regain.

The training, documentation, BI portal, reports, and support systems that we talk about in Chapter 14 need care and feeding, too.

Part V: Extending the DW/BI System

A key characteristic of the Kimball Method is that your DW/BI system development is iterative. Start with the most valuable business process, and keep looping back to bring in data to support additional business processes.

Chapter 16: Managing Growth

Maintenance is a critical task, but it's not the only ongoing effort. Growing the warehouse is really about adding value to the business. The more business information in the warehouse, the more valuable it becomes.

There is a common misconception among business and information systems management that developing a data warehouse is like most systems projects, with a large upfront development effort, followed by a small, ongoing maintenance task. This is not true because the data warehouse lifecycle is an iterative process. Once you finish with the highest priority business process subject area, you start on the next most important one, passing through the entire lifecycle again. Generally, the data warehouse team doesn't go away. In fact, it has more work to do maintaining and growing the data warehouse after the initial implementation, not less. We talk about longer term maintenance and growth issues in Chapter 16.

Chapter 17: Real-Time Business Intelligence

Chapter 17 takes on the topic of real-time business intelligence, discussing how to bring real-time data—loosely defined as data refreshed more frequently than daily—into the DW/BI system. SQL Server 2005 contains many features to enable real-time business intelligence. We talk about how to use these features, and the inevitable tradeoffs you face when implementing real-time BI.

Chapter 18: Present Imperatives and Future Outlook

Chapter 18 reviews the major phases of the DW/BI project and highlights where the most significant risks are to the overall success of the project. We finish the book with a wish list of features and functionality that we hope to see in the Microsoft BI toolset in the years to come.

Additional Information

This book includes most of the information you need to successfully build and deploy a basic DW/BI system using SQL Server 2005. In an effort to keep the book small enough to fit into a large backpack, we chose not to replicate tool instructions that could be easily found in SQL Server 2005 Books Online. Where appropriate, we provided search topics to assist in finding related materials. In several places, we recommend that you work through the tutorials that ship with SQL Server before you can expect to fully understand some technical material.

This book doesn't attempt to re-teach the fundamentals of data warehousing. We summarize many of the concepts and techniques found in the other volumes in the *Kimball Data Warehouse Toolkit* series rather than including all the details found in those books. We also provide references to key sections of those books as needed. Table 1 shows the core books in the *Toolkit* series, their major focus, and their primary audiences.

These books encapsulate the collective wisdom of the Kimball Group about data warehousing and business intelligence. We recommend that you add these books to your team's library.

We've laced this book with tips, key concepts, sidebars, and chapter pointers to make it more usable and easily referenced. We draw attention to some of these with the following formats:

REFERENCE Look for reference pointers to find other materials you can use to supplement your DW/BI library. This includes references to SQL Server Books Online, the Kimball Group *Toolkit* books, other books and articles, and online reference materials.

NOTE Notes provide some extra information on the topic under discussion, adding explanation or details to clarify the material.

Table 1 The Core Kimball Data Warehouse Toolkit Titles

TITLE	SUBJECT	PRIMARY AUDIENCE
The Data Warehouse Lifecycle Toolkit	Implementation guide	Good overview for all project participants; key tool for project managers, business analysts, and data modelers
The Data Warehouse Toolkit, Second Edition	Dimensional data modeling	Data modelers, business analysts, DBAs, ETL developers
The Data Warehouse ETL Toolkit	ETL System architecture	ETL architects and developers

TIP Tips offer shortcuts or hints that can make your work more productive.

WARNING Warnings help you avoid potential dangers that might cost you time, data, or sanity.

On the Web Site

We've collected most of the listings and examples and made them available on the book's web site: www.MsftDWToolkit.com. The web site's content is also available at www.wiley.com/go/MsftDWToolkit.

PART One

Requirements, Realities, and Architecture

Defining Business Requirements

Building the foundation

Business requirements are the bedrock of the DW/BI system. Business requirements guide the development team in making the biggest strategic choices, such as prioritizing subject areas for implementation, and in making the smallest tactical design decisions, such as how to present key performance indicators on the users' screens. In this chapter, we cover the process of gathering business requirements and converting them into a DW/BI system strategy. We describe the process of interviewing business and IT representatives, categorizing their requirements into analytic themes, converting those themes into incremental projects, and working with senior management to prioritize those projects. We also include a partial set of example requirements for the Adventure Works Cycles business.

As Figure 1.1 illustrates, the Business Requirements Definition is the foundation of the Lifecycle methodology. Business requirements and their associated business value give you the guidance you need to make decisions in all three downstream tracks. As you'll see, they influence the project scope and plan as well.

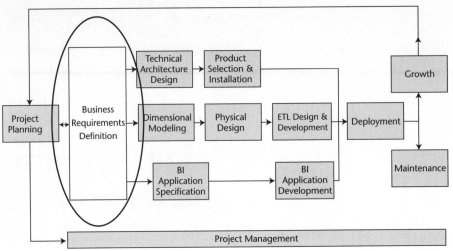

Figure 1.1 The Business Requirements Definition step of the Business Dimensional Lifecycle

This chapter is primarily about resisting temptation. Gathering business requirements is often outside a technical person's comfort zone. The overall success of the project is largely determined by your understanding of the business requirements and your relationships with the business people. Resist the temptation to just start loading data.

In this chapter you learn the following:

- The importance of understanding business requirements and securing solid business sponsorship

- How to define enterprise-level business requirements, including the interview process, developing analytic themes, linking themes to business processes, developing the data warehouse bus matrix, and prioritizing business processes with senior management

- How to plan the initial business process dimensional model implementation and gather project-level business requirements

- What a typical requirements summary document looks like and how it links to analytic themes and business process implementations

The Most Important Determinant of Long-Term Success

There is one common factor in successful business intelligence projects: delivering business value. Your DW/BI team must embrace the goal of enhancing business value as its primary purpose. This seems like an obvious statement, and we almost always get a chorus of agreements when we state this principle to the DW/BI teams with which we work. But most DW/BI folks are technologists at heart. We like the certainty of computers and programming. It works or it doesn't; if it doesn't, we can debug it.

You can't deliver business value unless you work closely with business people. You need to understand their language and learn to see the world from their point of view. You'll be working in a non-technical, highly ambiguous, politically sensitive environment. Are you feeling queasy yet? Many of us went into the computer trade specifically to avoid such discomfort. But this unsettled environment is what the DW/BI system is all about. You must develop the business knowledge and people skills right along with your technical skills in order to meet the needs of your business users. We realize the entire team will not become smooth-talking MBAs. However, someone on the team must have strong business and communications skills, and everyone will be more effective if they work to develop some of these skills.

So, while many DW/BI teams and consultants pay lip service to business value, the reality of their day-to-day behavior is that technology rules. Do not let this happen to you. Technology is important; business value is mandatory.

As you read this book, you'll encounter recommendations that may seem unnecessarily complicated or just plain unnecessary. Every time you're tempted to dismiss the authors as overly fond of their design methodology, or just overzealous, consider whether your reactions are driven by your technical convenience, or by the business users' needs. Never lose sight of the business.

Uncovering Business Value

If you're going to be driven by business value, you need to go out and identify, understand, and prioritize the needs of the business. This is easier said than done if your focus has historically been on technology. Fortunately, the Business Dimensional Lifecycle provides the tools to work through an entire development iteration of a data warehouse, beginning with business requirements.

Where do you start with your business intelligence system? What is the first step? The consultant in us immediately blurts out the standard consulting answer: "It depends." In fact, it does depend on a host of factors, such as how your organization works, what you already know about the business, who is involved in the project at this point, what kinds of DW/BI efforts came before, and many other factors. Let's talk about the most common scenario first, and then we'll address a few exceptions.

More often than not, the DW/BI system starts as a project hosted by the Information Technology (IT) organization. There is generally some level of business interest; in fact, the business folks may be the source of inspiration. But they are pushing for information in a form they can use, not specifically for a DW/BI system (unless, of course, they had access to a well-built data warehouse in their last job and they really miss it).

Most often, the IT-driven DW/BI project gets started because the CIO decides the company needs a data warehouse, so people and resources are assigned to build one. This is a dangerous situation. Please refer to the first point in this chapter: Focusing on business value is the most important determinant of long-term success. The problem with the IT-driven DW/BI system is that it almost always centers on technology. The team has been assigned the task of building a "warehouse," so that's exactly what they do. They get some hardware and some software and start extracting data.

We know some of you are thinking, "Oops, I already bought the ETL server and the user reporting tools." That's probably okay, but put those tools aside for the moment. Step away from the keyboard. If you get sucked into the technology, you're missing the whole point. You can build a technically great DW/BI system that provides very little business value. As a result, your project will fail. You have to start with business value, and identifying business value involves several major steps:

- Recruiting strong business sponsorship
- Defining enterprise-level business requirements
- Prioritizing business requirements
- Planning the project
- Defining project-level business requirements

We'll run through each of these steps in the following sections.

Obtaining Sponsorship

Developing solid business sponsorship is the best place to start the DW/BI project. Your business sponsors (it is generally good to have more than one) will take a lead role in determining the purpose, content, and priorities of the DW/BI system. You will call on them to secure resources and to evangelize the DW/BI system to the rest of the organization. This includes activities such as arranging for a planning meeting with senior staff, or speaking to a room full of business users at the project kick-off. You need to find at least one person in the organization who scores well in each of the following areas:

- *Visionary:* Someone who has a sense for the value and potential of information and some clear, specific ideas on how to apply it.
- *Resourceful:* Someone who is able to obtain the necessary resources and facilitate the organizational change the data warehouse will bring about.
- *Reasonable:* Someone who can temper his or her enthusiasm with the understanding that it takes time and resources to build a major information system.

Often, if you've been with your company for a while, you already know who these people are. In this case, your task is to recruit them onto the project. However, if you're new to the company, or you have not been out of the IT group much, you'll need to go out and find your business sponsors. In either case, the best way to find and recruit these people is by conducting an enterprise business requirements gathering project. It's worth the effort. Good business sponsorship can provide the resources and support you need to deliver real business value.

Defining Enterprise-Level Business Requirements

From a technical point of view, one long-term goal of the DW/BI team is to build an enterprise information infrastructure. Clearly, you can't do this unless you understand business requirements from an enterprise level. It is especially important in larger organizations to begin with this broad understanding because it is rare for the DW/BI team to have such an enterprise-level perspective. It's also particularly important for organizations that are just starting their first DW/BI system (or starting over) because getting the enterprise perspective built into the initial project helps you avoid painful and costly redesign down the road.

In these cases, the high-level version of the Lifecycle presented in Figure 1.1 doesn't give you quite enough information about how best to get started. In particular, the little arrow that goes both ways between Project Planning and Business Requirements Definition actually breaks down into several sub-activities, as shown in Figure 1.2.

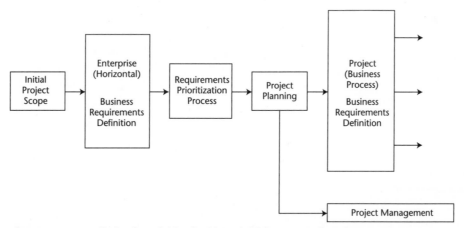

Figure 1.2 Detail of sub-activities between initial scope and project requirements

ENTERPRISE VERSUS PROJECT

Many organizations we've worked with have a clear understanding of which business process is their top priority right from the start. In these cases, we often combine the enterprise requirements definition step and the project requirements definition step into a single effort.

This does not lessen the importance of understanding the full range of enterprise requirements for information. In fact, we almost always go through the enterprise prioritization process with senior management. However, because the top priority is clear early on, we make sure we gather enough detailed information about that business process and the data it generates in the same interview set so we can create the design for the first business process in one pass instead of two.

In this subsection of the Lifecycle, defining the business requirements happens in several distinct steps. The rest of this section describes each of these steps in more detail.

NOTE We use the term "business process" throughout this section but do not describe it in detail for another few pages, when it makes more sense in the context of the requirements definition process. For now, think of it as a subject area or data source.

Establishing Initial Project Scope

Begin with the creation of an initial project scope based on the team's upfront knowledge of the organization's business needs and its experience in developing DW/BI systems, along with input from the business participants. The scope usually covers only the enterprise-level requirements definition and requirements prioritization steps in detail, leaving the initial project implementation plan for later when you have a much better idea of what the project needs to accomplish from a business perspective. The initial scope usually involves only user interviews, interview write-ups, a few meetings, and the creation of the final requirements document. It usually takes three to six weeks (or more) depending on how many interviews you do.

REFERENCE Additional information about project planning and management in the context of the Business Dimensional Lifecycle can be found in *The Data Warehouse Lifecycle Toolkit* (Wiley, 1998), Chapter 3.

Gathering and Documenting Enterprise-Level Business Requirements

The enterprise requirements definition step is designed to gather a broad, horizontal view of the organization from a business point of view. The process flow chart in Figure 1.3 breaks the Enterprise requirements definition box from Figure 1.2 down into its subtasks. As we see in Figure 1.3, the core part of defining business requirements involves gathering and documenting those requirements.

While the four steps that are circled on the left side of the figure are shown as separate subtasks, we usually do them in a pipeline fashion, conducting an interview, extracting its analytic themes, identifying their supporting business processes, and placing each business process in the initial bus matrix. We'll describe each of the core subtasks in Figure 1.3 in this section, leaving the senior management prioritization session for its own section.

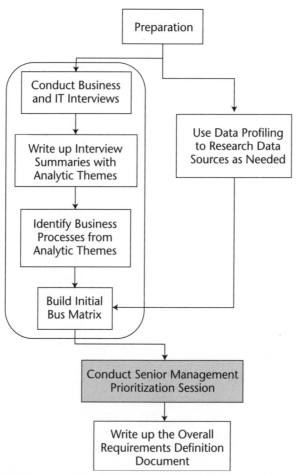

Figure 1.3   The enterprise requirements definition process flow chart

Preparation

Requirements definition is largely a process of interviewing business and technical people, but before you get started, you need to do a little preparation. Learn as much as you can about your business, your competitors, your industry, and your customers. Read your organization's annual report; track down any internal strategy documents; go online and see what's said about your organization, the competition, and the industry in the press. Find out what the big challenges are. Learn the terms and terminology the business people use to describe what they do. In short, do your homework.

Part of the preparation process is figuring out whom you should actually interview. This usually involves carefully examining an org chart with your sponsor and other key supporters. There are typically four groups of people you need to talk to early on: senior management responsible for making the strategic decisions for the organization; mid-management and business analysts responsible for exploring strategic alternatives and implementing decisions; source systems experts (the folks who really know what kinds of data issues are out there for you to trip over); and finally, people you need to interview for political reasons. This last group may not add any value, but if they're omitted, they could cause problems. Increasingly, there is a fifth group of people who may need the data warehouse—operational decision makers needing real-time or near real-time access to historical and integrated data. Your initial interviews should sample the operational community to see if such interest exists, and if so, a representative group of these users should be included in the interviews.

It's easy to start the interview list with the CEO and his senior staff. Add the analysts and managers who are known as leaders in the business intelligence area—folks whom senior management and co-workers turn to when they need information. They are also usually the folks who bug the IT organization the most. If you've been at your organization more that 12 months, you know who these people are. They have their own Access databases, they write SQL against the transaction system, and they create reports and charts with whatever tools they have available (mostly Excel and Access). Finally, add on a couple of the key IT folks who can educate you about the nature of the source systems.

> **NOTE** You are just making the list of whom to interview at this point, not the interview schedule. Start the schedule with a few people you know and trust before you turn to senior management. At the same time, make sure you get the elusive executives on the calendar as early as possible. Some of these folks can be tough to pin down.

A major goal during the interviews is to build positive working relationships with the business folks. These relationships will build on your understanding of the business issues your organization faces. In short, be prepared. Fortunately, gathering this information is not as difficult as it used to be, thanks to the Internet. However, you still have to read it.

Interviewing Business and IT

The next step in requirements gathering is actually talking to business users. Interview individuals or small groups (two to five people at most), rather than hold a large group design session. The individual interview allows each person to present his or her views on what the challenges are and what is required for success. It also gives the DW/BI team more opportunities to capture and clarify critical information. Finally, individual interviews are less work for the business folks. They take only an hour or so, rather than a whole day or two for group design sessions. On the downside, individual interviews collectively take longer and are more work for the DW/BI team.

In this first pass at gathering requirements, you will interview more senior level folks across the different departments and get a comprehensive list of the major challenges and opportunities your organization faces. We call these challenges and opportunities *analytic themes*. These themes often (but not always) line up with the strategic goals and initiatives of the organization. We talk about themes in more detail later in this section.

When you speak to the business users, you will often hear business requirements that sound really important and valuable, but end up being impossible to meet. A request such as "Sales data for our competitors by SKU by retail store by day would allow us to increase our market share by at least 5 percent" sounds great. The catch is that, for most industries, the data is not available. Even internal data might not be available, or it might be so dirty or poorly structured that it will take a major effort to make it presentable.

This is precisely why you need to interweave some interviews with source systems experts to understand the structure and content of the source systems and the nature of any data problems that might be lurking out there. You must also perform data profiling on all candidate data sources. (Data profiling is described in an upcoming section.)

At the end of each interview the interview team must take a few minutes to debrief. Review your notes, fill in the blanks, make sure you understand the terms you heard, and capture the key issues. The longer you wait to do this, the less you will remember. We've found ourselves staring at a sentence that reads, "The most important factor in our business is . . ." with no idea what came next. Debrief as soon as possible.

TIP Never ask the end user "What do you want in your data warehouse?" That puts them in the position of designing the system. That's your job. Besides, there is only one right answer to this question: "Everything." Instead, ask questions that help you learn what the end user does, and then translate this into what needs to go into the system. A question such as "How do you know when you have done a great job?" can get you started in the right direction.

Interview Summaries and Analytic Themes

It's a good idea to start writing up summaries of the individual interviews as you work through the interview schedule. This takes a bit of work because you don't want to simply transcribe the interview. Instead, summarize the various requirements and group them according to category or theme. This is where the analytic themes begin to appear.

Creating the list of analytic themes requires good categorization skills. It's like being able to look at each tree in the forest and group it by genus (and maybe even species). It gets easier with experience, but it's never simple. Start by grouping related requirements as you write up the individual interview summaries. Often, these groups are actually higher-level themes that include several sub-themes. In some cases, they're not really analytic themes at all, but represent a need for a new or improved operational process.

These are some example themes from a subscription business, such as MSN, grouped by the strategic goals they support:

A. Improve the effectiveness of the customer acquisition programs.

   1. Advertising

   2. Promotions

   3. Direct mail

   4. Online

B. Increase sales per customer by offering additional items of potential interest (cross-sell), or similar, higher value items (up-sell).

C. Improve margins by negotiating better prices and terms with suppliers.

D. Identify desirable profile(s) based on long-term customers and use them to create targeted acquisition programs.

This is a simple, enterprise list of goals and themes. Yours will need to be more detailed and extensive. Each theme should have examples of the specific analytic requirement you heard in the interview. It should also include some sense of the business value of meeting the requirement. In other words, how much is negotiating better prices and terms worth?

You may create an initial list of 20 or more major themes. Some of the themes on the list may represent new ways of doing business and will require new transaction systems, or at least significant changes to existing transaction systems. But even a quick review of the simple list provided begins to bring out ideas about how the DW/BI system can address some of these needs in the short term.

These analytic themes are a key input for the next step in the enterprise requirements process—identifying the supporting business processes. We'll get to this in a bit.

Meanwhile, the last step in creating the interview summaries is to validate what you heard. This can be done by sharing the interview summaries with the interviewees and asking for comments. Do this before you start working on the final overall requirements document. That way, any misunderstandings can be fixed and additions included. This validation step sends a positive message to your business users. It tells them you listened and understood their issues. In many cases, this is the first step in repairing damaged organizational relationships. It may be helpful to hold a findings review meeting where you invite everyone who participated in the interviews and have your business sponsor do the introductions.

Data Auditing/Data Profiling

At the same time you are interviewing people and creating the summaries, you will also need to do some queries against the source system data to get a firsthand understanding of the data issues. This kind of querying has come to be known as *data profiling* or *data auditing*, and there are several tools on the market designed to support it. There are three major points in the Lifecycle where data profiling is helpful. The first is here, during the requirements definition process where you should do a simple red light/green light assessment of your organization's data assets. You aren't looking for nuances at this point, but if a data source needs to be disqualified, now is the time. The second place to do data profiling is during the design of the dimensional model, and the third is during the design and implementation of the ETL process. You will want to do more in-depth data profiling once you select a specific business process and begin defining project-level business requirements. We describe data profiling in more detail when we discuss the dimensional modeling process in Chapter 2.

Identifying Business Processes That Support the Analytic Themes

As you extract the analytic themes for the interview summaries, you need to dig into each analytic theme to identify the business process (or processes) that generate the data needed to perform the desired analyses. You convert from themes to business processes because business processes are the units of work in building the DW/BI system. Each business process is usually measured by a single source system, which translates into a single pass through the Business Dimensional Lifecycle process. (See the related sidebar for more information.)

BUSINESS PROCESS: THE DW/BI SYSTEM UNIT OF WORK

We use the term "business process" to mean an operational activity the organization engages in to accomplish its primary goals. You can think of business processes as the links in the organization's value chain. Each business process typically has its own operational system or module that enables it, such as the order entry system, or the call tracking system, or the inventory management system. The information generated by these business processes measures only the business process itself, but that information usually has value well beyond the boundaries of the individual business process. Information from a single business process, such as orders information, could be of great interest to Sales, Marketing, Customer Service, and other groups across the organization.

   Each business process is a unique, coherent measurement system implemented as an operational system. If you need data from a given business process, you need to extract that data in its business context. In other words, you need to pull the measures and all of the associated descriptors in a careful, systematic fashion. This makes the business process the fundamental unit of work for the DW/BI system. Unless you have unlimited resources, your DW/BI team will concentrate on designing and loading data from one business process at a time. The business process is the DW/BI system unit of work.

While many analytic themes require information only from a single business process, one challenge you will face is that some themes require data from multiple business processes to meet the overall analytic needs. Customer and product profitability themes are good examples. They sound like a single analysis (the customer scorecard), but they actually require data from many separate business processes. We call these *consolidated* themes because they cannot be completely built until all prerequisite business processes are in place.

Converting from analytic themes to business processes helps determine the level of effort needed to support a given theme. If a theme must have data from more than one business processes, it will take more than one pass through the Lifecycle to enable that theme. While these passes can happen in parallel, there is no way around doing the work.

Converting from analytic themes to business processes involves thinking about which business processes are required to support each theme. For example, it may be possible to support the cross-sell and up-sell theme (B) from the example list based on data from a single business process: orders. With a data mining tool and orders data that indicates which products are bought together (the order, or "market basket"), you can identify the common relationships, which you can then use to influence sales. ("Would you like fries to go with that shake?")

On the other hand, a theme such as customer profiles (D) might draw on data from most of the major business processes. A profitable customer uses the web to get product information (low marketing costs), buys a lot (high sales), keeps what he buys (low returns), and doesn't need much help (few customer service calls). In this case, you'd need data from at least four business processes (or rows on the bus matrix, as described in the next section) to support theme (D). This is an example of a consolidated theme because it requires that data from more than one business process, such as orders or returns, be implemented first.

The worst case theme is often called a scorecard or executive dashboard. This deceptively simple application draws on data from almost all business processes in the organization. You can't create the entire dashboard until you've built the whole data warehouse foundation. Or worse, you end up building the dashboard by hand every day, manually extracting, copying, and pasting data from all those sources to make it work. It can be difficult to get business folks to understand the magnitude of the effort involved in creating this "simple" report.

Building the Initial Data Warehouse Bus Matrix

As you identify the business processes needed to support each analytic theme, you will also add those business processes to an enterprise data roadmap called the Data Warehouse Bus Matrix. This matrix maps your organizational business processes to the entities or objects that participate in those processes.

Each row in the matrix is a business process. Figure 1.4 shows a simplified example bus matrix for a retail company. Notice how the business processes down the left side of the matrix follow the organization's value chain. In this case, the company buys goods from their vendors and stores them in distribution centers. Then, as goods are demanded by consumers, they are moved out to the retail stores where they're held on shelves until the customer buys them and the goods leave the company's value chain. These business processes generally correspond to individual source systems or modules in the overall Enterprise Resource Planning (ERP) system.

Business Processes	Dimensions						
	Date	Product	Vendor	Shipper	Dist Ctr	Store	Promo
Purchase Orders	X	X	X		X		
Dist Ctr Deliveries	X	X	X	X	X		
Dist Ctr Inventory	X	X			X		
Store Deliveries	X	X		X	X	X	
Store Inventory	X	X				X	
Store Sales	X	X				X	X

(Value Chain — left side arrow)

Figure 1.4   Example enterprise bus matrix for a retail company

The columns in the bus matrix are the descriptive objects that participate in the various business processes, such as Store, Product, and Date. They contrast with the measurement-driven business processes that label the rows of the matrix. We call these objects *dimensions* in the dimensional model. Each dimension participates in one or more business process—we indicate this by placing an X in the intersecting cell in the matrix. For example, the Vendor dimension is involved in both the Purchasing and Delivery processes. The Store Sale business process, on the other hand, does not involve the Vendor or Distribution Center.

The bus matrix is essentially your enterprise dimensional data architecture. For each business process (row), you can see exactly which dimensions (columns) you need to implement. And for each dimension, you can see which business processes it must support. This dimension-oriented view is the visual representation of *conformed dimensions*—a concept we define in the next chapter.

The business processes in the bus matrix, and the themes they support (and the value those themes represent) become the major inputs to the next step in the requirements definition process: a prioritization session with senior management.

Creating the Overall Requirements Document

It's best to wait until after the prioritization session to write the overall requirements document so you can include the resulting list of prioritized business processes. The overall requirements document includes the business process summaries, the bus matrix, and the prioritized results. You might want to include the interview summaries as an appendix for those readers who want all the detail.

Once you've completed the overall requirements document, the conceptual foundation of the DW/BI system is in place. The rest of the Lifecycle depends on what you learned in these initial steps to make decisions and set priorities for all three tracks that follow, and on into the deployment, maintenance, and growth phases.

The Prioritization Process

If you're a technical person, it's safe to say the prioritization process is one of the most powerful business tools you'll ever use. This is a bold statement, but we have used this tool many times and have been repeatedly successful. We've conducted a few prioritization sessions where the client decided not to move forward with the DW/BI project right away. This decision is usually reached because the prioritization process helped senior management better understand the nature of the commitment or the size of the data problems. This is also a success because it means they will work to fix the problems rather than try to build a DW/BI system on shaky ground.

The prioritization process is a planning meeting involving the DW/BI team, the DW/BI project business sponsors, and other key senior managers from across the organization.

In this meeting, you describe the business processes you identified in the enterprise requirements gathering process so everyone has an understanding of the full list of possibilities. Go into this session armed with a PowerPoint presentation that describes each business process, gives a few examples of the associated analyses it will support along with a feel for the business value of those analyses, and includes an initial sense of level of effort needed to implement the business process (its feasibility). Be as crisp and clear as possible. Try to keep this presentation under two hours. As you describe each business process, you also describe the relative effort involved in supplying the needed data. Once everyone has an understanding of the business processes and terminology, take a break.

The second half of the session involves prioritizing the business processes. Lead the group in placing a sticky note for each business process onto a large version of a two-by-two grid like the one shown in Figure 1.5. This is an interesting exercise in negotiation and education and can easily take another hour and a half to two hours.

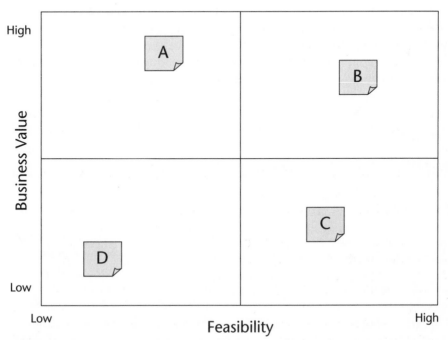

Figure 1.5 Example prioritization grid

The prioritization grid is deceptively simple: Study it carefully. The Y axis is about business value. The group needs to reach consensus on the relative impact of implementing each business process. The participants need to remember to take an organizational approach to assigning business value. There will always be someone who thinks any given business process is the absolute top priority. Gently remind them that there's more to the business than their little slice.

It helps to remind participants that the goal is to assign relative, not absolute, values on both axes. In Figure 1.5, we know that business process D is more difficult than business process A, but we don't need to know how many person-days it will take to implement either business process. The same goes for value. Figure 1.5 shows that business process A has more business value than business process B, but it's significantly less feasible to implement.

The X axis is about the level of effort each business process will take to implement. It is stated in terms of feasibility so the easier business processes go to the right (high feasibility) and the harder business processes go to the left (low feasibility). The DW/BI team leads the assignment of feasibility because team members have a better sense about the technical difficulties involved in each business process (although feasibility is not just technical—there are often organizational and political difficulties as well).

The true feasibility is not fully understood at this point. If you have someone on the team who's been in the organization long enough, she should have a good sense for the level of effort required to implement each business process. One obvious factor is when business processes must be implemented together to support a high value, consolidated theme.

The priority session is a good opportunity to educate the business folks about how bad things really are. You don't want to sound negative, but it's important to explain the level of effort it takes to gather the data and make it useful. For example, integrating customer IDs from two different source systems is a grind.

A CREDIBILITY BOOSTER

The prioritization process uses a common business school tool called the two-by-two matrix. This matrix was popularized in the early 1970s by the Boston Consulting Group. BCG used a "Growth-Share Matrix" to compare different business units in a portfolio by comparing Relative market share with industry sales growth rates. A business unit with high market share in an industry with high growth rate was called a "Star." By contrast, a business unit with low market share in a low-growth industry was a "Pet" (later referred to as a "Dog").

The great thing about the matrix is the positive impression the DW/BI team makes by cleverly adapting a classic MBA tool.

Sources: The Boston Consulting Group, *Perspectives on Experience and The Product Portfolio* (Boston, MA: The Boston Consulting Group, 1968)

Once all the business processes have been placed and everyone agrees on their relative locations, convert the matrix to a prioritized list of projects. One way to do this is to start in the upper-right corner of the prioritization grid and move to the lower-left corner, numbering the business processes as you encounter them. The two-dimensional nature of the matrix makes this a little difficult. Use the concept of concentric circles to establish a priority order, like ripples on a pond, centered in the upper-right corner.

The output of the prioritization process is a list of business processes in priority order. This list is your DW/BI roadmap; it tells you which row on the matrix, and which dimensions, to implement first. Less tangible, but equally important outcomes of the prioritization process are senior management consensus around the DW/BI roadmap, and a general improvement in the relationships between IT and the business.

In most cases, you will make only one pass at the enterprise requirements. Once the priorities are in place, the next pass and all subsequent passes will be at the level of the individual row on the bus matrix, the business process. Each row essentially becomes a project in the overall DW/BI program. From here on out, you will update enterprise business requirements and revisit priorities as the business changes, but most requirements definition efforts will be at the business process project level.

Revisiting Project Planning

Now that you have a clear idea of your business priorities and how they relate to the business processes (data sources), you can lay out a more detailed and precise project plan. This process is not much different from project planning for any major information technology project. The DW/BI perspective on project planning is described in detail in the Lifecycle Toolkit book and does not merit repeating here.

The plan will continue to evolve as you get more detail about the business requirements in the next step. There is a two-way arrow between project planning and project requirements definition in Figure 1.1, but the backward flow is not as major because you gained significant understanding of the nature of the opportunity in the enterprise requirements gathering and narrowed your scope in the prioritization process.

Gathering Project Requirements

Gathering project requirements follows the same basic process as the enterprise requirements gathering process described earlier. The difference is that now you have selected a particular business process on the bus matrix to implement. The enterprise requirements definition process should be a solid foundation for the project requirements. You now will deepen your understanding of the chosen business process.

The project requirements gathering step is about pulling together the information you need to be successful in the three tracks that follow. Specifically, you need enough detail to create real, practical, flexible data models that will support a broad range of analytic needs. You need a solid understanding of the technical issues around data volumes, data cleansing, data movement, user access, and a host of other issues so you can create a capable, flexible technical architecture to support the warehouse now and in the future. Finally, you need a clear understanding of the business analysis requirements to build the initial set of business intelligence applications to demonstrate value from the very start.

The same three steps you followed in the enterprise requirements process apply to the project requirements process: preparation, interviews, and documentation.

As we described in the enterprise requirements section, preparation is the critical first step. If you haven't already, do your homework. Study the particular business process in detail. Figure out as much as you can about how it works before you begin the interviews. Learn the business terminology, the steps in the business process, and how it is measured.

The goal with this round of interviews is to drill down on the selected business process in detail to understand the analyses, data models, and technologies required to make it work. This time you may take a more vertical slice of the organization, depending on the business process (some business processes have broader organizational appeal than others). Talk to the analysts, managers, report developers, and source systems people who can help you understand the intricacies of the business process in question. The actual interview process itself is generally the same as before.

ALTERNATIVES TO INDIVIDUAL INTERVIEWS

If interviews won't work in your situation, we have had success with group requirements gathering sessions, but they are more risky. If you must do group sessions, here are a few tips:

- ◆ **Preparation is even more important.** You have to know the business, and you also have to know what you want to accomplish and how you are going to go about it.

- ◆ **Have a clear agenda with times listed for each section, breaks, and food and drink.** Reserve a good room with plenty of space and comfortable chairs. Make sure you have all the tools you need—flip charts, markers, white boards, overheads, computers, and a projector—whatever makes sense for your plan.

- ◆ **Get a strong, experienced design meeting leader to run the meetings.** You have only a short time. If someone takes the meeting off course, you won't get what you need.

Depending on the business process selected, consider whether to interview your customers and suppliers. They are, or could be, business users of information in the DW/BI system. In fact, the need to offer information outside the organization is common enough that many of the front-end tool vendors include extranet access functionality as part of their product line. Listen carefully during the interviews to see if this is a likely source of significant business value for your organization.

Interviews with key source system people and data profiling play a bigger role in the project requirements gathering process. Strive to inform the dimensional modeling process as much as possible about both the business requirements and the data realities.

The documentation process for the project requirements is similar to that of the enterprise definition process, except it is more detailed. Where the analytic themes at the enterprise level ranged across all the business processes, at the project level, they should all be focused on the initial business process.

Although the project requirements definition task sounds a bit abbreviated here, it is actually the definition task you will repeat over and over, every time you iterate through the Lifecycle to bring the next priority business process into the DW/BI system. Let's hope you need to do the enterprise-level task only once, and then keep it updated.

REFERENCE **There is much more to the requirements definition process. For additional detail, please refer to the following sources:**

- *The Data Warehouse Lifecycle Toolkit* **(Wiley, 1998).**

- **Search kimballgroup.com for the topics "Business Requirements" and "Business Acceptance" for several related articles.**

Business Requirements Example: Adventure Works Cycles

The sample business intelligence databases in SQL Server 2005 are based on a fictitious company called Adventure Works Cycles (AWC), a multinational manufacturer and seller of bicycles and accessories. According to the descriptions in Books Online, the company is based in Bothell, Washington, USA and has regional sales offices in several countries. In this section we provide an example of the business requirements gathering process based on the Adventure Works Cycles business. Assuming the DW/BI system already has good business sponsorship, the first major step in the Lifecycle is requirements definition, and the first task in requirements definition is preparation.

Interview Preparation at Adventure Works Cycles

Typically, you'd carefully review all the information about Adventure Works Cycles that you could find, reading through strategy documents, annual reports, marketing plans, competitive analyses, and presentations from senior management's annual offsite planning meeting. Because Adventure Works Cycles is a fictitious company, you can't really do the kind of research you should. SQL Server Books Online (BOL) provides some background information about Adventure Works Cycles in the section "Sample Databases and Business Scenarios." You may want to review the materials in BOL to get a general sense for Adventure Works Cycles and the AdventureWorks transaction system database. In this section, we have enhanced the Books Online content by doing some analyses of data from the database itself. We also provide you with business requirements information from our imaginations.

Adventure Works Cycles Basic Business Information

There is an incredible amount of information about your organization buried in your transaction systems. Buried is the key word here—not many people can get at it, which is why you are building a DW/BI system in the first place. However, as a competent systems professional, you should be able to get at this data. A few queries against the transaction database can reveal much about the dynamics of the business and the nature of the data at the same time.

The Adventure Works Cycles transaction database is called Adventure-Works and is installed as part of the SQL Server samples. It holds data from January, 2001 through June 30, 2004. A few queries on this data reveal that Adventure Works Cycles is doing well, at least in terms of orders and growth. The Grand Total line in Table 1.1 shows that orders have been increasing rapidly, tripling in 2002 and increasing almost 50 percent in 2003. Based on the first six months, 2004 looks like another banner year. Table 1.1 also shows that Adventure Works Cycles sells products in four major product categories: bikes, components, clothing, and accessories. Bicycles account for more than 80 percent of orders, with clothing and accessories making up about 4 percent.

THE HISTORY OF ADVENTURE WORKS

The Adventure Works database has been evolving at Microsoft for several years. It's been used in various forms as a demo database for Microsoft's CRM solution, as a training database for .NET architecture courses, as an application to demonstrate Microsoft Transaction Server, and as an example to demonstrate online shopping using Commerce Server. In these last two incarnations, Adventure Works was a camping gear retailer.

Table 1.1 Adventure Works Cycles Product Orders by Category

CATEGORY	2001	2002	2003	2004 (YTD)
Bikes	10,985	28,854	38,026	24,160
Components	708	4,230	6,418	2,477
Clothing	35	501	1,031	589
Accessories	19	88	549	531
Grand Total	**11,746**	**33,673**	**46,023**	**27,757**

All figures in U.S. dollars

Adventure Works Cycles sells a lot of bikes. Additional database queries tell us where their bike orders come from. Table 1.2 reveals that AWC has sales in six countries, with about 60 percent of orders coming from the United States. The percentage of orders coming from outside the U.S. has increased from about 25 percent in 2001 to close to 40 percent so far in 2004.

Table 1.2 Adventure Works Cycles Product Orders by Country/Region

COUNTRY	2001	2002	2003	2004 (YTD)
United States	8,980	23,717	27,265	14,631
United Kingdom	467	2,348	5,683	4,232
Canada	1,340	4,359	4,721	2,278
France	27	1,542	3,915	2,576
Australia	814	1,186	2,142	1,917
Germany	119	521	2,298	2,123
Grand Total	**11,746**	**33,673**	**46,023**	**27,757**

All figures in U.S. dollars

In terms of sales channels, Table 1.3 shows that the bulk of orders come from bicycle stores and distributors, also known as Resellers. This channel accounts for about 70 percent of orders and is handled by a direct sales force of 18 people. Adventure Works Cycles broadened its business during the late 1990s by opening up a direct sales channel to consumers on the Internet. Oddly, Internet orders have been fairly constant at around 30 percent of sales across the four years of data we have available. While we don't know why this is so, we predict the VP of Sales will take credit for being able to grow the direct sales channel as fast as the Internet has grown.

Table 1.3 Adventure Works Cycles Product Orders by Sales Channel

SALES CHANNEL	2001	2002	2003	2004 (YTD)
Reseller	9,119	27,992	37,318	18,715
Internet	2,627	5,681	8,705	9,041
Total	11,746	33,673	46,023	27,757

All figures in U.S. dollars

Now you have a sense for what Adventure Works Cycles sells, where they sell it, and how they sell it. The next question is to whom do they sell? Table 1.4 gives a snapshot of customers broken down by sales channel. This split is vital to understanding AWC's customers because the two channels are very different.

Table 1.4 Adventure Works Cycles Customers by Sales Channel Snapshot

	TOTAL CUSTOMERS	ACTIVE CUSTOMERS	$US SALES (000)	ORDER COUNT	AVG $ PER ORDER
Reseller	701	467	18,715	901	23,751
Internet	18,484	11,377	9,041	13,050	827
Total	19,185	11,844	27,757	13,951	2,308

The Reseller channel has a total of 701 customers, 467 of whom are active (defined as having placed an order in the first six months of 2004). The Internet channel is much larger, with a total of 18,484 customers, 11,377 of whom have placed an order in 2004. The Reseller channel justifies a direct sales force in part because the average order is close to $24,000 compared with an average of $827 for the Internet. On the other hand, the Internet business should be significantly more profitable because the price would be closer to retail rather than wholesale, and the cost of selling would be much lower without a direct sales force. You may hear more about this during the business requirements interviews.

As the DW/BI system manager, you should continue from here, researching top reseller customers and their historical buying patterns (seasonality, product lifecycle, and so on). Investigate the Internet customers as well because you have demographic information on them that tells you who are they, what they buy, and where they come from.

These few reports demonstrate the power of analysis. They give you a general sense for the size and shape of Adventure Works Cycles. However, they do not give you enough information to build a DW/BI system. There is much more to learn in terms of the business, its strategies and plans, competitive environment, and key players. This is where you depart from the facts and venture into the fuzzy-edged land of organization and politics.

Interview Planning

The Adventure Works Cycles documentation doesn't include an org chart, but the HumanResources.Employee table in the AdventureWorks database lists a total of 290 employees. The Employee table is self-referencing with a ManagerID field that allows us to generate the company's org chart. The 290 employees are distributed across departments according to the org chart based on the Employee table shown in Figure 1.6. The org chart shows seven direct reports to the CEO.

The org chart should raise a few questions for you, such as why James Hamilton, the VP of Production, has only one direct report, and why Facilities and Maintenance (with seven people) is the only group reporting to him. Meanwhile, why does Peter Krebs, the Production Control Manager (not a VP) have all the rest of the 200-person manufacturing organization reporting to him? Why is David Bradley, the Marketing Manager, only a manager when Brian Welker is the Sales VP? If this were your organization, these would be important questions to get answered. This is why examining the org chart early on is generally a good idea.

Given the number of senior executives and the size of the organization, you would probably plan on more than 10 but fewer than 20 interviews at Adventure Works Cycles. Depending on availability, expect this to take a minimum of a week, more likely one and a half to two weeks.

The rest of this chapter highlights key parts of the requirements definition process in the context of the Adventure Works Cycles case study.

Once you've completed the project requirements definition step, you will be ready to begin designing your dimensional model, as covered in Chapter 2.

Adventure Works Cycles Enterprise Business Requirements

Begin with a series of enterprise requirements interviews to get a broad sense of the important business processes and their business value, and to identify potential sponsors. Summarize each interview by grouping the individual requirements into common analytic themes. This brings a useful structure to what is often a fairly scattered interaction. While the same analytic requirement may come up several times in the conversation, you need to summarize it only once. The typical summary for an hour-long interview takes about three to four pages. Each summary should include the business narrative along with example analyses and potential data problems. The narrative should capture an estimate of the value of each business process.

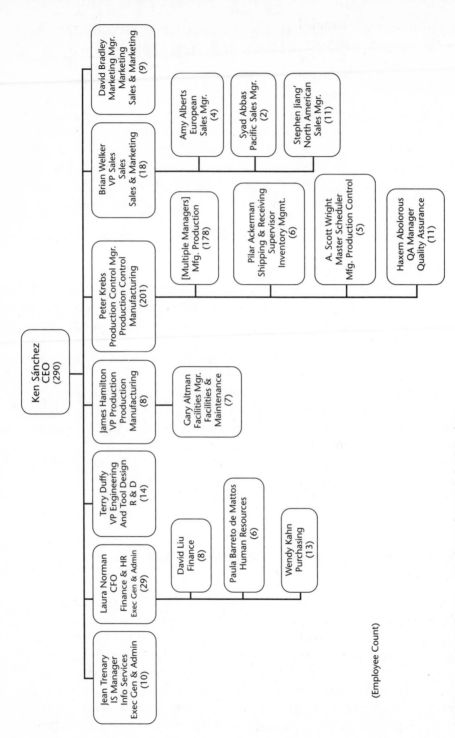

(Employee Count)

Figure 1.6 The Adventure Works Cycles organization chart

We've included an example interview summary for Brian Welker, the VP of Sales. The following summary gives you much of the information you need to understand the business processes and the dimensional modeling decisions made in the next chapter. To get a more complete understanding, read through the additional abbreviated interview summaries at the book's web site, www.MsftDWToolkit.com, for the following people:

- Ken Sanchez, CEO
- Peter Krebs, Production Control Manager
- David Bradley, Marketing Manager
- Mary Gibson, Internet Channel Analyst
- David Liu, Finance Manager

Adventure Works Cycles Vice President of Sales, Brian Welker, is a big believer in the power of information. He and his group have taken over one of the IT organization's analysts full time just to generate reports and analyses. The team decided to interview Brian early on to get some positive reinforcement.

After you've discussed roles and responsibilities, you might start the interview by asking Brian: How do you tell when you're doing a great job? If he's as smart as you think, his answer might be: "When my sales planning is accurate, when my sales grow, when I can leverage special offers, and when I have good customer satisfaction." That would be quite an answer, but it's a gold mine to drill down into his information needs. Your job is to react to his answer point by point, drawing out more detail. The following summary captures the results of that drill-down.

Example Interview Summary

Interviewee: Brian Welker, VP of Sales
Date: 7/25/2005
Interviewer: Joy Mundy
Scribe: Warren Thornthwaite
Additional attendees: Stuart Ozer, Carolyn Chau, Joy Byrd, Dave Wong

Roles and Responsibilities

Brian Welker is head of the sales organization. He's responsible for sales to Resellers, which was $37 million last year, or about 70 percent of total sales. He has 17 people who report to him, including 3 regional sales mangers. Brian is excited about his team and eager for them to be successful. They are all "bike freaks" who love to ride bikes and love to talk about them—perfect bike sales people. Brian is measured on achievement of the total Reseller sales target for the year.

Information Requirements

Brian is particularly frustrated with how difficult it is to get information out of the company's systems. When he asks for a report, it can take days or weeks to get the information. Often he's told "It can't be done." The major analytic areas that Brian works with are as follows:

- *Sales planning:* Planning for the year begins in the fall of the previous year with the Sales planning process. Sales territories are based on geography. All new customers are assigned to a sales territory when they place their first order based on where they are located. Sales planning includes looking at the following:

  - *Growth analysis:* Overall market, new products, new geographies, new sales people.

  - *Customer analysis:* Who are the top customers, how have they changed over the last year?

  - *Territory analysis:* Where are top customers located, what are the current sales territories, and how balanced are they? How does this map to sales regions?

  Brian and Ramesh Meyyappan (the analysts who work in IT) also look at sales by sales regions, which are groupings of customers based on the state where they're located. Regions overlap sales territories and are based on seasonal buying patterns and regional preferences. Being able to group historical sales like this helps the sales team do a better job of forecasting monthly sales. They usually look at regional sales a lot during the sales planning cycle and then compare actuals to the forecast during the year. Every year, they change the regions a bit to line up with changes in buying patterns.

  Ramesh does all of this data analysis for the Sales forecasting and quota assignment process in a spreadsheet. The spreadsheet includes territory growth factors, allocations, and manual adjustments. The planning process is totally manual and takes a couple of months in the fall, and maybe a week per month to do the reporting during the year.

  During the annual planning process, Brian wants to be able to see reseller customer orders by year by customer territory, regardless of the sales rep assigned to the territory. In previous jobs, Brian would adjust the size of the territories by moving customers from one territory to another with the goal of making the territories more even. He has not done this at AWC yet, so all customers are still assigned to their original territory. Sales reps can be reassigned to different territories, usually when a sales rep leaves.

- *Sales performance:* Once the planning process is done, Brian wants to see sales according to the new territory assignments, all the way back through history so he can compare with actuals as they come in. At any time, Sales must be able to re-create historical sales and commission reports based on what happened at the time of the order, not which territory gets credit today.

Brian also wants to look at orders from a sales rep perspective. The first thing he wants to see at the start of the week is how his sales reps are doing year to date. If Brian sees a problem in the higher level data, he wants to be able to drill down to detailed orders for individual reps. Of course, Brian has other reports he would like to see: for example, top 20 customers and orders by Reseller versus online.

■ *Basic sales reporting:* Brian wants to take better advantage of the customer information buried in the orders transaction system. The sales reps would really appreciate it if they could get a list of the customers in their territory ranked by orders. Because most sales go to a small percentage of Resellers, the sales reps would concentrate on making sure those important customers are happy.

Beyond this, Brian knows that 17 percent of 2002 customers did not reorder in 2003. And to date in 2004, he still has not heard from an additional 17 percent or so. His sales people could use this information to bring the best of these customers back to the business.

■ *Price lists:* The fact that the sales reps are out in the field most of the time makes it difficult for them to keep their price lists current. The price list changes fairly often, but only a few things on the list change. It would be great to get a report to the sales reps that flagged changes and special offers, and maybe even highlighted the relevant customers.

■ *Special offers:* The special offers could be a great sales tool. AWC just finished an inventory clearance sale on the silver Mountain 500s. The color didn't sell as well as others, resulting in too many in stock at model changeover. Mary Gibson, the marketing assistant for mountain bikes and David Liu in Finance put their heads together to come up with ideas to stimulate demand and came up with a 40 percent off offer. This is something the sales people can work with, but it's a random process. They'd like a report that shows which of their customers bought a lot of the product that is on special offer to see if they're interested in more at a great price.

Brian would like his sales people to start with the biggest potential customers first and keep selling down the list until they run out. Actually, Brian thinks the business would be better served if they contacted the more profitable customers about special offers first. Some of the biggest customers are big because they scoop up specials, which don't make a lot of money for AWC. That's another thing: The sales reps need to know when out of stocks occur on special offers.

- *Customer satisfaction:* Brian would like to create some measures of customer satisfaction and has been trying to get more information out of the customer care system lately, with limited success. He would love to be able to track calls by complaint type, product, sales region, and customer to get a sense for customer satisfaction and product quality. He also thinks comparing order date and ship date in the sales data to identify late orders, and determining the percentage of returned items might be indicators of customer satisfaction. This would make a great start at a customer satisfaction scorecard.

- *International support:* The company has been growing internationally, but the transaction systems haven't kept up. The systems do take orders in multiple currencies, but none of the descriptions has been translated from English. This is a problem for the sales people, who have split up the product list and done the translations themselves. This doesn't work in the long run because no one knows if they've translated the information correctly. All materials must be bilingual to comply with Canadian law. The product tags and documents are already bilingual, but the sales materials are not.

Additional Issues

Brian expressed a frustration on the part of his sales force about the difficulty they have using existing reports. It is our sense that Brian would like an analytic system that provides his sales reps most of the information they need in a standard format with just a few keystrokes. The time zone differences make it hard for some of them to get live support from headquarters. If they need to get custom information, he would like it to be easy for them to get it themselves.

Success Criteria

Brian would like the system to provide him and his team with:

- Easy access to basic sales data for the whole field organization
- Flexible reporting and analysis tools
- All the data in one place (especially sales and forecast data)

Requirements Summaries: What's Missing?

The short answer to "what's missing" is "a lot." This particular summary doesn't include much indication of business value. And one summary will never provide the range of business requirements you get from a full set of interviews. In addition, you would need IT and business analyst representation to get a sense for the level of effort or even availability of some of the data requested. However, there is enough information here to help you make sense of the next few steps.

Analytic Themes and Business Processes

The interview summaries have already grouped similar requirements into common analytic themes. We've found that it's easiest to identify the business processes that support each analytic theme as you write the summary. For example, Sales Planning is an analytic theme that is supported by information from the orders business process. Figure 1.7 is an example of how you might distill Adventure Works Cycles' business processes from the analytic themes based on Brian Welker's interview summary. Your final list will include many more themes and business processes.

The Supporting Business Process column in Figure 1.7 allows you to group themes that rely on data from the same business process and to identify themes that require data from multiple business processes. Recall that themes that rely on data from multiple business processes, or second level themes, are more difficult to implement. Look for the highly leveraged opportunities where several themes can be delivered with data from a single business process. In most organizations, this opportunity is the sales business process, which Adventure Works Cycles calls *orders*.

Once you fill in the complete list of themes, re-sorting it by business process will reveal that many of the business requirements rely on data from a few business processes. For Adventure Works Cycles, data from the orders business process is all that is needed to enable a wide range of analytic requirements, many of which are not on Brian's list in Figure 1.7. As the full set of requirements would reveal, Sales is not the only department interested in orders data. This is important because it adds to the overall business value of implementing the orders business process. All or most of the following requirements could be met with data from the orders business process:

- Sales planning input
- Basic sales reporting
- Special offers
- Production forecast input
- Product planning and monitoring
- Internet customer demographics (with a well-designed customer dimension)
- Customer profiling
- Customer loyalty program
- Standardized currency reporting

Analytic Theme	Inferred or Requested Analyses	Supporting Business Process	Comments
Sales Planning	- Reseller historical orders analyses	- orders	By customer, by territory, by sales region (from state)
	- Sales forecast	- orders	Forecast is a business process that uses orders data as an input
Sales Performance	- Orders by current territory	- orders	
	- Orders by original territory	- orders	
	- Sales rep performance report	- orders - forecast	Orders and forecast by sales rep
Sales Reporting	- Resellers ranked by orders in a given territory	- orders	
	- Churned customer list	- orders	Customers who have not ordered in X months
Price Lists	- Current price list	- orders	This is a connectivity issue, not a data warehouse issue
Special Offers	- Relevant customers by territory based on orders history	- orders	
	- Inventory status (out of stock)	- inventory	
Customer (Reseller) Satisfaction	- Calls by complaint type, product and customer attributes	- call tracking	
	- Order metrics of satisfaction	- orders	e.g. due date versus ship date
	- Returns by reseller by return reason	- returns	
International Support	- Local language translations of Product descriptions	- n/a (product dimension)	This is a transaction system problem. We need to make sure we can handle multiple languages in the DW/BI system, but the source system has to capture them when new products are created.

Figure 1.7 Analytic themes and supporting business processes from the interview summary

---

THE NAME GAME IN ACTION

The business processes listed in Figure 1.7 do not necessarily match up with the terms we heard from Brian Welker in the interview. He's the VP of Sales, and tends to use the word "sales" to describe the information he'd like to track. As it turns out, the term "sales" has a specific meaning carefully defined by the accounting department based on order dates, ship dates, and accounts receivables. Brian is not actually measured on sales; he is measured on orders. The process of determining business process, table, and attribute names starts here. You need to be as precise as possible in your use of terms. In fact, as soon as you understand the distinction between sales and orders, you should rewrite the interview summary to reflect it. We left the ambiguity in our summary to make the point.

Brian also discussed a few consolidated analytic themes that require data from more than one business process (from Figure 1.7):

- *Sales performance:* Orders and forecast
- *Customer satisfaction:* Call tracking, orders, and returns

The prioritization process focuses on business processes because these are the coherent units of work for the DW/BI system. In describing each business process, you need to tie it back to the analytic themes it supports, so senior management can assess its business value. The business processes from Brian's interview are shown in Table 1.5. Brian's supported analytic themes are underlined; the rest came from other interviews.

Table 1.5   Business Processes Derived from Brian Welker's Interview

LETTER	BUSINESS PROCESS	SUPPORTED ANALYTIC THEMES
A	Orders	<u>Orders reporting and analysis</u>, <u>orders forecasting</u>, advertising effectiveness, <u>customer satisfaction</u>, production forecasting, product profitability, customer profitability
B	Orders forecast	<u>Sales performance</u>, business planning, production forecast
C	Call tracking	Call center performance, customer satisfaction, product quality, customer profitability, product profitability
D	Returns	<u>Customer satisfaction</u>, product quality, customer profitability, product profitability, net sales

By the time you're finished with the interviews and write-ups, you should have a list of business processes that represents the major activities of your organization: 25 to 50 is a reasonable count at this point. You'll leave some items off the list, even though they will be discussed in the document and with senior management. In Brian's case, price lists and international support are important issues to his organization, but they are transaction system problems because they involve enhancing transaction systems or building new IT infrastructure. You can help with better reporting, but you shouldn't be dealing with connectivity and data capture issues if you can avoid it.

Adventure Works Cycles Bus Matrix

Business processes are the units of work in building the information layer of the BI system. The bus matrix shows the business processes and the dimensions needed to support them. The more you know about how the business and its supporting systems work the easier it is to define the bus matrix. Your full version of Table 1.5 would be the starting point for an initial version of your bus matrix. Figure 1.8 shows a high-level version of the Adventure Works Cycles bus matrix for the business processes from Table 1.5.

The bus matrix gets another level of detail during the dimensional modeling process when you add in the different types of fact tables. You'll get more on this in Chapter 2.

Business Process	Date	Product	Employee	Customer (Reseller)	Customer (Internet)	Sales Territory	Currency	Channel	Promotion	Call Reason	Facility
Sales Forecasting	X	X	X	X	X	X	X				
Orders	X	X	X	X	X	X	X	X	X		
Call tracking	X	X	X	X	X	X				X	
Returns	X	X		X	X	X	X		X		X

Figure 1.8   The Adventure Works Cycles bus matrix

The Adventure Works Cycles Prioritization Process

As we described earlier in this chapter, the prioritization process is a facilitated session where the DW/BI team presents the preliminary project findings and facilitates discussion with key business representatives. The primary goals of the prioritization process are to ensure a common understanding of the requirements findings and business processes, and prioritize the business processes based on business value and feasibility. The top priority business process becomes the focus of the initial DW/BI project.

Figure 1.9 shows the resulting grid from the Adventure Works Cycles prioritization session. It includes a few more business processes than we listed in Table 1.5, but it's still not a full set.

Note that there are two items on the grid that are not actually business processes: Customer and product profitability are consolidated themes that senior management has expressed significant interest in analyzing. These have been included on the grid to show their importance, but they are far over to the left to indicate the difficulty involved in building all the needed business processes. Given the number of analyses supported by data from the orders business process, it should come as no surprise that orders is the top priority theme. The team should get to work on this right away!

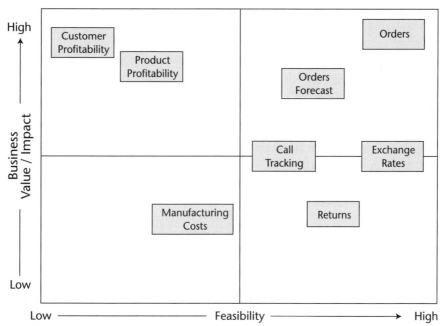

Figure 1.9 The Adventure Works Cycles prioritization grid

Business Requirements for the Orders Project

Getting to work on the orders business process requires holding an additional set of interviews to drill down on orders-related analyses. The team needs to understand several issues that were raised in the enterprise requirements process, such as what the different kinds of regions that people described are. The team would get more specific about the kinds of new reports and analyses people want to see as input to the BI Application track.

All of this information becomes the grist for the Adventure Works Cycles business dimensional modeling process case study in Chapter 2.

Summary

This chapter concentrated on the early tasks in the Lifecycle involving business requirements gathering, prioritization, and project planning. We gave special emphasis to the importance of understanding and documenting the business requirements.

The first part of the chapter described a process for gaining sponsorship, defining and documenting the enterprise-level business requirements, prioritizing the opportunities with senior business people, and gathering project requirements related to the top priority business process. This process also included the challenging task of distilling the analytic themes down to the business processes that provide the underlying information.

The second part of the chapter went through an abbreviated example of the business requirements gathering process at Adventure Works Cycles. The interview summary for the VP of Sales provided the analytic themes that tied to the business processes that fed into the bus matrix and the prioritization process.

These upfront business-related phases of the DW/BI project are by far the most important. Unfortunately, they can be intimidating for technologists. Do not resist or avoid the requirements gathering phase of the project. The resulting understanding of the business issues, their priorities, and the data that supports their solution is priceless for the DW/BI team. The requirements document will be your reference point for all major decisions from here on out. You get huge value just from the content of the document alone.

But wait, there's more! The requirements gathering process also helps you build positive working relationships with the business people. As the business people participate in the requirements process, they see that you've done your homework. You understand them, you speak their language, you want to help solve the problem—in short, you get it.

If that's not enough to convince you, there are even more benefits to this process. Not only do you get documented requirements and better relationships, you gain active user support. As the business folks begin to understand your vision for an information solution, they see how your success ultimately leads to their success. They begin to see how their involvement will improve the chances of success.

Designing the Business Process Dimensional Model

To arrive at the simple is difficult—Rashid Elisha

This chapter is about the basic concepts of dimensional modeling and the process of designing a business process dimensional model. Designing the dimensional model falls within the central section of the Lifecycle, as shown in Figure 2.1. This middle row of the Lifecycle's central section focuses on data, hence the clever name: *the data track*. The main objective of the data track is to make sure users get the data they need to meet ongoing business requirements. The key word in this objective is *ongoing*: Your goal in this step is to create a usable, flexible, extensible data model. This model needs to support the full range of analyses, both now and for the foreseeable future.

Because most of the work in building a DW/BI system happens in the data track, and the track builds on the dimensional model, it should be well designed. The first part of this chapter is a primer on dimensional modeling, including an overview of facts, dimensions, the data warehouse bus matrix, and other core concepts. The second major section of the chapter delves into more detail on several important design techniques, such as slowly changing dimensions, hierarchies, and bridge tables. Once the basic concepts are in place, the third section presents a process for building dimensional models. You should begin with a bit of preparation that involves reviewing the business requirements and determining naming conventions, setting up the modeling environment and data research tools. The modeling process itself starts with a design session which results in an initial high level model, an attributes list, and an issues list. This is followed by a detailed model development phase and a review and validation phase.

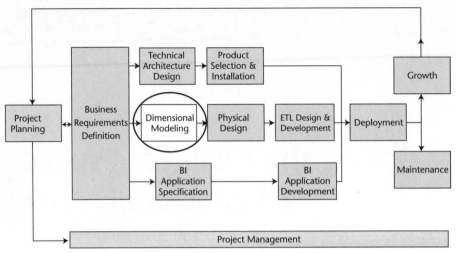

Figure 2.1 The dimensional modeling step in the Lifecycle context

The fourth part of the chapter applies the modeling concepts and process to the Adventure Works Cycles example to get a real-world feel for what it takes to create a dimensional model. Creating the Adventure Works Cycles model gives us an excellent opportunity to explore several common dimensional modeling issues and their solutions.

REFERENCE This chapter describes what a dimensional model is, why it's a useful design technique for a DW/BI system, and how to go about designing a strong data foundation. You cannot possibly learn everything you need to know about dimensional modeling in a single chapter—even a long one like this. For additional detailed guidance on the techniques, including industry case studies, we refer you to *The Data Warehouse Toolkit, Second Edition*, Ralph Kimball and Margy Ross (Wiley, 2002).

Dimensional Modeling Concepts and Terminology

There is broad agreement in data warehousing and business intelligence that the dimensional model is the preferred structure for presenting information to users. The dimensional model is the best way to meet our primary design goals:

- To present the needed information to users as simply as possible
- To return query results to the users as quickly as possible
- To provide relevant information that accurately tracks the underlying business processes

Albert Einstein captured the main reason we use the dimensional model when he said, "Make everything as simple as possible, but not simpler." As it turns out, simplicity is relative. The dimensional model is much easier for users to understand than the typical source system normalized model even though a dimensional model typically contains exactly the same content as a normalized model. It has far fewer tables, and information is grouped into coherent business categories that make sense to users. These categories help users navigate the model because entire categories can be disregarded if they aren't relevant to a particular analysis.

Unfortunately, *as simple as possible* doesn't mean the model is necessarily simple. The model must reflect the business, and businesses are typically complex. If you simplify too much, typically by presenting only aggregated data, the model loses information that's critical to understanding the business. No matter how you model data, the intrinsic complexity of the data content is ultimately why most people will use structured reports and analytic applications to access the DW/BI system.

In the relational environment, the dimensional model helps query performance because of the denormalization involved in creating the dimensions. By pre-joining the various hierarchies and lookup tables, the optimizer considers fewer join paths and creates fewer intermediate temporary tables. Queries against the SQL Server relational database generally perform better—often far better—against a dimensional structure than against a fully normalized structure.

In the Analysis Services OLAP environment, the engine is specifically designed to support dimensional models. Performance is achieved in large part by pre-aggregating within and across dimensions.

So what is a dimensional model, anyway? A dimensional model is made up of a central fact table (or tables) and its associated dimensions. The dimensional model is also called a *star schema* because it looks like a star with the fact table in the middle and the dimensions serving as the points on the star. We stick to the term dimensional model in this book to avoid confusion.

From a relational data modeling perspective, the dimensional model consists of a normalized fact table with denormalized dimension tables. This section defines the basic components of the dimensional model, facts and dimensions, along with some of the key concepts involved in handling changes over time.

Facts

Each fact table contains the measurements associated with a specific business process, like taking an order, displaying a web page, printing a book, or handling a customer support request. A record in a fact table is a measurement, and a measurement event can always produce a fact table record. These events usually have numeric measurements that quantify the magnitude of the event, such as quantity ordered, sale amount, or call duration. These numbers are called *facts* (or *measures* in Analysis Services).

The key to the fact table is a multi-part key made up of a subset of the foreign keys from each dimension table involved in the business event.

Just the Facts

Most facts are numeric and each fact value can vary widely depending on the business process being measured. Most facts are additive (such as dollar or unit sales), meaning they can be summed up across all dimensions. Additivity is important because DW/BI applications seldom retrieve a single fact table record. User queries generally select hundreds or thousands of records at a time and add them up. A simple query for Sales by Month for the last year returns only 12 rows in the answer set, but it may sum up across hundreds of thousands of rows (or more!). Other facts are semi-additive (such as market share or account balance), and still others are non-additive (such as unit price).

Not all numeric data are facts. Exceptions include discrete descriptive information like package size or weight (describes a product) or customer age (describes a customer). Generally, these less volatile numeric values end up as descriptive attributes in dimension tables. Such descriptive information is more naturally used for constraining a query, rather than being summed in a computation. This distinction is helpful when deciding whether a data element is part of a dimension or fact.

Some business processes track events without any real measures. If the event happens, we get an entry in the source system; if not, there is no row. Common examples of this kind of event include employment activities, such as hiring and firing, and event attendance, such as when a student attends a class. The fact tables that track these events typically do not have any actual fact measurements, so they're called *factless fact tables*. Actually, we usually add a column called something like EventCount that contains the number 1. This provides users with an easy way to count the number of events by summing the EventCount fact.

Some facts are *derived* or computed from other facts, just as a Net Sale number is calculated from Gross Sales minus Sales Tax. Some semi-additive facts can be handled using a derived column that is based on the context of the query. Month End Balance would add up across accounts, but not across date, for example. The non-additive Unit Price example could be avoided by defining it as a computation done in the query, which is Total Amount divided by Total Quantity. There are several options for dealing with these derived or computed facts. You can calculate them as part of the ETL process and store them in the fact table, you can put them in the fact table view definition, or you can include them in the definition of the Analysis Services database. The only way we find unacceptable is to leave the calculation to the user.

NOTE Using Analysis Services to calculate computed measures has a significant benefit in that you can define complex MDX calculations for semi-additive facts that will automatically calculate correctly based on the context of each query request.

The Grain

The level of detail contained in the fact table is called the *grain*. We strongly urge you to build your fact tables with the lowest level of detail that is possible from the original source—generally this is known as the *atomic level*. Atomic fact tables provide complete flexibility to roll up the data to any level of summary needed across any dimension, now or in the future. You must keep each fact table at a single grain. For example, it would be confusing and dangerous to have individual sales order line items in the same fact table as the monthly forecast.

NOTE Designing your fact tables at the lowest practical level of detail, the atomic level, is a major contributor to the flexibility of the design.

Fact tables are very efficient. They are highly normalized, storing little redundant data. For most transaction-driven organizations, fact tables are also the largest tables in the data warehouse database, often making up 95 percent or more of the total relational database size.

Dimensions

Dimensions are the foundation of the dimensional model, describing the objects of the business, such as employee, subscriber, publication, customer, physician, vehicle, product, service, author, and article. The dimensions are the nouns of the DW/BI system—they describe the surrounding measurement events. The business processes (facts) are the verbs or actions of the business in which the nouns (dimensions) participate. Each dimension table links to all the business processes in which it participates. For example, the product dimension will be involved in supplier orders, inventory, shipments, and returns. A single dimension that is shared across all these processes is called a *conformed dimension*. We'll talk more about conformed dimensions in a bit.

Think about dimensions as tables in a database because that's how you'll implement them. Each table contains a list of homogeneous entities—products in a manufacturing company, patients in a hospital, vehicles on auto insurance policies, or customers in just about every organization. Usually, a dimension includes all instances of its entity—all the products the company sells, for example. There is only one active row for each particular instance in the table at any time, and each row has a set of attributes that identify, describe, define, and classify the instance. A product will have a certain size and a standard weight, and belong to a product group. These sizes and groups have descriptions, like a food product might come in Mini-Pak or Jumbo size. A vehicle is painted a certain color, like white, and has a certain option package, such as the Jungle Jim sports utility package (which includes side impact air bags, six-disc CD player, DVD system, and simulated leopard skin seats).

Some descriptive attributes in a dimension relate to each other in a *hierarchical* or one-to-many fashion. A vehicle has a manufacturer, brand, and model (such as GM Chevrolet Impala, or Toyota Lexus RX330). Most dimensions have more than one such embedded hierarchy.

It may help to think of dimensions as *things* or *objects*. A thing such as a product can exist without ever being involved in a business event. You might make a product that never sells, which is not good for business, but the point is the product can exist outside of a business process. On the other hand, a business *process* cannot occur without its associated dimensions. You can't sell a product without having a product to sell.

The underlying data structures for most relational transaction systems are designed using a technique known as *normalization*. This approach removes redundancies in the data by moving repeating attributes into their own tables. The physical process of recombining all the attributes of a business object, including its hierarchies, into a single dimension table is known to DBAs as *denormalization*. As we described earlier, this simplifies the model from a user perspective. It also makes the join paths much simpler for the database query optimizer than a fully normalized model. The denormalized dimension still presents exactly the same information and relationships found in the normalized model—nothing is lost from an analytic perspective except complexity.

You can spot dimensions or their attributes in conversation with the business folks because they are often the "by" words in a query or report request. For example, a user wants to see sales *by* month *by* product. The natural ways users describe their business should be included in the dimensional model as dimensions or dimension attributes. This is important because many of the ways users analyze the business are often not captured in the transaction system. Including these attributes in the warehouse is part of the added value you can provide.

THE POWER OF DIMENSIONS

Dimensions provide the entry points into the data. Dimensional attributes are used in two primary ways: as the target for constraints and for the labels on the rows of a report. If the dimensional attribute exists, you can constrain and label. If it doesn't exist, you simply can't.

Bringing Facts and Dimensions Together

The completed dimensional model has a characteristic appearance, with the fact table in the middle surrounded by the dimensions. Figure 2.2 shows a simple dimensional model for the classic example: the retail grocery sales business process.

This model allows users across the business to analyze retail sales activity from various perspectives. Category managers can look at sales by product for different stores and different dates. Store planners can look at sales by store format or location. Store managers can look at sales by date or cashier. While this model is reasonably robust, a large retail grocer would have a few more dimensions, customer, in particular, and many more attributes.

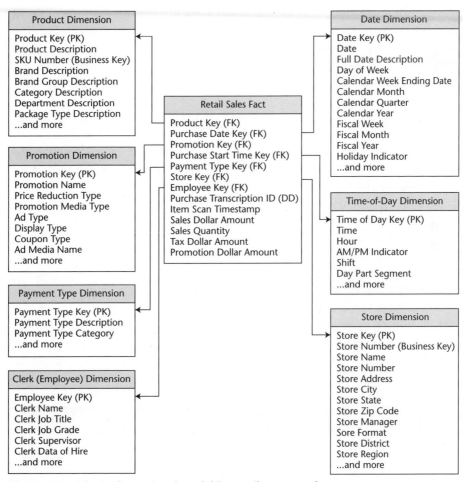

Figure 2.2   A basic dimensional model for retail grocery sales

In Figure 2.2, fields labeled PK are primary keys. In other words, these fields are the basis of uniqueness for their tables. In a dimensional model, the primary keys of dimensions are always implemented physically as single fields. The fields labeled FK are foreign keys, and must always match the corresponding PKs in the dimensions in order to ensure referential integrity. The field labeled DD is a special degenerate dimension, which is described later.

To grasp the concept of dimensions and facts, it's helpful to see examples of dimensional models from a variety of industries and business processes. The model shown in Figure 2.3 comes from *The Data Warehouse Toolkit, Second Edition* (Wiley, 2002). The business process is airline flight activity. The grain is at the flight segment/ticket level.

The dimensions have been filled out enough to give a sense of their contents. Like the retail grocery sales model, this model is valuable across the business. Route planners can look at activity by airport, logistics can look at aircraft utilization, Marketing can look at frequent flyer behavior, and flight activity by class and fare basis. Sales can assess the relative performance of the various sales channels. There is something for everyone in the airline organization in this dimensional model.

The Bus Matrix, Conformed Dimensions, and Drill Across

We spoke about the bus matrix in Chapter 1 as one of the deliverables from the enterprise requirements gathering process. Because it's the starting point for the dimensional modeling process, we revisit the concept here. The idea of re-using dimensions across multiple business processes is the foundation of the enterprise DW/BI system and the heart of the Enterprise Data Warehouse Bus Matrix concept. In the retail grocery example, a dimension such as product will be used in both the retail sales and the store inventory dimensional models. Because they are exactly the same products, both models must use the same dimension with the same keys to reliably support true, cross-business process analysis. If the logistics folks at the grocer's headquarters want to calculate inventory turns, they'll sum the total sales quantity by product from retail sales, sum the inventory quantity at the end of the period by product from store inventory, and divide the two to get inventory turns by product. This works only if the two business processes use the exact same product dimension with the same keys; that is, they use a *conformed* dimension. Conformed dimensions are the cornerstone of the enterprise-enabled DW/BI system. This kind of analysis involving data from more than one business process is called *drill-across*.

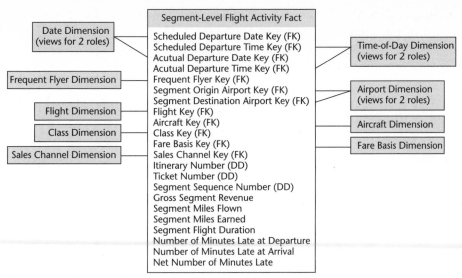

Figure 2.3   Segment-level flight activity dimensional model

NOTE The precise technical definition of conformed dimensions is that two dimensions are conformed if they contain one or more fields with the same names and contents. These "conformed fields" must then be used as the basis for the drill-across operation.

Note that this idea of drilling across multiple fact tables and combining the answer sets requires a front-end tool capable of supporting this function. A powerful reason to use Analysis Services is that conformed dimensions are part of the system architecture, so its calculation engine smoothly supports drill-across.

Examine the Adventure Works Cycles high-level bus matrix shown in Figure 2.4. Each row of the bus matrix represents a business process and defines at least one fact table and its associated dimensions. Often, a row in the matrix will result in several related fact tables that help track the business process from different perspectives. The Orders business process might have an orders transaction fact table at the line-item level and an orders snapshot fact table at the order level. Both of these orders-based dimensional models belong to the Orders business process. We call this grouping a *business process dimensional model*. The fully populated enterprise DW/BI system contains sets of dimensional models that describe all the business processes in an organization's value chain. As you create the business process dimensional models for each row in the bus matrix, you end up with a much more detailed version of the matrix. Each dimensional model has its own row grouped by business process. Order Transactions and Order Snapshot would be separate rows under the Orders business process.

Adventure Works Data Warehouse Bus Matrix — Business Process	Business Priority	Date (Order, Start, Ship)	Product	Promotion	End Customer	Employee	Reseller	Page	Internet Registered User	Part	Vendor	Shipper	Problem	Account	Department	Currency (Source, Dest.)	Benefits Plan
Advertising																	
TV		x	x	x													
Print		x	x	x													
Online		x	x	x	x												
Promotions		x	x	x	x		x										
Co-op programs		x	x	x		x	x										
Web Site Marketing		x	x	x	x			x	x								
PR		x	x	x													
Orders Forecasting	2	x	x	x		x	x										
Reseller Orders	1	x	x	x		x	x										
Internet Orders	1	x	x	x	x			x	x								
Purchasing		x	x		x	x				x	x	x					
Parts Inventory		x	x	x						x	x						
Manufacturing	6	x	x							x							
Finished Goods Inv.		x	x	x													
Shipping		x	x	x	x	x	x					x					
Returns	5	x	x		x	x	x					x					
Registration cards		x	x		x												
Customer Calls	4	x	x	x	x	x	x			x			x				
Web Support		x	x		x	x	x	x	x				x				
Financial Forecasting		x	x	x	x	x	x				x			x	x		
Exchange Rate Mgmt.	3	x														x	
GL-Revenue & Expense		x												x	x		
Cost Accounting		x	x											x	x		
Payroll		x			x										x		
Benefits Enrollment		x			x												x

Figure 2.4   Adventure Works Cycles high-level enterprise bus matrix

The bus matrix is the enterprise business intelligence data roadmap. Creating the bus matrix is mandatory for any enterprise-wide DW/BI effort. Getting enterprise agreement on conformed dimensions is an organizational challenge for the data modeler and data steward. Having a single dimension table to describe the company's products, customers, or facilities means the organization has to agree on how each dimension table is defined. This includes the list of attributes, attribute names, hierarchies, and the business rules needed to define and derive each attribute in the table. This is politically hard work, and the effort grows as a function of the number of employees and divisions. But it is not optional. Conformed dimensions ensure that you are comparing apples to apples (assuming you are selling apples).

REFERENCE *The Data Warehouse Toolkit, Second Edition* (Wiley, 2002) has more information and examples on dimensions, facts, conformed dimensions, and the bus matrix, along with example dimensional models from many different industries and business processes, including retail sales, inventory, procurement, order management, CRM, accounting, HR, financial services, telecommunications and utilities, transportation, education, health care, e-commerce, and insurance. We include references to specific pages for the concepts and techniques in the following section.

Additional Design Concepts and Techniques

Even though the dimensional modeling concepts we've described are fairly simple, they are applicable to a wide range of business scenarios. However, there are a few additional dimensional modeling concepts and techniques that are critical to implementing viable dimensional models. We start this section with a couple of key concepts: surrogate keys and slowly changing dimensions. Then we look at several techniques for modeling more complex business situations. Finally, we review the different types of fact tables. We briefly describe each concept or technique and provide references so you can find more detailed information if you need it.

Surrogate Keys

For your DW/BI system, you will need to create a whole new set of keys in the data warehouse database, separate from the keys in the transaction source systems. We call these keys *surrogate keys*, although they are also known as meaningless keys, substitute keys, non-natural keys, or artificial keys. A surrogate key is a unique value, usually an integer, assigned to each row in the dimension. This surrogate key becomes the primary key of the dimension table and is used to join the dimension to the associated foreign key field in the fact table. Using surrogate keys in all dimension tables reaps the following benefits (and more):

- Surrogate keys protect the DW/BI system from changes in the source system. For example, a migration to a new software package will likely create a new set of business keys in the transaction system.

- Surrogate keys allow the DW/BI system to integrate data from multiple source systems. Different source systems might keep data on the same customers or products, but with different keys. (Some of you might be shocked to hear that the same customer can be issued more than one customer ID, but it does happen.)

- Surrogate keys enable you to add rows to dimensions that do not exist in the source system. For example, there may be order transactions that come to the warehouse without an assigned sales rep. You can replace the NULL sales rep value in the fact table row with a surrogate key from the sales rep dimension that points to a row with the description of "Sales Rep not yet assigned."

■ Surrogate keys provide the means for tracking changes in dimension attributes over time. Generally, keeping track of history requires that you add new rows to the dimension table when an attribute changes. This means there will be multiple rows in the dimension with the same source system transaction key. The surrogate key provides the unique key for each row. We discuss attribute change tracking in an upcoming section on slowly changing dimensions (SCDs).

■ Integer surrogate keys are an efficient key in the relational database and Analysis Services. Using them improves query and processing performance, and because of their compactness, substantially reduces the size of the fact tables in the relational database.

The ability to track changes in dimension attributes over time is reason enough to implement surrogate keys. We've regretted it more than once when we decided not to track changes in attribute values over time, and later found out the historical values were important to support certain business analyses. We had to go back and add surrogate keys and re-create the dimension's change history. This is not a fun project; we encourage you to do it right the first time. If you use surrogate keys for all dimensions at the outset, it's much easier to change a dimension so that it tracks history.

NOTE The *date dimension* deviates slightly from the rules by using a surrogate key based on the date rather than a completely meaningless key. We discuss this further in the upcoming section on the date dimension.

The biggest cost of using surrogate keys is the burden it places on the ETL system. First you need to assign the surrogate keys to the dimension rows, and then you need to substitute the surrogate keys from the dimensions for the transaction system keys in the fact table rows. An extract for a fact table row generally is a list of transaction system keys and facts. We call the transaction system key the *business* (or *natural*) key, although it is usually not business-like. Because the dimension tables are accessed by surrogate keys, the fact table rows will not join to the dimensions until the business keys are replaced by surrogate keys. The ETL process uses each business key in the fact table extract to look up the current associated surrogate key for every dimension linked to the fact table. In other words, when you load fact table rows, you need to look up the source system key in each dimension table and substitute the corresponding surrogate key in what we call the surrogate key pipeline. Integration Services will help you with this work, as we describe in Chapter 6.

REFERENCE The following resources offer additional information about surrogate keys:

- *The Data Warehouse Toolkit, Second Edition* (Wiley, 2002), pp. 58–62.

- The MSDN Library for Visual Studio 2005: Search for a topic called "Dimension Tables" under the main topic "Creating a Data Warehouse."

Slowly Changing Dimensions

Although we like to think of the attribute values in a dimension to be fixed, it turns out that some change over time. In an employee dimension, the date of birth should not change over time (other than error corrections, which your ETL system should expect). However, other fields, such as the employee's department might change several times over the length of a person's employment. Many of these changes are critical to understanding the dynamics of the business. The ability to track these changes over time is one of the fundamental reasons for the existence of the DW/BI system.

If the value of an attribute can change, you need to be prepared to deal with that change. We call dimensions that have changeable attribute values *slowly changing dimensions* (SCDs). However, just because something changes, it doesn't mean that change has significance to the business. The choice of which dimensions and attributes you need to track and how you track them is a business decision. The most common techniques to deal with changes the business doesn't care about and changes the business wants to track respectively are called Type 1 and Type 2 slowly changing dimensions. Most of the popular ETL tools, including Integration Services, have these techniques built-in.

HOW SLOW IS SLOW?

We call this concept a *slowly* changing dimension because the attributes that describe a business entity generally don't change very often. Take customer address, for example. According to the US Census Bureau (www.census.gov/population/www/pop-profile/geomob.html), 16.8 percent of Americans move in a given year, and 62 percent of these moves are within the same county. If a change in zip code is considered to be a significant business event, a simple Customer dimension with name and address information should generate less than 16.8 percent change rows per year. If an attribute changes rapidly, causing the dimension to grow at a dramatic rate, this usually indicates the presence of a business process that should be tracked separately, either as a separate dimension or as a fact table rather than as a dimension attribute.

A Type 1 SCD overwrites the existing attribute value with the new value. Use this method if you don't care about keeping track of historical values when the value of an attribute changes. The Type 1 change does not preserve the attribute value that was in place at the time a historical transaction occurred.

If you need to track the history of attribute changes, use a Type 2 SCD. Type 2 change tracking is a powerful technique for capturing the attribute values that were in effect at a point in time and relating them to the business events in which they participated. When a change to a Type 2 attribute occurs, the ETL process creates a new row in the dimension table to capture the new values of the changed item. The attributes in the new row are in effect as of the time of the change moving forward. The attributes in the previously existing row are marked to show they were in effect right up until the appearance of the new row.

> **NOTE** A third change tracking technique, called Type 3, keeps separate columns for both the old and new attribute values—sometimes called "alternate realities." In our experience, Type 3 is less common because it involves changing the physical tables and is not very scalable.

The best way to understand the concepts of Type 1 and Type 2 change tracking, and the substantial impact of accurately tracking changes, is with an example. As we'll see in the case study, Adventure Works Cycles collects demographic information from its Internet customers. These attributes, such as gender, homeowner status, education, and commute distance, all go into the customer dimension. Many of these attributes will change over time. If a customer moves, her commute distance will change. If a customer bought a bike when he went to college, his education status will change when he graduates. These attributes all certainly qualify as slowly changing, but should you treat them as Type 1 or Type 2 attributes?

If you've been paying attention, you know the correct answer is to ask the business users how they'll use this information. You already know from the requirements gathering information in Chapter 1 that Marketing intends to use some data mining techniques to look for demographic attributes that predict buying behaviors. In particular, they want to know if certain attributes are predictive of higher-than-average buying. They could use those attributes to create targeted marketing campaigns. Let's examine some example customer-level data to see how decisions on handling attribute changes can affect the information you provide your users.

Table 2.1 shows the row in the customer dimension for a customer named Jane Rider as of January 1, 2006. Notice that the customer dimension includes the natural key from the transaction system along with the attributes that describe Jane Rider. The natural key allows users to tie back to the transaction system if need be.

Table 2.2 shows some example rows from an abridged version of the AWC Orders fact table in the data warehouse database. We have used surrogate keys for customer and product, but we left the order date as a date for the sake of clarity. These rows show all of Jane Rider's AWC orders.

A marketing analyst might want to look at these two tables together, across all customers, to see if any of the customer attributes predict behavior. For example, one might hypothesize that people with short commute distances are more likely to buy nice bikes and accessories than people with long commute distances. They might ride their bikes to work rather than drive.

Overwriting Values: The Type 1 Change

A few additional details help demonstrate the importance of appropriately handling attribute changes. To the untrained eye, attributes such as commute distance and homeowner flag might not seem important to the business, so you might treat them as Type 1 attributes and overwrite the existing values when changes occur. As it turns out, Jane took advantage of low mortgage interest rates and moved into a new home on January 2, 2006, changing her commute distance to 31 miles. If you do a Type 1 overwrite, Jane's commute distance value in Table 2.4 will change to 31, and her homeowner flag will change to Yes.

The timing of the attribute change events is important to understanding their impact on the analysis. If the marketing analyst decided to investigate the relationship between commute distance and orders on March 1, 2006, after the overwrite took place, all of Jane Rider's orders would be counted as occurring with a commute distance of 31 miles. By overwriting commute distance when a change occurs, you're no longer tracking the actual commute distance that was in effect at the time the order was placed. Instead, you're assigning all historical orders to the current attribute value. This means that any time your analysts try to do historical correlation analysis, they risk drawing incorrect conclusions.

Does this matter? Only the business users can say. If there aren't a significant number of rows that change, or if the attribute is not considered relevant, it probably doesn't matter if you overwrite the old value when a change occurs. However, you must be extremely careful in making this decision—it requires detailed exploration of the potential impact with knowledgeable business folks.

The short answer is it usually does matter. In the example case, the analyst may find a significant correlation between long commute distances and larger orders. This finding might then be used to design a marketing campaign targeted at people with long commute distances; a campaign that will likely be ineffective. In this case, the errors introduced by the Type 1 overwrite mainly costs money and time. In some cases, as in health care, overwriting attribute values might cost even more.

Tracking Historical Values—the Type 2 Change

Let's see how the same example data looks if you tracked the changes using the Type 2 approach. This will affect both the fact and dimension tables. Let's consider the dimension table first: When Jane Rider moves on January 2, 2006, add a new row to the customer dimension, with a new surrogate key, as shown in Table 2.3.

The customer dimension table has been augmented to help manage the Type 2 process. Two columns have been added to indicate the effective date and end date of each row. This is how you can tell exactly which row was in effect at any given time.

As Table 2.4 shows, the fact table has to change as well because it has a row that occurred after the Type 2 change occurred. The last row of the fact table needs to join to the row in the dimension that was in effect when the order occurred on February 22, 2006. This is the new dimension row with customer_key = 2387.

The correct assignment of dimension keys to fact table rows is handled as a matter of course in the ETL process. Integration Services even has a wizard to define this process. We have to go back and update the fact table in our example because we didn't start with Type 2 attributes in the first place. It would have been much better if we had designed the customer dimension as a Type 2 SCD originally. This should give you a feel for what you will have to do if you don't use Type 2 change tracking as well.

Now when the marketing analyst does the analysis, the data will show $2,276.20 in orders associated with a 3-mile commute distance and $19.95 associated with a 31-mile commute distance. The way to decide whether to track attribute changes as Type 1 or Type 2 is to ask, "Does it matter?" From the marketing analyst's perspective in this example, accurately tracking changes over time obviously matters a lot.

REFERENCE The following resources offer additional information about slowly changing dimensions:

- *The Data Warehouse Toolkit, Second Edition* (Wiley, 2002), pp. 95–105.

- Books Online: Search for the topic "Changing Dimension Support (SSAS)."

Table 2.1 Example Customer Dimension Table Row as of Jan 1, 2006

CUSTOMER_KEY	BKCUSTOMER_ID	CUSTOMER_NAME	COMMUTE_DISTANCE	GENDER	HOME_OWNER_FLAG
1552	31421	Jane Rider	3	Female	No

Table 2.2 Example Order Fact Table Rows for Jane Rider as of Feb 22, 2006

DATE	CUSTOMER_KEY	PRODUCT_KEY	ITEM_COUNT	DOLLAR_AMOUNT
1/7/2004	1552	95	1	1,798.00
3/2/2004	1552	37	1	27.95
5/7/2005	1552	87	2	320.26
8/21/2005	1552	33	2	129.99
2/21/2006	1552	42	1	19.95

Table 2.3 Example Customer Dimension Table Row as of Jan 2, 2006 with a Type 2 Change

CUSTOMER_KEY	BKCUSTOMER_ID	CUSTOMER_NAME	COMMUTE_DISTANCE	GENDER	HOME_OWNER_FLAG	EFF_DATE	END_DATE
1552	31421	Jane Rider	3	Female	No	1/7/2004	1/1/2006
2387	31421	Jane Rider	31	Female	Yes	1/2/2006	12/31/9999

Table 2.4 Updated Order Fact Table Rows for Jane Rider as of Feb 22, 2006

DATE	CUSTOMER_KEY	PRODUCT_KEY	ITEM_COUNT	DOLLAR_AMOUNT
1/7/2004	1552	95	1	1,798.00
3/2/2004	1552	37	1	27.95
5/7/2005	1552	87	2	320.26
8/21/2005	1552	33	2	129.99
2/21/2006	2387	42	1	19.95

Dates

Date is the fundamental business dimension across all organizations and industries, although many times a date table doesn't exist in the operational environment. Analyses that trend across dates or make comparisons between periods (that is, nearly all business analyses) are best supported by creating and maintaining a robust Date dimension table.

Every dimensional DW/BI system has a Date (or Calendar) dimension, typically with one row for every day for which you expect to have data in a fact table. Calling it the Date dimension emphasizes that its grain is at the day level rather than time of day. In other words, the Date table will have 365 or 366 rows in it per year.

> **NOTE** The Date dimension is a good example of a *role-playing* dimension. It is common for a Date dimension to be used to represent different dates, such as order date, due date, and ship date. To support users who will be directly accessing the relational database, you can either define a synonym on the view of the Date dimension for each role, or define multiple views. The synonym approach is simple, but it allows you to rename the entire table only, not the columns within the table. Reports that can't distinguish between order date and due date can be confusing.
>
> If your users will access the data through Analysis Services only, you don't need to bother with views or synonyms to handle multiple roles. Analysis Services understands the concept of role-playing dimensions.

Earlier in this section we said that all dimensions should use surrogate keys and we emphasized the importance of surrogate keys in tracking attribute changes. We recommend surrogate keys for the Date dimension, even though Date is unlikely to have attributes that require Type 2 change tracking, nor will it face interesting integration challenges from multiple systems—two of the key arguments for using surrogate keys for other dimensions.

Use a surrogate key for Date because of the classic problem often faced by technical people: Sometimes you don't have a date. While we can't help the technical people here, we can say that transactions often arrive at the data warehouse database without a date because the value in the source system is missing, unknowable, or the event hasn't happened yet. Surrogate keys on the Date dimension help manage the problem of missing dates. Create a few rows in the Date dimension that describe such events, and assign the appropriate surrogate date key to the fact rows with the missing dates.

In the absence of a surrogate date key, you will probably end up creating Date dimension members with strange dates such as 1-Jan-1900 to mean *Unknown* and 31-Dec-2079 to mean *Hasn't happened yet*. Overloading the fact dates in this way isn't the end of the world, but it can confuse users and cause erroneous results. Besides, it's pretty hokey.

The Date dimension surrogate key has one slight deviation from the rule. Where other surrogate keys are usually a meaningless sequence of integers, it's a good idea to use a meaningful value for the Date surrogate key. Specifically, use an integer that corresponds to the date in year-month-day order, so September 22, 2005 would be 20050922. This can lead to more efficient queries against the relational database. It also makes implementing date-based partitioning much easier, and the partition management function will be more understandable.

Just to prove that we're not entirely dogmatic and inflexible, we don't always use surrogate keys for dates that appear as dimension attributes. Generally, if a particular date attribute has business meaning, we use the Date surrogate key. Otherwise we use a smalldatetime data type. One way to spot a good candidate for a Date surrogate key is if the attribute's date values fall within the date range of the organizational calendar, and therefore are all in the Date table.

REFERENCE The following resources offer additional information about the date dimension:

- *The Data Warehouse Toolkit, Second Edition* (Wiley, 2002), pp. 38–41.

- Books Online: Search for the topic "Time Dimensions (SSAS)" and related topics.

Degenerate Dimensions

Transaction identifiers often end up as degenerate dimensions without joining to an actual dimension table. In the retail grocery example, all the individual items you purchase in a trip through the checkout line are assigned a transaction ID. The transaction ID is not a dimension—it does not exist outside the transaction and it has no descriptive attributes of its own as they've already been handled in separate dimensions. It's not a fact—it does not measure the event in any way and is not additive. We call attributes such as transaction ID a *degenerate dimension* because it's like a dimension without attributes. And because there are no associated attributes, there is no dimension table. We include it in the fact table because it serves a purpose from an analytic perspective. For example, you can use it to tie all the line items in a market basket together to do some interesting data mining, as we discuss in Chapter 10. It can tie back to the transaction system if additional orders-related data is needed.

Snowflaking

In simple terms, snowflaking is the practice of connecting lookup tables to fields in the dimension tables. At the extreme, snowflaking involves re-normalizing the dimensions to the third normal form level, usually under the misguided belief that this will improve maintainability, increase flexibility, or save space. We discourage snowflaking. It makes the model more complex and therefore less usable, and it actually makes it more difficult to maintain, especially for Type 2 slowly changing dimensions.

In a few cases we support the idea of connecting lookup or grouping tables to the dimensions. One of these cases involves rarely used lookups, as in the example of joining the Date table to the DateOfBirth field in the Customer dimension so we can count customers grouped by their month of birth. We call this purpose-specific snowflake table an *outrigger* table. You will see several examples of outrigger tables in the following sections and in the Adventure Works Cycles example. When you're building your Analysis Services database, you'll see this same concept referred to as a *reference dimension*.

Sometimes it's easier to maintain a dimension in the ETL process when it's been partially normalized or snowflaked. This is especially true if the source data is a mess and you're trying to ensure the dimension hierarchy is correctly structured. In this case, there's nothing wrong with using the normalized structure in the ETL application. Just make sure the business users never have to deal with it.

> **NOTE** Analysis Services 2000 had a slight preference for normalized dimension hierarchies for complex models. Analysis Services 2005 really doesn't care. If anything, the preference tilts slightly to the denormalized star structure. In either case, it's completely hidden from business users, which is the important thing.

REFERENCE The following resources offer additional information about snowflaking:

- *The Data Warehouse Toolkit, Second Edition* (Wiley, 2002), pp. 55–57.

- Books Online: Search for the topic "Dimension Structure (SSAS)" and other Books Online topics.

Many-to-Many or Multivalued Dimensions

The standard relationship between a dimension table and fact table is called *one-to-many*. This means one row in the dimension table will join to many rows in the fact table, but one row on the fact table will join to only one row in the dimension table. This relationship is important because it keeps us from double counting. Fortunately, in most cases this relationship holds true.

There are two common instances where the real world is more complex than one-to-many:

- Many-to-many between the fact table and a dimension
- Many-to-many between dimensions

In both cases, we introduce an intermediate table called a *bridge table* that supports the more complex many-to-many relationship.

Many-to-Many Between a Fact and Dimension

A many-to-many relationship between a fact table and a dimension occurs when multiple dimension values can be assigned to a single fact transaction. A common example is when multiple sales people can be assigned to a given sale. This often happens in complex, big-ticket sales such as computer systems. Accurately handling this situation requires creating a bridge table that assembles the sales rep combinations into groups. Figure 2.5 shows an example of the sales rep group bridge table.

The ETL process needs to look up the appropriate sales rep group key in the bridge table for the combination of sales reps in each incoming fact table record, and add a new group if it doesn't exist. Note that the bridge table in Figure 2.5 introduces a risk of double counting. If we sum Dollar Sales by Sales Rep, every sales rep will get credit for the total sale. For some analyses, this is the right answer, but for others you don't want any double counting. It's possible to handle this risk by adding a weighting factor column in the bridge table. The weighting factor is a fractional value that sums to one for each sales rep group. Multiply the weighting factor and the additive facts to allocate the facts according to the contribution of each individual in the group.

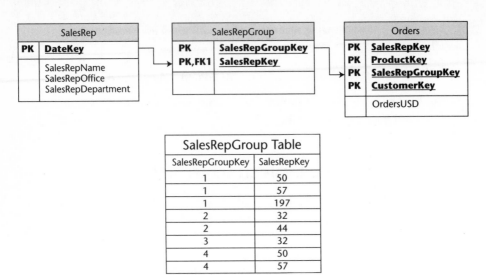

Figure 2.5 An example Sales Rep Group bridge table

Many-to-Many Between Dimensions

The many-to-many relationship between dimensions is an important concept from an analytic point of view. Most dimensions are not entirely independent of one another. Dimension independence is really more of a continuum than a binary state. At one end of the continuum, the store and product dimensions in a retail grocery chain are relatively independent, but not entirely. Some store formats don't carry certain products. Other dimensions are much more closely related, but are difficult to combine into a single dimension because of their many-to-many relationship. In banking, for example, there is a direct relationship between account and customer, but it is not one-to-one. Any given account can have one or more customers as signatories, and any given customer can have one or more accounts. Banks often view their data from an account perspective; the MonthAccountSnapshot is a common fact table in financial institutions. The account focus makes it difficult to view accounts by customer because of the many-to-many relationship. One approach would be to create a CustomerGroup bridge table that joins to the fact table, such as the SaleRepGroup table in the previous many-to-many example. A better approach takes advantage of the relationship between Account and Customer, as shown in Figure 2.6.

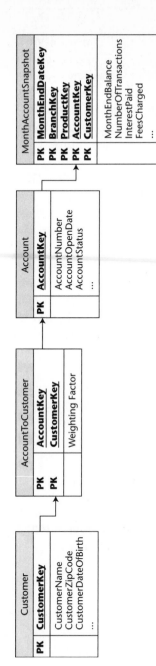

Figure 2.6 An example many-to-many bridge table between dimensions

An AccountToCustomer bridge table between the Account and Customer dimensions can capture the many-to-many relationship with a couple of significant benefits. First, the relationship is already known in the source system, so creating the bridge table will be easier than the manual build process required for the SalesRepGroup table. Second, the Account-Customer relationship is interesting in its own right. The AccountToCustomer bridge table allows users to answer questions such as "What is the average number of accounts per customer?" without joining to any fact table.

Bridge tables are often an indicator of an underlying business process. This is especially true if you must keep track of changes to bridge tables over time (that is, the relationship itself is Type 2). For customers and accounts, the business process might be called account maintenance, and one of the transactions might be called "Add a signatory." If three customers were associated with an account, there would be three Add transactions for that account in the source system. Usually these transactions and the business processes they represent are not important enough to track in the DW/BI system with their own fact tables. However, the relationships and changes they produce are important to analyzing the business. We include them in the dimensional model as slowly changing dimensions, and in some cases as bridge tables.

NOTE Analysis Services 2005 has new functionality to support many-to-many dimensions. Analysis Services expects exactly the same kind of structure that we described in this section. They call the bridge table an *intermediate fact table*, which is exactly what it is.

REFERENCE The following resources offer additional information about many-to-many relationships:

- *The Data Warehouse Toolkit, Second Edition* (Wiley, 2002), pp. 262–265 for many-to-many between fact and dimension and pp. 205–206 for many-to-many between dimensions.

- Books Online: Search for the topic "Many-to-Many Dimension Relationships (SSAS)" and other Books Online topics.

Hierarchies

Hierarchies are meaningful, standard ways to group the data within a dimension so you can begin with the big picture and drill down to lower levels to investigate anomalies. Hierarchies are the main paths for summarizing the data. Common hierarchies include organizational hierarchies, often starting from the individual person level; geographic hierarchies based on physical location, such as a customer address; product hierarchies that often correspond to merchandise rollups such as brand and category; and responsibility hierarchies such as sales territory that assign customers to sales reps (or vice versa). There are many industry-related hierarchies, such as the North American Industrial Classification System (replacement for the Standard Industrial Classification [SIC] code) or the World Health Organization's International Classification of Diseases—Tenth Modification (ICD-10).

Simple hierarchies involving a standard one-to-many rollup with only a few levels should be denormalized right into the granular dimension. A four-level product hierarchy might start with product, which rolls up to brand, then to subcategory, and finally to category. Each of these levels would simply be columns in the product dimension table. In fact, this flattening of hierarchies is one of the main design tasks of creating a dimension table. Many organizations will have several different hierarchies in a given dimension to support different analytic requirements.

Of course, not all hierarchies are this simple. The challenge for the dimensional modeler is to determine how to balance the tradeoff between ease of use and flexibility in representing the more difficult hierarchies. There are at least two common hierarchy challenges: variable-depth (or ragged hierarchies) and frequently changing hierarchies. Both of these problems require more complex solutions than simple denormalization. We will briefly describe these solutions here, and refer you to more detailed information in the other *Toolkit* books if you should need it.

Variable-Depth Hierarchies

A good example of the variable-depth hierarchy is the manufacturing bill of materials that provides the information needed to build a particular product. In this case, parts can go into products or into intermediate layers, called subassemblies, which then go into products, also called *top assemblies*. This layering can go dozens of levels deep, or more, in a complex product (think about a Boeing 7E7).

Those of you who were computer science majors may recall writing recursive subroutines and appreciate the efficiency of recursion for parsing a parent-child or self-referencing table. In SQL, this recursive structure is implemented by simply including a parent key field in the child record that points back to the parent record in the same table. For example, one of the fields in an Employee table would be the Parent Employee Key (or Manager Key).

RECURSIVE CAPABILITIES

SQL 99 introduced recursion into the "official" SQL language using the `WITH` Common Table Expression syntax. All the major relational database products provide this functionality in some form, including SQL Server 2005. Unfortunately, recursion isn't a great solution in the relational environment because it requires more complex SQL than most front end tools can handle. Even if the tool can recursively unpack the self-referencing dimension relationship, it then must be able to join the resulting dataset to the fact table. Very few of the query tools are able to generate the SQL required to navigate a parent-child relationship together with a dimension-fact join.

On the other hand, this kind of recursive relationship is easy to build and manage in the Analysis Services dimensional database. Analysis Services uses different terminology: *parent-child* rather than variable-depth hierarchies.

The Data Warehouse Toolkit, Second Edition describes a navigation bridge table in Chapter 6 that solves this problem in the relational world. But this solution is relatively unwieldy to manage and query. Fortunately, we have some powerful alternatives in SQL Server 2005. Analysis Services has a built-in understanding of the parent-child data structure, and Reporting Services can handle the parent-child hierarchy in the front-end tool. If you have variable-depth hierarchies and expect to use the relational database for reporting and analysis, it makes sense to include both the parent-child fields and the navigation bridge table to meet the needs of various environments.

Frequently Changing Hierarchies

If you need to track changes in the variable-depth hierarchy over time, your problem becomes more complex, especially with the parent-child data structure. Tracking changes, as you recall, requires using a surrogate key. If someone is promoted, they will get a new row in the table with a new surrogate key. At that point, everyone who reports to that person will have to have their ManagerKey updated. If ManagerKey is a Type 2 attribute, new rows with new surrogate keys will now need to be generated for these rows. If there are any folks who report to these people, the changes must ripple down until we reach the bottom of the org chart. In the worst case, a change to one of the CEO's attributes, such as marital status, causes the CEO to get a new surrogate key. This means the people who report to the CEO will get new surrogate keys, and so on down the entire hierarchy.

Ultimately, this problem is really about tracking the human resources business process. That is, if keeping track of all the changes that take place in your employee database is a high priority from an analytic point of view, you need to create a fact table, or a set of fact tables that track these events. Trying to cram all this event-based information into a Type 2 dimension just doesn't work very well.

REFERENCE The following resources offer additional information about hierarchies:

- *The Data Warehouse Toolkit, Second Edition* (Wiley, 2002), pp. 161–168.

- *The Data Warehouse Lifecycle Toolkit* (Wiley, 1998), pp. 226–237.

- Books Online: Search for the topic "Hierarchies" (search key words: Attribute Hierarchies).

Heterogeneous Products

Many organizations have several product lines or lines of business that share only a few high-level attributes. In banking, for example, the mortgage products have very different attributes from the checking products. The challenge here is designing a solution that allows business folks to analyze the entire organization across lines of business and go into the details of any given line of business. To accomplish this, you need to create two different forms of the fact table, one that has shared facts for all products across all lines of business and another that has all facts, including product-specific and shared facts. Create one of these product-specific fact tables for each line of business. The same is true for the product dimensions—split the product dimension into a core product dimension table that contains only the shared attributes and as many custom product dimension tables as are needed, each with its own specific, extended attribute list. The core product dimension has a row in it for every product across the entire business. The custom product dimensions share the same surrogate keys, but have only as many rows as there are products in each product line.

It is possible to put all unrelated attributes into a single product table, but it becomes difficult for users to understand because all of the product line–specific attributes are empty for products where they don't apply. Only one out of five rows will have values for a given column in a combined product table for an organization with five different lines of business. The product table can get excessively wide because each product line has a full set of attributes to define its products. The same is true for a combined fact table. Most of the lines of business will have facts specific to their own business processes that will need to be added onto the core fact table. These will also be empty (zero) for all products where they don't apply. In a complex business, the best compromise is to create a family of business process dimensional models with core fact and product tables and a set of fact and product tables specific to each line of business.

NOTE There are no magic features in Analysis Services that solve the heterogeneous dimension problem. It works about as well as it does in a purely relational deployment. Analysis Services does simplify navigation between the multiple fact tables in the family of business process dimensional models.

REFERENCE The following resources offer additional information about heterogeneous product models:

- *The Data Warehouse Toolkit, Second Edition* (Wiley, 2002), pp. 210–215.

- The kimballgroup.com: Search for the topic Heterogeneous Products for an article on an insurance business heterogeneous product dimensional model.

Aggregate Dimensions

You will often have data in the DW/BI system at different levels of granularity. Sometimes it comes to you that way, as with forecast data that is created at a level higher than the individual product. Other times you create it yourself to give the users better query performance. There are two ways to aggregate data in the warehouse, one by entirely removing a dimension, the other by rolling up in a dimension's hierarchy. When we aggregate using the hierarchy rollup, we need to provide a new, shrunken dimension at this aggregate level. Figure 2.7 shows how the Adventure Works Cycles Product table can be shrunken to the Subcategory level to allow it to join to forecast data that is created at the Subcategory level.

Each subcategory includes a mix of color, size, and weight attributes, for example. Therefore, most of the columns in the Product table do not make sense at the Subcategory level. This results in a much shorter dimension, hence the common term *shrunken dimension*.

The keys for aggregate dimensions need to be generated in the ETL process and are not derived from the base tables. Records can be added or subtracted from the base table over time and thus there is no guarantee that a key from the base table can be used in the aggregate dimension.

NOTE The Analysis Services OLAP engine automatically manages all this behind the scene. This is one of the reasons why Analysis Services is helpful.

Previous versions of Analysis Services required that you pre-build the aggregate dimensions in the relational database. Analysis Services 2005 has removed that requirement: You can easily hook in a fact table at any level of a dimension. Of course you may still need aggregate dimensions to support business process metrics (such as forecast), which live at the aggregate level only.

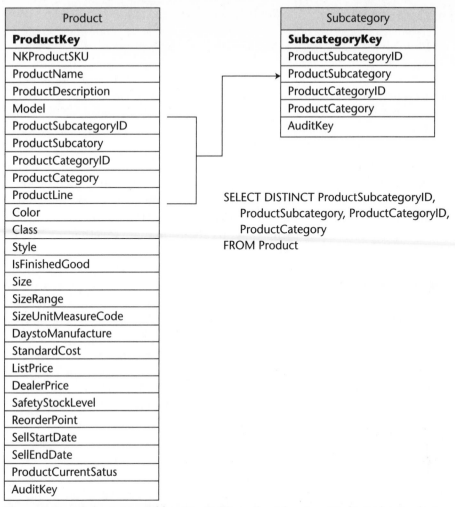

Figure 2.7   A Subcategory table extracted from the Adventure Works Cycles Product
              dimension table

REFERENCE The following resources offer additional information about
heterogeneous product models:

- *The Data Warehouse Toolkit, Second Edition* (Wiley, 2002), pp. 154–157
  for information about building minidimensions.

- The kimballgroup.com: Search for the topic Shrunken Dimensions for
  an article on aggregate dimensions.

Junk Dimensions

It's common to end the initial design pass with a handful of miscellaneous attributes that don't belong to any existing dimension. These are typically flags or indicators that describe or categorize the transaction in some way. They're usually low cardinality, with a dozen distinct values or less. Even though the name is a bit disrespectful, the contents of the *junk dimension* are often important. (We've also called them *miscellaneous* or *mystery dimensions* in previous writings.)

There are four alternatives for dealing with these extra attributes, and the first three don't count. You can leave them in the fact table, significantly expanding the fact table. You can create a separate dimension for each attribute, cluttering up the model with many new dimensions. You can omit these attributes and hope no one misses them. Or, you can group them together in a single junk dimension. This is obviously our preferred alternative.

With a little additional information, the grocery store data model shown in Figure 2.2 could be expanded to include a junk dimension. Many transaction systems have multiple transaction types as part of the same business process. Generally, 99 percent or more of the transactions fall into one transaction type; in the grocery business, the receipt would be the "Regular Sale" transaction. There also might be a "No Sale" transaction that allows the clerk to open the drawer to make change and a "Refund" transaction. If you recall, the Payment Type dimension already included in the model is a similar, low cardinality dimension. It has a handful of distinct values, such as "Cash," "Check," "Credit," or "Debit." You could combine these two dimensions into a single junk dimension. The name of the dimension needs to be generic enough to include all of its contents, so something like RetailTransactionInfo might work.

This example TransactionInfo dimension would have two columns, TransactionType and PaymentType. Figure 2.8 shows what the dimension and its contents might look like. You need to include all the combinations of TransactionType and PaymentType that occur in the fact table. Here, we listed three transaction types and four payment types. In the worst case, the total number of rows would be a Cartesian product of the cardinality of each column—implemented as a CROSS JOIN in T-SQL or the Crossjoin function (or "*" operator) in MDX. For our example, this would be $3 \times 4 = 12$ rows—these are the 12 rows shown in Figure 2.8. This is easy enough to build once and use forever, or at least until another value shows up. The ETL process will need to watch for new values and handle them appropriately by adding into the table.

DimTransactionInfo	
PK	**TransactionInfoKey**
	TransactionType PaymentType

TransactionInfo Dimension		
TransactionInfoKey	TransactionType	PaymentType
1	Regular Sale	Cash
2	Regular Sale	Check
3	Regular Sale	Credit
4	Regular Sale	Debit
5	Refund	Cash
6	Refund	Check
7	Refund	Credit
8	Refund	Debit
9	No Sale	Cash
10	No Sale	Check
11	No Sale	Credit
12	No Sale	Debit

Figure 2.8 An example junk dimension for the Retail Grocery Sales dimensional model

In many cases, if the junk dimension has several columns, the list of all possible combinations can be too large to pre-calculate. Ten columns, each with 100 unique values would give us a very big dimension table (100,000,000,000,000,000,000 rows). These codes are seldom completely independent, so it's rare for all possible combinations to occur in the real world. In any case, the upper bound on the number of junk value combinations is the number of rows in the fact table. In our grocery example, the "No Sale" transaction type occurs only with the "Cash" payment type. While this reduces our dimension table only from 12 to 9 rows, the reductions in the real world are often dramatic. A recent project had a junk dimension with a theoretical size of over a trillion rows, but a count from the last five years of data showed the actual set of combined values was closer to 70,000 rows. The ETL process would have to watch this dimension during the fact table lookup process to identify new combinations and add them in to the dimension. The junk dimension is also similar to the aggregate dimension in terms of its creation and maintenance.

> **NOTE** In Analysis Services, each of the different attributes included in the junk dimension becomes a separate attribute hierarchy. As in the relational data model, the disparate attribute hierarchies would be grouped together under one dimension, TransactionInfo in our example. You'd hide the bottom level of the dimension that has the surrogate key representing the intersection of the codes.

> **REFERENCE** The following resources offer additional information about junk dimensions:
>
> - *The Data Warehouse Toolkit, Second Edition* (Wiley, 2002), pp. 117–119.
> - The kimballgroup.com: Search for the topic Junk Dimensions for a relevant article.

The Three Fact Table Types

There are three fundamental types of fact tables in the DW/BI system: transaction, periodic snapshot, and accumulating snapshot. Most of what we have described thus far falls into the transaction category. *Transaction* fact tables track each transaction as it occurs at a discrete point in time—when the transaction event occurred. The *periodic snapshot* fact table captures cumulative performance over specific time intervals. Periodic snapshots are particularly valuable for combining data across several business processes in the value chain. They also aggregate many of the facts across the time period, providing users with a fast way to get totals. Where snapshots are taken at specific points in time, after the month-end close, for example, the *accumulating snapshot* is constantly updated over time. Generally, the design of the accumulating snapshot includes several date fields to capture the dates when the item in question passes through each of the business processes or milestones in the value chain. For an Orders Accumulating Snapshot that captures metrics about the complete life of an order, these dates might include the following:

- Order Date
- Requested Ship Date
- Manufactured Date
- Actual Ship Date
- Arrival Date
- Invoice Date
- Payment Received Date

The accumulating snapshot provides the status of open orders at any point in time and a history of completed orders just waiting to be scrutinized for interesting metrics.

NOTE Transaction fact tables are clearly what Analysis Services was designed for. Your Analysis Services database can accommodate periodic and accumulating snapshots, but you do need to be careful. The problem is not the model, but the process for updating the data. Snapshot fact tables—particularly accumulating snapshots—tend to be updated a lot in the ETL process. This is expensive but not intolerable in the relational database. It's far more expensive for Analysis Services, which doesn't really support fact table updates at all.

For snapshot facts to work in Analysis Services for even moderate-sized data sets, you'll need the Enterprise Edition feature that allows dimensional database partitioning.

REFERENCE The following resources offer additional information about the three fact table types:

- *The Data Warehouse Toolkit, Second Edition* (Wiley, 2002), pp. 128–130 and 132–135.

- The kimballgroup.com: Search for the topic Snapshot Fact Table for articles on the different fact table types.

Aggregates

Aggregates are precalculated summary tables that serve the primary purpose of improving performance. If the database engine could instantly roll the data up to the highest level, you wouldn't need aggregate tables. In fact, precalculating aggregates is one of the two reasons for the existence of OLAP engines such as Analysis Services (the other reason being more advanced analytic capabilities). SQL Server Analysis Services can create and manage aggregate tables in the relational platform (called relational OLAP or ROLAP) or in the OLAP engine. The decision to create aggregate tables in the relational versus OLAP engines is a tradeoff. If the aggregates are stored in Analysis Services' format, access to the data is limited to tools that generate MDX. If the aggregates are stored in the relational database, they can be accessed by tools that generate SQL. If your front-end tool is adept at generating MDX, using Analysis Services to manage aggregates has significant advantages. If you must support relational access, especially ad hoc access, you need to create and manage any aggregate tables needed for performance, along with the associated aggregate dimensions described earlier.

> **NOTE** SQL Server uses the term "aggregates" to mean the rules that define how data is rolled up. It uses the term "aggregation" to mean the resulting summary table.

In this section we have covered several of the common design challenges you will typically run up against in developing a dimensional model. This is not an exhaustive list, but it should be enough to help you understand the modeling process. If you are charged with the role of data modeler and this is your first dimensional modeling effort, we again strongly encourage you to continue your education by reading *The Data Warehouse Toolkit, Second Edition*.

The Dimensional Modeling Process

With a basic understanding of dimensional modeling and the core techniques under your belt, this section shifts focus to describe the process of building a dimensional model. Creating a dimensional model is a highly iterative and dynamic process. After a few preparation steps, the design process begins with an initial graphical model pulled from the bus matrix and presented at the entity level. This model is critically scrutinized in a high-level design session that also yields an initial list of attributes for each table and a list of issues requiring additional investigation. Once the high-level model is in place, the detailed modeling process takes the model table by table and drills down into the definitions, sources, relationships, data quality problems, and transformations required to populate the model. The last phase of the modeling process involves reviewing and validating the model with several interested parties. The primary goals of this process are to create a model that meets the business requirements, provides the ETL team with a solid starting point and clear direction, and verifies that the data is available to fill out the model.

Designing a dimensional model is a series of successive approximations, where you create more detailed and robust models based on your growing understanding of the source systems, the business needs, and the associated transformations. This series of iterations usually stops once the model clearly meets the business needs in a flexible and extensible way. This iterative process typically takes a few weeks for a single business process dimensional model, but can take longer depending on the complexity of the business process, availability of knowledgeable participants, existence of well-documented detailed business requirements, and the number of pre-existing reusable dimension tables.

Figure 2.9 shows the dimensional modeling process flow; the modeling process runs down the left side, and the inputs and deliverables from each task run down the right. This process flow will be our roadmap as we cover each of the major steps both in this section and in the Adventure Works Cycles case study that follows. Note that the inputs to the dimensional modeling process are the deliverables from the requirements definition step.

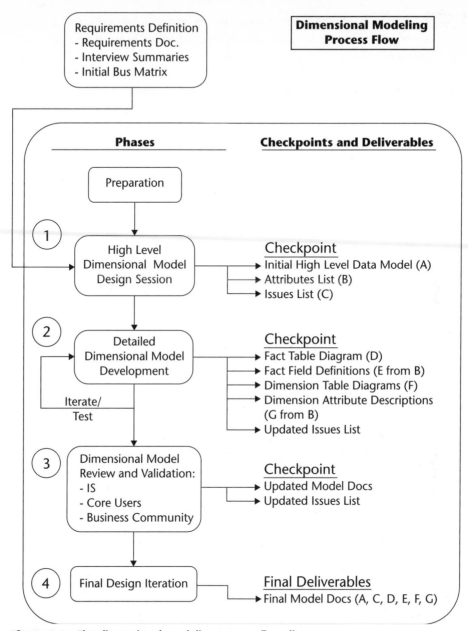

Figure 2.9 The dimensional modeling process flow diagram

The linear nature of the graphic can give the wrong impression. You will make many passes through the dimensional model, filling in blanks, adding detail, and changing the design over and over. Often we've made changes that sounded clever at the time, but ended up changing them back because they didn't work, either from the user or technical perspective, or both!

NOTE Creating the dimensional model is where an expert can help. If your team is new to the dimensional modeling process, bringing in someone who has extensive experience creating dimensional models can save you weeks of time, pain, and suffering. However, do not let the consultant take over the process—make them lead the team and facilitate the effort so everyone can participate in the design process and learn why various design decisions were made. Don't let the consultant disappear for a few days or a week or two and bring you back a completed model. The goal is to learn what goes into a dimensional model and why, so you know how to maintain and improve your model over time. More important, you need to know how to do the next one, so you don't have to pay someone to do this for you forever.

Preparation

All the major steps in the Lifecycle involve an initial preparation phase. For dimensional modeling, preparation includes identifying the roles and participants in the modeling process, determining a data architecture strategy, reviewing the requirements document, setting up the modeling environment, and determining naming conventions. This section covers each of these areas in turn.

Identifying Roles and Participants

Creating the dimensional model is an iterative and interactive process. As Table 2.5 shows, several roles are involved in the modeling step, but a core modeling team of two or three people usually does most of the work. The core modeling team includes a data modeler with a strong technical background and solid experience with the source systems, and a business analyst who brings a solid understanding of how the data is used in the analysis process and how it could be made more useful or accessible. The core modeling team often includes someone from the ETL team with extensive source systems development experience and an interest in learning. The *data modeler* has overall responsibility for creating the dimensional model.

The *data steward* role is tightly linked to the modeling process because this role is responsible for driving enterprise agreement on the names, definitions, and business rules of the data elements that are used in reporting and analysis across the organization. This is a non-trivial effort that often gets mired in politics and personalities. The person who takes on the data steward role must be adept at interpersonal communications and organizational politics.

Try to include a *business power user* who has a particular interest or expertise in a business process. This person is usually very helpful in interpreting the data from a business perspective and can help speed the design. Also, this business power user can play the role of data steward in a pinch.

Table 2.5   Major Participants in Creating the Dimensional Model

PARTICIPANT	PURPOSE/ROLE IN MODELING PROCESS
Data modeler	Primary responsibility
Business analyst	Analysis and source expert, business definitions
Data steward	Drive agreement on enterprise names, definitions and rules
Business power user	Describe and refine data sources and business rules from a user perspective
Source system developer	Source expert, business rules
DBA	Design guidance, Early learning
ETL designer	Early learning
ETL developer	Early learning
Steering Committee	Naming, business definitions, model validation

The core modeling team works closely with source system developers who can explain the contents, meaning, business rules, timing, and other intricacies of the particular source system involved in the dimensional model. You may need more than one source system expert to unravel the complexities of a given source system. You will almost certainly need to call on different experts as you model the different business processes on the bus matrix.

In addition to these participants, we suggest you include the DBA who will be implementing the physical database and the ETL designer and developer in the modeling process. These folks do so much better if they understand the business rationale for the model. Often the DBA comes from a transaction system background and wants to apply transaction system database design rules. In other words, the DBA wants to normalize the dimensions, which as we've described, does not work well for business intelligence queries. We find a similar tendency in the ETL designer. Without a full appreciation for the business requirements, the ETL designer often tries to simplify the ETL process by assigning certain calculations to the front-end tool, or skipping a description lookup step, or any of a number of time-saving shortcuts. While these do save time during the ETL development phase, they cost significant time whenever a user has to compensate for the omission.

There are generally a few additional participants as well. Although you risk slowing down the design process a bit by including more people, the benefits of a more robust design and engaged partners are almost always worth the price.

Understanding the Data Architecture Strategy

There are as many approaches to building a DW/BI system as there are consultants who dream them up. We will discuss the overall technical architecture of the Microsoft solution in Chapter 3. However, one of the big arguments centers on the issue of how you structure and manage your data. The questions are: What data do you keep, where do you keep it within your technical architecture, and how is it structured. Our standard approach is to build atomic-level dimensional models in the relational database platform that holds the lowest level of detail. This atomic level database provides for consistent data definitions, business rules, and tracking of history. It also supports the integration of data from multiple sources across the enterprise and from external sources such as vendors, customers, and third-party data providers. This atomic level also provides a means for including value-added data that is important to the analytic process but that currently exists only in spreadsheets on users' desktops (if anywhere). The atomic-level dimensional data warehouse is designed to be queried by users and built to meet their analytic needs and performance expectations. As we will describe in Chapter 3, this is generally true even though we encourage you to build atomic-level Analysis Services databases from the atomic-level relational warehouse and use Analysis Services as the primary query platform.

   We believe both the relational and Analysis Services databases are key components of a successful enterprise Microsoft DW/BI system. The goal of this chapter, and of all the chapters that focus on the data track of the Lifecycle, is to make sure we build the system in a way that leverages the strengths of both tools. The good news is that a solid, well-designed dimensional model is the best foundation for both platforms.

Revisiting the Requirements

After the modeling team and the data strategy are in place, the team's first step will be to pull out the detailed requirements documentation and carefully comb through it. If you skipped to this chapter with the idea that you could avoid all that business stuff, sorry, but you need to go back and do the work. The modeling team must understand the business problems the users are trying to solve and the kinds of analyses they perform to solve them. It's the team's job to translate those requirements into a flexible dimensional model that can support broad classes of analysis, not just re-create specific reports. This isn't an easy job. The data modeler must be able to function at an advanced level in both the business and technical areas. In fact, much of the initial dimensional modeling effort actually begins as part of the requirements definition process.

DATA-DRIVEN MODELS VERSUS BUSINESS REQUIREMENTS–DRIVEN MODELS

An experienced dimensional modeler can build a reasonable dimensional model based on the source system data structures. However, this model will inevitably fall short of meeting the business needs in many small but substantive ways. These little shortcomings add up to a weak dimensional model. We recently worked with a client whose requirements gathering had revealed a need for a field called PricingCategory. It turns out there is no such thing as PricingCategory in the source system. However, there was a Rate_Code field that in combination with some other status flags was the basis of what the business users called PricingCategory. A dimensional model based on the source system would have included Rate_Code (maybe) and left the users to re-create the business rules for determining PricingCategory every time they built a query that needed the field.

In short, you must understand the business requirements in detail before you dive into the task of designing the dimensional model.

The detailed business requirements document discussed in Chapter 1 has several sections that describe the high-priority business processes in detail. That document identifies analytic requirements supported by each high-priority business process. It describes the broad classes of questions and problems that management and business analysts have been trying (or would like to try) to answer. The requirements document should include a list of data elements, example questions, and even a list of desired reports that would help answer the analytic questions. These all play a central role when it comes time to defining the dimensional model. Your dimensional model must be able to answer these questions easily when it is finished, although the dimensional model is not built to provide a single target report.

Setting Up the Modeling Environment

It helps to get a few tools in place before you dive into the modeling process. We often start the modeling process using a spreadsheet as our initial tool because it allows us to make changes easily. Figure 2.10 gives a good example of the basic starting point for a model development spreadsheet. It captures the key elements of the logical model plus many of the physical attributes you'll need later. It also gives you a place to begin capturing some of the ETL information, such as source system table and column(s), and a brief description of the extract and transformation rules. Finally, it includes the initial set of business metadata in the form of the names, descriptions, example values, and comments. In our ETL Toolkit book, we call this the "logical data map." Regardless of the name, the central idea is to associate the original sources with the final targets.

Table Name: DimOrderInfo

Table Type	Dimension
View Name	OrderInfo
Description	OrderInfo is the "junk" dimension that includes miscellaneous information about the Order transaction
Used in schemas	Orders
Generate script?	Y

Target

Column Name	Description	Datatype	Size	Key?	FK To	NULL?	Default Value	Unknown Member	Example Values	SCD Type	Source System
Extended Property?	Y				Y				Y	Y	Y
OrderInfoKey	Surrogate primary key	smallint		PK ID		N		-1			ETL Process
BKSalesReasonID	Sales reason ID from source system	smallint				N		-1	1, 2, 3, 4...		AW
Channel	Sales channel	char	8					Unknown	Reseller, Internet	1	AW
SalesReason	Reason for the sale, as reported by the customer	varchar	30					Unknown		1	AW
SalesReasonType	Type of sales reason	char	10					Unknown	Marketing, Promotion, Other	1	AW
AuditKey	What process loaded this row?	int		FK	Audit Dim	N		-1		1	Derived

Source

SCD Type	Source System	Source Schema	Source Table	Source Field Name	Source Datatype	ETL Rules	Comments
Y		Y	Y	Y	Y	Y	Y
	ETL Process					Standard surrogate key	
	AW	Sales	SalesReason	SalesReasonID	int	Convert to char; left-pad with zero. R for reseller row.	We need to insert a single row for Reseller
1	AW	Sales	SalesReason	Derived		Internet' for real sales reasons. 'Reseller' for reseller row.	
1	AW	Sales	SalesReason	Name	nvarchar(50)	Convert to varchar; 'Reseller' for reseller row.	
1	AW	Sales	SalesReason	ReasonType	nvarchar(50)	Convert to varchar; 'Reseller' for reseller row	
1	Derived					Populated by ETL system using standard technique	

Figure 2.10 Example dimensional model development spreadsheet

TIP You can get a copy of this spreadsheet at the book's web site, www.MsftDWToolkit.com. Unhappy about the prospect of rekeying the model, we wrote a simple macro to generate the DDL to create the tables in SQL Server. We can then use the reverse-engineering capabilities of our modeling tool to pull the model out of the database. Our spreadsheet also writes the metadata info, such as the column description, transformations, and comments columns, into extended properties fields in the database system tables. Afterward, you can move this information into the metadata schema.

This spreadsheet can be extended to include other columns that may be useful in your environment, such as physical name (if it will be different from the logical or business name), a short description that can easily fit into a tooltip, and a long description that fully captures the definition of the column or table.

Once the model gets fairly firm, typically after a few weeks, you can convert to your standard modeling tool. Most of the popular modeling tools (such as ERwin, PowerDesigner, Oracle Designer, E/R Studio, and Visio) allow you to lay out the logical model and capture physical and logical names, descriptions, and relationships.

TIP If you are using the spreadsheet mentioned previously, you can transfer its contents to your modeling tool by generating the script to create the database, building it in SQL Server 2005, and using your modeling tool to reverse engineer the database. A good tool will pull in all the elements you've already defined.

Many of the tools are becoming dimensionally aware and have functions to support the creation of a dimensional model. For example, some tools can distinguish between a fact and dimension table; they can handle role-playing dimensions; and they can create multiple business process "layers" that correspond to the rows in the bus matrix. They also capture the information in their metadata stores and generally have a way to export or exchange that metadata with other systems or even with a centralized metadata catalog. Look for these features and take advantage of them.

Once the design is considered complete (for the first round, anyway), the modeling tools can help the DBA forward engineer the model into the database, including creating the tables, indexes, partitioning, views, and other physical elements of the database. Chapter 4 discusses these physical design issues. If you start using your modeling tool early on, things will be easier later.

Establishing Naming Conventions

Naming conventions are the rules you use to consistently name the objects in your dimensional model, and ultimately in the physical database. Spending time determining your naming conventions is one of those irritating tasks that feels like make-work. But it is definitely worth it in the long run.

Fortunately, it doesn't have to become your life's work. There are ways to abbreviate the process. First, don't start from scratch. Use whatever naming conventions your organization has in place. Almost all large organizations have a group of data modelers and/or DBAs somewhere—they might be called Data Administration, or Data Management. Somewhere in that group is the holder of the organization's official naming conventions. Given that you are reading the dimensional modeling chapter, you are likely either one of the folks in this group, or very close to them. Find the document and see if you can make them work for the DW/BI system. Existing naming conventions don't always work because sometimes they are not oriented toward user-friendly, descriptive names.

If you're in a smaller organization, don't despair. Several examples of naming conventions are available on the Internet. The web site for this book, www .MsftDWToolkit.com, has an example along with links to a few other examples. The point is, you don't need to start from scratch.

Data Profiling and Research

Once you've done your prep work, you can get started on the model. Throughout the modeling process, the modeler needs to dig into the under-layers of the data to learn about its structure, content, relationships, and derivation rules. You need to verify that the data exists (or can be created), that it is in a usable state, or at least its flaws are manageable, and that you understand what it will take to convert it into the dimensional model form. You don't have to find every piece of bad data or completely document every transformation at this point. Leave a little bit for the ETL folks to do.

This is not your first trip into data exploration. The requirements definition process in Chapter 1 included initial data profiling and data audit tasks to aid in the assessment of feasibility. The findings from those tasks are the starting point for this one.

Although data profiling is listed here as part of the preparation step, it is actually an ongoing process. As you work through the model table by table, filling in the list of attributes, you will find yourself returning to these data profiling and research tasks many times to resolve issues and clearly define each attribute.

There are several useful sources for detailed information about an organization's data, including the source system, data experts, and existing reporting systems.

Data Profiling and Source System Exploration

The data modeler usually has the benefit of both first-hand observation and documentation from the source system under investigation. Unfortunately, these two don't always line up. Gather and carefully review whatever documentation is available for the source systems. This might include data models, file definitions, record layouts, written documentation, and source system programs. More advanced source systems may have their own metadata repositories with all this information already integrated for your convenience. Don't count on this.

Perusing the source system data itself usually provides a quick jolt of reality. First, what you see typically does not match the documentation you carefully gathered and reviewed. Second, it usually is more difficult to unravel than you would hope. The older the system, the more time it's had to evolve. This evolution, usually driven by short-term business needs, often takes the form of one or more of these standard data quality problems:

- *Substituted fields:* "We needed a place to store the new product group, and rather than re-org the table, we just used the product weight field since it really hadn't been used in a couple of years anyway."

- *Overloaded fields:* "We don't have any available fields in the database, so let's just append the product group on the product description field. We can separate the two with a '/'."

- *Variable Definition fields:* "This field means product group unless we manufacture the product ourselves, in which case it lists the factory where it was manufactured."

- *Free form entry fields:* "Of course the Parent Customer data is in the database. The sales reps have been entering it into AddressLine5 for the last three years."

This is only a short list—there are plenty of other problems to be discovered. You can discover many of the content, relationship, and quality problems first-hand through a process that has come to be known as *data profiling* or *data auditing*. Data profiling is about using query and reporting tools to get a sense for the content of the system under investigation. Data profiling can be as simple as writing some SQL SELECT statements with COUNTs and DISTINCTs. An experienced modeler with a decent query tool and a source system data model can develop a good understanding of the nature of the source system data required for a given business process dimensional model in a few days.

On the other hand, data profiling can be a sophisticated study. Data profiling has become a product sub-category in the DW/BI software market. There are tools to make the data profiling task easier and probably more complete. These tools are available in stand-alone versions from data profiling tool companies, and the major ETL tool vendors include data profiling modules in their product offerings. The tools provide complex data analysis well beyond the realm of simple queries. They can reveal the following kinds of information:

- The domain and distribution of the data in each column in a table
- Relationships between columns, such as hierarchies and derivations
- Relationships between tables, such as hidden foreign key relationships or columns with similar content
- Common patterns in the data, such as telephone numbers, or zip codes, or money
- Data quality problems, such as outlier values or exceptions to a common pattern, or exceptions to a relationship

Figure 2.11 shows a simple version of a data profile report for the Production.Product table from the Adventure Works Cycles transaction database. It gives a good sense for what the data in the Product table looks like. Starting at the top of the report, we see that there are 504 rows in the table. There are 504 distinct ProductIDs, Names, and ProductNumbers. It's interesting to note the ProductNumber isn't really a number at all. Moving down the list, only about half the products have a Color, the rest are NULL, and there are only nine distinct values for Color. A commercial tool would give us more information at the table level, and allow us to select on a column and drill down into its detail. But even this simple report gives us a good start on understanding the contents of the table.

> **NOTE** The stored procedures and reporting services project that were used to create the data profiling report shown in Figure 2.11 are available at the book's web site at www.MsftDWToolkit.com. They work on SQL Server tables only, but they do give you a place to start.

Your goal is to make sure the data exists to support the dimensional model and identify business rules and relationships that will have an impact on the model. Write down any interesting complexities you uncover so the ETL folks won't have to re-discover them. You may not understand the exact business rules and derivation formulas as part of the modeling phase, but the modeling team should all agree that what you are proposing is reasonable, or at least possible.

Adventure Works BIS

Table Name: Product   Total Row Count: 504

Column Name	Ordinal Position	Data Type	Max Length	Min Value	Max Value	Distinct Values	Null Count	Pct Null	Avg Length Or Value	Max Char Length
ProductID	1	int(10)	10	1	999	504	0	0.0%	673	
Name	2	nvarchar(50)	50	Adjustable Race	Women's Tights, S	504	0	0.0%	18	32
ProductNumber	3	nvarchar(25)	25	AR-5381	WB-H098	504	0	0.0%	8	10
MakeFlag	4	bit	1	n/a	n/a	0	0	0.0%		
FinishedGoodsFlag	5	bit	1	n/a	n/a	0	0	0.0%		
Color	6	nvarchar(15)	15	Black	Yellow	9	248	49.2%	5	12
SafetyStockLevel	7	smallint(5)	5	4	1000	6	0	0.0%	535	
ReorderPoint	8	smallint(5)	5	3	750	6	0	0.0%	401	
StandardCost	9	money(19)	19	0.00	2171.29	114	0	0.0%	259	
ListPrice	10	money(19)	19	0.00	3578.27	103	0	0.0%	439	
Size	11	nvarchar(5)	5	38	XL	18	293	58.1%	1	2
SizeUnitMeasureCode	12	nchar(3)	3	CM	CM	1	328	65.1%	2	2
WeightUnitMeasureCode	13	nchar(3)	3	G	LB	2	299	59.3%	1	2
Weight	14	decimal(8)	8	2.12	1050.00	127	299	59.3%	74	
DaysToManufacture	15	int(10)	10	0	4	4	0	0.0%	1	
ProductLine	16	nchar(2)	2	M	T	4	226	44.8%	1	1
Class	17	nchar(2)	2	H	M	3	257	51.0%	1	1
Style	18	nchar(2)	2	M	W	3	293	58.1%	1	1
ProductSubcategoryID	19	smallint(5)	5	1	37	37	209	41.5%	12	
ProductModelID	20	int(10)	10	1	128	119	209	41.5%	37	
SellStartDate	21	datetime(8)	8	Jun 1 1998 12:00AM	Jul 1 2003 12:00AM	4	0	0.0%		
SellEndDate	22	datetime(8)	8	Jun 30 2002 12:00AM	Jun 30 2003 12:00AM	2	406	80.6%		

Report Name: Column List
Report Folder: /Data Profiler   Last run date: 11/4/2004 6:08 PM   1

Figure 2.11   A simple data profile report for the Adventure Works OLTP Product table

Source System Experts

The best data profiling tools are generally not as complete or accurate as actually working with the people who maintain the source systems (although sometimes the exact opposite is true). If you're lucky, the person who actually built or originally installed the source system is still around. For any given dimensional model, there are usually several source system people you need to pull into the modeling process. There might be a DBA, a developer, and someone who works with the data input process. Each of these folks does things to the data that the other two don't know about. Even with the best database design and the greatest programs, the data entry group could decide to enter a middle initial of Z for every customer who was unpleasant to work with. There also might be different people you need to go to for different parts of the source system, even for different tables in some cases. Get to know these folks; develop good relationships with them. Help them understand how the DW/BI system will make their lives better. You will need their full cooperation.

Core Business Users

The core business users, often called power users, are the ones who have figured out how to get data out of the source system and turn it into information. They typically know how to build their own queries, sometimes by actually writing SQL. They are particularly valuable to the modeling process because they understand the source systems from a business point of view, and they've created the business rules needed to convert the data from its form in the source system to something that can be used to support the decision-making process. Again, cultivate good relationships with these people. One or two of them should already be on the data modeling team. The rest should be brought in to work through the tight spots in defining individual dimensions or facts, and of course, participate in the dimensional model reviews.

Existing Reporting Systems

Existing reporting systems are often an excellent resource for information about the source systems and business rules needed to present information to the user community. Unfortunately, most of this information is buried somewhere in the code—either in the reporting system's ETL process, if it has its own database, or in the report definitions themselves. Usually the best way to get this information out is to find the main developer of the reporting system and get him or her involved in the modeling process.

Building Dimensional Models

After a round of data exploration, the process of building dimensional models typically moves through three phases. The first is a high-level dimensional model design session that defines the boundaries of business process dimensional model. This first phase is labeled (1) in the process flow diagram in Figure 2.9. The second phase, labeled (2) in Figure 2.9, is detailed model development that involves filling in the attributes table by table and resolving any issues or uncertainties. The third phase is a series of model review, redesign, and validation steps labeled (3) in Figure 2.9.

High-Level Dimensional Model Design Session

The first dimensional modeling design session is meant to put several major stakes in the ground in terms of the basic structure and content of the dimensional model. This session is facilitated by the lead data modeler, and involves the core modeling team and any interested participants from the source system group and the ETL group. It can take a day or more to work through the initial model, so set expectations accordingly.

TREAD LIGHTLY

It is extremely valuable to learn from the experience of those who went before you, but be very careful not to frighten or offend them. They may be threatened by the fact that they will no longer be needed. They might be angry or offended that you, not they, are building the DW/BI system. This is where your interpersonal skills will save you. Work to include them as part of the team early on. Keep them informed as the project moves forward. Involve them in the design of the database. Teach them how to use the reporting tools and include them in the development of new reports and applications from the DW/BI system. Let them (and their boss) know how much you appreciate their help.

The session has two distinct parts and three intermediate deliverables, more properly thought of as early versions of the ultimate deliverables. The first part is creating the high-level dimensional model—a graphical representation of the dimension, fact, and utility tables involved in representing the business process. As we describe in the next section, you should follow a four-step process for creating this high-level dimensional model. The second part of the session is creating the initial list of attributes for each dimension. The three checkpoints are: 1) the high-level graphical model; 2) the initial attribute list; and 3) the initial issues list. We describe the process of creating the high level dimensional model in this section and the two lists in the case study section.

Creating the High-Level Dimensional Model: The Four-Step Modeling Process

The initial task in the design session is to create a high-level dimensional model for the top priority business process. Creating the first draft is straightforward because the bus matrix from the detailed requirements document gives the team an excellent starting point (refer back to Figure 2.9). The high-level dimensional model is a data model at the entity level. You may also include any utility tables, such as lookup tables or user hierarchies, but usually these don't surface until later in the process. The process generally flows through four steps in this design session: choosing the business process, declaring the grain, choosing the dimensions, and identifying the facts.

> **Step 1: Choosing the business process.** The first step in the four-step modeling process is to pick the subject area to be modeled. This is a business decision and it normally occurs after the high-level business requirements have been gathered and the analytic themes have been synthesized out. Recall from Chapter 1 that these themes are the central discussion points in a session with senior business management, the goal of which is to prioritize the themes and select the top-priority business process. If the analytic themes were well defined, selecting the initial business process is essentially picking a row on the bus matrix. This

incremental approach allows you to carve off a piece that a) has significant value to the organization, b) can be built in a reasonable amount of time—typically about nine months for the initial business process, and c) lays the data foundation for the enterprise view by creating reusable, or conformed, dimensions.

By the time you get to this point, you should already know the initial business process to be modeled. If you don't, please return to Chapter 1 and work through the requirements gathering and prioritization process with your business folks. In the Adventure Works Cycles case study, the prioritization process clearly identified orders as the top-priority business process (see the prioritization chart in Figure 1.9 for a reminder).

Step 2: Declaring the grain. The second step in creating the high-level dimensional model is to decide on the level of detail, or the grain, needed for the selected business process. Choosing the grain is a combination of what is needed to meet the business requirements and what is possible based on the data collected by the source system. We've seen cases where the business would like more detail than is available, and we've seen cases where the source system collects more detail than is relevant to understanding the business process. In general, our recommendation is to start out with the goal of building the dimensional model at the lowest level of detail available—the atomic level. It's easy to roll up from the detail, but impossible to drill down from summary without underlying detail. This is one of the cornerstones of design flexibility in the dimensional model.

Part of declaring the grain is figuring out how to describe it. If you're pulling the lowest level of detail available, the grain can be thought of as one row in the fact table per source system transaction row. We usually describe this as "one row per X" where X is the business event, one row per customer call, one row per time sheet entry, one row per employee status change, and one row per order line item.

For Adventure Works Cycles, the grain of the orders business process clearly needs to be at the order line item level.

Step 3: Choosing the dimensions. The third step in the design session is a brainstorm discussion about the dimensions. Several major dimensions fall out naturally once you've determined the grain. The bus matrix usually provides a general idea of the major dimensions.

Scrutinize the dimensions to make sure they make sense (you will do this several times). Would certain dimensions be easier to work with or easier to understand if they were combined? How about if they were split apart? Look for hidden foreign key relationships, normalized hierarchies (one-to-many relationships). Ask hard questions about the assumptions behind each dimension—is it this way because it represents the true nature of the business process, or because it reflects the specific idiosyncrasies built into the transaction system? Revisit the bus matrix and test other dimensions to see if they fit. Any dimension that takes on a single value at the grain of the fact table is a candidate.

This step is where you begin to face the complexities of the real world. What you originally thought of as one dimension may really end up being two or three dimensions. Often an organization has strong preconceived notions about the data based on how it's represented in the transaction system. These notions are etched in the corporate understanding because the source system, in all its transactional complexities, is the only window people have had on the data. In banking, for example, the account is a central organizing concept. In the source system, the account is actually a high-level entity that contains several other business objects, or dimensions. Once you know the account, you know the product, such as checking or savings. Once you know the account, you know the primary customer because the account carries its own primary customer name and address. In many banking systems, once you know the account, you also know the branch because the account number includes a branch indicator. Teasing out these hidden dimensions can be a challenge because they force people to re-think their understanding of the data and organization.

Choosing the dimensions may also cause you to realize your grain declaration was incorrect. You may have thought you were working at the atomic level of detail, when all of a sudden, the identification of a useful dimension that participates in the target business process forces the grain down to a lower level of detail. For example, a typical call detail record for a phone company usually includes the originating phone number and called phone number. However, the business users in a cellular phone company may want to include the cell tower IDs connected to the originating phone and the receiving phone. Because this could change many times during the phone call, what was one record now becomes several. Adding the tower IDs forces the grain down to a lower level of detail, and adds a lot more rows to the fact table.

Step 4: Identifying the facts. The fourth step in the modeling process is to identify the facts or measures generated by the business process. The facts usually tie directly to the grain declaration. For many transaction-oriented business processes there are only a few fundamental facts, such as quantity and sale amount, to measure business process performance. There are many combinations and calculations that can be derived from these fundamental facts, and which are used to monitor the business. These calculated measures are important but are not necessarily part of the atomic fact table itself. As we said when we defined these derived or computed facts at the beginning of this chapter, they're usually best handled in Analysis Services or in the relational views. At this early point in the design, you're working to identify the fundamental facts. However, keep track of all the computed facts you come up with—you'll need them soon.

The High-Level Graphical Model

Graphically summarize the initial design session in a deliverable called the high-level graphical model (or the *bubble chart*, for short). The model shown in Figure 2.12 is an example of a starting point dimensional model for Adventure Works Cycles' orders business process based on the bus matrix from Chapter 1. We improve on this model in the next section.

Once this high-level dimensional model is completed, the hard work of filling in the dimension attributes and hierarchies, identifying and validating data sources, and defining names begins. At this point, the process gets specific to each individual organization. The rest of this chapter explores the process of identifying dimension attributes and facts, and validating the model in the context of the Adventure Works Cycles business.

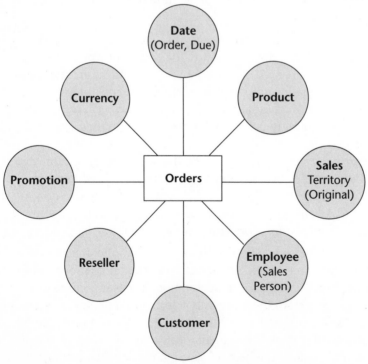

Figure 2.12   Initial Adventure Works Cycles High-Level Orders
dimensional model

Identifying Dimension and Fact Attributes

The second part of the initial design session involves filling in each table with a robust *attribute list*. The attribute list is a list of all the relevant attributes needed by the business, grouped according to the dimension or fact table to which they belong. If you're working with the dimensional modeling spread-sheet shown in Figure 2.10, create one worksheet per table in the model, and fill in its attribute list. The initial list for dimension and fact table attributes is identified as checkpoint (B) in phase (1) of Figure 2.9. We use the modeling spreadsheet shown in Figure 2.10 to keep track of our attribute lists.

The team will identify a large number of attributes coming from a wide range of sources. List them out brainstorm-style, grouping them by the dimen-sion or fact table to which they belong. Don't get caught up in naming or derivation yet; just pick a name and make a note of the alternatives names and the controversy on the issues list.

Speaking of the issues list, the last checkpoint from the high-level modeling session is the dimensional model *issues list*. This document comes to life in the high-level model design session, but it's constantly updated throughout the detailed modeling process. It's the best way we've found to remember all the little details about the problems we encountered and how we decided to resolve them. You'll see an example issues list in Figure 2.15 as part of the Adventure Works Cycles case study.

Assign someone the role of list keeper in every meeting. This person notes every data-related issue that comes up during the meeting and marks off pre-vious issues that have been resolved. It helps to save time at the end of each meeting to review and validate the new entries and their assignments. The data modeler can be the keeper of the issues list, but we've often seen it fall into the hands of the project manager. This is in large part because keeping the list updated and encouraging progress on resolving issues are usually strengths of a good project manager.

The results of this initial design session, the high-level dimensional model, the attributes list, and the issues list, are the foundation for the logical and physical business process dimensional models. At this point, you've identified the dimension and fact tables, each with a list of its associated attributes or measures. This model, along with the issues list, gives the data modeling team enough guidelines to carry the process into the next level of detail.

We will work through the steps in creating these lists in the context of the Adventure Works Cycles case study in the next section. This brings us to phase (2) in the dimensional modeling process shown back in Figure 2.9.

Developing the Detailed Dimensional Model

Detailed dimensional model development is primarily about filling in all the missing information in the dimensional model and testing it against the business requirements. Shown as phase (2) in Figure 2.9, this is where the team works through the issues list, resolving as many as possible, and identifying alternative solutions for the remaining issues. The goal is to identify all the interesting and useful attributes and determine the locations, definitions, and business rules that specify how these attributes are populated. This process is ultimately about *defining the contents of the DW/BI system*, table by table and column by column. Because the DW/BI system is an enterprise resource, these definitions must work for the entire enterprise. The data definition task is a business task—the BI team usually drives the process, but the business folks must determine and approve the standard names and definitions. This is another one of those organizational processes that can be difficult for the technically minded.

The team should meet on a regular basis, perhaps daily or every other day, to discuss the proposed alternatives and make decisions on open issues. Use these meetings to critically explore the progress, review any recommendations, and update the issues list. Focus these meetings on one or two tables at a time—too many and the meeting starts to get bogged down.

If there are enough competent dimensional modelers, the modeling team should divide and conquer. The model can be split out by table, with its associated attribute list and issues list.

If you aren't already using it, try the modeling spreadsheet mentioned in the Preparation section of this chapter and shown in Figure 2.10. It provides a place to capture most of the important descriptive information about each table and attribute. It allows the modeler to quickly move or copy attributes around the model as needed. It is a spreadsheet, after all.

This is the point where the data steward needs to drive consensus on table and attribute naming, descriptions and definitions. This will take some time, but it is an investment that will provide huge returns in terms of users' ability to understand and willingness to accept the dimensional model.

The model will go through some major shifts during this phase. You'll identify additional attributes, along with new dimensions and facts. If this is the primary focus of the dimensional modeling team, the model should begin to settle down with a week or two of intensive work.

REFERENCE See the following resources for additional information about developing the detailed model:

- *The Data Warehouse Lifecycle Toolkit* (Wiley, 1998), Chapter 7, "Building Dimensional Models."

- The kimballgroup.com: Search for the topic Naming Game for an article on the process of driving organizational agreement on attribute names.

Testing the Model

Once the model is fairly stable, step back and test it against the business requirements. The requirements are an integral part of the model development process, but a separate test step helps you think at a more practical level. Approach the test by asking the question "How would I actually get this information out of the model?"

The requirements document should have a bundle of test materials, including a candidate list of structured reports, example user reports, and ad hoc or future-oriented questions people would like to investigate. Pull these out and go through them one by one. For each request, decide how it could be answered (we often think up the SQL it would take) and assign it an effort score: low, medium, or high. A low effort query would be a simple SQL SELECT statement—no sub-selects or case statements or unions—that would be easy to construct in any desktop query tool. At the end of the test, most of the questions should fall into the low effort category—shoot for 75 percent.

Invariably, this testing process leads to several refinements in the model. You may identify missing attributes or hierarchies. Occasionally, you'll make major structural changes to the model based on a deeper understanding than you had before you created the detailed model.

Reviewing and Validating the Model

Once you're confident in the model's stability, the process moves into the review and validation phase, labeled (3) in Figure 2.9. This phase involves reviewing the model with successive audiences, each with different levels of technical expertise and business understanding. Get feedback from interested people across the organization. At a minimum, plan on talking to three groups. In the IT organization, the source system developers and DBAs can often spot errors in the model very quickly. (You may need to teach these folks about dimensional modeling before they start normalizing your dimensions.) Get feedback from any core business users who were not directly involved in the model development process. After each meeting, incorporate the feedback into the dimensional model.

Finally, review the model with the broader user community. Do this more in the form of a presentation and tie the model back to the business requirements. A series of statements that show how a user might get answers to a range of questions pulled right from the requirements document can be very powerful.

The modeling team will get valuable feedback from the review and validation process. The DW/BI team also gets value from these reviews in the form of a more informed and engaged user community. This feedback should be incorporated into the final model, labeled (4) in Figure 2.9.

Case Study: Creating the Adventure Works Cycles Orders Dimensional Model

This fourth major section of this chapter is meant to impart a sense for how the modeling process might work in the real world. We draw from the Adventure Works Cycles business requirements from Chapter 1 and source system data in the AdventureWorks transaction database for examples of each of the deliverables. The initial design session starts with the knowledge that the modeling team is designing a dimensional model for the Orders business process. According to the four-step process for creating a high-level dimensional model, step two is to choose the dimensions.

Choosing the Dimensions

In order to give you a richer context for the process of choosing dimensions, we'll go all the way back to step (1) in Figure 2.9: the high-level dimensional model design session. Using the dimensional model shown in Figure 2.12 as our guide, we'll summarize the Adventure Works Cycles DW/BI team's discussion and conclusions for each dimension, starting with the Date dimension. The dimensional model shown in Figure 2.12 is based on the initial bus matrix we developed as part of the requirements definition process in Chapter 1. The model in Figure 2.12 provides a rough starting point for the high-level dimensional model discussion. At the end of this section, we show the resulting updated high level Orders dimensional model.

Date

There are two important dates in the orders business process: order date and due date. The Date dimension will play two roles in the Orders dimensional model. Recall that a role-playing dimension means the same table will be used multiple times, either through views, synonyms, or physical copies of the table. Analysis Services has the concept of role-playing dimensions built in and doesn't need views or copies.

Take care to include each of the role-playing dimensions in the logical design documentation to facilitate a clear and concise understanding with your business partners and DBAs.

Product

The discussion about product was fairly easy until it became clear that product means different things in different business processes. In Orders, it means the thing that was sold to the customer—the "finished good." In manufacturing, it could mean a part or a finished good because manufacturing works with the entire bill of materials (BOM) that make up a given product. To them, every element in the BOM is a product of some process. In order for the Product dimension to be useful across the organization (that is, conformed), it must take the concept down to the lowest granularity. Therefore, the team decided that the Product table will include all product-related items. This decision was made easier when one of the source systems folks pointed out that that is how product data was kept on the source system, and there are only 504 rows in the table.

Sales Territory

The Sales Territory was confusing for the team. Initially, they felt there was no need to keep a separate Sales Territory dimension because Sales Territory is really an attribute of the Sales Rep and Customer. According to the requirements, the Sales organization needs to look at historical orders according to which sales rep got credit at the time of the order and which sales rep will get credit for current orders. The VP of Sales also might want to look at customers by territory in order to realign territories in the future. When they created the initial bus matrix, the team discussed different ways to handle the different requirements.

Adding a separate Sales Territory dimension ties the sales territory directly to the transaction. This locks in the territory to which the order was originally assigned, seemingly meeting the historical orders requirement.

Meanwhile, keeping a Type 1 attribute called Current Sales Territory associated with the sales rep allows the design team to provide current performance reports that show historical orders according to the current territory assignments.

This approach seemed to be the best way to meet the business needs, but the team felt further investigation was needed.

Employee

The Orders business process involves sales reps only. No other employees should appear in the Orders fact table (that can't happen, right?). However, rather than creating a limited use table just for sales reps, the modeling team decided to broaden it to include all employees. After all, building the Employee dimension supports the enterprise view of the bus matrix. A fully loaded Employee table can be used to support other business processes that involve employees.

The initial discussions categorized the employee table as a Type 1 table, containing current values only. The group decided this for two reasons. Changes in the Employee attributes really are a separate business process under Human Resources, so tracking the changes will be part of implementing that business process area and is out of scope of the Orders dimensional model. Second, it was unclear where the data to re-create the history of employee attribute changes would come from.

TRACKING HISTORY—ONCE MORE WITH FEELING

To emphasize the importance of tracking attribute changes over time, let's examine the impact of Type 1 versus Type 2 changes for Employee attributes. For example, if the VP of Sales wanted to do some headcount planning and needed to know the productivity of senior sales reps compared to junior sales reps, the information would be incorrect because several of the senior sales reps were hired as junior sales reps. When they got promoted, their old titles would have been overwritten in a Type 1 dimension. This is the same problem presented in the customer commute distance example earlier in this chapter.

The data in the following table shows the different answers Type 1 and Type 2 might give us in the Adventure Works Cycles case. Unfortunately, all the sales reps in the database have the same title: There is no indication of seniority. For the sake of analysis, we can assign seniority with a business rule that says sales reps are considered junior for their first 12 months. In a Type 1 tracking case, the VP of Sales would not be able to create a model because there are no sales for sales reps who were hired in the last 12 months. With Type 2 tracking, the title change generates a new row in the Employee dimension, and all new sales are associated with the new row. Type 2 tracking gives the VP the information he needs.

AVERAGE MONTHLY ORDERS BY SALES TITLE			
TYPE 1 REPORT		**TYPE 2 REPORT**	
Position	Avg Monthly	Position	Avg Monthly
Senior	166,354	Senior	195,153
Junior	0	Junior	119,447

One of the attributes of the Employee table will be the Current Sales Territory to which each employee is assigned (although all employees who are not sales people will be assigned to the HQ sales territory). Reporting orders with this Territory will show all the Sales Rep's historical sales aligned by their current Territory.

At this point in the discussion, a few of the team members noted their concern about not having Employee be a Type 2 slowly changing dimension. Several business requirements had been voiced about tracking the impact of organizational changes, and about basic employee counts. (Note that these are questions about the Human Resources business process.) Without a Type 2 dimension, it would be impossible to relate the employee attributes that were in effect at the time a transaction occurred with the actual transaction itself. Only current attribute values could be used to analyze history.

Based on this discussion, the team decided to treat the Employee dimension as a hybrid SCD dimension, with most of the attributes tracked as Type 2 attributes. This decision had significant ripple effect on the model. First, it revealed a weakness in the Sales Territory dimension. Having a Type 2 attribute called Historical Sales Territory in the Employee dimension tracks the same information as the Sales Territory table, only better: It locks in both the sales territory and the sales rep that got credit at the time of the sale. Therefore, the Sales Territory dimension can be removed from the model. Second, there is still a need to apply the currently assigned sales territory to all of history, which means keeping the Current Sales Territory attribute in the Employee dimension as a Type 1 attribute. The ETL process will have to change all historical rows for the Current Sales Territory when the sales territory changes for a given employee. Fortunately, this is one of the standard options in Integration Services' Slowly Changing Dimension Wizard.

NOTE The decision to include Type 2 attributes in the Employee dimension really means expanding the scope to include a second business process: Human Resources transactions. In a large organization, the ETL process will essentially create an employee transaction fact table that can then be used to build the Employee dimension. For Adventure Works Cycles, with fewer than 300 employees, this decision is probably not too onerous. For a larger organization with thousands of employees, this could be a lot of work.

The team also noted the issue of finding reliable historical information for employee changes will have to be researched, but lack of historical data is a bad reason to avoid implementing Type 2 tracking. The sooner you get started, the more history you will have.

Customer and Reseller

Next around the circle in Figure 2.12, we run into two related dimensions: Customer and Reseller. As the design team reviewed the business requirements related to customer, it became clear that there were multiple ideas of who the customer was, and that these ideas overlapped. Internet customers are direct-sale individuals, and Reseller customers are mostly wholesale or retail businesses. While they do share some attributes, like an address, the company has certain information about each that it doesn't have about the other. The sense when the bus matrix was created was that the two customer types are different enough to be split into separate dimensions.

During the design session, the design team recognized these heterogeneous customers as a variation on the heterogeneous products idea described earlier in this chapter. The heterogeneous products technique would say to create a separate MasterCustomer dimension that contained only the shared attributes for all customers—both Reseller and Internet. Then create two subset dimensions, one for Internet customers and one for Resellers, with all their unique attributes. These subset dimensions should have the same surrogate keys as their equivalent rows in the master customer dimension.

As it turns out, the design team modified the concept a bit because the reality they face is a bit different. First, there is a clear need to report total sales across both customer types in the same report, so the model must include an integrated MasterCustomer of some kind. Second, there are fewer than 20,000 customers in total, and the distribution is highly imbalanced: Less than 4 percent are resellers. Third, only 10 or so attributes are unique to Reseller (items such as StoreAnnualSales and NumberEmployees). The design team decided to combine all the attributes of the two customer types into a single, master Customer dimension. This decision allows much greater reporting and analysis flexibility and simplifies the dimensional model. However, it means the users need to understand and be able to work with the idea that both customer types are in the same table. When they want a count of Internet customers, they will need to limit the customer type field to "Internet."

At the end of the customer discussion, there was still some concern for whether the single customer table would be flexible enough to hold new customer types as Adventure Works Cycles add new distribution channels. The team noted this on the issues list with a reminder to investigate both possible new customer types and usability of a single customer table with the business folks.

Promotion

The requirements document clearly identified promotions as an important element in the marketing mix. However, promotions have not been a major marketing tool for Adventure Works Cycles in the past. In fact, there are only 16 promotions in the source system promotion table. At this point, it is enough to identify promotion as its own dimension and note on the issues list that more research is needed to define promotions because Marketing is planning to do more promotions of greater complexity. The data steward pointed out that tracking more information on promotions may involve enhancements to the source system.

Currency

Every sale in the source system is captured in its original, local currency. The system relies on a currency conversion table for translating currencies and reporting in US dollars. This table tracks the conversion rate between the local currency and US dollars both at the end of each day and as an average for each day. Getting standardized reports in US dollars to compare across countries requires a fairly complicated query and has long been a sore point for most of the folks in headquarters. At the same time, sales people in the field want to create reports in local currency to show their customers. Finance, of course wants both, along with the conversion table so they can assess the impact of exchange rates on budget variances.

Based on these requirements, the design team decided to include both local currency and U.S. dollar fields in the fact table, with a Currency dimension to indicate the currency of the local data. This means the ETL process would have to bring in the currency conversion table to convert non-U.S. sales into U.S. dollars.

Although it was out of scope for the initial cycle, the design team also decided to include the Exchange Rate table. The Exchange Rate table is essentially a fact table, which when combined with the Date table as the Exchange Rate Date and the Currency dimension forms its own business process dimensional model. Making this available to the users was an easy political decision because it is incrementally very little work. The Exchange Rate table must be brought into the ETL staging area in order to support the currency conversion in the Orders table. Besides, the Director of Finance is particularly interested in getting access to this data.

> **NOTE** This is already the second piece of scope creep in the design, the first being treating employee as a Type 2 dimension. We don't encourage this kind of scope creep in real life. In our experience, almost all DW/BI teams are overly ambitious in their first iteration. We're constantly coaching our clients not to over-commit—your mantra should be under-promise and over-deliver.

That brings us full circle around the initial high-level dimensional model. We have enough information to generate the Adventure Works Cycles initial high-level dimensional model for Orders, which is the checkpoint labeled (A) in step (1) of Figure 2.9. Before we show the updated model, let's complete the second part of the design session because there still might be a few changes.

Identifying Dimension and Fact Attributes for the Orders Business Process

The second half of the initial design session involves creating an initial data element list. This list is an attribute list for each dimension and a list of fact-related data elements. The starting point for this list is the detailed requirements document—one of its appendices should be a list of key data elements (attributes) that people specifically identified as important.

Figure 2.13 shows what a portion of the attributes list might look like for the Adventure Works Cycles Orders business process dimensional model. The Sample Values column is helpful in identifying attributes.

> **NOTE** Creating a stand-alone attribute list can be helpful, but if you are using the modeling spreadsheet we described earlier in the chapter, you already have a place to keep your attribute lists.

Promotion

Attribute Name	Description	Alternate Names	Sample Values
Special Offer ID	Source system key		
Special Offer Name	Name / description of the Special Offer	Promotion name, Special offer description	Volume Discount 11 to 14; Sport Helmet Discount 2002
Discount Percent	Percent item is discounted		
Special Offer Type	Description of the type of promotion, special offer or discount.	Promotion Type	Volume Discount; Discontinued Product
Special Offer Category	Channel to which the Promotion applies	Promotion Category	Reseller; Customer
Start Date	First day the promotion is available		6/15/03
End Date	Last day the promotion is available		12/31/04
Minimum Quantity	Minimum quantity required to qualify for the promotion		0
Maximum Quantity	Maximum quantity allowed under the promotion		NULL

Notes: The main table that Promotion information comes from is called SpecialOffer in the source system, but the business users refer to the general class as promotions. We may need to replace the Null value in the Maximum Quantity field.

Attributes Not Elsewhere Classified

Attribute Name	Description	Alternate Names	Sample Values
SalesReasonID	Sales reason ID from source system		
Sales Reason	Reason the customer bought the product, as reported by the customer (Internet only)		Demo Event; On Promotion; Price; Review; Sponsorship
Sales Reason Type	Grouping for Sales Reason		Marketing; Promotion; Other
Channel	Channel through which the item was ordered		Customer; Reseller

Notes: This attribute list is a good candidate to be a junk dimension.

Figure 2.13 Promotion dimension portion of the Adventure Works Cycles initial Orders attribute list

The process of creating the attribute list can trigger changes to the initial high-level dimensional model. The Adventure Works Cycles modeling team came across two attributes that did not have an obvious home: Sales Reason and Channel. To borrow a heading from the taxonomy experts, these attributes are shown under the Attributes Not Elsewhere Classified table in Figure 2.13. Users mentioned a couple of fields that are entered by Internet customers to describe why they bought an Adventure Works Cycles bike: Sales Reason and Sales Reason Type. After some exploration, the team found that customers could select one or more reasons for their purchase from a list of reasons. This is an example of a many-to-many relationship, and a good candidate for a bridge table. However, discussions with the business users revealed that they were interested in the primary reason only, which can be identified in the ETL process. In an effort to avoid additional scope creep, the team decided to include only the primary sales reason.

Users also mentioned Sales Channel several times—usually referring to Resellers or the Internet. If Sales Channel refers only to Reseller and Internet, the Customer Type field can handle this distinction. However, it was clear during the requirements interviews that there is a drive to open up new sales channels, including opening Adventure Works Cycles retail stores and providing private label bikes for large retailers.

A quick query of the source system revealed there are only ten sales reasons and two sales channels so creating two separate dimensions seemed inefficient to the design team. They opted to create a junk dimension called OrderInfo that would contain both concepts. The ETL process will have to manage the assignment of surrogate keys and watch for new entries in the source systems.

The Adventure Works Cycles attribute list included several versions of something called Region. People in different parts of the organization expressed a need to track orders by various groupings of the state the order came from, which they called "region." The different organizational units each had different definitions of which states made up any given region. After some discussion, the team decided to incorporate the different regions directly in the dimension tables. The data steward needs to push for conformed definitions of the different regions.

It's easiest to start the list of Date dimension attributes from a standard set of attributes and adjust them according to your business requirements. The Analysis Services business intelligence wizard provides a checkbox list of dozens of potential attributes.

One of the groups on the attribute list represents the fact table. This list includes all the ways people measure the business, from dollars to counts to weight to minutes. The fact list should capture any known information about the nature of the measure, such as its aggregation type (such as sum, count, or average). You'll hear users describe a frequently used measure that's actually a derived measure. In other words, it's calculated from other measures and formulas. Note that it's a derived field and identify its derivation rules if possible. Whatever is not completed here will be filled in during the detailed modeling process.

Revisit the source system tables at this point, as a final check to make sure you haven't left anything useful behind. This is meant to be a validation step, not a starting point.

Not all of the data elements on the attribute list will necessarily be attributes of the final dimensional model. Some of them are not really attributes; rather they're aggregates or constraints. Others are the same attribute masquerading under a different name. Still other attributes are missing altogether, either because they were so obvious people didn't think to mention them, or they were so little used, people didn't know to mention them. As you build the lists, keep an eye out for these kinds of redundancies and omissions. Start to boil down all this information to create the master attribute list for each table.

The Final Draft of the Initial Model

At the end of the initial design session, the team has created a good high-level dimensional model. The high-level model shown in Figure 2.14 is the result of merging the changes identified in the process of creating the attributes list (adding the OrderInfo dimension) along with the changes from the model design session itself (merging Reseller and Customer, removing the Sales Territory dimension, and adding the Exchange Rate tracking business process). This dimensional model contains all the elements needed to meet Adventure Works Cycles' orders-related business requirements in a simple, powerful, flexible form—at least as far as the team understands them at this point. This model will change, but it is a strong first pass.

We encourage you to compare this model with the initial model in Figure 2.12 to see how it evolved during the initial design session. We also encourage you to review the business requirements described in Chapter 1 to get a sense for how well the model will meet the needs.

The Issues List

The last checkpoint from the initial modeling session is the issues list. Figure 2.15 shows an example of the issues list from the Adventure Works Cycles orders business process design session.

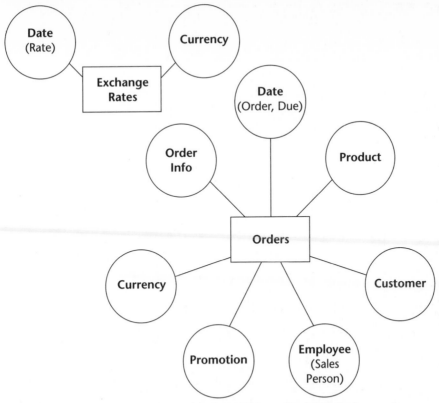

Figure 2.14   The high-level dimensional model from the initial design session

Detailed Dimensional Model Development

Develop the detailed dimensional model one dimension at a time. Begin with the attribute information you captured in your modeling spreadsheet in the initial design session (see Figure 2.13). Start with an easy dimension such as OrderInfo or Date, and fill in as much of the spreadsheet as possible based on current information. Source tables and columns are often fairly clear for most of the attributes. Transformations for most of the attributes are direct copies from the source. Target data types can be inferred based on the source system as well, although the data warehouse DBA will have the final say in determining the data types.

Once the known information is filled in, the open issues are more obvious. At this point, it's time to continue with the data exploration/data profiling process described earlier in this chapter.

Chng Flag	Issue #	Task / Topic	Issue	ID Date	Rptd By	Resp	Date Closed	Status	Priority
	27	Employee	Research availability of historical data.	3/8/06	Team	JM	-	Open	High
	28	Sales Territory	Research relationships and history among Sales Territory, Sales Rep, and Customer tables in the source system.	3/8/06	Team	JM	-	Open	High
	29	Customer	Assess projected impact of combined Internet and Reseller on data size and growth of Customer table.	3/8/06	Team	WT	-	Open	High
	30	Customer	Verify understanding of and support for combined Customer table with core users.	3/8/06	Team	WT	-	Open	High
	31	Promotions	Discuss special offer / promotions with marketing to understand how these might change.	3/8/06	Team	DK	-	Open	Med
	32	Order_Info	Verify concept of Channel with Marketing and Sales.	3/8/06	Team	DK	-	Open	High
	33	Order_Info	Verify usability of combined Channel and Sales Reason fields in the same table.	3/8/06	Team	DK	-	Open	High
	34	Order_Info	Determine list of possible combinations between Channel and Sales Reason.	3/8/06	Team	DK	-	Open	High

Figure 2.15 Adventure Works Cycles Orders dimensional model issues list

Identifying SCD Change Types

One of the columns in the modeling spreadsheet is the SCD Change Type. The data modeler will use this to identify how each attribute needs to be tracked over time and flag it appropriately. Remember, this is a business question. It's okay to make a first pass and flag all the attributes whose changes obviously must be tracked over time, or whose changes have no impact on the business whatsoever. All of the less obvious attributes should be discussed with the modeling team. Review all of these change-tracking decisions with the core business users before you make a final decision.

The ETL process must re-create the historical changes for every Type 2 SCD attribute in each dimension, at least as far back in time as the oldest fact table rows the dimension will support. The ETL process will load historical fact rows with the dimension surrogate keys that were in effect when the fact row occurred. The ETL developer has to go back into the transaction system to find all relevant historical transactions that apply to the dimension in question. While this is not the data modeler's task, it's helpful to look for indicators as to whether or not re-creating historical dimension data will be difficult or even possible.

Reviewing the Issues

Even though you may have filled in most of the spreadsheet, there will still be several issues that require a second or third opinion. In some cases, you can resolve these issues using the research tools described earlier in the chapter. In other cases, you need a sounding board to explore alternative solutions. Bring up open issues in the next data modeling team meeting and work them through.

Then move on to the next dimension.

Identifying the Facts

Filling in the detailed fact table description is much like filling in the dimensions. Start by copying in the list of measures and filling in all the easy items. Then use the research tools to address as many of the open items as possible. Finally, work with the data modeling team to resolve the remaining issues.

There are several issues that are specific to fact tables. These include:

- *Derived columns:* Identify the formula and indicate whether the derivation is additive or semi-additive, as in a month end account balance.

- *Allocations:* In the case of the Adventure Works Cycles Orders dimensional model, the grain is at the order line item level. The team must decide how to handle the handful of facts that are collected at the order level. Sales tax can easily be allocated to each line item. Other facts, such as shipping costs, might need to be allocated based on weight or size.

> **NOTE** Don't avoid the allocations! If you leave shipping costs in a fact table at the order (not line item) level, all your product-related financial rollups will omit the shipping costs. Grit your teeth and allocate!

- *Conformed facts:* The dollar sales field is a good example of creating a conformed fact. As the team discussed in the design session, there's a need to have all transactions stated in a single currency (US dollars), as well as the original local currency from the source system.

- *Degenerate dimensions:* While no transformations need to be applied to any degenerate dimensions in the dimensional model, you do need to indicate which fields in the fact table are degenerate dimensions. In the Orders dimensional model, there are degenerate dimensions for Order number, Order Line Item Number, and the Sales Order Revision Number. The data modeler will identify another potential degenerate dimension that comes in as part of the order: the Customer PO Number.

Final Dimensional Model

When all the design reviews are finished, the user meetings over, the source systems carefully scrutinized, and the requirements reviewed, it's time to physically instantiate the dimensional model. This is a job for the DBAs, but we usually set up a test database and run the script from the spreadsheet. (You will probably already have done this several times by now so you could reverse engineer the model into your modeling tool to create a presentable data model.) You can find the completed modeling spreadsheet we used to create the MDWT_AdventureWorks database at www.MsftDWToolkit.com.

At this point, you're ready to take on the real database physical design process and start thinking about designing the ETL system.

Summary

Designing dimensional models for business intelligence is no simple trick. The first part of this chapter concentrated on defining and describing the basic concepts of dimensional modeling: facts, dimensions, the bus matrix, and conformed dimensions. The next section expanded the description of dimensional modeling with key concepts such as surrogate keys and tracking changes with Slowly Changing Dimensions. We described several techniques to model a broad range of common (and uncommon) business processes and relationships like many-to-many relationships, hierarchies, heterogeneous products, and junk dimensions.

The third part of this chapter covered the process of dimensional modeling. Begin with a preparation step to identify the team, set up the modeling environment, and determine naming conventions. Begin the modeling process by using our four-step approach to create a high-level business dimensional model, along with attributes and issues lists. The next step is to develop the detailed model, table by table and column by column, filling in all the needed information and addressing all the issues. The last step in the process of creating the dimensional model involved reviewing the proposed model with several interested parties, including other IT people and core business users.

The last part of the chapter applied the dimensional modeling concepts and process to the Adventure Works Cycles case study, resulting in a dimensional model for the Orders business process. This dimensional model will be the target for the physical database creation and the ETL system described over the next several chapters.

The Toolset

When you have a hammer, everything looks like a nail.

In this chapter, we describe the architecture and product selection for the Microsoft data warehouse/business intelligence (DW/BI) system. It may seem pointless to talk about architecture alternatives and product selection for a Microsoft system, but Microsoft offers enough software components that there actually is an element of product selection.

Figure 3.1 repeats the familiar Business Dimensional Lifecycle diagram, highlighting the Architecture and Product Selection boxes that are the focus of this chapter. In this version of the diagram, we've included a mapping between the Lifecycle boxes and the Microsoft products and components you may use during your development and management processes.

This chapter continues with a description of the two main tools that you'll use to develop and operate your DW/BI system. You'll use a single integrated environment called the Business Intelligence Development Studio to develop most of your DW/BI system, and a second environment called the SQL Server Management Studio to manage it. We introduce the two tools here and provide an overview of the elements that are the same no matter what part of the DW/BI project you're working on.

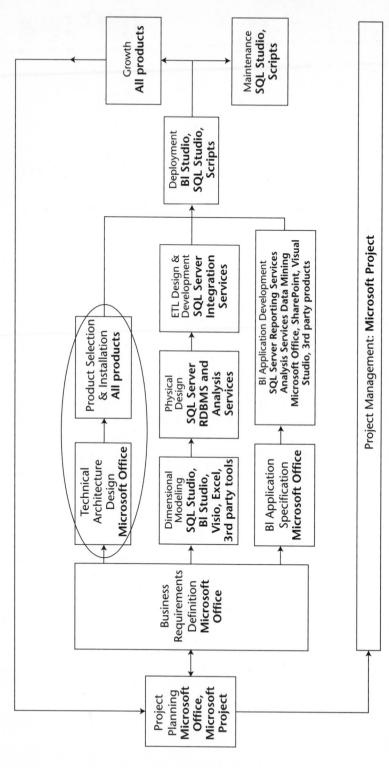

Figure 3.1 Business Dimensional Lifecycle and Microsoft technologies

The Microsoft DW/BI Toolset

The core set of DW/BI tools that Microsoft Corporation sells is Microsoft SQL Server 2005. SQL Server includes several major components of primary interest for DW/BI projects:

- The *relational engine (RDBMS)* to manage and store the dimensional data warehouse database.

- *Integration Services* to build the extract, transformation, and load (ETL) system.

- An OLAP database in *Analysis Services* to support users' queries, particularly ad hoc use.

- *Analysis Services data mining* to develop statistical data mining models, and also to include those models in advanced analytic applications.

- *Reporting Services* to build predefined reports. Most of the Reporting Services features are most appropriate for the DW/BI team, but you may provide some ad hoc query and report building functionality with *Report Builder.*

- Development and management tools, especially SQL Server BI Development Studio and SQL Server Management Studio, to build and manage your DW/BI system.

The SQL Server product contains the software necessary to build, deploy, populate, manage, and access your DW/BI system. A second significant set of Microsoft tools are designed for the business user. These include Microsoft Office, notably Excel, Office Web Components, Data Analyzer, and SharePoint Services.

Office and SharePoint provide tools that you can use to build end-user applications to access the data warehouse databases. Many DW/BI systems supplement Microsoft end-user tools with third-party software.

An increasingly important set of software developed by Microsoft is packaged analytic applications. Examples of these packaged analytic applications are:

- The analytic functionality that Microsoft is increasingly adding to transaction systems like Commerce Server and Microsoft Business Systems Great Plains

- Standalone analytic applications, which will be released after this book goes to print

Microsoft Visual Studio is a fundamental tool for the DW/BI development team. The SQL Server DW/BI development tools are hosted in Visual Studio. The necessary Visual Studio components are installed for you, and you may not even realize that you are using the standard Microsoft development environment.

You can use Visual Studio to build a custom application, such as an analytic application that connects your DW/BI system back to transaction systems. The heavy lifting of such an application may occur within your Analysis Services data mining model, but you'd still need to develop a bit of plumbing to connect the two systems.

Why Use the Microsoft Toolset?

Before we go on to describe how to build a DW/BI system using Microsoft technologies, it's worth asking the question: What is interesting about the Microsoft toolset?

- *Completeness:* From the operating system, database engines, and development environment to the Office and Excel desktop, you can build a complete DW/BI system using only Microsoft software. You have an extra margin of confidence that all the components work together effectively.

- *Low cost of ownership:* The licensing cost of SQL Server has been less than comparable product suites from other vendors, but total cost of ownership depends as much on ongoing support, training, and operations costs as on licensing costs. Microsoft asserts that SQL Server systems need fewer administrative resources than competitive products. Your organization may already have .NET programming skills. If so, it may be really easy for you to customize and extend your DW/BI system.

- *Openness:* Although you can build a complete DW/BI system with Microsoft software—and this book describes how to do it—you don't have to. Any component of the Microsoft DW/BI framework can be swapped out for a third-party product, and many customers build Microsoft DW/BI systems in heterogeneous environments.

- *High performance and scale:* At the time of this writing, DW/BI systems with data volumes in the terabytes are fairly common, and 10–20TB is not rare. As DW/BI systems are built on sub-transactional data like clickstreams and RFID data streams, even moderate-sized organizations may find themselves in the "terabyte club." Microsoft recognizes this trend, and has engineered and tested their products, especially the SQL Server components, to perform well at high data volumes.

■ *Microsoft investment in business intelligence:* The SQL Server 2005 business intelligence suite consists of real tools that work together, if not seamlessly, then at least with seams that have been professionally sewn. Some of the tools—notably Analysis Services—are best of breed. All of the tools are competitive on their own merits with standalone products. Microsoft is clearly committed to building tools to enable you to build great business intelligence applications. And you can be reasonably confident that Microsoft will remain in business for a long time.

Architecture of a Microsoft DW/BI System

All DW/BI systems consist of several major components, as pictured in Figure 3.2: sources of data, an ETL system, data warehouse databases, and a wide variety of uses. Metadata is the glue that binds together the complete DW/BI system.

As we explained in Chapter 2, the data warehouse databases should be in a dimensional form, consisting of fact tables and their associated dimension tables. Dimensions should be conformed across the enterprise. All business processes that are described by the customer dimension should use the same customer dimension with the same keys.

The primary place to store and manage the dimensional model is in the relational data warehouse database. In Microsoft terms, this is the SQL Server 2005 database engine. You will write an ETL system that populates that database, performing inserts and updates, and perhaps also managing system resources such as disk space and indexes.

The second place to store and manage the dimensional model is in the OLAP data warehouse database. In Microsoft terms, this is the Analysis Services OLAP engine. We recommend that you always build the OLAP database from a clean, conformed relational data warehouse database.

As we describe in Chapter 8, there are many kinds of BI applications, ranging from standard predefined reports to complex analytic applications that use data mining technology to affect business operations. Microsoft offers many technologies here, from Reporting Services for predefined reports, to Analysis Services data mining and the Visual Studio development environment to build custom applications.

The other kind of usage is exploratory or ad hoc. Here, Office Excel continues to be popular, although many organizations struggle with the data anarchy that comes with extensive use of Excel in the enterprise. Many organizations use non-Microsoft tools to deliver more structured, yet still highly flexible, ad hoc query functionality. As we discuss in Chapter 9, the Report Builder component of Reporting Services is designed to provide some ad hoc functionality. Data mining is another kind of exploratory use, delivered by the Analysis Services data mining features.

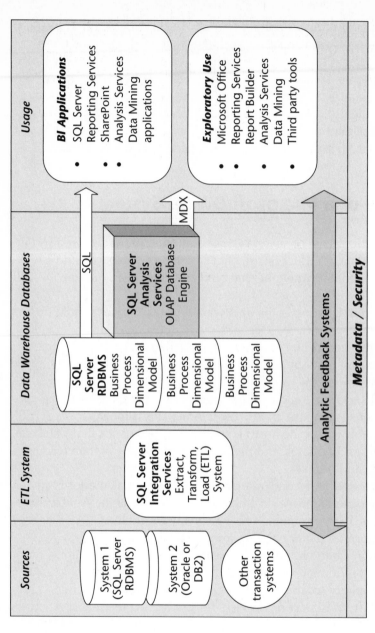

Figure 3.2 Microsoft DW/BI system architecture

> ### USE BOTH RELATIONAL AND OLAP DATA STORES
>
> Your Microsoft DW/BI system should contain both a relational data warehouse database and an OLAP database. You *could* build a DW/BI system with only a relational database to hold the dimensional data; you *could* build a system with only an Analysis Services OLAP database. But the majority of DW/BI systems should plan to store dimensional data in the relational database, with an Analysis Services layer on top.

All these tools use metadata for development and operations, but there's no specific metadata feature that we can point to. That doesn't mean the metadata is missing or even that it's unavailable; it's just not as easy to get to, nor as integrated as we'd like.

Most readers understand why the relational data warehouse database is important. Let's talk first about why your architecture should include Analysis Services.

Why Analysis Services?

What functionality is addressed by the OLAP database engine? Why would you want an OLAP engine—an Analysis Services implementation—in addition to the dimensional model stored in the relational database?

All DW/BI systems need a user-oriented layer on top of the dimensional data stored in the relational database. This layer could simply be a set of predefined reports. But for successful ad hoc access by business users, you need a layer that performs the following basic functions:

- *Easy user navigation:* User-oriented names for database objects, and transparent join paths between dimensions and facts and between multiple fact tables.

- *Complex calculations:* Centralized storage of calculation logic, and execution of calculations.

- *Fast user query performance:* Usually accomplished through aggregate navigation and aggregate management.

- *Data security definition and enforcement:* Preferably managed on a server rather than on users' desktops.

For many years people have used relational techniques like views and client-side query tools to deliver this functionality. An OLAP engine like Analysis Services provides a better way. There are two key characteristics of the best OLAP engines that make them superior to the classic approach of using a client query tool atop relational views:

- *Query language:* OLAP engines use a different—and better—query language than SQL to express complex calculations.

- *Computational performance:* An OLAP engine has been designed as a high-performance server—its ability to resolve the most complex calculations far outstrips any client-based tool (even those client-based tools that run on a shared file server).

Analysis Services meets our definition of an OLAP engine. It provides the following features:

- *User-oriented metadata:* The structure of the Analysis Services database explicitly defines dimensions, facts, and hierarchies. These structures have user-oriented names that can be localized into different languages for different users. Query and reporting tools provide an interface to browse the data and generate complex analytics using the familiar slicing, dicing, and drilling metaphors.

- *Complex analytics stored in the database:* The Analysis Services database stores information about calculations, from simple information about calculations, such as whether an inventory balance is calculated as an average or period-end, to the definition of complex calculations such as corporate profit or revenue allocation. Such calculations belong within the definition of the database itself, and Analysis Services provides many mechanisms for doing so, including calculated members, calculated cells, scripts, and key performance indicators.

- *Richness of the analytic language:* SQL is a set-oriented query language; it is not and will never be an analytic language, even with the ANSI-99 OLAP extensions. Query tools for Analysis Services generate MDX (Multidimensional Expressions) instead of SQL. MDX's greatest strength is its understanding of the dimensional metadata: facts, dimensions, attributes, hierarchies, parents, siblings, and children.

- *Query performance:* Ad hoc query performance is significantly improved over the "same" queries issued directly against the relational data warehouse database. This is especially true when you use the Analysis Services storage for most of the OLAP database.

- *Aggregate management:* Aggregate or summary tables are vital for query performance of any relational data warehouse database, but building, populating, and updating those aggregates is painful. Analysis Services is a great aggregate management and navigation system.

REFERENCE   Chapter 14 of *The Data Warehouse Lifecycle Toolkit* discusses relational aggregate management in great detail.

The concepts introduced here are discussed more thoroughly in Chapter 7, which describes how to design an Analysis Services database.

Arguments Against Analysis Services

Although Analysis Services has become an extremely popular component of SQL Server 2000, there are still several common objections to using Analysis Services:

- *Scalability:* What if your relational database contains several terabytes of data? Analysis Services 2000 scaled to this level, although like its relational cousin it scaled better with simple schemas than complex ones. Analysis Services 2005 has been designed for improved scalability. We wouldn't hesitate to implement systems with several terabytes of data in Analysis Services. This isn't to say Analysis Services won't scale higher than several terabytes, just that we'd be more cautious.

- *Duplication of data:* Many users dislike the notion of duplicating all the relational data warehouse data into a second database management system. First, you should recognize that using an Analysis Services database does not require duplicating the data—the data can continue to be stored only in the relational database. Even if you choose an implementation that duplicates the data, the technologies self-manage so that the duplication behaves like an index or cache.

- Changing the user applications: Your business users are accustomed to using a SQL-based query and reporting tool, which might not work the same way (or at all) against an Analysis Services database. There is significant cost in purchasing new tools and retraining your users. This is the best argument against Analysis Services, especially in companies that have made significant commitments to a SQL-based tool vendor. In many cases, however, the query and reporting tools require periodic expensive upgrades and re-licensing. If a solution based on Analysis Services and Microsoft Office meets most of your users' needs, and Office is already licensed for basic desktop use, you may minimize the cost of retooling.

Of the three common arguments against using Analysis Services, we find only the third to be broadly compelling. Worries about scalability and data duplication shouldn't prevent the vast majority of SQL Server implementations from reaping the very real benefits of a DW/BI system that's built on Analysis Services.

Why a Relational Store?

Perhaps you're convinced that Analysis Services is a vital part of your DW/BI system architecture. Your next question may be: why do you need to store the dimensional data in the relational database? You aren't required to do so:

Microsoft provides several mechanisms for populating Analysis Services cubes directly from non-dimensional source systems. Why go to the trouble and expense of implementing a relational data warehouse database? Here's why:

- *Disaster recovery:* The tools and knowledge for managing a relational database for easy recovery are better than those for Analysis Services. It's worth noting that Analysis Services management tools are much improved from SQL Server 2000.

- *Conforming dimensions and facts:* In a hypothetical, simple example you could conform data on the way into the Analysis Services database. In the real world, you will have to update and delete some data in the ETL pipeline, and you really want to do this in a relational database.

- *Query performance:* Insofar as users' queries are resolved from the relational database rather than the Analysis Services multidimensional cache, those queries will perform much faster against a dimensional source than against the normalized transaction system sources. This is an order of magnitude more important if the sources are on multiple servers.

- *Database flexibility:* If you want to modify an Analysis Services database, you usually need to redeploy and reprocess a large chunk of the database. It's much easier to "join and go" in the relational world.

- *Comfort:* DBAs and power users are very familiar with SQL and relational databases, and will violently resist the elimination of the relational layer.

- *Future flexibility:* The notion of eliminating the relational data warehouse database and populating the Analysis Services database directly from transaction systems may sound appealing. But if you choose this architecture, you're committing to an architecture that's especially Microsoft-specific.

There are scenarios, particularly around the real-time delivery of analytic data, where the best choice is to skip the relational storage of the dimensional data and populate the Analysis Services database directly from transaction systems. But these are edge cases. Most of us, most of the time, should plan to store and manage the dimensional data in the relational database, and use that store to feed Analysis Services. Think of the Analysis Services layer as metadata for the OLAP engine, which possibly includes a data cache.

Overview of the Microsoft Tools

Many readers will start to work with SQL Server 2005 by experimenting with its functionality in a single machine sandbox. If you have the time and bandwidth to do so, this is a great way to determine which product features are important to your business and users. In this environment, we recommend that you acquire a true sandbox machine: a new or rebuilt machine with a clean operating system and no other applications. You can use virtual PC technology to simulate a clean machine and run SQL Server well enough to evaluate functionality (although not performance).

Other readers are launching real projects and need to be more rigorous and thoughtful in setting up their environments. As we discuss in Chapter 14, plan from the outset for the standard three-tier system, with separate servers for development, test, and production. Your test system should be as similar to the production system as you can possibly make it. The more different your test and production systems are, the more difficult it is for your database administrators to evaluate alternative approaches to tuning and configuration before rolling those changes into production.

Most teams set up their development environment with a central server or two to hold relational and Analysis Services databases. Developers install the development tools—the studio workbenches described in the next section—on their own machines, and point those tools to the development database server. Early in the development cycle, developers may have personal databases, either on the shared server or on their own machines.

Which Products Do You Need?

At the time of the SQL Server 2005 launch there are three editions available that are interesting for DW/BI projects:

- Enterprise Edition
- Standard Edition
- Developer Edition

INTEGRATE DEVELOPMENT DATABASES EARLY

Don't delay for too long the integration of the development databases, as there are usually all sorts of surprising differences between databases that are supposed to be the same. The project manager should encourage developers to move to shared databases as soon as they can do so without harming productivity.

You will need to purchase and run either SQL Server 2005 Enterprise Edition or Standard Edition on your production servers. Enterprise Edition contains the entire product feature set, and—unsurprisingly—costs several times as much as Standard Edition.

REFERENCE You can find detailed information on each edition at www. microsoft.com/sql, and in Books Online. See the Books Online topic "Features Supported by the Editions of SQL Server 2005."

Besides Standard versus Enterprise Edition, you need to decide on the 32-bit platform versus the 64-bit platform. As we discuss in Chapter 4, almost everyone should use the 64-bit platform for DW/BI projects.

There is no hard and fast rule for which edition you should purchase. A simple rule of thumb suggests that Standard Edition is probably sufficient for most small and some medium implementations. If your data volume, measured as data only without indexes, is 50 gigabytes (GB) or less, then you can do without the scalability features in Enterprise Edition. Depending on incremental load volumes, frequency, and uptime requirements, a medium-sized implementation of up to 250GB can also work on Standard Edition. Any large, real-time, or otherwise challenging implementation should plan to use Enterprise Edition.

Whichever edition you use in production, your developers should use Developer Edition. Developer Edition is extremely inexpensive (approximately $50 at the time of publication); it will run on desktop operating systems such as Windows XP; and it contains all the functionality of the Enterprise Edition.

EDITIONS AND FEATURES OF SQL SERVER 2005

Enterprise Edition features that are excluded from Standard Edition support scalability in the enterprise. Mostly, scalability refers to data volumes, and often has more to do with maintaining and operating very large systems than actually storing and querying them. Another dimension of scalability is complexity; some of the excluded features would help your business users navigate a complex enterprise-level system more easily.

Here we'll list, and comment on, our favorite enterprise edition features:

◆ Relational database engine

- Relational database partitioned tables are a key feature for fast loading and improved maintainability of large tables. We talk about partitioning in Chapter 4.

- Relational database maintenance functionality, including online index operations and parallel index operations, is particularly important for loading new data into large tables in a short time frame and performing periodic maintenance.

- Relational database failover clustering beyond two nodes is important for improving the availability of your relational data warehouse database.

◆ Integration Services

- Integration with Analysis Services dimensions, cubes, and data mining models is a really nice feature, but not absolutely necessary. You could have Integration Services launch a script that updates the cube or data mining model.

- Advanced transforms such as fuzzy lookup and text mining are very cool, but they may be too complicated for most small projects to deal with anyway.

◆ Analysis Services OLAP engine

- Scalability and performance features, such as automatic parallel processing and partitioned cubes, are very important for delivering great performance with medium and large data volumes, greater than 100GB of source data.

- Proactive Caching is a feature that automates the flow of data into the cube database. It improves system manageability, and is particularly important for real-time applications.

- Features such as Account Intelligence, Writeback Dimensions, and particularly Perspectives, Semi-additive Measures, and Translations let you build more usable and complex OLAP databases.

◆ Analysis Services data mining

- Parallelism for processing and prediction is important for large data volumes and heavy usage scenarios.

- The statisticians in your organization will appreciate the advanced tuning and configuration options for the algorithms.

- The integration with Integration Services, as we've already described, is useful but usually not absolutely necessary.

◆ Reporting Services

- Scale-out report servers are an important feature for large-scale deployments. This is basically creating a web farm for the report servers.

- Data-driven subscriptions may be useful for a large enterprise. With this feature, you can email each manager his or her personalized budget variance report, run from a single report definition.

SQL Server 2005 Development and Management Tools

Two toolsets are installed as part of the client tools installation. The SQL Server Management Studio (Management Studio) is used to *operate* and *manage* your DW/BI system. The Business Intelligence Development Studio (BI Studio) is used to *design* and *develop* your business intelligence system.

SQL Server Management Studio

Management Studio is the primary tool for database administrators. It replaces and extends the operations and management functionality from SQL Server 2000 Enterprise Manager and Analysis Manager. In most cases, the Management Studio client tools are the only component of SQL Server that is installed on database administrators' workstations. The Management Studio screen is pictured in Figure 3.3.

When you launch Management Studio for the first time, you are faced with a screen that is mostly empty. On the left, under the toolbar, is the Registered Servers window. (If this window is not showing, you can choose View → Registered Servers.) In this window, you register all the servers that you manage. If you have the necessary permissions, you can start, stop, and rename those servers. Note that there are little icons at the top of the Registered Servers window that let you flip between managing relational, Analysis Services, SQL Server CE, and Reporting Services servers. In Figure 3.3, we're looking at the registered Analysis Services servers. Developers and designers will not use the Registered Servers window very much; you can close or hide it to save screen real estate.

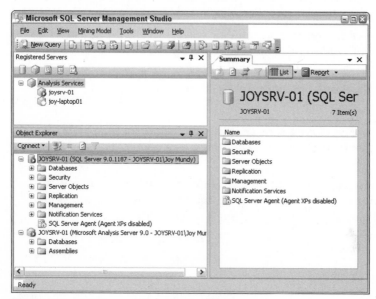

Figure 3.3   SQL Server Management Studio

The Object Explorer Window is also on the left. In this window you can connect to a database server (SQL, Analysis, CE, or Reporting) and browse its contents. The user experience for browsing a database server is very familiar to users of earlier versions of SQL Server. While browsing a SQL Server instance, notice that user databases and tables have been separated from system objects. Notice also the new sample databases called AdventureWorks and AdventureWorksDW—these databases replace the old Pubs and Northwind. AdventureWorksDW is Microsoft's dimensional DW/BI version of the AdventureWorks transactional database. Once you connect to an Analysis Services instance in the Object Explorer window, you can browse the corresponding Analysis Services demo database, Adventure Works DW.

The right-hand pane of Management Studio serves as the viewing area. The information that displays in the pane depends on what you're doing. In Figure 3.3, we've just launched Management Studio, and the right-hand side shows the objects in the database. In this area you'll write and execute queries, and you can have multiple documents open at the same time. Figure 3.3 shows a very small screen. On your workstation, the right-hand side will probably dominate the display.

From within Management Studio you can script any object in your relational, Analysis Services, or Reporting server—any table, cube, database, data mining model, package, or report. The scripts for relational database objects are generated as familiar CREATE statements. Scripts for other BI objects such as cubes, packages, and reports are generated as XML.

It is technically possible to edit and re-issue the BI object creation XML. In fact, it is technically possible to write a complete Analysis Services cube definition or Integration Services package by typing an XML file. Just because something is possible doesn't mean it's a good idea. Use BI Studio to design and debug BI objects (except for the relational database). In the rare cases when you need to automatically generate an object, you should use the appropriate programming object model rather than attempt to manipulate the XML directly.

If you generated a script for a database object, the first thing you probably noticed is that the query pane is integrated into SQL Manager, and supports SQL for the relational database; MDX, DMX, and XMLA for Analysis databases; and even XQuery for querying XML.

Readers who use Visual Studio will have noticed that Management Studio bears a strong resemblance to the Visual Studio development environment. Indeed, it is not just a resemblance: Management Studio and BI Studio are hosted in the Visual Studio shell. The integration with Visual Studio is particularly important for the BI Studio development environment.

NOTE Microsoft ships a short tutorial for SQL Server Management Studio, which you should run through. The tutorials—and sample databases, for that matter—aren't installed by default when you install SQL Server. If you didn't install them initially, run Add or Remove Programs, and modify the SQL Server installation.

Business Intelligence Development Studio

BI Studio is designed for all BI system designers and developers, with user interfaces for designing and debugging Analysis Services databases, data mining models, Integration Services packages, and Reporting Services reports. The obvious omission from this list is the design and development of the relational data warehouse database. Use SQL Studio for the relational part of the project and BI Studio for the rest.

Like SQL Studio, BI Studio is integrated with Visual Studio. This is great news for developers who already use Visual Studio because the interface will already be somewhat familiar. Even though the Visual Studio environment appears complex at first, everyone benefits from this integration. Your team can use integrated source control to manage project files; you can set breakpoints and debug Integration Services packages and MDX scripts; any code you may need to develop is integrated in the same environment; and all projects benefit from a unified approach to separating development from deployment.

Launch BI Studio from the Start menu (Start → All Programs → Microsoft SQL Server 2005 → SQL Server Business Intelligence Development Studio). Once you use BI Studio, your recent projects will be listed for you to choose from. But the first time you launch BI Studio you'll need to create a new project (File → New → Project), as illustrated in Figure 3.4. Ensure that the Business Intelligence Projects project type is selected on the left-hand side. The kinds of new projects available to you depend on what components of SQL Server (Analysis Services, Integration Services, Reporting Services) are installed on your workstation. If you use Visual Studio for programming in a language such as Visual Basic or C#, these projects will also show up on that list. In general, we'll assume that all components are installed locally, although we know many developers will install only the components they are actively working on.

You can name both the solution and the project within the solution. Directories get created, by default at ..\My Documents\Visual Studio 2005\Projects. The directory name will correspond to the name of the solution. It's very easy to click on a new Analysis Services project and then hit OK . . . and you've just created folders with names like Solution 1 and Project 1. The names can be changed, but it's easier to name them intelligently from the outset. You can (and should) include multiple projects in a solution—for example a project for the Analysis Services database, one for data mining models, several for Integration Services packages, and one for reports. Use a simple naming convention: prefix the project name with AS, DM, IS, or RS as appropriate.

DW/BI development teams should manage their files under source control, and BI Studio makes that very easy to do. You won't see this functionality unless you've installed a source control product like Visual Source Safe, and integrated it into Visual Studio. You can add other kinds of files, such as a Word or Excel document, by right-clicking on the project in the Solution Browser and choosing Add . . . Existing Item, and locating the file in the file system. The file will be copied into the project directory.

The files in the project folder completely define the project: They are the source code for the project. During the development process (especially if you're not using source control!), you may want to share your project definition with a colleague so she can view your work. You can simply send her a copy of the project folder, ensure she has appropriate database permissions, and she is set.

BI Studio shows different windows depending on whether you are working on an Analysis Services, Integration Services, or Reporting Services project. Figure 3.5 illustrates the BI Studio window for a Report Builder project. This is a new project that doesn't have much content yet.

All the different types of projects use a similar layout, imposed by Visual Studio. The Solution Explorer window, located by default in the upper right, lists the project files in the project and lets you navigate between them The Properties pane, located by default in the lower right, shows all the properties associated with an object; read-only properties are gray. As you'll see in subsequent chapters, BI Studio contains extensive wizards whose job, in effect, is to help you set these properties.

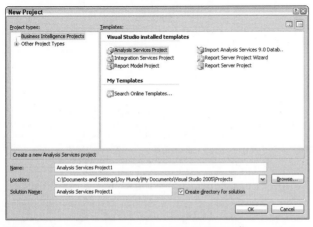

Figure 3.4 Creating a new project in BI Studio

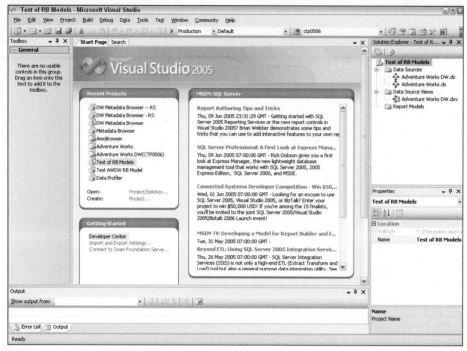

Figure 3.5 Basic layout of the BI Studio windows and panes

BI Studio gobbles up screen real estate. It officially requires a screen resolution of at least 1024×768, but we cannot get anything done on less than 1280×1024. BI Studio is a good excuse to get an upgraded monitor and video card. You can maximize screen real estate by setting windows such as the Solution Explorer and Properties pane to "auto-hide."

Many of the BI Studio components use the Toolbox pane on the left-hand side. The toolbox is empty for the start page displayed here, but Integration Services uses it a lot. The big section in the middle, which currently displays the start page, is used as a design surface. In here you'll design Integration Services packages, Analysis Services dimensions, cubes, and data mining models, Reporting Services reports, and so on. You generally want this central area to be as big as possible.

Finally, the BI Studio tools use Visual Studio's build, deploy, and debugging features such as watch windows. Sometimes it feels like there are dozens of extra little windows, located by default at the bottom of the screen where Error List and Output are displayed in Figure 3.5.

The other chapters in this book focus on the specific BI features such as Analysis Services and Integration Services. In those chapters, we spend more time describing how to use BI Studio, although this book is not intended to be a product tutorial. The tutorials that ship with SQL Server do a very good job of explaining how to use the product.

Summary

In this chapter we described how the Microsoft BI toolset maps to industry standard terminology. We made a compelling argument that you can build your entire business intelligence system using software only from Microsoft. You're not tied to Microsoft for your entire project, however: the components are "open," in the sense that they are linked together by published interfaces. If you wish, you can use a non-Microsoft product for any component of your BI system. Many people will develop a heterogeneous BI system—it's particularly common for an enterprise to require the relational database or front end tools to use the corporate standard.

We described the basic recommended architecture of a Microsoft BI/DW system and introduced the studio tools—SQL Server Management Studio and BI Development Studio. We will provide much more information about these tools in upcoming chapters.

PART Two

Developing and Populating the Databases

Setup and Physical Design

Where the rubber meets the road

Up to this point, we've been talking about project management, business requirements, logical data models, and system architectures. Until now, you haven't needed an instance of SQL Server 2005 installed in your organization. That changes in this chapter, as we discuss issues surrounding the setup of your development, test, and production systems, and get you ready to start the development process.

As you can see in Figure 4.1, the physical design issues addressed in this chapter fall squarely in the middle of the Data Track of the Business Dimensional Lifecycle.

We begin by helping you get a handle on the size of your business intelligence system, so you can make decisions about its basic physical configuration. Will you install all the server software components for your DW/BI system on a single machine or several? Will you use clustering or web farms? Do you need to budget for 64-bit hardware or expensive storage networks? We can't answer these questions for you, but we've provided some guidance that should help you answer them for yourself.

The decisions you make about your production hardware and software configuration should be reflected, as much as economically feasible, in your test or quality assurance system. It may seem wasteful to spend money on test systems, but if you're serious about delivering good-quality service to your existing business users, you need to be serious about testing before you roll system changes into production.

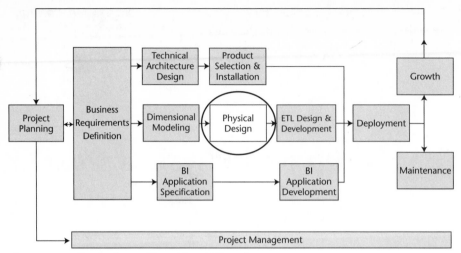

Figure 4.1 The Business Dimensional Lifecycle

The next section of this chapter discusses some of the issues in moving from the logical data model to the physical data model, particularly for the relational data warehouse database. As we described in Chapter 2, the dimensional logical model should be nearly identical to its corresponding physical model. However, when you actually create the database you need to worry about the placement of files on disk, as well as the creation of some housekeeping tables and columns that might not show up in your logical design. We also discuss exciting design issues such as index creation and key constraints.

One of the important considerations of the physical design of your relational data warehouse database is whether to partition the fact table. Table partitioning is a new feature in SQL Server 2005, and it's important for large-scale DW/BI systems. Finally, we discuss the physical design issues around aggregate, staging, and metadata tables.

We suspect many readers will be tempted to skip this chapter. At least one person on your project team should read it, even if you have very extensive experience in managing a SQL Server 2000 DW/BI system.

In this chapter, we address the following specific questions:

- Early in the design process, how can you determine how large your DW/BI system will be? What are the usage factors that will push you to a larger and more complex configuration?

- How should you configure your system? How much memory do you need, how many servers, what kind of storage and processors?

- How do you install the SQL Server software on the development, test, and production servers? What do different members of the DW/BI team need to install on their workstations?

- How do you convert the logical data model into a physical data model in the relational database? What's a good initial indexing plan? Should you use relational table partitioning?

System Sizing Considerations

We're sure that all readers of this book are hoping for a simple chart that will specify what kind of server machine they should buy. Sorry, it's not going to happen: The problem is too difficult to reduce to a simple matrix or tool. The best we can do is describe the different options and parameters, and the kinds of operations that will push you to require bigger and more expensive hardware.

There are four main factors that will push your project to more expensive hardware: data volumes, usage complexity, number of simultaneous users, and system availability requirements. These factors are illustrated in Figure 4.2, and discussed in the following sections.

Calculating Data Volumes

The first and most obvious characteristic of your DW/BI system that will affect your hardware purchases is data volumes. By the time you've finished your logical model and initial data profiling, you should have enough information to estimate how big your DW/BI system is going to be. Later in the project your DBAs will calculate database sizes in great detail, but for now you can just think about fact table row counts. Unless you have a monster dimension of 50–100 million rows, dimension sizes are insignificant.

For starters, just figure out what order of magnitude number of rows you'll have for your initial historical load of fact data. Multiply that number by 100 bytes, which is our generous rule-of-thumb for fact row sizes. You can get more precise if you like, but we like arithmetic that we can do on our fingers. One hundred million fact rows require about 10GB as stored in the relational database, measured as atomic data only, no indexes. It might be 7GB; it might be 12GB; it won't be 100MB or 100GB. When you add relational indices and Analysis Services indices and MOLAP storage, multiply that base number by 2 to 4. In the early stages, before we have a specific design, we use a factor of 3. The requirements for the ETL staging area could conceivably add another factor, although most often the staging area is small.

Overall System Size	Small	Medium		Large
Range of Configu- rations	One "Commodity" 32-bit or 64-bit 4-way	One high-end (8 or more processors) 64-bit system with max memory, or distribute components to multiple commodity servers		Distributed system on high-end 64-bit servers; some clusters
Data Volume	< 500 M fact rows, < 50 GB atomic fact data	< 5 B fact rows, < 500 GB atomic fact data		Billions and billions...
Usage Complexity	> 60% Simple use 30% Medium complexity < 10% Demanding use		50% Simple use 35% Medium 15% Demanding	35% Simple 40% Medium 25% Demanding
Number of Users	< a dozen simultaneous users	< 200 simultaneous users		Thousands
Availa- bility	Several hours of downtime each night acceptable	< 1 hour downtime or query slowdown each night		24x7 with excellent query performance

Figure 4.2   Factors influencing DW/BI system hardware requirements

The incremental daily or monthly load volume is important, too. From the incremental volumes, you can compute expected data volumes for each fact table one, three, and five years out, which will help you decide what class of storage system to buy today.

Although we've talked in this section about counting all the fact rows in your system, not all fact tables are created equal. A single billion-row fact table is going to be more demanding of system resources than ten 100 million–row fact tables would be. We don't have a scientific way to quantify this difference, but you should list the fact table sizes by fact table, in addition to an overall count.

In Figure 4.2, a small system is characterized by less than 500 million rows of fact data, or 50GB using our simple multiplier. A large system is more than 5 billion fact rows, into the terabyte range and above.

Determining Usage Complexity

The next key factor in deciding how big your hardware needs to be is to consider how your business users are going to use the data. There are two main questions: how many users will be working simultaneously, and what will they be doing? The usage patterns of a business intelligence system are quite different from the familiar workload of a transaction system. Even the simplest DW/BI query—for example, a query browsing a dimension—is more complex than most transactional queries. And the most complex DW/BI query is several orders of magnitude more complex, and touches more data, than any operational transaction.

COMPARING DATABASE SIZES

We wish all vendors would use fact table rowcounts and row sizes as their metrics for reporting the size of their customers' DW/BI systems. There's so much variety in size reporting that the information is effectively useless. We've seen reports ranging from the smallest possible number as we're discussing here (atomic data only, no indexes), all the way to the total storage attached to the system. The latter is fine for marketing purposes, but not useful for education or planning. Our measure reduces the likelihood that your system will put you in the Terabyte Club, but trust us when we tell you that you don't really want to be there.

You can't expect to already have a great understanding of system usage during the design phase of the DW/BI system. But you do need to think about different kinds of usage, and the approximate volume of use in each category. The data model tests we described in Chapter 2 are a good place to start. Your business requirements document should contain additional information.

Simple or Controlled Access

The more simple or predictable the users' queries, the more simultaneous users can be supported on the same size system. Examples of simple use include:

- *Predefined queries and reports based on a relatively small set of relational or Analysis Services data:* Because these queries are relatively simple and predefined, the system can easily be tuned to support them. It's particularly hard to understand what's simple and what's challenging to Analysis Services OLAP databases. Please refer to the related discussion in the following two subsections.

- *Reporting Services scheduled and cached reports:* As described in Chapter 9, scheduled reports may be extremely complex. But because they are run at night and cached, the load placed by users of these reports during business hours is relatively light.

- *Data mining forecasting queries:* Another kind of predefined query. As we discuss later, training a data mining model is most definitely *not* simple access. But performing a forecasting query on new information about a customer is straightforward.

Moderate Complexity

Examples of moderately complex use include:

- *Predefined reports based on a broad set of relational data,* such as all sales for the past year. On the positive side, the report is predefined and so it can be tuned. On the negative side, the underlying query touches a lot of data and so is expensive. Consider scheduling and caching these reports in Reporting Services to move them into the Simple category, or using Analysis Services as the report's data source.

- *Ad hoc query and analysis using Analysis Services,* where the analysis does *not* need to look at a large portion of the atomic data. If a lot of business users are performing ad hoc queries, the odds are good that they're hitting different parts of the OLAP database. In this case, the server's data cache will be of limited use (unless you have a *lot* of memory). Contrast this moderately complex ad hoc use of Analysis Services with the highly complex situation described following.

Highly Demanding Use

Examples of highly complex use include:

- *Ad hoc query and analysis using the relational data warehouse database:* The business users aren't experts, so they may make mistakes. It's not really feasible for them to use query hints. Queries typically join many tables and often access a large volume of data.

- *Ad hoc query and analysis on Analysis Services:* The analysis requires wide queries that access a large portion of the atomic data. There is a class of analytic problems that by definition must touch very detailed data. For example, a query that counts the unique values in a large set is unavoidably expensive because it must touch detailed rows. Similarly, a query that returns a median or top N percent must also touch many more rows than are handed back in the result set.

- *Training of a data mining model:* As we discuss in Chapter 10, creating the case sets for a data mining model often involves several full table scans of the fact tables.

Most DW/BI systems will be used in all these ways. A normal DW/BI system will have 60 percent simple, 30 percent moderately complex, and 10 percent demanding usage, as illustrated in Figure 4.2. A challenging usage profile has 35 percent simple, 40 percent moderate, and 25 percent demanding usage.

Estimating Simultaneous Users

The number of potential users of the DW/BI system provides only the roughest possible estimate of how many people are using the system at the same time. One analyst doing very complex work can use as many resources as dozens of users who are accessing simple reports. It's as important to know the system usage characteristics as it is to know how many people access the system.

If you currently have no DW/BI system in place, it will be difficult for you to forecast usage frequency and timing. Even our old standby recommendation, that you interview the business users, will be of little value. During the design and development phase, business users are not able to guess how much they'll use the system, and during what times of day.

A few broad patterns are easy to predict. There is usually a surge of demand in the morning, when people arrive at work and check the reports run on yesterday's data. Other cycles may be based on obvious work patterns, like month-end, quarterly, or year-end financial reporting calendars. Even with these patterns, however, remember that a DW/BI workload is quite different from the fairly constant stream associated with a transaction system. In most cases, a business user executes a query or report, and then examines and thinks about the information before executing a followup query. You should be careful to incorporate this think time into your understanding of simultaneous usage. If you buy or develop a performance testing suite, make sure it uses randomly generated think times of between 30 seconds and several minutes.

If you have an operational DW/BI system, the current usage statistics will provide a more certain estimate of future use. But if the current DW/BI system performs poorly, you'll find increased use with a new higher performance system than with the old. A lot of DW/BI queries and reports are somewhat optional for business users. If the current system is painful to use, they won't use it.

A small system may have only a dozen simultaneous users—people who are issuing queries and reports at more or less the same time. A challenging system, by contrast, will have hundreds or even thousands.

Assessing System Availability Requirements

The final factor affecting system size and configuration is the business requirements for system availability. These requirements can range from an 8-hour load window (midnight to 8 a.m.) during which the DW/BI system can be offline, to the opposite extreme of 24 hours a day, 7 days a week. If your business users require high availability, you may need to purchase a substantially larger and more complex system than you'd otherwise need.

The stronger the business need for a high availability system, the more likely you will be to cluster some of the components, notably the relational database and Analysis Services database, and to set up a web farm for Reporting Services.

System Configuration Considerations

One of the big configuration decisions is whether to use one large machine or distribute your DW/BI system across multiple servers. A small company can run a DW/BI system on a single server that runs the relational database, Integration Services, Analysis Services, and Reporting Services with IIS. A large enterprise's DW/BI system will be broken apart over multiple servers, some clustered. How can you possibly determine what configuration is going to be most appropriate for your workload? It helps to break the question down into the major system components and configuration options. These include memory, processors, storage, monolithic or distributed systems, and high availability systems.

How Much Memory?

All of the SQL Server DW/BI components love physical memory. The relational database uses memory at query time to resolve the DW/BI style of query, and during ETL processing for index restructuring. Analysis Services uses memory for resolving queries and performing calculations, for caching result sets, and for managing user session information. During processing, Analysis Services uses memory to compute aggregations, data mining models, and any stored calculations. The whole point of Integration Services' data flow pipeline is to avoid temporarily writing data to disk during the ETL process. Depending on your package design, you may need several times as much memory as your largest incremental processing set. Reporting Services is probably the least memory-intensive of the four major components, but rendering large or complex reports will also place a strain on memory resources.

Because all the DW/BI system components are memory intensive, the obvious solution is to buy hardware that supports a lot of memory. You can purchase a four-way 64-bit server with 8 to 16GB of memory for surprisingly little money. A commodity 64-bit four-way machine can be an all-in-one server for smaller systems, and the basic workhorse system for more complex configurations. The largest and most complex DW/BI systems will need one or more high-performance systems sold directly by the major hardware vendors. The operating system and SQL Server software are so similar between 32-bit and 64-bit hardware that the management of 64-bit systems is not a huge additional burden. We find no compelling reason to use 32-bit hardware, unless you're doing a proof of concept on a shoestring.

Monolithic or Distributed?

An all-in-one configuration is appealing for the cost conscious: You'll minimize operating system and SQL Server licensing costs, and one server is easiest to manage. If you decide to distribute your system, the first way to do so is by putting one or more SQL Server components onto separate servers. This architecture is much easier to manage than distributing the load by the business process dimensional model, placing all the server components for each dimensional model on a different machine. You need a high-bandwidth network between the DW/BI system servers, as significant volumes of data are shipped back and forth between the components.

The all-in-one configuration illustrated in Figure 4.3 has all server components, including possibly SharePoint Portal Services as a reporting portal, running on a single machine. Most users (clients) will access the DW/BI system by connecting to Reporting Services, either directly or through SharePoint. Some analytic business users will connect directly to Analysis Services or the relational database for ad hoc and complex analyses.

Figure 4.4 illustrates a common step up from the all-in-one configuration by creating a reporting server. Consider this configuration if your business users make heavy use of standardized reports built primarily from Analysis Services, and your DW/BI system processing occurs at night when users are not on the system. In this configuration, the Reporting Services catalog database will probably work best on the reporting server, although it could be placed on the SQL Server database server. In the reporting server configuration, some business users access the SQL Server data store directly.

All-in-One

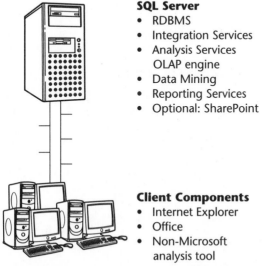

SQL Server
- RDBMS
- Integration Services
- Analysis Services
  OLAP engine
- Data Mining
- Reporting Services
- Optional: SharePoint

Client Components
- Internet Explorer
- Office
- Non-Microsoft
  analysis tool

Figure 4.3 All-in-one business intelligence system

Separate Reporting Server

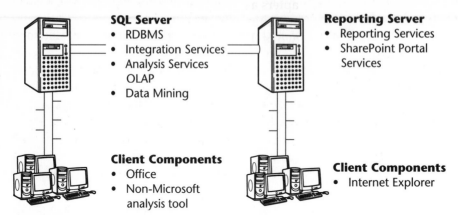

SQL Server
- RDBMS
- Integration Services
- Analysis Services
  OLAP
- Data Mining

Reporting Server
- Reporting Services
- SharePoint Portal
  Services

Client Components
- Office
- Non-Microsoft
  analysis tool

Client Components
- Internet Explorer

Figure 4.4   SQL Server data store and separate reporting server

If your system is allowed only a relatively short downtime, you should separate Analysis Services from the relational database, as pictured in Figure 4.5. In this configuration, the ETL process will not compete with Analysis Services queries, most of which will use the data cache on the Reporting and Analysis server. The Reporting Services catalog, located on the data store server, will compete with the ETL process for resources, but this is almost certainly better than having it compete with the reporting and analysis services. This configuration is not appropriate for a very high availability operation, which requires the use of clusters as discussed later in this chapter.

Separate Reporting and Analysis Server

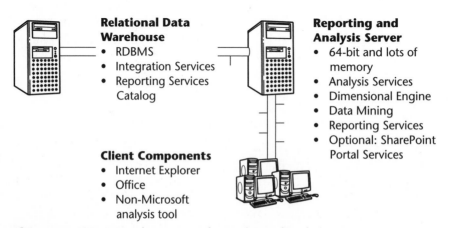

Relational Data Warehouse
- RDBMS
- Integration Services
- Reporting Services
  Catalog

Reporting and Analysis Server
- 64-bit and lots of
  memory
- Analysis Services
- Dimensional Engine
- Data Mining
- Reporting Services
- Optional: SharePoint
  Portal Services

Client Components
- Internet Explorer
- Office
- Non-Microsoft
  analysis tool

Figure 4.5   SQL Server data store and reporting and analysis server

As your system grows larger and places more demands on the hardware, you may end up at the logical end point: with each SQL Server component on its own server. Each of the chapters about the different components discusses some of the issues around distributing the system. But in general there is no built-in assumption that any two of the components are co-located on a single physical server.

You can even push the SQL Server architecture past the point of one server per component. Analysis Services can distribute the partitions of an OLAP database across multiple servers—a feature that was available in SQL Server 2000, although it was seldom used. Reporting Services can run on a web farm, which can greatly enhance scalability. Your network of Integration Services packages can also be distributed across multiple servers, although we expect only the most extreme ETL problems would need to use this architecture.

After you've reached the limit of distributing the SQL Server components to multiple machines, you can think about partitioning along the lines of business process dimensional models. Usually, when a DW/BI system is distributed throughout the organization, it's for political rather than performance reasons. Only for really large systems is it technically necessary to partition the DW/BI system along dimensional model boundaries. Also, various components may employ varying approaches to achieve uptime guarantees. We discuss how to make a horizontally distributed system work, but we prefer and recommend a more centralized architecture.

In the development environment, a common configuration is for developers to use a shared instance of the relational database and Analysis Services database on a two- or four-processor server. Some developers may also choose to run local instances of the database servers, in order to experiment in isolation from their colleagues.

What Kind of Storage System?

There are two kinds of storage systems to consider for your DW/BI system: Storage Area Network (SAN), or directly attached storage. You should plan to use RAID to provide some data redundancy whether you use a SAN or direct disk. We discuss alternative RAID configurations in the following section.

RAID

Almost all DW/BI system servers use a Redundant Array of Independent Disks (RAID) storage infrastructure. RAID-1, also known as mirroring, makes a complete copy of the disk. RAID-0+1, also known as a mirror of stripes, uses two RAID-0 stripes, with a RAID-1 mirror over top. RAID-1 and RAID-0+1 are used for replicating and sharing data among disks. They are the configurations of choice for performance-critical, fault-tolerant environments, but require 100 percent duplication of disks. RAID-1 has the same write performance as single disks, and twice the read performance. RAID-5's read performance is good, but its write performance suffers in comparison to RAID-1.

The RAID array needs to be managed, either by hardware or by software. A wide variety of hardware RAID-controlling technologies are available, including the Fibre Channel used by many SAN solutions. Use hardware to control the RAID. If you let the operating system control the RAID, those activities will compete with the operation and performance of the DW/BI system.

Don't skimp on the quality and quantity of the hardware controllers. To maximize performance you may need multiple controllers; work with your storage vendor to develop your requirements and specifications.

Storage Area Networks

The best, although most expensive, approach is to use a Storage Area Network (SAN). A SAN is strongly recommended for large DW/BI systems and for high availability systems. SAN disks can be configured in a RAID array.

A storage area network is defined as a set of interconnected *servers* and *devices* such as disks and tapes, which are connected to a common communication and data transfer infrastructure such as Fibre Channel. SANs allow multiple servers access to a shared pool of storage. The SAN management software coordinates security and access. Storage area networks are designed to be low-latency and high-bandwidth storage that is easier to manage than non-shared storage.

A SAN environment provides the following benefits:

- *Centralization of storage into a single pool:* Storage is dynamically assigned from the pool as and when it is required, without complex reconfiguring.

- *Simplified management infrastructure.*

- *Data can be transferred directly from device to device without server intervention:* For example, data can be moved from a disk to a tape without first being read into the memory of a backup server.

These benefits are valuable to a DW/BI system environment. As the DW/BI system grows, it's much easier to allocate storage as required. For very large systems, a direct copy of the database files at the SAN level is the most effective backup technique. Finally, SANs play an important role in a DW/BI system with high availability requirements.

> **NOTE** Directly attached RAID disks can offer better performance than SANs, particularly for sequential I/O. However, the advantages of the SAN technology usually, although not always, outweigh the difference in performance for DW/BI applications.

Processors

To make a gross generalization, DW/BI systems are more likely to hit bottlenecks in memory or I/O than in processing power. However, all of the SQL Server components individually are designed for parallelism, so systems will benefit—often significantly—from additional processors. It's hard to imagine anyone taking the time to build a DW/BI system that wouldn't at least benefit from a dual processor box, and most systems use four or more processors.

The additional processing capacity that comes from the 64-bit platform can be very useful. As we've already discussed, the greatest benefit of 64-bit comes from its ability to address very large memory.

Setting Up for High Availability

What does high availability mean for a DW/BI system? The answer, as you might expect, lies with the business users' requirements. The job of the DW/BI team is to gather requirements, evaluate and price technical options, and present the business sponsor with a recommendation and cost justification.

Relatively few DW/BI teams deliver 24x7 availability for the entire DW/BI system. Very high availability for the entire system is most common for multinational companies with business users spread throughout the globe. Even so, extremely high availability is seldom a mandate. If you move your DW/BI system to real time, you'll need to design more rigorously for high availability. Typically, although not always, real time affects a relatively small set of the data, and the high availability requirements might not affect the bulk of data and operations.

For most DW/BI systems, the business users are happy to use the system from approximately 7 or 8 a.m. to 10 p.m. local time. A DW/BI system that's used primarily for strategic and tactical decision making can tolerate an occasional downtime during the day.

No matter what your availability requirements, the most important thing that you can do is use redundant storage for all your data. As described previously, disk mirroring with a RAID-1 technology is best, but RAID-5 is acceptable for many situations. Disk failure is far more common than other types of system failures; it's a good thing that redundant storage is so easy and inexpensive.

It may be necessary to cluster your Analysis Services and relational database servers in order to deliver the highest availability. A properly configured cluster can provide failover in the event of an emergency. A cluster can also provide scalability under normal circumstances. You can run Reporting Services in a web farm configuration, which provides similar advantages for both scalability and availability for that portion of your DW/BI system. SQL Server Books Online provides clear instructions for clustering databases and installing Reporting Services on a web farm. But if high availability is mission critical, you should seriously consider contacting Microsoft for references to highly qualified consultants who can help with the system design and configuration.

REFERENCE   See the SQL Server Books Online topic "How to: Configure a Report Server Scale-Out Deployment (Reporting Services Configuration)."

For the vast gray area between needing 24x7 availability and having an 8-hour load window, there are a lot of things that you can do to minimize the system's downtime. The easiest thing to do is to use Analysis Services as the primary or only presentation server. The heavy lifting of the ETL processing occurs in Integration Services and in the relational database. Once the data is cleaned and conformed, the process of performing an incremental OLAP database update is generally quite fast. And even better, Analysis Services performs updates into a shadow partition so the database remains open for querying during processing. You can't expect query performance to remain at quite the same level while the database is being processed, but in most cases you can schedule the update at a time when the system is lightly used.

Even if you use the relational data warehouse database to support queries and reports, you can minimize the amount of downtime. Dimension updates are seldom the problem; it's the fact table inserts and especially updates, for example for a rolling snapshot fact table, which are most problematic. As we discuss later in this chapter, you can use partitioned fact tables to load current data without affecting the availability of yesterday's fact table. If your fact table is small and you're not using partitioning, you can use a similar technique to perform inserts and updates on a copy of yesterday's fact table, and then quickly switch it into production with an extremely short downtime. See the "Partitioned Fact Tables" section later in this chapter for a longer description of this technique.

NOTE   Partitioning for Analysis Services and relational databases are features of SQL Server 2005 Enterprise Edition. These features are not available in Standard Edition.

If you need very high availability for the relational data warehouse database, you may need to use the database snapshot feature. Users would query the snapshot while the underlying database is being loaded. This approach is most likely to be useful for those delivering 24-hour access to a global enterprise.

Software Installation and Configuration

The basic installation of the SQL Server and other Microsoft components is straightforward and well documented in Books Online. We won't discuss the installation experience here. Instead, we'll describe which pieces of software need to be installed on different developers' workstations, depending on what part of the DW/BI Project they're working on. Next, we'll describe some best practices for the initial configuration of the various SQL Server components, including the relational database, Analysis Services, Integration Services, and Reporting Services.

Most multi-person development teams share one or two database servers, and install only the development tools on their personal machines. A common development team configuration is illustrated in Figure 4.6.

Depending on their roles, different members of the development team will need to install different components of SQL Server, and some will need to install other Microsoft and third-party software. These requirements are outlined in the next section.

Development Environment Software Requirements

The following section outlines the software to be installed on the development database server, and the workstations for different common development roles.

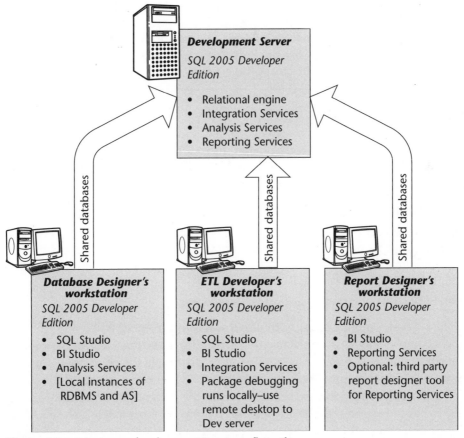

Figure 4.6 A common development team configuration

HOW POWERFUL SHOULD DEVELOPMENT AND TEST SYSTEMS BE?

In a perfect world, the test system will be physically identical to the production system. The test system plays two key roles. First, it's the system on which modifications are tested. In this first role, it's as important to test the scripts that deploy the system changes as it is to test the changes themselves. For testing the deployment process, the test system doesn't need to be identical to the production system. The second major role of the test system is to serve as a place to experiment with performance optimizations, such as indexes and aggregates. For performance tests to be valid, the test system should have similar physical characteristics as production. Many hardware vendors have Technology Centers, and may make those resources available to help validate system sizing prior to production deployment.

Development often takes place on a subset of data. If so, the developers' systems, including shared development database servers, can be much less powerful than the test and production servers. Memory is important. Install at least 2GB of RAM on any computer that's running one of the database services.

The ETL system developer should work on the development server by way of a Remote Desktop session because Integration Services packages run in debugging mode on the machine where BI Studio is running. With significant data volumes, package execution can overwhelm a typical developer's desktop.

Finally, the screenshots in this book should convince you that team members who use BI Studio will need big monitors. The screenshots in this book were taken at 1024 × 768, and that's really not big enough.

Development Database Server

As we described in the previous sidebar, most DW/BI teams share a database server for development purposes. The SQL Server components to install on the development database server are:

- Relational engine
- Integration Services
- Analysis Services
- Reporting Services
- BI Studio for remote use by ETL developers

Most development occurs with small data volumes, so co-hosting all the server components on a single machine is usually fine from a technical point of view. If you have access to plenty of servers, distribute the components in the same way for development as is planned for production.

The development database server requires the Internet Information Service (IIS) to be running in order to install and operate Reporting Services.

Database Designer

BI Studio is the main design tool for Analysis Services databases. The relational data warehouse database is primarily developed in Management Studio. Relational database designers may choose to install the relational database server on their local workstation. The SQL Server components to install on the database designer's workstation are:

- Management Studio
- BI Studio
- Analysis Services
- Relational database engine (optional)

In addition, the database designer should install Visual SourceSafe, or any other source control product that can be integrated with Visual Studio.

The relational database designer may want a data-modeling tool such as ERWin or Microsoft's Visio Enterprise Architect Edition. These tools support visual modeling of the database, with excellent forward engineering capabilities.

> **NOTE** At this time, the version of Visio that most of us buy packaged with Office can *reverse* engineer a database, but cannot *forward* engineer it. In other words, you can slurp a database definition into Visio and make a pretty picture. You can't edit that database and instantiate the changes. The only way to do the forward engineering piece is to purchase Visual Studio Enterprise Architect. Confused? Perplexed? Talk to Microsoft.

Development Database Administrator

Development databases are usually not managed very well—they are for development, after all. However, someone needs to perform some basic DBA tasks like ensuring the database has enough space. Backups are a really good idea, too. Management Studio is the tool for operating and maintaining databases (relational and OLAP), and managing the operation of Integration Services packages. The only SQL Server component required on the development DBA's workstation is Management Studio.

The development DBA should install and use the team's source control system for the management of any database maintenance scripts.

ETL System Developer

The ETL system developer will create Integration Services packages. BI Studio is the tool for developing and debugging Integration Services, and the Integration Services components also need to be installed on the developer's workstation. The SQL Server components to install on the ETL developer's workstation are:

- Management Studio
- BI Studio
- Integration Services

In addition, the ETL system developer should install source control such as Visual SourceSafe. Depending on how complex and unusual your ETL problems are, the ETL system developer may need to install the full Visual Studio 2005 product in order to develop custom objects in C# or VB. This is relatively unusual; the vast majority of ETL systems can be developed without any need for custom coding in a Visual Studio .NET language.

The ETL system developer often uses the development server to work on packages because packages run in debug mode on the same machine where BI Studio is running. Some teams start developing packages on the development server from the outset. Others may start on the developer's workstation but move packages to the development server when it's time to test with a reasonable volume of data. Still other teams find that it's easiest to simply buy a bigger workstation for the ETL developers.

Report Designer

The DW/BI team members who develop reports need the following software on their workstations:

- SQL Server BI Studio.
- Source control software such as Visual SourceSafe.
- Microsoft Office, especially Office Web Components and Excel. Your business users live in Office; you need to confirm that the reports you create look good when rendered to Excel.
- Optional: A non-Microsoft relational ad hoc query tool. It's a matter of taste, but we dislike the Microsoft-standard query generator that's part of Visual Studio. We recommend that you use your favorite third-party tool to formulate the query and then paste the SQL into the report designer. Microsoft's Report Builder can also be used to create datasets in the Report Designer.
- Optional: A non–Microsoft Analysis Services query tool. As we have discussed elsewhere in this book, many Microsoft-based DW/BI systems use a third-party Analysis Services query tool to circumvent the limitations of the Office suite. Look for future versions of Microsoft Office (after Office 2003) to fill in this hole in Microsoft's product offering.

Reporting Portal Developer

As we discuss in Chapter 9, many DW/BI systems will embed Reporting Services into a reporting portal built using SharePoint Services or some other portal software. The reporting portal developer needs the following software:

- SQL Server BI Studio
- Source control software such as Visual SourceSafe
- Microsoft Office Excel and Office Web Components
- Microsoft Office SharePoint Services

It would be unusual for the reporting portal developer to need Visual Studio .NET to implement functionality not included with SharePoint Services.

Data Mining Model Developer

As we discuss in Chapter 10, the first major step in building a data mining application is to develop and train data mining models. This is an activity that requires knowledge of statistics, of the business problems, and of the data, but it does not require actual coding skills. The software required includes:

- SQL Server BI Studio for developing the data mining models
- Analysis Services
- Relational and Analysis Services query tools for investigating the data
- Source control software

Analytic Application Developer

Analytic applications embed domain expertise and best practices into a guided analytic activity. Although some analytic applications are just a collection of predefined reports, sometimes they're more structured than that. The more structured the analytic application, the more likely the analytic application developer is writing code, perhaps integrating the data mining model described previously with the operational systems. The analytic application developer needs the following software:

- SQL Server Client and Developer tools. The application developers typically work with databases and data mining models that others have developed. You will need the SQL Server object models, which are installed by default with the Client Components.
- Source control software.
- Visual Studio 2005, with one or more .NET languages such as C# or VB.

Test and Production Software Requirements

In a perfect world, your test and production machines will have the same physical configuration. We recognize that's not always realistic, but it *is* realistic and mandatory that they have the same software configuration. They must have the same operating system with the same configuration. They must have the same components of SQL Server, with the same versions including service packs.

If you're using your test system only for testing, and not for any production use, you can use Developer Edition on the test systems. This is extremely appealing for components that use Enterprise Edition in production, not only because Enterprise Edition is expensive but also because the feature set of Developer Edition is the same as that of Enterprise Edition. But it's problematic to use Developer Edition on test machines where the production machines are running Standard Edition. That's because the Developer Edition feature set is richer, and you might not discover a dependency on an Enterprise Edition feature until too late. This issue is discussed at greater length in Chapter 14.

Earlier in this chapter we discussed how a small system might build an all-in-one server, with all SQL Server DW/BI components on a single machine. A large system will distribute the components across multiple machines.

Database Server

The database servers, unsurprisingly, require the SQL Server components:

- Relational database and/or
- Integration Services and/or
- Analysis Services and/or
- Reporting Services. Reporting Services requires Internet Information Services (IIS) in order to install and operate.

To manage the system effectively, you should install the following Windows Server components:

- Performance Monitor (also known as System Monitor) is installed automatically with Windows. It is the tool that exposes the performance counters that are published by the database servers, and is an invaluable tool for monitoring system performance.

- Microsoft Operations Manager (MOM) is an add-on to the Windows Server System that provides system monitoring and management services. Large or complex systems should evaluate whether they should purchase MOM or use alternative systems operations software.

Database Administrator

The DBAs for the test and production machines will use SQL Server Management Studio (Management Studio) to operate and maintain the DW/BI system, and manage the operation of Integration Services packages.

Operating Systems

SQL Server requires a Windows Server operating system in production: Windows Server 2000 (Service Pack 4), Windows Server 2003, or later. You can purchase a 64-bit version of SQL Server to install on a 64-bit operating system. You can use a wider variety of operating systems on your development machines. Most developers use Windows XP Professional. The SQL Server setup program will not let you install on a machine that is not configured appropriately.

Server operating systems and software are usually installed on a RAID-1 array, for data redundancy and failover. Internet Information Services (IIS) must be running in order to install and operate Reporting Services.

SQL Server Relational Database Setup

Use the following guidelines when installing, configuring, and securing SQL Server.

Install the relational database component of SQL Server Enterprise Edition or Standard Edition. You may choose to install the Management Studio tools on a server; often the server is managed remotely from a DBA's workstation. Go to the Microsoft SQL Server web site at www.microsoft.com/sql to learn if any service packs are available. In the past, service packs have been made available without charge. Upgrade the instance to the latest service pack. You can install the relational database as either a default instance or a named instance. The only compelling reason we've come up with for installing multiple instances on a single server is to test multiple scenarios on a single machine.

> **NOTE** Multiple SQL Server components can be installed on the same machine. Most organizations use per-processor licensing for DW/BI systems rather than licensing based on the number of users. Your licensing cost is the same if you install and use all SQL Server components on a machine, or only one component such as the relational engine.

The SQL Server relational database is resource intensive and you'd seldom choose to share the physical server that holds the data warehouse database with another data application. In production, you usually create the data warehouse databases in the default instance. In the development and test environments, multiple named instances may be very useful.

The SQL Server relational database is a Windows service just like any other Windows service. Use the Management Studio tool to start, stop, administer, and manage a SQL Server relational database instance. The SQL Server database engine service has no dependencies on any other component of SQL Server. As we describe in Chapter 11, you can choose to install and use the relational database as the only component from the SQL Server product suite.

Security Options During Installation

Install and run the SQL Server relational database in Windows Authentication mode. The mixed authentication mode is inherently less secure and should be avoided if possible. During installation, you are asked to provide a Service Account to run each service. It's easiest to manage if you use the same account for all the services, but you are not required to do so. You can modify this choice later by using the SQL Server Configuration Manager utility.

WARNING Use the SQL Server Configuration Manager utility to change the characteristics of the service account, rather than the Administrative Tools → Services tool from the Control Panel.

Restrict access to SQL Server data and log files to system administrators and the SQL Server and SQL Server Agent service accounts. The system databases are secured by default by the SQL Server setup program, but we still like to check.

After you've installed the SQL Server database engine, you may need to run the Surface Area Configuration tool, available from the Start menu, to turn off and on some features and services. If you've found that the "." or LocalHost connections to the local machine don't work as expected, you need to go into this utility to enable local and remote connections.

Security issues are discussed in detail in Chapter 12.

Files, Filegroups, and RAID

SQL Server data is stored in files, which can be grouped into *filegroups*. One of the main reasons to use filegroups is to make it easier to balance I/O across multiple disks. If you place database files on RAID drives, this I/O balancing is handled for you. Unless you're partitioning your fact tables, simply place database files in the default filegroup on a RAID drive. (Later in this chapter we discuss partitioning in detail.)

We strongly recommend that all relational database files be placed on RAID arrays, either RAID-1 or RAID-5, preferably with hardware controllers rather than managed by the operating system. RAID-1 is significantly better than RAID-5, although predictably more expensive, because it's faster both for writes and for recovery after a disk failure.

The SQL Server system databases *master*, *model*, and *msdb* can be placed on the RAID-1 array that holds the operating system. These databases are typically very small, and there's usually plenty of room for them on that array. Alternatively, place them on their own small RAID-1 array. A third alternative is to place them on the same RAID array as user databases. It is vital that these databases, especially *master*, be placed on a fault-tolerant array.

The fourth system database, *tempdb*, could grow significantly as the data warehouse database is being used. You should pre-allocate *tempdb* to a large size to avoid auto-growth during query operations. Don't place *tempdb* on the system RAID-1 array which is usually small. Use at least one file per CPU for high-performance *tempdb* operations. Be sure to spread *tempdb* out over many drives to maximize I/O performance. If the total number of drives on your system is limited, you can place *tempdb* on the same RAID array as the user databases, especially if you use RAID-1 or RAID-0+1 for the user databases. However, if you set up the user databases on a RAID-5 array, you should consider separating out *tempdb* onto its own RAID-1 array to minimize potential bottlenecks.

You'll likely have at least three user databases: the data warehouse database, a staging database, and a metadata database. Reporting Services has a separate database, which in some circumstances can grow to be quite large. You can put all these databases together on a single RAID-1, RAID-0+1, or RAID-5 array. Because of the size of the data warehouse database and possibly the Reporting Services catalog, the size of this array will dwarf the other databases' arrays.

Assuming you're using RAID, you could put all of the data warehouse's data into a single file. But long before you reach 2TB, the maximum drive size that SQL Server can address, you'll want to break the database into multiple files in order to simplify management and backup. You can use filegroups to ensure data is spread evenly across all the drives in use. In the absence of partitioning, discussed later in this chapter, consider creating a file all for dimensions and a file for each fact table. A single file should be adequate for the staging database and the metadata database, unless your DBAs have strong feelings about an alternative configuration.

NOTE The file layout discussion in this section was directed primarily at small- to medium-sized systems. If you have huge data volumes, in the terabyte range and above, you should work with your storage vendor to lay out your files and disks very carefully.

Database Recovery Model

SQL Server provides three recovery modes: Full, Bulk Logged, and Simple. A database that is operated with Simple recovery mode can be recovered only to the point of the last backup. The Simple model may be appropriate for the staging database, which is often designed to be emptied of data at the start of each load.

> **NOTE** Even if you empty out the staging database at the beginning of each load, keep a copy of the extracted data somewhere. We often keep a copy of the extracts in the file system, in a file whose name includes the date and time of the extract. These extracts should be backed up, as should any permanent data in the staging database. More often than not, the kinds of backups you can do with the Simple recovery model meet the needs of backing up the staging database.

The Bulk Logged recovery model sounds very appealing for a data warehouse database, as we know we're going to use bulk inserts as much as possible. But the sad reality is that, other than the initial historical load of data, your ability to perform bulk inserts into the data warehouse database is limited. Bulk inserts work fast only on a table empty of data or on a table without indexes—an unlikely state of affairs after the initial loading is complete. A possible exception occurs when you're using partitioned tables, as we discuss later in this chapter. Unless you're using partitioned tables, you should set the data warehouse database to the Full recovery model once the historical load is complete.

Database Initial Size

Set up your SQL Server database with an initial size adequate to hold the initial historical load. You might have permitted automatic growth up to a certain maximum, but you should monitor the database size carefully and increase the database's file size during a period of slow usage. That's because the initial allocation and subsequent increases are resource-intensive. It's better to pay this file initialization price at a time managed by the DBAs than during the DW/BI system's load processing window.

Windows Server 2003 includes a feature called Instant File Initialization that improves the performance of database allocation. However, "instant" is a bit of a misnomer; it's still a resource-intensive process. For best performance, especially for very large databases, avoid auto-grow. Instead, set up an automated process to check for needed file space and programmatically increase file sizes if necessary.

As we discuss in Chapter 15, you should set up an automated process to check for disk space on a weekly, daily, or load-by-load basis.

> **REFERENCE** See the Books Online topic "Database File Initialization" for more information.

After the database tables' physical design has been finalized, as we discuss later in this chapter, you can accurately assess the storage requirements for the initial database setup and storage layout.

Analysis Services Setup

The Analysis Services server machine must have at least the Analysis Services component of SQL Server installed on it. Other components, including the relational database engine and the Studio tools, are not required on that server. Often, especially in locked down production environments, the server is always managed remotely from the DBA's workstation. Make sure you keep up to date with service packs.

You can run Analysis Services alone, if you wish, without using any other SQL Server technology. You don't need even a small instance of the relational database engine to run an Analysis Services database. See Chapter 11 for a discussion of running Analysis Services by itself.

NOTE Remember that if you install the Relational database on one machine and Analysis Services on a second machine, you have to pay for two licenses.

Like the relational database, Analysis Services supports multiple instances on a single server machine. In a standard production environment, we don't see a compelling argument for using multiple instances rather than multiple databases within the same instance. Multiple instances may be useful during development and testing. If you're building a solution for external parties such as vendors, you may find that multiple instances provide an extra level of security or comfort to your customers.

Analysis Services File Locations and Storage Requirements

The main configuration choice to make at or soon after installation time is where the program, data, and log files are located. These choices are made for an instance; all cubes and databases within that instance use the same default location. A RAID array, either RAID-1, RAID-0+1, or RAID-5, is the best choice for all file locations. The program files for a production system should be installed on a RAID-1 array, often the operating system array.

The best place for the log files is their default location, near the SQL Server program files. We recommend using RAID-1 or RAID-0+1 for these files, as you would probably use for the program files.

Analysis Services data files are by far the largest kind of files. It is nearly impossible at design time to estimate with any degree of accuracy how big the Analysis Services data files will be. Let's start with a simple rule of thumb: an Analysis Services database that's built at the same grain as a relational fact table will take approximately 25 percent of the space of that fact table (atomic data only, no indexes). This 25 percent rule includes Analysis Services data and indexes, before aggregations are added, and again it's worth emphasizing that this is at the same grain as the fact table. We have seen Analysis Services atomic data at 15-40 percent of its corresponding relational data, but 25 percent is a reasonable midpoint.

When you add well-designed aggregations, the total data size is usually 35–100 percent of the relational data. You will be at the high end of that range if you use distinct count measures. In our experience, Analysis Services databases including indexes and aggregations typically take 35–50 percent of the data of the corresponding relational table at the same grain, data only, no indexes. This factor was included in the very high-level storage space guesstimate that we discussed at the beginning of this chapter.

For small- and medium-sized installations, a 50 percent factor should suffice for disk planning. For very large installations, you should partition your Analysis Services database. Build a test database with several partitions, and then scale that storage requirement by the number of partitions.

We recommend that you use RAID-0+1 to store the data files. Use a SAN for large installations. To maximize processing speed, use a different RAID array, with a different physical controller, than the location of the relational data warehouse database that feeds the Analysis Services database.

If you're too cost conscious to use RAID-0+1 for the data files, but don't want to take the write performance hit of RAID-5, it's not as important to use redundant storage for the Analysis Services database as for the relational database. After all, you can always reprocess the Analysis Services database from the relational data warehouse database, or restore it from backup. Be warned, however, that it could take many hours to process an Analysis Services database that covers multiple terabytes of relational data. We strongly recommend using some level of redundant storage.

When you create a partition for an Analysis Services cube, you can place that partition anywhere in your storage system. Assuming you're using RAID, we see no compelling reason for placing data files anywhere but in the default location.

SQL SERVER 2000/2005 CHANGE: ANALYSIS SERVICES METADATA

Readers who are familiar with Analysis Services 2000 may be asking when and where they should migrate the metadata repository. There is no formal repository for Analysis Services 2005. Instead, the metadata consists of the XML files throughout the OLAP Data directory, such as *DatabaseName*.db.xml, *CubeName*.cub.xml, *DimensionName*.dim.xml, and so on.

This change may sound dramatic, but the main implication for Analysis Services administrators is improved manageability, particularly for backups and restores, as described in Chapter 15.

Analysis Services and Memory

Analysis Services loves memory. Analysis Services 2005 has been redesigned to solve the most intractable memory problems associated with Analysis Services 2000. Nonetheless, the more data you can cache in physical memory, the happier you and Analysis Services will be.

Those familiar with Analysis Services 2000 probably know that Analysis Services required that all of a server's dimensions always be resident in memory. If the server didn't have enough memory, Analysis Services 2000 wouldn't run. This is no longer true; in Analysis Services 2005, dimensions do not need to be memory resident. Information about dimension members will move in and out of memory cache as needed. This is great, for certainly a server should handle memory contention gracefully. Nonetheless, for excellent query performance you want plenty of memory for dimension members, a result set cache, the computation engine's cache, and other uses. Don't skimp on memory, and seriously consider using 64-bit hardware for the Analysis Services component of your DW/BI system infrastructure.

Integration Services Setup

Integration Services has two major components: a design environment, which is part of the BI Studio; and a runtime environment, which is what you install on your production servers. The design environment is where you create and edit packages. You can see a visual representation of the package's tasks, and run the package in debug mode on the development machine, and only on the development machine. The only way to remotely execute an Integration Services in development/debugging mode is to use a remote desktop connection to the remote machine.

On the production server, install the Integration Services component of SQL Server Enterprise Edition or Standard Edition. You may install the Management Studio tools on your production server, although often production instances of SQL Server are managed remotely from an administrator's workstation.

You can use Management Studio to interactively execute a package that's been deployed to test or production. But for the ETL system, you will use SQL Agent to schedule the execution of the DTExecUI or DTExec utility. Using these utilities, you can run on one server a package that is stored on a second server. In production, Integration Services packages can be located anywhere, and can be run on any server that has the Integration Services runtime executables.

As we describe in Chapter 5, you can design your ETL system to run multiple Integration Services packages on multiple servers. If you choose this architecture for your high scale ETL problem, install Integration Services executables (and pay SQL Server licenses) on all of the servers on which the packages are running.

Integration Services has no dependency on any other component of the SQL Server product suite. It could be used as the ETL tool for an otherwise non-SQL Server DW/BI system.

Integration Services presents the option of storing package definitions in the SQL Server. This is not something you need to decide at installation time.

As we described earlier in this chapter, most DW/BI systems will run Integration Services on the same server as the relational data warehouse database. It is easy to change package locations as your warehouse matures and your requirements change.

Integration Services File Locations and Storage Requirements

You may use a relational database to stage data during ETL processing. As we describe in Chapter 5, you will probably use both a relational staging area and a file system staging area. You may use the file system staging area to rest data after it has been extracted from the source systems but before the heavy duty ETL processing begins; you may also use this staging area for intermediate storage, and for a kind of backup of changed data before launching an update. Many people hold on to the source system extracts for days, weeks, or months before deleting them or moving them to offline storage. The volume of disk space you'll need for the file-based and relational staging areas depends completely on the design of your ETL system.

Many people use non-redundant storage for staging areas. RAID-1 or RAID-0+1, as always, is recommended, but it's the least important data to store redundantly.

Reporting Services Setup

Like all the other components of SQL Server, Reporting Services can be installed on a standalone reporting server, or it can share a server with one or more other components of SQL Server.

When you install Reporting Services, you must supply several pieces of configuration information:

- *The location of the report server catalog database:* The report server catalog is a relational database that Reporting Services needs in order to run. It is where report definitions, metadata, histories, and snapshots are stored. The installation program will create the report server database for you. The report server database can be located on a different machine, but you must have the appropriate privileges. This catalog database must be a SQL Server relational database.

- *Configuration options for email delivery of reports:* You will probably want to run a subset of standard reports, and use email to deliver either the report or a link to the report. The email account information and other configuration options are well documented in Books Online.

You may choose to install the client-side report authoring tool, Report Designer, on the server. Report Designer is integrated into BI Studio, and most developers use it on their workstations rather than on the server.

Reporting Services is a Windows service just like the SQL Server relational database or any other Windows service. It is also implemented as an ASP.NET Web service that runs on Internet Information Services (IIS). Both the Windows service and the Web service are implemented on the report server. Use the Management Studio tool to start, stop, administer, and manage a Reporting Services instance.

Reporting Services doesn't require any significant file storage other than the report catalog database. Issues around the potential size and placement of the report server catalog were discussed earlier in this chapter, in the section on the SQL Server relational database setup.

> **NOTE** Like the other components of SQL Server, Reporting Services can be installed in isolation. However, it does need access to a SQL Server relational database server for the report catalog.

Physical Data Warehouse Database Design

Before you start the relational database physical design process, you should have completed the logical model. There is very little to do between the logical and physical models. Here are the basic steps, which we discuss in greater detail in the pages to follow:

- Ensure that object names match the naming conventions. Your logical model should already be using good, clear, sensible names that conform to your naming conventions. You should already have defined naming conventions for database objects such as tables and columns.

- Ensure that each column has the correct data type. Start off with the column definitions from the modeling process, but you may need to modify data types later, after you've completed the data profiling discussed in Chapter 2. For example, you may learn that some customer surnames take more than the 35 characters you originally assumed would suffice.

- Specify how to handle a changed value for each dimension attribute.

- Identify the levels of natural hierarchies, such as the familiar Year to Quarter to Month to Day.

- Decide whether you will declare foreign keys in the database for all, some, or none of the logical foreign key relationships.

- Develop your initial indexing plan.

- Develop your fact table partitioning plan.

■ Specify dimension and fact metadata: process-related metadata that you may choose to include in each dimension and fact row. These metadata elements were introduced in Chapter 2, and are discussed further in Chapters 6 and 13.

The best tool for developing the physical model is a data modeling tool such as ERWin or Visio. These tools can forward engineer the SQL Server database, which makes it very easy to modify the database during the early, iterative design phases. (As we have already described in this chapter, the only way to get the version of Visio that will forward engineer the database is to purchase Visual Studio Enterprise Architect.)

These data modeling tools are expensive, and some small companies will balk at purchasing them. In Chapter 2 we introduced the Excel workbook and macro for logical modeling. You can use the workbook and macro to generate your own database if you don't have a data modeling tool. We provide this spreadsheet because not all readers will have a specific data modeling tool.

Surrogate Keys

The primary key for dimension tables should be a surrogate key assigned and managed by the DW/BI system. The most common method for creating surrogate keys is to use the IDENTITY property on the surrogate key column. Every time a row is inserted, the identity column populates itself by incrementing.

Check to ensure the surrogate key column is an integer data type. Choose the appropriate integer type given the anticipated size of the dimension:

■ *Tinyint* takes values in the range 0 to 255, and requires 1 byte of storage

■ *Smallint* ranges from -2^{15} (-32,768) to $2^{15}-1$ (32,767), and takes 2 bytes

■ *Int* ranges from -2^{31} to $2^{31}-1$, and takes 4 bytes

■ *Bigint* ranges from -2^{63} to $2^{63}-1$ and takes 8 bytes

Choose the smallest integer type that will work for your dimension. This isn't very important for the dimension table itself, but it's vital for the fact table's storage and performance. These same surrogate keys show up as foreign keys in the fact table. Using the small data types is also important for minimizing memory use during data processing. Make sure you use the same integer types for the fact table as for the corresponding dimension tables.

We usually frown on using meaningful surrogate keys—which is something of an oxymoron—but we make an exception in every DW/BI system we build. The Date dimension should use a surrogate key. That surrogate key should be an integer. But it's awfully convenient for it to be a meaningful integer of the form year-month-day, such as 20050723. Developers are people, too.

String Columns

When we're building the logical model, we tend to be careless about string column lengths. During the modeling process, we're focusing on business meaning, not on how long a string column should be. In fact, we tend to use just two or three string column lengths: 50 for names of things, 100 for descriptions.

We need to clean this up in the physical model. This is particularly true for columns in very large dimensions, and the occasional string column in fact tables. The relational database stores variable length string columns, type varchar, efficiently. It doesn't pad these columns with spaces. However, other parts of the SQL Server toolset will pad columns. Notably, Integration Services and Analysis Services pad string columns with spaces under the covers. Both Integration Services and Analysis Services love physical memory, so there's a cost to declaring string columns that are far wider than they need to be.

> **TIP** Start by making the string columns in the data warehouse database the same length as in the source database. But we've seen systems that routinely use varchar(100) for all string columns. In this case, investigate the actual lengths of string data. Make the data warehouse columns wider than any historical width, just for insurance. As we illustrate in Chapters 5 and 6, add a data quality screen to your ETL application to catch especially long strings in the future.

Don't get carried away by the varchar data type. Any column smaller than 5 (some people say 10) characters should just be a char data type, even if the data length varies somewhat. If the string length varies little, say from 10 to 13 characters, simply use the char type.

We have seen many people confused by the nchar and nvarchar data types that Microsoft uses in its sample databases such as AdventureWorks. These string data types are exactly analogous to char and varchar, but they hold 2-byte Unicode data. Microsoft uses them because the same sample database structure works worldwide. Use char and varchar unless your data actually uses Unicode characters because you have string data in, say, Korean.

To Null, or Not to Null?

Avoid null values in the data warehouse tables. They are confusing to business users, especially when constructing queries that filter on an attribute that's sometimes null. If you decide to let a column be null, document your rationale in your system documentation.

It's not strictly necessary to enforce nullability in the database. The data warehouse tables are loaded through an ETL process and only through the ETL process. As long as you don't actually load any null values, you should be okay.

But let's be professional here. If a column isn't supposed to be null, it should be declared NOT NULL in the database.

Insert an Unknown Member Row

A corollary to forbidding nulls, especially for the fact table foreign keys, is how to handle a fact row that does have a null or bad foreign key. For example, how would we load a fact row that has a missing Customer ID? We talk about the specifics of this scenario in some length in Chapter 6, but one of the answers is to add an Unknown Member row to each dimension table. We habitually do this as soon as we create the table, and we use -1 as the unknown member's surrogate key.

If you use the identity column property to generate dimension surrogate keys, you can add the unknown member row by using the following logic:

```
SET IDENTITY_INSERT OFF
INSERT Dim_MyDim (MyDim_Key, MyDim_TK, Attribute1, Attribute2)
VALUES (-1, NULL, 'Unknown', 'Unknown')
SET IDENTITY_INSERT ON
```

Table and Column Extended Properties

When you developed the DW/BI system's logical model, you specified how each dimension tracked history. You should also have thought about how the dimension's primary hierarchies were going to be structured, and whether you will enforce those hierarchical relationships in the data. We like to annotate these decisions in the physical database, using column extended properties. For tables and views, we recommend storing a business description, and possibly a second technical description, as table extended properties.

- For each table, create a table extended property called *Description* to hold the business description of the table.

- For each column in each dimension table, create a column extended property *Description* to hold the business description of the column. Create a column extended property called *Source System* to hold a business-oriented summary of the source system.

- For each non-key column in each dimension table, create a column extended property called *SCD Type*. The value of the *SCD Type* extended property should be 1-Restate History or 2-Track History.

The Excel spreadsheet that we've already talked about, and which is posted on the book's web site at www.MsftDWToolkit.com, automatically creates these extended properties for you.

Housekeeping Columns

There are several columns that should be added to the physical model, if they're not already included in the logical model. For dimensions, add columns to track the date range for which the dimension row is valid.

NOTE You don't have to add these columns to a dimension table that has no Type 2 (track history) slowly changing dimension attributes in it.

The RowStartDate and RowEndDate columns indicate the date range for which the dimension row is valid. Make these dates be inclusive, so that a SQL statement that includes a BETWEEN clause works as expected. For the current row, you could leave RowEndDate as a NULL, but it works better if you make it the maximum date for your data type. These maximum dates are 12/31/2079 for *smalldatetime*, and 12/31/9999 for *datetime*. Populate a third column, RowIsCurrent, with the value yes or no (Y/N). Although this column could be inferred from the row's end date, sometimes it's easier to use the current indicator. In the MSFT_AdventureWorksDW case study data model, the Customer and Employee dimensions include Type 2 columns. Their table definitions include these columns.

Occasionally it's interesting to the business users to be able to easily tell which of several columns propagated a Type 2 change in the dimension. A simple way to do this is to add a column to track the RowChangeReason: the columns that changed on the date this row was added. The Customer and Employee dimensions in our case study database include this column.

The Audit dimension is a dimension that keeps track of when and how a row was added to the DW/BI system. It is closely tied to the ETL system, and keeps track of the package and step that loaded the data. Using an Audit dimension for both fact and dimension rows is becoming more important, as increasingly strict compliance regulations mean we must track the lineage of the data in our warehouse. In Chapter 6, we provide examples of how to populate a simple Audit dimension. All dimension and fact tables in our case study database include a key to the Audit dimension. In fact, we use two Audit dimension keys: one for the process that initially loaded a row, and one for the latest update to that row.

REFERENCE *The Data Warehouse ETL Toolkit* (Wiley, 2004) outlines more complex auditing procedures. You need to evaluate your business and auditing requirements against the cost and complexity of maintaining a richer data auditing system.

Consider adding one or more sorting columns to your dimension tables. There may be some sort order other than alphabetical that makes sense to your business users. This is especially true of Chart of Accounts dimensions.

Indexing and Column Constraints

In this section we provide a simple indexing plan for your relational data warehouse database. You should think of this as a starting point. You need to evaluate your query load against your data on your test system, in order to optimize your indexing plan.

Dimension tables with a single-column integer surrogate primary key should have a clustered primary key index. A clustered index is embedded with the data rows; it actually becomes the physical table itself. Unless the dimension is tiny, you should also create an index on the natural key.

For small dimensions, the only other index you might want to define at the outset is a single column index on any foreign keys. In the case study database, all dimensions have two foreign keys to DimAudit, and the Customer dimension has a foreign key to DimGeography, so we created indexes on those columns. All of the dimensions in our sample database are small enough that it's unlikely to be worthwhile to create any additional indexes.

For larger dimensions, your indexing plan depends on how the relational data warehouse database will be used. The hardest case to tune for is if the relational data warehouse will support significant reporting and ad hoc queries. Insofar as you know what that query and reporting load will be, you can tune the index plan for the expected use. You should already have identified the hierarchical relationships in your dimension. For a large dimension supporting direct queries, these hierarchical attributes are probably the first non-key attributes that you'll want to index. A very simple dimensional model is illustrated in Figure 4.7. If DimProduct is large and heavily used, consider single-column indexes on ProductCategory, ProductSubcategory, and ProductName.

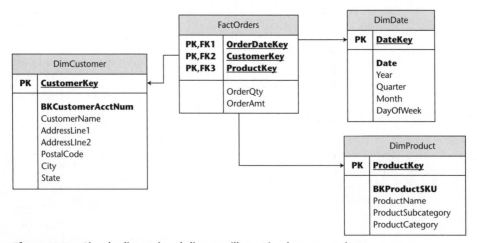

Figure 4.7: Simple dimensional diagram illustrating key constraints

INDEXING VERY LARGE DIMENSIONS

A very large dimension that contains some Type-2 slowly changing dimension attributes should have a four-column index on the business key, row begin date, row end date, and the surrogate key. The row end date and surrogate key can be created as INCLUDE columns in the index. This index will speed the performance of surrogate key management during the ETL process.
    See the Books Online topic "Indexes with Included Columns."

Microsoft SQL Server's query engine will use multiple indexes on a single table when resolving a query. With a specific workload of predefined queries, you can probably define multi-column indexes that are very useful. However, if you know very little about how users will access the data, the single-column index approach is the most sensible starting point.

For fact tables, the standard starting point is to create a single column clustered index on the date key. If your fact table has multiple date dimensions, choose the one that's most often used in queries or, if your fact table is partitioned, the one that's used in the partitioning strategy. Next, create a single column index on each of the other foreign keys to the dimension tables. In the simple database illustrated in Figure 4.7, you would create a clustered index on OrderDateKey and single column indexes on CustomerKey and ProductKey in the FactOrders table. Most DW/BI systems do use the relational database for some queries and reports, so the simple fact table indexing described here is a good starting point. As with the dimensions, you should tune the indexing plan with your data and query mix.

NOTE If your relational data warehouse is being used only to stage the Analysis Services database, you can get away with building fewer indexes. You'll certainly want to keep the primary key index on dimensions. Fact tables can be left largely unindexed. Because the queries Analysis Services uses to find data for processing are always the same, you can run the Index Tuning Wizard and tune the relational database exactly for that set of queries.

What about the primary key on the fact table? And what about the foreign key constraints between the fact table and the dimension tables? Our first answer is that of course you should declare the fact table keys, both primary and foreign. Even though you should do so, a few paragraphs from now we'll talk about why you often don't.

Let's start with what should happen. Declaring keys in the database is the right thing to do. Any professional database administrator will look at you funny if you suggest anything different. In the case of a fact table, there is virtually no value in defining a surrogate (integer) primary key on the fact table.

Create a unique index over the set of columns, usually dimension keys, that makes a fact row unique. In Figure 4.7 it's all three dimensions, but that's not always the case. Put the DateKey as the first column in the primary key index, as it's frequently used in query filter conditions.

> **NOTE** The unique, primary key index on a fact table should never be a clustered index. The primary key index is a big, multi-column index. If it's a clustered index, all other indexes on the fact table will be huge and inefficient because they will use the clustered index as their row identifier.

You have already created single-column indexes on the individual foreign key columns in the fact table, and their primary key reference columns in the corresponding dimension tables. Add a foreign key reference between the fact table and its dimensions. You need to let SQL Server check referential integrity, usually when you add the constraints, but you could schedule this task for later. If SQL Server doesn't check referential integrity, the constraints are just window dressing and don't do anything.

In practice, we often do not create the primary key and foreign key constraints on the fact table. Maintaining these structures is extremely expensive and slows down the data loads. As we describe in Chapter 6, one of the most important jobs of your ETL system is to prevent referential integrity violations—and using surrogate keys is a nearly foolproof way to do that. With foreign key constraints in place, every time a row is added to the fact table the SQL Server engine will check that each dimension key exists in its corresponding dimension table. This is a very expensive check for something that you did just moments before when you looked up the fact table's surrogate keys. Along the same lines, for SQL Server to maintain a multiple-column unique index is obviously expensive. Since SQL Server resolves most queries by using the single-column indexes that you've created on each dimension key in the fact table, this unique index provides very little value for its cost of maintenance.

> **NOTE** Build your fact tables the right way, with primary and foreign key constraints defined and enforced in the database. For the initial historical load, disable the constraints, load all the data, and then re-enable and check the constraints. Test your incremental load process. If it's too slow, and you're positive the slowness is occuring during the INSERT step, test the performance gains that result from removing the primary key index and foreign key constraints. If you decide to run this way, check periodically (weekly or daily) for referential integrity violations, which can creep in no matter how beautifully you've designed your ETL system.

Create Table Views

All business-user access to the relational data warehouse database should come through views. Similarly, Analysis Services databases should be defined on views, rather than the underlying tables. In both cases, the rationale is to provide a protective layer between the users and the underlying database. This layer can be very helpful if you need to modify the DW/BI system after it's in production.

All user access should be through views rather than to the underlying tables. The table names shouldn't even show up in a user's list of database objects. In the simplest case, a table's view would simply select all the columns from the underlying table. You may want to drop some columns from the view, especially some of the housekeeping columns described previously.

If you have snowflaked a dimension, create a single view for the dimension that collapses the multiple tables into a single logical table. To improve performance, you may choose to make this an indexed view.

All of your database object names should be business-user friendly. But the view definition is an opportunity to rename a column, especially for role-playing tables, discussed in Chapter 2.

Partitioned Fact Tables

In SQL Server 2005, Microsoft introduced partitioned tables. Partitioned tables are important for the scalability of the relational data warehouse database. The improved scalability comes not so much from improved query performance against partitioned tables, although improved query performance is possible. Rather, the big win comes from greatly increased manageability of very large tables. With a very large partitioned table, everything from loading data, to indexing, and especially to backing up the data, can be much easier and faster than with a single monolithic table.

In a relational data warehouse database, you will typically partition the fact tables. Dimension tables, even very large dimension tables, seldom benefit from partitioning. From the point of view of a user or application issuing a query, a partitioned table looks and behaves the same as a non-partitioned table.

Analysis Services databases can also be partitioned. Most people use the same partitioning scheme for Analysis Services as for the relational database, and create, merge, and delete partitions from the two data stores on the same schedule. This is just a convenience; there is no requirement that Analysis Services partitions be synchronized with relational partitions.

Relational and Analysis Services partitioning are both features of SQL Server Enterprise Edition only.

How Does Table Partitioning Work?

A partitioned table is a lot like a set of physical tables that are combined with a UNION ALL view. The classic partitioning scheme is to partition by month. Each month of fact data goes into a separate physical table, which is tied together with the other months' identically structured tables. We expect that most readers could define the UNION ALL view that does this task. A partitioned table works pretty much the same way, but there is a special syntax for defining it. There are some specific requirements, discussed shortly, for how the partitions are physically structured. The benefits are substantial, and the old UNION ALL approach should no longer be used in your relational data warehouse database.

> **NOTE** In this chapter we illustrate an extremely simple partitioned table and load it with a handful of rows. These scripts are available on the book's web site at www.MsftDWToolkit.com.

The first step in defining a partitioned table is to define a partition function, using the CREATE PARTITION FUNCTION syntax that's well defined in Books Online. If you're creating monthly partitions for a DateKey surrogate key, you would use syntax like:

```
-- Create the partition function
CREATE PARTITION FUNCTION PFMonthly (int)
AS RANGE RIGHT
FOR VALUES (20040101, 20040201, 20040301)
GO
```

In this very simple example, the first partition holds all data before January 2004, the second partition holds January data, the third holds February data, and the fourth holds all data for March onward. Note that a partition function automatically creates partitions to hold all possible values. Three boundary points, as in the preceding example, create four partitions. If you're using surrogate date keys, you need to create an integer function that uses the appropriate key ranges. You can create complex partition functions, but most people will just create simple functions like the one illustrated here. (This is the main reason to use a meaningful surrogate key for Date.)

The next step is to define a partition scheme, which maps each partition in a partition function to a specific physical location. A simple example is illustrated here:

```
-- Add the partition scheme
CREATE PARTITION SCHEME PSMonthly
AS PARTITION PFMonthly
ALL TO ( [PRIMARY] )
GO
```

Although we're creating all the partitions on the database's Primary filegroup for this example, in the real world you would specify which partition goes on which filegroup. Aged partitions that no longer receive data or updates can have their filegroups set to Read Only, which will greatly speed backups. See Books Online for details.

NOTE If you plan to use Read Only filegroups, it makes most sense to put each partition on its own filegroup. That way you have the most flexibility for rolling a partition into and out of read-only status.

Finally, create your partitioned table on the partition scheme. The syntax is really simple: Basically you're replacing the standard ON <filegroups> syntax with an ON <PartitionScheme> clause. Here is a very simple table:

```
-- Create a simple table that we can partition
CREATE TABLE PartitionTable
(DateKey int NOT NULL,
CustomerKey int NOT NULL,
SalesAmt money,
CONSTRAINT PKPartitionTable PRIMARY KEY NONCLUSTERED
(DateKey, CustomerKey)
)
-- The ON clause refers to the partition scheme
ON PSMonthly(DateKey)

GO
```

NOTE The partition key (DateKey in our example) must be NOT NULL.

You can insert data into the partitioned table simply by using an INSERT statement. SQL Server uses the partition function to determine where the inserted data should go. A corollary to this statement is that this partition function should be simple and high-performance. Although you can define a partition function that performs a lookup or calculation, you should try to avoid doing so.

In the data warehouse database, we most often partition fact tables by date. Let's add a few rows to our partitioned table:

```
-- Add some rows
INSERT INTO PartitionTable (DateKey, CustomerKey, SalesAmt)
VALUES (20031201, 1, 5000)
INSERT INTO PartitionTable (DateKey, CustomerKey, SalesAmt)
VALUES (20040101, 2, 3000)
INSERT INTO PartitionTable (DateKey, CustomerKey, SalesAmt)
VALUES (20040215, 55, 6000)
INSERT INTO PartitionTable (DateKey, CustomerKey, SalesAmt)
VALUES (20040331, 5, 3000)
```

```
INSERT INTO PartitionTable (DateKey, CustomerKey, SalesAmt)
VALUES (20040415, 57, 6000)
GO
```

If you query PartitionTable, you should see all these rows. There are some system views that you can query to see how your partitioned table is set up.

REFERENCE   See the Books Online topic "Querying Data and Metadata from Partitioned Tables and Indexes."

Run the following query to see how many rows are in each partition:

```
-- Query the system views to see what happened
SELECT $partition.PFMonthly(DateKey) AS [Partition#],
COUNT(*) AS RowCnt, Min(DateKey) AS MinDate, Max(DateKey) AS MaxDate
FROM PartitionTable
GROUP BY $partition.PFMonthly(DateKey)
ORDER BY [Partition#]
GO
```

As you should expect, the first partition, which contains all data before 1/1/2004, contains a single row, as do the partitions for January and February 2004. The fourth partition, which starts on 3/1/2004, contains all rows after that date, so it includes two sample rows for 3/31/2004 and 4/15/2004.

Changing the Partitioning Scheme

Our very simple example raises an interesting point. How do we add a new partition for April? And what happens to our existing row for April when we do that?

Use the ALTER PARTITION FUNCTION command:

```
-- Add a new partition for April

ALTER PARTITION FUNCTION PFMonthly ()

SPLIT RANGE (20040401)
```

Re-run the query that counts the rows in each partition; you'll see that SQL Server automatically moved the row dated 4/15 into the new partition. There are a few issues to be aware of here. First, this works great on a partition that contains two rows. But what if your partition contained 10 million, 100 million, or more rows? Although it will work, it probably will take more resources than you wish.

TIP Always leave yourself at least one empty partition that covers the date range that you plan to split later. Create new partitions well before you need them, so that you are always splitting an empty partition. In most cases, you want the first and last partitions always to be empty.

A second syntax for the ALTER PARTITION FUNCTION command will merge two partitions. As with splitting partitions, you'd prefer to merge empty partitions. We'll discuss how to do so most effectively.

In the real world, you will want to be careful about the filegroup on which the next partition is created. Use the ALTER PARTITION SCHEME command to specify which filegroup to use for the next partition that will be created.

TIP Issue the ALTER PARTITION SCHEME command before executing the ALTER PARTITION FUNCTION command.

Using Table Partitions for Fast Data Loads

As you saw in the simple example in the preceding text, you can insert data directly into a partitioned table. It shouldn't surprise you to learn that this is not a fast loading process: At best it's as fast as an insert into a normal table. Especially for your initial load, you'll want to know how to load the partitioned fact table as fast as possible. There's an elegant trick that works great.

The trick is to load data into a separate table that's structured exactly the same as the table partitions—same columns, datatypes, indexes, filegroups, and so on. We'll call this separate table a pseudo-partition. Note the CREATE TABLE script that follows is exactly the same as we used for the partitioned table, excluding the ON <PartitionScheme> clause:

```
-- Create an empty table nearly identical to the partitioned table
CREATE TABLE PseudoPartition_200405
(DateKey datetime NOT NULL,
CustomerKey int NOT NULL,
SalesAmt money,
CONSTRAINT PKPseudoPartition_200405 PRIMARY KEY NONCLUSTERED
(DateKey, CustomerKey),
CONSTRAINT CKPseudoPartition_200405 CHECK
(DateKey >= 20040501 and DateKey <= 20040531)
)
-- We don't want the ON <PartitionScheme> clause
--ON PSMonthly(DateKey)
GO
```

PSEUDO-PARTITION CHARACTERISTICS

The pseudo-partition table must be defined on the same filegroup as the partition it's destined to replace. Everything about the pseudo-partition table must be exactly the same as the target partitioned table, with one exception. You must define a check constraint for the partition key (DateKey in our example), to ensure that the pseudo-partition table contains only data appropriate for the partition.

If you have indexes on keys other than the partitioning key, you must INCLUDE the partitioning key in the indexes of the pseudo-partition. SQL Server automatically adds the partitioning key as an INCLUDE column to any partitioned index that doesn't already have it included, but it's better to do it in advance so the partition switch can be very fast.

See the Books Online topic "Index with Included Columns."

Go ahead and create empty partitions for May and June:

```
-- Create empty partitions for May and June
ALTER PARTITION SCHEME PSMonthly
NEXT USED [PRIMARY]
GO
ALTER PARTITION FUNCTION PFMonthly ()
SPLIT RANGE (2004501)
GO
ALTER PARTITION SCHEME PSMonthly
NEXT USED [PRIMARY]
GO
ALTER PARTITION FUNCTION PFMonthly ()
SPLIT RANGE (20040601)
GO
```

Use standard fast-load techniques to load the data into that pseudo-partition:

- Set the database to Bulk-Logged or Simple recovery mode.
- Confirm the table is empty and/or disable all indexes and constraints.
- Bulk Insert or BCP from a file, or develop an Integration Services package using a SQL Server Destination task in the data flow.
- Enable (or create) indexes and constraints.
- Return the database to the desired recovery mode.
- Perform appropriate backups.

But in our example, we'll skip all these steps and simply add a few rows by hand to our new partition for May 2004:

```
-- Insert a few rows by hand. In the real world we'd use
-- a bulk loading technique.
INSERT INTO PseudoPartition_200405 (DateKey, CustomerKey, SalesAmt)
VALUES (20040505, 33, 5500)
INSERT INTO PseudoPartition_200405 (DateKey, CustomerKey, SalesAmt)
VALUES (20040515, 27, 6000)
GO
```

Once the data is loaded, the indexes rebuilt, and the constraints re-enabled, switch the pseudo-partition into the partitioned fact table. This switch is a metadata operation and executes very quickly.

```
-- The magic switch - very fast even with large data volumes

ALTER TABLE PseudoPartition SWITCH TO PartitionTable PARTITION 6

GO
```

You can re-run the query that examines the rowcounts in partitions to confirm that this actually works. Examine the PseudoPartition table: It now contains zero rows. When we executed the ALTER TABLE ... SWITCH TO command, no data actually moved. Instead, the system's metadata logically swapped the places of the empty partition and the populated pseudo-partition. This is why they have to be structured identically.

NOTE For populating the initial historical data, it's usually fastest to create all indexes after the entire partitioned table is populated and stitched together. SQL Server will build the indexes in parallel.

This technique minimizes overall load time and system resources because we can perform a fast, non-logged load of large volumes of data. At the same time, we're minimizing the impact on the database's users. The data is loaded into a table that's invisible to users; during that load the partitioned table remains available for query; and the switch step executes extremely fast. In addition, the pseudo partition can be backed up as a separate table, improving system manageability.

Dropping Old Data from a Partitioned Table

One of the great advantages of a partitioned table is that it makes it so easy—and fast—to drop aged data. It's a common practice to keep a rolling window of data in the fact table, usually in multiples of a year plus one month (for instance, 37 months). Without table partitioning, dropping the oldest month (or year) of data requires a resource intensive DELETE FROM statement.

The best way to drop an old partition is to create an empty pseudo-partition, and swap it into the partitioned table for the old partition. As before, the pseudo-partition table must be structured identically to the partition it replaces, although in this case you don't need to add a check constraint on the DateKey:

```
-- Create another pseudo partition table, this one to swap out
CREATE TABLE PseudoPartition_200312
(DateKey datetime NOT NULL,
CustomerKey int NOT NULL,
SalesAmt money,
CONSTRAINT PKPseudoPartition2 PRIMARY KEY NONCLUSTERED
(DateKey, CustomerKey),
)
GO
```

Now, swap this empty table into the partitioned table, replacing partition 1:

```
-- The Switcheroo - very fast move offline of aged data

ALTER TABLE PartitionTable SWITCH PARTITION 1 TO PseudoPartition_200312

GO
```

Examine both the partitioned table and the pseudo-partition. The partitioned table has an empty partition 1, and the PseudoPartition_200312 table now contains a row. As above, this is a metadata operation and occurs very quickly. Now, PseudoPartition_200312 can be backed up and dropped from the database if you wish.

Using Partitioned Tables in the Data Warehouse Database

If you've read this whole section on partitioned tables, you've already figured out that partitioned tables are too complicated to use unless you really need them. So when do you need them? If you have a fact table that contains a billion rows, you certainly want it to be partitioned. You should seriously consider partitioning for smaller fact tables if you can't find a better way to reduce your backup window or load window to an acceptable target. At the low end, it's hard to imagine that a 10 million row fact table would truly need to be partitioned.

If you decide to partition your fact table, you must automate the process of loading and managing the table and partitions. Your ETL system should be partition-aware, and automatically add new partitions as needed to accommodate new data. Books Online provides examples of best practices for how to do this.

PARTITIONED TABLE LIMITATIONS

We really like the partitioned table feature. But there are some limitations that it's important to know about.

- ◆ As we mentioned, there's a limit of 1,000 partitions per table.

- ◆ Partitioned tables cannot have indexed views defined on them.

- ◆ Issue the ALTER PARTITION FUNCTION... MERGE RANGE and SPLIT RANGE commands only against empty partitions. SQL Server will let you issue the command against a populated partition, and it will move the data around, but it will do it very slowly. If you have enough data that you're using partitions, you need to move the data yourself, most likely with an Integration Services package.

Most systems with partitioned fact tables will partition monthly by date. Most will implement the fast load and partition switching technique for the historical load, but not bother to do so for the daily incremental loads. If your DW/BI system has extreme data volumes, on the order of 10 million new fact rows a day, you may need to play this game on your daily loads.

If you're in this situation, the easiest thing to do is to partition by day instead of by month. However, you want to keep the total number of partitions for any one table to several hundred. There's a limit of 1,000 partitions per table.

However, keeping even one year of data, or 365 daily partitions, is a bit worrisome. You may consider consolidating daily partitions into weekly or monthly partitions as they age. Obviously you want to do this the fast way, using partition switching, rather than by merging populated partitions. The recommended approach is to build an Integration Services package that selects from daily partitions into a weekly pseudo-partition table, and then modifies the partitioning scheme. Have fun.

Aggregate Tables

Aggregates are the single most useful way to improve query performance on a dimensional DW/BI system. An aggregate table summarizes data at a higher level than the atomic data maintained in the detailed fact table. You would create aggregate tables at a parent level in a dimension, say at Product.Category, Geography.Country, or Date.Month. Some or all of the other dimensions would remain at their leaf levels.

REFERENCE The process of designing and maintaining aggregate tables in the relational data warehouse database is discussed in the books *The Data Warehouse Toolkit* (Chapter 14) and *The Data Warehouse ETL Toolkit* (Chapter 6).

Microsoft has a few tools to help you maintain aggregate tables. We've seen people use indexed views as a substitute for aggregate tables. You can define an indexed view on the business process dimensional model, to summarize the detailed data and store the summary in the view's index. This approach is most appealing to people who have done a lot of data warehousing in Oracle, which has a similar feature. We haven't seen any large SQL Server DW/BI systems make extensive use of indexed views in this way, and we don't recommend it as a best practice.

Most Microsoft DW/BI systems that would benefit from aggregates use Analysis Services to manage those aggregates. As we describe in Chapter 7, the Analysis Services OLAP functionality has a host of features for designing and maintaining aggregates. This is one of the core features of Analysis Services. Even if Analysis Services provided no other benefits, its usefulness as an aggregate manager makes implementing it worthwhile.

If you just can't do OLAP, and really need to maintain relational aggregate tables, we recommend that you maintain them the old-fashioned way: in your ETL process. If you only ever add rows to your data warehouse database, and you only build aggregates on Type 2 slowly changing dimensions, then maintaining aggregate tables isn't at all difficult. In the real world, it's a painful process. Again, see the books referenced above for a more complete description of the issues and approaches.

Staging Tables

One of the last steps in your physical design process is to develop staging tables. Staging tables are relational tables that are used to hold data during the ETL process. Use staging tables for data that you want to use as a lookup for other processing. You may create a staging table based on each dimension that contains today's version of the key lookups, for use during the fact table surrogate key assignment process. You may create a staging table to tie together similar members such as people from multiple source systems.

Because staging tables are intimately tied to the ETL process, the ETL developer is usually the person who specifies the requisite structure. A defining characteristic of a staging table is that it is not available to business users for querying. Best practice puts staging tables in a separate database from the relational data warehouse.

During your staging area design process, it's important to remember to stage in relational tables only data that is used for lookups, and to index it appropriately to speed those lookups. You should use the file system, and especially the Integration Services raw file format, to stage data that's not used for lookups. Writing data in the raw file format is orders of magnitude faster than writing it to relational tables. Use the relational database only as appropriate.

Metadata Setup

At this point in the process, when you are setting up your other databases and file system, you should also define your metadata database. We have an entire chapter devoted to metadata, in which we suggest some structures that integrate with the way we like to build Microsoft DW/BI systems. See Chapter 13 for details.

Aside from the data model for metadata that you define, the other issue with metadata is where it is stored. We like to store user-defined metadata in its own relational database. Usually this database is on the same server as the data warehouse database. The reason you want it in a separate database is that the metadata database is more transactional than the data warehouse or staging databases. You should back it up frequently—which is easy to do because it's small.

Summary

We began this chapter by discussing various options for configuring your DW/BI system. System sizing is challenging because it depends on so many factors—some of which you won't have much information on until your system is in production. The easy factors to predict are data volumes and system availability requirements. It's harder to guess how many simultaneous users you'll have, and how many of them will be performing challenging ad hoc queries. Nonetheless, we conclude that the vast majority of systems will use one or several commodity 4-way 64-bit servers. High-end systems will use one or more 8-way, 16-way, or even larger 64-bit servers. The 64-bit architecture is appealing because it allows so much more addressable memory. All the BI software components love memory.

We discussed storage architecture, and came down firmly on the side of using a Storage Area Network with some level of hardware-controlled redundant RAID.

We briefly described the SQL Server software installation issues for the development, test, and production servers. General installation and setup issues are well documented in SQL Server Books Online. This chapter is long enough that it makes no sense to repeat that information here. Instead, we focused on issues that are specific to data warehousing.

The second half of this chapter discussed setup and design issues for the relational data warehouse database. We described how to convert the logical data model into a physical data model in the relational database. We discussed indexing and foreign key enforcement. Finally, we described relational table partitioning, which can greatly improve the manageability of large fact tables.

CHAPTER 5

Designing the ETL System

Measure twice; cut once

Some people like to plan, specify, and document systems; most don't. We've observed that Extract, Transformation, and Load (ETL) system development draws folks in the latter category. We've found so few people who write adequate design specifications for their ETL systems that we've practically stopped asking to see our clients' planning documents. Either they're unaware of the impending complexity, or they don't have the planning tools. We intend not to let this happen to you.

In this chapter we begin by providing an overview of SQL Server Integration Services, including a description of the processing and transformation tasks that are available. The purpose of this introductory material is to provide you with enough background about how Integration Services works so you can make informed decisions about the design of your ETL system. The next chapter, "Developing the ETL System," provides more detailed guidance on how to use Integration Services.

The second half of this chapter describes how to develop the specification for your ETL system. Begin with high-level planning; make some system-wide decisions about how to approach various issues; and then perform a thorough analysis of the source data. We'll talk about how to set up the ETL system and staging areas. Finally, you will have gathered enough information and made enough decisions to develop the detailed ETL system specification. Throughout, we will be referring to the Adventure Works Cycles case study.

As Figure 5.1 illustrates, and common sense dictates, the ETL portion of the project is part of the data track. Remember, however, that these boxes aren't to scale. The ETL effort requires the most time invested in the data track, and often in the entire project.

In this chapter, you learn:

- What SQL Server Integration Services is, and its role in the DW/BI system. You'll receive an overview of its most important features for ETL system design.

- The components of a solid ETL design specification, and how to create this document:

  - High-level map

  - Detailed data profiling report

  - Source-to-target mapping

  - Strategy document for extracting data

  - Strategy document for updating Analysis Services database

- The details of ETL system physical design and architecture.

An Introduction to SQL Server Integration Services

We begin this chapter with an overview of SQL Server 2005 Integration Services. The goal of the introduction is to familiarize you with the ETL toolset so that you can understand its features and grow comfortable with its vocabulary. This overview is not a tutorial on Integration Services; we're focusing more on the "what and why" of the tool than on the "how."

> **SQL SERVER 2000/2005 CHANGE: DATA TRANSFORMATION SERVICES**
>
> SQL Server 7.0 and SQL Server 2000 included a product called Data Transformation Services, DTS for short. Many customers used DTS to build part or all of their ETL systems. DTS's primary appeal—perhaps its only appeal—was its price: Included with SQL Server, it was free. The most effective use of DTS was as a framework for an ETL system that was primarily SQL-based. In other words, people mostly wrote SQL statements or scripts to perform transformations, and used DTS to define the success/failure workflow between those scripts. Most DTS-based ETL systems were not substantively different than the old SQL-and-Perl-script custom systems of decades past, except the scripting part was replaced by the DTS model and design palette.

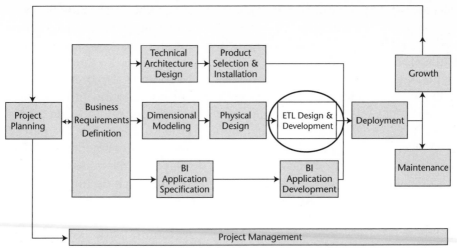

Figure 5.1   The Business Dimensional Lifecycle

The new Integration Services, which replaces Data Transformation Services (DTS), is a lot more than a name change: It's a completely new product. Integration Services has nothing in common with its predecessor. It's important to emphasize this point, especially to those readers who were familiar or even expert with the old DTS. Integration Services is more than just an ETL tool. You can use it to manage and maintain your databases and to integrate data among applications or perform complex calculations in real time. In this chapter, we focus on using Integration Services for ETL.

Your ETL team will develop one or more Integration Services packages to populate your DW/BI system. A package is analogous to a computer program or a script. When your DW/BI system is in production, you can execute a package to perform a database maintenance task, to load a table, or to populate an entire business process dimensional model.

An Integration Services package contains one or more tasks. In the ETL application you'll primarily use control flow tasks, like manipulating files, sending email to an operator, or bulking insert data from a file. By far the most interesting task is called the Data Flow task, in which most of the real ETL work is done. We'll talk a lot more about the Data Flow task later in this chapter.

Overview of BI Studio Integration Services Tool

During the design and development phases of your DW/BI project, you'll use Integration Services in its design and debugging mode. You'll develop Integration Services packages in the Business Intelligence Development Studio tool (BI Studio), which as we described in Chapter 3 is part of the Visual Studio development toolset.

The easiest way to become familiar with the BI Studio Integration Services designer is to open an existing package, like the *Master_Dims* package illustrated in Figure 5.2. This package is included on the book's web site, www.MsftDWToolkit.com.

In the upper right of the BI Studio screen is the Solution Explorer. The Solution Explorer provides a mechanism for navigating between the different components of your Integration Services project: the data sources and data source views that you've defined; the Integration Services packages that are part of this project; and other files, which may include documentation. The *Master_Dims* package is open and currently displayed in the middle of the BI Studio. This project is part of a solution, which could include multiple Integration Services projects, Analysis Services projects, and Reporting Services projects.

In Figure 5.2, our solution is called MDWT_AdventureWorks, and contains several Integration Services projects, an Analysis Services project, and several reporting projects. Because the window is small, you can see only the opened Integration Services project, MDWT_AdventureWorks_Hist.

On the left-hand side of the BI Studio screen is the toolbox, which lists, in this view, the control flow items that you can add to your package. The large area in the center of the screen is the design surface, on which you place control flow tasks. You can connect tasks with precedence constraints, specifying whether to execute a downstream task upon success, failure, or completion of an earlier task or tasks. You can define expressions on the precedence constraints, which is a powerful feature for system automation. As you'd expect, precedence constraints can contain OR conditions as well as AND conditions.

There are several components of the design surface: Control Flow, Data Flow, Event Handlers, and Package Explorer. Each of these is represented by its own tab across the top of the design surface. During and after package execution in BI Studio, you'll be able to examine execution progress in the Progress tab, which doesn't appear until you run the package. (The Progress tab is renamed Execution Results once you exit execution mode.) Navigate between the design components by clicking on the appropriate tab. You'll use the Control Flow and Data Flow tabs most often. The Control Flow is the outer layer of the package, in which all the package's tasks and dependencies are defined.

The Package Explorer tab presents a navigation interface for you to examine the objects that have been defined in the package. Here you can browse the variables that are defined at the overall package level, or scoped down to a task or container. Similarly, you can view the event handlers that you've defined for the overall package or for any task or container. Variables and event handlers are discussed in more detail in the sections that follow.

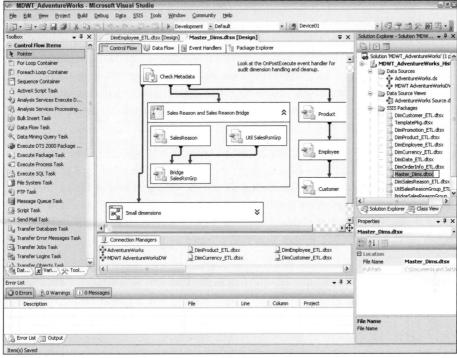

Figure 5.2 Editing the Master_Dims package in BI Studio

Control Flow

The toolbox on the left-hand side of the screen in Figure 5.2 shows the available control flow tasks. There are two categories of control flow tasks: Control Flow Items and Maintenance Plan tasks. In the small screen pictured in Figure 5.2, only some of the control flow tasks are visible. You might use some of the maintenance tasks in your ETL packages, but their main use is for automating operations and maintenance.

The control flow items are more relevant for building an ETL system. The most important is the Data Flow task, which we discuss in much greater detail in the text that follows. As you design your ETL system, you should be aware of the other predefined tasks that are available to you:

- *Bulk Insert task:* The Bulk Insert task lets you perform a fast load of data from flat files into a target table. It's similar to using BCP to bulk copy a file into a table, and is appropriate for loading clean data. If you need to transform data that's stored in a flat file, you should instead use a data flow task that uses the flat file as a source.

■ *Execute SQL task:* The Execute SQL task, as you might expect, will execute a SQL statement against a specified database. The database need not be SQL Server, but the statement must be written in the appropriate dialect of SQL. Use this task to perform database operations like creating views, tables, or even databases. A common use of this task is to query data or metadata, and to put the query results into a variable. We used the Execute SQL task in the package illustrated in Figure 5.2.

NOTE The Execute SQL task, like many other tasks and objects in Integration Services, uses an interface—usually OLE DB—to execute SQL even against SQL Server. You may find that a statement that you develop and test in Management Studio will generate an error inside the Execute SQL task: OLE DB syntax is more restrictive than that allowed in Management Studio. Declaring a variable is the most common SQL syntax that's disallowed by OLE DB.

■ *File Transfer Protocol and File System tasks:* Use the File Transfer Protocol task to transfer files and sets of files. Use the File System task to perform file system operations like copying, moving, or deleting files and folders.

■ *Execute Package, Execute DTS2000 Package, and Execute Process tasks:* The Execute Package task executes an Integration Services package. With it you can (and should) break a complex workflow into smaller packages, and define a parent or master package to execute them. The Master_Dims package from Figure 5.2 is a master package used only for workflow. Its work is handled by the subpackages it calls. Create a separate package to populate each table in your data warehouse database. The use of parent and children packages enables the modularization and reuse of complex logic. If you have DTS2000 packages running already in your production system, you can run them with the Execute DTS2000 Package task. The Execute Process task will run any operating system process. For example, you may have a custom process that will generate the source system extract, or you may invoke a non-SQL Server relational database's bulk loader.

■ *Send Mail task:* The Send Mail task sends an email message. You will almost certainly use this task in an event handler, for example to send a message to an operator about a processing failure.

■ *Script and ActiveX Script tasks:* These tasks are available to perform an endless array of operations that are beyond the scope of the standard tasks. The ActiveX Script task is provided for backwards compatibility to DTS2000; use the Script task for new work. The Script task uses Visual Basic .NET from the Visual Studio for Applications environment.

Or, you can use any .NET language to create a custom task that will become available in the list of control flow tasks. Defining a custom task is a programming job, rather than simply scripting, but has the significant benefit of re-use.

- *Data Mining and Analysis Services Processing tasks:* The Data Mining task runs an Analysis Services data mining query and saves the results to a table. The Analysis Services Processing task will launch processing on Analysis Services dimensions and databases. Use the Analysis Services DDL task to create new Analysis Services partitions, or perform any data definition language operation. There are Data Mining and Analysis Services Data Flow transforms, as well as these control flow tasks. Use the Analysis Services control flow tasks to fully or incrementally update your databases and models. The use of the corresponding Data Flow transforms is discussed in the next section.

- *XML and Web Services tasks:* The XML task retrieves XML documents and applies XML operations to them. Use the XML task to validate an XML document against its XSD schema, or to compare or merge two XML documents. Use the Web Services task to make calls to a web service.

- *Message Queue, WMI Data Reader, and WMI Event Watcher tasks:* These tasks are useful for building an automated ETL system. The Message Queue task uses Microsoft Message Queue (MSMQ) to manage tasks in a distributed system. You can use the WMI tasks to coordinate with the Windows Management Interface, and automate the execution of a package or set of tasks when a specific system event has occurred.

- *ForEach Loop, For Loop, and Sequence containers:* Use containers like the ForEach Loop and For Loop to execute a set of tasks multiple times. For example, you can loop over all the tables in a database, performing a standard set of operations like updating index statistics. The Sequence container groups together several tasks. Use it to define a transaction boundary around a set of tasks so they all fail or succeed together. Or, use it simply to reduce the clutter on the design surface by hiding the detailed steps within the sequence. We used a sequence container in the package illustrated in Figure 5.2, for the Sales Reason and Sales Reason Bridge tables. You can also group control flow objects, and collapse or expand those groups. There's no task for grouping. Simply select several objects, right-click, and choose *Group*. In Figure 5.2 we grouped the Execute Package tasks for several small dimensions, and collapsed that into the Small dimensions group.

- *Data Flow task:* The Data Flow task is where most ETL work is performed. The Data Flow task is discussed in the next section.

Data Flow

The Data Flow task is a pipeline in which data is picked up, processed, and written to a destination. The key characteristic of the pipeline is defined by the task's name: The data *flows* through the pipeline in memory. An implication of the data flow pipeline architecture is that avoiding I/O provides excellent performance, subject to the memory characteristics of the physical system.

In the control flow design surface, the Data Flow task looks like any other task. It is, however, unique in that if you double-click on the Data Flow task, you switch to the data flow design surface where you can view and edit the many steps of the data flow, as illustrated in Figure 5.3.

The toolbox on the left now displays the list of Data Flow transforms. You can re-order the transforms so that your favorites are at the top.

A data flow task contains one or more data sources, zero or more transformation steps, and zero or more data destinations. The simplest useful data flow task would have one source and one destination: It would copy data from one place to another. Most data flow tasks are a lot more complicated than that, with multiple sources, transformations, and even destinations.

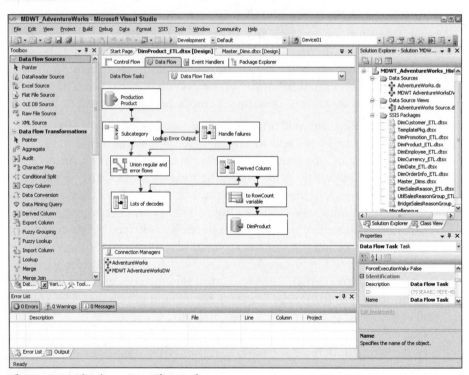

Figure 5.3 Viewing a Data Flow task

Data Sources

There are several kinds of predefined source adapters, called Data Flow Sources in the toolbox pane:

- Use the *OLE DB Source adapter* to extract data from any source that has an OLE DB provider, including SQL Server, Oracle, and DB2. You can source from a table or view, or from a SQL query or stored procedure. You may source from a query or stored procedure if your source table is huge and you want only a relatively small number of rows. Figure 5.3 depicts a data flow that uses an OLE DB data source.

- Use the *DataReader Source adapter* to extract data from a .NET Provider like ADONET:SQL or ADONET:ORACLE. You'll probably use an OLE DB provider instead, even for sourcing data from SQL Server because it has a nicer user interface. If performance is vital, use the DataReader source adapter, which has slightly better performance than the OLE DB adapter, but only the most basic user interface.

- The *Flat File Source adapter* pulls data from a flat file. You could use an OLE DB or ODBC flat file driver, but we prefer the Flat File Source because it has a better UI and handles bad data more flexibly.

- The *Raw File Source adapter* pulls data from a raw data file, which is a format unique to Integration Services. Integration Services writes data to and reads data from the raw format very efficiently. Raw files are a great format to use for data staging, for example to store data extracts during the day (or month) until the main transformation logic kicks off. Also use raw files to hold a fast "backup" of the dimension tables or fact rows that will be updated during an ETL operation.

- The *XML Source adapter* pulls data from an XML source. The XML source can be either in a file or in a package variable (which, presumably, you set in an earlier task in the package). You can optionally apply an XSD schema definition against the XML data. You should hesitate to take any XML data that doesn't have a schema! Because XML data is so unstructured, the source adapter lets you break out the data into multiple destinations. These might flow into different tables, or be handled in different ways before being recombined into a single table.

- You can define a *custom source adapter* to consume data from a unique source, like a file whose rows have different formats under different conditions. For a single-time use, you could use the Script transform to write the source adapter. To easily re-use the custom adapter, develop it in any VS.NET language and install the custom adapter into the list of data flow transformations, as described in Books Online.

All of the source adapters except the raw file source use connection information that is shared across the package. If you plan to pull data from 25 tables in a database, you define one shared connection, including login information, to that database. If you need to change the connection information, for example when you change servers, you have to modify only the single shared connection. Within one or more data flow tasks, define the data source steps to use the shared connection to extract the data from those 25 tables. You can see the example connections in Figure 5.3 in the Connections Managers pane in the lower-middle section of the screen.

All of the source adapters, except the raw file source, support an error flow in addition to the normal output data flow. The ability to define error flow logic on the source is particularly useful for unstructured data sources like Excel workbooks or flat files, where malformed data is very common. We'll discuss error flows in greater detail later in this chapter.

Data Destinations

There are several kinds of predefined destination adapters, called Data Flow Destinations. These are available in the same toolbox illustrated in Figure 5.3, simply by scrolling down in the toolbox list.

- The *OLE DB destination adapter* will load data into any OLE DB target database or table, like SQL Server, Oracle, DB2, or even Excel. If you are loading a large volume of data into non-SQL Server OLE DB destination, it's usually more efficient to write the data as a flat file and use the Execute Process control flow task to invoke the target database's bulk loader.

- You can use the *SQL Server destination adapter* to load data into the SQL Server relational database, instead of the OLE DB adapter. There are several differences between the two adapters:

  - The SQL Server adapter can write data only to a SQL Server relational database running on the same machine as Integration Services.

  - The SQL Server adapter requires that data be formatted perfectly; it skips some data checking and conversion steps that the OLE DB adapter performs for you.

  - The SQL Server adapter can perform faster than the OLE DB adapter because it skips those data checking and conversion steps.

  - Unlike the OLE DB adapter, the SQL Server adapter doesn't let you set a batch size or commit size for bulk loading. In some scenarios, setting these parameters optimally enables the OLE DB adapter to out-perform the SQL Server adapter.

Use OLE DB during the early stages of development because it's more forgiving of data type mismatches. Late in the development cycle, test the performance of the two adapters to determine which you want to use in production.

■ The *Flat File and Raw File destination adapters* write the data stream to the file system. Use raw files if the data will be consumed only by Integration Services. Flat files are a standard format appropriate for many uses.

■ Use the *Data Reader destination adapter* to generate a Reporting Services report directly from an Integration Services package. This feature enables an interesting use of Integration Services for real-time DW/BI systems, as we discuss in Chapter 17.

■ The *Recordset destination adapter* populates an ADODB recordset object held in memory.

■ The *SQL Mobile destination adapter* is appropriate for pushing data down to SQL Server Mobile Edition databases.

■ The *Dimension and Partition Processing destination adapters* push the pipeline data into an Analysis Services dimension or fact partition, without the usual intermediate step of writing the data to a relational database. In this scenario, the Analysis Services database is populated directly from the ETL data stream. This feature is most interesting for real-time DW/BI systems.

■ You can define a *custom destination adapter* to write data to a custom target, just as you could develop a custom source adapter. We hope someone will develop a flexible, high-performance Oracle destination.

Data Transformations

Between sources and destinations are the data transformation steps. These include:

■ *Sort and Aggregate transforms* perform high performance sorting and aggregation. The Aggregate transform can generate multiple aggregates in a single step. The Sort transform can optionally remove duplicate rows. Both the Sort and Aggregate transforms are asynchronous, which means they consume all the data in the flow before they generate an output flow. When you think about what they're doing, this makes perfect sense. The performance of the Sort and Aggregate transforms is excellent, and should meet most applications' sorting and aggregation requirements. In exceptional circumstances you may need a third-party sort or aggregation utility that integrates with Integration Services.

SORTING AND AGGREGATING LARGE DATASETS

Exercise caution in using the Sort and Aggregate transforms for large datasets. These transforms will use virtual address space, and can create memory pressure on other applications running on the server. In Chapter 15 we describe how to monitor your DW/BI system to watch for memory pressure.

- *Conditional Split and Multicast transforms* create multiple output streams from one data stream. Use Conditional Split to define a condition that divides the data stream into discrete pieces, for example based on a column's value being greater or less than 100. You can treat the split streams differently and recombine them later, or you can use the Conditional Split to filter the data. The Multicast transform efficiently replicates a stream, perhaps for parallel processing. The Conditional Split transform sends each input row to one and only one output stream; Multicast sends each input row to each output stream.

- The *Union All, Merge, Merge Join, and Lookup transforms* all join multiple data streams. Use Union All to combine multiple streams with similar structures, perhaps from an upstream Conditional Split, or for Customer records from multiple source systems. Merge is very similar to Union All, but it interleaves sorted rows. If you don't care about the order of the rows in the output stream, Union All is both more forgiving and more efficient. Merge Join is a lot like a database join: it merges rows based on columns in common, and can perform a left, full, or inner join. The Lookup transform is very useful for decoding a code from the source data into a friendly label using information stored in a database table. You'll make heavy use of the Lookup transform in performing the surrogate key assignment on your incoming fact data. The operations performed by these four transforms could all be performed using SQL queries. But if the data is in the pipeline it's easier and almost always more efficient to use these transforms than to write to a table and potentially index that table before performing a SQL query. We use the Lookup transform in the data flow illustrated in Figure 5.3.

- The *Character Map, Copy/Map, Data Conversion, and Derived Column transforms* all do basic transformations. Character Map works only on string data, and will perform transformations like changing case, and changing character width for international strings. Copy/Map simply creates a second copy of an existing column in the stream. Data Conversion changes the data type of one or more columns, for example translating a date string to a true date. Finally, the Derived Column transform is where the most interesting transformation logic occurs. Use Integration Services variables and expressions, discussed in the text that follows, to develop complex transformations on one or more columns, like parsing or concatenating strings, calculating a mathematical expression, or performing a date/time computation. The Derived Column transform dialog box calls the expression editor to help you construct your expressions. We use the Derived Column transform in Figure 5.3.

■ The *Slowly Changing Dimension transform* does a lot more for you than most of the other transforms. It launches a wizard that generates a bunch of objects to manage dimension changes. You'll use the wizard to specify which columns take a Type 1 change, a Type 2 change, or which can never be changed. The generated objects automatically compare the incoming dimension rows with the existing dimension, propagate a new row for the Type 2 dimension if necessary, update Type 1 attributes, and manage the common slowly changing dimension metadata attributes. You could do all this by hand using more atomic Integration Services objects, but the Slowly Changing Dimension transform is a lot easier.

■ Use the *OLE DB Command transform* to update or delete rows in a target table, based on the data in the data flow. The OLE DB Command transformation executes a SQL statement for each row in a data flow; the SQL statement is usually parameterized. The OLE DB Command is the only way to execute an UPDATE statement from within the Data Flow. If your ETL process requires a large number of updates—most common for snapshot fact tables—you should consider writing the target rows to a staging table and performing a bulk UPDATE statement from the Execute SQL task in the Control Flow instead.

■ The *Row Count and Audit transforms* are most useful for developing process metadata about the data flow. Use the Row Count transform to efficiently count the rows that will be loaded to the target, or that flow into the error handler. Audit captures information about the system environment at the time the data flow task is run, including the computer name, user id, and execution start time.

■ You can use the *Percentage Sampling and Row Sampling transforms* during package testing, to operate against a subset of the source data. You'll also use sampling to choose a random sample for deep analysis and data mining, and for building your sandbox source system as described later in this chapter.

■ The *Pivot and Unpivot transforms* will reduce or increase, respectively, the number of rows in the data stream. Use the Unpivot transform to create 12 rows of data from a single source row that has 12 columns holding a year's worth of monthly values.

■ Use the *Data Mining Model Training and Data Mining Query transforms* to incorporate Analysis Services data mining technology into your ETL application. For example, you may have a Customer Score attribute in the Customer dimension, whose value comes from a data mining model. These transforms will compute that model and return the results into the data flow pipeline.

- *Fuzzy Grouping and Fuzzy Lookup transforms* employ fuzzy logic algorithms that were developed by Microsoft Research. These are useful transforms for data cleansing and de-duplication. Fuzzy Lookup, like the Lookup transform, compares and matches two sets of data, but with a measure of confidence based on semantic similarity. Fuzzy Grouping acts much the same way, but is used to de-duplicate data on fuzzy criteria. Unlike third-party tools that perform name/address matching based on a detailed history of addresses, these fuzzy algorithms are based on semantics. You have to experiment with the settings, but the transforms are valuable for a wide range of data cleansing problems.

- *Term Extraction and Term Lookup transforms* employ text-mining algorithms that were also developed by Microsoft Research. Term Extraction is a text-mining component which returns key terms from a document in a text column. Term Lookup matches a document to key terms in a reference table.

- The *File Extractor and File Injector transforms* are used primarily to strip out (extract) text and image data from a data flow and put it into a file or files, or to add such data from files into the data flow.

- The *Script component* provides a simple mechanism for creating a custom transformation in the Visual Studio for Applications environment. We include a simple example of using the Script component in Chapter 6.

Error Flows

Most of the data flow source adapters and transformations support two kinds of output flows: normal flows (green) and error flows (red). The error flow from a flat file source would include any rows with a type mismatch, for example string data in a numeric field. The error flow is a data flow just like the normal flow. You can transform the data to fix the error, and hook it back up with the normal flow. You can write the error flow to a table or file. You can see an illustration of error flows in Figure 5.3, extending to the right of the Subcategory lookup.

The most important characteristic of the error flow construct is that an error in some data rows does not halt the entire data flow step unless you design the flow to do so. And, you can perform arbitrarily complex transformations to the error flow, to correct the data or to log the bad rows for a person to examine and fix.

WARNING By default, all steps in the data flow are set up to fail if an error is encountered. To make use of error flows, you'll need to modify this default behavior by setting up an error flow and changing the error flow characteristics of the transform.

Concepts for Dynamic Packages

There are many tools available to modify the actions that a package takes when it's executing. As we describe in the following subsections, expressions and variables work hand in hand. Integration Services implements a rich expression language that is used in control flow and also in the data flow transform. The results of expressions are often placed into variables, which can be shared throughout the network of packages.

Configurations are a way to change the way a package executes at runtime. You will use configurations most often to set connection information like server names.

Expressions

As you'd expect, Integration Services includes an expression language for specifying data flow transformations. Surprisingly, that expression syntax is neither TSQL nor VBScript, but something unique to Integration Services.

Most expressions are simple: A + B, or A > B, a function like GETDATE(), or a constant like ABC. The two places where you're most likely to use expressions, including complex expressions, are in the Conditional Split and Derived Column data flow transforms. The dialog boxes for these two transforms provide the Expression Builder, which is a graphical tool for building expressions. The Expression Builder provides a list of available data columns and variables, and a list of functions and operators, which you can use to construct an expression. The Expression Builder automatically adds needed syntax elements, like the @ prefix on variable names.

In addition to the Conditional Split and Derived Column transforms, you can use expressions in the following contexts:

- A variable's value can be set to an expression.
- Many container task properties can be set to a variable or expression. Perhaps you're manipulating files whose names are affixed with a date and time. Create an expression to generate the file names in, say, the FTP task, and iterate over the expression.

- Data Flow transforms cannot be reconfigured dynamically. This is different from DTS2000, where such dynamic reconfiguration was often necessary. However, many of the transforms can source from a query or data passed in from a variable. This feature, combined with the Script transform, meets a lot of the needs for dynamic configuration.

- A For Loop container's initialization, evaluation, and increment statements are expressions.

- A precedence constraint can use an expression to specify whether the downstream tasks run. For example, you can set a precedence task to evaluate to TRUE if some value (like an error rowcount) is less than a specified maximum.

Variables

You can define variables within your package. Variables can be scoped to any object: package-wide, within a container like a sequence, or scoped down as specific as a single task. Variables that are defined at the package level are available to all objects and tasks within the package.

You'll frequently set a variable to a constant expression like 1000, but the full power of the expression syntax is available to you. As a simple example, near the beginning of your package you may set a variable you've defined to track the package start time, to the expression GETDATE().

WARNING There are several ways to get the current time. In addition to GETDATE(), you could use the Integration Services variable StartTime. Unless all your servers' clocks are synchronized, you should use a consistent method to get the current time.

You'll find more uses for variables than we can list here. Some of the common uses are to:

- Control execution of container loops
- Populate a variable from a SQL query, and then use that variable to control the package's execution
- Build expressions using variables, for use in data flow transforms like Derived Column

You can examine the values of variables while the package is executing in debug mode.

User-defined variables are the most interesting, but there are a ton of system variables available for you to examine and, possibly, log to your metadata tables.

You can create a new variable from within many dialog boxes that use variables. But it's better to think about the variables you'll need during design time, and create them by choosing the SSIS → Variables menu and working in the Variables taskpad.

Configurations

Configurations help your Integration Services packages respond gracefully to changes in your operating environment. You can overwrite most of the settings for Integration Services objects by supplying a configuration file at runtime. Variables' initial values can also be set from a configuration file.

The single most powerful use of configurations, which everyone should use, is to change server connection settings for sources and destinations. At runtime, without editing the package, you can point all connections to the production servers, or easily change server names or database names. It makes sense to use configurations to change other properties in the production environment, like a disk space threshold, or a threshold for how many rows are processed at a time.

Multiple packages can use the same configuration file, which makes it very easy to deploy a server name change in the production environment. A single package can use multiple configurations. You control the order in which the configuration files are applied; if multiple configurations affect the same property, the last configuration wins.

Integration Services can load configurations from various sources: SQL Server, an XML file, a parent package variable, or a Windows environment variable or registry entry. XML configuration files are easily managed in your source control system. As database people, we generally prefer to use SQL Server to store configurations in production. In Chapter 6 we describe how to use configurations to communicate between packages using a parent package variable.

Use the Configuration Wizard to create the basic structure of a configuration file. Launch that wizard by choosing the SSIS → Package Configurations menu item in BI Studio. The Configuration Wizard generates the configuration as an XML file in the file system with the file extension .dtsConfig. To change the values of an item in the XML file, use your favorite editor. You may want to add the configuration file into the project, as a miscellaneous file. This last step isn't necessary, but it makes the configuration file easy to find and edit from within BI Studio. Don't forget to put the configuration files under source control!

In the test and production environments, you will use the DTExecUI or DTExec utilities to execute your packages, rather than the debugging environment in the BI Studio. With those utilities, you can specify which configuration file or files to use for this execution. We talk more about these utilities in Chapter 15.

Event Handlers

The Integration Services package, container, and task objects will raise events during package execution. You can create custom event handlers for these events. These event handlers are just like a separate package or subpackage, and will contain tasks just like the main package does. You can write a different event handler for many different kinds of events, including OnError, OnPreExecute, or OnPostExecute.

Write an OnPostExecute event handler to clean up temporary storage and other settings when a package or task finishes. Write a package OnPreExecute event handler to check whether there's enough disk space available for the package to run. Write an OnError event handler to restore the data warehouse database to a consistent state, and notify an operator of the problem.

Events percolate up until they find an event handler. For example, if you define an OnProgress event handler at the package level, the individual tasks in that package will use that same event handler unless they have an OnProgress event handler of their own.

You can design and edit event handlers from the Event Handler tab on the Integration Services design surface. The easiest way to see which event handlers have been defined for a package object is to switch to the Package Explorer tab.

High-Level Planning

Now that you're familiar with the features and architecture of Integration Services, this chapter returns to the process of planning the ETL system. The end goal of this chapter is to describe how to write a detailed ETL specification. Before you dig into the details, it's best to start at a high level, by developing the first draft high-level map from the information that was gathered during the business process dimensional modeling effort.

After you pull your very high-level thoughts together into a high-level map, it's time to do detailed data profiling to learn about the characteristics of your data and what the transformation rules will need to be. These profiles will feed into the detailed source to target maps.

You will need to develop some system-wide approaches and rules, for example how to extract data and maintain conformed dimensions. For each fact table you'll need to decide how much history to load initially, and how much historical data to keep live in the DW/BI system.

A summary of the high-level planning process includes the following items:

- Develop a high-level map.
- If helpful, build a sandbox source system.

- Perform detailed data profiling and complete the source-to-target mapping.

- Determine how often you'll load each table.

- Determine how much historical data you'll load for each table.

- Develop a strategy for partitioning the relational and Analysis Services fact tables.

- Design a strategy for extracting data from each source system.

- If necessary, de-duplicate key data elements like person and organization.

- If necessary, develop a strategy for distributing dimension tables across multiple database servers.

Develop the First Draft High-Level Map

One of the early steps of the ETL system design process is to develop an overall map. Draft the map at a higher level of detail than the source-to-target mappings, with a box for each source table, file, spreadsheet, or other source, and a box for each table in the business process dimensional model. Visio, PowerPoint, or even your whiteboard are good tools to use for illustrating the high-level map. We really mean for this map to be at a high level. As a rule of thumb, a map for a simple subject area consisting of a primary fact table and related dimensions can, with a small font, fit on a single sheet of paper.

The high-level map serves several goals:

- It forces you to think about the big issues early. Which tables need to be populated first? What are the big and expensive transformation problems? What data are you missing? How will you create historical Type 2 dimension changes? Trying to fit everything on a page helps focus your attention on what is important and what is noise.

- It provides a succinct mechanism for communicating with management, and other interested parties who aren't all *that* interested. The ETL system is difficult and expensive to build. It's good to have an overview that helps explain why that's so, without overwhelming nontechnical folks with details.

- It serves as an outline for the detailed ETL design specification.

- If the detailed ETL design specification never gets written, it provides the bare minimum of direction to the ETL system development team. People tend to skimp on the design phase of the ETL system. If you can't take the time to think through and draw a one-page picture of what you plan to do, it's hard to see how you can possibly pull together an ETL system that does what's necessary, in the time allotted and without errors.

The high-level map should be aligned around the business process dimensional model. It should illustrate which sources feed each table in the model, and highlight dependencies between tables. A fact table can't be populated before its associated dimension tables, and sometimes one dimension table has a dependency on another.

An example high-level map is included as Figure 5.4. This is a portion of the map for populating the case study database. This map illustrates the population of the Customer dimension table.

At the top we have a list of the tables that provide data to each dimension table. Customer uses data from seven tables in the transaction database. The shaded (source) box illustrates a condition on an extract from the main source table, including the method for finding new or changed rows.

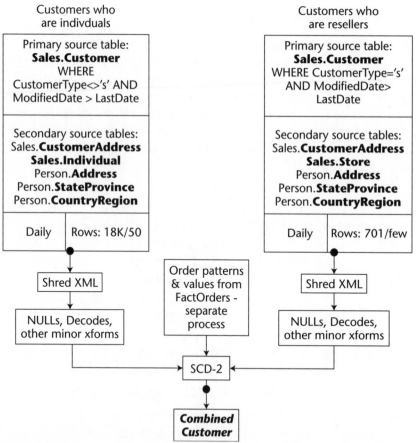

Figure 5.4   High-level map for Customer (both individual and reseller)

Just below the shaded boxes are three small boxes that contain the same information for each table: What is its update cycle; what type of dimension change logic does it require; and approximately how many rows do you expect initially and during each periodic (daily) load? The rowcounts should be very approximate; the goal is to provide a pointer to any troubling data volumes.

The next section describes, at a very high level, what needs to be done to the data. Highlight steps that you're a little worried about, like shredding XML or applying complex logical rules. The high level model in Figure 5.4 shows that information on individuals and resellers flow into the final combined Customer dimension.

In Figure 5.4, the data flow arrows begin and end with a red dot (visible as a filled circle in this black-and-white figure). This dot represents a data quality check, which should be included in every table's processing. We discuss data quality checks in greater detail in Chapter 6. Even though every table's process should include data quality checks, we like to call them out in the high-level diagram because we find that people often forget this important step.

Figure 5.4 is a relatively small section of the full high-level ETL diagram for the case study. The complete diagram is available on the book's web site.

Create the high-level map soon after you've developed your dimensional model. However, as we discuss in the next sections, you still have a lot of investigative work to do. You'll learn more about the requirements of the ETL system and will need to refresh the high-level map to reflect changed plans. At the end of this chapter we talk about what the detailed ETL specification should look like. That specification includes an accurate high-level map. Once the detailed specification is complete, the high-level map serves as a communication tool with people who are not fascinated by the gory details of the ETL system.

Build a Sandbox Source System

During the ETL development process, you'll need to investigate the source system data. If your source system is heavily loaded, and you don't already have some kind of reporting instance for operational queries, the DBAs may be willing to set up a static snapshot of the database for the DW/BI team. Early in the ETL development process, it's convenient to be able to poke around the source systems without worrying about launching the kind of killer query that, presumably, your project is supposed to prevent.

Some source systems require data to be extracted through their programming interfaces. In this situation you need to check with the vendor to ensure your sandbox system is not in violation of their license.

The simplest way to build the sandbox source is to restore the source database or databases from a consistent point-in-time backup. If your source data is very large, consider using Integration Services and the sampling transforms to grab a random subset of fact data. Many people pull over only the most recent few months of data into their sandbox, but this approach omits the inevitable problems that you'll encounter with older data.

NOTE The Integration Services sampling transforms will pull over all the data and then perform the sampling on the Integration Services box. So don't try this on your laptop. If you have the computing resources and bandwidth, random sampling is a good idea. You really do want to pick data from throughout a wide range of time and other conditions.

You can often make a first cut of sampling on the source system query by choosing something pretty random, like customer numbers that end in 7. It's a good idea to do a random sample of a core dimension, like customer, and then pull all transactions associated with only those customers. This helps you get a complete and consistent subset of the source system.

Most large databases contain only a few tables that are very large. These usually feed fact tables, although they can become monster dimension tables. If you don't have the disk space to restore the entire source database and then prune away the unwanted data, instead create a consistent subset using a process like the following:

1. In Management Studio, script the creation of all relevant table and view objects in the source database, including keys and indexes. You probably do not want to script triggers.

2. Create the sandbox database and run the script to instantiate empty versions of all the objects.

3. In Management Studio, use the Import/Export Data Wizard to quickly generate an Integration Services package that will load data from each table in the source database to its corresponding table in the sandbox database. Be sure to omit moving data for the very large tables.

4. Enable identity insert if any column uses the IDENTITY keyword.

5. For the handful of very large tables, develop a custom Integration Services package that pulls over only the desired subset of data.

6. For the large tables, drop indexes and constraints so the load can proceed as fast as possible. Be sure to restore constraints and indexes later. If you don't restore constraints you may spend a lot of time chasing down referential integrity violations that exist only in your sandbox.

7. Check your work by generating a CREATE script for both the source and sandbox databases. Use windiff or your favorite tool to compare the two scripts. This will ensure all keys, indexes, and constraints are the same.

8. Further check your work by comparing table sizes and rowcounts.

You can't stick with the sandbox system throughout the entire ETL design and development process. Sooner or later—and better sooner than later—you'll need to tackle the issues surrounding the arrival of new and updated data.

You don't have to build a sandbox system. If your source system doesn't have major performance problems, and you coordinate with its DBAs about when and how to run queries, you don't need this extra step. In many small companies, the source system DBAs are intimately involved with the DW/BI team and can easily facilitate careful use of their operational databases.

Perform Data Profiling

Data profiling is a methodology for learning about the characteristics of your data. As we described in Chapter 2, you should have begun profiling your data during the dimensional modeling process. You should already have a good idea of domains, relationships, and data quality problems.

REFERENCE   The excellent book *Data Quality: The Accuracy Dimension* by Jack Olson (Morgan Kaufmann, 2003) is largely devoted to the subject of data profiling. You can also find a lot of information about data profiling by performing an Internet search on a term like "data profiling tool."

The best way to perform data profiling is to purchase a tool to run against your sandbox source system. An Internet search will show several good candidates, although you'll notice that Microsoft is not currently included in the vendor list. Nor does SQL Server 2005 include data profiling technology.

Whether you profile your source data in a formal way at the start of your ETL project, or piece by piece after you've started developing, you *will* end up profiling your data. Perform this task at design time so that you can better scope your development effort.

Refer to Chapter 2 for a longer discussion of data profiling. The data profiling that you perform now, for the ETL system design, is similar to the data profiling performed earlier. Now, you focus exclusively on the data sources for the ETL system and keep working with the data until you're satisfied you completely understand it.

Include the results of your data profiling efforts in the ETL system detailed specification. As you work through the results of the data profiling effort, you should first consider if it's possible to correct some of the data errors in the source systems.

It's often difficult to get the source system owners to pay attention to your concerns about data quality. You'll strengthen your negotiating position by presenting a complete data profile report that highlights where, when, and how often bad data has entered the system. We can't tell you how often source system DBAs have told us "you just can't get that kind of error," only to wither into silence when presented with the evidence. It makes most sense to correct historical data in the source system if data checks are now in place, or can now be added, to prevent new errors of this sort from occurring. There's not much use in correcting the historical data if tomorrow's transactions are going to create new junk.

You're unlikely to get all the problem data corrected historically, and even more unlikely to get the source systems modified to prevent all new data errors. The data profiling results will inform the design of your ETL system, both for the historical load and for where to expect and how to handle the inevitable errors that show up on the incremental load.

Complete the Source-to-Target Mapping

The source-to-target mapping is a textual description of how to populate each table and column in the business process dimensional model. The data profile analysis is the single most important input into the source-to-target mapping. The mapping outlines *what* needs to happen, without going into the details of *how*.

Most mappings are simple: CUSTNM in a source system gets mapped to CustomerLastName in the Customer dimension table. Make a note of any transformations that you know about already, like:

- Parsing a source column into multiple target columns: for example, breaking out area code from phone number
- Combining multiple source columns into a single target column: for example, constructing a customer's full name
- Correcting any data errors discovered during data profiling
- Changing case: for example, changing a name field from all capitals to proper case

Make overall notes at the table level about sequencing, like noting that the Customer dimension must be processed after the Geography dimension.

In Chapter 2 we introduced an Excel workbook that illustrates a reasonable level of detail for the source-to-target mappings. At this point in the ETL system design process, ensure the map is completely and accurately filled in.

Load Frequency

Most people load their DW/BI system on a daily basis, and that's primarily what we talk about in this book. The design of your ETL system doesn't change significantly as long as you're loading in batches, be they monthly, weekly, or daily. As soon as you start loading more frequently than daily, the characteristics of your ETL system change. These real-time issues are discussed in Chapter 17.

The main reason to load data monthly rather than daily is if your source system performs some complex business logic at month-end, for example an accounting system. Even so, your business users will probably gain significant value from seeing numbers as they accrue during the month, even if the month-end load supersedes the daily increments. Other data sources, especially external data sources, may be available only monthly.

In our consulting practice we occasionally encounter companies that fully refresh their DW/BI system during each load. If you really had to perform a full refresh for each load, that would be a good reason for loading only monthly. A DW/BI system that's fully refreshed for each load is typically one that was developed as a prototype and moved directly into production. We have seen very few cases where such a design was truly necessary, and in fact, this design usually creates significant problems for the business users' ability to track history.

Some companies load their DW/BI system weekly in order to have the entire weekend to complete processing. While it's not unheard of to need so much time to perform processing, it ought not be necessary. If you're in this situation, and your business users are clamoring for yesterday's data, evaluate whether a redesign of the system—or, more to the point, the system's current bottlenecks—can greatly reduce processing time.

More business users are asking for access to data at even lower latency than daily. It's much easier to deliver low latency data with SQL Server 2005 than ever before. However, as soon as you move to intraday processing, there are some user experience issues that you need to understand. These issues are discussed in Chapter 17. If you are working on Phase 1 of your first DW/BI system, you should load data no more frequently than daily.

How Much History?

There are two questions relating to history that affect the design of your ETL system. The first is forward-looking: How much history do you plan to keep in your DW/BI system on an ongoing basis? Analyze the costs and benefits of keeping data forever. The business community must provide the justification. The technical folks can formulate the costs, including not just hardware (storage, memory, and processors required to manipulate large datasets), but also the complexity of managing a large system.

A CAUTIONARY TALE

Kimball Group recently reviewed a large system that performs a full refresh of billions of rows every month. It takes seven days to reload the system at the end of the month. They can't track history: Everything, including facts, is treated as a Type 1 change and updated in place.

This design resulted from an ETL team taking shortcuts. They didn't want to take on the hard work of figuring out how to recognize incremental loads, and weren't given enough time by management to do it right. Now they have tens of millions of dollars invested in a system that doesn't meet the users' needs. Nobody wants to deliver the message that the ETL system needs to be redesigned, for millions more dollars.

If you decide not to keep data indefinitely but instead to maintain a moving window of data, you—and the business users—need to decide what that time period is, how frequently data is pruned, and what happens to it when it's pruned. Some systems keep a minimum of, say, 37 months of data and let it accumulate to 49 months before performing an annual pruning. Others prune monthly. (Note that the examples we provide are one month longer than a year. That extra month is valuable for month-to-month comparisons—37 months of data provides a 36-month time series of deltas.)

A second decision is how much historical data to load into the DW/BI system for its launch. Some DW/BI systems begin with zero historical data, and simply start accruing information as time goes by. We find this approach difficult to justify, as the benefits from the DW/BI system come largely from having a reasonably long time series. It certainly has a negative impact on the project's ROI and user appeal.

Loading historical data can be quite expensive, as source systems may have changed multiple times over the years. You may end up writing several transformation steps to cover different time spans. We've even seen companies whose historical data was completely unavailable, because their backup tapes were—and had always been—empty.

TIP Thoroughly test both backup and restore procedures.

The DW/BI team can't make the decision about how much history to load. Develop a proposal and cost/benefit analysis based on the business requirements. Present the proposal to the project sponsor and business users, for their review and approval.

Using Partitions

The SQL Server 2005 RDBMS has a new feature that makes it much easier to maintain large fact tables: partitioned tables. Partitioned relational tables are especially useful in the rolling window scenario described earlier. Most medium to large fact tables should be partitioned, at least by year and typically by month. In Chapter 4, we discussed partitioned relational tables in some detail.

The Analysis Services database can also be partitioned, and it's common although not required to partition along the same lines as the relational database. Most often the Analysis Services database keeps the same rolling window as the relational database, although sometimes the window is shorter. You typically wouldn't manage an Analysis Services database with a *longer* timeframe than the corresponding relational database because you always want to be able to reprocess the database if necessary. If you fully understand the conditions under which a partition may need to be reprocessed, and are willing to accept the risk of data loss—or have developed plans for restoring the relational partitions if necessary—then you can leave orphaned Analysis Services partitions.

As far as the design of the ETL system is concerned, the use of partitioned tables and Analysis Services partitions requires that you implement logic to ensure the appropriate partitions exist before you try to load data into them. Because you almost always partition by date, for example month, you need to create a partition for each new date period before you try to load data into the partitioned table. Although you always define a failsafe partition to hold data that doesn't belong in any other partition, you really don't want to use that partition. Instead, you want to create a new partition before you need it.

Another issue to consider at design time is whether you can fill a relational partition in a single load. Doing so is highly desirable, especially during the historical data load, because you can use fast loading techniques that increase data load performance by an order of magnitude compared to inserts into an indexed table. If your daily fact table insert volume is extreme, you may want to define daily partitions for the most recent week of data, in order to benefit from these fast loads. On a weekly or monthly cycle, with virtually zero downtime, you can consolidate these daily partitions into weekly or monthly partitions. A table can't have more than 1,000 partitions, so you need to set up this consolidation process if you design daily partitions.

WARNING Setting up a partition consolidation process is not a simple task. Although SQL Server will consolidate partitions for you automatically, it does so with intolerably slow performance, assuming your data is large enough that you're using daily partitions. Instead, write an Integration Services package or SQL script that bulk-copies data from multiple daily partitions into a weekly table and then switches the weekly table into the partitioned fact table. Chapter 4 describes this partition-switching process.

Analysis Services performs incremental partition processing very swiftly so you shouldn't need to set up corresponding daily partitions in Analysis Services.

If your ETL system performs fast loads into relational partitions, presumably because you need the performance boost, you may still face a few thorny problems. The first is late-arriving data. Hopefully today's load contains *all* data for yesterday (or last month), and *only* data for that prior period. If data for earlier periods can show up in the current period's load, split the data flow to handle that late-arriving data in a different way. This situation is most likely to occur with distributed source systems. You will need to handle updates and deletes separately from inserts. But since Integration Services requires that anyway; this isn't an incremental burden. Late-arriving data is discussed in more detail in Chapter 6.

Historical and Incremental Loads

By the time you've developed the high-level plan, you should have a fairly good idea about how different the historical and incremental load processes need to be. Sometimes the ETL process for dimension tables can be the same for the historical and incremental loads. The simplest case is when your source, like a customer table, has been updated in place. You have a list of all customers "since time began," but have information about only the current attributes of those customers. In this case, your customer dimension table will have to begin as of the date the DW/BI system goes live, and it can capture future Type 2 changes. You don't have the information to recreate history. If this is your situation, you should educate your business community about this issue.

Business users will be happier if history can be recreated. This may be possible if the source system archives changes in a history table, an older data warehouse, some other easily accessible store, or even old database backups. Recreating history is, be warned, a tedious and time-consuming task. It sounds difficult, and usually turns out to be even harder than expected. Nonetheless, it's vital that the DW/BI team not make the decision about whether to recreate history without consulting with business users. The executive sponsor should make the decision based on the cost estimates you present, together with the benefits voiced by the business.

As hard as it may be to recreate history now, it's far more difficult to do so after the DW/BI system is in production. All of the fact rows will be associated with the version of the dimension member as of the date the DW/BI system went live. If you later decide to go back and recreate history, your dimension table will have more members and different surrogate keys. You must rebuild any fact tables that use that dimension to ensure they get the correct keys. This is deeply unpleasant.

Fact table data is fairly likely to require different ETL logic for the historical and incremental processing. The most common differences you'll encounter are:

- *Data volumes differ.* This point is so obvious it's hardly worth making. But the techniques for extracting, transferring, and loading huge volumes of data are substantially different than for the incremental loads, which are several orders of magnitude smaller. During the historical data loads, where you might be loading hundreds of gigabytes or terabytes of data, you should put the database in Simple or Bulk-Logged recovery mode, drop all indexes, and bulk load the data as swiftly as possible. Fast bulk loads are often impossible on incremental updates, for reasons we discussed in Chapter 4.

- *If you have any dimensions with Type 2 attributes, the historical load logic must associate each fact row with the correct dimension member.* Build the full, historical dimension table first, before processing any facts. Then, you have a design choice. Either you can perform the fact table lookup by joining business keys where the fact transaction date is between the dimension row effective dates. Or, you can design the fact table package to process data a day at a time. During each iteration, create an image of the dimension mapping that would be current as of that date; the surrogate key lookup joins only on the natural key since the correct dates have already been selected.

- *Sources may differ.* Historical data may be saved off in a separate area, like a previous generation data warehouse, a static sandbox as we described previously, a reporting instance, or another data store. Source data structures may differ as well.

- *Transformations may differ.* As with dimensions, you sometimes can gain information about fact transactions as they occur, information that is lost when you examine the historical record. You may have to implement additional logic for the transformation of historical data. This is relatively uncommon, but it certainly happens.

A solidly designed ETL system parameterizes any value that might change. For small databases it's often possible to use the same design and even the same Integration Services packages for the historical and incremental loads. For large databases or those with different transformations for historical and incremental data, design both ETL processes in tandem for maximum re-use of complex components.

Develop Strategies for Extracting Data

You'll use different strategies to extract data from different source systems, and even different entities in the same source system. Choosing the best extraction technique depends more on the characteristics of the source system than on the requirements of the ETL system.

From the ETL point of view, your ideal is an extraction system—written by someone else—that identifies and passes into your world only the rows that have been inserted or changed since the last load. In the real world it's seldom so simple.

Extracting Data from Packaged Source Systems

Most companies that are building BI systems these days use packaged systems for some, most, or all of their transaction systems. Some packaged systems require, or at least strongly recommend, that you use their custom API for accessing the data managed by their transaction system. We don't always like to use the APIs for extracting the data to load into the DW/BI system. First, we might not have (or want to pay for) the scarce talent that's familiar with those APIs. Second, even if we're comfortable with the coding, these APIs were often developed for message-level traffic and perform quite poorly for bulk extracts, especially for the historic data.

Many of these packaged systems offer an analytic system, often as an add-on feature at additional expense. Most of these packaged analytic systems are not entirely satisfactory, which is probably why you're reading this book. However, they often excel at extracting the data from their own systems. The packaged analytic add-on to a transaction system can make a great source to your ETL system. You should investigate whether the advantages are worth the cost, but be sure to verify that the packaged system collects data at the grain you desire.

THE IDEAL PACKAGED BI MODULE

The ideal Business Intelligence module of your packaged system should include the following characteristics:

- ◆ Packaged BI data model is dimensional.
- ◆ Data is stored at the atomic grain.
- ◆ Data model is clear and comprehensible.
- ◆ Attribute changes can be tracked over time (Type 2 slowly changing dimensions are supported). The attribute tracking method is something you should be able to change for each attribute.
- ◆ Ability to easily integrate non-packaged data sources like external demographics or data from another transaction system.
- ◆ Ability to act as a dimension subscriber or manager.

We've never seen a packaged BI system implement all this functionality.

THE SAP .NET PROVIDER

SQL Server 2005 ships with a .NET provider for SAP, which provides two methods of accessing SAP R/3 data:

♦ Write a SQL statement against a single SAP table. You can access column data from all types of SAP tables.

♦ Execute BAPI/RFC. With this access method you can execute a BAPI or custom RFC in the SAP server.

With either approach, the results of your query or call are surfaced by the ADO.NET DataReader interface. What this means to you is that the resulting rowset is available from within Integration Services, Reporting Services, or any other tool that consumes managed sources.

At initial release, the provider does not contain a user interface for constructing a query or a BAPI call. It's your job to type in the correct syntax.

We certainly expect to see Microsoft, and third-party vendors, create additional tools and functionality for integrating with packaged systems.

An alternative to working directly with system APIs is to use a tool that simplifies the extraction of data from many popular source systems. Such a tool effectively substitutes for the expertise we described previously. Some ETL tools have packaged common source system mappings or wizards into their products, usually as connectors available at an extra cost. SQL Server 2005, at its initial release, offers basic connector functionality only for SAP.

If this basic functionality doesn't meet your requirements—clearly the case if your source system is not SAP R/3—there are some third-party tools that you can use. Try an Internet search on "business integration software" for some likely candidates. Research possible tools carefully. Many, especially those that talk exclusively about Enterprise Application Integration (EAI), are oriented much more toward messaging than toward the large data volumes of the BI world.

For many packaged systems, you may be able to extract directly from the database tables. The vendors discourage this approach, but if your packaged system does not have a complete data access API, you have no choice but to extract directly from the database. The major risk in this approach is that the vendor will change the structure of the database in a future release, thereby breaking your extracts. A second risk is that the packaged system might hide some business logic that is difficult or impossible to reconstruct from the database alone.

We have helped to reverse-engineer any number of packaged systems, and it has always turned out to be harder than anticipated. Nonetheless, direct extracts can be a cost-effective approach, especially if you can find a consultant who has performed the task for your source system already.

WARNING We strongly discourage this approach for complex, enterprise-class source systems. We know someone—a smart guy!—who managed a DW/BI system that pulled data from SAP tables. They never got the extract right. At the close of every month, the controller was in the manager's office, screaming about how the data warehouse was wrong again. Do yourself a favor. Don't even try.

Extracting Directly from the Source Databases

Many organizations have custom-built systems to manage a portion of their operations. Usually, these custom-built systems exist to support unique characteristics of the organization, often providing real competitive advantage. Sometimes, they're just old, legacy systems that have not yet been migrated to more modern platforms. Many DW/BI systems are populated, wholly or in part, from these custom source systems. Custom extracts are the only way to pull data from a custom source.

If the custom source is relational, defining the custom extract is generally pretty easy. There are probably people in your organization who are expert on the system, data model, and data. They can help you define the queries to extract the desired data with minimal impact on the systems.

If you have very old, mainframe-based source systems, you may have to develop a custom extract in a language like COBOL. If you're in this situation, let's hope there is still someone around that knows the system. If not, be sure to add additional time to your ETL design and development estimates. Get your extracts written quickly before the last skilled programmer retires.

Most of the projects we've worked on have had a hidden source of data: business analysts' desktops, usually Excel spreadsheets. For example, the interesting characteristics of promotions are very often not entered into the source system but instead are managed in Excel by a Marketing analyst. It's tempting, when you uncover these hidden systems, to design a small applet to better manage the data and process. We recommend that you keep your focus on building the DW/BI system, and accept these spreadsheets and similar sources as the raw material for Phase 1. It's not difficult to use Integration Services to pull data directly from spreadsheets. You should ask the spreadsheet's owner to build an image of the interesting data—usually in a separate sheet of the workbook—that has been structured in a simple table format with column names in the first row. Usually this can be done very simply with Excel formulae and references to the sheet(s) that the user maintains directly.

We've worked with several teams who had huge data volumes fed from proprietary file formats. These were online systems or services, and the data source was system logs whose volume required a custom design for extremely efficient storage. In such cases, the system's developers will have to decode the proprietary file sources for you. They could write a program to consume log files and spit out nicely formatted flat files for Integration Services to pick up. A more elegant and scalable solution for SQL Server 2005 Integration Services would be to have the developers write a custom source adapter for Integration Services. The parsing logic would be exactly the same as before, but the source adapter would be embedded within Integration Services, eliminating the expensive middle step of writing data to flat files. SQL Server 2005 ships with a sample source adapter project, and Books Online includes extensive documentation on the subject. A third, similar alternative would be to write a custom ADO.NET provider. A custom adapter is easier to write and performs slightly better, so you'd write a custom ADO.NET provider only if there's a second (non-Integration Services) use for the output data. With any of these approaches, the hardest programming effort and the most resource-intensive processing will be in the logic to parse the proprietary files.

You may be able to shift some of the burden of transformation to the query that extracts data from the source system, for example by defining the extraction query to join multiple tables or filter rows. This is a tempting path for those of us who are very comfortable with SQL, but it should be used judiciously. If you put transformations in the source query, those transformations can be hard to find. More important, the source queries should always be designed to place the minimum possible burden on the transaction systems. Best practice says to keep the source queries as simple as possible, and explicitly perform transformations in the Integration Services data flow.

As we described earlier in this chapter, Integration Services can extract data from practically any relational database system. The only requirement is that an OLE DB provider (or ADO.NET provider) be available. Because SQL Server includes an OLE DB provider for ODBC, practically every source is readily available. You should always look for a native OLE DB provider rather than use the double layer of middleware. A well-written OLE DB provider is only marginally less efficient than using the database's native interface, like Oracle's SQL*Net. But poorly performing OLE DB providers definitely exist; we've seen instances where the OLE DB for ODBC combination actually performed better than the native OLE DB provider. Microsoft doesn't write most OLE DB providers; they are written and supported by the source database company or a third party.

ANOTHER CAUTIONARY TALE

A recent client had a business-critical, production mainframe application that was over 30 years old and written in Assembler. Only one former employee, now retired, knew anything about the system. The DW/BI system development project timeline depended on how many hours a week this retired programmer cared to work.

If your data volumes are quite large, and your source system extracts are a bottleneck, you should test alternative drivers and providers. For most situations, however, this isn't such a big problem and even the OLE DB for ODBC combination performs adequately for most systems' incremental updates. If you're worried that your historical extract will not finish before the next ice age, consider dumping the large historical tables to flat files. Integration Services' flat file source adapter performs very well.

Extracting Data for Incremental Loads

If you're lucky, your source systems are reasonably modern, well designed and carefully implemented. The ideal source system is ledgered, with updates entered as changes. For example, changes to order quantities after the order was created would be entered as new rows with positive or negative quantities, rather than updating in place the original order row. This is particularly important for fact data and large dimensions with more than a million members.

> **TIP** In most systems, new rows are relatively easy to find. There is usually a transaction date that is trustworthy and we just pull those rows. The trick is finding the rows that have been updated or deleted in the source system. We particularly enjoy it when the source system folks tell us "Oh, no, we never update facts. It can't happen."

In the real world, we don't always have this situation. Usually we at least have a way to find which rows in the source system were changed yesterday—typically a column that keeps the last modified date and time. In Integration Services, the source extract query for fact data should dynamically filter for rows changed "yesterday."

If your source system's fact data doesn't keep track of when rows were last changed, incremental loads are extremely challenging. If the data volumes are small you can pull the entire dataset and compare it to the image in the DW/BI system. If changes are limited to recent months, you can do this comparison over a limited date range. We have also seen systems that do a full refresh of the fact table at certain intervals like quarterly, or whenever the DW/BI system deviates too far from the source system. All of these approaches are painful.

If data volumes are large, you should work with the source system DBAs to craft a solution. Alternative approaches include using change data capture tools on the source system, adding triggers to the source system tables, or defining transactional replication on the source system. Replication is a particularly effective option if your DBAs have expertise in managing a replicated system, or are willing to develop that expertise. Be careful about how to track source system deletes. We almost never delete data from the DW/BI system, with the exception of pruning sets of aged data from a rolling window.

It is much less of a problem to find dimension changes. Most dimensions are small enough that it's perfectly fine to pull all the dimension data into the ETL system on each incremental load and compare with the existing dimension. It's more efficient to pull over only new and changed rows, but it's generally not a problem if you have to extract the entire table. The Integration Services Slowly Changing Dimension Data Flow transform gracefully handles the full table comparisons for you and updates only dimension rows that have actually changed.

Extracting Historical Data

You may choose a different strategy for extracting data for the historical load than for the daily incremental load. It's common to extract the large datasets to flat files, usually one file for each month of data. Often, although not always, you need a different Integration Services package to extract and process historical data than the one that handles incremental loads.

Small datasets, especially the data for dimension tables, are usually extracted in the same Integration Services data flow task that performs transformations and loads the target tables in the data warehouse database.

De-Duplication of Person and Organization

One of the most valuable services that the DW/BI system can provide is de-duplication of people and organizations. De-duplication is particularly important when information about people comes from multiple source systems. Although we would love it if the source systems were modified to use a master person or organization directory service, in many cases that's just not realistic. Nor is developing that master data management part of the DW/BI project.

Some teams face severe data quality problems around the identification of unique people, organizations, and addresses. Although Integration Services includes valuable data cleansing technology, you may need to implement third-party name and address cleansing software. You should investigate this requirement during the ETL system design process.

Integration Services includes two general-purpose transforms that help you address data quality and de-duplication: Fuzzy Lookup and Fuzzy Grouping. These transforms do a surprisingly good job at identifying similar data and assigning a probability to the match's correctness. However, these transforms work best if the data has been standardized first.

To standardize information about a person's name and address, break the source systems' rows into tiny parts, like title, first name, middle name or names, last name, suffix, street number, street name, street type like Avenue, and so on. We've all received mail addressed to strange permutations of our names, so even without the inevitable misspellings we all understand the various ways in which different source systems might hold similar information. It's not a trivial task to correctly parse a name that may be stored as "Warren Thornthwaite" in one system, "Thornthwaite, Warren" in a second, and "Warren N. Thornthwaite, Jr." in a third. The mess related to addresses is even more profound. Add in country-specific standards for names and addresses, and you have a difficult problem indeed.

Some source systems standardize names and addresses for you already. For example, the Person.Contact table in AdventureWorks has broken the name into Title, First Name, Middle Name, Last Name, and Suffix. But the Person.Address table holds address as Address Line 1, Address Line 2, City, Postal Code, and State. To standardize the addresses in AdventureWorks, you'd parse the address lines and change all instances of "Ave." or "Ave" or "Av" to "Avenue." You'd almost certainly find strange additional information in these fields, like "Leave package at side door."

If de-duplication of person and organization is vital to your business, and especially if your source systems don't standardize names and addresses, use a third-party data-cleansing tool. These tools solve the standardization problem for you, and many include different rule sets for different countries. These tools will also de-duplicate the standardized data. They may do a better job than the fuzzy transforms of Integration Services if their algorithms are written specifically for name and address problems. The authors have found the Integration Services fuzzy transforms work well on standardized data.

If your source system data about person and organization are fairly clean, and the business users can accept less complete de-duplication, you can get away without purchasing a data-cleansing tool. For example, in the case of AdventureWorks, the person data looks pretty clean and standardized already. With a few days effort to write a script to standardize the addresses, you will have a high-quality set of data to feed into the Fuzzy Lookup and Fuzzy Grouping transforms. Note that the AdventureWorks data is not realistic enough to make a good case study for the fuzzy transforms.

We'd prefer to use a third-party data-cleansing tool that has been integrated into the Integration Services data flow pipeline. This integration is possible because Microsoft publishes an API for writing a custom transform. The data-cleansing tool vendor would need to write a wrapper around its tool that accepts a stream of dirty data and returns standardized and/or de-duplicated data. You should certainly ask prospective vendors if they have integrated with the Integration Services pipeline. If your tool of choice has not or cannot perform this integration, you can always write the data to a flat file or table and use the Execute External Process task to launch the data cleansing tool from the control flow.

Develop a Strategy for Dimension Distribution

The key to the Kimball Method architecture, and to designing an enterprise DW/BI system, is to conform dimensions across multiple business process dimensional models. This is easy if all the dimensional models are on the same system. We expect the majority of DW/BI teams can build their enterprise DW/BI system without having to distribute the relational data warehouse database.

In Chapter 4 we talked about distributing your system horizontally, with different business process dimensional models on different physical servers. If you must distribute the system horizontally, because of data volumes or political pressures, you'll need to build a single ETL system that processes all dimensions. This system, called the *dimension manager*, is simply a set of Integration Services packages that manages the processing for all of your organization's dimension tables. Distributed databases use local copies of the master dimensions provided by the dimension manager. By isolating the processing of dimensions and facts as we described in this chapter, you'll build a more solid, flexible, and scalable ETL system, even if you don't need to distribute dimensions.

If you have a horizontally distributed DW/BI system, you need to copy the completed dimensions to the distributed business process dimensional models that will use them for fact table processing. For the vast majority of dimensions, it's easiest to just copy/replace the entire dimension to the distributed databases. You need some metadata that describes which databases subscribe to which dimensions, when the master version of a dimension was last updated, and when the master dimension was copied to each business process dimensional model. Then simply create an Integration Services process to push the dimensions out, or have the distributed databases' Integration Services packages pull the dimensions when they are ready for them. Consider using an Integration Services OnPreExecute event handler to pull the dimension tables required by a dimensional model.

WARNING To copy the entire dimension over to the distributed database, you need either to have no foreign key constraints defined between the fact table and dimension tables, or you need to disable and re-enable those constraints. For large dimensions, use replication to propagate only the changes.

It's much easier to manage a non-distributed environment, so we certainly encourage you to challenge any political forces driving you toward complexity. Distributing your DW/BI system vertically, say by having a server devoted to ETL, to the relational data warehouse, to Analysis Services, or to Reporting Services, is nowhere near as complex as the horizontal distribution discussed here.

Updating Analysis Services Databases

We recommend that you use Analysis Services as the main presentation server for your DW/BI system. All the hard ETL work goes into populating the relational dimensional data warehouse database. The Analysis Services database is then built from the relational data warehouse database, and should always consume cleansed and conformed data.

We've seen many installations where Analysis Services is treated not as part of the DW/BI system, but instead as a kind of client tool that doesn't need to be managed in a professional way. This attitude sets you up for trouble. Your team should clearly understand that Analysis Services is a server, with significant requirements for availability and recoverability.

The first thing to understand about Analysis Services is that there are two basic units of processing: dimension processing and fact processing. Just as you have already defined the structure of your relational database before you run the ETL job to populate it, you have already defined your Analysis Services database structure and are ready to add the same data you've just added to the relational data warehouse database.

The standard method of updating the Analysis Services database is to use the Analysis Services Processing task in Integration Services. You could add this task to the end of each package's control flow. Once the table is correctly updated in the relational database, kick off the associated Analysis Services processing. You can even define an Integration Services transaction to roll back the relational changes if the Analysis Services processing encounters a severe error.

An alternative, and usually better, approach is to create one package to perform all Analysis Services processing. Execute this package as the final step in the master package's control flow. This way you can easily bind all the Analysis Services work together into a single transaction.

If you have SQL Server Enterprise Edition, you could set up the Analysis Services database with Proactive Caching. Proactive Caching, which we discuss at greater length in Chapter 17, is a new feature of Analysis Services 2005 that basically monitors the relational database and automatically populates the Analysis Services database. With this approach, the Integration Services packages would ignore Analysis Services. Proactive Caching is most useful for low latency scenarios, where you're adding data to the cube throughout the day.

ETL System Physical Design

The last information to document before pulling together the detailed ETL system specification is the details about the ETL system physical design. Consider where Integration Services will run in test and production; where and how big the staging area will be; and where package definitions will be stored and how they will be named.

It may surprise you to learn that there aren't any global configuration parameters for Integration Services. Beyond installing Integration Services and the BI Studio tools, there's really nothing else to set up.

System Architecture and Integration Services

Integration Services has two major components: a design environment that's part of the BI Studio, and a runtime environment. The design environment is where you create, edit, and debug packages. The only way to remotely execute an Integration Services package in development/debugging mode is to use a remote desktop connection to the remote machine.

On test or production systems, use the DTExecUI or DTExec utility to execute packages. You can run on one server a package that is stored on a different server. In production, Integration Services packages can be located anywhere, and can be run on any server that has the Integration Services runtime executables.

You need a SQL Server 2005 license on any server that has the Integration Services runtime executables installed on it. Chapter 4 includes a discussion of how you may configure your SQL Server 2005 system, and concludes that most often the ETL system will run on the same physical server as the data warehouse relational database.

Design your ETL system with no assumptions about where Integration Services will be running. In other words, build in the concept of (and variables for) an ETL server that may or may not be co-located with another component of the DW/BI system. As much as we try to provide you with practical advice during the design phase, the only way to know for certain whether your ETL system needs a dedicated server is to build it and test it.

You can even design your ETL system to run multiple Integration Services packages on multiple servers. For example, if your enterprise DW/BI system consists of several distributed but conformed business process dimensional models, you would have one central ETL server manage the dimensions, which are then distributed to the conformed dimensional models. Each distributed database could perform its own fact processing on its own ETL server, reporting back to the central server the details of processing success or failure.

Staging Area

Earlier books in the Toolkit series, particularly *The Data Warehouse Lifecycle Toolkit* and, to a lesser extent, *The Data Warehouse ETL Toolkit*, talk extensively about a staging area. The staging area is a *non-user-queryable* place to rest data after it's extracted from the source systems and before it's loaded into the DW/BI system.

STAGE FACT DATA FOR RECOVERABILITY

We recommend that you stage fact data, if only to provide a buffer between the source systems and the ETL system. If a load fails (What? Impossible!), you can always go back to the recovery area rather than have to touch the source systems again. It's a good idea to store a copy of dimension extracts as well, especially if they get overwritten in the source system. Set up your staging process to keep copies as far back as you might need them. We've kept anywhere from seven days for some tables to all of history for others. It depends on how easy it is to go back and get the exact same data set.

In systems with high-performance requirements, you may store the data in the recovery area in parallel with transforming the data, rather than to perform these steps in series. The Integration Services multicast transform makes it easy to develop such parallel flows.

Some Integration Services ETL systems will not use a staging area at all. They will kick off a package at some predetermined time often in the middle of the night. The package pulls data from the source systems, performs all necessary transformations, populates the relational data warehouse database, and launches Analysis Services processing.

Other systems may execute a process on the source system to extract data to files, and then use Integration Services to move those files to the ETL server for processing. In this case the staging area would consist of some file space on both the source and ETL servers.

Another common architecture will be to design a set of Integration Services packages to perform extracts, and a second set of packages to perform transformations and loads. You might choose this architecture if you want to extract data more frequently than you want to transform and load it. In this case, the extract packages write the data as flat files or raw files (an Integration Services-specific format), and the staging area would consist of file space on the ETL server.

Fewer new ETL systems will use a relational staging area than previously. The flat file and raw file storage is efficient and relatively easy to manage. However, a staging relational database is a concept that's comfortable and familiar to many ETL architects. There's nothing wrong with using a database rather than files, if your load window can handle the overhead.

Package Storage

An Integration Services package is an XML file, and has the file extension .dtsx. If you open an Integration Services package file in Notepad or any other text editor, you can verify this is so. And yes, if you're curious, you can theoretically develop a package simply by writing a correctly structured XML file. You would be crazy to do it this way. If you need to build or modify packages programmatically, use the object model.

During development, when you're working with packages in BI Studio, those packages are stored in the file system, ideally under your source control system. After you've developed your ETL system, you will deploy it to your test and then production systems. When you install a set of packages on the target system, you can store the packages in the file system or in the *msdb* database in an instance of SQL Server 2005. We prefer to store production packages in the file system Package Store. The Package Store is a special file system folder in which Integration Services can find packages.

> **NOTE** Readers who are experienced with DTS 2000 are usually biased against storing packages in SQL Server. In DTS 2000, there was no way to categorize packages stored in the database. Integration Services solves that problem. There are two reasons we continue to prefer file system storage:
>
> - **Integration with source control**
> - **Flexible backup and restore, compared to objects inside the msdb database**

Package Naming Conventions

Develop a set of naming conventions for the packages. Our convention is to start with the table name, and append an acronym for the major sets of processing that the package handles. Some examples follow:

- DimCustomer_ETLPi performs incremental extraction, transformation, load, and Analysis Services dimension processing (P) for the customer dimension (DimCustomer table).

- DimCustomer_Eh performs historical extraction only for the customer dimension.

- DimCustomer_TLh performs historical transformation and loading for the customer dimension.

- FactOrderLineItem_ETLPi performs incremental extraction, transformation, loading, and Analysis Services partition processing for the Orders fact table.

- Master_Orders_i runs subpackages for the incremental processing of any dimension tables used by the Orders business process, and then runs subpackages for the incremental processing of the one or more related fact tables in that dimensional model.

We start the file name with the name of the table, so that all the packages that have to do with any one table are sorted together.

Alternatively, group all the packages that do only historical loads into a separate project, as we illustrated earlier in this chapter.

Developing a Detailed Specification

In this chapter we've talked about the features of Integration Services, and walked through some general strategies for high-level planning and the physical design of your ETL system. Now it's time to pull everything together, and develop a detailed specification for the entire ETL system.

All the documents you have developed so far—the source to target mappings, data profiling reports, physical design decisions—should be rolled into the first sections of the ETL specification.

Document all the decisions we have discussed in this chapter, including:

- The default strategy for a package error handler
- The default strategy for extracting from each major source system
- The default approach for handling partitioning
- The design of the dimension manager
- Locations of staging areas
- Data model of the ETL process metadata
- Requirements for system availability, and the basic approach to meeting those requirements

The next section of the ETL specification describes the historical and incremental load strategies for each table. A good specification will include between two and ten pages of detail for each table, and document the following information and decisions:

- Table design (column names, data types, keys, and constraints).
- How much historical data to load (for example, 37 months).
- Historical data volumes (row count).
- Incremental data volumes, measured as new and updated rows/load cycle.
- How to handle late-arriving data for facts and dimensions.
- Load frequency, like daily.
- How changes in each dimension attribute will be handled (like Type 1, 2, or 3).
- Fact table and associated Analysis Services partitioning strategy. Discuss how to implement partitioning if today's load can include fact data for aged partitions.
- Overview of data sources, including a discussion of any unusual characteristics of the sources, like an unusually short access window.
- Detailed source-to-target mapping.

- Source data profiling, including at least the minimum and maximum values for each numeric column, the count of distinct values in each column, and the incidence of NULLs.

- Extract strategy for the source data (source system APIs, direct query from database, dump to flat files).

- Dependencies: Which other tables need to be loaded before this table is processed?

- Document the transformation logic. It's easiest to write this section as pseudo-code, rather than trying to craft complete sentences. The more familiar you are with Integration Services, the more you can use short-hand like *Conditional split on ColA>1000*.

- Preconditions to avoid error conditions. For example, should the package check for file or database space before proceeding.

- Cleanup steps, for example deleting working files.

- Package error handler, if it differs from the default described previously.

- The packages you will create to handle the table's processing, and the scope of work for each package.

- An estimate of whether this portion of the ETL system will be easy, medium-difficulty, or difficult to implement.

The final section of the ETL specification describes any master packages, and provides a first cut at job sequencing. Create a dependency tree that specifies which tables must be processed before others. Whether or not you choose to parallelize your processing, it's important to know the logical dependencies that cannot be broken.

Summary

The goal of this chapter is to encourage you to plan your ETL system. To develop a good plan, you need a basic understanding of how an ETL system is built in SQL Server 2005. The main ETL tool is Integration Services, which contains a rich set of functionality for developing and executing an ETL system. This chapter introduces you to Integration Services' features, without going into any details about how exactly to use them.

The first step in developing your ETL system specification is to start from the draft source to target mappings that are created during the modeling process. While you're developing your data model, you must be looking at the source systems in order to validate that your data model is feasible. At this point you haven't done detailed examination of the source systems, but you've identified source tables for your dimensional model, and you've identified some data quality issues. Document these relationships and issues in a high-level map. You'll edit this map throughout the specification process in order to correct your early assumptions.

The next big step is to profile the source system data. We recommend that you purchase a tool to perform data profiling, as it's very tedious to do by hand. The data profiling results are the main set of information that you need to complete the source-to-target mapping on a detailed level, table by table and column by column.

There are several system-wide decisions to make and document: How often will you load data, and how much history will you maintain? Will you partition your fact tables, and if so how will you maintain those partitions? What strategies will you use for extracting data from the source? How will you handle de-duplication of people and organizations? How will you manage your dimension processing? And what strategy will you use for updating your Analysis Services databases and predefined reports?

All of the information we've described here should be collected into an ETL system design specification. This doesn't have to be a fancy document; just collect the information we've described and slap a table of contents on it. A few years from now, when the team needs to revise the system, your protégé will marvel at your foresight in pulling together all of this information.

Developing the ETL System

What could possibly be more fun?

The Extract, Transformation, and Load (ETL) application is the foundation of the DW/BI system. Business users don't see the ETL system, and they don't care about it. That is, they don't care unless the data isn't available first thing in the morning. They don't care unless the data is unreliable. If the business users care about ETL, it's probably bad news for the DW/BI team.

Building an ETL system is largely a custom process. ETL tools, like SQL Server 2005 Integration Services, provide a huge productivity boost over hand-coding. But there's no getting around the fact that companies have diverse source systems. Integrating and aligning the data from those systems is an exercise in accounting for idiosyncrasies.

When Microsoft decided to rebuild Data Transformation Services (DTS), it took an "If it ain't broke, don't fix it" approach. Comparing DTS with Integration Services, we can infer that the pale yellow background in the designer wasn't broken. Other than that, Integration Services is astonishingly different from DTS. Integration Services is a real ETL tool, and you can use it to build real, enterprise-class ETL systems. This chapter describes how to do exactly that.

Integration Services can be used in a wide variety of scenarios beyond ETL. In this chapter, we focus exclusively on how to implement the ETL system for a Kimball Method data warehouse. We come back to other Integration Services features and uses in Chapters 15 and 17. Still other uses of Integration Services fall outside the scope of this book, as of course do other uses of the relational database.

Although we expect readers to skip around in this book, you should read Chapter 5 before you start this chapter. And before you start developing your ETL system, you should think through most of the design issues discussed in that chapter. Look back at Figure 5.1 to re-orient yourself to where ETL system development falls in the Kimball Method Business Dimensional Lifecycle methodology.

This chapter makes significant use of the Adventure Works case study, and the associated packages available on the book's web site at www. MsftDWToolkit.com. You can read the chapter on its own, but sample code is worth ten thousand words: You'll learn more if you pick through the sample packages. This is a long chapter, as befits the area that takes the majority of project implementation resources. Most readers will get a good enough idea of how Integration Services works by reading the first 15-20 pages of the chapter. ETL architects and developers should read it all.

REFERENCE There's more to say about ETL and Integration Services than we can possibly fit into a single chapter, however lengthy. Two key resources are *The Data Warehouse ETL Toolkit* (Kimball and Caserta, Wiley, 2004) and *Professional SQL Server 2005 Integration Services,* by Knight, Chaffin, Barnes, Warren, and Young (Wrox, 2006).

The chapter sections reference the Kimball Method 38 Subsystems of ETL ("The 38 Subsystems of ETL" by Ralph Kimball, *Intelligent Enterprise*, December 4, 2004). You can find a link to this article at www.kimballgroup.com/html/articlesbydate/articles2004.html.

This long chapter contains four main sections:

- *Getting Started:* In the first portion of the chapter, you learn how to use BI Studio to create Integration Services projects, data sources, and connections. You also learn about package templates and create a master package.

- *Dimension Processing:* This section shows you the basics of dimension processing—extract, transform, and load—and walks you through the steps to build a package to populate a simple dimension. You learn how to manage slowly changing dimensions in Integration Services.

- *Fact Processing:* This part of the chapter helps you understand how fact table extracts and cleaning differ from dimension processing. You learn about how to implement the surrogate key pipeline in Integration Services, and how to design alternative approaches to managing challenging fact table loads, like snapshots and late-arriving facts. This section presents the two most important approaches for incrementally processing Analysis Services databases.

- *Tying It All Together:* See the details of our recommended audit system, and learn how to use package configurations to communicate between master and child packages.

Getting Started

If you're an ETL system developer, you're ready to start moving some data around. If you're like most ETL developers, you've experimented with Integration Services and quickly decided it's both cool and exciting. When you start doing real work, you'll get frustrated because it's not as easy as it looks. Fortunately, after a—hopefully short—learning curve, it starts to be almost as fun and productive as it appeared in the demos. We'll try to keep that learning curve as short and gentle as possible.

We start this section by talking about the development environment, which we've already introduced in Chapter 4. We then encourage you to create a template package early in your development cycle, to make it easier for all your packages to use similar objects and styles. On the subject of development styles, we also encourage you to modularize your package development, creating a system of master and child packages. Don't try to stuff too much functionality into a single package.

Create Solution, Project, and Data Sources

Your ETL development process may well be the first time you use BI Studio. If you haven't already created a solution for your DW/BI project, do so now. Most teams will share a single solution for the Integration Services, Analysis Services, and Reporting Services components of their solution. You may keep all your Integration Services packages in a single BI Studio project. If you create separate packages for the historical load and ongoing incremental loads, you might separate these into separate BI Studio projects. Projects exist for your convenience during development. Use source control in a team development environment to help manage multiple people working on the same files.

KIMBALL METHOD ETL SUBSYSTEM This section describes techniques relevant to Kimball Method ETL Subsystems:

- **#38 *Project Management System:* Comprehensive system for keeping track of all ETL development.**

- **#31 *Version Control System:* Consistent "snapshotting" capability for archiving and recovering all the metadata in the ETL pipeline. Check-out and check-in of all ETL modules and jobs. Source comparison capability to reveal differences between different versions.**

We introduced solutions and projects in Chapter 3. Data Sources and Data Source Views are the package's links to the outside world. A Data Source includes connection information in its properties, like the name of the server, the source database, and logon credentials. A Data Source View is a metadata layer that you can use to redefine the data structures in a Data Source to make it easier for your ETL task to work with. Define Data Sources and Data Source Views once in your solution, for use across all the solution's projects. For your Integration Services project, define a Data Source to your source system(s) and to your relational data warehouse database. Data Source is a confusing name for this object in the context of Integration Services because you need to define Data Sources on target databases as well.

Data Source Views are useful for projects that are built from a complex source database. Imagine a source database that contains thousands of tables, which is common in purchased ERP systems. Probably you'll access only dozens or at most several hundred tables during the course of any one DW/BI project. Set up a Data Source View that contains only the tables of interest. Everyone benefits by having to look at only this small table subset.

HANDS-ON EXAMPLE If you're working through the examples in this chapter, you need to set up your environment. First, create a database called MDWT_AdventureWorksDW. You can obtain the database create script from the book's web site. Next, create a new BI Studio solution called MDWT_Examples and add an Integration Services project called MDWT_AWDWHist to that solution. Finally, add two Data Sources to that project. Set up the first source to the AdventureWorks database that contains the source data. Set up the second source (which is really a target) to the newly created database MDWT_AdventureWorksDW.

The AdventureWorks source database is simple enough that there's no value in creating a Data Source View for it.

NOTE It would be helpful if you work through the tutorials that ship with SQL Server 2005 before reading this chapter. Although we're walking you through a case study, this chapter is not a tutorial.

Package Template

Define a package template that you use as the starting point for all Integration Services packages in your solution. A package template is simply a starter package that contains objects that you frequently use. With a package template, you'll spend less time tediously recreating the same objects.

Until you read this chapter and experiment with your own designs, you won't be able to set up a complete package template. The template will evolve over time. At the outset you can create a template with the following components:

- *Start with an empty package:* Use the Add New Item by right-clicking on the project name in the Solution Explorer. Add a new IS Package to your project to serve as the template package.

- *Set up package connections:* The Data Sources and Data Source Views are shared components across the project. Integration Services packages need an additional communication layer called a connection. These live on the Connection Managers tab that opens under the package designer. The easiest way to create a package connection is to right-click on the Connection Managers tab and choose New Connection from Data Source to create a package connection from an existing Data Source or Data Source View. It's only a few mouse clicks, but it's a little perplexing that Integration Services doesn't do this for you automatically. Build a package connection into your template for each Data Source that you'll use in your ETL system, including package connections for the data warehouse database and the staging and metadata databases.

- *Create standard variables:* Until you've designed several packages, you won't know which variables you will use a lot. At the outset, create a variable called RowCount as an Int32 (default value = 0). You'll use this variable during the debugging process. In the longer run, you'll create variables to hold information passed down from the master package to the child packages. Create variables in the Variables window, which you can always get to from the View → Other Windows → Variables menu choice.

- *Put an OnPostExecute breakpoint in the template package body:* The breakpoint pauses package execution when the specific event occurs: in this case, when the package finishes (technically, when the OnPostExecute event is thrown). This breakpoint is useful because you can examine only the condition of variables during a breakpoint. It's very annoying to run the package but not be able to examine variables' values—especially if the package takes some time to execute! Add a package breakpoint by right-clicking in the background of the Control Flow design surface and choosing Edit Breakpoints.

Once you have greater experience with Integration Services, and have made some solution design decisions, you can add the following components to the template:

- *Define common configurations:* A configuration defines the default values of package objects' properties, including package variables' values. Use master and child packages, and always push a standard set of auditing information from the master package to the child packages. In the configuration definition you specify how the master package communicates with the child package. We'll walk through an example of this later in this chapter.

- *Define a standard starting sequence, if you use one:* A starting sequence is a set of tasks that you usually execute at the beginning of every package. In our sample package we begin all child packages by setting up auditing dimension rows for the package processing. You can put these sequences in the body of the package, or you can be fancy and hide them away in an event handler.

- *Define standard event handlers, like what to do if the package fails during execution:* We discuss event handlers near the end of this chapter.

- *Define standard logging configurations:* We discuss logging in Chapter 15.

Save the template package with an obvious name, like MyTemplatePackage. You'll need to save it to a convenient place. We keep the template packages in a SQL Server database that the development organization manages, but you could just as easily designate a separate file system folder for template packages.

TIP To save the template package to SQL Server, choose File → Save Copy of [Package.dtsx] As, and select SQL Server as the package location. (The Save Copy choice will not appear if the package is highlighted.) You can use SQL Studio to add directories and manage packages saved in SQL Server. To do this, open the Registered Servers window in SQL Studio, select the Integration Services icon and double-click the server name. This opens the Integration Services directory structure in the Object Explorer window.

When you want to create a new package from your template package, you have to do something less obvious than choosing the menu item to create a new package. Instead, right-click in the Solution Explorer and choose Add → Existing Package to add a copy of the template package to the current project, and then immediately change its name.

Using template packages seems a bit convoluted at first, but you'll soon get into the habit of working this way. After you've created the same connections the umpteenth time, we think you'll welcome this suggestion.

HANDS-ON EXAMPLE If you're working through examples while reading this chapter, create a template package called MDWTTemplateSimple. Create the RowCount variable, create an empty Data Flow step, and define package connections to the AdventureWorks and MDWT_AdventureWorksDW Data Sources.

Master Packages and Child Packages

As we discussed in Chapter 5, develop a separate package to load each table. Develop a master package that calls each of these table-specific packages. The master package contains one Execute Package task for each child package. Many of the dimension packages can execute in parallel, but some dimension tables may have a dependency on another table. Use Control Flow precedence arrows to define these dependencies.

KIMBALL METHOD ETL SUBSYSTEM This section describes techniques relevant to Kimball Method ETL Subsystem #26 Job Scheduler: System for scheduling and launching all ETL jobs. Able to wait for a wide variety of system conditions including dependencies of prior jobs completing successfully. Able to post alerts.

Start your system development by creating all the child packages. Remember to add a copy of your template package rather than create a new package. Create a child package for each table in your dimensional model, and name them appropriately. Create a master package from the template package. Later, you may decide to create a different template for a master package than for a child package.

Refer to Figure 5.2 for an illustration of a master package. This package, Master_Dims, first checks some metadata to figure out which set of data it should run. Then it launches a bunch of Execute Package tasks, some of which are grouped together into sequences and groups. In this example the sequences and groups are optional; we're using them simply to reduce the clutter on the design surface.

Your master package consists primarily of Execute Package tasks. The only property to set for an Execute Package task is the location of the child package. During development, the child package is located in the File System, not the default SQL Server location. Change the Location property to File System, and then select the Connection property box. Click the pull-down arrow and select <New connection . . . > to define a connection to the appropriate package. Rename the task to include the name of the child package the task will execute.

In Figure 5.2 you can see that each of the child packages has its own connection at the bottom of the screen. You created these connections when you set up the Execute Process tasks. In the production environment, you can reconfigure the package at run time to change the location where Integration Services will look for the child packages.

You can disable any task by right-clicking it and choosing Disable. A disabled task won't run when you execute the Master_Dims package, which is useful for debugging.

It may seem like make-work to break out each table's processing into a separate package. Some tables are so simple and fast to populate that it hardly seems worthwhile to build a separate package. Using a master package and a child package for each table greatly increases your system's flexibility and understandability. As your DW/BI system evolves and grows, you can easily modify the master package and leave the child packages untouched.

A child package is nothing special. It's just a package that you execute from another package, the master package, instead of executing it directly. You often communicate between a master and children by passing variables back and forth, but communication isn't necessary. We like to perform initial development and debugging on a child package in isolation. Only after it seems to work do we hook it up to the master package and pass the variables back and forth.

The communication between master and child is easy, but we've deferred the description of the details to the end of this chapter.

HANDS-ON EXAMPLE To follow along, create two new child packages from the simple template: DimPromotion_ETL.dtsx and DimProduct_ETL.dtsx. Create the master package Dim_Master, and add two Execute Package tasks: one for each new, still mostly empty, package. Disable the Product_ETL package task for now. We'll begin with the DimPromotion_ETL package.

Dimension Processing

Dimension tables provide the structure and context for the fact tables and measurements in the DW/BI system. Dimension tables are much smaller than fact tables, which is good because their processing is complex.

Dimensions are updated over time, either by updating in place (Type 1), or by adding new rows to track history (Type 2). Sometimes you're lucky enough to be handed separate streams of new rows and changed rows. Often you need to figure out what changes have occurred, and handle them appropriately.

This section presents examples related to the AdventureWorks databases. You'll be able to follow along simply by reading the text and looking at the figures. But if you want to experiment with the packages from this chapter, you need to go to the book's web site. We're populating a modified version of the AdventureWorksDW database that ships with SQL Server 2005: We call our versions MDWT_AdventureWorksDW. The web site (www.MsftDWToolkit.com) has copies of the packages that populate MDWT_AdventureWorksDW.

Dimension Processing Basics

KIMBALL METHOD ETL SUBSYSTEM This section describes
techniques relevant to Kimball Method ETL Subsystems:

- *#1 Extract System:* Source data adapters, push/pull/dribble job
  schedulers, filtering and sorting at the source, proprietary data format
  conversions, and data staging after transfer to ETL environment.

- *#9 Surrogate Key Creation System:* Robust mechanism for producing
  stream of surrogate keys independently for every dimension.
  Independent of database instance, able to serve distributed clients.

Start with a simple dimension: Promotions. In the Adventure Works Cycles
case study, the DimPromotions table is sourced from the [Sales].[SpecialOffer]
table, with no transformations necessary. You should be so lucky in the real
world.

Even though this is the simplest possible example, we're still going to
develop a data flow diagram in Visio, which is illustrated in Figure 6.1. As you
can see, even a trivial example has several steps. Ignore the Audit dimension
for now, and focus on the basics. We discuss the auditing subsystem later in
this chapter.

First, define the extract from the source system. There's a grand total of 16
promotions in our source system, so simply select all the rows from the source
table. In the section on Slowly Changing Dimensions, we describe how to compare them against the Promotion dimension table before deciding whether to
insert them or update any changed values.

HANDS-ON EXAMPLE This section walks you step by step through the
process of creating, modifying, and running the simple Promotions package.
After this section, we abandon the step-by-step approach.

Extract Promotions Data

To extract the Promotions data from the SQL Server source in Adventure-
Works, set up a connection and define the extraction query. Open the DimPro-
motion_ETL package that you created earlier and add a Data Flow task if you
don't have one already. In the Data Flow task, add an OLE DB Source, and set
the connection to your source database (AdventureWorks). Specify that you'll
be extracting from a table, and choose [Sales].[SpecialOffer], as you see in Figure 6.2.

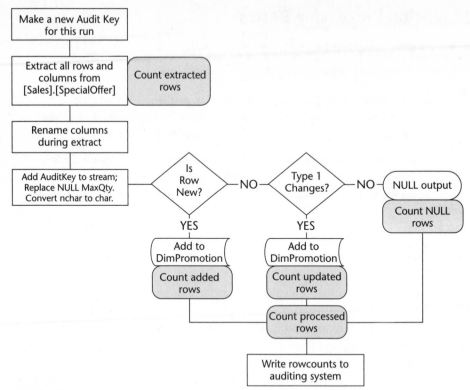

Figure 6.1 Logic flow diagram for populating DimPromotions

NOTE If you source from a table or view, Integration Services extracts all the rows in that object. To extract only the rows changed today, you need to change the Data Access Mode to a SQL command. We show how to do that later in this chapter.

Choose all the columns in the table except the last two: rowguid and ModifiedDate. This step is optional, but it's a good practice to extract only the data you really need. Remember that data is resident in memory within an Integration Services Data Flow task. Keep the data stream as small as possible. Memory is not a concern for our 16 promotions, but you should develop good habits from the outset.

Change column names to match target columns as soon as possible. You can do so in the OLE DB Source Editor, as illustrated in Figure 6.3.

You may wonder, in Figure 6.3, what the column names that end in "_U" are all about. These columns are in Unicode format, and our target tables are single-byte character strings. By creating the extract columns with the "U" suffix, you're saving the correct column name for later on, when you perform this conversion.

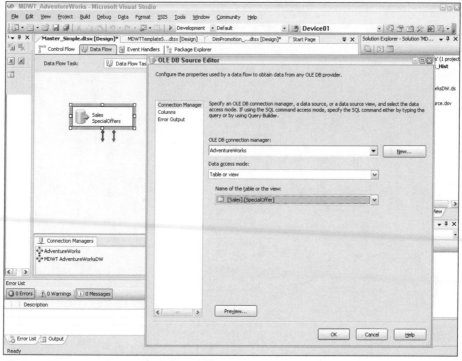

Figure 6.2   Promotion package OLE DB source

You may never run into this Unicode to single-byte string conversion in the real world. Typically, source systems are defined correctly to support the data that is stored in them. Microsoft uses Unicode by default in all of its demo databases to support localization of the AdventureWorks database. But you will definitely use this trick: There's always something to convert.

The third section of the OLE DB Source Editor is where you configure error outputs. We're hard pressed to understand how a relational source could have malformed data. Error outputs make a lot of sense for a flat file source, but they're seldom useful for a relational source.

> **NOTE**   If you look closely back at Figure 6.2, you'll see that we renamed the OLE DB Source transform to "Sales SpecialOffers." We like to name source transforms to indicate the data source table, in this case the SpecialOffers table in the Sales schema. You should rename all objects and descriptions in your packages, and add text annotations to the package surface as well. As we describe in Chapter 13, package object names and descriptions are a part of your metadata. There aren't many ways to decorate packages with custom metadata, and you should use every option you have.

Figure 6.3 OLE DB Source Editor column configuration for DimPromotions

Transform Promotions Data

Although we claimed that no transformations were necessary on the promotions data, a quick look at Figure 6.1 tells you that was an exaggeration. You want to get rid of the null values for the maximum quantity applicable to a promotion. If you leave this as null, business users will have to construct a complicated filter condition: where the quantity sold is between the minimum and maximum quantities, or where it's greater than the minimum, and the maximum is null. Instead let's take the simple step of replacing null with a large number. Because this is an integer column, use the maximum value an integer can take: 2,147,483,647.

TIP The maximum value for a smallint is 32,767; the largest tinyint is 255. The largest bigint is a really big number: 9,223,372,036,854,775,807.

If you often replace null values, add a MaxInt variable to your template package.

Add a Derived Column transform to the data flow diagram, and hook it up to the SpecialOffers Source. Add two columns here. First, add a new column for the AuditKey, and set it equal to zero for now. We'll come back and fix this later. Next, add a derived column that replaces `MaxQty`. Set its value to the following expression:

```
ISNULL(MaxQty) ? 2147483647 : MaxQty
```

This expression checks to see if `MaxQty` is null. If so, it replaces its value with our new maximum value; otherwise it keeps the existing value of `MaxQty`.

REFERENCE The Books Online topic "Data Types (Transact-SQL)" contains information about relational data types.

The Books Online topic "Integration Services Expression Reference" is an important reference for creating expressions.

Figure 6.4 illustrates the Derived Column transform. In addition to the AuditKey and MaxQty columns, trim all of the string columns. String columns often have extra spaces, usually to the right. These spaces are undesirable, and are really hard to debug because they're invisible.

TIP Trim all string columns immediately after the data source step.

Figure 6.4 Derived Column transform

You could convert the Unicode strings to single-byte in this same transform. This is probably what we'd do in a real package, trimming and converting in the same step. But in this case add a third transform to the data flow, a Data Conversion transform. Set it up to convert PromotionName_U, PromotionType_U, and PromotionCategory_U to single-byte strings of the appropriate lengths (50, 20, and 20, respectively). Remove the "_U" when you specify the Output Alias.

> **TIP** Readers who are working with a localized version of SQL Server 2005, localized to a double-byte language, might find that the data in the demo AdventureWorks database has been translated and actually does use double-byte strings. In this case, the conversion step will throw an error.

We like to test packages incrementally, and although we usually build up a bit more logic before testing, let's start small. Test your logic at various points by setting up a flow to the Row Count transform. The only thing to set up in the Row Count transform is the package variable to write the row count to. Your template package has a `RowCount` variable already.

> **WARNING** Package variable names are case sensitive.

The point of writing to the Row Count transform for debugging purposes is not so much for counting the rows, although that's useful. The greater value is that it lets you add a data visualizer to the pipeline. You want to examine the rows as they flow out of the Derived Column transform. You need one additional transform in order to check the output of the Derived Column transform. Any transform will do. We usually use the Row Count transform to serve the role of low-cost pipeline endpoint for debugging purposes.

Add the data visualizer by right-clicking the flow arrow between the derived column and row count transforms. Choose Data Visualizers → Add. There are several options for types of visualizers, including histograms, scatter plots, and column charts, but we use the grid most often.

Figure 6.5 illustrates our simple package at this point. Execute the package by highlighting it from the list of packages in the Solution Explorer; right-clicking, and choosing Execute Package. BI Studio automatically saves the package when you execute it.

> **TIP** Always execute packages by right-clicking in the Solution Explorer. Get into this habit from the outset. If you've done any Visual Studio development, you know that pressing the F5 key will start execution. But in an Integration Services project, this can, and usually does, launch a package other than the one you're looking at.

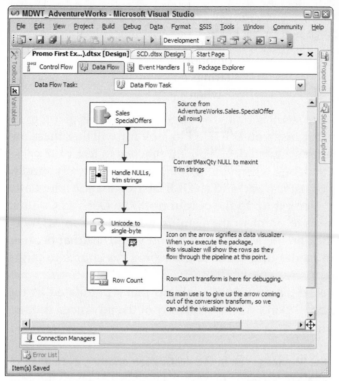

Figure 6.5 Ready to run the Promotions Package for the first time

The BI Studio environment provides a lot of information to the developer while the package is executing. Transforms turn yellow while they're executing, green when they've succeeded, and red if they throw an error. You can see how many rows have flowed through each step. And you can actually see the data in any data visualizers in the package. The data visualizer pauses the package's execution; you need to detach it (or press the green arrow button) to proceed. When a package finishes executing in BI Studio, it's left in a debugging state. You need to stop the execution by pressing the blue square box in the debug toolbar, or by selecting Stop Debugging in the Debug menu to edit any package.

TIP Maximize the useful design surface by setting the Solution Explorer, Toolbox, Variables, and Properties windows to auto-hide. You can get them back by moving the mouse over the window tab.

If you followed our suggestion to add an `OnPostExecute` breakpoint to the package template, the package will pause for you to examine package variables. You can see the RowCount along with a list of system variables by selecting the Locals tab that opened up in the lower left corner during execution. When you are finished, simply continue or stop the package's execution.

> **TIP** If you close the Locals window, you can get it back by choosing Debug → Windows while the package is in Debug mode.

Load Promotions Data

The next step is to write the result set into the target table. This is going to be another throwaway step because you still need to look for whether these are new or changed rows. But it's a good development practice to test your package bit by bit. It's easiest to debug when you're doing something really simple.

Delete the Row Count transform and add an OLE DB Destination adapter to your data flow diagram. Hook it up to the output from the Derived Column transform, and configure it to point to the DimPromotion table in MDWT_AdventureWorksDW. Click on the Mappings tab, and you'll see that because you changed the column names in the source transform, the source-to-target mappings come up correctly by default. The surrogate key, PromotionKey, has no mapping. That's because it's an identity column that's populated as the data is inserted into the table. Don't worry about any of the advanced properties for now.

> **TIP** You have to go to the Mappings tab in the destination adapter, even if you know the default mappings are going to work. It's tempting to set up the connection and then click OK, but that doesn't set up the adapter correctly. You have to click on the Mappings tab.

Now, execute this package. You'd expect to see 16 rows processed and added to DimPromotion. After the package finishes executing, run a query on DimPromotion; the 16 rows should be in there.

> **HANDS-ON EXAMPLE** This version of the Promotion package is available on the web site. It's called Promo v.1.dtsx.

You can execute the new package as often as you like. Each time, you add 16 rows to the target table DimPromotion. Obviously, this isn't what you want to happen. You need to modify the package to check for whether rows exist and add them only if they are new. You also need to look for whether an existing row has been changed. We discuss these modifications in the following sections.

> **TIP** The example in this section uses the OLE DB destination adapter. You could have used the SQL destination instead. In Chapter 5 we discuss the tradeoffs between the two destination adapters. In general, use OLE DB during development. If the performance of the insert is a problem, consider switching to the SQL destination, which is sometimes faster.

Extract Changed Rows

KIMBALL METHOD ETL SUBSYSTEM This section describes techniques relevant to Kimball Method ETL Subsystem #1 Extract System: source data adapters, push/pull/dribble job schedulers, filtering and sorting at the source, proprietary data format conversions, and data staging after transfer to ETL environment.

Whether you're processing dimensions or facts, you either need to be told which rows might have seen changes, or you need to figure it out in your ETL process. In Chapter 5 we discuss some of the many ways that source systems can be designed to flag changed rows. AdventureWorks, luck for us, uses a ModifiedDate column in each table.

WARNING Explore the ModifiedDate columns or their equivalents in your organization's source systems. We have seen many systems where ModifiedDate is managed in application logic. Any bulk updates by the DBA do not necessarily set the ModifiedDate correctly. You really want ModifiedDate to be maintained by a database trigger, as is done in AdventureWorks.

Each of your packages should have two package-level variables to bracket the date range for which the package is to be run. We call these `ExtractStartDate` and `ExtractEndDate`. Set the initial values of the variables to a useful range for the initial stages of development and testing. In production, you'll set the variables' values dynamically at runtime. Because most or all of your packages will use these variables, you should add them to your package template. We use a convention that the data range for the package's run starts on `ExtractStartDate`, for example 2000-01-01 00:00:00.000 and runs to but excluding the `ExtractEndDate`, for example 2004-08-01 00:00:00.000. In other words, by putting the end date of 2004-08-01 in the variables value, use a "less than" on the comparison. This guarantees that you'll get all transactions that occurred on July 31 no matter how close to midnight, and no transactions that occurred on August 1.

TIP The variable editor taskpad tries to be helpful when you create a date variable. It puts up a calendar date dropdown and forces you to use it. We find that more annoying than helpful. If you go to the variable's property pane, you can just type in a date.

You could get clever and put a dynamic default value for the end date, equal to today's date at 00:00. That way, by default the package will pull all changes up until yesterday midnight. There are two tricks to accomplishing this that are worth discussing:

- Set the variable's default value to an expression. Open the property pane for the variable, and set `EvaluateAsExpression` to `True`. Now you can enter an expression, like `getdate()`. The function `getdate()` includes the time part of today's date, so you need to strip that out.

- Strip out the time part of the date by using some cast functions. The expression should be:

    ```
    (DT_Date)(DT_I4)(DT_Date)getdate()
    ```

> **WARNING** In the real world, you don't always set the end date to yesterday. You need to be able to run the package for two days ago, in case you missed a load. Use a package configuration to set the value of the variable at runtime. When setting the date from a configuration, you don't want the variable to be set to an expression: The expression will override the configuration value. Don't get so clever that you hurt yourself.

If you have a reliable row modified date from the source system, and some package variables with the date range you want to extract, simply parameterize the query from the source system so that it filters on the row modified date. Figure 6.6 illustrates a parameterized source system query.

Figure 6.6　Parameterized source system query

The Parameters button on the right side of the SQL command text box brings up a small window titled Set Query Parameters where you map package variables to the parameters in your query. The user interface is fine here, where there are only two parameters. But if your SQL statement has many parameters, you'll improve readability by making that SQL statement into a stored procedure.

This query will extract only the rows that changed during the date range of interest. For daily processing, that date range refers to yesterday. In a small dimension like Promotions in the demo database, we'd expect that most days would deliver zero changes to dimension rows. You can continue to execute the rest of your package with zero rows, which shouldn't take long, or add a check to halt package execution. Later in this chapter we discuss how to design your package so that it halts execution at appropriate points.

If no one tells you which rows have changed, you have to figure out the changes by brute force: by comparing the new rows with the existing data. For dimension tables, the easiest way to develop this logic is to use the Slowly Changing Dimension transform.

Slowly Changing Dimensions

In Chapter 2, we talked about the two main types of slowly changing dimensions:

- *Type 1:* Restate history by updating the dimension row when attributes change.

- *Type 2:* Track history by propagating a new dimension row when attributes change.

KIMBALL METHOD ETL SUBSYSTEM This section describes techniques relevant to Kimball Method ETL Subsystems:

- **#9 Surrogate Key Creation System: Robust mechanism for producing stream of surrogate keys, independently for every dimension. Independent of database instance, able to serve distributed clients.**

- **#10 Slowly Changing Dimension Processor: Transformation logic for handling three types of time variance possible for a dimension attribute: Type 1 (overwrite), Type 2 (create new record), and Type 3 (create new field).**

- **#11 Late Arriving Dimension Handler: Insertion and update logic for dimension changes that have been delayed in arriving at the data warehouse.**

■ *#12 Fixed Hierarchy Dimension Builder:* Data validity checking and maintenance system for all forms of many-to-one hierarchies in a dimension.

Standard Handling for Slowly Changing Dimensions

Any dimension that contains a Type 2 attribute should track the date range for which each dimension row is valid. For any dimension with a Type 2 attribute, add three columns: RowStartDate, RowEndDate, and IsRowCurrent. For every dimension member like customer, there should be one and only one current row at any one time. Older rows have their RowStartDate and RowEndDate set appropriately. Figure 6.7 illustrates the logic for handling updates to a dimension with both Type 1 and Type 2 attributes.

We've seen companies get so intimidated by this complexity that they decide to manage all dimensions as Type 1, even if that's not what the users want. The Integration Services Slowly Changing Dimension transform is a great feature. It does most of this work for you.

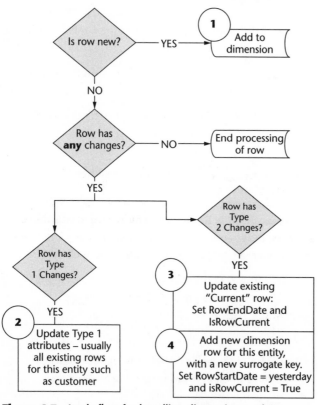

Figure 6.7 Logic flow for handling dimension updates

When you drag the Slowly Changing Dimension (SCD) transform into the Data Flow design palette, it consists of a single rectangle like all the other transforms. When you edit it, it launches a wizard with several pages of questions. And when you finally press Finish, the wizard generates a bunch of transforms and flows for you. The generated transforms and flows do the work that's outlined in Figure 6.7.

The wizard starts by asking you to specify the dimension table you'll be loading. Next, identify the business key, used to tie together all the instances of a particular entity. In a customer dimension the business key is usually the account number or customer ID. Map the other columns in the input flow to the attributes in the target dimension.

The wizard next has you identify how to manage the changes in each attribute. In addition to the Types 1 and 2 (restate and track history) described previously, Integration Services includes a Fixed attribute, which should never be updated. Set the attribute change type for all the columns in your target table.

On the next screen you're asked several housekeeping questions. Do you want the processing to fail when you encounter a change to a fixed attribute? Answer No (you rarely want processing to fail outright). Do you want the bad row to go into an error flow? Answer Yes. You're also asked if a Type 1 change, when encountered, should update all the historical rows for the dimension entity, or just the current row. The textbook definition of a Type 1 attribute indicates you should update all the rows, and this is the recommended setting. This is a characteristic that's set for the whole table, not for each column, which is too bad.

If you have any Type 2 attributes in your dimension, you're next asked how to identify the current row. Do you use row start and end dates, or an indicator like IsRowCurrent?

NOTE You can't have the SCD Wizard maintain both the row start and end date and the row current indicator. It's one or the other. As we discuss in the next section, you can edit the results of the wizard, and you can generally make it do what you want. We find it easier to generate the SCD Wizard using the row current indicator technique, and then edit the resulting transforms to add the row date handling.

When you reach the wizard's screen about inferred members, you are almost at the end. Inferred members are an Integration Services innovation, and help you handle the late arrival of a dimension member generated by an early arriving fact. Early arriving facts appear in your incremental processing stream before you have any dimensional data for them. If you expect to have early arriving facts, design your fact table load so that it will generate a dummy dimension row. That way you can load all of your fact data.

Creating that dummy dimension row creates a problem during dimension processing. If the dimension contains any Type 2 attributes, then as soon as you get the real information about the new dimension member, you'll automatically propagate a new dimension row. What you really wanted to happen was to update all the missing values in the original row with the new information. And that's exactly what the inferred dimension member support does: If all the attributes are missing it will update them in place even if it's a dimension with Type 2 attributes.

Perhaps you're exasperated with the complexity of this wizard, although we'll point out that it's a complex problem. Your reward comes when you press the Finish key and see all the transforms that have been created for you, as illustrated in Figure 6.8. These objects are exactly what's been generated by running through the wizard for a hybrid dimension with Type 1 and Type 2 attributes and inferred member support. We rearranged and renamed the transforms to improve readability, and labeled the data flow diagram branches with 1, 2, 3, and 4 to correspond to the branches in our logical flow in Figure 6.7.

HANDS-ON EXAMPLE Set up the Slowly Changing Dimension Wizard on the Promotions package. Delete the target transform to DimPromotion, and set up the SCD transform in its place. Because the Promotion dimension attributes are all Type 1, the output isn't as interesting as the customer example illustrated in Figure 6.8. Go through the wizard again, setting up one of the attributes as Type 2. You can see how different flows are created.

The Slowly Changing Dimension transform will meet many projects' requirements without any further changes. However, there are circumstances where you need to do something tricky, or circumvent the wizard altogether. The next few sections discuss some advanced topics around handling dimension changes.

Custom Handling for Slowly Changing Dimensions

You will probably want to customize the output from the SCD Wizard. There are even a few cases where it makes sense for you to develop custom handling for dimension changes.

The SCD Wizard will identify the current row for an entity like customer in one of two ways: with a True/False (or Yes/No) indicator, or with a range of dates for which the row is valid. If you choose the date range approach, the SCD transform will look for the single row for each natural key that has a null end date.

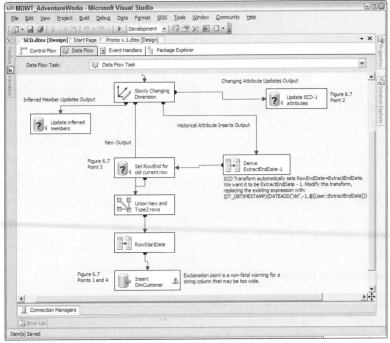

Figure 6.8 Results of running the Slowly Changing Dimension Wizard

We recommend that you use both the row current indicator technique and the valid date range technique. Also, set the end date to a date far in the future, rather than leave it null. Can you still use the SCD Wizard? Yes you can, but you need to modify the generated objects in order to populate your dimension the way you want. Use the row current indicator to identify the active row, and then modify the computed column transform that's between the Union All and the OLE DB transforms, in such a way that it calculates the row start and end dates the way you want them. This is easy to do, but be warned: If you need to go through the wizard again, perhaps to switch an attribute from Type 1 to Type 2 handling, you'll lose any customizations you've made to the generated objects.

> **NOTE** The objects generated by the SCD Wizard are standard Integration Services transforms. You can edit them to do whatever you like.

The only logic that you can't modify is the comparison logic that's hidden in the SCD transform itself. Under the covers, this transform takes a row in the pipeline and compares it to the current row in the dimension table; determines if the pipeline row is new or an update; and sends the row to the correct downstream path or paths. Except by going through the wizard again, you can't change any of the logic in this transform.

Row Changed Reason

The Type 2 Slowly Changing Dimension logic doesn't explicitly track which attributes changed when it creates a new row for an entity like customer. All you know is that something changed. Our Type 2 dimension tables include a Row Changed Reason column. This column should indicate which attributes changed, causing the creation of a new dimension row.

The SCD transform does not supply this information. If you use the wizard—which you almost always want to do—you can't populate this column. If this information is really important to your business users, you must do one of the following:

- Develop a post-processing step that runs through the dimension rows added today and figures out what changed.

- Abandon the SCD transform, and manage dimension changes using fundamental Integration Services transforms.

REFERENCE For additional detail on tracking the row changed reason, please refer to the following sources:

- **Search kimballgroup.com for the topic Row Changed Reason for a related article.**

- **Visit the book's web site (www.MsftDWToolkit.com) for a few simple examples of the options described.**

Performance of the Slowly Changing Dimension Transform

It makes sense that you can't modify the internal logic of the SCD transform, but this restriction presents a problem for large dimensions. Unfortunately, the comparison logic is not blazingly fast. Use the SCD transform for as many dimensions as you can. It's well thought out and tested, and using it will simplify your development process. For very large problems, you may have to custom code the dimension change logic.

The best way to find out if the SCD transform works for you is to test it against your data in your environment. But we can provide some guidance. There are two main parameters: the size of the data flow you're sending through the SCD transform, and the size of the target dimension.

TIP Minimize the number of rows going into the SCD transform. The SCD transform can handle rows in the pipeline that are unchanged: neither inserts nor updates. But if you can efficiently filter out those rows in advance, do so.

If the flow and the target dimension are both small—say less than 10,000 rows—use the Slowly Changing Dimension transform. If the input rowset is small and the dimension is large, the SCD transform should still work acceptably quickly.

If the input rowset is large and the dimension is small, it's probably because this is a first time load of the dimension table. You might want to build a separate package to handle the historical load of a dimension with Type 2 changes, and simply circumvent the SCD Wizard during the historical load. Other circumstances where the input rowset is large yet the dimension is small are also probably better handled by cleaning up the input rowset using custom logic.

Finally, we reach the tough problem: The input rowset and the dimension are both large. The most obvious solution is better hardware, especially 64-bit with large memory. But that may be too expensive, or not speed the processing sufficiently. You may have to build dimension change logic by hand, as people have done for ages past.

To hand-craft the dimension change logic, use a hash or checksum function to speed the comparison process. Add to your dimension table two new housekeeping columns: HashType1 and HashType2. Soon you'll have more housekeeping columns than real attributes! Into the HashType1 column place a hash of a concatenation of the Type 1 attributes; similarly for HashType2. Hashing algorithms are commonly used for encryption. The algorithms convert a very long string into a much shorter string that is guaranteed to be almost unique. (Computer scientists, forgive me.) This is a common technique for high performance dimension change management. Compute the hashes and store them in the dimension table. Then compute the hashes on the incoming rowset and compare to the stored values. The comparison on a single, relatively short string column is far more efficient than pair-wise comparison on dozens of separate columns.

> **NOTE** By far the easiest way to compute the hashes is to use the Checksum transform available for download from www.sqlis.com.
>
> Alternatively, use one of the many algorithms for computing hashes. Among those available to you from within Integration Services are:
>
> - System.Security.Cryptography.KeyedHashAlgorithm
> - System.Security.Cryptography.MD5
> - System.Security.Cryptography.SHA1
> - System.Security.Cryptography.SHA256
> - System.Security.Cryptography.SHA384
> - System.Security.Cryptography.SHA512

These algorithms have different performance and uniqueness characteristics. Experiment in your own environment. If you use a System.Security algorithm, you'll implement Script Transform. Later in this chapter we walk through an example of creating a Script Transform. Script Transforms are easy to develop, extremely powerful, and are not inherently slow (although you could certainly code a slow transform!).

Here is an outline of the logic flow for custom-coded dimension change management:

1. Filter out unchanged rows as early in the flow as possible.

2. Identify new rows as cheaply as possible. Some source systems keep track of the date an entity (like customer) was added to the system, let's hope in addition to the date the row was last modified. If this information is reliable, by all means use it to separate new rows into a separate stream for insert into the target dimension table.

3. Compute HashType1 and HashType2 on the incoming stream, as described previously.

4. Perform an Integration Services Lookup to the active dimension rows in the dimension table, matching on the natural key. Keep the columns from the incoming rowset, plus the surrogate key and hashes from the dimension table.

   a. Create an Error Flow on the Lookup transform to handle failures from the lookup.

   b. Lookup failures are new dimension members not already in the dimension table. Flow the error stream into the dimension table.

5. Write a script component that creates streams for Type 1 and Type 2 changes. The script component will create two output streams.

   a. Compare the incoming HashType1 to the HashType1 that you picked up in the Lookup or Merge Join.

   b. If the incoming and stored hashes differ, output to the Type 1 output flow.

   c. Repeat for the Type 2 comparison.

   d. You must write a script rather than use the Conditional Split transform because some rows will go to *both* the Type 1 and Type 2 output flows. Conditional Split sends a row to one output or the other, but not both. Writing this script component sounds really ugly, but it's approximately 20 lines of code.

6. Recreate the logic to perform the updates and inserts, similar to what is automatically generated by the SCD transform.

We can think of even more complicated strategies to improve dimension processing performance and functionality. If nothing else, we expect this discussion has convinced you what a great feature the SCD transform is. We didn't discuss Fixed attributes or Deferred Members in this custom example. That logic is left as an exercise for the reader.

REFERENCE The book *Professional SQL Server 2005 Integration Services,* by Knight, Chaffin, Barnes, Warren, and Young (Wrox, 2006), is an important reference if you need to further improve the performance for processing dimension changes.

An example package that implements the custom dimension change handling logic is available on the book's web site, www.MsftDWToolkit.com.

Recreating Dimension Change History

If your dimension has one or more Type 2 attributes, you should recreate history for the dimension's initial load. Some source systems keep track of all the historical addresses associated with a customer, for example, and the date ranges for which those addresses were active. Working with the business users, decide at the outset whether you will recreate dimension changes. Once the dimension is built and associated facts are loaded with the appropriate surrogate keys, it is usually too expensive to go back and rebuild.

As usual, there are many possible solutions to this problem. One alternative is to create a package with a loop that executes the incremental dimension load Data Flow task for each day in the historical time period.

Alternatively, construct a data flow that contains the current image for each dimension member and all the historical changes as well. In the case of a customer dimension that triggers a new row when the address changes, the data flow pipeline would contain one row for each combination of customer and address. Include the date the address became effective. Usually multiple attributes trigger Type 2 changes: include as many as you have historical data for.

Use the Sort transform to sort by natural key and by RowStartDate descending.

Next, develop a Script transform that works through the set of rows associated with each dimension entity like customer. Because the data is sorted descending by RowStartDate, the first row that the script encounters for a new customer will become the active row. Use one row's start date to set the end date for the next row in the sequence.

Sample Script Transform

In the preceding sample, we blithely talked about creating a script transform. This may sound intimidating, but it's really easy. Here is an example of the script transform code to set the end dates and row current indicators:

```
Public Class ScriptMain
    Inherits UserComponent

    'These variables retain their values from row to row
    Dim CurrentEntity As String = ""  ' Change data type to match BusinessKey
    Dim NextEndDate As Date

    Public Overrides Sub Input0_ProcessInputRow( ByVal Row As Input0Buffer)
        '
        ' Kimball Group, Microsoft Data Warehouse Toolkit
        ' Example script component used to set row end dates and row current
        ' indicators for the historical load of a dimension with type 2
        ' attributes.
        '
        Dim FirstEndDate As Date

        If Row.BusinessKey <> CurrentEntity Then
            CurrentEntity = Row.BusinessKey        'We have a new group
            NextEndDate = Row.StartDate.AddDays(-1)     'Set next end date
            Row.IsRowCurrent = "Y"
            'We set all row end dates to 9999-12-31 in a computed column
            'before we run this script transform. Leave that value for
            'this row, which is the currently active row.
        Else
            'Fix up end date and is current indicator for the inactive rows
            Row.EndDate = NextEndDate
            Row.IsRowCurrent = "N"
        End If

    End Sub

End Class
```

Listing 6.1   Script transform to set end dates

As you can see, the code is simple. This same logic will work for any dimension, except you'll need to rename the columns like Row.NaturalKey as appropriate. You may want to do something more complex in your script, but this sample provides the basic structure.

It's more complicated to set up a Script transform than most Integration Services transforms. In the Input Column setup tab, you must choose which columns will flow through the transform. If you don't choose a column, it's thrown away. Also note that you can choose whether an input column is

ReadOnly or ReadWrite. In the example illustrated here, we made the End-Date column be ReadWrite.

To add columns to your flow, go to the Column Properties setup tab. Add an output, and then add columns to that output. If you're simply replacing a ReadWrite input attribute you don't need to do this, but if you want a new column, you do.

Finally, go to the Script tab of the Script Transform Editor, and click the Design Script button. Integration Services launches a VB.NET editor for you, and autogenerates a bunch of code. Compare the sample script here to what's automatically generated; you can see how few lines of code—eleven!—we wrote in order to solve this little problem.

Integration Services keeps track of the code you've written, integrating it into the package. If you were ambitious enough to open an Integration Services package in Notepad or your favorite XML editor, you'd see it in there. The point is that you don't need to worry about where to store the source code; it's part of your package.

REFERENCE You can learn more about scripts and the script transform in the book *The Rational Guide to Scripting SQL Server 2005 Integration Services Beta Preview,* (Rational Guides, 2005) by Donald Farmer.

SCRIPTS WITH MULTIPLE INPUTS OR OUTPUTS

If you play around with the Column Properties tab, you'll come to realize that a Script transform can have multiple inputs and outputs. You can also adjust the grain of the flow by outputting a different number of rows than are input.

If your Script transform needs multiple outputs, or needs to adjust the grain of the flow, you'll need to break the connection between the input and output. Click on an output, like Output 0, in a Script transform. It has a SynchronousInputID property, which by default points to the ID of the first input. To break the synchronicity, set the output's SynchronousInputID property to zero. Now you'll have to add, by hand, an output column for each input column. Make sure you get the data types correct.

In your script you'll now need to distinguish between the input buffer and the output buffer. You can refer to a single input buffer as Row, but you'll refer to your output buffer as Output0Buffer. To figure out the correct name for the buffer, poke around in the BufferWrapper module that Integration Services autogenerates for you. You'll need to explicitly add a row to the output buffer, using syntax like Output0Buffer.AddRow(). You will also need to explicitly set the value of each output column; they don't automatically get set as they do in the simple case.

For most scripts, the output is synchronized with the input, the columns flow automatically from the input to the output, and you don't need to worry about this technical note.

De-Duplication and the Fuzzy Transforms

A great ETL challenge is to de-duplicate information, like customer accounts. A common situation is a retail operation that's operated by phone and direct mail now opens a web ordering application. It's easy to have the same customer or family have many account numbers. Similarly, if your business has grown by acquisition you're likely to have the same customer—and even product—reflected in the source systems of the different business entities. If your business users are interested in analyzing the history of a customer's purchases, some de-duplication may be necessary. De-duplication is also necessary when you integrate data from multiple source systems even within a single company, or combine multiple individuals' accounts into a family or household group.

KIMBALL METHOD ETL SUBSYSTEM This section describes techniques relevant to Kimball Method ETL Subsystem #4 Data Cleansing System: Typically a dictionary-driven system for complete parsing of names and addresses of individuals and organizations, possibly also products or locations. "De-duplication" includes identification and removal usually of individuals and organizations, possibly products or locations. Often uses fuzzy logic. "Surviving" using specialized data merge logic that preserves specified fields from certain sources to be the final saved versions. Maintains back references (like natural keys) to all participating original sources.

IT'S NOT OUR PROBLEM

The need for de-duplication is really an artifact of stovepipe transaction systems—systems that were developed independently but that deal with the same customers, products, employees, or other entities. Historically, the transaction systems were not required to make an effort to integrate their data; if payroll correctly generated the paychecks and benefits correctly tracked program enrollments, it didn't really matter that the two systems used different IDs for the same employee.

Most organizations have long known this is the wrong approach, but they were unwilling to invest in fixing it because they didn't understand the full cost. The emergence of DW/BI systems has shown that this lack of integration makes accurate analysis impossible. Organizations are beginning to see the direct cost of integrating the data downstream; it's an expensive, ongoing effort. Even worse, this stovepipe approach puts the burden of maintaining correct attribute values in multiple systems on the employee (or worse, the customer), a hidden cost that could be greater than the direct cost.

Many organizations are assuming the responsibility to create and maintain an integrated data store as part of the transaction system. Most of the major ERP vendors and several specialty software companies have built modules or systems to address data integration at the source, before it becomes a problem. Search the Internet for "master data management" to find some examples.

SIMILARITY VERSUS CONFIDENCE

What's the difference between *similarity* and *confidence*? If you had a lot of U.S, customers, and ran Jo Smith through the algorithm, you might find a match to Joe Smith with high similarity. The confidence rating would be relatively low, however, because J. Smith, John Smith, Joe Smith, and many other similar names are all very common.

De-duplication of existing data is usually done as an analytic project, often as part of the development of a customer-oriented DW/BI system. It's a labor-intensive process. Tools help a lot, but a person needs to be looking at results and making judgments about where correlations exist and what techniques are working. At the end of this process of trial and error, you'll have a handful of techniques, and an order in which to apply those techniques that work well with your data. You'll make a one-time pass to de-duplicate existing data and integrate these de-duplication transforms into your incremental loads.

Integration Services is a productive environment in which to conduct a de-duplication project. The Data Flow task visualizers and Data Source View data viewers are hugely valuable for investigating the data. The Fuzzy Lookup and Fuzzy Grouping transforms are particularly valuable for de-duplication. These transforms find one or more matches in an incoming row to a second data set, using one or more columns in each data set. The underlying algorithm is sophisticated. Unlike some similar algorithms, it's not specific to a language (like English), but instead is based on pattern matching. The Fuzzy transforms return both matches and measures of similarity and confidence.

Microsoft has published a number of excellent examples on using the Fuzzy transforms, so we won't repeat usage details here. However, we can't refrain from mentioning one important best practice. The algorithm used by the Fuzzy transforms is efficient, but it's not magic. Always use a standard lookup first to find perfect matches. Then use a conditional split to divide your data flow diagram and use Fuzzy matching only on the unmatched data.

REFERENCE Search on MSDN (www.msdn.com) for "fuzzy lookup" to find articles and examples about the fuzzy transforms and de-duplication.

Fact Processing

We've been describing how to build packages to perform dimension processing. Now it's time to turn our attention to fact processing. Extracting fact data, consolidating it, and loading it into the data warehouse is generally less complex than managing dimension changes. Most fact tables are at the grain of a transaction. During normal processing of a transaction grain fact table, rows are inserted but not updated. Later in this chapter, we discuss exceptions to this general rule.

There are three main things to worry about when processing facts:

■ *Cleaning data and synthesizing data from multiple sources*: This task is dependent on your environment. The greatest challenge is the design step: What data needs to be cleaned and synthesized, and how will you go about doing it? Integration Services has many tasks and transforms to use in building your custom logic. For example, the fact table in the MDWT_AdventureWorksDW dimensional model keeps orders data in both U.S. dollars and the original local currency. The source system holds only the local currency, so the fact table ETL process must pull conversion rates and calculate the U.S. dollars amount for each row.

■ *Performing the surrogate key lookups:* The greatest burden of cleaning and conforming is in the dimension processing. By the time you process the facts, you have well-formed dimension tables or staging tables against which to perform the lookups that swap out the natural keys from the extracts for the surrogate keys that get stored in the fact table.

■ *Moving and processing large data volumes:* A characteristic of fact table processing is that the data volumes are typically much larger than for dimension table processing. Although you want all processing to be efficient, it's particularly important for fact tables. Techniques that work just fine for a dimension table with ten thousand rows—even a million rows—just aren't practical for a fact table with billions of rows.

As with dimensions, you should set up an Integration Services package for each fact table's normal processing. You might include the fact package as another child package in the same master package that calls the dimension table packages. Alternatively, create a separate master package for fact processing. A complex enterprise DW/BI system covering many business processes might have several master packages, especially if some fact tables are populated on different schedules.

Extracting Fact Data

Because you're building transactional fact tables at an atomic grain, new facts are usually easy to find. Most source systems include a transaction date on a fact table record. Work closely with the source system DBAs to develop the fact table extract queries or reports, and the precise schedules and conditions under which the extracts are run. In an ideal world you can specify what you need and when, and it's the transactional DBA's job to provide it. More likely, it will be a joint effort. These issues are discussed in Chapter 5.

KIMBALL METHOD ETL SUBSYSTEM This section describes techniques relevant to Kimball Method ETL Subsystems:

- **#1 *Extract System:*** Source data adapters, push/pull/dribble job schedulers, filtering and sorting at the source, proprietary data format conversions, and data staging after transfer to ETL environment.

- **#2 *Change Data Capture System:*** Source log file readers, source date and sequence number filters, and CRC-based record comparison in ETL system.

You can probably develop a single Data Flow task to perform fact processing. While this is theoretically possible, it's not advised. You should extract data from the source system and immediately write it as a flat or raw file, with minimal or zero transformations. This staged data provides a restarting point, without having to go back to the source database. The staged data also provides a data quality milestone so the Data Steward can investigate the source of a data problem.

INTEGRATION SERVICES RAW FILES

The raw file format is unique to Integration Services: Only Integration Services can read and write a raw file.

The only required configuration property in the raw file destination is the name and location of the file. We set up a directory called c:\SSIStemp, where we dump temporary files. When debugging, use the default WriteOption, CreateAlways. If you use raw files in your real ETL system, perhaps to hold an image of the extracted data, you might prefer to use a different WriteOption to be sure you don't clobber existing valuable data.

The other trick to the Raw File Destination is that you have to specify the columns to go into the raw file. You might expect the default would be to write all columns from the pipeline into the raw file, but instead the default is to write no columns.

Integration Services reads and writes raw files so fast that you should generally use raw files instead of flat files, unless an external process needs to read the data. You can always set up a trivial Integration Services package to read the data if you need to. Once you've done it once or twice, it's much easier than using flat files . . . especially if you've ever tried to open a million-row flat file in Notepad!

There are circumstances in which reading and writing raw files is slower than using flat files. Raw files are bigger than the corresponding flat files because they allocate space that corresponds to the data types in the Integration Services data flow. If your data types are wide but the actual data is small, a flat file is smaller. Depending on your disk subsystem, the raw file's advantage in not having to parse the data can be eaten up by disk I/O from the larger file. Raw files are usually faster, but if your disk subsystem is slow and performance is an issue, test how flat files perform in your environment.

Figure 6.9 illustrates a Data Flow task that extracts from a source table, counts the rows, and then writes the flow into a raw file. The Row Count transform puts a count of rows into a package variable created for that purpose. You may recall that we recommend you use a template package that predefines, among other elements, a package variable called RowCount. Ignore the Multicast transform and the second output from it in Figure 6.9 for now. We discuss these elements in the next sections.

You may use technology that's native to the source system, rather than Integration Services, for this extract step. For example, a mainframe-based source system may use reporting functionality to generate a flat file. Communicate clearly and completely between systems, so that you can be confident that the source system is extracting data for the date range that you're expecting in your packages. You can use the Integration Services Execute Process task to launch the extract. Alternatively, ensure the source system extract writes a clear message that you can pick up in Integration Services. The most common method of communication is to have the source system extract write a row to a metadata table that you design. But there are many alternative methods, including making a web service call or sending a message via MSMQ.

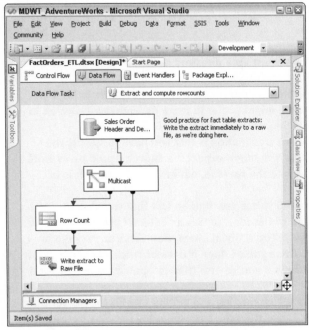

Figure 6.9   Data Flow task to extract and check data

Extracting Fact Updates and Deletes

Although new rows to be inserted into the fact table are usually easy to identify, updated and deleted rows can be more challenging. For a transactional fact source table, as opposed to a snapshot fact table, true updates and deletes are, we hope, abnormal events.

In the best case, updates and deletes are handled in the source system as ledgered entries as we described in Chapter 5. A ledgering source system would handle a change by making a change entry, like increasing quantity by +2 or canceling an order by entering an offsetting transaction. Your normal fact processing sees these offsetting entries as new fact rows, and should handle them smoothly and correctly as inserts.

It shouldn't surprise you to learn that not all transaction systems act this way. If your source system generates updates to historical transactions, let's hope it tags those rows as changed. Many transaction systems flag each row with a last modified date column, on which you can place a filter condition. You need to be diligent in your data exploration, as this column may not be properly maintained. We've often found the column to be well maintained through the source system application logic, but if a DBA performs a bulk operation the last modified date is not reset.

Unless your fact data volume is tiny, these un-audited updates are a problem you cannot overcome. The only solutions are extremely unattractive:

- Ask the source system to fix the problem.
- Grab the history of facts, and perform a column-by-column comparison to find rows that have changed.
- Rebuild the entire fact table every load cycle.

The right solution is to push the problem onto the source system DBAs. If they can't properly maintain the last modified date in the transaction fact data, and are unwilling to set up triggers or replication, you should seriously consider refocusing your project on a different subject area.

Deletes present a similar problem. Most often, transaction systems perform a soft delete, which simply flags the row as inactive. It would be a poorly designed transaction system that performs hard deletes on business process data without logging that deleted information—but that doesn't mean it never happens. We like to ask the transactional DBAs if they perform non-logged hard deletes, and gauge their level of horror at the notion.

> **NOTE** The source system in the AdventureWorks sample database does not behave nicely. The SalesOrderHeader table, which is a source for the Orders fact table, gets a new row when an order is placed. That row is updated with the ShipDate when the order ships. We can probably agree that this isn't a great design for a transaction system, but it's not terribly uncommon either. If you extract updates based on ModifiedDate, you'll get these changed rows— even though the Orders fact table does not contain shipping information. Evaluating these changed rows is an unavoidable cost of managing the DW/BI system, but it's lucky that you can expect to encounter only one update per row. In the case of AdventureWorks, we know from discussions with the source system DBAs that no changes occur to a fact row that are relevant to the Orders subject area. In the case of AdventureWorks, we don't need to look for updates or deletes at all.

If your transaction grain source system allows updates and deletes, you should convert these into ledgered transactions for your dimensional model. In other words, even if the source system will physically update an order quantity in place, say from five to three, you should convert that update into an insert of -2 in the fact table. This is even more important for deletes. This means you will need a transaction date in addition to the order date in your fact table.

If you don't convert hard updates and deletes into transactions, your DW/BI system will be un-auditable. In addition, hard updates and deletes create a terrible management problem for aggregates and Analysis Services databases. Analysis Services can't process hard updates or deletes in the facts except by reprocessing the entire associated partition. That may sound harsh, but think about what the logic would be for maintaining aggregate tables by hand. Dropping and rebuilding is a reasonable strategy. By contrast, ledgered entries are easy to manage for aggregate tables and Analysis Services cubes. Ledgered entries are simply incremental data.

Cleaning Fact Data

As with dimension data, cleaning fact data is idiosyncratic to your source systems. Initially, most DW/BI systems need relatively little cleaning of fact data. The fact data sources are usually the core systems used to run the business, and are in pretty good shape. The dimensions are often a mess, but by the time it comes to process the facts, the dimension cleaning has been done. Most of the work of the fact table processing is in looking up the surrogate keys from the cleaned dimensions, as we discuss in the next section.

KIMBALL METHOD ETL SUBSYSTEM This section describes techniques relevant to Kimball Method ETL Subsystems:

- ■ *#7 Quality Screen Handler:* In-line ETL tests applied systematically to all data flows checking for data quality issues. One of the feeds to the error event handler (see subsystem 8).

- ■ *#8 Error Event Handler:* Comprehensive system for reporting and responding to all ETL error events. Includes branching logic to handle various classes of errors, and includes real-time monitoring of ETL data quality.

The exception to the rule about significant cleaning of fact data is when those facts come from some type of logging system rather than a transaction system. A clickstream system is a good example: The data source is web logs. In this case, you may need to perform significant filtering, cleansing, and scoring of the fact data to determine its quality and prepare it for loading.

REFERENCE Chapter 4 of *The Data Warehouse ETL Toolkit* has an extensive discussion of these issues.

Checking Data Quality and Halting Package Execution

KIMBALL METHOD ETL SUBSYSTEM This section describes techniques relevant to Kimball Method ETL Subsystem #28 Recovery and Restart System: Common system for resuming a job that has halted, or for backing out a whole job and restarting. Significant dependency on backup system (see subsystem 36).

A critical but often-neglected step in fact data processing is to verify that the data in today's extract is valid. Look for evidence that the extract executed correctly. The most obvious metric is the count of rows in the extract. If there are zero rows, abort fact table processing. Design the package to throw an error condition, unless this is a source for which zero activity is plausible.

You can apply increasingly stringent tests. It's probably not sufficient to test for zero rows: Instead, test for whether the count of rows today is within several standard deviations of the expected daily row count. Another test is to compare row counts from the beginning and end of the transformation process to make sure you didn't drop any rows. You may also want to sum the sales activity for the day, for comparison to an expected value. Apply these simple tests immediately after the extract and transformation steps, before loading the data into the data warehouse database.

REFERENCE Chapter 4 of *The Data Warehouse ETL Toolkit* includes a discussion on the kinds of reasonableness checks that might cause you to halt package execution.

The article "Is your Data Correct??" by Ralph Kimball, *Intelligent Enterprise*, December 2000, includes a longer discussion on this technique. You can find a link to this article at www.kimballgroup.com/html/articlesbydate/articles2000.html.

Figure 6.10 shows the same data flow task as Figure 6.9, but we've moved the transforms around so you can see how to compute aggregate values to check for reasonableness. At the same time as the data flows into the raw file for staging and backup, a copy of that data flows into the Aggregate transform. That transform computes how many customers are in today's extract, how many products, and how many days of data, with rowcounts by day. You'd expect these counts to be fairly consistent over time, subject to some seasonal or cyclical variation.

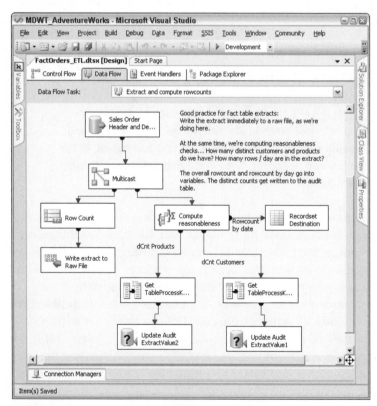

Figure 6.10   Computing reasonableness checks

In Figure 6.10, we're planning to perform some more transformations on the data. A second Data Flow task will pick up the data from the raw file, and continue processing it.

Figure 6.11 illustrates details of the Aggregate transform. The Aggregate transform is a high-performance method for computing multiple aggregate measures. Here, the Aggregate transform performs three calculations in parallel:

- Count of rows by date (illustrated)
- Count of distinct customers
- Count of distinct products

The row count by date will produce a stream with multiple rows; the other two aggregations are single-valued.

NOTE When you first open the Aggregate transform, it presents a simplified user interface to support a single aggregation. In Figure 6.11 you see the Advanced user interface that shows the different aggregations defined to run in parallel within this single transform.

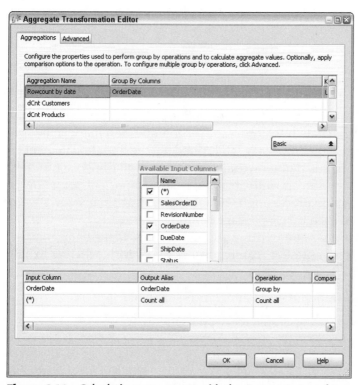

Figure 6.11   Calculating row counts with the Aggregate transform

The next step is to get the customer and product counts back to the Control Flow in order to make a decision about whether to continue processing, or abort the package. Remember, the Control Flow is aptly named: It's where you can control the flow of the package's execution. There are several possible methods for transferring the information back out to the Control Flow, including the values into package variables, or writing the values out to an audit table. Figure 6.10 illustrates both of these options.

- The Row Count transform writes the count of rows to a variable named RowCount.

- The Recordset Destination transform writes the count of rows by day to a variable named RowCountByDay. This variable will hold a recordset rather than a single value.

- The distinct count of customers and products is written to an audit table in the two OLEDB Command transforms called Update Audit ExtractValue1 and Update Audit ExtractValue2.

The OLE DB Command transform labeled Update Audit ExtractValue1 performs an update to an auditing table. For the customer count, that update statement is:

```
UPDATE AuditTableProcessing

SET ExtractCheckValue1 = ?

WHERE TableProcessKey = ?
```

The first question mark in the script picks up the customer count value that is output from the Aggregate transform. The second question mark is the primary key for the AuditTableProcessing table, directing the update statement to the correct row. Later in this chapter we talk about the Audit dimension and its supporting tables, so we don't go into details here. The important point now is that the system maintains processing metadata about how many rows were extracted and inserted each time a package is run.

This Data Flow task ends after writing the aggregations to the database. The next step is to test these values for reasonableness, and decide whether to halt execution:

- Read the values from the AuditTableProcessing table

- Compare to the average counts for the past month

- Determine whether today's counts are reasonable

Depending on the quality of your data and the workings of your business, the rule you use to evaluate reasonableness might be simple or complex. A good yet simple rule is to evaluate whether today's value is within three standard deviations of the past 90 days' values.

MORE ON THE OLE DB COMMAND TRANSFORM

The OLE DB Command transform is a little complicated to set up. Read Books Online carefully. You can find a helpful walkthrough of setting up the transform at www.sqlis.com. Examine the completed package FactOrders_ETL, available on the book's web site.

The Derived Column transforms in Figure 6.10 are a trick worth explaining. The OLE DB Command transform cannot access package variables. (We assume this is a product oversight that will be fixed in a future version.) In order to use a package variable—the primary key for AuditTableProcessing in this case—you need to create a derived column in the data flow diagram and populate it with the package variable. It's inelegant, but it works.

The Control Flow is the place to gracefully stop package execution, and launch an event like notifying an operator. In this chapter we've worked with the Data Flow, which is just a task—a complex task—within the package's Control Flow. The design of a Data Flow task is analogous to a pipe manifold through which data will flow. In order to launch some event other than the flow of data, you need to put the data somewhere so you can exit to the Control Flow. In the current example, we've put the extracted data in a raw file, written some reasonableness checks to a database table, and stored other reasonableness checks in package variables.

Figure 6.12 illustrates the Control Flow for the fact table extract. The first Data Flow task, labeled Extract and compute rowcounts, is the one from Figure 6.10. In this Control Flow, the system stops all processing and emails Warren if the extract fails, or if it succeeds but contains too few rows. We also want to check the reasonableness of the extract by verifying whether the counts of distinct customers and products in the extracts are within three standard deviations of the recent history. If the reasonableness checks fail, the system stops and emails Warren.

Notice that several of the precedence constraints, displayed as arrows in the Control Flow, have a function notation (*fx*). This notation signals that the precedence constraints are more complicated than simply Success, Failure, or Completion. Figure 6.13 shows the Precedence Constraint Editor for the precedence constraint at the top right of Figure 6.12 (with the dashed line). In this case, the system hands control to the Send Mail task if one of two things happened in the first Data Flow task: It failed, or it generated fewer than 5,000 rows. (In the real world, you should use a standard deviation calculation rather than hard-coding a row count limit.) The precedence constraint leading to the Sequence container is the opposite condition.

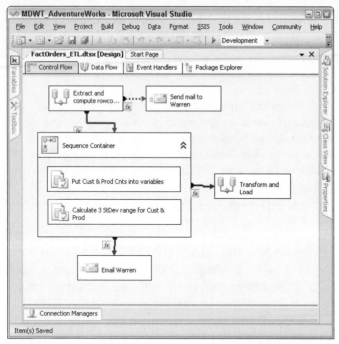

Figure 6.12   Control Flow for fact extract, clean, and check

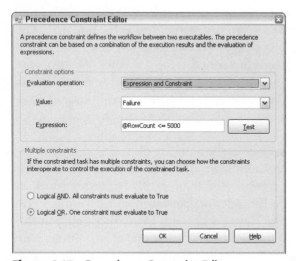

Figure 6.13   Precedence Constraint Editor

PRECEDENCE CONSTRAINT CONDITIONS

When you set up a conditional flow between tasks, you often want the control to pass to one and only one downstream task. In other words, you want the flow to be exclusive. When the precedence constraints are just "success" or "failure," that's simple. When the precedence constraints have expressions in them, as illustrated in 6.13, it's easy to introduce gaps where either no downstream task is executed, or where multiple tasks are executed. There's no built-in catch for this; you need to be careful and test thoroughly.

Next in the Control Flow of Figure 6.12 are two SQL tasks grouped together in a Sequence Container. The first reads today's counts and puts the results into package variables. The second is a bit more complicated. The task reads the series of customer and product rowcounts from the auditing table, and computes the reasonableness ranges as:

```
SELECT
    isnull(convert(int, avg(Extract_Check_Value1) -
        3*stdev(Extract_Check_Value1)),0) As CustCountMin,
    isnull(convert(int, avg(Extract_Check_Value1) +
        3*stdev(Extract_Check_Value1)),0) AS CustCountMax,
    isnull(convert(int, avg(Extract_Check_Value2) -
        3*stdev(Extract_Check_Value2)),0) As ProdCountMin,
    isnull(convert(int, avg(Extract_Check_Value2) +
        3*stdev(Extract_Check_Value2)),0) AS ProdCountMax
FROM AuditTableProcessing
WHERE TableName = 'FactOrders'
AND SuccessfulProcessingInd = 'Y'
```

Every time the package runs, it logs the count of distinct customers in the audit table. This query calculates a range plus or minus three standard deviations from the mean, since the package started logging this information to the audit system. In the real world, you'd make this query more complex, perhaps limiting to the last 60 days, or performing some kind of seasonal adjustment. Put the values of the range minimums and maximums into four package variables.

Placing the tasks inside a Sequence Container makes it easier to define a precedence constraint. This precedence constraint is similar to the one described earlier in this chapter. If the count of distinct customers or products is outside their expected ranges, control will pass to the Email task.

Fact data cleansing is as varied as the possible source systems. More often than not, you'll have data as clean as that in the Adventure Works sample, and you won't have any fact data cleansing to do. In that case, you can check row counts as we did here to confirm that the extract worked as expected.

In a more complex situation, you might not choose to fail processing when you encounter anomalies. You may be able to apply a logical rule to fix the data.

REFERENCE Chapter 4 of *The Data Warehouse ETL Toolkit* talks about the kind of actions you might take when you encounter data anomalies.

The data quality checks that we walked through in this section were performed on the data as it was extracted. You should perform similar checks just before loading the data, to confirm your processing hasn't introduced anomalies.

Transforming Fact Data

We've already discussed the first part of the fact data ETL process: extracting, cleaning, and checking the fact data. In this section, we talk about a second set of work: performing transformations. Cleaning data requires transformations, of course. This section focuses on other kinds of transformations that you may make to fact data.

Aggregating Data

You may wonder why we're talking about aggregating data before loading it. After all, the Kimball Method strongly recommends that transaction fact tables be developed at the finest possible grain. Why would we aggregate data before loading it? Sometimes you just have to. As hardware and software grows more powerful, what we think of as extreme scale has grown substantially. At the time of this writing, a DW/BI system that captures telephone network call detail records is no longer extreme, although five years ago it was. But call detail records are created from call event details, which few telecommunications companies would keep for more than a short while. Similarly, a clickstream or RFID DW/BI system may throw away or aggregate a lot of data . . . and what it keeps may still be a very large data store.

In a lot of these cases, custom applications already exist to prune and aggregate the data stream. You should certainly use those applications if they do what you need them to do. But if your ETL system needs to do this work, you can use Integration Services to aggregate your data.

Use the Aggregate transform to aggregate the data. We've already used the Aggregate transform to perform distinct counts used for determining whether the extract worked correctly. That same transform could be used to aggregate the entire stream of data that will flow into the fact tables. The Aggregate transform is high performance and automatically parallelizes its operations across multiple processors.

> **WARNING** The Aggregate transform, like the Sort transform, works in memory. Performance is excellent as long as the data flow fits in memory. Consider increasing server memory, or using an alternative method of aggregating data, if you see memory pressure. You may be able to find a third-party aggregation routine that plugs into the pipeline. Or, you could stage the data to a table and use GROUP BY.

Disaggregating Data

Disaggregating data, the opposite of aggregation, sounds like a strange concept, but we do it all the time. The Orders fact table has an example of disaggregating data. The Orders fact grain is at the order line item level, so that users can see sales information by product. But several dollar amounts are stored in the transaction system at the order header level, Freight and Tax in particular. You need to allocate these amounts to the order line item grain of the Orders fact table.

Your business users provide the business logic for allocating these amounts to the line item. There is certainly an algorithm for computing sales tax, usually as a flat rate on some categories of products. (In many states, food items are exempted from sales tax, unless they are intended to be consumed on the premises.) Freight is often calculated based on product weight, which is a common attribute in the Product dimension.

We'll illustrate an example here, allocating sales tax and freight to all the products in the order based on the line item total sale amount as a percentage of the order total sale amount. Here's the logic flow:

1. Pick up the fact data from the post-extract staging area.

2. Aggregate by order number, summing total sale amount to serve as the divisor in the allocation computation.

3. Join the aggregates back in to the original data flow.

4. Compute line item freight and tax.

Figure 6.14, from the FactOrders_ETL package, illustrates this common design pattern. Source the data from a raw file and then sort it by OrderId (these two steps are not shown). Then the data flows into the Multicast transform, which copies the pipeline into two or more identical streams. One stream goes into an Aggregate transform, which sums amounts by OrderId.

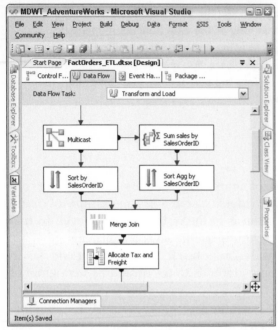

Figure 6.14 Data Flow for allocating tax and freight

The only slightly tricky element of this design pattern is the Merge Join transform. Merge Join works just like a database join, except it requires that the input data be sorted in the same order. You can do an inner or outer join; in this case an inner join is appropriate. The Merge Join transform, unlike most other transforms, does not automatically map all the input columns to the output flow. Instead, you need to select the columns you want by checking their boxes. This is a good opportunity to drop unneeded columns to keep the pipeline as small as possible.

Finally, calculate the Freight and Tax at the line item level. In the Derived Column transform replace Freight and Tax by their existing amounts (from the Order Header), divided by the total sale amount for each order.

Although this transformation occurs before the surrogate key lookup and assignment, sometimes it's more efficient to do the surrogate key assignment first. If you want to use a dimension attribute like Product Weight in the calculation, pick up that attribute during the ProductKey lookup step of the key assignment.

Other Transformations and Calculations

There are several kinds of common transformations and calculations that we make to fact data. These fall into the following categories:

- *Within-row calculations,* like computing the ratio of two columns. The vast majority of computational requirements can be met with the Derived Column transform. Anything else can be met by writing a Script transform. A common transformation of this type is to replace nulls with a default value. This is particularly useful when the null value is in one of the natural key columns you need to join to a dimension. In some source systems, a column is null most of the time and has a code only if a specific event occurred. For example, a null promotion code means the sale did not use any promotions; or a null currency code means the transaction used the home country's currency. Although you could handle these null violations in the surrogate key pipeline, it's best to replace the null with a default value that is the natural key of its corresponding dimension member.

- *Between-row calculations,* like the tax allocation problem described in the previous section. Once again, any logic that can't be met by the expression language in the Derived Column transform can be handled via custom Script transform.

- *Mapping,* for example collapsing information about several accounts to a single household ID. Most of the complex mapping logic—determining which accounts are linked together in a household—is handled before the fact table processing, when you're working on the dimensions. The outcome of that dimension processing is a straightforward mapping table for use when processing the facts. The mapping table identifies which set of account numbers maps to a single household. The steps required to run the fact data against the mapping table in order to look up the household ID are essentially the same as you'll use for surrogate key assignment, described next.

Surrogate Key Pipeline

Everyone who follows the Kimball Method must load fact data by looking up surrogate keys from the conformed dimensions. Your extract contains natural keys; the fact table contains the substituted surrogate keys. The dimension tables contain the mapping between natural keys and surrogate keys that you use to do the substitutions.

KIMBALL METHOD ETL SUBSYSTEM This section describes techniques relevant to Kimball Method ETL Subsystems:

- *#19 Surrogate Key Pipeline:* Pipelined, multithreaded process for replacing natural keys of incoming data with data warehouse surrogate keys.

- *#29 Parallelizing/Pipelining System:* Common system for taking advantage of multiple processors, or grid computing resources, and a common system for implementing streaming data flows. Highly desirable (eventually necessary) that parallelizing and pipelining be invoked automatically for any ETL process that meets certain conditions, like not writing to the disk or waiting on a condition in the middle of the process.

Type 1 Dimensions

As usual, we'll start with the easiest possible case: dimensions whose attributes are all updated in place. Type 1 dimensions have a one-to-one mapping between natural keys and surrogate keys.

The heart of the surrogate key pipeline is to look up the natural key in the fact stream and replace it with the surrogate key from the dimension table. You won't be surprised to learn that we'll use the Lookup transform to do the heavy lifting.

The Lookup transform supports a single or multiple column equi-join between the data in the pipeline and data in an OLE DB source like a dimension. By default, the entire lookup table or query is cached. To minimize memory pressure, use a query that returns only the columns of interest—for dimensions that only have Type 1 attributes, this is usually just the natural key and the surrogate key. If you don't have enough memory, you can set up the transform to use partial or even zero caching.

Figure 6.15 illustrates a piece of the surrogate key pipeline that includes three lookups for Type 1 dimensions: Date, Promotion, and Product. These use the default settings in the Lookup transform, except we used a source query instead of the entire table, as we just described.

It looks like this pipeline will execute the lookups in series, one after the other. Not so: On a multi-processor system, multiple lookups will execute in parallel. You don't need to set up anything; Integration Services handles parallelism for you automatically.

Note the error flows to the right from each Lookup transform, labeled Lookup Error Output. These flows handle the cases where the fact has no corresponding value in the lookup table. Never insert a fact that has no corresponding dimension member. The way you choose to handle the error rows depends on your business requirements, technical environment, and data realities. We list several possibilities here, and Figure 6.15 illustrates the first three:

- *Throw away the fact rows.* This is seldom a good solution, but we illustrated it for the Product dimension. The error flow for the Product dimension counts the error flows but doesn't transform them or store them anywhere.

- *Write the bad rows to a file or table.* This is a common solution, and we illustrated it for the OrderDate dimension lookup.

- *Map all the bad fact rows to the Unknown member for that dimension by supplying a key of -1 (or whatever your Unknown Member key is).* We illustrated this solution for the Promotions dimension. This is seldom a good solution because the fact row is difficult to fix if you receive better information about what the promotion was supposed to be.

- *Insert a dummy row into the dimension.* This case is discussed in the following subsection, "Early Arriving Facts."

- *Fail the package and abort processing.* This is the default if you don't set up an error flow. It seems a bit draconian.

Logging to a file or mapping to the Unknown member (or both) are the most common approaches. Whatever you do, be sure to place each error row count into its own package variable. When you get back out to the Control Flow, you'll log these error counts, shoot off email about the events, and potentially halt processing.

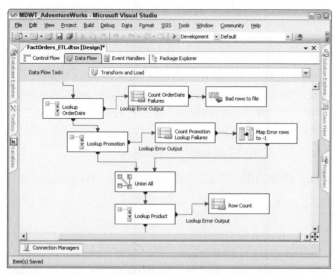

Figure 6.15 Surrogate key pipeline, Type 1 dimensions

Early Arriving Facts

An early arriving fact is a fact row that arrives before its associated dimension member has been created. If you always process dimensions before facts, how can you get a fact before its dimension member? In some systems this is a possible (non-error) scenario. The best example is when you sign up for a grocery store loyalty card. They generate a member number right there at the register and tag that first purchase to you. You take home the form, fill it out, and send it in. In this case your purchase facts will arrive long before the new customer dimension member.

If this scenario fits your business, you really want to create a skeleton dimension member and load the facts. In due time you'll get the attributes for this dimension member, and can update the appropriate dimension row. We discussed the dimension part of this issue earlier in this chapter, when we talked about inferred members in the Slowly Changing Dimension transform.

The logic flow for handling the early arriving facts is to:

1. Send the lookup failure errors into an OLE DB Command transform.

2. Set up the OLE DB Command transform to insert a row into the dimension table with only three columns populated: the natural key, the surrogate key (which is automatically populated if you use table identity columns), and the audit key for the current package. Once again, we're trying not to talk in detail about the audit subsystem until later in this chapter, but it makes sense that you'd want to flag this dimension row as having been inserted during a fact table's lookup process.

3. If you defined the dimension table to generate default values for the non-key columns, these attributes will be populated automatically as you insert each row. The SCD transform identifies an inferred member in one of two ways: either all the non-key attributes are null, or you explicitly specify a column that identifies an inferred member.

4. Send the data flow into a new Lookup transform. Don't cache the second Lookup, to ensure the data flow picks up the new dimension member that you just added. On the Advanced tab of the Lookup editor, choose Enable memory restriction.

5. Add error handling to this second Lookup—just in case.

6. Finally, Union this flow back with the package's main flow.

Type 2 Dimensions

Fact table lookups against a dimension that tracks historical change are more complicated because the dimension table has multiple rows for each natural key. A simple lookup against the dimension table, joining on the natural key, will not give the results you need.

If today's load includes data only from yesterday, this is only slightly more complicated than the surrogate key pipeline for Type 1 dimensions. In this case, the source query for the lookup limits the results to the currently active row for the dimension, like:

```
SELECT CustomerKey, BKCustomerID

FROM DimCustomer

WHERE RowIsCurrent = 'Y'
```

All the error handling, and handling of early arriving facts, is exactly the same.

Loading Fact Data

The next step of fact processing is—at long last—to load the data into the fact table. This section describes how to load data for the three main kinds of fact tables: the common transaction grain, and the periodic and accumulating snapshot fact tables. We discuss some extra things to worry about during the initial load of historical data. And we discuss how you should modify your fact table packages to automate the creation of relational table partitions.

KIMBALL METHOD ETL SUBSYSTEM This section describes techniques relevant to Kimball Method ETL Subsystems:

- *#16 Transaction Grain Fact Table Loader:* **System for updating transaction grain fact tables including manipulation of indexes and partitions. Normally append mode for most recent data. Uses surrogate key pipeline (see subsystem 19).**

- *#17 Periodic Snapshot Grain Fact Table Loader:* **System for updating periodic snapshot grain fact tables, including manipulation of indexes and partitions. Includes frequent overwrite strategy for incremental update of current period facts. Uses surrogate key pipeline (see subsystem 19).**

- *#18 Accumulating Snapshot Grain Fact Table Loader:* **System for updating accumulating snapshot grain fact tables including manipulation of indexes and partitions, and updates to both dimension foreign keys and accumulating measures. Uses surrogate key pipeline (see subsystem 19).**

ADVANCED TOPIC: LATE ARRIVING FACTS

A late arriving fact is one that arrives after its transaction date. Under normal operations, you expect to load today the fact data from yesterday's transactions. Most systems work this way, but some sources have late data trickling in days or even months after the event date. If you have only Type 1 dimensions, late arriving facts don't need special processing. But if you have any Type 2 dimensions, you need to look up the dimension key that was active at the time the fact event occurred, not the key that's current today.

If you used SQL to perform the lookup, the join between a fact and dimension table would look like the following:

```
SELECT d.DimSurrogateKey, d.DimNaturalKey
FROM FactStream f INNER JOIN DimTable d
ON (f.DimNaturalKey = d.DimNaturalKey
AND f.EventDate BETWEEN d.RowStartDate AND d.RowEndDate)
```

But the Lookup transform doesn't support this kind of complex join.

We don't have a single recommended strategy to solve this problem because no single strategy dominates the others. Your solution is going to depend on business requirements, whether you have large data volumes or very large dimensions, and whether late arriving data trickles in over months or just a few days. We describe three techniques next, but we can think of dozens of variations of these techniques. This is a good opportunity for some design creativity.

STRATEGY 1: LOOP OVER DAYS

The first strategy is to create a loop out in the Control Flow that runs all or part of the fact table surrogate key pipeline for each date represented in the fact table's incremental load. If you look back to Figure 6.10, you'll see that when we were testing for reasonable row counts, we also ran a check to see how many dates contain data. In the Control Flow, you could set up a For Loop container to iterate over this rowset.

To support late arriving facts, define a view on the Type 2 slowly changing dimensions, and update that view at the start of each iteration. The view selects the dimension rows that were active at a specific date in the past. For example, the iteration for June 1, 2004 would redefine the dimension view as:

```
CREATE VIEW v_MyDimKeyLookup AS
SELECT DimSurrogateKey, DimNaturalKey
FROM DimTable
WHERE '06/01/2004' BETWEEN RowStartDate AND RowEndDate
```

This view will return a single row for every dimension member active on June 1. In the Lookup transform for this dimension, use the view as the source. When you're processing fact rows for June 1, they'll get assigned the correct dimension surrogate keys that were active on that date.

As you can see, it's vital that you correctly maintain dimension row start and end dates. You need a complete set of rows for a dimension member, with ranges that contain neither overlaps nor gaps.

At the beginning of the Data Flow step, use a Conditional Split to pull out the data you're working on for that iteration. Depending on relative data volumes, it may be efficient to write the older data to a raw file, rewriting over the same file each time. If you work through the data from newest to oldest, you'll rewrite the least data.

This technique will work well if your data arrives just a few days late. If you have late fact data arriving for dozens of dates, this technique will probably not perform well enough. This would be especially true if your dimensions are large.

STRATEGY 2: USE THE RELATIONAL DATABASE

Use a Conditional Split to split off the late arriving facts just before you're faced with the Type 2 lookups, and write them to a staging table. Complete the processing of yesterday's facts as normal.

Back out in the Control Flow, use an Execute SQL task to create indexes on the staging table. Index each natural key.

Write a second Data Flow task to handle the late arriving data. You will have a single source, which is a query that joins the staging table to the Type 2 dimensions, joining on the natural key, and using the correlated BETWEEN clause that picks up the correct dimension surrogate keys. One query could pick up all the dimension keys. This is effectively a star query on the natural keys, returning the surrogate keys. Write the resulting flow into the fact table.

This approach has the significant disadvantage of not handling errors well. You'll need to write code to handle referential integrity violations—late arriving facts whose dimension natural keys don't exist in the dimension tables.

STRATEGY 3: ACCUMULATE LATE FACTS AND PROCESS WEEKLY

Once your fact data is late, it may be less urgent to add that data into the DW/BI system immediately. It may be acceptable to the business users if you stage late arriving facts until the weekend. A week's worth of late data will benefit from economies of scale in processing—and weekends typically have longer load windows.

As a variation on this theme, you might immediately load the data that's one or two days late, and defer the rest until the weekend.

Loading Transaction Grain Facts

For the incremental load into a non-partitioned transaction grain fact table, use the OLE DB or SQL Server destination as the final step in the data flow diagram. The fast load options are usually irrelevant for incremental loads. Of course you want the load to be fast, but the fast loading path requires either that you load into an empty table, or that you load into an unindexed table. For a daily incremental load, it usually doesn't make sense to drop and rebuild indexes because of the way SQL Server handles indexes during inserts, and obviously there's already data in the table. Unless you're using partitions, the

only time you can realistically perform a fast load is during the initial historical load of the fact data.

As with the Lookup transform, always redirect errors generated by the Destination adapter. Count errors and dump the rows to a file or staging table.
This is vital during package development; by the time you're in production
you hope to have found and fixed the myriad errors that could cause the insert
to fail. But you never know.

Aside from using relational table partitions, the only way to improve the
performance of incremental loads is to not enforce referential integrity
between the fact and dimensions. It's common practice to rely on the surrogate
key pipeline to maintain the all-important referential integrity. Always try to
finish processing within your load window with the foreign key constraints in
force; remove them only if you must.

Most systems will be able to finish processing within the allotted time, even
without the fast path for table inserts.

Incremental Loads and Table Partitions

The most common table partitioning strategy is to partition by month. A
monthly partitioning strategy is easy to maintain (see the related discussion in
Chapter 4) but doesn't help you with the performance of the daily incremental
load. Only if you process facts monthly could you load into an empty monthly
partition, and hence use the fast load path.

In this most common case, specify the partitioned table as the destination
for the OLE DB or SQL Server destination adapter, just as if the table were not
partitioned. The data will be inserted at approximately the same speed as into
a non-partitioned table.

If you have extreme daily fact table volumes and a short load window, create daily partitions. In theory this is no more difficult to manage than monthly
partitions. In practice, you can't have more than 1,000 partitions, so you'll need
to create a process to consolidate partitions on a weekly or monthly basis.

The Historical Load

The historical fact table load is the process in which you are manipulating the
greatest volume of data. If you have only Type 1 dimensions, or if you're not
recreating history for your Type 2 dimensions, the historical load is simply a
big version of the incremental load. It's common to run the historical load in
chunks of months, quarters, or years.

In this simple case, you have two things in your favor: You can perform fast
loads, and you will be loading the data before the DW/BI system goes online.
So if it takes a week, it takes a week.

PARTITIONED FACT TABLES

If your fact table is partitioned, load partitions in parallel for best performance. There are many ways to load in parallel. You could design your package to load a month of data. Parameterize the month, and launch several versions of the package at the same time. Alternatively, set up a conditional split to create multiple streams within a single Data Flow task.

We discussed partitioned tables in Chapter 4. Table partitioning is a feature of SQL Server Enterprise Edition.

For the historical load or loads, do the following:

1. Completely load all dimensions.

2. Back up the data warehouse database.

3. Make sure you have enough disk space, and that your database files are set big enough, or are set to autogrow.

4. Put the data warehouse database into Simple recovery mode.

5. Drop the indexes on the fact table. Drop (or disable) any foreign key constraints.

6. Use the OLE DB or SQL Server destinations as appropriate. With the OLE DB destination, make sure you choose the data access mode of Table or view—fast mode.

7. Turn on Table Lock.

8. Handle insert errors appropriately in your error flow.

9. After all the historical data is loaded, rebuild the indexes.

10. Recreate and check any foreign key constraints, if you're using them.

The historical load process is more likely to fail than the incremental loads—probably because of the inherent challenges of dealing with large data volumes and the reality that source systems change over time. And because you're dealing with so much data, restarting the load is so much more expensive.

With DTS 2000, we would commit every 10,000 rows as a best practice. With Integration Services, set up an error flow to catch bad data. The error flow will also catch data that arrives after a database runs out of room, in the unlikely event that you've miscalculated your space requirements. Error flows minimize the importance of periodic commits for the purpose of recoverability. However, if the batch size and commit level are set to zero, the relational database will consume valuable memory. It's still a good idea to batch and commit at reasonable intervals.

TIP The optimal commit level is application dependent—it depends on what else is happening on your machine. The best way to find the appropriate commit level is through trial and error: Set it at different levels, and watch memory usage. At some point, buffering the load in memory constrains the server performance. Set the commit batch size a bit smaller than that level.

You can't set the commit level and batch size on the SQL Destination, but you can on the OLE DB Destination.

If you've been able to recreate history for your Type 2 dimensions, you now face the challenge of matching the historical fact data with the correct Type 2 dimension surrogate key. This is exactly the same problem we discussed at length with late arriving facts.

Because you'll be processing a full day of data for each date, your best bet is almost certainly to load historical data by using the looping strategy discussed previously.

Loading Periodic Snapshot Fact Tables

A periodic snapshot fact represents a span of time, regularly repeated. This style of table is well suited for tracking long-running processes like bank accounts. The facts are things like end-of-month account balances, and total deposits and withdrawals during the month.

REFERENCE Issues around loading periodic snapshot fact tables are well described in Chapter 6 of *The Data Warehouse ETL Toolkit*.

Periodic snapshots, and periodic snapshots with a current hot rolling period, are particularly easy to load if the fact table is partitioned. In either case, load into an empty partition and then swap that loaded partition into the fact table. These processes can use fast path loading.

An Analysis Services database measure group that's built from a periodic snapshot fact table can be incrementally processed each month. If the measure group also contains the current rolling period, the Analysis Services database should be partitioned by month. Plan to reprocess the current month's partition each day; older partitions need not be touched. See Chapter 15 for more information on Analysis Services partitions.

Loading Accumulating Snapshot Fact Tables

The accumulating snapshot fact table is used to describe processes that have a definite beginning and end, like order fulfillment, claims processing, and most workflows. The accumulating snapshot fact table is characterized by many date dimensions for different roles of the date. For example, an order fulfill-ment fact table might have dates for when the order was placed, shipped, delivered, and paid for.

The nature of the accumulating snapshot means that each fact row will be updated several times, as the underlying process moves through its lifecycle. Microsoft SQL Server offers no special magic for managing an accumulating snapshot. Here are two ways to improve performance in an environment with a high volume of updates:

- Conditionally split the flow of updates in order to spin up several par-allel update transforms. For example, split the stream into four flows based on an arbitrary column like product. Each of the four flows ends in an OLE DB Command transform that performs simultaneous updates on the fact table.

- Write the set of fact rows to be updated into staging tables, and update in a bulk transaction rather than row by row. This SQL-based approach cannot take advantage of the error handling that Integration Services provides. However, it's likely to perform far better than using the OLE DB Command transform.

An Analysis Services database or measure group that's built against an accumulating snapshot fact table is challenging to process. It's difficult to avoid a scenario where you are reprocessing the entire structure each load cycle.

Analysis Services Processing

The processing of Analysis Services databases is usually a part of the ETL sys-tem. You usually want to trigger Analysis Services database processing upon successful completion of the relational data warehouse loads.

KIMBALL METHOD ETL SUBSYSTEM This section describes techniques relevant to Kimball Method ETL Subsystem #22 Multi-Dimensional Cube Builder: Creation and maintenance of star schema foundation for loading multidimensional (OLAP) cubes, including special preparation of dimension hierarchies as dictated by the specific cube technology.

Integration Services provides Analysis Services Processing and Analysis Ser-vices DDL Control Flow tasks. These are easy to integrate into your ETL sys-tem, at the master package or table-specific package level, and are described in Chapters 7 and 15.

Analysis Services provides several ways of processing its databases, includ-ing an automated proactive caching system that self-processes. We'll defer detailed discussion of Analysis Services processing to Chapter 7.

Tying It All Together

Throughout this chapter we've been focusing on the details of data flows and Control Flows. We've continually deferred discussion about over-arching issues like the audit system, and communication between master packages and child packages. It's finally time to tackle these topics.

The Audit System

A decade and more ago, our DW/BI systems had primitive or, more often, no auditing systems. In the current regulatory environment, we need to do better. You could spend almost as much time and energy developing an auditing a system as building the core system itself. The auditing system that we present here is better than most systems we've seen, but by no means is it as extensive as we can envision. It strikes a balance between ease of implementation and robustness, and will be good enough for most DW/BI systems.

> **KIMBALL METHOD ETL SUBSYSTEM** This section describes techniques relevant to Kimball Method ETL Subsystem #6 Audit Dimension Assembler: Assembly of metadata context surrounding each fact table load in such a way that the metadata context can be attached to the fact table as a normal dimension.

We have several design goals for the audit system. We want to be able to answer the following questions:

- How did each row initially enter the DW/BI system?
- What process most recently updated each fact row?
- How can you locate all the fact rows loaded today? How would you back out a load?
- Was this row loaded through the standard process, or through an exception-handling branch of the ETL process?
- How many rows were loaded today? How many error rows were logged?
- Was today's processing successful?
- How many rows did the table have before and after the load?

NOTE These aren't the only interesting questions you can ask about the processing. There's a whole set of important information about the process, like how long the entire load took, and how long each package took to run. These process questions are much easier to answer because you can set up Integration Services logging to collect the information automatically. The logging information can join to the data auditing information that we discuss in this section. We discuss Integration Services logging in Chapter 15.

Figure 6.16 illustrates the data model for the basic audit system to answer these questions. The first table, AuditPkgExecution, receives a row each time a package is executed. Generate a surrogate primary key, and keep track of basic information like the package name, ID, version information, and the time that execution began. All of this information is available to you from Integration Services system variables. When the package finishes, update this row with the stop time. You should also track the parent package, as most of your packages will be called from a master package.

Use stored procedures to insert and update the audit tables. Use the Execute SQL Control Flow task to execute the stored procedures, and pass in parameters from system and local package variables.

TIP The best way to understand how to configure the components of the audit system presented here is to explore the sample packages from the book's web site, www.MsftDWToolkit.com.

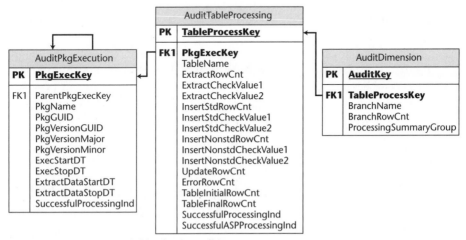

Figure 6.16   Data model for basic auditing system

Listing 6.2 lists the stored procedure to insert a new row.

```
CREATE PROCEDURE [dbo].[Insert_AuditPkgExecution]
    @PkgName varchar(50) ,
    @PkgGUID uniqueidentifier ,
    @PkgVersionGUID uniqueidentifier,
    @PkgVersionMajor smallint,
    @PkgVersionMinor smallint,
    @ExecStartDT datetime,
    @ParentPkgExecKey int
AS
BEGIN
    SET NOCOUNT ON;

    IF @ParentPkgExecKey = 0 SET @ParentPkgExecKey = NULL

    INSERT INTO AuditPkgExecution (
            PkgName, PkgGUID, PkgVersionGUID, PkgVersionMajor,
            PkgVersionMinor, ExecStartDT, ParentPkgExecKey)
    VALUES (@PkgName, @PkgGUID, @PkgVersionGUID, @PkgVersionMajor,
            @PkgVersionMinor, @ExecStartDT, @ParentPkgExecKey)
END
```

Listing 6.2 Sample stored procedure to insert an audit row

The next table, AuditTableProcessing, gets a row for every table that's manipulated during a package's execution. Much of the time there's one row in AuditTableProcessing for each row in the AuditPkgExecution table because you usually build a package for processing each table. But some packages touch several tables, so you can't assume a one-to-one relationship between packages and tables.

At the start of each child package, add a row for each table the package manipulates. As above, use the Execute SQL task and pass in parameters to a stored procedure. When you first add each row, you know only the table name and the initial row count. Update the other counts and values after the package finishes. In this case, you need to create a package variable to hold the TableProcessingKey for each table the package touches.

You could include this Execute SQL task in a transaction with the Data Flow task, so that a failure in the Data Flow task will back out the audit row. We don't discuss Integration Services transactions in this book. A better design than including the task in the Data Flow transaction is to explicitly update the audit row with a failure indicator.

REFERENCE See Books Online and *Professional SQL Server 2005 Integration Services,* by Knight, Chaffin, Barnes, Warren, and Young (Wrox, 2006) for a complete discussion of Integration Services transactions.

You may wonder what the check value columns are for. Use these columns to store important information about each table. Make these columns a numeric, non-integer data type so you can store either integers such a row counts, or a sum of transaction amounts. For example, earlier in this chapter when we talked about checking for data reasonableness, we stored row counts by customer and product in these fields. You might need more than two; for some tables you won't use any at all.

> **NOTE** If you check a lot of different data characteristics during package execution, you should create a separate auditing table for each table. You'd have AuditCustomer, AuditProduct, AuditOrders, and so on. Then you can name the check columns with sensible names that reflect their contents. This is a better design, although more complex.

If you don't care about whether a row was inserted during standard processing, or through an exception handling branch of the package, these two tables will meet your auditing needs. Put TableProcessKey on each dimension and fact row, instead of the AuditKey (or call the AuditTableProcessing table AuditDimension instead). This is a perfectly reasonable approach for many applications.

If you do want to track whether a row was inserted during normal or non-standard processing, you need one more auditing table: AuditDimension. For every branch of your package that you want to track separately, come up with a branch name. For a fact table, examples of branch names are *Normal/Clean*, *Adjusted out of bounds amount*, and *Forced Referential Integrity*. At the start of each child package, you'll add several rows to AuditDimension. Each gets its own key, which you'll hold in package variables.

The final step of the audit system is to put the audit key into the dimension and fact tables. Recall from the dimensional model in Chapter 2 that every table has an AuditKey column. Add a derived column transform to your data flow, adding a column AuditKey (type integer) that you set equal to the appropriate system variable.

> **TIP** If you look back at Figure 6.4, you'll see where we added AuditKey to the flow. We set it to zero only because we didn't want to explain the audit system at the beginning of the chapter. The final version of these packages, which you can download from the book's web site, correctly sets the AuditKey to the corresponding package variable.

In the book's sample packages, we track dimensions only at the package execution level. We do insert a row into the audit dimension, just to stay consistent. It's important for a fact table row to track both its original insertion and the most recent update, so fact rows contain two audit keys.

AN EVEN SIMPLER AUDITING SYSTEM

The simplest audit system outlined here, using AuditPkgExecution and a stripped-down AuditTableProcessing table, is easy to implement. If even that seems like too much trouble, there is one extremely simple solution. Add two columns to each table: PkgName and PkgExecutionDatetime. You can use the Audit transform to populate these columns in the Data Flow. We don't recommend this approach as a best practice because we don't think it captures enough information. . . and the information it does capture is stored inefficiently. But it's better than nothing and should be considered the absolute minimum level of auditing information.

REFERENCE Chapter 4 of *The Data Warehouse ETL Toolkit* contains a much more complete list of the kinds of information you might track in a fact audit system.

The Master Package

At the beginning of this chapter we talked about the master package. We were pretty cavalier back then about what goes into the master package. Now it's time to pin down a few more details.

KIMBALL METHOD ETL SUBSYSTEM This section describes techniques relevant to Kimball Method ETL Subsystems:

- *#8 Error Event Handler:* Comprehensive system for reporting and responding to all ETL error events. Includes branching logic to handle various classes of errors, and includes real-time monitoring of ETL data quality.

- *#26 Job Scheduler:* System for scheduling and launching all ETL jobs. Able to wait for a wide variety of system conditions including dependencies of prior jobs completing successfully. Able to post alerts.

Initialize the Master Package

When the master package launches it should initialize the audit system by adding a row to AuditPkgExecution. Because this is the master package, this row's ParentPkgExecKey is null. Store the newly generated row key in a package variable.

In the master package, set up a package variable or variables to hold the date or date range for which you'll be extracting and processing data. You'll need a watermark metadata table (or tables) to hold the dates that have been successfully processed. Every time you complete processing for a date, add that date as a row to the watermark table. If you process tables on different schedules, maintain a separate watermark table for each schedule.

The master package should check whether the date it's being asked to process has already been processed successfully, in which case it should exit gracefully. If the requested date is not the next date in the schedule, you could either design the master package to loop (filling in the date range), or exit gracefully.

All of this checking can be performed with the Execute SQL task, parameterized if necessary. Place results into package variables, as we've described elsewhere.

Call the Child Packages

Calling the child packages is as simple as connecting a bunch of Execute Package tasks with the appropriate precedence constraints.

The only trick is passing variables from parent to child. Set up the communication from within the child package, by setting up a configuration in the child package. As Figure 6.17 illustrates, specify that the configuration comes from a parent package. Specify the name of the parent package variable, and map that name to the corresponding variable's value in the child package. Set up a configuration for each of the variables passed from parent to child.

> **NOTE** Communicating by way of configurations seems unnecessarily awkward. Even worse, there's no straightforward way of passing information between child and parent. The best approach is to have the child package put information in a metadata table, and then have the parent package read that variable.

> **REFERENCE** See Books Online for other important information about calling child packages. Relevant topics include "Implementing Logging in Packages," "Incorporating Transactions in Packages," and "Inherited Transactions."

Master Package Cleanup

After the master package has called all the child packages, and they have completed—let's hope successfully—the master package needs to perform some cleanup.

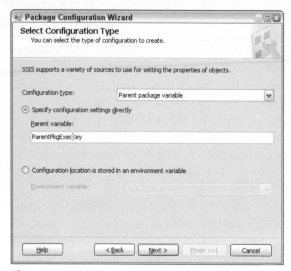

Figure 6.17   Set up a configuration from a parent package

The master package should update its row in AuditPkgExecution with its execution stop time and whether the processing was successful. It should also update the watermark table with a success or failure indicator.

If the processing was not successful, the master package should send email or alert an operator. Use the Send Mail or Notify Operator tasks.

Halting the Master Package

If the child package fails with a hard error, it's trivial to communicate that failure up to the master package. But we hope we've provided enough techniques that your package is relatively unlikely to fail: Try to plan for the likely events so that the package ends gracefully.

Several times in this chapter we've discussed how to build complex precedence constraints so that a package will stop executing if, say, your extracted data looks unreasonably small. We haven't described how to communicate this soft failure up to the parent package. If we don't communicate up, the master package thinks we succeeded: After all, we didn't throw an error condition.

Refer back to Figure 6.12. In the Control Flow for handling the failure of the reasonableness, you can see that the package sends an email if the test fails. But this is just a conditional flow, not necessarily an error condition. If you want the master package to stop all execution when the reasonableness test fails, you need to set the child package's error condition yourself. Do so by writing a Script task that contains a single line:

```
Dts.TaskResult = Dts.Results.Failure
```

Set the FailPackageOnFailure property of the Script task to True. When the script runs, it immediately fails the task, which fails the package. Up in the parent package, catch the child package failure and handle it however you wish. In the scenario we're discussing, you may want to halt all execution of the master package, set off alarm bells, and hunker down. If you've bound steps into a transaction, you could even roll back some of the earlier steps of the master package.

TIP In the packages available on the book's web site, we hid this Script task in an OnPostExecute event handler for the Send Mail tasks. That's why you don't see the Script task in Figure 6.12.

Package Event Handling

KIMBALL METHOD ETL SUBSYSTEM This section describes techniques relevant to Kimball Method ETL Subsystems:

- *#8 Error Event Handler:* Comprehensive system for reporting and responding to all ETL error events. Includes branching logic to handle various classes of errors, and includes real-time monitoring of ETL data quality.

- *#26 Job Scheduler:* System for scheduling and launching all ETL jobs. Able to wait for a wide variety of system conditions including dependencies of prior jobs completing successfully. Able to post alerts.

In the earlier section on the master package, we talked about initialization, error handling, and cleanup logic that should be in the master package. If you've looked at the sample packages posted on the book's web site, you may be wondering where we've hidden this logic.

The initialization, cleanup, and error handling are all in event handlers. You can find all the event handlers for a package in the tab compellingly titled Event Handlers, next to the Control Flow and Data Flow tabs. You can create handlers for any kind of event like pre-execute or error, for a task or for the package as a whole. An event handler can contain the same kinds of tasks as the main package.

OnError and OnPostExecute are the most important event handlers to set up at the package level. These event handlers will run no matter where an error occurs, or in which branch the Control Flow terminates normally. The biggest issue with the event handlers is discoverability: there's no visual clue in the main package Control Flow that event handlers have been defined for the overall package or a specific task. Developers, and others who are looking at packages, should get into the habit of looking in the Package Explorer tab to identify the event handlers that have been defined.

Unit Testing

The ETL system developer must test every path that data can take through the packages. You hope that many of the packages' branches will never be encountered during normal execution. But you need to test the logic before moving even to the test system, much less into production.

The only way to unit test data flows is to create test data sets that contain all the different types of errors, and combinations of errors, that you can think of. Creating those data sets is hard enough, but the real challenge is in keeping track of the data, the test cases that each data set addresses, and the expected and observed results.

You will need to create different versions of source and target tables. In a simple system, you can create multiple test databases. Use package configurations to change the package's connection, so that you're using the appropriate test databases during each test run.

For more complex systems and testing scenarios, it might be easier to write a package that assembles test data from data stored in flat files and in other working databases. By the time you reach this point, you should be expert enough with Integration Services that such a package will present no serious challenges.

It's almost universally true of developers that they hate to document anything. If you can't force yourself to document your unit testing procedures and results, the project team leader must assign someone to do this for you. This is a key part of the project's documentation in a regulated world, and your test logic and procedures will be very helpful in the deployment process.

Summary

In this chapter, we presented the ETL system as the core of the business intelligence system's reliability. ETL system development is the most time-consuming and resource-intensive activity of your DW/BI project.

We described at a high level what your ETL system will look like: a system of master packages calling child packages. Actual data manipulation occurs in the child packages. We talked about how to set up a template package to simplify development.

We walked slowly through some simple packages, to become familiar with the toolset and the way SQL Server Integration Services works. We extracted data, performed some simple transformations, and loaded that data into a dimension table.

Developing the logic to manage dimension changes is one of the challenges of an ETL system. That challenge is greatly simplified by Integration Services' SCD Wizard. We also discussed how to modify the results of the SCD Wizard and how you might go about replicating that logic using more basic Integration Services transforms.

Fact table processing usually has more to do with data volumes than with the complexity of the transformations. We showed how to aggregate and allocate data, and perform other calculations.

The surrogate key pipeline, where the fact table's natural keys are replaced by surrogate keys, is the core fact table processing element. We described how to build the surrogate key pipeline, focusing on alternative methods of handling errors. Next, we described some of the issues around loading transactional fact data, both for the historical load and the ongoing incremental load.

We finished the chapter with a detailed view of the topics we began with: master packages, intra-system communication and event handling, and the auditing system.

Our goal with this chapter was to describe how to use Integration Services to build an ETL system. In Chapter 7, we'll talk about the next step in the DW/BI system: Analysis Services databases. Later, in Chapters 14 and 15, we'll return to Integration Services to discuss issues of Deployment and Operations. And in Chapter 17 we'll return to talk about how to populate a low latency DW/BI system.

Designing the Analysis Services OLAP Database

The tip of the iceberg

You've designed, built, and loaded the relational data warehouse database; now it's time to think about building your Analysis Services OLAP database. This part of the project straddles the data track of the Lifecycle, as illustrated in Figure 7.1. There's a substantial component of dimensional and physical design and a modest extension of the ETL system for populating the database.

The business process dimensional model drives the design of the Analysis Services database. Start with an OLAP database that's nearly indistinguishable from the underlying dimensional design. Use Analysis Services' wizards to get started, and you can develop a decent prototype in a few days.

It'll take more than a few days to polish that prototype, adding complex calculations and other decorations, making the physical design decisions, and setting up and testing the process to keep the Analysis Services database up-to-date. But you're starting from a clean and conformed dimensional model, so it's really not that hard. The investment in building and populating the OLAP database is typically measured in person-weeks, not person-months.

This chapter starts with a plug for why you should include an Analysis Services OLAP database in your DW/BI system. What it comes down to is this: It's substantially easier, and lots more fun, to deliver fast query performance and complex analytics in Analysis Services than in a relational database. Analysis Services works well. Especially when you consider its price, it's the obvious choice of OLAP technology on the Microsoft platform.

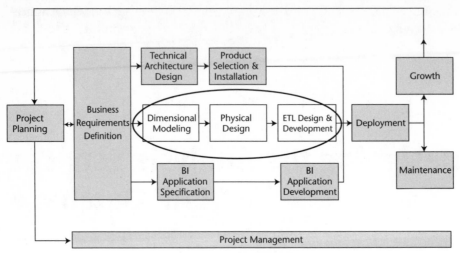

Figure 7.1   Business Dimensional Lifecycle: The Data Track

We spend most of the chapter discussing how to develop your Analysis Services dimensions and measures. We end with a discussion of physical design considerations, including pre-computed aggregations and partitions, along with an overview of the approaches for keeping your Analysis Services database up-to-date.

In Chapter 10, we look at the other part of Analysis Services' functionality: data mining.

Why Analysis Services?

The relational database is a great place to store and manage the data in your DW/BI system. But the relational database doesn't, by itself, have enough intelligence. To build a great DW/BI system, you need an analytic server to deliver excellent query performance and provide analytic capabilities beyond those provided by the SQL language.

Aggregation Management

The single most important thing you can do to improve the query performance of any DW/BI system is to define aggregations. Aggregations are pre-computed and pre-stored summarizations of the detailed data in the fact table. They're nothing mysterious: They're simply summary tables at different grains, for example monthly, or by geographic region, or both. Defining a good set of aggregations is more valuable to query performance than indexing and cheaper than upgrading your hardware.

The first challenge in aggregation management is figuring out which aggregations are most useful. The best way to do this is to monitor how business users are querying the system. You need to consider which aggregations will benefit you the most: Aggregating daily data to monthly reduces data volume by thirty-fold, whereas aggregating monthly to quarterly provides only a three-fold improvement. The problem gets much more complex when you think about aggregating multiple attributes across multiple dimensions. This is a task that software can help you with, as Analysis Services does.

The next challenge is to populate and maintain the aggregations. If you've read Chapters 5 and 6, you'll have a good idea about how to maintain summary tables in the relational data warehouse database. Incremental data is pretty easy to handle, but any deletions or updates—including updates to Type 1 dimension attributes that are used in aggregations—are very tricky to handle. It's not rocket science, but again it's a task that software should be able to handle for you, as indeed Analysis Services does.

Aggregation Navigation

Once you build and maintain your aggregations, you need to use them appropriately. To do so, you need a logical layer. The simplest approach is to depend on the business user: Train users which summary table to use, and when. This approach has obvious flaws.

You could build the aggregation navigation into the reporting front end. This common approach works adequately for many applications, but it means you have to go through that reporting client in order to use the aggregations. It's a much better design to put this logic into a server that all clients, however simple or complex, can seamlessly use.

Again, Analysis Services provides this service. It uses pre-stored aggregations where it can, accessing the smallest possible set of stored or cached data necessary to answer a query. Some relational database engines build aggregation navigation into the relational database server, as indexed or materialized views. This can be an effective approach, but even if you assume that aggregation navigation using indexed views works as well as it does in an OLAP server like Analysis Services, there are many other reasons to use Analysis Services.

NOTE The SQL Server relational database has an indexed views feature which performs some aggregation navigation. However, we've not found it to be particularly useful for dimensional schemas. Analysis Services works so well that almost no one uses SQL Server indexed views for aggregation navigation on dimensional schemas. DW/BI systems built using the Oracle RDBMS make heavy use of their similar materialized views and query rewrite features.

Summarization Logic for Each Measure

Most of the facts or measures in your dimensional model are additive: Total Sales this year is the sum of all sales for all products for all days for all regions. Non-additive and semi-additive measures require more attention.

The best example of a semi-additive measure is any kind of period-ending balance, like inventory level. If you track the quantity of products by day in your warehouse, you can't sum each of those daily inventory levels to get the monthly level. The definition of monthly inventory levels is driven by business requirements, but it's typically either the month-end or an average of the daily levels. In the relational database, how do you ensure business users don't attempt to add these facts across time?

Even worse, business users may use period-end levels for queries up to monthly, but use averages for quarterly and annual queries. The relational database has no structure in which to store this default summarization logic. When you combine this complexity with the goal of reading data from the smallest possible aggregation table, you can no longer hope that business users will get it right without software to help them out.

You can create predefined reports that present the data accurately, but that's not a very flexible solution. Plus, this approach places a huge burden on the report builders who, like the business users, are only human.

NOTE Semi-additive facts are the simplest example of a wider problem of complex calculations. One of the most compelling reasons for using Analysis Services is that the effort it takes to get SQL to perform analytics ranges from frustrating to impossible, depending on the level of complexity. The Q in SQL stands for query, not analysis.

Even if a client-side query and reporting application can handle the computation logic, the best system design folds this functionality into a server. With a server, you define the logic once and use it many times. A server has an engine that can perform complex calculations on a large volume of data with a good chance of acceptable performance. With an Analysis Services server you also have a language that can handle these calculations: MDX.

Query Performance

Query performance is the first reason most people are attracted to Analysis Services OLAP. In general, Analysis Services offers excellent dimensional query performance, in a way that's cheaper and easier to manage than is possible from the relational database alone. You can get good query performance from a pure relational DW/BI system, but it requires a lot of work that Analysis Services does for you.

Analysis Services' query performance comes from four primary areas:

- Smart aggregations, used intelligently.

- Effective data compression reduces I/O. You might think that the cost of compressing and decompressing the data would outweigh the benefits of reduced I/O. Empirically, this is not the case.

- Analysis Services' storage structures, indexes, query optimizer, and language are optimized for analytic use.

- Effective data caching keeps data in server memory longer, again reducing disk I/O.

Calculations

In addition to storing summarization logic, you can define business calculations like [Profit], [Sales year to date], and [Sales same period last year]. You can define sets like [Top 10 customers] and a host of other calculations. Once these calculations are defined, all business users—no matter what tool they use to access Analysis Services—will use the same formula. Complex calculations can be challenging to define correctly, but the work is done once by the development team and shared by all.

Many business intelligence tools define business calculations in the front end, like in report definitions. This approach leads to several difficulties:

- *Manageability and consistency:* By embedding logic in client tools and report definitions, you're setting the stage for different reports to calculate a measure differently. This is one of the problems you're building the DW/BI system to solve. Store calculations' definitions on the server, and queries and reports will be consistent.

- *Query performance:* SQL is a limited language. To perform calculations that cannot be expressed in SQL, you need a query engine. Some calculations need to access a lot of detailed data. You really don't want this work done by your reporting server or, worse yet, by your client tool. The Analysis Services calculation engine is designed for complex analytics on large data volumes.

Other Reasons for Using Analysis Services

There are other reasons for using Analysis Services as the primary query server for your business intelligence application:

- Analysis Services efficiently calculates and loads predefined aggregations. We've already discussed that Analysis Services simplifies aggregation management. It also calculates and stores those aggregations very efficiently.

- Security, particularly complex row-level security, is awkward and difficult to define in the relational database. Analysis Services easily supports very sophisticated security models, as we describe in Chapter 12.

- It's relatively simple to manage an Analysis Services system with minimal downtime. The relational part of the ETL process is the most time-consuming part of the load cycle. Incrementally loading the OLAP database and calculating aggregations is usually fast. Analysis Services can cache a shadow copy of data being updated so the system is available for querying while it's being updated. You certainly don't need Analysis Services to provide this functionality, but it's a lot easier.

- Analysis Services clients reveal metadata to business users. The dimensional structure is defined by the Analysis Services metadata, and is easily extended to include user-oriented descriptive information. This metadata—what is available and what does it mean—is extremely valuable to business users.

WHAT'S NEW IN ANALYSIS SERVICES 2005 OLAP ENGINE?

For readers familiar with Analysis Services 2000, here's a list of what we consider the most important changes. Most of these changes are discussed in greater detail in this chapter.

- ◆ In Analysis Services 2000, dimensions were strongly tied to hierarchies like Year, Quarter, Month, Day. Non-hierarchical attributes like DayName or IsWeekend were second-class citizens and difficult to work with. In Analysis Services 2005, dimensions are attribute-based, and behave like relational dimensions. We talk more about this change later in this chapter, when we discuss how to design the dimensions.

- ◆ Analysis Services 2005 no longer requires that dimensions be cached in memory. You'll be able to build cubes with extremely large dimensions— possibly beyond 100 M members. For those who don't have extreme dimensions, the main implication of this important change is that although the server will still benefit from lots of physical memory, it should no longer fail if memory is tight.

- ◆ Proactive caching is used for BI applications with low latency. We discuss proactive caching in Chapter 17.

- ◆ The metadata repository is gone, replaced by XML data definition files.

- ◆ You can use the standard management tools to process partitions in parallel. Parallel processing occurs by default.

- ◆ Calculations are computed on the server, rather than distributed between client and server. This has the effect of reducing the performance of simple queries—probably by an amount that's not noticeable to people. On the upside, complex queries will resolve much faster because the server rather than the client is always operating on the data.

◆ You can capture the text of users' queries, which makes it much easier to understand what users are doing and to debug problematic queries.

◆ The Key Performance Indicator (KPI) framework lets you define corporate measures on the server. A KPI consists of expressions for value, goal, current status, and trend, which are displayed using simple graphics like gauges and stoplights.

◆ Analysis Services 2005 lets you present one database in multiple languages, including both metadata (the names of dimensions and levels) and data (dimension member contents and measure calculation and display).

◆ The administrative security model is richer than in Analysis Services 2000.

◆ MDX Scripts are the new mechanism for defining Calculated Members, Named Sets, and Cell Calculations. MDX Script syntax is simplified and improved, and can actually be debugged.

◆ You can write stored procedures for Analysis Services, using popular languages like VB.NET or C++. Stored procedures will perform far better than the old user-defined functions because stored procedures execute on the server.

◆ Data writeback, which was a flawed feature in Analysis Services 2000, is much better. Writeback performance has improved dramatically.

◆ There are new features for developers, like web services and the XMLA protocol. Analysis Services 2005 continues support for the old protocols and object models: OLE DB for OLAP, ADOMD, and ADOMD.NET. A new management object model, Analysis Management Objects (AMO), replaces DSO. AMO's most important new feature is the ability to script an object's creation or modification.

◆ There are new features to improve system management, like server trace events for monitoring and auditing system usage and performance. The Flight Recorder feature makes it much easier to debug problems.

Why Not Analysis Services?

We recommend that most DW/BI systems use Analysis Services as the primary query server. The relational version of the dimensional schema serves as the permanent store of the cleaned and conformed data, and feeds data to the OLAP database.

Some systems will close the relational data warehouse database to most business users. This is an appealing architecture, for in this case the relational database can be lightly indexed. The Analysis Services database, including data, indexes, and a reasonable set of pre-computed aggregations, is smaller than the relational indexes it replaces. Standard reports, KPIs, analytic reports, and ad hoc analyses can all be sourced from Analysis Services, using Reporting Services, Excel, SharePoint Portal Server, and possibly a non-Microsoft ad hoc query tool.

Other systems will permit user access to both Analysis Services and the corresponding relational database. And others don't use Analysis Services at all. What are some of the common reasons to commit less than fully to Analysis Services?

- The Analysis Services development market is immature. There is more than a 20-year history of tools, books, articles, consultants, and classes to help implement a relational DW/BI system. There are fewer tools, experts, and informational material about how to work with Analysis Services.

- The query and reporting tool market is confusing and immature. Reporting Services is the first report publishing server that can source from Analysis Services—and Reporting Services is itself a young product. On the ad hoc query and analysis side, the tools are maturing but it's still a confusing market.

- Companies have a large investment in existing client tools and developer and user skills.

- Some kinds of analysis are intrinsically difficult in OLAP. This is particularly true for analyses that align data not by dimension attributes but by an event that's buried in the facts.

NOTE Most ad hoc analyses are easier to construct with MDX and OLAP than with SQL. A counter-example from a clickstream business process is to analyze how users behave after they first visit a certain page. First you need to go into the facts to find who visited the page (and when). Then you may want to align all the users' page clicks by time to see patterns in behavior. This is moderately difficult in SQL but extremely challenging in OLAP and MDX. In truth, this kind of analysis is best handled by data mining. But sometimes we just want to poke around, and for this kind of problem we prefer SQL.

Designing the OLAP Structure

If you've followed our instructions to build a DW/BI system with surrogate keys, conformed dimensions, and well-managed dimension changes, then building an Analysis Services OLAP database is straightforward. There are several major steps:

1. Set up the design and development environment

2. Create a Data Source View

3. Create and fine-tune your dimensions

4. Run the Cube Wizard and edit the resulting cube

5. Deploy the database to your development server

6. Create calculations and other decorations

7. Iterate, iterate, iterate

Later in the chapter, we discuss physical storage issues, which are largely independent of the database's logical design.

NOTE Analysis Services contains features to help you overcome flaws in the design of the source database, like referential integrity violations, but we're not going to talk about those features. Instead, build your DW/BI system correctly, as described in this book.

Getting Started

There are several steps in the setup process. First, you need to install and configure one or more Analysis Services development servers. You need to ensure the correct software is installed on developers' desktops. You should have some clean data loaded into the data warehouse database, and you should have created a set of views on those database tables.

Setup

As the Analysis Services database developer, the only SQL Server components you must have on your desktop PC are the development tools, notably BI Studio and Management Studio. Many developers run the server components on their desktop PCs, but it's not required. You can point to a shared Analysis Services development server, just as you would share a development relational database server.

Use BI Studio to design and develop the Analysis Services database, and Management Studio to operate and maintain that database. The way the tools have been broken apart may be confusing at first: After all, there's no such distinction for the relational database. With the appropriate permissions, you can enter DDL against a production relational database from within Management Studio. We all know that's a really stupid thing to do (although how many of us do it?). The new BI tools strongly discourage it for Analysis Services. From within Management Studio you can perform only the actions necessary to maintain the database: Add partitions, process partitions, backup, and so on.

Any design change must occur within the BI Studio and be deployed into production. Deployment issues are discussed in Chapter 14. But when in doubt, remember: Use BI Development Studio for development, and use the Management Studio for management.

Analysis Services Tutorial

Work through the tutorial that ships with SQL Server 2005 before trying to design and build your first OLAP database. It's a good tutorial, and not only teaches you which buttons to push but also provides information about why. This chapter is not a replacement for the tutorial. Instead we assume you'll learn the basics from the tutorial. Here, we focus more on process and advanced design issues.

Create Relational Views

In Chapter 4, we talked about creating a database view for each table in the dimensional model. End users' and Analysis Services' access to the relational database should come through the views. The views provide a layer of insulation, and can greatly simplify the process of making future changes to the DW/BI system. Give the views and columns user-friendly names: These names become Analysis Services object names like dimensions and attributes.

> **TIP** Analysis Services does a pretty good job of turning the common styles of database object names into friendly names. It will parse CamelCase and Underscore_Case names, stripping underscores and inserting spaces as appropriate. It's not perfect; you do need to review the friendly names in the Data Source View.

The downside of using views is that you obscure any foreign key relationships defined in the data. Many tools automatically create join paths based on these relationships; these join paths must be added by hand when you use views. On the other hand, as we discuss in Chapter 4, it's common to drop the foreign key relationship between fact and dimensions anyway.

> **TIP** Creating the view layer sounds like make-work. But we've always regretted it when we've skipped this step.

Populate the Data Warehouse Database

You don't need to wait until the ETL system is finished, and the relational data warehouse fully populated with historical and incremental data, before you start working on the Analysis Services database. Technically, you don't have to populate the database at all. But that's just a theoretical point: In practice, you want to look at the data as you're designing the OLAP database.

It's helpful during the design process to work from a static copy of the warehouse database. It's much easier to design and debug the cube if the underlying data isn't changing from day to day. Most people fully populate the dimensions and several months of data in the large fact tables. Small fact tables, like the Exchange Rates fact table in the Adventure Works Cycles case study, can be fully populated.

Fully populate most of the dimensions because that's where most of the design work occurs. Dimensions are usually small enough that you can restructure and rebuild them many times, without an intolerable wait to see how the modified dimension looks. If you have a larger dimension, say 100,000 to 1 million members, you may want to work on a dimension subset for the early phases of the design cycle. Define your dimension table view with a WHERE clause so that it subsets the dimension to a reasonable size, iterate on the design until you're satisfied, and then redefine the view and rebuild the dimension at its full size. We can almost guarantee you'll still tweak the design a few more times, but you should be past the worst of the iterations.

We mentioned that most people use a few months of fact data. This works great for structural design tasks like setting the grain, dimension usage, and base measures for that fact data. But defining complex calculations is often easier to do with a longer time series. As a simple example, consider a measure that compares sales this month to the same month last year.

If you have really big dimensions and facts, you should take the time to build a physical subset of the relational database. Keep all small dimensions intact, but subset large dimensions to less than 100,000 members. Randomly choose leaf nodes rather than choose a specific branch of the dimension. In other words, if you have 5 million customers, randomly choose 100,000 of them rather than choose all of the customers from California (who may not be representative of your full customer base). Choose the subset of facts from the intersection of your dimensions. Be very careful to avoid grabbing facts for the dimension members you've excluded from the test database. In other words, load facts for the 100,000 selected customers only.

Chapter 5 describes how to build a sandbox source system for developing the ETL system. That same subset, in the relational dimensional structure, may serve you again during Analysis Services design.

TIP Yes, this is a lot of work at a time when you're anxious to get started with Analysis Services. You'll be thankful later, when you're iterating on your cube design for the hundredth time. Also, this small database may be useful again for end user training.

Create a Project and a Data Source View

Finally, you're ready to use the tools to get started on the design process. Create an Analysis Services project in BI Studio, usually within the same solution as your Integration Services and Reporting Services projects.

TIP For those of you who would like to follow along as we create the Analysis Services database, first create the relational data warehouse database. You can download this database, MDWT_AdventureWorksDW, from the book's web site, www.MsftDWToolkit.com.

By default, BI Studio points to the default instance on the local server—the developer's desktop. To specify a different Analysis Services instance or server, right-click on the project name in the Solution Explorer, and choose Properties. As illustrated in Figure 7.2, you can identify a server for development.

TIP Most DW/BI teams will use SQL Server Developer Edition, which contains all the functionality of Enterprise Edition. If you're using Standard Edition in production, change the Deployment Server Edition property of the project to Standard. That way, you'll get warnings if you attempt to use functionality that's not available in Standard Edition.

The next step in designing the Analysis Services database is to create a Data Source View (DSV) on the relational data warehouse database. We introduced DSVs in Chapter 6, where they were optional. The Analysis Services database is built from the Data Source View, so you must create a DSV before designing the database.

Right-click on Data Source Views and choose New Data Source View. The Data Source Wizard prompts you to choose or create a Data Source. If your Analysis Services project is part of the same solution with your Integration Services or Reporting Services project, you should re-use the appropriate Data Source. Shared data sources are easier to manage in production because you have to go to only one place to change the characteristics of the connection.

STARTING THE ANALYSIS SERVICES SERVER

If you're running Analysis Services on your desktop computer, you may want to have the service start manually. Write a one-line batch file to start the service:

```
net start MSSQLServerOLAPService
```

Create a shortcut to this .bat file from your desktop. Create a similar command file to stop the service (`net stop MSSQLServerOLAPService`).

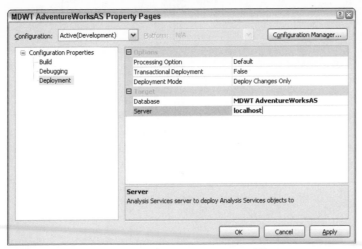

Figure 7.2   Deploy development projects to a different server

TIP There's an option on the first screen of the Data Source Wizard to create a data source based on another object. Click this radio button to pick up the data source from another project rather than creating a new one.

Choose a subset of tables or views to include in the DSV. You can always add and delete tables from a DSV after it's been built, so don't worry too much about getting the subset correct the first time through the wizard. The Select Tables and Views page of the Data Source View Wizard has a filter utility to make it easier to find the objects you want. Exclude any metadata tables, staging tables, or utility tables that you won't want in the cube you create.

Figure 7.3 illustrates the DSV for the MDWT_AdventureWorksDW database in the DSV Designer. The Properties pane for Customer is showing; notice that we've copied in the table description that we created in the Excel workbook way back in Chapter 3. Use the list of tables on the left-hand side to quickly find a table.

Edit the DSV in the BI Studio DSV Designer. Within the schema pane of the DSV Designer, you can view the tables, columns, and relationships. You can also view the tables and columns in a tree view. The Diagram Organizer pane is useful for very complex DSVs. In it you can create subdiagrams for viewing smaller sets of tables.

Add tables (or views) and relationships to the DSV. You can change object names here, although your dimensional model should have friendly names already. When you create the Analysis Services database, it will take default names from these objects in the DSV. You can also add tables from the existing data source, or from additional databases and servers including non-SQL Server sources.

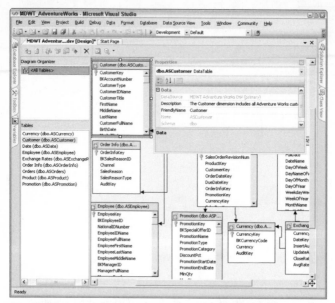

Figure 7.3 DSV for the MDWT_AdventureWorksDW database

WARNING Avoid using the DSV to cobble together an Analysis Services database from a variety of heterogeneous sources. First, unless you've scrubbed all the data, it's not going to join well at all. Second, there's a considerable performance cost to joining remotely. You're almost certainly better off cleaning and aligning the data and hosting it on a single physical server before building your cube. Yes: You're better off building a data warehouse.

However, if you're careful and judicious, you can use this distributed sources feature to solve some knotty problems. A distributed DSV uses the SQL Server engine under the covers to resolve the distributed query. At least one SQL Server data source must be defined in order to create a distributed DSV.

You must construct the relationships correctly in the DSV because these relationships help define the Analysis Services database. A relationship between a fact and dimension table should appear, as in Figure 7.4. Make sure you set the relationship in the correct direction.

The Description attribute for tables and columns in the DSV are picked up by the Cube Wizard and incorporated into the definitions of dimensions, attributes, and other cube objects. From there, most ad hoc query tools can show the descriptions to the business users. You'll run the Cube Wizard many times, so it's really nice to get the descriptions populated in the DSV. Otherwise, the descriptions will get wiped out every time you re-run the Cube Wizard.

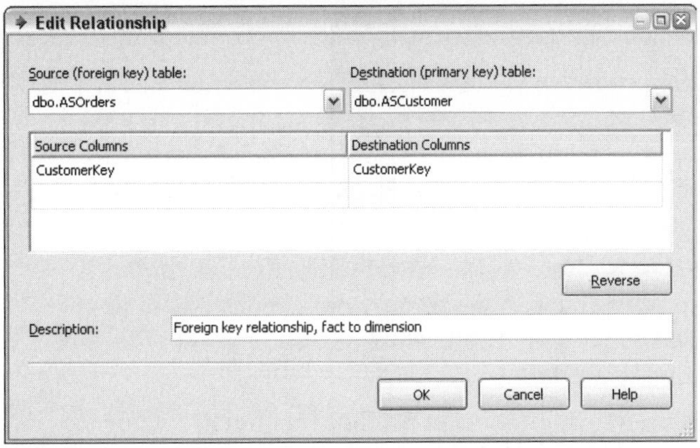

Figure 7.4   A Data Source View relationship between fact and dimension

Dimension Designs

The database that you design and build in Analysis Services will be very similar to the relational data warehouse that you've built using the Kimball Method. This section describes how Analysis Services handles dimensions in general, and how it handles several of the dimension design issues we discussed in Chapter 3.

After we've talked about how OLAP dimensions correspond to the dimension tables in your relational data warehouse, we talk about the actual process of creating and editing those dimensions.

RUNNING THE CUBE WIZARD: THE ONE-CLICK CUBE

In most materials about Analysis Services 2005, including Books Online and the tutorials, you're encouraged to start building your OLAP database by running the Cube Wizard after you've defined the DSV. The Cube Wizard reads the relationships you've defined in your Data Source View, and automatically generates the definition for the entire OLAP database, including all dimensions.

We've found that most people will take this route two or three times. It certainly makes a fun demo. But if you're trying to get work done, you'll probably find an alternative process more productive. Create dimensions one at a time, as we describe in the next section. Work on each dimension, setting its attributes and properties correctly, processing and browsing it until you like the way it looks. Move down the list of dimensions until you've defined all the dimensions associated with a fact table. Only then should you run the Cube Wizard.

ANALYSIS SERVICES DIMENSION TERMINOLOGY

The terminology around dimensions in SQL Server 2005 Analysis Services is similar to the familiar Kimball Method terminology. Here's a brief list of vital Analysis Services vocabulary having to do with dimensions. These concepts are discussed in more detail later in this chapter. This sidebar introduces them so you can understand the vocabulary.

- ◆ *Dimension:* The concept is effectively identical to the Kimball Method usage of the term. In normal use, Analysis Services dimensions correspond exactly to a relational dimension. Some decorations are different, but the core concepts are the same.

- ◆ *Attribute:* An Analysis Services dimension attribute is directly analogous to a Kimball Method dimension attribute.

- ◆ *Dimension hierarchy:* A common drilldown path in the dimension, predefined by the system developer for the benefit of users.

  - ■ *Natural hierarchy:* A drilldown path with referential integrity between attributes at different levels, like Year to Month to Day.

  - ■ *Navigation hierarchy:* A drilldown path between unrelated attributes, like Gender to Age. This is sometimes called a *reporting hierarchy*.

    You won't find the terms "natural hierarchy" or "navigation hierarchy" in Books Online. But the distinction is very important for query performance, as we'll discuss in this chapter.

- ◆ *Attribute hierarchy:* Each dimension attribute is exposed as a single-level attribute hierarchy. You optionally define one or more multi-level dimension hierarchies from those attributes.

- ◆ *Attribute relationship:* An attribute relationship is, effectively, a declaration of referential integrity between two attributes. All attributes have an attribute relationship to the key of a dimension. You can and should define other attribute relationships.

- ◆ *Member:* A member is an item in a dimension level or attribute hierarchy. Examples are January 2006 in the Month level of the Date dimension, or Rural Cycle Emporium in the Customer level of the Customer dimension. A member is analogous to a row in the dimension table.

  - ■ *Leaf member:* A leaf is a member at the finest grain of the hierarchy, like a date, customer, or employee.

  - ■ *All member:* A member, usually defined only in Analysis Services, that represents the aggregation of all the leaf members: All customers, All products, and so on. The All member is optional.

  - ■ *Default member:* The member that's included by default if a query does not reference the dimension. By default, the Default member is set equal to the All member—and behaves exactly as the relational database would if you exclude a dimension from the query.

◆ *Many-to-many dimension:* What the Kimball Method calls a multivalued dimension. A standard dimension has a one-to-many relationship between a dimension key and the fact table. A multivalued dimension has a many-to-many relationship. Common examples are patient hospital visits and diagnoses (one patient visit can have multiple diagnoses), and purchase reasons (a customer could have multiple reasons for purchasing your product). Multivalued or many-to-many dimensions are directly (and rather elegantly) supported in Analysis Services 2005.

◆ *Parent-child hierarchy:* What the Kimball Method calls a variable depth hierarchy. A variable depth hierarchy is characterized by a self referencing join. Canonical examples are an organizational hierarchy (employee to manager) or a bill of materials.

◆ *Reference dimension:* The Kimball Method doesn't have a name for this concept. A reference dimension is a dimension that's referenced by others. For example, many dimensions like Customer, Vendor, and Shipping Destination could all use the same Geography table. All you need is to put the Geography surrogate key into those primary dimensions. We haven't found reference dimensions to be particularly useful, and we don't discuss them in this chapter.

◆ *Fact dimension:* A fact dimension is what the Kimball Method calls a degenerate dimension. It's a dimension that's populated from the fact table. The common example is a Purchase Order and Line Item Number from a sales transaction fact table. We don't expect users to slice and dice by PO numbers, but it's often very convenient to have them available in both the relational data warehouse and the cube. However, we almost never build a separate relational dimension table from this kind of entity. Any interesting attributes of the purchase order have been pulled out into one or more dimension tables. This entity is halfway between fact and dimension, so we call it a degenerate dimension. There are several ways to support degenerate dimensions in Analysis Services.

Standard Dimensions

A standard dimension contains a surrogate key, one or more attributes and attribute hierarchies, and sometimes zero or more multi-level hierarchies. Analysis Services can build dimensions from dimension tables that:

- Are denormalized into a star structure, as the Kimball Method recommends

- Are normalized into a snowflake structure, with separate tables for each hierarchical level

- Include a mixture of normalized and denormalized structures

- Include a parent-child hierarchy
- Have all Type 1 (update history) attributes, Type 2 (track history) attributes, or a combination

Even though Analysis Services doesn't require a surrogate key, recall that surrogate keys are a cornerstone of the Kimball Method; build a permanent, enterprise Analysis Services database only from a dimensional relational source with surrogate keys.

TIP Analysis Services 2005 has built in many features to help you live without surrogate keys. For example, you can set up the database so that it automatically finds and "fixes" referential integrity violations. In our view, this activity should be done during the ETL process. Build Analysis Services databases from clean, dimensional data in the relational database.

Your business users will tell you whether dimension attributes should be tracked as Type 1 or Type 2. We've found that most dimension attributes are tracked as Type 2. In Chapter 6 we talked extensively about how to set up your ETL process to manage the propagation and assignment of surrogate keys for Type 2 dimension attributes. Although Type 2 dimensions seem harder to manage in the ETL system, the payoff comes with your Analysis Services database. Analysis Services handles Type 2 attribute changes gracefully. The larger your data volumes, the more you should be relying on Type 2 changes, where they make sense for the business user.

Type 1 attributes can cause some problems for OLAP databases for the same reason they're troubling in the relational world: pre-computed aggregations. When a dimension attribute is updated in place, any aggregations built on that attribute are invalidated. If you were managing aggregations in the relational database, you'd have to write logic to fix the historical summary table when an attribute changes. Analysis Services faces the same problem. You don't have to do anything to fix up the historical attributes—Analysis Services does that for you. But this is an expensive operation. If you have a lot of Type 1 changes in a very large database, you're going to be unpleasantly surprised by the incremental processing performance. Later in this chapter we talk about some choices you can make in your design to minimize the cost of managing Type 1 dimension changes.

Variable Depth or Parent-Child Hierarchies

Variable depth or parent-child hierarchies are a useful way of expressing organization hierarchies and bill of materials explosions. However, as we discussed in Chapter 6, these dimension structures are difficult to maintain in the relational data warehouse. This is especially true if the dimension has Type 2 attributes.

If you can maintain your parent-child hierarchy in the relational database, either as a Type 1 or Type 2 dimension, then Analysis Services can consume it. It's straightforward to set up a Parent-Child dimension in Analysis Services. It's straightforward to query that dimension—far more so in Analysis Services, by the way, than using standard SQL.

TIP Parent-child hierarchies are a valuable feature in Analysis Services. However, it's not a trivial exercise to get them to perform well in a very large database, or with many members in the Parent-Child dimension. If your system is large, you may want to bring in an expert, or launch Phase 1 using a standard dimension. Add the parent-child relationship when your team has developed more expertise.

When you build a parent-child hierarchy in Analysis Services, you don't need a bridge table. You may have built a bridge table to facilitate relational queries, as described in Chapter 3. If so, you should eliminate that bridge table from the DSV for the Analysis Services database.

Multivalued or Many-to-Many Dimensions

The relational design for a multivalued dimension includes a bridge table between the fact and dimension tables. This bridge table identifies a group of dimension values that occur together. The example in the Adventure Works Cycles case study is the sales reason. Adventure Works Cycles collects multiple possible reasons for a customer purchasing our product, so each sale is associated with potentially many reasons. The bridge table lets you keep one row in the fact table for each sale, and relates that fact event to the multiple reasons.

This same structure serves to populate the Analysis Services database. The only nuance is that the bridge table is used as both a dimension table and a fact table, or as just a fact table, within Analysis Services. This seems odd at first, but it really is correct. The fact the bridge table tracks is the relationship between sales and sales reasons—you could think of it as the Reasons Selected fact table.

Keep the bridge table from your relational data warehouse in your DSV. The designer wizards correctly identify the structure as a multivalued dimension, which Analysis Services calls a many-to-many dimension.

Creating and Editing Dimensions

Create dimensions one by one, by right-clicking on the Dimensions node in the Solution Explorer window and choosing New Dimension to launch the Dimension Wizard.

In the first screen of the Dimension Wizard, change the selection from the default choice of Create attributes and hierarchies. Instead, choose Create attributes only, as illustrated in Figure 7.5. We've never kept the hierarchies that the wizard recommends.

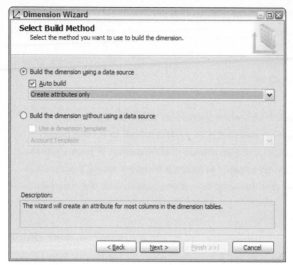

Figure 7.5 The Dimension Wizard: Select Build Method

BUILD THE DIMENSION WITHOUT USING A DATA SOURCE

You may be perplexed by the second major option: building a dimension without a data source. The Kimball Method, as you know from reading this book, moves the development project through a structured sequence, from requirements gathering to design, creating and populating the relational database, and then here to building the Analysis Services database. This option in the Dimension Wizard turns that sequence on its head, effectively jumping directly from the business requirements to the cube and dimension design. From there you create the relational data warehouse by auto-generating tables that exactly support the Analysis Services database design.

This is a good idea, as it keeps the designer's focus on the business requirements rather than the existing data. However, it removes you too far from the data realities. When you go back to populate the relational data warehouse from the source systems, and browse the cube with data in it, you'll probably find that you'd prefer to restart the cube design from scratch.

This alternative path through the Dimension Wizard (and a similar path through the Cube Wizard) will have significant value in the future, assuming Microsoft develops a market in predefined BI templates. Several generic templates are shipped with Analysis Services, but the real value will come from a template closely targeted to a specific industry's business intelligence requirements and metrics. Even a very small consulting company, with expertise in a specific area, can build a template that will give you a huge head start for developing a shrink-wrapped or custom business intelligence application.

In the absence of good templates, this path through the wizard is most useful for prototyping, and as a learning aid. Consultants may use this feature for quickly building a proof of concept.

CONFORMED DIMENSIONS

People new to Analysis Services are often confused by the admittedly subtle distinction between a cube dimension and a database dimension. Dimensions are defined at the database level and shared across multiple fact tables. In the Dimension Designer, you're editing database dimensions.

Later, you'll build a cube and associate dimensions with that cube. There are a handful of dimension properties that apply to the dimension in the cube. We won't discuss these properties until later in the chapter, when we're discussing cubes. But keep this distinction between database dimensions and cube dimensions in the back of your mind.

After you choose the build method, the Dimension Wizard asks you to identify the main table for the dimension. On the bottom of this same screen of the wizard, you can identify a column to use as the member name. Usually you choose the business key here because users never want to see the data warehouse surrogate key. After this point, unless you have one of the unusual types of dimensions described in the previous section, you can usually accept all the defaults. Name the dimension, and click Finish.

BI Studio generates the metadata for the dimension and leaves you looking at the basic dimension structure in the Dimension Designer. Next, you need to edit your dimensions in the Dimension Designer, getting each dimension the way you like it before moving on to the next one. At this point in the process, you have only metadata—the definition of the dimension. Later we describe how you build, deploy, and process the dimension so you can actually look at the dimension's data.

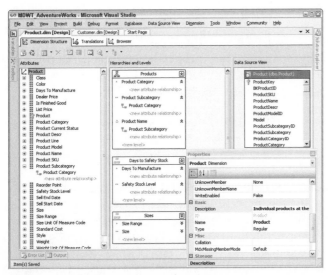

Figure 7.6   The Dimension Designer

Figure 7.6 shows the final version of the Product dimension. In the rightmost pane of the Dimension Designer is a representation of the tables or views that underlie the dimension. This pane is linked to the Data Source View; if you try to edit the entities in this pane, you're flipped over to the DSV Editor. When you edit the DSV and return to the Dimension Designer, the changes follow.

The left-hand pane of the Dimension Designer is the Attributes pane, and shows the list of attributes within the dimension. Within the Attributes pane, you can rename and delete attributes, and change the properties of those attributes. To create a new attribute, drag a column from the data source in the DSV. You may need to create a calculated column in the DSV.

In the central pane of Figure 7.6 is the view of Hierarchies and Levels. Create a new hierarchy by dragging an attribute into the background area. Add levels to hierarchies by dragging and dropping.

The final pane in Figure 7.6 is the Properties pane, which is sometimes docked below the Solution Explorer. We set it to float in order to maximize screen real estate. Some of these properties are very important; others you might never change.

Figure 7.6 includes the properties of the Product dimension. If the Properties pane isn't showing, you can launch it by right-clicking on the Product dimension in the Attributes pane. In Figure 7.6 you can see that the Product dimension is highlighted, and the Properties pane title clarifies that you're looking at the dimension's properties. All the objects in the dimension—each attribute, hierarchy, and level—also have properties.

When you're editing a new dimension, take the following steps:

- Edit the names of the dimension and each attribute within the dimension.
- Edit the properties of the dimension.
- Edit the properties of each attribute.
- Create attribute relationships and edit their properties.
- Create hierarchies. Edit the hierarchies' properties and the properties of each level.
- If necessary, define dimension translations.
- Build, deploy, and process the dimension so you can look at the dimension's data.
- Iterate, iterate, iterate.

The order of these steps isn't very important, but it helps to have a checklist. As you can see by reviewing the preceding list, the process of editing the dimension is largely a process of editing object properties. There are only a few other tasks, like creating attribute relationships and creating hierarchies.

In the next few sections, we'll run through the properties of dimensions, attributes, hierarchies, and levels. We'll talk only about the most important properties that you can change; see Books Online for the details. In all cases, the Properties pane shows the properties for the highlighted item. Properties that you've changed from the default values are highlighted in boldface.

Editing Dimension Properties

A dimension has several editable properties. The most important are:

- *Name:* The name shows up in the user interface, so keep it short yet descriptive.

- *Description:* Most query tools for Analysis Services have a way of showing the description to the user, usually as a tool tip. As discussed previously, populate the Description metadata from the information you collected during your requirements gathering process.

- *Type:* Type is a frustratingly vague name for a property, but it's hard to think of a better name. Type is a classification of the dimension that's used by Analysis Services only in a few special cases (Time and Account). Most of the time, if you set the dimension type to anything other than Time or Account, nothing happens. Set your Date dimension's Type to Time, so Analysis Services knows to use the dimension in time-related calculations.

> **TIP** If you're a software developer building a packaged application on Analysis Services, you can use the dimension Type property to identify dimensions that are important to your application. The user can name the dimension whatever they want.

- *AttributeAllMemberName:* This label will show up to users when they start drilling down in the dimension and are looking at the All member of the dimension. By default, this property is blank, but that doesn't mean the All member's name is blank. Instead, the default All member name is All (on English language systems).

- *ErrorConfiguration:* Analysis Services provides a lot of different options for handling problems with the dimension data, like duplicate keys and referential integrity violations. You can see the options if you set ErrorConfiguration to (custom). If you're sourcing your dimension from a solid Kimball Method dimension table, as we've described in great detail in this book, you shouldn't have to worry about this property. You shouldn't have bad dimension data; shame on you if you do.

TIP Though you shouldn't have duplicate surrogate keys—or bad data anywhere in your dimension—it's not unheard of between levels of a dimension hierarchy. For example, Postal Code should roll up to State, but in the source data there may be a handful of violations. If your ETL process doesn't catch and fix these violations, it should be modified to do so. If you change the ErrorConfiguration from its default to custom, and change the KeyDuplicate property from IgnoreError to ReportAndContinue or ReportAndStop, you'll enlist Analysis Services' help in figuring out where your data problems are. We usually turn on at least this level of error checking on dimensions.

- *ProcessingMode:* Sometimes, all of the aggregations associated with a dimension need to be recalculated. With this property, you can specify how quickly after an update the new cube data is available for users to query. We discuss this issue later in this chapter, in the section on Planning for Updates to Dimensions.

- *ProactiveCaching:* This property is useful for low latency population of the dimension. We discuss proactive caching in Chapter 17.

- *StorageMode:* Dimensions can be stored in Analysis Services format (MOLAP), or in the relational database (ROLAP). The vast majority of Analysis Services implementations should use MOLAP for all dimensions.

REFERENCE See the Books Online topic "Dimension Properties (SSAS)" for a complete list and extremely brief description of all the dimension properties.

Editing Attribute Properties

As with the dimension properties, most of the important properties of an attribute are set correctly by the Dimension Wizard. A few useful properties aren't set by the wizards. And if you add attributes within the Dimension Designer, you need to be aware of how to set these important attributes correctly.

- *Name, Description,* and *Type:* Ensure these properties are set correctly, as we discussed above for the dimension.

- *Usage:* This property is usually set correctly by the Dimension Wizard. One attribute for the dimension can and should have its usage set as Key. This is, obviously, the surrogate key for the dimension. Almost always, the other attributes are correctly set as Regular. The two exceptions are:

- The parent key for a Parent-Child dimension (set to Parent)
- A column in a Chart of Accounts dimension that defines the account type (set to AccountType)

- *Source KeyColumns:* By default, the KeyColumns property is correctly set to the appropriate column in the relational dimension table. The KeyColumns can be made up of more than one column, but in a Kimball Method system they always use the single-column surrogate key.

- *NameColumn:* You have an opportunity to set the NameColumn for the Key attribute in the Dimension Wizard. If you forgot to set it there, set it here. Users don't ever want to see the surrogate key; worst case, show them the business key. NameColumn is usually blank, unless you set it in the Dimension Wizard. Sometimes you set the NameColumn for other attributes of a dimension, especially levels that you will make into a natural hierarchy.

- *OrderBy* and *OrderByAttribute:* You can easily set an attribute to be ordered by either its key or its name. For example, we usually want to sort months not alphabetically (by month name), but by the month number. Occasionally, you want to sort one attribute not by its key or name, but by some other attribute in the dimension. To do this, you need to make the other attribute a Related Attribute of the first attribute, as we describe in the next section. Then you can set the sort order to that attribute. Alternatively, you could set AttributeHierarchyOrdered to False, in which case there'd be no sort order at all.

- *IsAggregatable:* This property of an attribute specifies whether the attribute can be aggregated. It should almost always be set to the default value of True. If you set this property to False, the attribute hierarchy will not contain an All level.

- *AttributeHierarchyDisplayFolder:* You can add a lot of value to your Analysis Services database by adding display folders for the Attribute Hierarchies. If you have more than 10 to 12 attributes in your dimension, you should create multiple display folders and assign attributes to them. Creating a display folder is as simple as typing a name into the attribute's AttributeHierarchyDisplayFolder property.

- *AttributeHierarchyVisible:* You can also prevent a specific attribute from appearing in the list of Attribute Hierarchies, by changing AttributeHierarchyVisible to False. Hiding the attribute hierarchy doesn't prevent you from exposing the attribute in a multi-level hierarchy. In fact, it's common to hide the attribute hierarchy for attributes that are available through multi-level hierarchies, especially if the dimension has a lot of attributes.

ATTRIBUTE HIERARCHIES

Earlier in this chapter we noted that one of the biggest changes with Analysis Services 2005 is that dimensions are attribute-based rather than hierarchy-based. This is mostly a good thing because most dimension attributes, like Color, Size, and Cost, are not hierarchical.

With Analysis Services 2005, an Attribute Hierarchy is created by default for each attribute. Attribute Hierarchy isn't a great name for this object because it's a flat hierarchy that consists only of the attribute and its All member. However, Attribute Hierarchies behave like, and show up in lists with, the multi-level hierarchies that you create for your users to navigate the dimension.

This improvement to Analysis Services, like most improvements, comes with a cost. The cost is reduced simplicity, both to the end user and to the developer. The end user now has to navigate many attributes rather than a few simple hierarchies. And the developer has to do whatever she can—like create Display Folders—to simplify the users' view of what is, at its heart, a more flexible, and therefore more complicated database.

TIP The usefulness of the Display Folder depends on the client tool you're using to access the Analysis Services database. As we discuss in Chapter 13, the Display Folder shows up in a Report Builder Report Model that you build atop the Analysis Services database. In this case, using Display Folders substantially improves the user experience.

- *DefaultMember:* Each Attribute Hierarchy has a default member. Unless you change it here, the default member is the "All member" for the dimension. This leads to the behavior you'd expect: If you're not including an attribute in your query, you get all members just as a relational query would do. Occasionally, you might want to set the default member to something else. For example, in a Date dimension, you could set the default member for Year to the current year. You can even enter an MDX expression for the default member, if you really want to get fancy. But be warned; you may end up confusing your users more than helping them.

- *Parent-child properties:* If the dimension has a parent-child hierarchy, you need to set up several properties. The most important one is the identification of the parent-child relationship. Just as one attribute in all dimensions is the key, in a Parent-Child dimension one attribute is identified as the Parent (set the Usage property to Parent for that attribute). The Dimension Wizard usually sets these properties correctly. You can look at the Employee dimension of the AdventureWorksAS sample database shipped with SQL Server for an example of a parent-child hierarchy. Other, less important, parent-child properties include:

- *RootMemberIf:* How do you identify a member that's at the top of the tree? This would be the CEO in an employee hierarchy. There are several options, all self-explanatory.

- *NamingTemplate:* How do you know what level of a parent-child hierarchy you're on? Many parent-child hierarchies don't have meaningful levels, but some do—employee organization is again a good example. For example, the top levels could be called Executive, VP, Senior Management, and then the remaining levels just called Level4, Level5, and so on. Use the NamingTemplate property to name these levels.

REFERENCE See the Books Online topic "Attribute Properties (SSAS)" for a complete list of attribute properties, and a terse description of each property. There are many more attribute properties than we've listed here.

Related Attributes

Related Attributes is one of the most important characteristics of dimensions that you'll need to edit. Related Attributes is the mechanism for declaring referential integrity between different attributes in a dimension. The declaration of attribute relationships is very important in the design of pre-computed aggregations and the Analysis Services indexes that are vital to query performance.

The only places to see this relationship in BI Studio are buried in the Attributes pane and Hierarchy pane of the Dimension Designer. Click on the plus sign next to an attribute to see its Related Attributes. (Don't ask the authors' opinion of a user interface that hides such an important property!) When you create a dimension, the wizards automatically add all the dimension's attributes as Related Attributes of the key. This makes perfect sense: The key is unique, and all other attributes must by definition have a many-to-one relationship to it. Thus, all other attributes are Related Attributes of the key. The wizards also do a good job with snowflake dimension levels and the Date or Time dimension.

Create an attribute relationship by dragging an attribute from either the Attributes pane or the Hierarchy pane and dropping it under the attribute with which it has a one-to-many relationship. You can see some attribute relationships in Figure 7.6.

You should define Related Attributes between levels of a natural hierarchy. A great example that everyone understands is the Date dimension. All attributes are Related Attributes of the day, which is the grain of the Date dimension. Month is a Related Attribute of Day: Each day belongs to one and only one month. But Month is not a Related Attribute of Week: Each week may span multiple months. Quarter is a Related Attribute of Day and Month. Year is a Related Attribute of Day, Month, and Quarter.

CAUTION Indirect attribute relationships are preferred to direct attribute relationships. When you define an attribute relationship between two attributes, remove the relationship with the key, or any other attribute. In other words, when you make Year a related attribute of Month, you should remove it as a related attribute to Day. Month is still a related attribute of the key Day, and Year picks up that indirect relationship.

Let's suppose you just remembered that Quarter belongs between Month and Year. You add Year as a related attribute of Quarter, and Quarter as a related attribute of Month. As before, remove Quarter as a related attribute of Day. But also remove Year as a related attribute of Month.

This is really important for query performance. It's not even remotely obvious, nor is it well documented in Books Online.

The other important thing to remember about Related Attributes is that member keys must be unique, and defined to be unique. Returning to our Date dimension example, you would not want the Month attribute key to be January, February, and so on because these values are repeated each year. Even though they're unique within the context of a hierarchy—there's only one January each year—they are not unique across the level. Instead, in this case, the correct key for the Month attribute is something that includes the year, like 200503.

TIP Add only the relationships that are truly many-to-one. Analysis Services sees an error if you define the relationship but the data violates that relationship. Unfortunately, Analysis Services by default will ignore that error. Sigh. A few pages back, in the section on Dimension Properties, we talked about changing the ErrorConfiguration setting. It's for exactly this reason that we like to change the dimension's KeyDuplicate error handling to ReportAndContinue or ReportAndStop.

By declaring Related Attributes correctly, you're informing Analysis Services that it can index and aggregate the data and rely on that relationship. Query performance will improve relative to a dimension whose Related Attributes are not set correctly. For medium and large data volumes, especially with very large dimensions, query performance improves substantially, largely because of improved design of aggregations that are based on the Related Attributes.

There's a second reason for declaring Related Attributes correctly. This reason has to do with multiple fact tables at different levels of granularity: for example, quota data at a monthly level. In order to correctly define an Analysis Services database with data at different grains, the Related Attributes must be set properly. We talk about this issue again in the next section on hierarchies.

WARNING Unless your OLAP database is tiny, it's extremely important to set attribute relationships correctly.

There is one vital property associated with a Related Attribute: RelationshipType, which can be Rigid or Flexible. RelationshipType is where Analysis Services manages Type 1 and Type 2 dimension changes. Rigid means the relationship is fixed over time: The Related Attribute is managed as a Type 2 slowly changing attribute. Flexible means the relationship can change over time: The Related Attribute can be updated in place. As you might expect, Flexible is the default, and this setting works well and is easy to manage for small- to medium-sized cubes. The appropriate setting for this property is a business decision, but the choice has implications for cube load times. We talk about this issue later in the chapter, in the section on incremental cube processing.

If your cube is built on hundreds of gigabytes or terabytes of data, you need to pay careful attention to the settings for RelationshipType, and the aggregations that are built on attributes with flexible relationships. The issue, as we discuss later in the chapter, is about whether aggregations are dropped during incremental processing. Aggregations build really quickly, so this isn't a big deal for small cubes. But it's an important tuning consideration for large cubes.

REFERENCE See the Books Online topic "Attribute Relationships (SSAS)" for a description of attribute relationships.

See the Books Online topic "Attribute Relationship Properties (SSAS)" for a complete list of the properties of attribute relationships.

Check the Microsoft Project Real web site at www.microsoft.com/sql/bi/ ProjectREAL for information about performance tuning Analysis Services databases.

Creating Hierarchies and Editing Hierarchy Properties

Creating hierarchies is incredibly easy. Just drag and drop attributes from the Attribute pane to the Hierarchies pane. You can create as many hierarchies as you want, or none at all.

As we mentioned previously in this chapter, multi-level hierarchies can be natural like Year, Month, Day. But a hierarchy doesn't have to be natural. You can create a hierarchy just for navigational or reporting purposes. In Figure 7.6 you can see a navigational hierarchy of Days to Manufacture and Safety Stock Level. There's no relationship between the two attributes in this navigational hierarchy.

We've just finished discussing attribute relationships without discussing hierarchies at length. But it should be clear that a natural hierarchy is one in which you can—and should—define attribute relationships between levels.

Hierarchies have few interesting properties:

- *Name* and *Description:* Ensure these properties are set correctly, as we discussed earlier for the dimension.

- *AllMemberName:* The name of the All member of the hierarchy. This property of the hierarchy is very much like the AttributeAllMemberName property of the dimension. All attribute hierarchies of a dimension share the same All Member name. User-defined hierarchies can have unique All Member names.

- *DisplayFolder:* Usually we want the hierarchy to show up in the top level when the user is browsing the dimension, so we leave DisplayFolder blank. If you have a really complicated dimension, it may make sense to put hierarchies into a display folder, as discussed earlier for attributes.

- *Display order for hierarchies:* A subtlety of the Dimension Designer interface is that the order in which the hierarchies are displayed in the hierarchy pane is the same order in which they'll appear in most query tools' user interfaces. You can drag and drop the hierarchies to re-order them. This isn't an official property that you can edit, except by re-ordering the hierarchies.

Levels are constructed from attributes. Most of the interesting properties are associated with the underlying attribute, and you hardly ever have to change the properties of levels.

- *Name* and *Description:* Ensure these properties are set correctly, as we discussed earlier for the dimension.

- *HideMemberIf:* Usually, you want this property set to its default value of Never. You might want to hide a member if you have an unbalanced hierarchy that doesn't have members at all levels. The easiest example of an unbalanced hierarchy is a worldwide geography hierarchy. Small countries like Luxembourg don't have states, so you'd usually just carry the country name down to the state level. In this case, you may choose to set HideMemberIf to ParentName or OnlyChildWithParentName. Be warned: Not all client query tools respect the HideMemberIf setting.

REFERENCE See the Books Online topic "Multilevel Hierarchy Properties (SSAS)" for a complete list of the properties of a multilevel hierarchy.

See the Books Online topic "Level Properties (SSAS)" for a complete list of the properties of hierarchy levels.

Translations

Looking back to Figure 7.6, notice that there are three tabs at the top of the Dimension Designer. We've been working in the Dimension Structure tab; the other two are Translations and Browser.

Translations are a very nice feature of Analysis Services 2005 Enterprise Edition. If your company is multinational, business users will probably prefer to view the cube in their native languages. A fully translated cube will have translations for its metadata (names of dimensions, attributes, hierarchies, and levels) as well as the dimension data itself (member names and attribute values). In other words, the dimension name Date needs to be translated, the attribute name Month, and the attribute values January, February, and so on.

The Translations tab is where you do this translation. You can add a new language by right-clicking in the window and choosing New Translation. Then you can type in the translations for the metadata.

If you want to translate the attribute values, your relational dimension table or view needs to have additional columns for the new languages. Typically, you remove these columns from the list of attributes in the Dimension Structure tab. The translations are populated from the source table rather than from attributes in the dimension.

The AdventureWorksAS database that ships with SQL Server has a good example of translations in the product dimension. Here, they've chosen to translate only a few columns (Name, Category, and Subcategory); you can translate as many as you wish.

Browsing Dimension Data

The third tab across the top of the Dimension Designer is labeled Browser. This is where you can look at the dimension's data and hierarchies, as illustrated in Figure 7.7.

Before you browse the dimension's data, you need to process the dimension. Up to now we've been dealing at the logical level, refining the dimension's structure without reference to its data.

Later in this chapter we talk more about building and deploying the Analysis Services database. But for the purposes of looking at a dimension whose attributes you've been editing, it's sufficient to know that you don't need to build, deploy, and process the entire database in order to look at the dimension. You can right-click on the dimension in the Solution Explorer, and choose to build and deploy the changes to the project, then process the changed dimension.

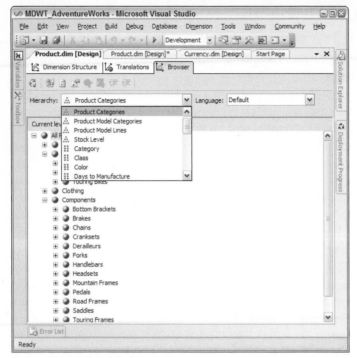

Figure 7.7   Browsing dimension data

Take time to look at the dimension in the browser. Look at the different hierarchies, available from the dropdown list as highlighted in Figure 7.7. If you've defined translations, you can view them here. Drill around the different levels and attributes in the dimension to ensure everything looks the way you want it to. It's a good bet that you'll need to adjust something. On the first time through, you're fairly likely to have to go back to your ETL team and talk about improving the cleaning of the dimension's data. You should get detailed feedback from a representative of the business user community before you decide that a dimension is correctly defined.

> **TIP**   It's hard to overemphasize the importance of ensuring that the dimension's data and structure are clean and make sense to the business users. The dimension attributes are used for drilling down in queries; they also show up as report column and row headers. Spend time now to get them right, or you'll be stuck with ugliness and confusion for years to come.

Keep working on your dimensions, hierarchies, and dimension data until you're pleased with them. Be sure to at least define the key level of each dimension correctly, before moving on to the Cube Designer.

Creating and Editing the Cube

After you've created and perfected your dimensions, it's time to run the Cube Wizard to create the cube structure. The Cube Wizard looks a lot like the Dimension Wizard.

The Auto-Build feature of the Cube Wizard does an excellent job of reading the DSV and determining which tables are dimensions, which are fact tables, and which are bridge tables for many-to-many dimensions. You can examine the wizard page titled Identify Fact and Dimension Tables, but we've almost never found a mistaken identification. On the wizard page titled Review Shared Dimensions, specify that you want to use the existing dimensions, rather than have the Cube Wizard design new dimensions for you.

The next page of the wizard, Select Measures, offers an opportunity to review and rename the measures that will be created. You can edit and deselect measures here, or wait and do it in the Cube Designer. If the wizard finds dimensions in the DSV that you haven't already created, it will list them and provide an opportunity to rename them on the Review New Dimensions page. When you finish with the Cube Wizard, you're dropped into the Cube Designer interface, illustrated in Figure 7.8. Anything you did in the Cube Wizard, you can do in the Cube Designer. You can—and will!—modify the objects that were created by the Cube Wizard. Use the Cube Designer to improve the cube, add new dimensions to a measure group, and add new measure groups.

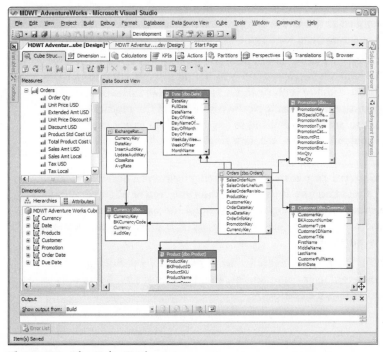

Figure 7.8   The Cube Designer

ANALYSIS SERVICES CUBE TERMINOLOGY

Earlier in this chapter we saw that Analysis Services' terminology about dimensions is pretty similar to the Kimball Method terminology. The terminology around facts is quite different, although the concepts are roughly analogous. Here is a brief list of vital Analysis Services vocabulary having to do with facts and schemas:

◆ *Measure:* An Analysis Services measure is what the Kimball Method calls a fact.

  ■ *Physical measures* are defined from a column in the relational fact table view. Because you're sourcing from a view, you can create simple calculations in the view definition.

  ■ *Calculated measures* are defined using Multidimensional Expressions (MDX). We discuss this topic in much greater detail later in the chapter.

  ■ An *aggregate function* is associated with each measure. The default is to sum measures, but you can count, min, max, count distinct, or summarize by account. Some of the more complex aggregate functions, like by account, are available only in Enterprise Edition.

◆ *Measure group:* A measure group is directly analogous to a Kimball Method fact table. A measure group contains data at a grain specified by its dimensionality. If you have a relational fact table, you should expect to have a corresponding measure group.

◆ *Cube:* An Analysis Services cube is roughly analogous to a set of Kimball Method business process dimensional models. You could define a cube that encompasses the entire enterprise dimensional model, although that may be impractical for large and complex organizations.

  This definition of a cube differs from Analysis Services 2000. The best practice in Analysis Services 2005 is to define a single cube for a database. To those familiar with Analysis Services 2000, this would be like defining a virtual cube that logically combines all the physical cubes in a database. You are still permitted to create multiple cubes in a database, but you shouldn't. Instead, create a single cube with multiple measure groups.

◆ *Analysis Services database:* As discussed, an Analysis Services 2005 database should be one-for-one with the cube. You're allowed to create multiple cubes within a single database, but the best practice is to create a database with a single cube. If you follow this practice, database and cube are synonymous.

◆ *Perspective:* Simplify the overall view of the cube by defining perspectives for different user communities. Perspectives are available only in SQL Server Enterprise Edition.

◆ *Cells:* A cell is a location in the cube.

- A leaf cell is analogous to a row in a fact table—although more accurately it's a column in a row.

- A non-leaf cell is a location that corresponds to a summarized value, like Total Sales in November 2005 for Brand X. A cell is, effectively, the address of a number that you could bring back in a query. A cell represents a single coordinate from each dimension hierarchy, including the Measures dimension.

- A cell's contents can be calculated, as we discuss later in this chapter.

- A cell can be empty. An empty cell takes up no space in an Analysis Services cube.

◆ *Measure dimension:* Analysis Services automatically creates a dimension called Measures where it stores all the fact-related attributes (called measures in Analysis Services). Users can locate measures by navigating to the Measures dimension.

There's a lot going on in the Cube Designer, but it's organized logically. Note the tabs going across the top of the window of Figure 7.8, titled Cube Structure, Dimension Usage, and so on. We'll examine these tabs in greater depth, but first we'll quickly describe what each is for.

- *Cube Structure:* Use this view to examine the physical layout of the cube's sources. This is the active pane in Figure 7.8.

- *Dimension Usage:* Use this view to refine the dimensionality of each measure group.

- *Calculations*: Use this view to define, edit, and debug calculations for the cube.

- *KPIs*: Use this view to create and edit the Key Performance Indicators (KPIs) in a cube.

- *Actions:* Use this view to create and edit drillthrough and other actions for the cube. Actions are a powerful mechanism for building an actionable business intelligence application that does more than just view data.

- *Partitions:* Use this view to create and edit the partitions for a cube. Partitions are the unit of storage for cube data. You can specify different storage locations, storage modes, and refresh frequencies for different cube partitions. You can define different pre-computed aggregations for different partitions. Once a cube has been moved into production, you no longer edit partitions here. Instead, you manage partitions either from the Management Studio or your Integration Services packages.

- *Perspectives:* Use this view to create and edit the perspectives in a cube, to provide a simplified logical view of the cube for a set of business users.

- *Translations:* Use this view to create and edit the translated names for objects in a cube, like measure groups, measures, and calculations.

- *Browser:* Use this view to look at the data in the cube, once the cube has been deployed and processed.

Edit the Cube Structure

Figure 7.8 illustrates the Cube Structure tab of the Cube Designer. In the center pane is a representation of the Data Source View of the relational tables or views on which the cube is built. This is similar to the source data pane in the Dimension Designer, but a lot more complicated because it includes all the tables used in the cube. As with the Dimension Designer, if you want to edit the Data Source View you're flipped into the DSV Editor. Changes in the underlying DSV are reflected here immediately. In this view, fact tables are coded in yellow and dimensions in blue.

As with dimensions, the main activity in editing the cube structure consists of editing the properties of objects. In the case of the cube, edit the properties of measure groups, measures, and cube dimensions.

Edit Measure Groups and Measures

The small pane in the top left is where the cube's measure groups are listed. Open a measure group to see its measures. The most important properties for a measure group are:

- *Name* and *Description:* Ensure these are set correctly. Most Analysis Services client query tools reveal the Description as a tooltip.

- *StorageMode* and *ProactiveCaching:* Usually during development, these are set to MOLAP and Off respectively. We talk about these properties later in this chapter, when we discuss physical design considerations. Early in the development process, you'll be iterating on the design. Using MOLAP storage now—even if later you'll be moving to a different kind of storage—keeps the development cycle faster and simpler.

- *StorageLocation:* You can point the cube's MOLAP storage to a location other than the default.

We discuss the other properties of the measure group later, in the discussion of physical design considerations. For the initial iterations of the design and development, these settings are not very important.

The most important properties for a measure are:

■ *Name, Description,* and *FormatString:* Ensure these are set correctly. Most Analysis Services client query tools automatically format data correctly, according to the FormatString.

■ *DisplayFolder:* By default, measures are grouped by, well, measure group. Since each measure group can have dozens of measures, DisplayFolders give you an extra grouping layer within a measure group. They don't exist anywhere else. You make them up by typing them in the property window.

■ *AggregateFunction:* Most measures are defined to summarize by summing or counting; less frequently by distinct count, min, or max. You can also define options for semi-additive or non-additive measures: averaging, beginning of period, end of period, and so on.

TIP You could set this behavior by right-clicking on the cube in the Solution Explorer and launching the Business Intelligence Wizard. The option to define semi-additive behavior sets the measure's AggregateFunction.

■ *Visible:* It's surprisingly common to hide a measure. Many measures are used for calculations but aren't very interesting on their own. Hiding them reduces clutter for the business users.

Edit Dimensions in the Cube

The small pane in the lower left is where the cube's dimensions are listed. You can launch the Dimension Editor from here, or from the Solution Explorer as we discussed earlier.

The primary editing activity in the Dimensions pane of the Cube Structure tab is to add a new dimension or to re-order dimensions. The order of the dimensions in the cube, as they appear here in this pane, is the same as they'll show up to the users. Put the obscure dimensions at the bottom!

TIP There is a second implication of the order of the dimensions in this list, which is vital if you have complex calculations. The order of dimensions in this list affects the application of dimension calculations, like unary operators. This is particularly important for a financial model, where you might allocate along one dimension before calculating along a second dimension (usually the Account dimension). You can see this in the AdventureWorksAS database. The Organization dimension in that database must be listed before the Accounts dimension for the calculations to work properly. Try reordering the dimensions and recalculating the measure group to see how important the ordering is.

Dimensions are defined first at the database level, then optionally added to the cube. As we discussed earlier in the sidebar on cube terminology, the recommended practice is to have one cube in an Analysis Services database. This one cube contains multiple measure groups.

So, if you add new dimensions to your database after your initial run through the Cube Wizard, you may need to add them to your cube as well. Do so here.

The properties of a cube dimension that you might edit are:

- *Name* and *Description:* The dimension name as created in the database is usually the correct name. The only time you're likely to want to edit the name of the dimension in the cube is if the dimension has multiple roles. This is very common with the Date dimension: Order Date, Due Date, Ship Date, and so on are different roles of the Date dimension. Similarly, adjust the Description property for dimension roles.

You can also edit the properties of the hierarchy of a cube dimension, and attributes of a cube dimension. It's unlikely that you'd want to do this.

Cube Properties

There are a few properties of the cube that you might want to adjust during development. You can see the list of these properties by clicking on the cube in either the Measures or Dimensions panes of the Cube Structure tab.

- *Name* and *Description:* Edit the cube's name and description as appropriate.
- *DefaultMeasure:* One measure will come up by default, if users don't specify a measure in a query. You should choose which measure that is, rather than letting Analysis Services choose it for you.
- *StorageLocation:* You can set the StorageLocation here, rather than for each measure group individually.

Most of the other options have to do with physical storage and processing, and are discussed later in the chapter. During the first part of the development cycle, the defaults are usually fine.

Edit Dimension Usage

You specify exactly how dimensions participate in measure groups on the next tab of the Cube Designer. Figure 7.9 illustrates the Dimension Usage tab for the MDWT_AdventureWorksAS sample cube. Our simplification of the Adventure Works schema presents a simple display. To see a more realistic display of dimension usage in a complex system, check out the AdventureWorksAS sample database that ships with SQL Server.

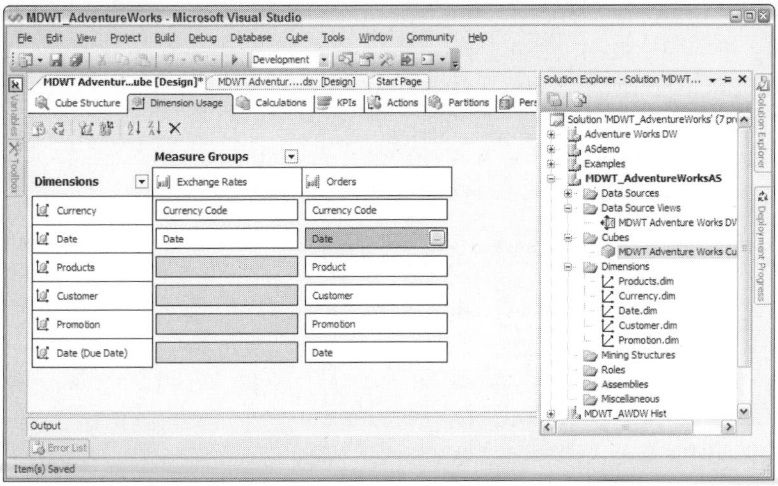

Figure 7.9   Dimension usage

The Dimension Usage tab's summarization of dimension usage is very similar to the Kimball Method bus matrix with the rows and columns flipped. At a glance you can identify which dimensions participate in which measure group, and at which cardinality.

The dimensionality of the Orders measure group displayed in Figure 7.9 has been modified from the defaults generated by the Cube Wizard. There are three date keys in the two fact tables, each with a different name. Originally, Analysis Services defined three roles for the Date dimension: Date from the Exchange Rates measure group, and Order Date and Due Date from the Orders measure group. However, the business users think of the Order Date as the main date key in the Orders table. Therefore, we deleted the Order Date role, and reassigned the OrderDateKey to the main Date role, using the Define Relationship window shown in Figure 7.10.

Measure Groups at Different Granularity

Measure groups, and their underlying relational fact tables, may hook into a conformed dimension at a summary level. The most common scenario is for forecasts and quotas. Most businesses develop forecasts quarterly or monthly, even if they track sales on a daily basis. The fundamentals of dimensional modeling tell you to conform the Date dimension across uses, even if those uses are at different grains. By re-using the dimension, you're making it easy to compare quarterly data from multiple measure groups.

Analysis Services makes this conformation easy for you. All you have to do is correctly define the granularity attribute in the Define Relationship dialog box (set to DateKey in Figure 7.10). Make sure you set the Related Attributes properly in any dimension for which some measure groups join in above the grain.

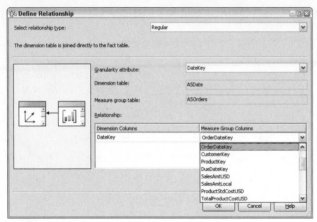

Figure 7.10 Editing dimension usage

Complex Relationships Between Dimensions and Measure Groups

There are several kinds of relationships between dimensions and measure groups, which you can set in the Dimension Usage tab. Most dimension relationships are Regular, but you can also specify Fact, Reference, Data Mining, and Many-to-Many relationships here.

The Cube Wizard does a good job of setting up these relationships correctly, but you should always check them.

Build, Deploy, and Process the Project

At this point in the development cycle, you've worked on your dimensions, and you've built and processed them several times. You've defined the basic structure of your cube, including the relationships between measure groups and dimensions.

Now is a good time to perform the first processing of the OLAP database. The easiest way to do this is to right-click on the project name in the Solution Explorer, and choose Process. By choosing Process, you're doing three things:

- Building the project, looking for structural errors.
- Deploying that project to the target Analysis Services server, creating a new database structure (or updating an existing database structure).
- Processing that database, to fully or incrementally add data.

It makes sense to look at the data after processing has completed. See the discussion in the following section on the Browse Data tab.

> ### THOSE PESKY ATTRIBUTE RELATIONSHIPS AGAIN
>
> It's absolutely critical to set the Related Attributes properly in any dimension that's used at multiple granularities. You need to inform Analysis Services that it can expect referential integrity between various attributes in the dimension. If you aren't careful here, you can see inconsistent query results because aggregations are computed and stored incorrectly, or will not show up at all.
>
> Unfortunately, it's easier to set up measure groups with different granularity wrong than it is to do it right. Review the Analysis Services tutorial topic "Defining Dimension Granularity within a Measure Group" before you develop your first summary measure group. And check your work (and the numbers) carefully.

Create Calculations

The third tab of the Cube Designer is where you'll create calculations using the Multidimensional Expression language, or MDX. Most BI teams we've worked with have resisted learning MDX as long as they can. No one wants to learn a new language, but all eventually agree that at least one person on the team needs to step up to this challenge. The good news is that the BI Studio tools make it easy to define common calculations. And you can learn a lot about MDX by looking at how these calculations are defined for you.

You have opportunities to sprinkle MDX throughout the definition of the cube. The most obvious place is here, on the Calculations tab, where you can create calculated measures, other calculated members, sets, and calculated sub-cubes. You'll greatly improve the usefulness and user-friendliness of your Analysis Services database by defining common calculations that benefit all business users regardless of how they're accessing the cube.

- Calculated measures will show up under the Measures dimension. Many calculated measures are quite simple, like the sum or ratio of two other measures. To a business user browsing the cube, calculated measures are largely indistinguishable from physical measures. Some query tools, including the Cube Browser integrated with BI Studio, will show a different icon for calculated measures and physical measures. A calculated measure is really just a calculated member, assigned to the Measures dimension. A very complex calculated measure may perform less well than a physical measure because calculations are performed at runtime.

- Calculated members can be created on any dimension. Non-measure calculated members can be very powerful. They're a way to create a kind of calculation that applies for some or all members. For example, you could create a calculated member Year To Date on the Date dimension, to automatically calculate multiple measures year-to-date.

TIP The Add Business Intelligence Wizard will create a wide variety of calculations for you, including the Year To Date calculated member.

- Named sets are a set of dimension members. A really simple named set would specify the set explicitly, perhaps as a list of important products. More complicated set definitions locate the set of products with a high price, products that sold well this year, and so on.

- Calculated sub-cubes are a way to calculate an arbitrary portion of the cube's data and summarizations. A common use of calculated sub-cubes is to allocate summary data (like monthly quotas) down to more fine-grained data. Or, calculated sub-cubes can provide a complex summarization method, if your business rules are more complicated than can be supported by the standard Aggregate Functions. If you're among the handful of people who are intimately familiar with calculated cells from Analysis Services 2000, you'll dig into calculated sub-cubes and readily understand the improvements that MDX scripting and scoped assignments provide.

TIP How do you know whether you need a calculated member or a calculated sub-cube? A calculated member changes the visible structure of the cube; you can see the calculated member in the list of dimension members. A calculated sub-cube doesn't change the list of members or attributes in a dimension. Instead, it changes the way the numbers inside the cube are calculated.

The Calculations Tab

The Calculations tab of the Cube Designer is illustrated in Figure 7.11. As you can see, this is another complicated screen. But let's face it: Calculations are complicated.

TIP In Figure 7.11 we're illustrating the Calculations tab for the AdventureWorksAS database that ships with SQL Server, rather than our simplified version. Microsoft's sample database contains a rich set of calculations, KPIs, and Actions. Exploring this database is an easy way to become familiar with using MDX to create calculated objects.

In the upper left is the Script Organizer. This pane lists the calculations that have been defined for this cube. The selected calculation is a calculated measure called [Growth in Customer Base], which calculates the change in the number of customers from one period to the next. The main area of the Calculations tab shows a form where this calculation is defined. The lower-left pane shows three tabs that contain a list of objects in the cube; a list of available functions, which you can drag into your calculation; and a set of templates, which can provide a starting point for some kinds of calculations.

This calculated member is defined on the Measures dimension; it's a calculated measure. The next area contains the MDX for the calculation. Even without knowing anything about MDX, we probably can all parse this statement.

- If you're currently at the "All Time" level—if the level of the [Date].[Calendar Time] hierarchy is zero—you want to display NA.

- If you're currently at the beginning of the dataset—if there is no previous member of the Date dimension—you want to display NULL.

- If you're anywhere in the Date dimension other than these two edge cases, you want to display the Customer Count for this period minus the Customer Count for last period, divided by the Customer Count for last period, in other words, the percentage change in the number of customers.

We could have illustrated a simpler calculated member in Figure 7.11, but this one has the advantage of being realistic. It's a nice example because it illustrates the important concept of defining your calculations relative to where the user is in the cube.

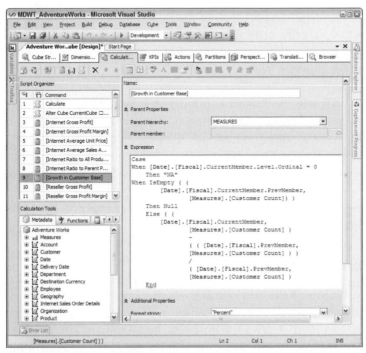

Figure 7.11   The Calculations tab

> **NOTE** If you're defining lots of similar calculations, like [Annual Change for 2005] and [Annual Change for 2004], you should step back and figure out how to generalize. Probably you really need a single [Annual Change] calculation that computes relative to the current position in the cube: a far more elegant solution.

The calculation form also provides a place for you to add properties like formatting, color, and font. These properties can be conditional, which is particularly valuable for color: Display the measure in green if it's positive, and red if it's negative. You can also identify the Display Folder and Associated Measure Group for a calculation from within the Calculation Properties window.

> **TIP** The Calculation Properties window is absurdly hard to find. Launch it by choosing Cube → Calculation Properties, or click the Calculation Properties toolbar icon.

The calculation form view is a good way to create new measures and named sets. The form view is an item-by-item view of an underlying script. If you want to look at the entire script, switch to the script view by choosing Cube → Show Calculations in → Script (or click the Script toolbar icon).

Adding Business Intelligence

Unless you're already an MDX expert, one of the best places to get started in adding calculations to your cube is by using the Business Intelligence Wizard. This wizard will build for you the most common kinds of calculations. You can launch the Business Intelligence Wizard in several ways, including from the first icon on the Calculations toolbar.

Most applications will use the Business Intelligence Wizard to add "time intelligence" to their cube. This wizard option will automatically create for you calculations like [Year to Date], [12 Month Moving Average], and so on. These calculations appear on the Date dimension. They're non-measure calculated members. As such, they can apply to multiple underlying measures in one fell swoop.

A second advantage of the Business Intelligence Wizard is that you can pick apart the calculations to learn how they were done.

Define Key Performance Indicators

Key Performance Indicators (KPIs) are numbers or displays that are intended to measure the health of the organization. When KPIs are based on a clear understanding of the factors that drive the business, and a robust DW/BI platform, they can be an extremely powerful organizational management tool. Unfortunately, most KPIs are either brain-dead simple, divorced from the underlying data, or both. Really, who cares that sales are down 0.1 percent today unless we know that today is a Friday and Friday's sales are usually up 0.1 percent? And even if we did know the context, simply telling the executive that sales are down doesn't provide any understanding about why.

We hope that the definition and display of KPIs with Analysis Services will help address these shortcomings. The KPI implementation is well thought out. Because KPIs are defined in the cube, the supporting data can be made available in useful ways.

Analysis Services 2005 defines a KPI on the KPIs tab of the Cube Designer:

- *Name of the KPI:* And the measure group with which the KPI is associated.

- *Value to be measured:* The underlying measure for the KPI. Most often you'll use a physical measure or a calculated measure that you've already defined. You can enter an MDX expression here, but it usually makes more sense to create a calculated measure and use that. In the very simple example we used in this section, the value to be measured might be [Sales Revenue].

TIP Whenever you specify an MDX expression when you create a KPI, the server will create a hidden calculated measure.

- *Goal for the value:* An MDX expression that defines the target for the measure. A trivial goal would be a number: The sales target is $100,000. That would give a stupid KPI. More interesting would be a goal to increase sales 0.1 percent from the same day the previous week, or a goal that's based on sales quotas

- *Status:* A graphic and an MDX expression that describe how the business is doing relative to its goal. Analysis Services provides several built-in graphic gauges, including thermometers, traffic lights, and happy faces. The MDX expression needs to evaluate to numbers between -1 (very bad) to +1 (very good). If you're clever about defining the status expression, you can do a good job of conveying important information about wide deviations from the goal, and keep minor deviations quiet.

- *Trend:* A graphic and an MDX expression that describe whether you're moving toward or away from your goal. Is the situation getting better or worse? As with the status graphic, Analysis Services provides a few built-in trend graphics, notably a trend arrow. The MDX expression must evaluate to numbers between -1 (going south in a hurry) and +1 (getting better fast).

WHERE TO GO FOR HELP

Like so much we've introduced, Calculations and MDX are rich and complex topics about which entire books are written. We've barely scratched the surface here.

The first place to go for help is the excellent section on Calculations in the SQL Server Analysis Services tutorial, which is part of Books Online. This tutorial walks you through the process of creating several calculated members, named sets, and calculated sub-cubes. The tutorial shows you how to debug your Calculation Script by setting breakpoints, stepping through calculations, and watching how each step modifies the cube's structure and data.

The debugger is a great feature. Learn how to use it, especially if you have any MDX scripts. The debugger is absolutely vital if you have multiple calculations that overlap one another.

The MDWT_AdventureWorksAS database is available on the book's web site. It contains a handful of calculated members and sets, for the same simplified version of the AdventureWorks case study that we've used throughout this book.

The AdventureWorksAS database that's shipped with SQL Server is a good learning tool. It contains a lot of fairly complex calculations, especially for the finance module.

There are several books that the MDX expert on your team should own:

◆ *MDX Solutions* by Spofford, Harinath, Webb, and Civardi (Wiley, 2005). This is the new edition of the popular MDX Solutions edition for Analysis Services 2000. The new edition covers not only Analysis Services but also Hyperion Essbase, which now speaks MDX as well.

◆ *Professional Analysis Services 2005 with MDX* by Harinath and Quinn (Wrox, 2005). This book covers a lot more than MDX.

◆ *Fast Track to MDX* by Whitehorn, Pasumansky, and Zare (Springer, 2003). This introductory text was written for Analysis Services 2000, but it remains relevant for Analysis Services 2005. We expect it to be updated for 2005.

To display your KPIs, you need some client software that understands KPIs. An ad hoc query and reporting tool that's been designed to work well with Analysis Services 2005 will expose the KPI functionality. Your organization may have developed a reporting portal using Windows SharePoint Services, as discussed in Chapter 8. If so, you can embed KPIs in that portal by writing custom code to the APIs.

Widespread use of KPIs must wait until the client tool market matures, and especially until Microsoft releases new versions of information worker tools, like Excel and SharePoint, that are designed to work with Analysis Services 2005. Software vendors who are building packaged analytics on Analysis Services will probably be the first to use KPIs extensively in their front ends.

Create Actions

An Analysis Services Action is a command that's stored on the server. Actions are defined using MDX, which means that the command is context-sensitive. In other words, you can define an Action that executes when the user right-clicks on a cell in a report. The Action knows the values of each of the dimensions that make up the address of the cell and can execute a customized command for that address.

Like KPIs, the server-side definition of an Action is only half of the solution. You need a client tool that implements Actions. It's the job of the query tool to intercept the "right-click" on a report cell, and present (and execute) the appropriate list of Actions.

The most obvious use of an Action is to execute a relational query. As we've already described, the majority of SQL Server 2005 Analysis Services databases are built at the same grain as the underlying dimensional model. An interesting BI application could include an Action that drills back to enterprise data, perhaps even back to the original transaction system. This query Action can easily be implemented as an Action that launches a Reporting Services report.

Analysis Services provides for three kinds of Actions:

- Drillthrough to the cube's leaf-level data.
- Execute a Reporting Services report.
- Execute a generic Action. Actions can bring up a URL, return a rowset or dataset, or execute a command. An Action is defined as an MDX statement, and can be attached to specific parts of the cube. For example, you can have one Action that executes when someone right-clicks on the Month label in the Date dimension, and a second Action that launches when someone right-clicks on a data cell.

TIP Two kinds of Actions—HTML scripts and Command Line Actions—pose security risks and should be avoided. Microsoft has moved these Action types out of the BI Studio interface. You'd have to create the Action by writing a script without the benefit of the UI.

Under the covers, the Drillthrough Action is simply a kind of rowset Action that's common enough that Microsoft built a simple user interface for defining it. Similarly, the Report Action is just an instance of a URL Action.

Drillthrough and Reporting Services Actions are very easy to set up. Generic Actions, like launching a parameterized web page, are pretty tricky. Start with something really simple, like launching a static web page (like Google or MSN). Add complexity a bit at a time. Process the cube and try out the Action in the browser window before adding another layer of complexity. If you change only an Action definition between processing, the processing step refreshes only metadata (not data), so processing occurs tolerably quickly.

Partitions

Use the Partitions tab of the Cube Designer to define the physical storage characteristics of your cube. During the first part of your development cycle, don't bother with this tab. Use the default settings so you can focus on getting the cube structure and calculations correct.

In the next section of this chapter, we discuss physical design considerations. We return to this tab and its settings, and talk at some length about what's going on under the covers, so you can make informed decisions about how to deploy your Analysis Services database in production.

Maintain Perspectives

You'll almost certainly define a few Perspectives if you follow the best practice recommendation of creating a single Analysis Services cube that contains multiple measure groups. Unless your implementation is really simple, this single-cube approach will lead to a structure that's challenging for business users to navigate.

An Analysis Services Perspective is like a big view on top of the database, limiting a user's view to a set of related measure groups and dimensions. A Perspective is analogous to a business process dimensional model in the Kimball Method vocabulary. It's a very nice approach because you're not replicating data into multiple cubes: You're simply providing different users with different views of the same data.

Use the Perspectives tab of the Cube Designer to define your cube's Perspectives. You can create as many Perspectives as you like; it's a simple matter of choosing which portions of the overall cube to hide in each Perspective. You can also specify which measure is shown by default in each Perspective.

Most users will see only a few Perspectives, rather than the entire cube containing all measure groups. You can hide the cube itself, by setting its Visible property to False, and reveal only the Perspectives that contain the information your user communities are interested in.

It may feel as though Perspectives are a security mechanism. Not so! As we discuss in Chapter 12, Analysis Services security is applied at the database object level.

Unfortunately, Perspectives are not available in SQL Server 2005 Standard Edition. Many organizations don't have the users or data volumes needed to justify Enterprise Edition, but almost all organizations could benefit from Perspectives.

Define Translations

We introduced the notion of Analysis Services translations in the discussion of the Dimension Designer. This Translations tab in the Cube Designer is where you finish up the translating work. You can provide translations for the objects you've created in the Cube Designer: Display Folders, Measures, Cube Dimensions, Perspectives, KPIs, Actions, and Calculations.

When you use the Browser tab to browse the data, you can view the data with different Translations. This is fun to do, and if your organization is multilingual, it is certainly worth including in any demos you create for senior management. The AdventureWorksAS sample database that ships with SQL Server 2005 includes a rich set of translations.

The Translation feature works really well. It leverages the Localization technology in all Microsoft products. It picks up the locale ID from the user's desktop and automatically displays either the appropriate translation, if it exists, or the default language. Most client tools don't need to do anything special.

Translations are not available in SQL Server 2005 Standard Edition.

Browse Data

The last tab of the Cube Designer is where you browse the data in the Analysis Services database. You don't need to work through all the other tabs before you take a look at the data. After you've defined the basic cube structure and verified the relationships with the dimensions, you generally want to check your work.

As we described earlier when talking about browsing the dimensions, you need to build, deploy, and process the cube before you can browse the data. The browser tab will remind you to do that if necessary.

Earlier in this chapter we talked about starting your Analysis Services development against a much reduced dataset. As you process the cube for the umpteenth time to check the implications of an edit, you'll recognize why this was a good idea.

Physical Design Considerations

Up to this point in this chapter we've been discussing the logical design process for the Analysis Services OLAP database. We've recommended that you work with a small subset of data so that you can concentrate on the structure, calculations, and other cube decorations, without worrying about the physical design.

CUBE PHYSICAL STORAGE TERMINOLOGY

Readers who are familiar with Analysis Services 2000 will already be familiar with most of the terminology for the physical storage and processing of the Analysis Services database. This sidebar merely defines these concepts. Recommendations and implications are discussed in detail elsewhere in the chapter.

- *Leaf data:* Leaf data is the finest grain of data that's defined in the cube's measure group. Usually, the leaf data corresponds exactly to the fact table from which a cube's measure group is sourced. Occasionally you'll define a measure group at a higher grain than the underlying fact table, for example by eliminating a dimension from the measure group.

- *Aggregations:* Pre-computed aggregations are analogous to summary tables in the relational database. You can think of them as a big SELECT. . . GROUP BY statement whose result set is stored for rapid access.

- *Data storage mode:* Analysis Services supports three kinds of storage for data.

  - *MOLAP:* Leaf data and aggregations are stored in Analysis Services' MOLAP format.

  - *HOLAP:* Leaf data is stored in the relational database, and aggregations are stored in MOLAP format.

  - *ROLAP:* Leaf data and aggregations are stored in the source relational database.

- *Dimension storage mode:* Dimension data, corresponding to the relational dimension tables, can be stored in MOLAP format or left in the relational database (ROLAP mode).

- *Partition:* Fact data can be divided into partitions. Most systems that partition their data do so along the Date dimension; for example, one partition for each month or year. You can partition along any dimension, or along multiple dimensions. The partition is the unit of work for fact processing. Partitions are a feature of SQL Server Enterprise Edition.

- *Fact processing:* Analysis Services supports several kinds of fact processing for a partition.

  - *Full processing:* All the data for the partition is pulled from the source system into the Analysis Services engine, and written in MOLAP format if requested. Aggregations are computed and stored in MOLAP format if requested, or back in the RDBMS (ROLAP mode).

  - *Incremental processing:* New data for the partition is pulled from the source system and stored in MOLAP if requested. Aggregations—either MOLAP or ROLAP—are updated. It's your job to tell Analysis Services how to identify new data.

> ◆ *Proactive caching:* **Proactive caching is an important new concept for Analysis Services 2005. It's particularly interesting for low latency databases—for populating the cube in real time (or near real time). When you set up proactive caching, you're asking Analysis Services to monitor the relational source for the measure group's partition and to automatically perform incremental processing when it sees changes.**

Now it's time to start addressing the physical issues. Most of the time, physical implementation decisions are made independently of the logical design. That's not completely true, and in this section we discuss how some design decisions can have a large impact on the manageability and performance of your cube.

Storage Mode: MOLAP, HOLAP, ROLAP

The first question to resolve in your physical design is the easiest one. Should you use MOLAP, HOLAP, or ROLAP mode to store your Analysis Services data? The answer is MOLAP.

We're not even being particularly facetious with this terse answer, but we will justify it a bit.

Analysis Services MOLAP format has been designed to hold dimensional data. It uses sophisticated compression and indexing technologies to deliver excellent query performance. All else being equal, query performance against a MOLAP store is significantly faster than against a HOLAP or ROLAP store.

Some people argue that MOLAP storage wastes disk space. You've already copied data at least once to store it in the relational data warehouse. Now you're talking about copying it again for the cube storage. To this argument we reply that a relational index also copies data. No one asserts you shouldn't index your relational database.

MOLAP storage is highly efficient. The leaf data in MOLAP mode (data and indexes) tends to require about 20 percent of the storage of the relational source (data only, no indexes). The MOLAP store of the leaf data is comparable in size to a single relational index on the fact table—and buys a lot more for you than any single relational index could possibly do.

Another common argument against MOLAP is that it slows processing. ROLAP is always the slowest to process because writing the aggregations to the relational database is expensive. HOLAP is slightly faster to process than MOLAP, but the difference is surprisingly small.

Dimensions also can be stored in MOLAP or ROLAP mode. Use MOLAP.

> **NOTE** Why does Microsoft offer these alternative storage modes, if they're inferior to MOLAP storage? The main answer is marketing: It's been an effective strategy to get Analysis Services into companies that would never countenance an instance of the SQL Server relational database in their data center. The multiple storage modes make the initial sale. Often, the DW/BI team figures out how much faster MOLAP is, and convinces management that it's okay. It's also a hedge against the future. It's possible that improvements to relational technology could make HOLAP or ROLAP storage more appealing. Certainly we'd love to see Analysis Services' indexing, aggregation, compression, and processing abilities integrated into the SQL Server RDBMS, although we don't think that's particularly likely in the near future.

In Chapter 17 we back off slightly from the strong recommendation to use MOLAP. If you have a compelling business need for near-zero data latency from the cube, you may set up a ROLAP partition for data for the current hour or day.

Designing Aggregations

The design goal for aggregations is to minimize the number of aggregations while maximizing their effectiveness. You don't have to define every possible aggregation. At query time, Analysis Services will automatically choose the most appropriate (smallest) aggregation that can be used to answer the query. Aggregation design is a difficult problem, and Analysis Services provides several tools to help you out.

Before we talk about designing aggregations, however, it's worth pointing out that very small cubes don't really need aggregations at all. During your development cycle, you're probably working with a small enough dataset that you don't need to worry about aggregations. Systems with small data volumes may not need to create any aggregations even in production. If you have only a hundred thousand rows in your measure group's partition, you don't need to worry about aggregations. Even large enterprises can find that many of their measure groups—for example for quotas and financial data—are so small that aggregations are unnecessary.

Large data volumes, of course, do require thoughtful aggregation design. You should be experimenting with different aggregation plans in the later part of your development cycle, when you start to work with realistic data volumes. During development, you can design aggregations with the BI Studio, by launching the Aggregation Design Wizard from the Partitions tab of the Cube Designer. Figure 7.12 shows the Aggregation Design Wizard.

In the Partitions tab you can see the partitions in each measure group. Launch the Aggregation Design Wizard displayed in Figure 7.12 by clicking on the Aggregations column for the partition.

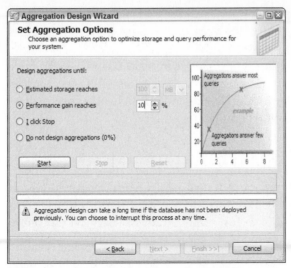

Figure 7.12 The Aggregation Design Wizard

The Aggregation Design Wizard will design aggregations based on the cardinality of your data. It looks at your dimensions and figures out where aggregations are going to do the most good. As a simplification of what it's doing, consider that aggregating data from a daily grain up to monthly creates an aggregation that's one-thirtieth the size of the original data. (This isn't strictly true, but suffices for explanatory purposes.) But summarizing from monthly to quarterly gives an aggregation that's one-fourth the size. The Aggregation Design Wizard has reasonably sophisticated algorithms to look at the intersection of hierarchical levels to figure out where aggregations are best built.

We recommend that you use the Aggregation Design Wizard during development. Set the "performance gain reaches" number very low: 5 to 20 percent, as illustrated in Figure 7.12.

TIP One of the most common physical design mistakes is to build too many aggregations. The Aggregation Design Wizard positively encourages you to build too many aggregations, with its default setting of 30 percent. The first several aggregations provide a lot of benefit. After that, the incremental benefit at query time is slight; and the cost during processing time can grow substantially.

As clever as the Aggregation Design Wizard is, and as good as its recommendations are, it's missing the most important information in aggregation design: usage. The aggregations that you really want are those based on the queries that business users issue.

At the end of the development cycle, and as you move your Analysis Services database into the testing process, you should have developed the common queries and reports, as described in Chapters 8 and 9. Even in a test environment, running these common queries and reports against the database will provide much better information for aggregation design than the Aggregation Design Wizard uses.

We discuss how to develop a plan for ongoing tuning of usage based aggregations in Chapter 15. For the time being, remember to use the Aggregation Wizard during development, if your data is big enough to need aggregations. Plan to use usage-based aggregations in production.

Partitioning Plan

You can define multiple partitions for a measure group. Multiple partitions are a feature of SQL Server Enterprise Edition, and are very important for good query and processing performance for large Analysis Services measure groups. If you have a measure group with more than 50 million rows, you really should be using partitioning.

Partitioning is vital for large measure groups because partitions can greatly help query performance. The Analysis Services query engine can selectively query partitions: It's smart enough to access only the partitions that contain the data requested in a query. This difference can be substantial for a cube built on, say, a billion rows of data.

The second reason partitioning is valuable is for management of a large cube. It's faster to add a day's worth of fact data to a small partition than to incrementally process that same day of data into a huge partition that contains all of history. With a small partition for current data, you have many more options to easily support real-time data delivery.

Partitioning also makes it possible—even easy!—to set up your measure group to support a rolling window of data. For example, your users may want to keep only 90 days of detailed data live in the cube. With a partitioned measure group, you simply drop the dated partitions. With a single partition, you have no option for deleting data other than reprocessing the entire measure group.

Partitioning improves processing performance, especially for full processing of the measure group. Analysis Services automatically processes partitions in parallel.

The largest measure groups, containing hundreds of millions or even billions of rows, should be partitioned along multiple dimensions: say by Month and Product Group. More partitions are better for both query and processing performance, but at the cost of making your maintenance application more complicated.

TIP If you've defined a lot of partitions, say a thousand, Management Studio will be slow. It'll take a few minutes to populate the lists of database objects.

You can always set up partitioning on your development server because SQL Server Developer Edition contains all the functionality in Enterprise Edition. But those partitions won't work on your production server if you use Standard Edition in production. As we described previously in this chapter, be sure to set the project's Deployment Server Edition property, so Analysis Services can help you avoid features that won't work in production.

Set up the initial partitioning plan in BI Studio, from the Partitions tab. Figure 7.13 illustrates the Partitions tab, this time for multiple partitions of the Orders measure group. The Orders measure group is partitioned by half-years. The first partition should always be empty; it's been defined to hold all data before the first row that exists in the source system. Each subsequent partition is defined to select only the rows for contiguous six month blocks. The source query for one partition is shown. Analysis Services automatically generates most of the query. You need simply add the WHERE clause.

TIP You need to be very careful to define the WHERE clauses correctly. Analysis Services isn't smart enough to see whether you've skipped data or, even worse, double-counted it.

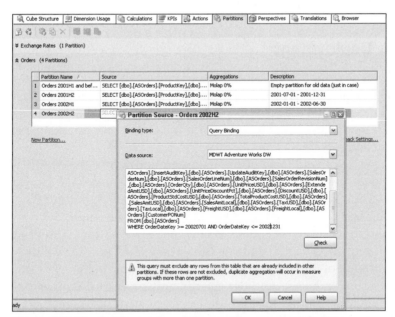

Figure 7.13 The Partitions tab and the partition source definition

There are several critical pieces of information to set correctly whenever you create a new partition:

- *Source:* It's your job to ensure that the data that flows into each partition doesn't overlap. In other words, the partition for year 2005 needs a source query that limits its data only to 2005.

- *Slice:* The Slice is where you tell Analysis Services which partitions to selectively access when resolving a query. Analysis Services 2005 sets this property automatically for you for MOLAP partitions. If you have a ROLAP partition—which is relatively unlikely unless you have a very low latency partition—set the slice by hand.

- *Aggregations and storage:* One interesting feature of Analysis Services partitions is that storage mode and aggregation design can differ for each partition. The most common intentional use of this feature is to add new kinds of aggregations only to current partitions as the aggregation plan changes over time.

When you're working with your database in development, you set up the partitions by hand in BI Studio. In test and production, you need to automate the process of creating a new partition and setting its source and slice. These issues are discussed in Chapter 15.

Planning for Deployment

After you've developed the logical structure of your Analysis Services database using a subset of data, you need to process the full historical dataset. This is unlikely to take place on the development server, unless your data volumes are quite small. Instead, you'll probably perform full cube processing only on the test or production servers.

In Chapter 4, we discussed some of the issues around where the Analysis Services data should be placed. We discussed using RAID and SAN arrays; you should have your hardware vendor assist with the detailed configuration of these technologies.

One of the biggest questions, of course, is how to size the system. Earlier in this chapter we mentioned the 20 percent rule: The leaf level MOLAP data tends to take 20 percent of the space required by the same data in the relational database (data only, no indexes). Another equally broad rule of thumb is that aggregations double that figure, up to a total of 40 percent of the relational data. This is still amazingly small.

TIP We've seen only one or two cubes whose leaf data plus aggregations take up more space than the relational data (data only, no indexes). That doesn't mean it's not possible, but it is a reasonable upper bound to consider during the early stages of planning.

Your system administrators, reasonably enough, want a more accurate number than this 40 percent figure pulled from the air. We wish we could provide you with a sizing tool, but we don't know how to solve that problem. Exact cube size depends on your logical design, data volumes, and aggregation plan. In practice, the way people perform system sizing for large Analysis Services databases is to process the dimensions and one or two partitions using the initial aggregation plan. The full system data requirements scale up the partitions linearly (ignoring the dimension storage, which usually rounds to zero in comparison to the partitions).

Historical Processing Plan

In an ideal world, you'll fully process a measure group only once, when you first move it into test and then production. But change is inevitable, and it's pretty likely that one or more necessary changes to the database's structure will require full reprocessing.

You can fully process a measure group from within Management Studio: right-click on the measure group and choose Process. Once you're in production, this is not the best strategy for full processing. Instead, you should write a script or Integration Services package to perform the processing.

TIP Don't get in the habit of using Management Studio to launch processing. This isn't because of performance—exactly the same thing happens whether you use Management Studio, a script, or Integration Services. The difference is in a commitment to an automated and hands-off production environment. These issues are discussed in Chapter 15.

You can create the basic processing script from the Management Studio Process Measure Group dialog by choosing the Script option. This option generates a script that you can execute in Management Studio, or use the Integration Services Execute Analysis Services DDL task.

We recommend that you use an Integration Services package rather than a script to perform measure group processing. This is especially true if you're using Integration Services for your ETL system, as you'll have a logging and auditing infrastructure in place. Integration Services includes a task to perform Analysis Services processing. A sample package for fully processing the MDWT_AdventureWorksAS database is included on the book's web site.

Incremental Processing Plan

Long before you put your Analysis Services database into production, you need to develop a plan for keeping it up-to-date. There are several ways to do this. Scheduled processing will continue to be the most common method of processing. Analysis Services 2005 offers a new processing method called Proactive Caching. Proactive caching is tremendously important and interesting for real-time business intelligence, and we discuss it in some length in Chapter 17.

You can also populate a cube directly from the Integration Services pipeline, without first storing it in a relational table. This is an interesting concept, especially if you multicast the flow to populate the cube and relational data warehouse at the same time. However, most mainstream applications will first store the data in a relational data warehouse.

Scheduled Processing

Scheduled processing of Analysis Services objects is basically a pull method of getting data into the cube. On a schedule, or upon successful completion of an event like a successful load, launch a job to pull the data into the cube. In this section we're providing an overview of techniques. We go into greater detail in Chapter 15.

Full Reprocessing

The simplest strategy is to perform full processing every time you want to add data. We're surprised by how many people choose this strategy, which is akin to fully reloading the data warehouse on every load cycle. It's certainly the easiest strategy to implement. Analysis Services performs processing efficiently, so this approach can perform tolerably well for monthly or weekly load cycles—or even daily for very small measure groups.

The same script or Integration Services package that you used for the initial population of the cube can be re-executed every week or month.

Incremental Processing

If your data volumes are large enough that full processing is not desirable, the next obvious choice is to schedule incremental processing.

Incremental dimension processing is straightforward and can be scripted in the same way as database, cube, or measure group full processing. In Chapter 6, we recommend that you create an Integration Services package for each dimension table. You can add the Analysis Services processing task to each dimension's package, to automatically start dimension processing when the corresponding relational dimension has successfully loaded. Alternatively, wait until the relational work is done and process all Analysis Services objects together in a single transaction.

Incremental measure group processing is more complicated than dimension processing because you must design your system so you process only new data. Analysis Services doesn't check to make sure you're not inadvertently adding data twice or skipping a set of data.

The best way to identify the incremental rows to be processed is to tag all fact table rows with an audit key, as we describe in Chapter 6. All rows that were added today (or this hour, or this month) are tied together by the audit key. Now, you just need to tell Analysis Services which batch to load. You could write a simple program that would redefine a view of the fact table that filters to the current batch. Or, define a static metadata-driven view definition that points Analysis Services to the fact rows that haven't been loaded yet.

TIP It's tempting to use the transaction date as the filter condition for the view or query that finds the current rows. In the real world, we usually see data flowing in for multiple days, so we tend to prefer the audit key method. If you're sure that can't happen in your environment, you can use the transaction date.

As before, once your view of the fact table has been redefined (if necessary) to filter only the new rows, it's simple to launch measure group processing from a script or package.

Incremental Processing with Multiple Partitions

If you're using SQL Server Enterprise Edition and are partitioning your measure groups, your incremental processing job is even more challenging. First, you need to be sure that you create a new partition or partition set before you need it. In other words, if you're partitioning your measure group by month, then each month you need to create a new partition designed to hold the new month's data.

TIP There's no harm in creating twelve monthly partitions in advance. But you still need to add some logic to your Integration Services package, to be sure you march through the partitions as each new month begins.

Make sure that the source query for the measure group's incremental processing has two filters:

- Grab only the rows that are new.
- Grab only the rows that belong in this partition.

This is particularly tedious if you have late-arriving facts—in other words, if today's load can include data for transactions that occurred a long time ago. If this is the case, you'll need to set up a more complicated Integration Services package. Query the data loaded today to find out which partitions you'll need to incrementally process; define a loop over those time periods.

REFERENCE SQL Server includes a sample Integration Services package that manages Analysis Services partitions. Explore and leverage this excellent sample. It's installed by default at `C:\Program Files\Microsoft SQL Server\90\Samples\Integration Services\Package Samples\ SyncAdvWorksPartitions Sample`.

Planning for Updates to Dimensions

Updates to dimensions generally happen gracefully and automatically in the dimension incremental processing. The easiest kind of dimension update is a Type 2 dimension change. Analysis Services treats a Type 2 change as a new dimension member: It has its own key, which the database has never seen before. From the point of view of dimension processing, there's no way to distinguish between a new set of attributes for an existing customer and a new row for a new customer.

Type 1 changes are picked up during dimension processing. Type 1 changes are potentially expensive because if any aggregation is defined on the Type 1 attribute, that aggregation must be rebuilt. Analysis Services drops the entire affected aggregation, but it can re-compute it as a background process.

Specify whether or not to compute aggregations in the background by setting the ProcessingMode property of the dimension. The ProcessingMode can be:

- *Regular:* During processing, the leaf-level data plus any aggregations and indexes are computed before the processed cube is published to users.

- *LazyAggregations:* Aggregations and indexes are computed in the background, and new data is made available to the users as soon as the leaf-level data is processed. This sounds great, but it can be problematic for query performance, depending on the timing of the processing. You want to avoid a situation where many users are querying a large cube at a time when that cube has no indexes or aggregations in place because it's performing background processing.

For many applications, use lazy aggregations, and choose the processing option on the dimension to Process Affected Objects. This processing option ensures that indexes and aggregations are rebuilt as part of the incremental processing transaction.

The place to worry about a Type 1 change is if you have declared the attribute to have a rigid relationship with another attribute: in other words, if you have declared there will never be a Type 1 change on the attribute. You do want to use rigid attribute relationships because they provide substantial processing performance benefits. But if you try to change the attribute, Analysis Services will raise an error.

Deleting a dimension member is impossible, short of fully reprocessing the dimension. Fully reprocessing a dimension requires that any cubes using this dimension also be fully reprocessed. If you must delete dimension members, the best approach is to create a Type 1 attribute to flag whether the dimension member is currently active, and to filter those dimension members out of most reports and queries. Monthly or annually, fully reprocess the database.

Planning for Fact Updates and Deletes

The best source for an Analysis Services cube is a ledgered fact table. A ledgered fact table handles updates to facts by creating an offsetting transaction to zero out the original fact, then inserting a corrected fact row. This ledgering works smoothly for the associated Analysis Services measure group, because the ledger entries are treated as new facts.

Sometimes it's not that easy. How do you plan for the situation where you mess up and somehow mis-assign a bunch of facts to the wrong dimension member? The only solution—unless you want to ledger out the affected rows—is to fully reprocess the affected partition.

TIP Multiple partitions are starting to sound like a really good idea.

There are several kinds of deleted data. The simplest, where you roll off the oldest month or year of fact data, is easily handled with a partitioned measure group. Just delete the partition by right-clicking it and choosing Delete in Management Studio or, more professionally, by scripting that action.

As with fact updates, deleting specific fact rows is impossible. The scenario is fairly common: You inadvertently load the same data twice into the relational database. It's unpleasant but certainly possible to back out that load from the relational tables, especially if you use the auditing system described in Chapter 6. But within Analysis Services, you're pretty much out of luck: Fully reprocess the affected partition.

TIP As we describe in Chapter 6, your ETL system should perform reasonableness checks to ensure you're not double-loading. If you have late-arriving facts, where you're writing data to multiple partitions during each day's load, you'll be especially motivated to develop a solid ETL system.

Summary

Analysis Services is one of the key components of the Microsoft Business Intelligence technologies. It's a solid, scalable OLAP server that you can use as the primary or only query engine for even the largest DW/BI system. In Chapter 10, we discuss how to use Analysis Services to build a data mining application.

In this chapter you learned:

- Once you've built a conformed dimensional relational data warehouse database, building the Analysis Services database is relatively easy.

- The tools and wizards in the BI Studio give you a good head start on the logical design of your cube database.

- There's still lots of editing to do when you've finished the wizards. And the more challenging your application—in data volumes or complexity— the more careful you need to be in your logical and physical design choices.

- There's still more work to do to integrate cube processing with the ETL system. These issues are discussed further in Chapter 15.

- You must set attribute relationships correctly to get good query performance. The user interface and documentation obscure rather than highlight the importance of attribute relationships.

- The single most important Analysis Services feature of SQL Server Enterprise Edition is measure group partitioning. Partitioning greatly improves the query and processing performance of your database, and provides greater flexibility in system management. These benefits come with the fairly substantial cost of increased system complexity.

- Some of the interesting features of Analysis Services, like KPIs and Actions, require work from client software in order to be useful additions to your system.

- Most features, like calculations, storage mode, advanced processing techniques, and even translations, are available to even the simplest Analysis Services client software.

Analysis Services is a complex piece of software. In this chapter we've presented only the bare essentials of the information necessary for you to be successful. The Analysis Services expert on your team should plan to purchase at least one additional book devoted to the subject of Analysis Services 2005.

PART

Three

Developing the BI Applications

Business Intelligence Applications

We're from the Data Warehouse, and we're here to help

We have struggled since the early 1980s with the belief that business people should be responsible for creating their own reports and analyses. In our view, they should be eager to dive in and explore the data that represents their business. After all, who knows better than the business person what information is needed and how the analysis should be created?

The problem with this belief is that most business people do not seem to agree. In fact, based on our experience, you will be lucky to get 10 percent of your user base to actually build their own reports from scratch. We suspect this is because learning the tools and learning the data is just too far outside the comfort zone of most business people. As part of the 10 percent, it's hard for us to understand this, but we have come to accept it.

A critical part of every DW/BI project is providing the other 90 percent of the user community with a more structured, and therefore easier, way to access the data warehouse. We provide this structured access through what we call *business intelligence (BI) applications*. This chapter describes the concept of BI applications along with a process for creating these applications in the context of the overall Lifecycle. (The next chapter gives an example of building a simple BI application using Reporting Services and other Microsoft tools.) Bottom line, we need to support as many users as possible, regardless of their ability or interest in learning how to build queries.

In this chapter you learn:

- The basic concepts of business intelligence applications, including standard reports and analytic applications, the value of BI applications, and delivery platform options.

- A BI application's development process that occurs in two major steps in the Business Dimensional Lifecycle. The first step is application specification, which immediately follows the requirements definition process. The second step is application development, which doesn't begin until data is available in the business process dimensional model, the end user tools have been installed, and basic business metadata is in place.

- The role of the BI application developer, and the importance of maintaining the content and performance of the BI applications.

Business Intelligence Basic Concepts

In the broadest sense, business intelligence has come to mean using information to make better business decisions. Many definitions list a term from the 1970s, decision support system (DSS), as a synonym. We've always liked this term because it is practical and descriptive of what we're trying to build. The term "business intelligence" began to rise in popularity at the end of the 1990s. It primarily referred to the structured data access layer between the users and the data warehouse—what we call the BI applications. However, at that time, the industry analysts were describing business intelligence as separate from the data warehouse, like you might build one without the other.

Although it is conceptually possible to build business intelligence applications without the benefit of a data warehouse, this rarely happens. A well-built data warehouse adds such incredible value to the data through the business dimensional model and the ETL process that it makes no sense to replicate this effort in order to build a stand-alone BI application. Most business intelligence applications are an integral part of the user-facing end of the data warehouse. In fact, we would never think of building a data warehouse without business intelligence applications—that's why one of the three tracks in the middle of the Lifecycle diagram in Figure 8.1 is dedicated to BI applications. That's also why we use the words "data warehousing" and "business intelligence" as a single term.

There's no commonly accepted definition of what constitutes a BI application, so we're offering our own. BI applications are the delivery vehicle of business intelligence—the reports and analyses that provide usable information to the business users. BI applications include a broad spectrum of reports and analyses, ranging from very simple, fixed-format reports to sophisticated analytic applications with complex embedded algorithms and domain expertise. It helps to split this spectrum into two categories based on the level of sophistication. We call these categories *standard reports* and *analytic applications*.

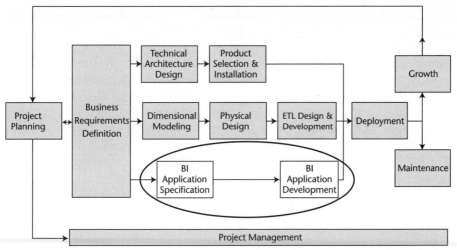

Figure 8.1   The BI application specification and development steps in the Lifecycle

Standard Reports

Standard reports are at the basic end of the BI application spectrum. They are typically relatively simple, predefined-format, parameter-driven reports. In the simplest case, they are pre-run, static reports. Standard reports provide users with a core set of information about what's going on in a particular area of the business. Standard reports may sound dull, but they're often the work-horse BI applications of the business. These are the reports people look at every day. Most of what people asked for during the requirements definition process would be classified as standard reports. That's why we encourage you to develop a set of standard reports as part of the Lifecycle approach. Some typical standard report titles might be:

- YTD Sales vs. Forecast by Sales Rep
- Monthly Churn Rate by Service Plan
- Five-Year Dropout Rate Time Series by School
- Direct Mail Response Rates by Promotion by Product
- Audience Counts and Percent of Total Audience by Network by Day of Week and Time of Day
- YTD Claims vs. Forecast by Vehicle Type
- Call Volume by Product as a Percent of Total Product Sales

Analytic Applications

Analytic applications are more complex than standard reports. They are usually centered on a specific business process and encapsulate a certain amount of domain expertise about how to analyze and interpret that business process. They may go so far as to include complex, code-based algorithms or data mining models that help identify underlying issues or opportunities. Another advanced feature in some analytic applications is the ability for the user to feed changes back into the transaction systems based on insights gained from using the application. At the far end of the spectrum, analytic applications are sold as black-box, stand-alone applications in part to protect the intellectual capital that went into their creation. Some common analytic applications include:

- Promotion effectiveness
- Web path analysis
- Affinity program analysis
- Shelf space planning
- Fraud detection
- Category management

The more targeted an analytic application is, the easier it is to justify a stand-alone implementation. In other words, you can do promotion analysis without having to spend all that time and energy building the BI system. This has the ring of truth, but that's because the justification applies the entire cost of building the BI system against the value of the specific BI application.

Build or Buy?

It is possible to build your own advanced analytic applications using standard front-end tools and custom code to capture and apply the best practice business rules. For example, we worked with a company that was building a custom fraud detection application to identify suspect transactions in an Internet-based business. They chose to build rather than buy because they felt their unique data sources and unusual business processes would make it difficult to use a purchased application. There are a lot of analytic application providers out there that would disagree with this decision.

Originally, vendors tried to sell packaged analytic applications as off-the-shelf solutions. This has not worked well for exactly the reasons our client chose to build: unique data sources and unusual business processes. However, purchased analytic applications can be a great starting point. If they align reasonably well with your industry, company, and business functions, they can add significant value with relatively low effort. This is particularly true if the vendor has built their applications on a well-designed dimensional model. This will make the mapping of your model to theirs relatively easy. Unfortunately, many of the applications we've seen are based on data models that are tightly tied to the applications themselves. As a result, packaged analytic application implementations typically involve a fair amount of customization.

Another limitation (and advantage) of purchased applications is that the internal business rules and calculations are often considered intellectual property by the companies that build these packages. This could be bad because it may mean you can't review or change the underlying business rules. However, it could be good because the company that created the applications may be better at the particular business process than your company is.

There are as many analytic application packages out there as there are business functions and industries. The most common analytic applications are budgeting and forecasting—primarily because these functions are the most standardized business functions and can be replicated across businesses and industries.

BI Application Developers

Including BI applications as part of the deliverables puts the DW/BI system team in the role of desktop application developers. This is very different compared to the ETL development role. Where the ETL developer is building a system that will be used strictly by other developers, the BI applications developer is creating a product that will be used by potentially hundreds or thousands of non-technical users.

In fulfilling the BI application developer role, you need to deal with many issues that may be unfamiliar. You need to be clear about the market demand—the need for and value of your product; you need to be clear about its specifications; you need to pay careful attention to the user interface, testing it to make sure it makes sense to users and they can easily find what they need. You must test and validate the content of the reports, including all computed fields and calculations. You need to document these applications, paying special attention to the definitions and descriptions you use. You need to offer support to the users when they are having difficulty. Finally, you need to maintain the BI applications and add new ones as the business evolves and business needs change.

THE DANGER OF DASHBOARDS

One common analytic application we often have to deal with is the Executive Dashboard. The Executive Dashboard is typically envisioned as the senior executive's window into the business. It's a collection of key measures (KPIs, BPMs, and so on) that are meant to tell the executive the current state of the business and its general direction. This sounds useful, and looks great in the vendor demo, but you need to be particularly careful of this type of analytic application for several reasons:

◆ It's hard to build and manage. The executive dashboard must pull information from across all the major business processes—otherwise you can't really tell what's going on in the business. This means either the DW/BI system must be substantially completed, or you will have to build custom extracts and manual feeds to generate the dashboard—and re-generate it every day, week, or month (depending on its time granularity).

◆ Dashboard information is often not that actionable. The tools don't give users a rich context for the information or any indicators of cause-and-effect. Without knowing the cause, you can't really determine what the appropriate response might be. While sales may be going down, it will still take analysts and frontline managers to figure out the likely causes and recommend appropriate actions. Features like the stoplight (red, yellow, and green indicators) or the speedometer are information poor. If the light turns red, what do we do, stop? If the sales speedometer starts slowing down, what do we do, hit the gas? The corporate equivalent might be for the CEO to call up the VP of Sales and start yelling.

◆ It's often not that useful. In many cases, the main value of the dashboard is as an early warning tool—management does not want to be caught by surprise. (Note that this could make it the most important project on your list.)

Some dashboards can bring huge value to the organization. Corporate performance management systems or balanced score cards can be great ways to tie an organization's performance to its goals. However, this means the organization has to clearly identify its goals and agree on how to measure them. Most of the work to create these systems is organizational and political. If you start with the dashboard first, you are starting at the wrong end of the animal.

The Value of Business Intelligence Applications

Developing BI applications sounds like a lot of work. Before we dive into the details of creating these applications, it's worth reviewing the value you get from them to help justify that work. As it turns out, they add significant value in several ways.

- *Business value:* The process of identifying and creating BI applications based on business requirements almost guarantees that you will provide something of significant value to the business.

- *Broad access:* These applications provide data warehouse access for a broad, important user community. Remember, 90 percent of your knowledge workers will not develop the technical skills and data acumen needed to build their own reports. You must provide them with a means to get the information they need to make informed decisions.

- *Early impact:* BI applications demonstrate the value of the DW/BI system from day one. Business users across the organization can take advantage of the initial business process dimensional model as soon as you deploy it.

- *Data validation:* BI applications help validate the data warehouse content because they represent real-world analyses that bring together dimensions and facts in a way that hasn't happened prior to this point. That is, the ETL developers and data quality folks have been mostly focused on tables and columns. The BI applications bring the whole business process dimensional model together from a business perspective. For example, a report that compares sales by product type, gender, and store format would pull from three different dimensions: product, customer, and store. If you've done the underlying development of the dimensions and facts correctly, there should be no problem. Typically, you will uncover some data irregularities at this point.

- *Query performance:* Similar to data validation, the BI applications generate more complex queries than the basic testing that has taken place prior to this point. So much so, you should capture the SQL and MDX queries from the BI applications and use them to generate some of the ongoing performance metrics.

- *Tool functionality:* Because the BI applications are real business analyses, it is important that your front-end tool be able to handle them easily. Building BI applications provides an opportunity to test the ability of the tools to meet the business needs. The team can bring in a development expert from the vendor's consulting organization (surely, you negotiated this as part of your purchase) to show them how to work around some of the rough edges of the product. In the worst case, the team may need to identify an alternative approach to create certain types of reports. At least this happens during development and testing, and not after the full rollout.

- *Relationship building:* Including your power users in the BI application development process is a great way to keep them excited about the DW/BI system and motivated to climb the learning curve. The users get early, supervised training on the reporting tool and the data, and the team gets extra help building the applications. (So maybe it isn't so helpful in terms of actually getting reports built, but the relationship part is worth the extra effort.) Make this process more fun by setting up a development lab where users and team members can all work and learn together. Bring donuts.

- *Feedback:* Finally, building BI applications helps the DW/BI team experience the impact of their design decisions. Many of the tradeoffs that were made during the design phase surface at this point. For example, it is now possible to estimate the full cost of decisions about pre-calculating a value versus letting the users calculate it in their reports. Consider having your data modelers and ETL developers participate in creating some of the BI applications. Experience is the best teacher.

We hope you were already planning to include BI applications as part of your DW/BI system development effort and this section has served only to highlight the wisdom of your plans. Now that you are appropriately motivated, let's dig into the application development process.

Delivery Platform Options

There are plenty of options for creating BI applications, but every viable option has to support a basic set of functions. At a minimum, the tool must provide the ability to:

- Define the contents, layout, and formatting of a report
- Provide user interaction controls for navigation, parameter setting, and drill down
- Define the execution options for a report—scheduled, interactive
- Define the distribution options for a report—web, email, file directory, and so on
- Participate in existing security systems, and potentially augment them at the user/report level
- Keep extensive metadata about each report
- Keep logs of report access and execution

There are several delivery platform options available from Microsoft, including Microsoft Excel and Access. In particular, SQL Server Reporting Services has been designed specifically to address the BI applications area. Most of our discussions here focus on Reporting Services. A typical DW/BI system chooses a platform to create the officially sanctioned standard reports, and that same platform often supports a range of other options for creating and accessing the BI applications set. Tools for organizing and navigating the report set, like

Windows SharePoint Services, or at least a basic web design tool like FrontPage, are a critical piece of the puzzle. Other add-ins or components like PivotTables in Excel or the .NET grid control might also play a significant role in the application environment. As we discuss in Chapter 9, Microsoft has also included a basic ad hoc reporting tool called Report Builder as part of Reporting Services.

> **NOTE** As we discuss in Chapter 9, Reporting Services includes basic portal functionality. We suggest you supplement this out-of-the-box functionality by integrating with Windows SharePoint Services or other portal technology. Nonetheless, many companies find the basic Reporting Services portal meets enough of their needs that they can't justify the additional expense of a fancier portal.

Our focus in this chapter and the next is on using the Microsoft reporting toolset to create standard reports. There are options other than Microsoft in this space. The market has consolidated in recent years, leaving two leading front-end tool vendors: Business Objects and Cognos. These two companies both have product functionality dedicated to meeting the BI application requirements. There are also front-end tool vendors who specialize in Analysis Services reporting. ProClarity and Panorama are leading providers in this area. Beyond these, literally dozens of companies offer tools in this space. If you don't find something that meets your specific needs, just keep looking. Whatever you choose, the process and principles for creating BI applications we describe here still apply.

The BI Application Development Process

In this section, we describe the process of developing BI applications. The discussion centers on developing the standard reports that make up the majority of BI applications. The process for more complex analytic applications is essentially the same, with more work in the application development phase.

As you saw in Figure 8.1, the Lifecycle divides the overall application development process down into two steps: Specification and Development. We separate the steps because of their dependencies on other sections of the Lifecycle. The Specification step needs to happen as soon as possible after the requirements definition process is complete, before you forget the details. On the other hand, the Development step cannot begin until the other two tracks are mostly complete. You cannot start application development until you have determined your front-end tool strategy and selected a tool. You also need to have data available, so the data modeling and most of the ETL work need to be completed. If you're sourcing reports from Analysis Services, that database should be designed and deployed. Since the two BI application steps are so separated in time, it's easiest to manage them as separate steps in the process.

Application Specification

The goal of the specification step is to capture what you learned about BI application needs during the requirements definition process in a way that can be quickly turned into real applications once the pieces are in place. Create these specifications as soon after gathering requirements as possible. The longer it takes, the harder it will be to remember the details. It's a good idea to include some of your key end users in this process of defining the applications, assigning priorities, and generally making sure you get it right. Application specification typically includes the following tasks:

- Creating a standard look-and-feel template
- Creating the target report list
- Creating a mock-up and documentation for each target report
- Designing the navigation framework
- Conducting the user review

Let's go through each of these tasks in a bit more detail.

Creating the Standard Template

People can find information more quickly if it is presented to them in a consistent fashion. If you read the newspaper at all, you are well aware of this (or at least you benefit from it). The information is grouped in categories: sports, business, lifestyle, and world news. Even though different newspapers generally carry much of the same information, each has its own format standards. You may even have had first-hand experience with the importance of standards and consistency. If your favorite magazine or newspaper ever changed its format, it probably caused you some level of discomfort. This is nothing compared to the discomfort the publication's management felt in making the decision to change the format.

The front-end team is basically in the publishing business. You need to have your own format and content standards and use them consistently. You'll need standards at the portal level and at the individual document level. (We deal with the portal level in the section on navigation structure.) At the individual report level, create a template to identify the standard elements that will appear every report, including their locations and styles.

It's helpful to define the standard template before you begin listing the individual reports because the template will give you some context for defining the reports. The following standard elements need to be defined and in most cases included on every report that comes out of the DW/BI system:

- *Report name:* Create a clear, descriptive name for the report that communicates the contents of the report to the viewer.

- *Report title:* Develop standards for the information that's included in the title and how it's displayed.

- *Report body:* Column/row layout of data, including:

  - Data justification: Right justified for numbers, left justified for row headers, right justified or centered for column headers.

  - Data precision: Dependent on data—figure it out for all your numeric fields.

  - Column and row heading format: Often bold or underlined to distinguish them from report data.

  - Background fills and colors.

  - Formatting of totals or subtotal breakout rows.

- *Header and footer:* The following items should be found somewhere in the header or footer. Create a standard layout, font, and justification scheme, and stick to it.

  - Report name.

  - Parameters used.

  - Navigation category.

  - Report notes: One of the most useful notes about a report is its exceptions, like "Excludes intercompany sales."

  - Page numbering.

  - Report run time and date.

  - Data source(s): Generally which business process dimensional model(s) in the warehouse contributed to the data in the report, and whether that source was relational or OLAP.

  - Confidentiality statement.

  - DW/BI reference: name and logo.

- *Report file name:* The report definition file name is based on your standard file-naming convention. The file itself and any associated code should be under source control.

Figure 8.2 shows one way to lay these elements out on a page. The angle bracket signs (<>) and curly brackets ({}) indicate elements that are context sensitive. That is, they may be system variables, or parameters specific to the report that is being run.

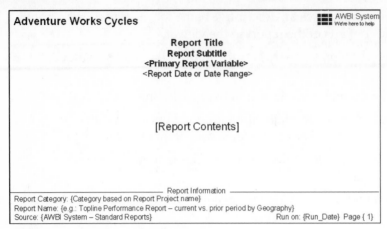

Figure 8.2   Example standard template

Not all report information is displayed on the report itself. You will also need to create the following information for each report:

- User variables and other user interactions like drill downs, links, and so on.
- Report metadata, including description, calculations, derivations, author, date created, and so on.
- Security requirements, including a list or description of the security groups that can see the report.
- Execution cycle, if the report is to run automatically on a periodic basis.
- Execution trigger event, if the report is to be executed in response to a system event like the completion of the nightly HR data load.
- Delivery mechanisms, like email, web site, file directory, or printer.
- Delivery list, which is generally the name of an email distribution list.
- Standard output format, like text, html, PDF, Excel, or Word.
- Page orientation, size, and margin settings.

Observe that all of these elements are essentially *report metadata*. Therefore, this information should be kept in a metadata repository at some point, so it can be used during report creation or accessed by the users on demand when they need to understand more about a given report. Meanwhile, you can use a spreadsheet or text document while you are creating the specs. Metadata structures for Reporting Services are discussed in Chapter 13.

Creating the Target Report List

The first step in creating the target report list is to go back through the user interview documentation and pull out every reporting/analysis request, desire, fantasy, or hope that anyone expressed. As you make this list of candidate reports, give each report its own name and description. In addition, capture your best sense of its business value and the effort it will take to build. It also helps to make note of who asked for it, (there may be several people), and any other parties you think might benefit from it. These are the folks who will help you further define the report should it make it on the target list.

It's easiest to capture this list in a spreadsheet, like the example shown in Figure 8.3.

You need to understand the content, format, and priority of all these reports, as you add them to the list. The business value and level of effort are on a 1-10 scale, where 10 is high value or high effort. These need to be only relative estimates at this point. They're not meant to be converted directly to dollars or work hours. It's worth spending time on the names and descriptions because the better these are, the more likely you'll be able to figure out what they mean later on. Part of creating the standard template includes coming up with some useful naming conventions for report types, like Topline, Trend, Time Series, Comparison, and so on. Figure 8.3 is a bit simplified in order to fit on the page. Your list will likely have more descriptive information.

Once you have a complete list of candidate reports, rank them in priority order. Group related reports that draw on the same data sources to speed the prioritization process. Conduct this prioritization with a small group of competent, interested business folks. Review the list with the group, making sure everyone understands the reports. In particular, spend some time reviewing (or assigning) the business value score. Some reports, like actual orders versus quota, might be particularly interesting to the VP of Sales, but they may get a lower priority than the reports that include only orders data because quota information may not be in the DW/BI system yet. If everyone agrees on the business value score, the rest is relatively easy.

After the whole list has been reviewed, re-sort the rows and set a cutoff point at about 10 to 15 reports down the list. This is your initial target list. Eyeball the results with the group to make sure all the reports on the target list deserve their success. Also, make sure all the reports that didn't make the target list deserved to be cut. Remember, this decision is often as political as it is logical, and just because a report doesn't make the initial list doesn't mean it won't get done. Many of these may be handed off to the experts from the departments (the power users) who were most interested in the reports.

You might need to expand the number of reports on the target list a bit, but make sure anyone who pushes for more reports understands that each report is a couple of days more work. Perhaps they would be willing to work on building those additional reports?

#	Report Name	Short Description	Report Category	Primary Owner	Business Value	Level of Effort	Report Type	Comments
	Doc Title: Candidate Report List	**Project:** AWBI System: Orders business process			**Prepared By:** Karen Berg		**Date Prepared:** 07/09/2005	
1	Sales Rep Performance Ranking	Total orders by Sales Rep for target year and prior year, with rank for each year and the change in rank.	Sales Performance	Brian Welker	9	3	Table	Add a drill down to sales details for a select Rep.
2	Product Topline Performance	Product Orders and Market Share by Current Period vs Prior by Geography	Marketing Results	Mary Gibson	8	4	Matrix / Pie Chart	List of Measures, calcs, drill downs, etc.
3	Territory Orders Time Series	Last 13 months Actual Orders vs Forecast by Territory	Orders Analysis	Amy Alberts	7	3	Line Chart	
4	Product Orders Time Series	Last 13 months Actual Orders vs Forecast by Product level	Marketing Results / Orders Analysis	Mary Gibson	8	3	Line Chart	
5	Product Cross-sell	...						

Figure 8.3   Example Candidate Report list

THE BASIC BUSINESS ANALYSIS CYCLE

Understanding how analysis is used to support decision making is a key part of being able to create useful reports. The BI team must be able to make meaningful contributions to the business, not just build reports from specs.

Business analysis usually happens in a repeating cycle. The following figure shows a progression from Plan to Implement to Monitor to Assess and back to Plan. The analysis cycle for any given business event can begin in any of the processes although it rarely starts in the Implement process.

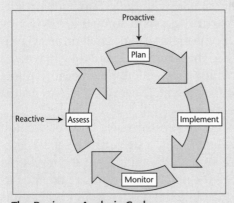

The Business Analysis Cycle

PLAN

When the analysis is proactive, the cycle typically starts with the planning process. Planning involves gathering data from various business processes and external sources to build a business model for a new product, service, program, or any significant business activity. This data could include costs and revenue growth curves for existing, similar items; time to market estimates; seasonal factors; or any other relevant measures. Much of this input is based on historical data that can be found in the BI system. The planning process is often ad hoc in nature, driven by the specific attributes of the new program.

IMPLEMENT

Once the program is approved, the various business processes that will make it come to life kick in. These are the actual tasks of marketing, manufacturing, field training, and so on across the organization's value chain. Most of this activity happens outside the scope of the BI system; however, it is critical that a BI representative be involved to help implement the program with the appropriate measurement systems in mind. This is particularly true in e-commerce when it often happens that a company rolls out a new online service and has no real way to measure its usage. They can tell how many people sign up for the service and how much revenue it generates, but the actual usage data may be buried in the web logs, or not even really collected. The implementation process usually does not involve a significant amount of analysis.

MONITOR

Everything in the ongoing business must be monitored, but most of the ongoing activity is routine and can be managed by exception. Even monitoring new program activity is not much more than answering the question "What is happening?" in the early stages. These numbers will get a significant share of management attention, but it is difficult to understand the implications of the numbers and to develop meaningful trends until some amount of time has passed. It usually makes no sense to react to a number that is less than expected on the first day. It may take longer than planned for the market to find and understand the new product. Alternatively, the initial marketing campaign may have been mis-targeted. The monitoring process for ongoing activity is the primary role of standard reporting.

ASSESS

Once enough data is available, it becomes possible to assess the impact of the new program. It requires a significant amount of exploration to root out the interesting relationships in the data. This may even extend beyond the ad hoc tools to include data mining functions.

All too often, the analysis cycle actually begins in the Assess phase when the business is reacting to an external change. For example, if a competitor cuts the price of its product, the first response of a clever organization would be to assess whether or not the price cut had any impact on market share. Even if it does, further analysis may show that it makes sense to hold the price and lose some amount of market share.

In any case, once the impact of the event is understood, the organization can plan a response, which takes us back around to the top of the cycle. If appropriate analytical applications are available, they can help make the assessment process much easier. Otherwise, assessment is primarily ad hoc in nature.

Creating Report Specifications and Documentation

It may sound obvious, but during the application specification step, you should create a specification for each report. The report specification consists of the following components:

- Report template information as outlined previously
- Report mock-up (optional, but most helpful)
- User interaction list
- Detailed documentation

The report mock-ups are a great way to communicate the content and purpose of the reports. Beyond the mock-up itself, create two additional items to complete the spec: a user interaction list and detailed documentation. We'll go through the report mock-up first, and then discuss the user interaction list and the detailed documentation.

Report Mock-Ups

The example report mock-up shown in Figure 8.4 is based on the standard template we created earlier. The difference is we've filled in the report structure for one of the reports on our target list (you can see another report mock-up example in Chapter 9).

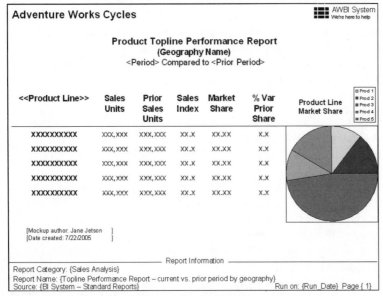

Figure 8.4 Example Product Topline Performance Report mock-up

It's helpful to indicate several user interaction functions on the mock-up. For example, the double angle bracket signs (<<>>) indicate drill-down capabilities—that is, a user could click on an entry in this column or row header and drill down to the next level of detail. We've found it useful to indicate the following functions on the mock-up. You may have additional needs, or prefer to use other indicators.

< >   User-entered variable

<< >>   Drillable field

{ }   Application entered variable (either from the system or metadata)

\\ \\   Link/URL—link to another report or documentation source

( )   Page or section break field

[ ]   Report template comments

User Interaction List

Although the function indicators on the report template tell you what kind of interaction is possible, they don't tell you what that interaction is like. The user interaction list identifies the nature and degree of interaction a user may have with a given report. This can range from None for a completely static, pre-run report to an extensive list of fields and behaviors for a fully interactive report. Capture the basic interactions: variable specification (and its sub-types: user entry or user selection), drill down, and field addition/replacement. Figure 8.5 shows an example user interaction list for the Product Topline Performance report shown in the mock-up in Figure 8.4.

Doc Title:	Project:			Prepared By:	Date Prepared:
User Interaction List	AWBI System – Orders business process			Karen Berg	07/09/2005
Report Number: 2	Report Name: Product Topline Performance				

#	Report Element	Source	Function Type	Default value(s)	Handled in:	Comments
1	Geography Name	Primary data query	Page/ Section break	N/A	Reporting tool	Sales wants this at the region level, but it may be helpful to have a version that allows user selection of the geography level.
2	Product Line	Data query	Drill down	Product Line Level	Reporting tool	SELECT DISTINCT from DimProduct
3	Period	Initial prompt screen	Pull down menu	Current month	Reporting tool	User can determine granularity of period (e.g. week, month, quarter, year)
4	Prior Period	Initial prompt screen	Pull down menu	Year ago month	Reporting tool	Note: Prior period must be before current period and must be at same grain as Period entry.
5	Report Category	Report metadata	Application entry	N/A	Hard coded	See if the tool can read this from the metadata at execution time, otherwise, hard code it in the report itself.
6	...					

Figure 8.5   Example user interaction list

Figure 8.5 shows a row on the user interaction list for each function indicator on the report mock-up. Include enough information so that someone who's building this report can use the mock-up and the user interaction list to do the job.

Most front-end tools provide a means for interacting with the user to gather user-specified values prior to report execution. In Figure 8.5, items 3 and 4 come from the initial prompt screen. Some tools are fairly rudimentary in their control choices; others allow you full control over the user interface. If your front-end tool has a great deal of flexibility, create a standard user interface template for user-provided values.

Detailed Documentation

Create detailed documentation to collect the information you haven't captured elsewhere. Note the report category, the sources of the data in the report, the calculations for each column and row, and any exceptions or exclusions to build into the query. Additional information about the report might include creation and modification tracking, and an expiration date, if the report has a limited useful life. A good place to keep this is at the end of the user interaction list.

Designing the Navigation Framework

Once you know which reports to build, you need to categorize them so the users can find the information they're looking for as quickly as possible. We call this organizing structure the *navigation framework*, or *navigation hierarchy*. Ideally, this structure is self-explanatory. That is, anyone who knows something about the business can generally find what they want fairly quickly.

The best approach we've found, and this may sound obvious, is to organize the reports by business process. If someone knows your business, even at a cursory level, they will be able to find what they need. There are a lot of additional design principles that come into play here, but we will leave them to the next chapter when we describe a simple navigation framework for Adventure Works Cycles.

Conducting the User Review

Once you have a solid set of application specs in place, it is extremely helpful to go over them with the user community. This design review covers a lot of ground. In it, you need to validate your choice of high-priority applications and test the clarity of the specifications—do they make sense to the business folks? It involves users in the process, emphasizing their central role and developing their commitment. It also can keep people engaged in the project by giving them a sense for what will be possible in just a few short months. Leave time in your project plan to make any modifications to the specs that come out of this design review.

Once the specs are complete and have been reviewed, you can put them on the shelf, so to speak. But keep them close by because they'll be useful if you do any front-end tool evaluations. Whatever tool you choose should be able to easily handle the range of reports in the initial report set. Other than that, there isn't much more you can do with the specs until you're ready to begin the report development process.

Application Development

It's difficult to start the application development process before a lot of the DW/BI system infrastructure is in place. You need a reasonably representative subset of the data in the presentation database in the final model. The front-end tools must be selected and purchased. And of course, you must have completed the BI application specifications. Typically, all of these events don't occur until some time close to the system test process we describe in Chapter 14. As a result, we usually do the application development as part of the system testing. This makes sense because these reports are excellent test cases for several reasons: They represent a range of analyses, they are typically more complex than fake test reports, and they are real-world in that they are based on how users want to see the data.

The application development process itself is a fairly typical development effort. We usually cover the following steps within the Prepare-Build-Test-Rollout framework:

Prepare
- Install front-end tool(s).
- Set up end user data access security system.
- Create business metadata.
- Capture process metadata.

Build
- Build applications.
- Create the BI portal.

Test
- Unit test.
- System test.
- User test.

Rollout
- Publish.
- Monitor and maintain.

Let's examine each of these tasks in a bit more detail.

Install Front-End Tool(s)

Each front-end tool has its own system architecture and technical complexities—getting it functioning in good working order is often less than trivial. Installation might include components located on a whole range of application servers, desktops, web servers, and even in the database server. We described some of these options for Reporting Services in Chapter 4. See your administration manuals or contact your vendor if you are using any other front-end tools.

Set Up End User Security

As we discuss in Chapter 12, you should push for a security policy that's as simple as possible for the DW/BI system. Encourage the decision makers to put information in the "open" category—available to everyone who can access the DW/BI system. Data is valuable only in context, and the richer the context, the more valuable the data.

There are legitimate reasons to limit access to certain data, especially personal information like credit card numbers or health care data. But often the drive to protect data is political: A sales manager doesn't want his colleagues to see how he's doing, for example. Data is an organizational asset and should be accessible to anyone who can use it to benefit the organization.

The ideal approach to security from the BI system perspective is to let someone else do the heavy lifting. As much as possible, leverage your IT organization's centralized security system when building your BI organization's security system. In a Microsoft environment, this typically means using Active Directory to create users and groups. Then the SQL Server database objects, Analysis Services database objects, Report Server objects, web pages, and front-end tools all work from the centralized security service. Users log on once and can move seamlessly from tool to tool and server to server without even knowing it.

We talk about some specific Reporting Services security techniques in Chapter 12.

Review Business Metadata

Business metadata is the descriptive information about the contents of the standard reports. You should already have the report-related metadata in the specs you created back in the application specification step. Pull these out and review the names, descriptions, titles, and other business metadata elements to make sure they still make sense. See Chapter 13 for more information on business metadata.

Capture Process Metadata

Process metadata is information about the execution of various processes in the DW/BI system. With regard to reporting, you need some way to monitor usage and performance of your standard report set. At a minimum, you need to know what reports are being used, and how long they take to execute. Over time, if certain reports are never used, you may want to take them out of the portal. If other reports are used often, and they do not perform well, examine them carefully to see how you can improve that performance. But if you don't capture usage statistics, you won't have any idea where to start.

Most of the front-end tools have their own logging system that you can tap into to monitor and tune the reporting process. Chapter 13 gives some basic metadata structures to hold Reporting Services process metadata. Make sure your logging mechanisms are in place and working properly. The earlier you do this, the better.

Build Applications

Finally, you get to have some fun! Actually building the applications takes relatively little time compared to the rest of the process. As we mentioned earlier, it also provides a great opportunity to build relationships with your user community. Set up a temporary lab (it could be the training room) and dedicate it to application development for as long as necessary. Bring in a group of power users to help build out the initial target list of reports. If you have managed expectations early on, these users should be excited about participating. They get early access to the tools and the data. Bring in donuts and lunch, and maybe have special hats or T-shirts made up. Start the day by conducting a brief training session on the tools, and reviewing the specs. Then start building. Encourage lots of interaction—interaction is the rationale for the lab—so everyone can learn from one another. Keep at least two lists of issues and difficulties: one for the data and one for the front-end tool.

If this is your first experience developing reports with your front-end tool, bring in an expert as a consultant toward the mid-point of the development process. Go through your list of issues and have the person show you how to solve or work around the problems you've encountered. You may have to actually pay for the consulting unless you negotiated it as part of the software purchase. Either way, get help from an expert. It's worth it.

Create the Navigation Portal

At the same time you are building the initial set of reports, you need to be building them a home as well. The question is what technology container you will put them in to present them to the user community. The simple answer is the web, but that doesn't narrow your choices too much. You could build your own web site from scratch, use a portal technology to give you the basic delivery infrastructure, or use the delivery vehicle provided by your tool of choice. The navigation portal is based on the navigation structure we outlined during the report specification process. Chapter 9 shows a simple example of a navigation portal for Adventure Works Cycles.

Unit Test

Test each report. Have someone else go through the report piece by piece, testing the calculations, report layout, user inputs, and results. If possible, compare the results to those from another, independent source from outside the DW/BI system. We cover testing in Chapter 14 when we describe the deployment process.

System Test

Once the report is deemed to work on a stand-alone basis, see how it works as part of the production process. Depending on your front-end tool, and the complexity of your warehouse environment, there could be a large number of elements that need to be tested. If it is supposed to run at a certain time or in response to a certain event, does it in fact do so? Does it publish its results properly? Can users see updated results where they expect to see them: on the web, on a file server, or in their email? If there is a problem with the process, do notifications go out on failure? Is there some indicator of successful completion, like an entry in the log files?

If you are supporting a large user community with these reports, you should plan for some stress testing as well. There are tools that will simulate multiple simultaneous users. Set them up and see what happens. Include ample time in your project plan to tune these applications for large user communities.

User Test

If users were involved in the development of the reports, this step may not be necessary. However, if the users have not yet seen the reports, or you'd like to get reactions from non-technical users, include a task in your process to give them a chance to inspect and approve them. This may take the form of a demo to a group of users with time for questions and answers. Or, it may be something users can do from their desks, with a simple web survey form or email response. Some IT organizations require a formal signoff from a user representative. This makes us nervous. While it can be useful to have an official acceptance mechanism, it is often an indicator of a lack of trust between the two groups. We usually document the acceptance by marking the application development task complete in a project status meeting with user representatives present. Sometimes we'll send an email to the business project lead to specifically note the completion of the application development and verify they are happy with the results; this is usually framed in celebratory terms.

Publish

The initial release is primarily a public relations process. You need to notify users that the BI portal is now available and give them a link to check it out. We encourage you to hold short, one-hour orientation classes to teach people how to use the BI portal. If you have a good navigation framework, this class is unnecessary, at least for its stated purpose. An overview session is still extremely valuable because it allows you to educate users—including senior management—about what data is available, what future plans are, where to go for help, and what they should expect from the BI system. In other words, this might be your only chance to indoctrinate them.

As soon as these reports are made available, users will begin to think of many other reports they would like to see. There are several ways to handle this. First, manage expectations up front by getting buy-in on the initial set during the specification process. This is much easier when you involve users in the definition of the original report set. Second, remind users they can learn to create their own reports. Have training classes scheduled as part of the deployment and encourage users to learn how to help themselves. Third, direct users to their departmental experts who may be able to create the reports they need. Fourth, if their requests look valuable, consider adding them to the candidate list. They may sort to the top in the second release. Finally, allocate hidden resources right from the start to create some of these additional reports.

As power users and departmental experts develop their own reports, they will want to share them with their co-workers. You will need to provide a place for them to do so, but it should be clearly identified as departmental reports. They do not carry the official BI system seal of approval.

These strategies allow you to be flexible and responsive at a crucial, early point in the user's experience with the BI system. Remember your motto: We're from the Data Warehouse, and we're here to help.

Maintenance

Maintenance is covered in detail in Chapter 15, but this section presents a few things to keep in mind. The first job in maintaining the BI applications is to make sure the existing report set is available and continues to perform as expected. There are plenty of reasons why their performance might degrade—changes in the database, increased usage, or other processes running on the report server. In one case, we had to build out a separate report server for our standard reports because the users were scheduling hundreds of their own reports to execute overnight. The server was limited to running eight reports at a time, so the standard reports were waiting in the queue every morning. We could have simply raised the priority for the standard reports, but we didn't want to seem like we were pushing the users around.

In addition to performance, you need to monitor the content of the standard reports. Over time, many will become stale—they are no longer useful from a business perspective. Sometimes the reports are still useful, but some of the definitions have changed. The business has refined its understanding of the data and newer reports reflect this, but the older reports need to be updated.

The front-end team will also be adding new reports all the time. In fact, you should consider every request for an ad hoc analysis to be an opportunity to add a new report to the library. The more reports in the portal, the more likely a user will find one that provides needed information, as long as the portal is well designed. The price of this wealth of information is that the maintenance job grows as the report library grows.

Plan to have a report "spring cleaning" every year or so. Go through the whole library with the usage statistics data and see what gets used and what doesn't. Look at each report to make sure it still works and that it still has value. Involve users in this process to help assess the value of questionable reports. This is definitely one of those activities like cleaning the refrigerator—it's unpleasant but important. If you don't do this, the BI system will begin to lose credibility with the users because more and more of the reports are out of date, or don't work. The portal begins to look like an abandoned property with broken windows and unsightly trash piled in the side yard. Not the image you're looking for.

Summary

We have learned to accept the reality that 90 percent of business users are unlikely to ever build their own query from scratch, and they need a more appropriate access method. Business intelligence applications provide the bridge most business users will take to access the data warehouse. In this chapter we described the nature and purpose of BI applications, ranging from standard reports to more complex, business process-specific analytic applications. We also talked about some of the tradeoffs involved in buying packaged analytic applications.

The bulk of the chapter described the Lifecycle's two-step process of specifying and building an initial set of standard reports to be included in the initial deployment of the BI system. The initial application specification step follows closely on the heels of the requirements definition process. The application development step must wait until the data is available, the tools are selected and installed, and the specs are completed. As a result, the two steps are separated by a fairly large time gap, usually measured in months.

Both the specification and development processes involve participation from the user community. This helps build an understanding of the strengths and weaknesses of the BI system, and an ownership of the decisions around which reports to build and the tools and data choices that went into the initial design.

The next chapter presents many of the techniques described here in the context of Microsoft's Reporting Services.

Building the BI Application in Reporting Services

Building a bridge for those who don't want to swim

Every user of your DW/BI system will access BI applications and standard reports. The vast majority of them—typically between 70 and 90 percent—will use only standard reports. To those users, the standard reports *are* the DW/BI system. After working through the database design, ETL system requirements, and OLAP database design, creating reports seems easy. If your designs are driven by business imperatives, creating reports is easy. But you won't know you've succeeded until you actually create some.

Reporting Services is Microsoft's offering for enterprise reporting. It was first released in January 2004 and has moved through a couple of development iterations since then. Reporting Services has been well received by the Microsoft customer base and has been successfully implemented in many large organizations. Given its reasonable level of functionality and its more than reasonable incremental cost, we expect that a large percentage of folks reading this book will choose Reporting Services as the delivery vehicle for their standard reports and analytic applications.

This chapter provides the basic information you need to build your initial set of standard reports. We start with an exploration of general business requirements for standard reporting and the architectural implications of those business requirements. We then examine the Reporting Services architecture to see how it matches up to the business requirements and to learn its terms and terminology.

> **NOTE** As we described in Chapter 8, analytic applications are a more sophisticated form of standard reports. Your initial set of standard reports may include some analytic applications, but that doesn't matter at this point. For the sake of simplicity, we refer to the general class of official, predefined reports as standard reports.

As Figure 9.1 illustrates, this chapter addresses the BI application development step of the Lifecycle methodology based on using Reporting Services as the application platform.

The bulk of the chapter describes how to work with Reporting Services to develop standard reports. We start with the usual planning and preparation steps—in this case, setting up the environment and the report templates. Then, we create one of the standard reports for Adventure Works Cycles based on the prioritized target report list from Chapter 8. Finally, we discuss the creation of a navigation portal to provide the framework for presenting these reports in a simple BI portal.

By the end of this chapter, you should be able to answer the following questions:

- What is Reporting Services? How does it work, and where does it fit in the overall DW/BI system?

- What tools does Reporting Services provide for report development?

- What does it take to create a standard report in the Reporting Services environment?

- Why is the BI portal important, and what information should be included in the portal? How can you design the portal so it's easy for users to understand, and easy for you to maintain?

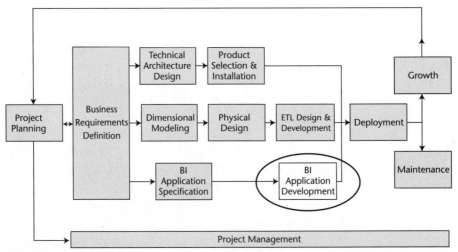

Figure 9.1   The BI application development step

> **LEARNING REPORTING SERVICES**
>
> This chapter is not a tutorial on Reporting Services. If you've been charged with the task of building the initial set of reports, you should first install Reporting Services and the examples on your development machine. Then review the documentation in Microsoft's Books Online and work through the tutorials. You may also want to get one of the many Reporting Services books available, or even take one of the many classes offered in Reporting Services.

A High-Level Architecture for Reporting

Remember, the initial step in any architecture effort is to understand the business requirements. The Lifecycle shows that business requirements determine the architecture, and the architecture defines product requirements. Standard report users' business requirements should determine the functionality of the tool you use.

This section begins with an overview of the high-level business requirements for standard reporting and the architectural or functional implications of each of these requirements. With these requirements as a guide, we examine Reporting Services to see how well it fits into your reporting architecture. It's important to step back to consider reporting and analysis requirements because it may turn out that Reporting Services doesn't provide all the functionality your users need. You will need to gather detailed requirements for reporting and analysis as part of the requirements definition process. The functional list we provide here is not enough for you to do a rigorous product evaluation.

Reviewing Business Requirements for Reporting

The real, detailed business requirements will come from the requirements-gathering process. The steps outlined in this section are not a substitute for that process. However, it's possible to identify some common, high-level business requirements for reporting. Create a mental image of your user community. The group includes people at all levels of the organization, with a broad range of technical skills. The common element is that they're business focused. They're generally not that excited by technology and will rarely build their own queries from scratch. They're more interested in getting a quick answer to a specific business question than in working through an analysis process or figuring out the correct SQL syntax for a query.

Table 9.1 summarizes the major, high-level requirements of this group related to standard reports. A few of the major functional implications are listed for each requirement. Look at the second row of the table: In order to meet the business need to find reports, the DW/BI team will need to provide navigation, metadata, and search functions. Table 9.1 serves as a roadmap for describing the basic requirements for reporting and their architectural implications.

Table 9.1 User Requirements and Functional Implications

BUSINESS REQUIREMENT	FUNCTIONAL IMPLICATIONS
Create reports	Variety of presentation formats (tables, charts, matrices, and so on) Powerful, easy, fast development tool to build reports
Find reports	Navigation framework Metadata Search
View reports	Access through a variety of methods User-initiated (for example, browser-based) System-initiated (for example, auto email)
Receive results in most useful way	Output to a variety of file types
Change report as needed	Parameters Drill down/additional attributes Linking
Solid, reliable system	Performance Scalability Management

Let's look at each requirement in turn:

- *Create reports:* As the business changes, business users will need new reports. These reports must present information in a way users can understand and use. Because we don't expect business users to create these reports themselves, the reporting tool must provide the developers with a range of alternative ways to display the information, including various tabular formats, pivots, and charts. The tool must be easy for the report developers and power users to use, allowing them to be as effective as possible. In most cases, only a few developers will be meeting the reporting needs of many users.

- *Find reports:* Standard report users must be able to find the published report that answers the question at hand. The reports must be presented in an intuitive framework with good descriptions and clear, concise, easily accessible documentation. We described the idea of the navigation portal in Chapter 8, which provides the framework for users to navigate to the report they're looking for. Users should be able to browse the metadata and search the report library for key words to identify reports that contain the information they seek.

- *View reports:* Users must be able to view the information when and where they need it. At the very least, this means providing access to the reports on the organization's intranet. Users must be able to view a report in a browser, and print it out to take to a meeting. It might be important in some organizations to provide email delivery, saving to a file share, printing to a remote printer, or sending a fax. In some cases, the users come to the reporting environment and request, or pull, a report. In other cases, users want to have the report sent, or pushed, to them as soon as it's ready or the underlying data has changed. Most organizations want both types of access.

- *Receive results:* Users need to receive reports in the file format that is most appropriate for their needs. In many cases, this could simply be an HTML file. If a user wants to integrate the report with other information like a planning model, she may prefer a more sophisticated format like Excel. Users often want to view the report in one format and export it in another. There are at least a dozen common target file formats. Each DW/BI team will need to make sure it provides the ones that are important for its users.

- *Change reports:* The term "standard report" doesn't mean completely fixed structure. Users need some flexibility in interacting with the reports. This is also true from a development point of view—it makes no sense to build a new report for every possible value of each attribute in the DW/BI system. The tool needs to provide the means to parameterize the report and customize its content to some degree. Parameters allow the user to enter a value or choose from a pulldown menu, and re-run the report to see the results based on the new selection. Parameterized reports let the user explore the data within the safety of the report structure.

Report linking provides a related level of flexibility. In a linked report, clicking on a row, column, or number will use the specific value selected to initiate a link to a related report or URL. The user can click on one of the product categories in a Sales by Product Category report that you have defined to link to a report displaying sales data for all the subcategories within the selected category.

The reporting tool should allow users to drill down to the next lower level of detail by letting them include additional attributes that were not displayed in the original presentation of the report. This drilldown may follow the natural hierarchies in the data, like drilling from year to month, or product category to product. It may also include the simple addition of another attribute, potentially even from another dimension in the business process dimensional model. For example, the report may start out showing sales by product. The user may want to include the gender attribute from the Customer table to see if certain products display gender preferences. A simple version of this drilldown involves showing and hiding data that's already included in the results set. A more complex approach allows the user to select additional attributes.

- *Solid, reliable system:* All the requirements listed so far come from directly stated user requirements. There's another list of requirements that users are generally unaware of, unless you fail to meet them. These requirements are about providing and managing an enterprise reporting service. They include functions like report library management, performance, and scheduling. Library management functions include providing ways for users to subscribe to a report (that is, sign up to have it pushed to them), and allowing users to check in their own reports (in a special area, of course). The reporting service must support processing functions like scheduling reports to run as soon as the data is available, and managing the performance of the report server. These management features are especially important if you have a heavy user load.

The business also has second-level requirements about things like security and reliability, but we are more concerned with direct business functionality at this point.

This brief business requirements and architectural implications review is one part of the architecture process described in this book's Introduction. Clearly, this is only the initial pass at reporting requirements, and your organization's requirements will include additional functionality. In practice, you need to back up each requirements section with a more detailed description of the required functionality. For example, if you ask any tool vendor a question like "Do you provide a variety of presentation formats?" the answer, spoken in a loud, confident manner, will be "Absolutely!" Instead, list several detailed examples of how people need to see information. Make them tough, real-world examples and use them to test out the tool's functionality and to give you a chance to see how difficult it is to work with the tool.

Examining the Reporting Services Architecture

The primary intent of Reporting Services is to provide a solid, scalable, extensible reporting infrastructure. This helps us understand the pieces of the architecture and how they fit together to become Reporting Services. Figure 9.2 shows the high-level architecture of Reporting Services and its operating environment.

The heart of Reporting Services is a stateless web service called the Report Server. It sits inside Internet Information Services (IIS) as an ASP.NET application. It was built from the ground up based on ASP.NET web services. (Web services are essentially applications hosted by a web server.) This means the functionality is accessible either through a browser pointed to the Report Server URL, or through an application using the SOAP API. The SOAP API allows developers to integrate reports seamlessly into other applications.

The Report Server communicates with its metadata store hosted in a SQL Server database called ReportServer. The ReportServer database stores all the information needed to define and manage reports. It is not the source for report data.

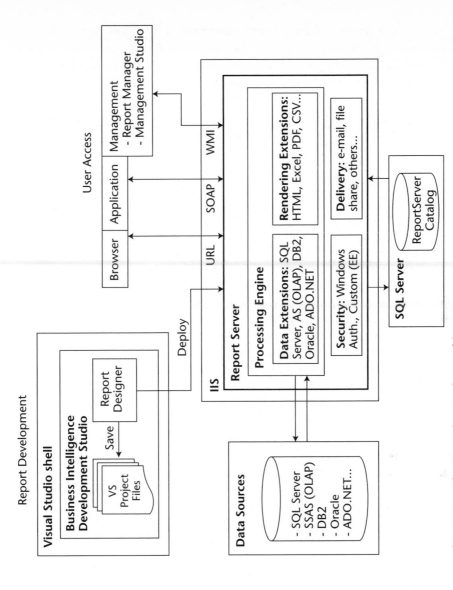

Figure 9.2 The Reporting Services architecture

At the core of the Report Server is a Processing Engine that supports functions like sorting, filtering, aggregations, and conditional formatting. It has several components that are designed to be extensible: Data, Rendering, Security, and Delivery.

- *Data:* A data extension allows the server to connect to a data source. Reporting Services ships with several data extensions, including SQL Server, Analysis Services, DB2, Oracle, and ADO.NET. ADO.NET indirectly provides access to a wide range of data sources that have OLE DB or ODBC drivers. Microsoft provides a set of APIs in the data extension space if you need to add a data extension of your own. If you have invested in an ADO.NET data extension, you can plug it into the Report Server.

- *Rendering:* The rendering extension allows the processing engine to take a report defined in the Report Definition Language (RDL) and output it to any number of formats including HTML, Excel, PDF, CSV, and others. You can write your own rendering extension and add it to the list, but it is non-trivial because of the complexity of the formatting options in RDL. We expect third parties to develop rendering extensions for specific products like charting packages.

- *Security:* The standard edition of Reporting Services relies on existing IIS and Windows authentication for security. If you have an application that is not using Windows Integrated security, you can support it through an extensible security component included in SQL Server 2005 Enterprise Edition.

- *Delivery:* Reporting Services supports the distribution of reports in ways other than direct access to the web server. The delivery function allows you to send reports through file shares and email. This, too, is extensible, and partners have built other delivery options like fax and networked printers.

From a user access perspective, the upper-right corner of Figure 9.2 shows how Reporting Services provides three major methods for directly interacting with the server. Most users access the server through the web browser using a URL that points to the reporting service. As we described earlier, it is also possible to access the server through an application using SOAP APIs. The management functions are accessible through the Windows Management Instrumentation (WMI) provider objects. This is what the Report Manager uses from the browser or from the Management Studio to manage Reporting Services.

Overall, the Reporting Services architecture accomplishes its primary intent—it is an extensible, scalable reporting infrastructure designed to meet the technical needs of a broad range of organizations, from small companies to large enterprises. While good technology is important, technical products succeed only if they meet business users' needs. The next section examines the architecture from a business requirements perspective.

Using Reporting Services as a Standard Reporting Tool

The first section in this chapter outlined the business requirements for standard reporting and the architectural implications of those requirements. The next section described the basic architecture of Reporting Services. This section uses the list of functional implications in Table 9.1 as a means to examine the Reporting Services architecture from a business requirements point of view. Each section that follows takes a row in the table and explores how Reporting Services provides the needed functionality.

Creating Reports

The Report Designer in BI Studio is Microsoft's primary development tool for creating Reporting Services reports. As we discussed in Chapter 3, the BI Studio lives in, and leverages the power of, the Visual Studio development environment. This means the person creating the reports is working in a software development environment. The report creator needs to know about words like debug, build, and deploy. He'll need to be able to create a data connection and write SQL. It's not a place for the faint of heart, and certainly not a place for the vast majority of end users. Report Designer allows developers to create reports, save them to the file system, and publish them up to the report server.

After the report is defined in Report Designer, the definition is saved in Report Definition Language (RDL), which is an open XML schema for defining all the components of the report. This includes the definition of the datasets; calculations like totals, expressions, conditional formatting, sorts, and filters; and layout of information including tables, pivots, charts, text, and formatting. When you publish, or deploy, a report to the Report Server, it writes the RDL out to the Reporting Services Catalog in an XML data type field in one of the metadata tables.

REPORT DEFINITION LANGUAGE

You can see what the Report Definition Language looks like by opening up a report in a browser (look for files ending in .rdl). If you want to see the full XML schema, go to the beginning of the .rdl file and look for the URL of the namespace. It should be right after "xmlns=". Copy the URL you see there into the address box of another browser window. You can see the entire XML schema of the Report Definition Language.

REPORT BUILDER

Microsoft includes Report Builder in Reporting Services. Report Builder is designed to allow business users to create simple ad hoc reports. Report Builder limits users to a simple tabular report, a simple matrix, or a simple chart. Are you seeing a simple pattern here? As Microsoft says in its marketing materials, Report Builder is not designed to be a full-featured data analysis tool. However, Report Builder reports are RDL files, so users can create reports and publish them to the Report Server (if they have permission). Reports created using Report Builder can be scheduled and managed just like any other Reporting Services reports. You can also use Report Builder as a query design tool to create the input datasets inside the Report Designer.

Using a standard like RDL has huge implications for the reporting architecture: It separates report design from report execution. It means that anyone can create a tool that saves its report definition in RDL. At that point, the tool writer can take advantage of the Reporting Services infrastructure to manage, publish, distribute, and render the report. In fact, there are already several alternative report design tools available, including one from Microsoft called Report Builder.

The Report Designer meets the basic requirements for creating reports. Because Report Designer is oriented toward programmers, the solution to many problems is to write code of some sort rather than making a selection, dragging and dropping, or checking a box, as with the more end user-oriented tools used for creating reports. Of course, this is the universal tradeoff: power and flexibility versus ease of use. The nature of this tradeoff will become clearer later in this chapter when we create an example report. It will become (painfully) obvious when you begin working with the tool firsthand.

Finding Reports

After the developers have created and deployed a set of standard reports, users need to be able to find a report they want when they want it. Start by organizing the reports into categories that make sense to users, as we described in the section on creating the navigation framework in Chapter 8.

Microsoft has included a basic navigation framework as part of the Reporting Services product called Report Manager. The Report Manager plays two roles. It allows the developer to set some of the parameters and properties of the report server and the reports themselves. It can also serve as a simple vehicle to deliver standard reports interactively to the users.

Figure 9.3 shows the top level of a simple Report Manager home page. The interface is essentially a list of directories that follow the basic tree structure of the projects that have been deployed to the report server. This simple three-level hierarchy (Home/Project/Report) serves as the navigation framework for the user. You can add levels to this hierarchy by adding folders in the Report Manager or in the TargetReportFolder property of the Project Properties under the View menu of the Report Designer. When the report is deployed to the server, the project name is used to create a directory. To view a report, the user clicks on the project name and then on the report name.

Figure 9.4 shows the three Sales by Product reports available when the user clicks on the 01 Marketing - Product Mgmt - Sales by Product directory shown in Figure 9.4.

Under the covers, Report Manager is a web application that uses the SOAP and WMI protocols to provide access to the Report Server and its contents. Management Studio provides the same basic report management functionality for the developer as Report Manager does, but in the server manager interface. Accessing the Report Manager through Management Studio allows the developer to manage server and report properties, security, shared execution schedules, and jobs all through the object browser window. Used in this mode, Management Studio is strictly a management tool for the Report Server—it does not display the contents of the reports or provide the other user-oriented functions that Report Manager in the browser does.

Report Manager does provide many useful functions. Because it's based on the file system directory structure, it allows the delivery of standard reports to the users as soon as they've been deployed. It also provides some means for users to set up their own reports, subscribe to reports, and publish their own reports if they have appropriate permission. There is a search capability within the report site, which searches both the file names and description metadata in the Reporting Services catalog. Report Manager will also display parameter entry boxes and dropdown choice lists in the Report Manager header area, allowing users to enter their own choices and re-run the report. There is a Find function to search within the body of a report, which can be particularly helpful in large reports. Finally, users have the ability to export the report to a file in any of several formats.

In spite of all this useful stuff, Report Manager is a limited report delivery solution. You can customize its appearance by changing the color scheme and displaying your own logo. But at the end of the day the reports are still grouped by project and ordered by name. Beyond this, all of the features and functions described earlier are available through the API. The web service nature of the product will allow ambitious customers or third-party companies to write better navigation portals to the report library.

While it is far from a full-featured information portal, it does provide enough functionality to be considered a viable delivery solution. Even in the face of these (and other) limitations, many companies have successfully employed Report Manager as their standard report delivery vehicle.

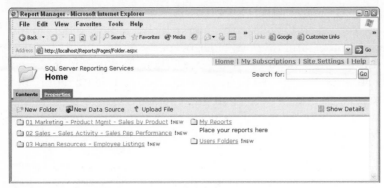

Figure 9.3 Report Manager home page

Viewing Reports

After a user has found a report that seems like it might contain the needed information, he has to have a way to view its contents. This is known as a "pull" model, where the user finds the reports and interactively pulls the data from the server.

Users can view reports through any application that can access the report server, either through a URL with an Internet browser or through an application that uses the SOAP methods, like the Report Manager interface. Both allow easy integration of Reporting Services reports into existing portals or into custom-built or third-party applications.

The browser is the most popular tool for viewing reports. Using a browser means users don't need additional software installed on their machines and IT doesn't need to manage the software distribution and upgrade process. (Unless, of course, your users have browsers other than Internet Explorer, or they have a version of Internet Explorer not supported by Reporting Services.)

Figure 9.5 shows what the user would see in the browser as a result of clicking on the Product Subcategory Trend link shown in Figure 9.4.

This example shows the report in the Report Manager interface. You can view the report directly in the browser without the Report Manager's organizing structure. You'll see this direct access when we include a report in a simple portal structure later in this chapter.

The custom application approach to accessing reports might be something like an ASP.NET application built to integrate reports into a larger system that provides additional functionality. For example, a customer care system might use Reporting Services to display a customer's purchasing and returns history to the customer care agent. On the same screen, there could be a button that would allow the agent to select a recent order and submit it to the transaction system to generate a Returned Merchandise Authorization.

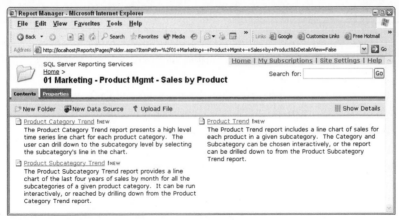

Figure 9.4 Reports in the Sales by Product directory

Receiving Results

Reporting Services offers several delivery methods and file formats other than the pull approach described in the Viewing Reports section. It's helpful to look at these options in two separate categories: first in terms of delivery methods, and then in terms of formats.

The idea of the push model is to deliver the report to the user based on a predefined schedule. A user visits the reporting web site and finds a report that she'd like to see on a regular basis. Clicking the New Subscription button takes the user to a set of pages for defining the nature and timing of the subscription. The subscription includes a schedule based on a time event or a data event. In the case of a time event, the report is distributed at a certain time on a periodic basis (at 8:00 a.m. every weekday, for example). In the case of a data event, the report is distributed whenever the underlying report snapshot is updated. The users can create their own subscriptions to reports they'd like pushed to them, or the Report Administrator can create shared schedules that send reports to a list of users. Initial releases of Reporting Services supported pushing reports out through email or to a file share. However, since this function is extensible, several companies are offering more push-style delivery options, like faxing and printing.

Reporting Services provides several output formats for exporting or subscribing to a report. These formats include Excel, XML, TIFF, PDF, CSV, and various HTML versions. Like the delivery mode, the format choices are extensible, although creating a new rendering extension is an involved project because the developer will need to translate the full set of RDL display capabilities into the target format.

Changing Reports

Static reports based on carefully identified business requirements often provide enough information to answer the question of the moment. In fact, some of the DW/BI projects we've been involved in provided user access only at the two ends of the flexibility spectrum: completely static HTML reports and blank slate ad hoc tools. This puts the BI front-end team in the business of continuously creating and publishing new reports to meet the changing needs of the business (but you often end up doing that anyway).

In many organizations, standard report users want the ability to make changes to a report without having to ask someone else to do it, or having to learn the complexities of the data model and the ad hoc tool. In most cases, it makes sense to provide users with the ability to customize the standard reports to meet their individual needs. Reporting Services includes several common functions that provide users with the ability to change a report, including parameters, report linking, drill-down, and content modification.

The report in Figure 9.5 includes a parameter at the top of the report section labeled Select Product Category. The parameter has been set to the value Bikes using a pull-down menu. A user can select a particular product category and then press the View Report button to re-execute the report. We'll discuss some of the other functions for allowing users to interact with reports in the second half of this chapter when we step through the process of building a report.

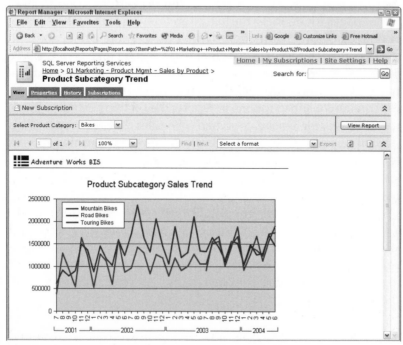

Figure 9.5   The Product Subcategory Sales Trend report

> **THE LIMITS OF SECURITY**
>
> Once someone has removed a report from the Reporting Services environment, either through email or by directly exporting the report, access to the data is no longer managed by Reporting Services. Once users have the information in a file format, there's very little the DW/BI team can do to control what they do with it. This is one of the reasons the DW/BI system must have a clear security and privacy policy, and compliance with that policy must be monitored. See Chapter 12 for more details.

Solid, Reliable System

Having a solid, reliable system is not the kind of business requirement you like to hear from your users. The only time they specifically mention this requirement is when previous efforts haven't performed well or have been unreliable. Regardless of the history, you want the new version of the DW/BI system to meet expectations. This involves setting up the standard reporting process infrastructure, securing access to reports, and managing performance.

The process infrastructure is a combination of Reporting Services functions like shared schedules, and process metadata connections with the rest of the DW/BI system. You need to create a mechanism for initiating the execution of a set of standard reports when a particular ETL process completes. The process should implement simple logic like, "When the nightly Orders update is finished, start these reports." Security is also part of a solid, reliable reporting system. After you've designed the report, you need to determine who has access to the report, when they can view it, and how they can interact with it. This can be accomplished through the Report Manager using role-based security. These roles can be managed through Windows security services in SQL Server 2005 Enterprise Edition, or through another security service by writing the appropriate extensions.

Performance is part of the system reliability job. If the report server is too slow, users will get frustrated. Reporting Services has several options for managing performance, including scheduling reports to be executed during low demand windows like early in the morning. You can set up a large report to execute on a regular schedule, and save its results in an intermediate snapshot structure. Users have fast access to the snapshot rather than re-executing the report itself. This option works well for the daily load cycle of the standard DW/BI system. Later in this chapter, we discuss ways to monitor performance over time to find opportunities for improvement.

Reporting Services Assessment

Overall, Reporting Services provides the basic functionality needed to create and deliver standard reports that will meet a majority of the business requirements.

Because it's oriented to developers, it's more difficult to use than other reporting tools. Creating reports will take a bit longer. This is balanced by the flexibility of the programming paradigm. You can generally create a work-around to solve most any problem.

Reporting Services has limited functionality, particularly in the area of report layout controls. However, Reporting Services has already improved in its short existence and will continue to get better over time. Microsoft has competent folks who are interested in creating the best product they can. They're receiving feedback from a large number of users who have been more than happy to provide a long list of desired enhancements. One unfortunate side effect of this feedback loop is that most of the feedback comes from developers who want more programmatic functionality. We encourage you to provide your own business requirements-based feedback on how to improve the tool.

In a way, Reporting Services is a "nobody ever got fired" choice. The incremental cost and reasonable functionality make it an easy decision. With the addition of Report Builder, Reporting Services offers basic ad hoc query functionality to business users. However, most organizations will need another tool so business users can create advanced ad hoc queries and reports. The DW/BI team will need to support at least two tools and their associated metadata.

In some cases, bringing a second tool into the picture complicates the Reporting Services decision because the major ad hoc query and reporting tool vendors also provide similar reporting services functionality, usually at an extra price. Buying both ad hoc and reporting service functionality from the same vendor means you have to support only one toolset. Additionally, ad hoc reports built in the vendor's front-end tool can generally be moved right into the tool's standard report environment without any conversion. Any reports developed in a third-party tool must be converted to Reporting Services in order to take advantage of Reporting Services' report server capabilities, unless they were designed to work with Reporting Services in the first place.

Some of the more focused tool vendors, like ProClarity and Panorama, are leveraging the Reporting Services infrastructure to provide enterprise report management for their products. In these cases, you can use these third-party query tools to create complex reports, and then save them out to Reporting Services for scheduling and distribution.

Selecting end-user tools is more than just a technical process. It is also highly political and personal. You need to get the end users deeply involved in this process.

Building and Delivering Reports

At last, it's time to put together a standard reporting environment. This section concentrates on the process of building the environment and the reports themselves. As always, our process starts with a bit of planning and preparation.

We then proceed to the creation of the initial set of standard reports based on the prioritized list presented in Chapter 8. Once the individual reports are in place, we examine an approach to creating the BI portal. This is followed by setting up the standard report operations process. Finally, we talk a bit about ongoing maintenance of the standard reporting system. Although this is not intended to be a step-by-step tutorial, we will build an example report based on the updated Adventure Works data warehouse relational and Analysis Services databases described in Chapters 3 and 7. You should be able to recreate the example report once you get a little Reporting Services experience.

Planning and Preparation

The temptation to dive in and start building reports is almost irresistible at this point. Be strong. Even if you're a Reporting Services pro, it's worth taking a few days to set up your reporting environment and figure out the overall reporting process before you start creating reports. You should also have done all the application specification work described in Chapter 8. The major items you need to address are setting up the development environment, creating standard templates and styles, setting up the delivery and notification metadata and processes, and setting up a usage tracking system.

Setting Up the Development Environment

We discussed setting up the development environment for Reporting Services in Chapter 4. The main challenge lies in finding the optimal combination of services and machines. Reporting Services keeps its metadata in a SQL Server database called ReportServer. While it is possible to have Reporting Services and the ReportServer database on the same machine, moving the catalog to a SQL Server instance on another machine is the easiest way to improve Reporting Services performance.

Creating Standard Templates

Once the development environment is in place, you need to set up the standard report layout templates we described in Chapter 8. The easiest way to create a report template is to create a blank report with the standard elements you and your business partners defined and laid out according to the specification from Chapter 8 (see Figure 8.2). We won't go through the step-by-step process of creating the template because it's the same process as creating a report, which we do in the next section. Figure 9.6 shows what the simple report template from Chapter 8 might look like in the Report Designer. It includes both a Table and Matrix with the appropriate styles (fonts, background colors, and the like) predefined, but there are no data fields in these items. Usually, the developer uses the appropriate item for the report and deletes the other item.

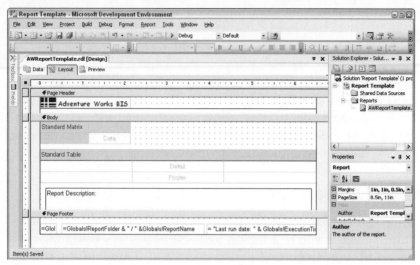

Figure 9.6 Example Adventure Works Cycles layout template in the Report Designer

After you've defined your layout template, use your source control system to make it available to the development team. If you'd like to have it appear in the dialog box as a choice when you use the Add/New Item . . . Report dialog box to add a new item, you need to save the template to a special directory. Save the completed layout template report to its project directory and copy the resulting .rdl file to the template directory.

TIP The location of the template directory depends on how your system is configured. It's usually located under the Visual Studio folder inside Program Files. Search for the ReportProject directory in the Program Files directory.

In most cases, experienced report designers will start each report from the standard layout template by selecting the Add/New Item . . . Report choice in the Project menu, or by right-clicking on the project in the Solution Explorer pane. One of the report item choices will be your standard layout template, if you put it in the right directory.

NOTE The Report Wizard is a great place to start if you are just learning Reporting Services because it provides a structured step-by-step framework for creating a report. However, you will soon move beyond its capabilities as you begin to create real-world reports. Also, the wizard does not provide the opportunity to select a layout template.

One drawback of the standard layout template in Reporting Services is that it does not include a master style sheet. The developer can define the style of each individual element in the template—bold type, font, color, and so on—but he or she cannot set defaults styles for any new elements that are added once the template is being used to create a specific report. New elements added to the report take on the bland styles of the generic report.

Interestingly enough, while the Report Wizard does not access the layout template, it does allow the selection of a style template. You can choose from at least four predefined styles in the Report Wizard: Bold, Casual, Compact, and Corporate. If these don't work for you, you can add to the XML document that defines the available styles. This XML document is called StyleTemplates.xml.

REFERENCE Look in Books Online in the "Creating a Report Using Report Wizard" topic for more information on finding and editing the StyleTemplates.xml document.

Creating Reports

Now that you're ready to build some reports, the question is where to start. The Business Dimensional Lifecycle provides the answer. Revisit the report specifications you created in the End User Application Specification step of the Lifecycle described in Chapter 8. These specifications list the standard reports in priority order along with mock-ups and documentation on the definitions and contents of the reports. After reviewing the specification document, start building the report set. When the set is complete, deploy them to the test server for testing. Finally, deploy them to the production server. We'll go through each of these steps.

Revisit the Report Specifications

In Chapter 8, the BI Application Specification step of the Lifecycle involved creating a list of candidate reports based on the requirements interviews and then prioritizing the list with the business folks. In reviewing the standard report specifications for Adventure Works Cycles, recall that senior management decided that orders data is the top priority. During the requirements gathering process, it became clear that everyone wanted to see orders data, but they all wanted to see it sliced differently. Because you did such a great job capturing the standard reporting needs, all you need to do at this point is pull out the prioritized list and the associated mock-ups and start at the top.

The specifications from Figure 8.3 in Chapter 8 list the Sales Rep Performance Ranking report as the top priority report. The specifications include a report mock-up for this report, illustrated in Figure 9.7.

This report is not very creative or clever and the fact that it's top priority could indicate who holds the most power in Adventure Works Cycles. It could also be first because the report provides a good demonstration of several Reporting Services features. As you'll see as you work through this section, even a straightforward report like this one presents some development challenges.

REPORTING SERVICES WORKAROUNDS

Your standard template should include both the layout of standard elements on the page (headers, titles, footers), and the standard formatting styles (fonts, sizes, colors). Reporting Services can use standard layout templates or custom report styles, but not both at the same time. If you're willing to go the extra mile, you can have both a layout template *and* a style template. Create a metadata table with the standard style entries in your database, and then create a dataset to retrieve the style information into your report. You can then use this to set style properties based on the query results. If the dataset is named StyleDataSet, and it has a column called FontFamily, then an expression to assign the FontFamily property of a Textbox might look like the following:

```
=First(Fields!FontFamily.Value,"StyleDataSet"))
```

This option is probably overkill for most DW/BI projects, but it does give you the best of both worlds. You can create a standard layout template and include a dataset that reads the style information along with the code that applies it. You need to create this only once and save it out to the template directory. From then on, all reports built from this template will have the standard layout and style. An extra benefit comes from the fact that the styles are applied dynamically, every time the report is run. When you change the standard styles in the metadata table, all the standard reports will automatically change to the new style the next time they are run.

TIP To get the most out of this section, you should be at your computer with SQL Server 2005 and the Adventure Works relational and Analysis Services sample databases installed. This section uses a walk-through format to describe the process of creating a report. We don't describe every mouse click, but if you've at least worked through the SQL Server 2005 Reporting Services tutorials, there should be enough information in each step for you to follow along.

Creating Your First Standard Report

Begin by creating a new report project in BI Studio. Rename the Solution to Sales Reports, and rename the Project to Sales Rep Performance. To add a new report to the project, right-click on the Reports directory in the Solution Explorer pane and select Add → New Item from the popup menu. Be careful not to use the Add New Report choice because it will bring up the Report Wizard, and you won't be able to select your standard template.

Adventure Works Cycles

Sales Rep Performance Ranking
<Year> Compared to {Prior Year}

| Sales Rep | | | <Year> | <Year> | Prior | Prior | Change |
ID	Last Name	First Name	Sales	Rank	Sales	Rank	in Rank
xx	xxxxxx	xxxxxx	\\xxx,xxx\\ [1]	xx.x	xxx,xxx	xx.x	x.x [2]
xx	xxxxxx	xxxxxx	\\xxx,xxx\\	xx.x	xxx,xxx	xx.x	x.x
xx	xxxxxx	xxxxxx	\\xxx,xxx\\	xx.x	xxx,xxx	xx.x	x.x
xx	xxxxxx	xxxxxx	\\xxx,xxx\\	xx.x	xxx,xxx	xx.x	x.x
xx	xxxxxx	xxxxxx	\\xxx,xxx\\	xx.x	xxx,xxx	xx.x	x.x

NOTES:
[1] The current Sales field links to the Sales Rep Detail report. Parameters: Sales Rep ID and Year.
[2] The background color of each row is conditionally set based on the Change in Rank field.
Rule: Change > 2 = light green, Change <-2 = light red.

_____ Report Information _____

Report Description: The Sales Rep Performance Ranking report lists each sales rep with their total sales in the selected Year and Prior Year. The report is ordered by the selected year rank and calculates a change in rank.

Report Category: {Sales Analysis}
Report Name: {Sales Rep Performance Ranking – current vs. prior year}
Source: {DW - Sales Performance}

Run on: {Run_Date} Page {1}

Figure 9.7 Sales Rep Performance Ranking report mock-up

Select your standard template in the Add New Item dialog window. When the report appears in the Solution Explorer, rename it Sales Rep Performance Ranking. Click the Add button, and the new report should open up in the Report Designer design surface with the Layout tab selected and all the standard report elements in place. At this point, it should look much like your version of the standard report template in Figure 9.6. If you haven't defined a standard template, just add a new blank report item.

Creating the Data Source and Query

Reporting Services uses the same kind of data sources that Integration Services and Analysis Services use. Share data sources across the projects in your solution to make it easy to change connection information. Create a shared data source called AdventureWorksAS that references the Adventure Works DW Analysis Services database that ships with SQL Server 2005. Be sure to test the connection before you proceed. While you're at it, create another shared data source called AdventureWorksDW that references the AdventureWorksDW SQL Server database.

> **TIP** In general, it makes sense to use the production data warehouse databases as the sources, even for report development (assuming the data has already been loaded into production). Report development is essentially the same as ad hoc querying and poses no significant additional risks to the database server. It makes the development job easier because the data used for creating the report is the final data. In addition, you don't need to change the data sources when you move from development to test to production.

Now create a dataset called SalesRankData for the Sales Rep Performance Ranking report based on the AdventureWorksAS data source. Click the Data tab in the upper-left corner of the report template, select the dropdown menu box in the header bar labeled Dataset:, and select <New Dataset . . . >.

Change the name of the dataset to SalesRankData, and make sure the data source for the dataset is AdventureWorksAS. When you click OK, BI Studio displays the Analysis Services query designer in the design surface. The Analysis Services query designer lets you build simple MDX queries with a drag-and-drop interface. You can view the MDS or enter it directly, by switching out of design mode in the upper-right corner of the designer.

If your data source was a SQL Server relational database, the query designer would allow you to enter SQL into the upper pane and view the results in the lower pane. The relational query design also has a more graphical interface mode called the query builder. It looks suspiciously like the Microsoft Access query builder. If the data source were a Report Builder model, you'd use the Report Builder tool to define datasets.

The query building tools in the Report Designer are not so great in the initial release of SQL Server 2005. In many cases, developers will end up creating the SQL or MDX in some other tool and pasting it in. Even in our simple example, the fields for the Sales Rep Performance Ranking report require the creation of calculated members in MDX.

WARNING If you enter your SQL or MDX directly, do not try to switch over to the query builder or into design mode. The designer will try to rewrite your query and may fail because of its complexity, ruining the SQL and the formatting in the process. In the MDX case, it doesn't even pay to rewrite the query. You have to start over.

According to the report specs and the mock-up for the Sales Rep Performance Ranking report, the VP of Sales wants to compare current year and prior year sales by sales rep. Like many business requests, this is conceptually simple, but it turns out to be not so easy to do in MDX, SQL, or the Report Designer. For purposes of the example, we'll create this report using an MDX query against the Analysis Services data warehouse database. The Data tab in the Report Designer shown in Figure 9.8 shows the completed dataset.

When you create a report, you need to break it down into subsets to make it easier to build. You usually need a minimum of two datasets: one for the report contents and one for the user input parameter prompt list. The report in Figure 9.8 requires identifying two subsets of data, current year sales and prior year sales by employee; ranking each of those subsets independently; and calculating the change in ranking from the prior year to the current year. Let us be clear at this point: We are not MDX experts. In MDX, the easiest way to accomplish the creation of subsets, as far as we can tell, is to create calculated members for each of the two sales subsets (in the Calculated Members pane in the lower-left corner), then create calculated members that rank those subsets, and finally, calculate the difference of the two rank members.

The current year sales calculated member is easy because it can simply be the sales measure. To create this calculated member, simply drag the appropriate measure from the Measures list in the Metadata pane in the upper-left corner into the MDX expression box in the Calculated Member Builder window. For this report, that expression would be:

```
[Measures].[Reseller Sales Amount]
```

Technically, you don't need a calculated member for this measure, but it helps clarify the contents of the report and subsequent calculations. Next, recall that the mock-up identified the target year as a user-entered parameter. If you limit the calendar year to CY 2004 in the filter pane at the upper part of the designer, you will see a check box to make this limit a parameter. When you check the box, the Analysis Services report designer creates a Reporting Services parameter along with the query needed to populate the choice list.

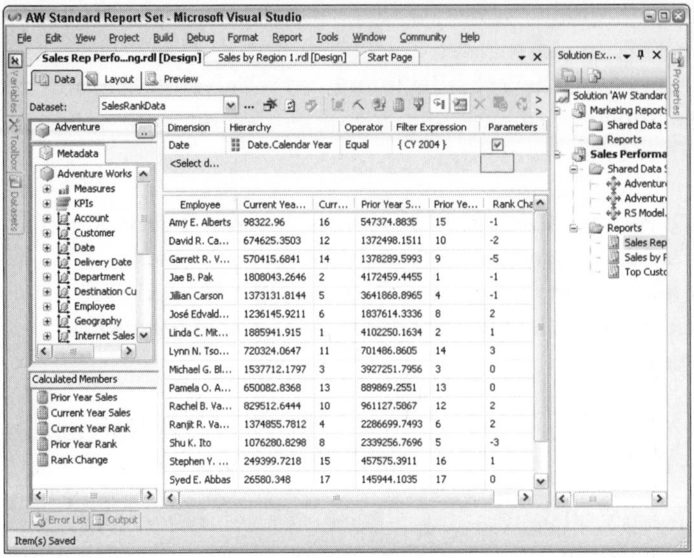

Figure 9.8   The completed data tab for the Sales Rep Performance Ranking report

The next calculated member is the prior year sales field. This is a bit more complex because it relies on the ParallelPeriod function:

```
SUM({ParallelPeriod([Date].[Calendar Year].LEVEL,1)},
        [Measures].[Current Year Sales])
```

This says to sum the measure for one year lagged behind the current year, or CY2002 based on the filter we previously set.

The next calculated measure, called Current Year Rank, does a rank on current year sales. Like so much of the MDX language, the RANK function in MDX is not like the RANK function in SQL, although it has the same name. The MDX RANK tells you the location of a member in its current set. For employees, the current set might be in alphabetical order. Therefore, a straight ranking of sales reps might rank Amy Alberts as number one, even though she's actually sixteenth on the list. When you use the RANK, you need to tell it what set it is part of, and what order the set is in, as follows:

```
IIF (ISEMPTY( [Measures].[Current Year Sales] ), NULL,
    RANK (
        [Employee].[Employee].CurrentMember,
        ORDER (
            [Employee].[Employee].[Employee].Members
            , ([Measures].[Current Year Sales])
            , BDESC
            )
        )
    )
```

This MDX first checks to make sure there are Current Year Sales before it does the RANK. This is because only a handful of employees are sales reps, and you don't want the report to list all 296 employees. Next, the expression ranks the current employee according to where it is in a set of employees ordered by Current Year Sales, descending. The Prior Year Rank is the same expression only ordered by Prior Year Sales.

The final column, Rank Change, is simply the difference in the two ranking calculated members:

```
[Measures].[Prior Year Rank] - [Measures].[Current Year Rank]
```

While this may seem complicated, there are two aspects to consider that might make it seem relatively easy. First, you can define commonly used calculated members, like Current Year Sales or Prior Year Sales, in the Analysis Services OLAP database once; then they become drag-and-drop fields in the Metadata pane, just like any other measure. Second, the SQL alternative to this query is even less attractive; it goes on for almost a page to accomplish the same results. (You can get a script for the equivalent SQL query at the book's web site: www.MsftDWToolkit.com.)

Even though the primary dataset is complete, you still have at least one more dataset to consider. When you select the parameter check box in the Date.Calendar Year limit, the MDX query designer automatically creates a second dataset, called DateCalendarYear, and links that dataset to a parameter also called DateCalendarYear. The dataset retrieves the distinct list of choices for the attribute selected and includes a value field and a label field. The label field is used to populate the choice list of a pulldown menu in the user interface, and the corresponding value field is passed to the DateCalendarYear parameter in the MDX query. If you use the SQL query builder, you have to create the dataset to populate the parameter choice list yourself.

TIP To toggle back and forth between the two datasets, select the name of the dataset you would like to see in the pulldown menu in the Data tab header bar in the Report Designer. Hit the exclamation mark button in the header bar to refresh the results set.

Design the Report Layout

Once your datasets are defined, switch over to the Layout tab in the Report Designer design surface and start putting the report together. Fortunately, the Sales Rep Performance Ranking report has a simple layout. Start with the standard layout, and then add a few subtle items like the DateCalendarYear parameter and some conditional formatting to highlight potential problem areas.

The design surface in the Layout view should look familiar to anyone who has created forms or reports with Access, Visual Basic, VBA, or Visual Studio. The basic process involves dragging various Report Items from the Toolbox onto the design surface and then specifying their properties as appropriate.

The standard template from Figure 9.6 already has predefined Table and Matrix items. The report mock-up looks like a good candidate for the Table control, so delete the Matrix control to clear up a little space. (If you're not using a standard template, just drag a Table from the Toolbox into the report area.) Fill in the Table control by dragging columns from the Fields list in the Dataset pane into the Detail row of the Table control. Once you have the columns in place, select the Preview tab to see how the initial report looks.

> **TIP** If the template doesn't have enough columns in the Table, you can add more by right-clicking in the gray header for any column. Select Insert Column to the Right or Left as needed. This will clone any pre-set formatting into the new column.

When you select Preview, the report should run and generate results for the default calendar year of 2004. Try changing the Date.Calendar Year parameter in the pulldown menu at the top of the report. You need to hit the View Report button to re-execute the query. Note that the pulldown menu allows you to select more than one year. This will break the prior year calculations, so go back and change this.

To improve the default settings, return to the Layout pane and select Report → Report Parameters to display the Report Parameters dialog box, as illustrated in Figure 9.9.

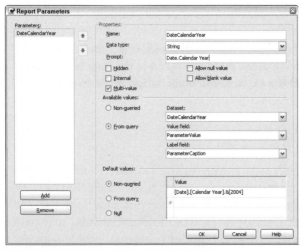

Figure 9.9 Report Parameters dialog box

Change the prompt string to make sense to your business users, and uncheck the multi-value box in the Properties section. Now, if you select the Preview tab, you should be able to select only a single year in the pulldown menu.

Creating reports is a classic 80/20 process, or even 90/10, in that it takes only 10 percent of the time to create 90 percent of the report. Most of the final 10 percent of creating a report is formatting, and it usually takes much longer than you would expect. In this case, the Sales Rep Performance report now has the key elements it will have when it's finished, but it doesn't look very professional. Go back to the Layout view and take a few minutes to clean up some of the following appearance problems:

- Change the column widths to make better use of the available space.

- Format the sales columns to get rid of all those decimal values and add some commas. Try selecting the field in the Detail row and putting an "N" in its Format property, or try a custom format string, like "#,##0." (See the "Predefined Numeric Formats" topic in Books Online for more options.)

NOTE You might think that number formatting would be easier if the data source is Analysis Services rather than SQL. One of the advantages of Analysis Services is that it contains metadata about such things as formatting for measures.

Alas, no. Reporting Services does not respect the formatting that's defined in the Analysis Services database.

- Verify the line spacing and borders.

Figure 9.10 shows the finished report in the Report Designer environment. Notice the Total Sales fields, which are expressions added to the Footer row of the table.

The guiding philosophy in laying out and formatting reports is that they should be as clear and self-explanatory as possible. Users will not take the time to look elsewhere for report documentation, nor should they be expected to. Clarity is one of the major challenges the DW/BI team takes on when it includes standard reports as part of its responsibilities. Involve someone who has solid graphic design expertise in the design process of the layout template and the initial report set. Experiment with alternatives and get feedback from users as to which one works best. A bit of extra work at this point will pay off massively in the long run.

TWEAKING THE REPORT LAYOUT

To create a clear, understandable, professional-looking report, you will need to go beyond these basic formatting items. Some additional improvements to consider include:

◆ *Add a report description to the report's metadata.* This description lives in the properties of the report itself. To access these properties, select the area outside the design surface in the Layout view and view the properties sheet, or right-click in the same area and select Properties.

◆ *Add conditional formatting.* Reporting Services supports expressions written in Visual Basic .NET. You can use this powerful capability to define most of the properties in the report programmatically. Conditional formatting is a good example of this capability. (See the "Common Expressions" topic in Books Online for more examples.)

For example, in the Sales Rep Performance Ranking report, the VP of Sales might want to highlight those sales reps that have risen or slipped more than two places in the rankings. You need a soothing green color for the rising stars and an ominous red color for the slackers. To accomplish this, apply conditional formatting to the entire Detail row. Select the row, and then select the pulldown menu for the BackgroundColor property in the Properties window. The first choice in the menu is <Expression . . .>. Select it and the Edit Expression dialog window opens. Delete the contents of the Expression box and enter the following expression:

```
=iif( Fields!Rank_Change.Value > 2, "LightGreen",
   iif(Fields!Rank_Change.Value < -2, "MistyRose", "White"))
```

Select OK, and then select the Preview tab. You should see some nice highlighting at this point. Can you tell who is going to be in trouble when you publish this report?

■ *Add parameterized labeling.* This is another useful application of expressions. Rather than have generic column labels that don't tell the user exactly what is in the column, you can use expressions to incorporate parameters right into the report text. This is particularly helpful for when reports are printed. Once you separate the report from the Reporting Service, it is unclear which parameters you used to generate the report. Labels can be made more descriptive by using expressions as follows:

Right-click the SalesAmnt header field and select Expression. In the Expression box, delete the text title and enter the following expression:

```
=Left(Right(Parameters!DateCalendarYear.Value,5),4) & " Sales"
```

- Select OK, and then select the Preview tab. If the TargetYear is still set to 2003, the Sales column header should now be 2003 Sales.

- Make appropriate, similar changes to the CurrentRank, PriorSalesAmnt, and PriorRank header fields. Remember, the parameter is a string value, so you may need to use the Val() and Str() functions to get the prior year into the titles.

- Add an interactive sort expression to the Current Ranking header field. This will allow your users to sort out the top or bottom performers.

- *Verify print layout.* It is rare that a report you have created to fit on the screen will also fit on the printed page the first time. You may need to change the column widths and font sizes to squeeze things in a bit. You can change the page setup as well, adjusting margins and switching from portrait to landscape. If you can't keep all the columns on a single page, you may need to change some of the properties of certain fields and groups to cause them to repeat on subsequent printed pages.

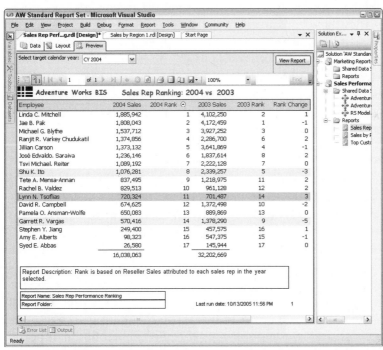

Figure 9.10   Final report layout for the Sales Rep Performance Ranking report

Unit Test

Report developers should do the first round of testing right in the development environment. At the very least, the developer should test the parameters and validate the results.

Test different parameters. For example, try the Sales Rep Performance Report with the year 2003. What happens? It looks like some of the rows are missing a few values. This makes sense in this case because you would expect some sales reps to have data in one year and not the other. Fortunately, Analysis Services does an outer join for you to make sure everyone in the target year is represented in the report.

Validate the numbers. Check the numbers as carefully as possible. Compare them to any known alternative sources for the same information. If the numbers should be the same and they are not, figure out why. Research the business rules in the alternative source and compare them to your own. The problem may be in your query, or all the way back somewhere in the ETL process. If there's a problem, resolving it is serious detective work and can take a lot of time and energy.

If the numbers are supposed to be different because they have been improved or corrected in the ETL process, carefully document the reasons for the differences. If possible, show how you can get from the data warehouse numbers back to the alternative source numbers. This documentation should be available in the BI portal, and the report description should refer to it.

Before you actually deploy the report, you may want to create a few more reports and deploy an entire project all at once. In this case, you can add a Sales Rep Detail report or a report that includes quota information and set up the ranking report to drillthrough to the detail.

Deploy to the Test Web Server and Test Some More

In large environments with hundreds or thousands of users pounding on the standard report set, it makes sense to deploy the reports to a test server environment that is as similar to the production environment as possible. This step allows the reporting team to stress test the new reports to ensure they don't reduce the performance of other reports before moving them into production. In medium-sized or smaller organizations where the user population is smaller, it may not be necessary for a full test server environment. The reporting team could deploy the reports to the production Report Server and test them there. You can minimize the risk of this move by limiting access to the new report directories, and by not publishing the new reports in the BI portal until you have completed testing.

This test phase typically involves several steps. The process begins with deploying the project to the target Report Server (either test or production). Once there, the reports need to be retested to ensure proper display and printing. The tester should make sure the reports all perform as expected in the target environment. If they are not working well enough, there are a number of tuning techniques available. These range from tuning the query to creating report snapshots to actually changing the server configurations.

Deploying the project or report to a Reporting Services instance is straightforward. Each project has its own configuration properties, so if you have multiple projects in a solution, you will need to set up the properties for each project. Within each project, there are several configurations and each can have its own target Report Server. The default configurations are DebugLocal, Debug, and Production. To set up the target server in the project properties, in the Project menu, select Properties. This opens a project-specific Properties pages window. To deploy the project, you need to provide a target server URL for the active configuration. In the simplest case, where the web server is on the same machine as the development environment, the target server URL can be http://localhost/ReportServer.

After you test the basics of appearance and performance, the next step is to integrate the new reports into the production process. If there are standard schedules these reports depend on, the reports should be linked to the appropriate schedules in the Report Manager. If there are standard distribution lists that should receive these reports, they should be set up at this point. The DW/BI team should also validate the subscription process to make sure the report is available for users to subscribe to and receive on a regular basis.

Deploy to Production

When there is an actual deployment to the production server, you will need to repeat many of the steps you went through to move the reports into test. These include schedules, snapshots, subscriptions, and email distribution lists. However, in most cases, the deployment to production has already taken place in the test step, so this step is more of an unveiling than anything else. This is especially true when the primary user interface with the reporting environment is through a web site or portal. In this case, the reports are not visible to the users until you make them available in the portal. On the other hand, if users access the reports through the Report Manager interface, the new directories and reports will appear as soon as you deploy them to the server (assuming they have appropriate access rights).

The BI portal is such a powerful tool for the DW/BI system that we explore it in detail in the following section. At this point, it is enough to say that if you are providing reports through a portal, you need to integrate this new set of reports into that portal as part of the production deployment.

An important part of deploying a report to production is setting the security for the report. Reporting Services has several options for managing security, as do the relational engine and Analysis Services. We discuss security in Chapter 12.

The BI Portal

In Chapter 8, we introduced the concept of the navigation portal as the organizing framework for the standard report set. Any time we use the word *portal*, it invokes visions of a major enterprise effort to collect and categorize all structured and unstructured information and make it available through a rich framework with intelligent search capabilities and the ability to personalize the experience. Building the enterprise information portal may be a useful and important task, but in most cases, it is someone else's task. For our purposes, think about the navigation portal as the web site for the DW/BI system: the BI portal.

The success of the DW/BI system is determined by whether or not the organization gets value out of it. For the organization to get value from the DW/BI system, people have to use it. Since the BI portal is the primary interaction most people have with the DW/BI system, the DW/BI team needs to do everything in its power to make sure the BI portal provides the best possible experience.

As you begin the design process, keep in mind that a significant component of the work a DW/BI team does is about managing organizational change (sometimes it feels like that is just another way to say "politics"). The BI portal plays a significant role in this change process, so it has to work at several levels. It must be:

- *Usable:* People have to be able to find what they need.
- *Content-rich:* It should include much more than just the reports. It should include as much support information, documentation, help, examples, and advice as possible.
- *Clean:* It should be nicely laid out so people are not confused or overwhelmed by it.
- *Current:* It needs to be someone's job to keep the content up-to-date. No broken links or 12-month-old items labeled "New!" allowed.
- *Interactive:* It should include functions that engage the users and encourage them to return to the portal. A good search tool, a metadata browser, maybe even a support-oriented news group are all ways for people to interact with the portal. A capability for users to personalize their report home page, and to save reports or report links to it, makes it directly relevant to them. It also helps to have new items appear every so often. Surveys, class notices, and even data problem warnings all help keep it fresh.
- *Value-oriented:* This is the organizational change goal. We want everyone who comes to the BI portal to end up with the feeling that the DW/BI system is a valuable resource, something that helps them do a better job. In a way, the BI portal is one of the strongest marketing tools the DW/BI team has and you need to make every impression count.

In short, the design principles that apply to any good web site apply to the BI portal.

Planning the BI Portal

The process of creating the BI portal requires a careful balancing of two basic design principles: density and structure.

- *Density:* The human mind can take in an incredible amount of information. The human eye is able to resolve images at a resolution of about 530 pixels per inch at a distance of 20 inches. Compare this with the paltry 72 pixels per inch resolution of the typical computer screen. Our brains have evolved to rapidly process all this information looking for the relevant elements. The browser gives us such a low-resolution platform that we have to use it as carefully and efficiently as possible. Every pixel counts.

- *Structure:* Although we need to fill the BI portal home page with information, it doesn't work if we jam it full of hundreds of unordered descriptions and links. Your brain can handle all this information only if it's well organized. For example, a typical major daily newspaper has an incredible amount of information but you can handle it because it's structured in a way that helps you find what you need. At the top level, the paper is broken up into sections. If you're looking for certain kinds of information, you know which section to start with. Some readers look at every section, but most skip a few that they deem irrelevant to their lives. The next level down within each section may be divided into subsections, but the most common organizing structure is the headline. Headlines (at least non-tabloid headlines) attempt to communicate the content of the article in as few words as possible. These headlines are the "relevant elements" that allow readers to quickly parse through the newspaper to find information that is interesting to them.

REFERENCE For interesting reading about image density, see the work of R. N. Clark:

- *Visual Astronomy of the Deep Sky*, Cambridge University Press and Sky Publishing, 1990.

- http://clarkvision.com/imagedetail/eye-resolution.html.

Edward Tufte's work provides a good general reference for structure and information display, including:

- *Visual Explanations: Images and Quantities, Evidence and Narrative*, Graphics Press, May, 1990.

Impact on Design

The idea of density translates to the BI portal in a couple of ways. Primarily, it means we flatten the information hierarchy. Categories are often represented as hierarchies in the browser. You see a list of choices, each representing a topic. Click on a topic, and you're taken to a page with another list of choices, and so on until you finally reach some content. Flattening the hierarchies means bringing as much information to the top-level pages as possible. Meaning that was captured in the hierarchy of pages is now collapsed down to an indented list of category and subcategory headings on a single page.

Figure 9.11 translates these concepts into the world of Adventure Works Cycles. The BI portal shown here demonstrates how two levels of report categories have been collapsed into one page. The portal is easy to navigate because you can identify major categories of information based on the headings and ignore them if they don't apply to your current needs, or examine them more closely if they seem relevant. Having the two levels on the same page actually gives the user more information because the two levels help define each other. For example, Sales helps group the sales-related subcategories together, but at the same time, each subcategory helps the user understand what activities are included in Sales.

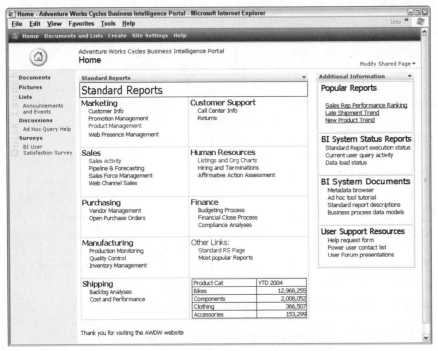

Figure 9.11 The Adventure Works Cycles BI portal home page

Business Process Categories

Every word you include on the portal—every header, description, function, and link—all need to communicate what content people will find behind it. Generally, the best way to organize the portal is to use the organization's business processes as the main outline. Look at Figure 9.11 from a business process perspective. The left column under Standard Reports includes Adventure Works Cycles major business processes. You can also think about this as the organization's value chain. In Adventure Works Cycles' case, Marketing and Sales business processes come early in the value chain, working to bring in new customers and new orders. Once the company has orders, they purchase materials from their suppliers, manufacture the bikes, and ship them out to the customers. Customer Support may interact with the customers at any point along the way, and even after the product has been shipped. There are also internal business processes that generate information that is useful across the organization, like headcount data from HR, or cost data from Finance.

Beyond business process categories, the BI portal needs to have a standard layout so people can easily find what they're looking for. If your organization has a standard page layout that you can adapt for the BI portal, use it. Your users won't have to learn a new interface when they come to the BI portal.

Additional Functions

Although one of the main points of the BI portal is to provide access to the standard reports, it must offer much more than just reports. In addition to the categories and reports lists, you need to provide several common functions:

- *Search:* The search tool serves as an alternative report locator if the business process categories aren't helpful. A good search tool that indexes every report, document, and page on the BI web site can dramatically shorten the amount of time it takes a user to find what she wants.

- *Metadata browser:* A metadata browser can be as simple as a few ASP.NET pages or even Reporting Services reports that allow the user to browse through the metadata's descriptions of the databases, schemas, tables, columns, business rules, load statistics, report usage, report content, and so on. In short, interested users can learn a lot about the DW/BI system through the metadata browser.

- *Newsgroup:* It may make sense to host a support-oriented news group on the BI portal. This can be a good way for users to find help when they need it. It can also create a record of problems and their solutions for future reference. It takes a fairly large user community to generate the critical mass of activity needed to make a newsgroup successful.

- *Personalization:* Users should be able to save reports or report links to their personal pages. This personalization can be a powerful incentive for people to return to the portal every day.

■ *Information center:* It helps keep things interesting to have new items appear on a regular basis. Offer a survey, have people sign up for tool training, or post a notice of an upcoming User Forum meeting.

There is also a whole set of support and administration content the BI portal needs to provide. This includes online training/tutorials, help pages, metadata browser, example reports, data cheat sheets, help request forms, and contact info for the DW/BI team. This information all goes in the lower-right corner, the least valuable real estate on the screen (at least for languages that read from left to right and top to bottom). We discuss this supporting content again in Chapters 14 and 15.

Creating and maintaining the BI portal is much more work than most DW/BI teams ever expect. The effort is worth it because the BI portal is the farthest-reaching tool the DW/BI team has for delivering value to the organization. It is also one of your best tools for marketing the DW/BI system.

SharePoint Portal Server

While it is possible to create a fine BI portal using FrontPage, several major enterprise portal players are on the market, offering an extended set of web functionality. Microsoft's SharePoint Portal Server and the supporting Windows SharePoint Services provide local and enterprise-level portal capabilities. The BI portal shown in Figure 9.11 was built in the Windows SharePoint Services environment. These technologies allow you to add a whole range of functionality to your BI portal, including:

■ Embedding live reports on web pages

■ User personalization capabilities (my reports, custom layouts, and so on)

■ Advanced search across the portal environment

■ News and Topics controls to provide information to users

■ Web-based surveys

■ Discussion groups

■ Alerts to notify users when documents or other items of interest change

Reporting Operations

The deployment process included steps to tie the new reports in with existing reporting operations processes like schedules and distribution. These operations processes will also need to be maintained on an ongoing basis, independent of the introduction of new reports.

In addition to building the reports themselves, you may need to cause a set of reports to run automatically when the data load for a business process dimensional model is finished. Reporting Services isn't directly tied to the ETL system, but it does have a control structure called a *subscription* that can help. Create a set of subscriptions that the main load processes will kick off as part of the regular update process.

One way to accomplish this is to invoke the subscription from within the data load Integration Services package. The problem with this approach is it hard-codes the link between Integration Services and Reporting Services, making it difficult to maintain and enhance.

An alternative solution is to create a metadata layer between the two components. You can use a simple set of tables to drive the relationships between your ETL and reporting systems. The table-driven approach described in the associated sidebar is easy for an administrator to manage.

As you deploy new standard reports to the Report Server, add them to the appropriate schedules and create any system subscriptions to distribute the reports as needed. The DW/BI team will also need to maintain any data-driven subscriptions that involve individual users and email lists. The team may need to add and delete users from these lists as they come and go from the organization.

The same goes for other distribution mechanisms, like file shares. Computers and networks have a tendency to change. For example, the Accounting department may have requested a set of reports distributed to their file server. Then they get a new file server and turn off the old one without telling you. At this point, you have a subscription failing on a regular basis, and a set of users not receiving scheduled reports.

TABLE-DRIVEN REPORT DISTRIBUTION

A simple example of event-based notification involves a Reporting Services component and an Integration Services component, with a metadata table in between to define the linkages. On the Reporting Services side, you need to do the following:

1. **Use Management Studio to create a shared schedule. Name the shared schedule in a way that describes the event it represents, like Orders Data Load Complete.**

2. **Link reports to the shared schedule by going to the Execution properties of the Properties tab of each report.**

3. **Set the Execution properties of the report to create a snapshot on the shared schedule created in Step 1 (for example, Orders Data Load Complete).**

4. **Set up subscriptions to distribute the report. To do this, go to the Subscriptions property tab of each report and create a new subscription set to "Notify me when the report content is refreshed."**

(continued)

TABLE-DRIVEN REPORT DISTRIBUTION *(continued)*

5. When the Shared schedule runs, it will cause all reports linked to it to execute, refreshing the snapshot contents and triggering the notification subscription.

6. The administrator could set up master subscriptions using the data-driven subscription feature to send reports to email distribution lists.

A table named LoadToScheduleMap sits between Reporting Services and Integration Services. The following figure shows how this table links a particular load name to any number of schedules. In the example dataset, the Orders Data Load Complete load is linked to three schedules. Each of these schedules is linked to several reports in the Reporting Services metadata. Fortunately, the linkage between reports and schedules is part of the Reporting Services infrastructure. Note that one of the LoadTypes is Test. This allows the Integration Services package to run in test mode to test the entire process. The schedule associated with the Test LoadType is linked to only a few reports that are sent to the developers. Without this flag, everyone will receive a full set of reports every time the IntegrationServices package is run, even if it's a test run.

LoadToScheduleMap	
PK	**LoadID**
PK	**ScheduleID**
	LoadName
	LoadType
	ScheduleName
	ScheduleStatus
	ModifiedDate

Load ID	Schedule ID	LoadName	LoadType	ScheduleName	ScheduleStatus	ModifiedDate
23	47	Orders Data Load Complete	Regular	Sales Org Orders Reports	Active	7/29/2004
23	52	Orders Data Load Complete	Regular	Product Orders Reports	Active	8/17/2004
23	37	Orders Data Load Complete	Test	Test Orders Reports	Active	6/29/2004
...						

The LoadToScheduleMap table and example rows

On the Integration Services side, each load package should execute a shared Notification package at the end of a successful completion. The Integration Services package will need to pass a few parameters, including LoadName, LoadType, and CompletionTimestamp. See Chapter 6 for a discussion of how to communicate between Integration Services packages.

The Notification package uses the LoadName and LoadType to select the list of Schedules that need to be initiated from the LoadToScheduleMap table. It then runs a script that calls the rs.exe utility to set each schedule to run in the next few minutes. You may want to get clever and include a priority value in the LoadToScheduleMap table. The script could then stagger the start time for each schedule, depending on its priority. You can find an example of these scripts and data structures on the book's web site at www.MsftDWToolkit.com.

Summary

Delivering a set of high-value standard reports is a major component of the DW/BI team's responsibilities. These reports are the primary interface to the DW/BI system for a large majority of the user community. In this chapter, we explored the viability of Reporting Services as the platform for developing the standard report set.

The basic business requirements for reporting include creating, finding, viewing, and changing reports. You need a solid, reliable reporting system foundation to support these requirements. With this broad set of requirements in place, we examined the Reporting Services architecture to see what functions it provides to meet these needs. This gave you a good sense for the components of the tool and how those components fit together. Comparing the Reporting Services architecture to the business requirements for reporting, we concluded that Reporting Services has a reasonable feature-cost ratio, especially considering its incremental cost.

With this understanding in place, the next section focused on actually creating a report in the Reporting Services development environment. Start with some preparation steps to get the development environment set up and to create a standard template that serves as a starting point for every new standard report. Next, revisit the standard report prioritization list, specifications, and mock-ups that you captured as part of the requirements gathering process early on in the Lifecycle. We walked through a case study that picked the top-priority report from the list and dove into the development process.

Development involves setting up the data source and writing the queries that feed the data into the report. Next, put together the report layout. The initial report display is quick, but tweaking the content and formatting takes more time and energy than the uninitiated might imagine.

After you've unit tested the report in the development environment, deploy it to the production server and test it in the real world. In large DW/BI environments, testing on a test server that mirrors the production server is a prudent step.

Delivering the reports is only half of delivering the information. The DW/BI team needs to provide a navigation framework to help users find the reports they need. You can build this framework using standard web tools, a web portal system like Windows SharePoint Services, or using the portal capabilities of a third-party BI tool.

The standard reports are a critical part of the DW/BI system, but they take a fair amount of work to build and maintain. The DW/BI team must plan for that work on an ongoing basis, as we describe in Chapter 15.

CHAPTER 10

Incorporating Data Mining

We dig up diamonds by the score
A thousand rubies, sometimes more
From Snow White by Walt Disney Company, music by Frank Churchill,
words by Larry Morey, ©1938

Data mining is not a single topic; it's a loosely related collection of tools, algorithms, techniques, and processes. This makes it a difficult subject area to tackle, especially in a single chapter. However, we must tackle it for two main reasons: First, data mining offers the potential of huge business impact; and second, SQL Server 2005 includes a suite of data mining tools as part of the product. In short, high value, low cost—the motivation is obvious.

The first part of this chapter sets the context for data mining. We begin with a brief definition of data mining and an overview of the business motivation for using it. We then look at the Microsoft data mining architecture and environment provided as part of SQL Server 2005, including a brief description of the data mining service, the algorithms provided, and the kinds of problems for which they might be appropriate. We next present a high-level data mining process. The process breaks into three phases: business, mining, and operations. The business phase involves identifying business opportunities and understanding the data resources. The data mining phase is a highly iterative and exploratory process whose goal is to identify the best model possible, given the time and resource constraints. Once you identify the best model, you need to implement it in a production form where, you hope, it will provide the intended business value.

The second part of the chapter puts these concepts and processes into practice by demonstrating the application of SQL Server 2005 data mining in two examples. The first example creates clusters of cities based on economic data, and the second creates a model to recommend products for the Adventure Works Cycles web site.

By the end of this chapter, you should have a good sense for what data mining is about, what the SQL Server 2005 data mining toolset includes, and for the high-level process for data mining. And although this is not a tutorial, you should also end up with a basic idea of how to use the SQL Server 2005 data mining toolset.

Defining Data Mining

We generally describe data mining as *a process of data exploration with the intent to find patterns or relationships that can be made useful to the organization.* Data mining takes advantage of a range of technologies and techniques for exploration and execution. From a business perspective, data mining helps you understand and predict behavior, identify relationships, or group items (customers, products, and so on) into coherent sets. These models can take the form of rules or equations that you apply to new customers, products, or transactions to make a better guess as to how you should respond to them.

The field of data mining is known more broadly as *Knowledge Discovery and Data Mining* (KDD). Both terms shed light on the purpose and process of data mining. The word "mining" is meant to evoke a specific image. Traditional mining involves digging through vast quantities of dirt to unearth a relatively small vein of valuable metallic ore, precious stones, or other substances. Data mining is the digital equivalent of this analog process. You use automated tools to dig through vast quantities of data to identify or "discover" valuable patterns or relationships that you can leverage in your business.

Our brains are good examples of data mining tools. Throughout the course of our lives, we accumulate a large set of experiences. In some cases, we're able to identify patterns within these experiences and generate models we can use to predict the future. Those who commute to work have an easy example. Over the weeks and months, you begin to develop a sense for the traffic patterns and adjust your behavior accordingly. The freeway will be jammed at 5:00 p.m., so you might leave at 4:30, or wait until 6:00, unless it's Friday or a holiday. Going to the movies is another example of altering behavior based on experience. Deciding when to arrive at the theater is a complex equation that includes variables like when the movie opened, whether it's a big budget film, whether it got good reviews, and what showing you want to see. These are personal examples of building a data mining model using the original neural network tool.

The roots of data mining can be traced back to a combination of statistical analysis tools like SAS (Statistical Analysis System) and SPSS (Statistical Package for the Social Sciences) that took form in the academic environment in the 1960s and 1970s and the Artificial Intelligence surge back in the 1980s. Many of the techniques from these areas were combined, enhanced, and repackaged as data mining in the 1990s. One benefit of the Internet bubble of the late 1990s is that it showed how data mining could be useful. Companies like Amazon began to mine the vast quantities of data generated by millions of customers browsing their web sites and making purchase selections, popularizing the phrase "Customers who bought this item also bought these items:"

Data mining has finally grown up and has taken on a central role in many businesses. All of us are the subject of data mining dozens of times every day—from the junk mail in our mail boxes, to the affinity cards we use in the grocery store, to the fraud detection algorithms that scrutinize our every credit card purchase. Data mining has become so widespread for one reason: it works. Using data mining techniques can measurably and significantly increase an organization's ability to reach its goals. Data mining is used for many purposes across the organization, from increasing revenue with more targeted direct marketing programs, and cross-sell and up-sell efforts, to cutting costs with fraud detection and churn/attrition reduction, to improving service with customer affinity recommendations. A charitable organization might use data mining to increase donations by directing its campaign efforts toward people who are more likely to give. More often, the goals are as base as "sell more stuff." Our goal here is to describe the technology, not judge the application; how you use it is up to you.

There are two common approaches to data mining. The first is usually a one-time project to help you gain an understanding of who your customers are and how they behave. We call this *exploratory* or *undirected* data mining, where the goal is to find something interesting. The second is most often an ongoing project to work on a specific problem or opportunity. We call this more focused activity *directed* data mining. Directed data mining typically leads to an ongoing effort where models are generated on a regular basis and are applied as part of the transaction system or in the ETL application. For example, you might create a model that generates a score for each customer every time you load customer data into the BI system. Models that come from the data mining process are often applied in the transaction process itself to identify opportunities or predict problems as they are happening and guide the transaction system to an appropriate response on a real-time basis.

While exploratory data mining will often reveal useful patterns and relationships, this approach usually takes on the characteristics of a fishing expedition. You cast about, hoping to hook the big one; meanwhile, your guests, the business folks, lose interest. Directed data mining with a clear business purpose in mind is more appealing to their business-driven style.

In Chapter 8 we defined an analytic application as a BI application that's centered on a specific business process and encapsulates a certain amount of domain expertise. A data mining application fits this definition perfectly, and its place in the Business Dimensional Lifecycle is pictured in Figure 8.1, in the boxes for BI Application Specification and Development.

Basic Data Mining Terminology

The data mining industry uses a lot of terms fairly loosely, so it's helpful for us to define a few of these terms early on. This is not an exhaustive list of data mining terms, only the relevant ones for our discussion.

- *Algorithm:* The programmatic technique used to identify the relationships or patterns in the data.

- *Model:* The definition of the relationship identified by the algorithm, which generally takes the form of a set of rules, a decision tree, a set of equations, or a set of associations.

- *Case:* The collection of attributes and relationships (variables) that are associated with an individual object, usually a customer. The case is also known as an observation.

- *Case set*: A group of cases that share the same attributes. Think of a case set as a table with one row per unique object (like *customer*). It's possible to have a nested case set when one row in the parent table, like "customer", joins to multiple rows in the nested table, like "purchases". The case set is also known as an observation set.

- *Dependent variable(s)* (or predicted attribute or predict column): The variable the algorithm will build a model to predict or classify.

- *Independent variable(s)* (or predictive attribute or input column): The variable with descriptive information used to build the model. The algorithm creates a model that uses combinations of independent variables to define a grouping or predict the dependent variable.

- *Discrete or continuous variables:* Numeric columns that contain continuous or discrete values. A column in the Employee table called Salary that contains the actual salary values is a continuous variable. You can add a column to the table during data preparation called SalaryRange, containing integers to represent encoded salary ranges (1 = "0 to $25,000"; 2 = "between $25,000 and $50,000"; and so on). This is a discrete numeric column. Early data mining and statistical analysis tools required the conversion of strings to numeric values like the encoded salary ranges. Most tools, including most of the SQL Server data mining algorithms, allow the use of character descriptions as discrete values. The string "0 to $25,000" is easier to understand than the number 1. Discrete variables are also known as categorical. This distinction between discrete and continuous is important to the underlying algorithms in data mining, although its significance is less obvious to those of us who are not statisticians.

■ *Regression:* A statistical technique that creates a best-fit formula based on a dataset. The formula can be used to predict values based on new input variables. In linear regression, the formula is the equation for a line.

■ *Deviation:* A measure of how well the regression formula fits the actual values in the dataset from which it was created.

■ *Mining structure:* A Microsoft data mining term used as a name for the definition of a case set in Analysis Services. The mining structure is essentially a metadata layer on top of a data source view that includes additional data mining-related flags and column properties, like the field that identifies a column as input, predict, both, or ignore. A mining structure can be used as the basis for multiple mining models.

■ *Mining model:* The specific application of an algorithm to a particular mining structure. You can build several mining models with different parameters or different algorithms from the same mining structure.

Business Uses of Data Mining

Data mining terminology has not yet become completely standardized. There are terms that describe the business task and terms that describe the data mining techniques applied to those tasks. The problem is, the same terms are used to describe both tasks and techniques, sometimes with different meanings.

REFERENCE The terms in this section are drawn from the book *Data Mining Techniques: For Marketing, Sales, and Customer Relationship Management* by Michael J. A. Berry and Gordon S. Linoff, Second Edition (Wiley, 2004).

Berry and Linoff list six basic business tasks that are served by data mining techniques: *classification, estimation, prediction, affinity grouping, clustering,* and *description and profiling*. We've added a seventh business task to the list called *anomaly detection*. We describe each of these business task areas in the following section, along with lists of the relevant algorithms included in SQL Server 2005 Data Mining. A word of warning: Some of these tasks overlap in what seems to be odd ways to the uninitiated because the distinctions between the areas are more mathematical than functional.

Classification

Classification is the task of assigning each item in a set to one of a predetermined set of discrete choices based on its attributes or behaviors. Consumer goods are classified in a standard hierarchy down to the SKU level. If you know the attributes of a product, you can determine its classification. You can use attributes like size, sugar content, flavor, and container type to classify a soda. Typical classes in business include Yes and No; High, Medium, and Low; Silver, Gold, and Platinum. What these are classes *of* depends on the business context; Good Credit Risk classes might be Yes and No. Classification helps organizations and people simplify their dealings with the world. If you can classify something, you then know how to deal with it. If you fly often with the same airline, you have no doubt been classified as an elite level, or Platinum customer. Knowing this classification allows the airline employees to work with you in a way that is appropriate for top customers, even if they have never met you before. The key differentiating factors of classification are the limited (discrete) number of entries in the class set and the fact that the class set is predefined.

A common example of classification is the assignment of a socioeconomic class to customers or prospects in a marketing database. Companies like Claritas, with its PRIZM system, have built an industry around classification. These systems identify classes of consumers who have common geographic, demographic, economic, and behavioral attributes and can be expected to respond to certain opportunities in a similar way.

Classification algorithms predict the class or category of one or more discrete variables, based on the other variables in the case set. Determining whether someone is likely to respond to a direct mail piece involves putting them in the category of Likely Responder or not. Microsoft Decision Trees, Microsoft Neural Network, and Microsoft Naïve Bayes are the first choice algorithms for classification when the predict column is a discrete variable.

Estimation (Regression)

Estimation is the continuous version of classification. That is to say, where classification returns a discrete value, estimation returns a continuous number. In practice, most classification is actually estimation. The process is essentially the same: A set of attributes is used to determine a relationship. A direct mail marketing company could estimate customers' likelihood to respond to a promotion based on past responses. Estimating a continuous variable called Response_Likelihood that ranges from zero to one is more useful when creating a direct marketing campaign than a discrete classification of High, Medium, or Low. The continuous value allows the marketing manager to determine the size of the campaign by changing the cutoff point of the Response_Likelihood estimate. For example, a promotions manager with a budget for 200,000 pieces and a list of 12 million prospects would use the predicted Response_Likelihood variable to limit the target subset. Including only those prospects with a Response_Likelihood greater than some number, say 0.80, would give the promotions manager a target list of the top 200,000 prospects. The continuous variable allows the user to more finely tune the application of the results.

Estimation algorithms estimate a continuously valued variable based on the other variables in the case set. Microsoft has built several algorithms that can be used for either discrete or continuous variables. Microsoft Decision Trees and Microsoft Neural Network are good choices for estimating a continuous variable.

Most of the estimation algorithms are based on regression analysis techniques. As a result, this category is often called regression, especially when the algorithm is used for prediction.

Prediction

Where classification and estimation are assignment of values that are "correct" by definition, *prediction* is the application of the same techniques to assign a value that can be validated at some future date. For example, you might use a classification algorithm to classify your customers as male or female based on their purchasing behaviors. You can use this classification as an input to designing various marketing programs.

> **TIP** Be careful not to reveal your guess to your customers because it could adversely affect your relationship with them. For example, it would be unwise to use this variable by itself to send out promotional pieces for a "For Women Only" sale. However, the variable is useful for the business even though you will never know for certain which customers are actually male or female.

Prediction, on the other hand, seeks to determine a class or estimate as accurately as possible before the value is known. This future-oriented element is what places prediction in its own category. The input variables exist or occur before the predicted variable. For example, a lending company offering mortgages might want to predict the market value of a piece of property before it's sold. This value would give them an upper limit for the amount they'd be willing to lend the property owner, regardless of the actual amount the owner has offered to pay for the given property. In order to build a predictive data mining model, the company needs a training set that includes predictive attributes that are known prior to the sale, like total square footage, number of bathrooms, city, school district, and the actual sale price of each property in the training set. The data mining algorithm uses this training set to build a model based on the relationships between the predictive variables and the known historical sale price. The model can then be used to predict the sale price of a new property based on the known input variables about that property.

One interesting feature of predictive models is that their accuracy can be tested. At some point in the future, the actual sale amount of the property will become known and can be compared to the predicted value. In fact, the data mining process described later in this chapter recommends splitting the historical data into two sets, one to build or train the model, and one to test its accuracy against known historical data that was not part of the training process.

> **TIP** The real estate sale price predictor is a good example of how data mining models tend to go stale over time. Real estate prices in a given area can be subject to significant, rapid fluctuations. The mortgage company would want to re-build the data mining model with recent sales transactions on a regular basis.

Microsoft Decision Trees and Microsoft Neural Network are the first choice algorithms for regression when the predict column is a continuous variable. When prediction involves time series data, it is often called *forecasting*. Microsoft Time Series is the first choice algorithm for predicting time series data, like monthly sales forecasts.

Association or Affinity Grouping

Association looks for correlations among the items in a group of sets. E-commerce systems are big users of association models in an effort to increase sales. This takes the form of an association modeling process known as *market basket analysis*. The online retailer first builds a model based on the contents of recent shopping carts and makes it available to the web server. As the shopper adds products to the cart, the system feeds the contents of the cart into the model. The model identifies items that commonly appear with the items currently in the cart. Most recommendation systems are based on association algorithms.

Microsoft Association is an association, or affinity grouping algorithm. Other algorithms, like Microsoft Decision Trees, can also be used to create association rules.

Clustering (Segmentation)

Clustering can be thought of as auto-classification. Clustering algorithms group cases into clusters that are as similar to one another, and as different from other clusters, as possible. The clusters are not predetermined, and it's up to the data miner to examine the clusters to understand what makes them unique. When applied to customers, this process is also known as *customer segmentation*. The idea is to segment the customers into smaller, homogenous groups that can be targeted with customized promotions and even customized products. Naming the clusters is a great opportunity to show your creativity. Clever names can succinctly communicate the nature and content of the clusters. They can also give the data mining team additional credibility with the business folks.

Once the clustering model has been trained, you can use it to classify new cases. It often helps to first cluster customers based on their buying patterns and demographics, and then run predictive models on each cluster separately. This allows the unique behaviors of each cluster to show through rather than be overwhelmed by the overall average behaviors.

One form of clustering involves ordered data, usually ordered temporally or physically. The goal is to identify frequent sequences or episodes (clusters) in the data. The television industry does extensive analysis of TV viewing sequences to determine the order of programs in the lineup. Companies with significant Internet web sites may use sequence analysis to understand how visitors move through their web site. For example, a consumer electronics product manufacturer's web site might identify several clusters of users based on their browsing behavior. Some users might start with the Sale Items page, then browse the rest of the e-commerce section, but rarely end with a purchase (Bargain Hunters). Others may enter through the home page, and then go straight to the support section, often ending by sending a help request e-mail (Clueless). Others may go straight to the e-commerce pages, ending with a purchase, but rarely visit the account management or support pages (Managers). Another group might go to the account management pages, checking order statuses and printing invoices (Administrators). A Sequence Clustering model like this one can be used to classify new visitors and customize content for them, and to predict future page hits for a given visitor.

Microsoft Clustering and Microsoft Sequence Clustering are segmentation algorithms. The Microsoft Sequence Clustering algorithm is primarily designed for sequence analysis (hence the clever name).

THE POWER OF NAMING

When Claritas originally created its customer segmentation system called PRIZM, they likely used clustering techniques to identify about 60 different groups of consumers. The resulting clusters, called lifestyle types, were numbered 1 through 60+. It's clear that someone at Claritas realized that numbers were not descriptive and would not make good marketing. So, they came up with a clever name for each cluster; a shorthand way to communicate its unique characteristics. A few of the names are: 02. Blue Blood Estates (old money, big mansions), 51. Shotguns and Pickups (working class, large families, mobile homes), and 60. Park Bench Seniors (modest income, sedentary, daytime TV watchers).

Anomaly Detection

Several business processes rely on the identification of cases that deviate from the norm in a significant way. Fraud detection in consumer credit is a common example of anomaly detection. Anomaly detection can take advantage of any of the data mining algorithms. Clustering algorithms can be tuned to create a cluster that contains data outliers, separate from the rest of the clusters in the model. Anomaly detection involves a few extra twists in the data mining process. Often it's necessary to bias the training set in favor of the exceptional events. Otherwise, there may be too few of them in the historical data for the algorithm to detect. After all, they are anomalies. We provide an example of this in the case studies later in this chapter.

Description and Profiling

The business task Berry and Linoff call *description and profiling* is essentially the same activity we earlier called undirected data mining. The task is to use the various data mining techniques to gain a better understanding of the complexities of the data. Decision trees, clustering, and affinity grouping can reveal relationships that would otherwise be undetectable. For example, a decision tree might reveal that women purchase certain products much more than men. In some cases, like women's shoes, this would be stereotypically obvious, but in others, like hammers, the reasons are less clear and the behavior would prompt additional investigation. Data mining, like all analytic processes, often opens doors to whole new areas of investigation.

Description and profiling can also be used as an extension to the data profiling tasks we described in previous chapters. You can use data mining to identify specific data error anomalies and broader patterns of data problems that would not be obvious to the unaided eye.

Business Task Summary

The definitions of the various business tasks that are suitable for data mining, and the list of which algorithms are appropriate for which tasks can be a bit confusing. Table 10.1 gives a few examples of common business tasks and the associated data mining algorithms that can help accomplish these tasks.

Roles and Responsibilities

Microsoft's Data Mining tools have been designed to be usable by just about anyone who can install BI Studio. After a little data preparation, a competent user can fire up the Data Mining Wizard and start generating data mining models. Data mining is an iterative, exploratory process. In order to get the most value out of a model, the data miner must conduct extensive research and testing. The data mining person (or team) will need the following skills:

- *Good business sense and good-to-excellent working relationships with the business folks:* This skill set is used to form the foundation of the data mining model. Without it, the data miner can build a sophisticated model that is meaningless to the business.

- *Good-to-excellent knowledge of Integration Services and/or SQL:* These skills are crucial to creating the needed data transformations and packaging them up in repeatable components.

- *A good understanding of statistics and probability:* This knowledge helps in understanding the functionality, parameters, and output of the various algorithms. It also helps to understand the data mining literature and documentation—most of which seems to have been written by statisticians.

- *Data mining experience:* Much of what is effective data mining comes from having seen a similar problem before and knowing which approaches might work best to solve it. Obviously, you have to start somewhere. If you don't have a lot of data mining experience, it's a good idea to find a local or online data mining special interest group you can use to validate your ideas and approach.

- *Programming skills:* To incorporate the resulting data mining model into the organization's transaction systems, someone on the team or elsewhere in the organization will need to learn the appropriate APIs.

Table 10.1 Examples of Business Tasks and Associated Algorithms

BUSINESS TASK	EXAMPLE	MICROSOFT ALGORITHMS
Classifying customers into discrete classes	Assigning each customer to an Activity Level with discrete values of Disinterested, Casual, Recreational, Serious, or Competitor.	- Decision Trees - Naïve Bayes - Clustering - Neural Network
Predicting a discrete attribute	Predicting a variable like ServiceStatus with discrete values of Cancelled or Active might form the core of a customer retention program.	- Decision Trees - Naïve Bayes - Clustering - Neural Network
Predicting a continuous attribute	Predicting the sale price of a real estate listing or forecasting next year's sales.	- Decision Trees - Time Series - Neural Network
Making recommendations based on a sequence	Predicting web site usage behavior. The order of events is important in this case. A customer support web site might use common sequences to suggest additional support pages that might be helpful based on the page path the customer has already followed.	- Sequence Clustering
Making recommendations based on a set	Suggesting additional products for a customer to purchase based on items they've already selected. In this case, order is not important. ("People who bought this book also bought . . .")	- Association - Decision Trees
Segmenting customers	Creating groups of customers with similar behaviors, demographics, and product preferences. This allows you to create targeted products and promotions designed to appeal to specific segments.	- Clustering - Sequence Clustering

SQL Server Data Mining Architecture Overview

Microsoft SQL Server 2005 Data Mining offers a rich, well-tuned, integrated, and easy-to-use data mining environment. For those of you who worked with data mining in SQL Server 2000, the 2005 release is a great leap forward. In this section we give an overview of the data mining environment using the high-level architecture drawing presented in Figure 10.1 as a guide.

From a system point of view, integrating data mining into the overall product allows the data mining service to take advantage of the functionality offered by the rest of the system. For example, point A in Figure 10.1 shows how data mining models are built using the dimensional engine, leveraging its ability to load data and quickly perform the base statistical calculations like sums, averages, and counts. The data mining server can also easily pull case data from both relational Analysis Services databases as seen at point B in Figure 10.1.

Point C in Figure 10.1 shows how the typical developer will first experience data mining by creating a BI Studio Analysis Services project and then using the Data Mining Wizard to create a new data mining structure and an initial data mining model. The mining structure is a new construct that provides a metadata layer allowing several mining models to work with the same input data. Each mining model in a mining structure can have different algorithms and parameters. The wizard provides model building guidance with auto selection and adjustment of variables based on the algorithm selected. The wizard also helps you create case sets, including complex, nested queries.

The Data Mining Design Environment

When the wizard is finished building the mining structure and the initial data mining model, it drops the developer into the data mining design environment. At this point, the mining model has not been built; the project contains only the metadata that defines the model. The Data Mining Designer is also significantly improved, with new model viewers to examine the models created by the different algorithms, validation checks, and direct access to column properties and model parameters. The Designer is broken up into five tabs to support the data mining process. (Refer to Figure 10.7 to see an example of the Designer.) Several of these tabs work with the completed mining model as it exists on Analysis Services, so they are not available until the model has been built and deployed. The first tab shows the Mining Structure with its underlying data source view. The second tab is the Mining Models tab, showing the source mining structure and all the data mining models that have been defined based on this structure. The third tab is the Mining Model Viewer that lets you select a model and a viewer type, and then provides several sub-tabs, each with a different graphic or tabular representation of the contents of the model.

The Mining Model Viewer tab is the primary tool the data miner uses to explore the various models. The fourth tab is the Mining Model Accuracy Chart. This tab provides two ways to compare the relative accuracy of certain kinds of predictive models: the Lift Chart and the Classification Matrix. Finally, the fifth tab is the Mining Model Prediction tab that allows the data miner to specify a prediction query using a rudimentary query builder interface.

Build, Deploy, and Process

Most of the functions in the Data Mining Designer work with the actual model as it exists in Analysis Services. This means once the wizard is complete, the developer must build and deploy the project (which includes processing the model cubes) before any more progress can be made. Building the project writes the metadata out to project files in the development environment. The actual model does not come into being until the project is deployed to an Analysis Services instance. At that point, BI Studio creates a database for the project in Analysis Services. It writes out the model structure metadata and the definition of each model. Finally, it creates a cube for each model and processes the models, inserting the training data so the algorithm can calculate the rules, correlations, and other relationships. Until the project is deployed and a model is processed, it cannot be viewed in the viewers.

TIP It is possible to process a single model rather than all models in a model structure by selecting the model in the Mining Models tab, and then selecting Process Model . . . from the Mining Model menu. This can save a lot of time if you are working with large case sets and complex models.

Accessing the Mining Models

As you see at Point D in Figure 10.1, Data Mining eXtensions to SQL language (DMX) is at the core of all the Microsoft data mining API. As the name suggests, DMX is an extension to SQL designed to create, train, modify, and query data mining models. DMX was introduced with SQL Server 2000 as part of the OLE DB for Data Mining APIs. It has been enhanced in SQL Server 2005 with additional options for data sources and more flexible SELECT functionality. An easy way to begin learning about DMX is to use the Mining Model Prediction tab in the Data Mining Designer and examine the syntax it generates for DMX queries. The code can be copied to a DMX query window in SQL Studio for further exploration. Although DMX is an extension to SQL, queries are submitted to the Analysis Services server—that's where the data mining services are.

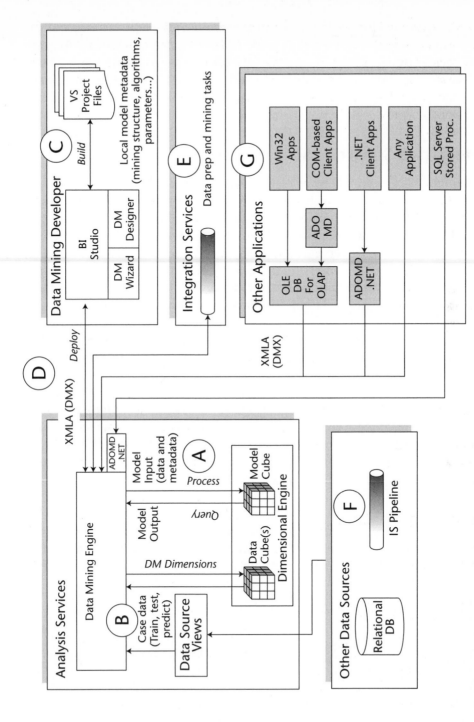

Figure 10.1 The SQL Server data mining architecture

When the development environment submits its DMX commands and queries to Analysis Services, it uses the XML for Analysis (XMLA) APIs. In fact, because Analysis Services is a native XMLA server, the data mining models are available to any application as a web service by using SOAP protocols. It is still possible to access the server with old OLE DB APIs, or ADO and ADO.NET.

Integration Services and Data Mining

Integration Services can play a major role in the data mining process as shown in Figure 10.1. Many of the standard transforms used for data cleansing and data integration are particularly valuable for building the training and test case sets. Besides the obvious tasks, like Data Conversion and Derived Column, tasks like the Percentage Sampling, Row Sampling, Conditional Split, Lookup, and Merge Join are powerful components the data miner can use to build a set of packages to prepare the case sets for the data mining process. This is shown at point E in Figure 10.1. In addition to the standard tasks, there are two Integration Services tasks that directly interact with the data mining models, shown at point F in Figure 10.1. The Data Mining Model Training destination task is the target for a training set used to train (or re-train) an existing mining model. This capability is perfect for the ongoing re-training required to keep certain mining models current—recommendation models, for example. The Data Mining Query task is specifically designed to do prediction joins against a model in the IS pipeline, once the model has been trained and tested. This could be used to add scores to the Customer table or identify significant data anomalies during the nightly ETL process. It could also be used in a real-time mode to flag transactions that were potentially fraudulent.

Additional Features

There are several additional features that will be important for certain applications. Most of these can be found at point G in Figure 10.1 and are listed briefly here:

- *Extensibility:* Microsoft has provided a set of COM APIs that allow developers to integrate additional data mining algorithms into the data mining engine. They can integrate custom viewers into the data mining designer as well. Someone could even create a new viewer for an existing Microsoft algorithm.

- *Analysis Management Objects (AMO):* AMO is a new API for managing the creation and maintenance of data mining objects, including creating, processing, backing up, restoring, and securing.

- *Stored procedures and user-defined functions:* A developer can create what are essentially stored procedures or user-defined functions and load them as managed assemblies into Analysis Services. This allows clients to work with large mining models through the intermediate layer of the server-based managed assembly.

- *Text mining:* It is possible to do some interesting data mining on unstructured text data, like the text in HTML files in a set of web directories, or even text fields in a database. For example, use the Integration Services Term Extraction transformation to build a dictionary of terms found in the text files. Then use data mining to create classification rules to categorize the documents according to the terms they contain. This is essentially a data mining application, not a new data mining algorithm, but it has value in certain areas.

REFERENCE To find more information about the text mining technique, see the Books Online topic "Term Extraction Transformation," or visit www.sqlserver datamining.com for a text mining tutorial.

Architecture Summary

Our goal in this section is to show how data mining fits into the overall SQL Server 2005 architecture, and to show how well data mining has been integrated into the SQL Server environment. It should be clear by now that data mining is a serious element of the BI toolset. Data mining and application developers will have a lot more to learn before they are proficient with all the data mining components. Fortunately, Microsoft's documentation is heavily weighted toward the development community. Additional help should be easy to find. A good place to start is a web site called www.sqlserverdatamining.com, maintained by the SQL Server data mining development team.

Microsoft Data Mining Algorithms

Data mining algorithms are the logic used to create the mining models. Several standard algorithms in the data mining community have been carefully tested and honed over time. One of the algorithms used to calculate decision trees uses a *Bayesian method* to determine the score used to split the branches of the tree. The roots of this method (so to speak) trace back to its namesake, Thomas Bayes, who first established a mathematical basis for probability inference in the 1700s.

The Data Mining group at Microsoft has been working diligently to expand the number of algorithms offered in SQL Server 2005 and to improve their accuracy. SQL Server Data Mining includes seven algorithms that cover a large percentage of the common data mining application areas. The seven core algorithms are:

- Decision Trees (and Linear Regression)
- Naïve Bayes
- Clustering
- Sequence Clustering
- Time Series
- Association
- Neural Network (and Logistic Regression)

The two regression algorithms set parameters on the main algorithm to generate the regression results. Some of these higher-level algorithms include parameters the data miner can use to choose from several underlying algorithms to generate the model. If you plan to do serious data mining, you need to know what these algorithms are and how they work so you can apply them to the appropriate problems and are able to get the best performance. We briefly describe each of these algorithms in the following list. The Books Online topic "Data Mining Algorithms" is a good starting point for additional information about how each of these algorithms work.

REFERENCE For more detailed information, see the book *Data Mining with SQL Server 2005* (Wiley, 2005) by ZhaoHui Tang and Jamie MacLennan, key members of the Microsoft SQL Server 2005 Data Mining team.

Decision Trees

The Microsoft Decision Trees algorithm supports both classification and estimation. It works well for predictive modeling for both discrete and continuous attributes.

The process of building a decision tree starts with the dependent variable to be predicted and runs through the independent variables to see which one most effectively divides the population. The goal is to identify the variable that splits the cases into groups where the predicted variable (or class) either predominates or is faintly represented. The best starting variable for the tree is the one that creates groups that are the most different from each other—the most diverse.

For example, if you're creating a decision tree to identify couples who are likely to form a successful marriage, you'd need a training set of input attributes for both members of the couple and an assessment of whether or not the partnership is successful. The input attributes might include the age of each individual, religion, political views, gender, relationship role (husband or wife), and so on. The predictable attribute might be MarriageOutcome with the values of Success or Fail. The first split in the decision tree—the one that creates the biggest split—might be based on a variable called PoliticalViews: a discrete variable with the values of Similar and Different. Figure 10.2 shows that this initial split results in one group (PoliticalViews=Similar) that has a much higher percentage of successful marriages than the other (PoliticalViews=Different). The next split might be different for each of the two branches. In Figure 10.2, the top branch splits based on the height difference between the two (calculated as height of husband minus height of wife). The lower branch also splits on height difference, but uses different cutoff points. It seems that couples can better tolerate a height difference if their political views are similar.

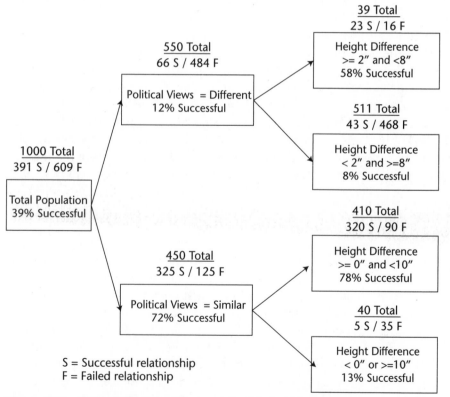

S = Successful relationship
F = Failed relationship

Figure 10.2 A simple decision tree to predict relationship success

The bottom branch of this tree indicates that the chances of having a successful marriage are more likely when the couple shares similar political views (.72). Following down that same branch, the chances get better when the husband is at least as tall as, but not more than 10 inches taller than the wife (.81). The group with the lowest probability of success (.08) is characterized by different political views and a height difference where the husband is either less than 2 inches taller or 8 inches or more taller than the wife. Once you build a decision tree like this, you could use it to predict the success of a given relationship by entering the appropriate attributes for both partners. At that point, you'd be well on your way to building a matching engine for a dating web site.

Naïve Bayes

The Microsoft Naïve Bayes algorithm is a good starting point for many data mining projects. It is a simplified version of Decision Trees, and can be used for classification and prediction for discrete attributes. Fortunately, if you select the Naïve Bayes algorithm in the data mining wizard, it will automatically "discretize" your data by converting any continuous variables in the input case set to discrete values.

The Naïve Bayes algorithm is fairly simple, based on the relative probabilities of the different values of each attribute, given the value of the predictable attribute. For example, if you had a case set of individuals with their occupations and income ranges, you could build a Naïve Bayes model to predict Income Range given an Occupation. The decision tree in Figure 10.2 could have been generated by the Naïve Bayes algorithm because all the variables are discrete (although the Tree Viewer is not available for Naïve Bayes models. The required probability calculations are almost all done as part of the process of building the mining model cube, so the results are returned quickly.

Clustering

The clustering algorithm is designed to meet the clustering or segmentation business need described earlier. Clustering is generally considered a density estimation problem with the assumption that there are multiple populations in a set, each with its own density distribution. (It's sentences like the previous one that serve to remind us that statisticians speak in a different language.) It's easier to understand clustering visually: A simple spreadsheet graph can be used as an eyeball clustering tool—especially when there are only two variables. It's easy to see where the dense clusters are located. For example, a graph showing per-capita income versus per-capita national debt for each country in the world would quickly reveal several obvious clusters of countries. We explore the idea of graphically identifying clusters further in the next section. The challenge is finding these clusters when there are more than two variables, or when the variables are discrete and non-numeric rather than continuous.

NOTE The Microsoft Clustering algorithm uses what's known as an Expectation-Maximization (EM) approach to identifying clusters. An alternative, distance-based clustering mechanism called K-means is available by setting parameters on the model.

Sequence Clustering

Sequence clustering adds another level of flexibility to the clustering problem by including an ordering attribute. The algorithm can identify common sequences and use those sequences to predict the next step in a new sequence. Using the web site example, sequence clustering can identify common click-paths and predict the next page (or pages) someone will visit, given the pages they have already visited.

Time Series

The Microsoft Time Series algorithm can be used to predict continuous variables, like Sales, over time. The algorithm includes time-variant factors like seasonality and can predict one or more variables from the case set. It also has the ability to generate predictions using cross-variable correlations. For example, product returns in the current period may be a function of product sales in the prior period. (It's just a guess, but we'd bet that high sales in the week leading up to December 25 may lead to high returns in the week following.)

Association

The Microsoft Association algorithm is designed to meet the business tasks described as association, affinity grouping, or market basket analysis. Association works well with the concept of nested case sets, where the higher level is the overall transaction and the lower level is the individual items involved in the transaction. The algorithm looks for items that tend to occur together in the same transaction. The number of times a combination occurs is called its *support*. The SUPPORT parameter allows the data miner to set a minimum number of occurrences before a given combination is considered significant. The Association algorithm goes beyond item pairs by creating rules that can involve several items. In English, the rule sounds like "When Item A and Item B exist in the item set, then the probability that Item C is also in the item set is X." The rule is displayed in this form: A, B → C (X). In the same way the data miner can specify a minimum support level, it is also possible to specify a minimum probability in order for a rule to be considered.

Neural Network

Neural network algorithms mimic our understanding of the way neurons work in the brain. The attributes of a case are the inputs to a set of interconnected nodes, each of which generates an output. The output can feed another layer of nodes (known as a hidden layer) and eventually feeds out to a result. The goal of the neural network algorithm is to minimize the error of the result compared with the known value in the training set. Through some fancy footwork known as back propagation, the errors are fed back into the network, modifying the weights of the inputs. Then the algorithm makes additional passes through the training set, feeding back the results, until it converges on a solution. All this back and forth means the neural network algorithm is slowest from a performance standpoint. The algorithm can be used for classification or prediction on both continuous and discrete variables.

Using these seven algorithms, separately or in combination, you can create solutions to most common data mining problems.

The Data Mining Process

There are probably as many ways to approach data mining as there are data mining practitioners. Much like dimensional modeling, starting with the goal of adding business value leads to a clear series of steps that just make sense.

You'll be shocked to hear that our data mining process begins with an understanding of the business opportunities. Figure 10.3 shows the three major phases of the data mining process and the major task areas within those phases.

ADDITIONAL INFORMATION ON THE DATA MINING PROCESS

We didn't invent this process; we just stumbled on it through trial and error. Others who've spent their careers entirely on data mining have arrived at similar approaches to data mining. We're fortunate that they have documented their processes in detail in their own publications. In particular, three sources have been valuable to us. The book Data Mining Techniques, 2nd Ed. by Michael J. A. Berry and Gordon S. Linoff (Wiley, 2004) describes a process Berry and Linoff call the Virtuous Cycle of Data Mining. Another, similar approach comes from a special interest group that was formed in the late 1990s to define a data mining process. The result was published as Cross Industry Standard Process for Data Mining (CRISP). Visit www.crisp-dm.org for more information. Also, the SQL Server Books Online topic "The Data Mining Process" presents a similar approach.

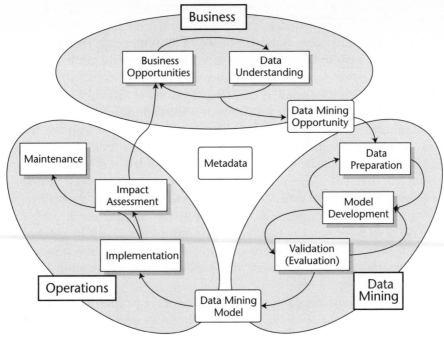

Figure 10.3 The data mining process

Like most of the processes in the DW/BI system, the data mining process is iterative. The arrows that point back to previous processes in Figure 10.3 are the most common iteration points. There are additional iteration points; for instance, it is also common to return to the Business phase tasks based on what is learned in the Data Mining phase. In this section, we examine the three phases and their task areas in order, beginning with the Business phase.

The Business Phase

The business phase is a much more focused version of the overall requirements gathering process. The goal is to identify an opportunity, or a list of opportunities and their relative priorities, that can have a significant impact on the business. The Business Opportunities and Data Understanding tasks in Figure 10.3 connect to each other because the process of identifying opportunities must be bounded by the realities of the data world. By the same token, the data itself may suggest business opportunities.

Identifying Business Opportunities

As always, the most important step in successful business intelligence is not about technology; it's about understanding the business. In data mining, this usually takes the form of a set of discussions between the business folks and the data miner about potential opportunities, and the associated relationships and behaviors that are captured in the data. The purpose of these meetings is to identify several high-value opportunities and think through each one carefully. First, identify the overall business value goal of the data mining project. It helps to describe this in as narrow and measurable a way as possible. A goal like "increase sales" is too broad. A goal like "reduce the monthly churn rate" is a bit more manageable. Next, think about what factors influence the goal. What might indicate that someone is likely to churn, or how can we tell if someone would be interested in a given product? While you're discussing these factors, try to translate them into specific attributes and behaviors that are known to exist in a usable, accessible form. The data miner may hold several of these meetings with different groups to identify a range of opportunities. At the end of these meetings, the data miner should work with the business folks to prioritize the various opportunities based on the estimated potential for business impact and the difficulty of implementation. These priorities will change as you learn more about the data, but this is an important starting point.

The data miner then takes the top-priority business opportunity and its associated list of potential variables back to the BI Studio for further exploration.

Understanding the Data

The data miner typically spends a significant amount of time exploring the various datasets that might be relevant to the business opportunities discussed. At this stage, the goal is to be reasonably confident that the data needed to support the business opportunity is available and clean enough to be usable. This exploration is generally not much more complex than the data exploration and data profiling that took place during the data modeling step in Chapter 2, and in designing the ETL process in Chapter 5. Any problems identified at this point should be noted so they can be included in the Data Mining Opportunity document.

Describing the Data Mining Opportunity

The data mining opportunity is a document that describes the top-priority opportunity discussed with the business folks. The opportunity description should include the following sections:

- Business Opportunity Description
- Expected Data Issues
- Modeling Process Description
- Implementation Plan
- Maintenance Plan

It's important to document the opportunity, and have the business folks review it to make sure you understand their needs, and they understand how you intend to meet them. The data mining opportunity document is also a milestone in the data mining process. Once the data miner has a solid, clearly described, approved business opportunity, the data mining process enters the second phase: the data mining phase.

The Data Mining Phase

Once you understand the business opportunities and data structures, you can move into the data mining phase of the project. The data mining phase is where you build the data mining model. The data miner works through the tasks of preparing the data, developing alternative models, comparing their accuracy, and validating the final model. As Figure 10.3 shows, this is a highly iterative process. Data preparation feeds the model development task, which often identifies the need for further data preparation. By the same token, the process of validating a model commonly indicates the need for further improvements, which loops the data miner right back to the model development task, and potentially back to data preparation. In some cases, when serious problems arise, the loop goes all the way back to the business opportunity step. We ignore all this iteration in our description and move sequentially through the tasks.

Data Preparation

The first task in the data mining phase is to build the data mining case sets. Recall that a case set includes one row per instance or event. For many data mining models, this means a dataset with one row per customer. Models based on simple customer attributes, like gender and marital status, work at the one-row-per-customer level. Models that include behaviors like purchasing work at the one-row-per-event level. A case set for customer purchases would have one row for each product purchased by a customer. This is called a *nested* case set with two components—the customer case set with one row per customer and all the applicable customer attributes, and the product case set, which includes the customer key and the products purchased by the given customer. Building the case set involves creating SQL scripts, MDX scripts, and/or Integration Services packages to clean and transform the data, and copy it into the datasets needed to support the model building process.

Cleansing and Transforming

Ideally, the variables in the case set are fully populated with only the appropriate values and no outliers or null values. The bulk of this book describes the incredible amount of work it takes to create that cleaned, conformed information infrastructure we call the data warehouse. This is why the data warehouse is the ideal source for data mining case data. In the easiest case, many of the variables identified in the business opportunity already exist as attributes in the data warehouse database. This is often true with fields like CustomerType, or ProductColor. The data miner's world gets even better when demographics and other external data are already loaded as part of the standard ETL process. While these variables can be directly extracted, it is always a good idea to verify that basic data quality rules have been appropriately applied.

Unfortunately, directly selecting variables from the data warehouse database rarely provides us with a rich enough dataset to build a solid mining model. You may have to transform the data to make it more relevant to the business opportunity. This might include converting variables into more useful forms, like using standard discrete ranges for continuous variables if your industry has them—audience age range in television programming and advertising is a common discrete range. If no standard ranges exist, the data mining designer can be used to automatically discretize these variables based on different methods, like a histogram of the values, or an even distribution. This can also be done in a SQL statement using the CASE function. Some attributes might need multiple conversions, like birth date might be converted to age, which could then be converted to age range. There are several common conversions, like combining fields and discretizing.

Unfortunately, these descriptive variables are generally not enough for many mining models, even after they have been transformed into more relevant forms. The most influential variables in a data mining model are typically behavior-based, not descriptive. Behaviors are generally captured as facts. What did customers do, how often did they do it, how much did they do it, and when did they do it are basic behavior questions. For example, knowing which web pages someone has viewed, what products they bought, what services they used, what problems they complained about, when the last time they complained was, and how many complaints they had in the last two months can help you build a clear picture of the status of your relationship with that customer.

These behavioral variables are painstakingly extracted from the detailed fact tables as part of the data preparation process. The choice of which behavioral variables to create is based on the business's understanding of behavior. Note that many of these behavior-based attributes require full table scans of the fact tables to create.

Integrating External Variables

Unfortunately, behavioral variables may still not be enough. Building an effective model often means bringing in additional data. These attributes, like demographics, come from various systems around the company or even from external sources. They will need to be merged together to make a single case set. When the source tables share a common key, this typically means joining them together to create a single row per case (usually per customer). However, it is not uncommon to have to map keys from the external source to the transaction system's natural keys, and then to the dimension's surrogate keys. In the worst case, the external data will not have a known key that ties to any field in the data warehouse database. When this happens, the relationship will need to be determined using matching tools. This is a tedious process, and it's another argument for using Integration Services and its fuzzy matching task for data mining data preparation.

WARNING Accurately tracking history is critical to successful data mining. If your DW/BI system or external sources overwrite changes in a Type 1 fashion, your model will be associating current attribute values with historical behavior. This is particularly dangerous when integrating external data that might have only current attribute values. See the section "Slowly Changing Dimensions" in Chapter 2 for an example of how this might create problems.

Building the Case Sets

Build these datasets by defining data cleansing and transformation steps that build a data structure made up of individual observations or cases. Cases often contain repeating nested or child structures. These case sets are then fed into the data mining service. It's helpful to manage these tables independent of the data warehouse itself. Keep the data mining case sets in their own database, on their own server if necessary. The process of building the case sets is typically very similar to the regular ETL process. It usually involves a set of transformations and full table scans that actually generate a resulting dataset that gets loaded into the data mining database.

There are two main approaches to data preparation in the SQL Server 2005 environment. Folks who come from an SQL/relational background will be inclined to write SQL scripts, saving the results to separate case set tables that become inputs to the DM process.

NOTE Creating case sets can also be done through views if you are creative enough with your SQL. We don't recommend this because if underlying data changes (like when new rows are added), the mining model may change for no apparent reason.

Folks who come from an ETL background will be more comfortable using Integration Services to merge, cleanse and prepare the data mining case sets. The Integration Services approach has some advantages in that there are many transformation components built into the Integration Services toolbox. Integration Services can also more easily pull data from external sources and in different formats and can be used to deposit the prepared case set wherever it is needed, in a variety of formats.

Table 10.2 The Primary Data Mining Datasets

SET	PURPOSE
Training	Used as input to the algorithm to develop the initial model.
Validation	Used to make sure the algorithm has created a model that is broadly applicable rather than tightly tied to the training set. (Used in certain circumstances only.)
Test	Data not included in the training sets—often called holdout data. Used to verify the accuracy or effectiveness of the model.

Depending on the business opportunity and the data mining algorithms employed, creating the initial datasets often involves creating separate subsets of the data for different purposes. Table 10.2 lists three common datasets used for data mining. The Percentage Sampling, Row Sampling, and Conditional Split tasks are particularly well suited to creating the training and test case sets. For example, use the Row Sampling transform to grab a random sample of 10,000 rows from a large dataset. Then use the Percentage Sampling transform to send 80 percent to the training set and 20 percent to the test set.

Most of the models we describe use only the training and test datasets. Working with the validation set requires an additional degree of data mining expertise.

One last advantage of Integration Services is that it allows you to build a package or project that contains all of the steps needed to prepare data for a given data mining project. Put this Integration Services project under source control, and re-use it to create new datasets to keep the model current. In our opinion, Integration Services is the best choice for data mining data preparation. SQL plays a role in defining the initial extracts and some of the transformations, and will be part of any data preparation effort, but building the whole flow generally works best in Integration Services.

Model Development

The first step in developing the data mining model is to create the mining model structure in the BI Studio. The mining model structure is essentially a metadata layer that separates the data from the algorithms. The data mining wizard creates the initial mining model structure which can then be edited as needed.

Once the mining structure is defined, the data miner builds as many mining models and versions as time allows, trying different algorithms, parameters, and variables to see which one yields the greatest impact or is most accurate. Usually this involves going back and redefining the data preparation task to add new variables or change existing transformations. These iterations are where SQL Server Data Mining shines. The flexibility, ease of use, range of algorithms, and integration with the rest of the SQL Server toolset allows the data miner to run through more variations than many other data mining environments. Generally, the more variations tested, the better the final model.

Model Validation (Evaluation)

There are two kinds of model validation in data mining. The first involves comparing models created with different algorithms, parameters, and inputs to see which is most effective at predicting the target variable. The second is a business review of the proposed model to examine its contents and assess its value. We will examine both validation steps in this section.

Comparing Models

Creating the best data mining model is a process of triangulation. Attack the data with several algorithms like decision tree, neural net, and memory-based reasoning. You'd like to see several models point to similar results. This is especially helpful in those cases where the tool spits out an answer but doesn't provide an intuitive foundation for why the answer was chosen. Neural nets are notorious for this kind of result. Triangulation gives all the observers (especially end users and management) confidence that the predictions mean something.

Analysis Services Data Mining provides two common tools for comparing the effectiveness of certain types of data mining models—a lift chart and a classification matrix. These can be found under the Mining Model Accuracy tab in the data mining designer. To use the Accuracy tab tools, first select the mining structure that supports the models you want to compare and join it to your test dataset. The lift chart works in a couple of different ways, depending on the models being compared. The basic idea is to run the test cases through all of the models, and compare the predicted results with the known actual results from the test dataset. The lift chart then plots the percentage of correct predictions for a given percentage of the overall test population, beginning with the most accurate portions of the model (the cases with the highest predicted probability). Figure 10.4 shows a lift chart that compares two simple models used to predict Income Range based on the other non-income demographics in the AdventureWorksDW Customer table.

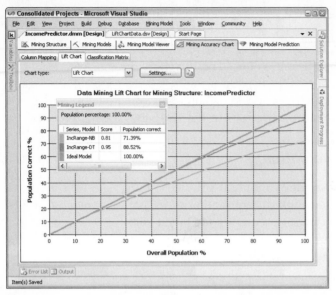

Figure 10.4   An example lift chart comparing two models designed to predict Income Range

The lines representing the two models are bounded by an upper limit that represents the best possible prediction. In the best case, the model would be 100 percent right for whatever percent of the population it processed. The best case is represented by the heavy, straight line between 0 and 100. The worst case would be a random guess. Because this model has only six possible values of predicted income ranges, a random guess would be right 16.67 percent of the time. The Decision Trees model called IncRange-DT is clearly more predictive than the Naïve Bayes model called IncRange-NB. At the 100 percent point, the Decision Trees model accurately predicts 88.52 percent of the cases while the Naïve Bayes predicts only 71.39 percent of the cases.

The second tool, called the classification matrix, is a matrix with the predicted values on the rows and the actual values on the columns. Ideally, you'd like to see a single vector down the diagonal of the matrix with values, and the rest of the cells should be zeros. This would represent the outcome where all of the cases the model predicted to be in a certain Income Range actually were in that Income Range. Figure 10.5 shows the classification matrix for the same Decision Trees and Naïve Bayes models.

In this example, the Naïve Bayes model clearly is incorrect more often than the Decision Trees model. For example, for cases where the actual range is 10,000-39,000 (the third data column), the Naïve Bayes model predicts an Income Range of 40,000-79,000 for 202 cases, while the Decision Trees model makes this error only 98 times.

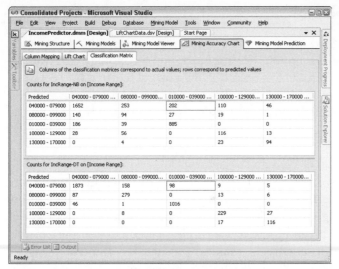

Figure 10.5   Example classification matrices for the Income Range models

Unfortunately, the Mining Model Accuracy tools work only for single-valued results in the initial release. They don't work for result lists, like recommendation lists. In those cases, you will need to build your own comparison tests using the Integration Services tasks to query the mining model with the test dataset and compare the results. We show an example of this in one of the case studies later in this chapter.

REFERENCE For more information about using lift charts and classification matrices, see "Validating Data Mining Models" in SQL Server Books Online.

Business Review

The data mining phase ends with the selection of the "best" model based on its performance in the model comparison process. Ultimately this is a business decision, so you need to review the contents and performance of the model with the business folks to make sure that it makes sense.

Prepare for this review by carefully combing through the selected model to understand and document the rules it uses, the relationships it defines, and the impact you expect it to have. The various tabs in the data mining designer are particularly helpful in developing this understanding. Present this documentation to the business users and carefully walk them through the logic behind the model. This presentation also includes evidence of the model's performance from the Mining Accuracy Chart tab tools and other sources. This helps all participants understand the expected impact of the model. Once the business review is complete, the next step is to move the model out into the real world.

The Operations Phase

The Operations phase is where the rubber meets the road. At this point, you have the best possible model (given the time, data, and technology constraints) and you have business approval to proceed. Now you get to put it into production and see what kind of impact it has. The Operations phase involves three main tasks: implementation, impact assessment, and maintenance.

Implementation

After all participants have approved the final model and the implementation plan, the team can move the model into production in the implementation task. Production can range from using the model once a quarter to assess the effectiveness of various promotions, to classifying customers as part of the nightly ETL process, to interactively making product recommendations as part of the web server or customer care transaction system.

Each of these alternatives involves a different cast of characters. At one end of the spectrum, the quarterly update of the customer dimension may involve only the data miner and the ETL developer. At the other end of the spectrum, making online recommendations will clearly involve the production systems folks. And, depending on the transaction volume, they will likely want a production Analysis Services server (or cluster) dedicated to providing recommendations. Moving the data mining model into production also involves significant changes to the transaction system applications to incorporate the data mining query and results into the business process and user interface. This is usually a big deal. You must figure out who needs to be involved in the implementation task for your data mining model and let them know as early as possible, so they can help determine the appropriate timeframes and resources. Deploy in phases, starting with a test version, to make sure the data mining server doesn't gum up the transaction process.

Assess Impact

Determining the impact of the data mining model can be high art. In some areas, like direct mail, the process of tuning and testing the marketing offers and collateral and the target prospect lists is often full-time work for a large team. They do test and control sets with different versions of the mailing before they do the full mass mailing. Even in the full campaign, often several phases with different versions and control sets are built in. The results of each phase help the team tweak subsequent phases for best results.

In general, the data miner should adopt as much of this careful assessment process as possible.

Maintain the Model

Almost all data mining models will need to be re-trained, or to be completely rebuilt over some period of time. As the world changes, the behaviors that have been captured in the model become outdated. This is particularly noticeable in a fast-changing industry like retail where new fashions, products, and models are announced on a daily basis. A recommendation engine that didn't include the most recent behavior and latest models would be less than useful to the customer. In a case like this, the basic model structure may still apply, but the rules and relationships must be re-generated based on new behavior data.

Metadata

In the best of all possible worlds, the final data mining model should be documented with a detailed history of how it came into being. What sources contributed to the case set? What kinds of transformations were applied to the variables, and at what points in the process were they applied? What was the initial model and what were the intermediate versions considered and discarded? What parameter values were used for which versions of the model? A professional data miner will want to know exactly what went into creating a model in order to explain its value, to avoid repeating the same errors, and to re-create it if need be. The data miner should also keep track of how and when the model is used, and when it should be maintained.

The problem with tracking the history of a mining model is that because Analysis Services makes it so easy to create additional versions of the model, it takes much more time to document each iteration than it does to actually do the work. Nonetheless, you still need to keep track of what you have and where it came from. We recommend keeping a basic set of metadata to track the contents and derivation of all the transformed datasets and resulting mining models you decide to keep around. This can get much more complex if you like, but the simplest approach is to use a spreadsheet, as pictured in Figure 10.6.

SECURITY

The data mining process takes place across the various DW/BI system platforms and relies on their security mechanisms. The data miner needs to have enough privileges on the data source servers to create new tables and/or cubes. Additionally, to create and modify data mining models, the data miner must be a member of the Analysis Services Administrators group on the data mining computer.

Data Mining Project Documentation Sheet

Project Information	Data Preparation SSIS Package Information
Project Name:	Package Name:
Project Owner:	Package Location:
Business Contact:	Data Mining Server Name:
Start Date:	Data Mining Database Name:
Expiration Date:	
Project Description:	

Data Mining Data Sources					
Source Name	Type	Create step	Version	Version date	Xforms and changes
...					

Data Mining Structures			
Structure Name	Version	Version Date	Xforms and changes
...			

Data Mining Models								
Model Name	Parent Structure	DM Algorithm	Version	Version date	Input Vars	Predict Vars	Parameter settings	Results
...								

Figure 10.6   A simple spreadsheet for tracking data mining models

Data Mining Examples

For many of us, the best way to learn something is by doing it. This is especially true for technical folks, and even more so for data mining. You really
need to work through the SQL 2005 Data Mining Tutorial before you run
through this example. This will give you a chance to get familiar with the tools
and the user interface, which will make these examples easier to understand
and follow. If you haven't already done so, please take the time to go work
through the data mining tutorials now.

In this section we start out with a simple example to get a feel for the data
mining tool environment and the data mining process. In fact, the first example is so simple that its case set of economic data can be presented on a single
page. Then we dig into a more detailed example based on the Adventure
Works Cycles data mining tutorial data. Both of these examples will follow the
general flow of the data mining process presented in the previous section.

Case Study: Classifying Cities

This first example is a small, simplified problem designed to provide a clear
understanding of the process. The dataset has only 48 cases total—not nearly
enough to build a robust data mining model. However, the small size allows
us to examine the inputs and outputs to see if the resulting model makes sense.

The scenario is based on a large non-governmental organization with a mission and operations much like that of the World Bank:

> (T)o fight poverty and improve the living standards of people in the developing world. It is a development Bank that provides loans, policy advice, technical assistance and knowledge sharing services to low and middle income countries to reduce poverty. The Bank promotes growth to create jobs and to empower poor people to take advantage of these opportunities. (http://web.worldbank.org/)

Classifying Cities: Business Opportunity

The data miner on the Bank's DW/BI team held meetings with key directors and managers from around the organization to identify business opportunities that are supported by available data and can be translated into data mining opportunities. During these meetings it became clear that there were not enough resources to properly customize the Bank's programs. The Bank had historically focused its efforts to provide financial aid at the country level. Several economists felt that targeting policies and programs at the city level would be more effective, allowing for the accommodation of unique regional and local considerations that are not possible at the country level.

A switch to the city level would mean the people who implemented the Bank's programs would need to deal with potentially thousands of cities rather than the 208 countries they were working with around the world. This switch would significantly expand the complexities of managing the economic programs in an organization that was already resource limited.

The group discussed the possibility of designing programs for groups of cities that have similar characteristics. If there were a relatively small number of city groups, the economic analysts felt it would be possible to design the appropriate programs.

Classifying Cities: Data Understanding

During the meetings, there was discussion about what variables might be useful inputs. The analysts had a gut feel for what the city-groups might be, and some initial guesses about which variables would be most important and how they could be combined. The group came up with a list of likely variables. The data miner combed through the organization's databases to see if these inputs could be found, and to see what other relevant information was available. This effort turned up 54 variables that the organization tracked, from total population to the number of fixed line and mobile phones per 1,000 people. This wealth of data seemed too good to be true, and it was. Further investigation revealed that much of this data was not tracked at the city level. In fact, there were only ten city-level variables available. The data miner reviewed this list with the business folks and the group determined that of the ten variables, only three were reliably measured. Fortunately, the group also felt these three variables were important measures of a city's economic situation. The three variables were average hourly wages (local currency), average hours worked per year, and the average price index.

At this point, the data miner wrote up a description of the data mining opportunity, its expected business impact, and an estimate of the time and effort it would take to complete. The project was described in two phases; the goal of the first phase was to develop a model that clusters cities based on the data available. If this model made sense to the business folks, phase two would use that model to assign new cities to the appropriate clusters as they contact the bank for financial support. The data mining opportunity description was reviewed by the economists and all agreed to proceed.

Classifying Cities: Data Preparation

The data miner reviewed the dataset and realized it needed some work. First, the average hourly wages were in local currencies. After some research on exchange rates and discussion with the economists to decide on the appropriate rates and timing, the data miner created a package to load and transform the data. The package extracted the data from the source system and looked up the exchange rate for each city and applied it to the wages data. Because the consumer price data was already indexed relative to Zurich, using Zurich as 100, this package also indexed the wage data in the same fashion. Finally, the package wrote the updated dataset out to a separate table. The resulting dataset to be used for training the cluster model, containing three economic measures for 46 cities around the world, is shown in Table 10.3.

NOTE This data actually comes from the Economics Research Department of the Union Bank of Switzerland. The original set contains economic data from 48 cities around the globe in 1991. It has been used as example data for statistics classes and can be found on many web sites. Try searching for "cities prices and earnings economic (1991) globe".

Table 10.3 The City Economic Data Training Set After Data Preparation

OBS.	CITY NAME	AVG WORK HRS	PRICE INDEX	WAGE INDEX
1	Amsterdam	1714	65.6	49
2	Athens	1792	53.8	30.4
3	Bogota	2152	37.9	11.5
4	Bombay	2052	30.3	5.3
5	Brussels	1708	73.8	50.5

OBS.	CITY NAME	AVG WORK HRS	PRICE INDEX	WAGE INDEX
6	Buenos Aires	1971	56.1	12.5
7	Cairo	NULL	37.1	NULL
8	Caracas	2041	61	10.9
9	Chicago	1924	73.9	61.9
10	Copenhagen	1717	91.3	62.9
11	Dublin	1759	76	41.4
12	Dusseldorf	1693	78.5	60.2
13	Frankfurt	1650	74.5	60.4
14	Geneva	1880	95.9	90.3
15	Helsinki	1667	113.6	66.6
16	Hong Kong	2375	63.8	27.8
17	Houston	1978	71.9	46.3
18	Jakarta	NULL	43.6	NULL
19	Johannesburg	1945	51.1	24
20	Kuala Lumpur	2167	43.5	9.9
21	Lagos	1786	45.2	2.7
22	Lisbon	1742	56.2	18.8
23	London	1737	84.2	46.2
24	Los Angeles	2068	79.8	65.2
25	Luxembourg	1768	71.1	71.1
26	Madrid	1710	93.8	50
27	Mexico City	1944	49.8	5.7
28	Montreal	1827	72.7	56.3
29	Nairobi	1958	45	5.8
30	New York	1942	83.3	65.8
31	Nicosia	1825	47.9	28.3
32	Oslo	1583	115.5	63.7
33	Panama	2078	49.2	13.8
34	Paris	1744	81.6	45.9
35	Rio de Janeiro	1749	46.3	10.5

(continued)

Table 10.3 *(continued)*

OBS.	CITY NAME	AVG WORK HRS	PRICE INDEX	WAGE INDEX
36	Sao Paulo	1856	48.9	11.1
37	Seoul	1842	58.3	32.7
38	Singapore	2042	64.4	16.1
39	Stockholm	1805	111.3	39.2
40	Sydney	1668	70.8	52.1
41	Taipei	2145	84.3	34.5
42	Tel Aviv	2015	67.3	27
43	Tokyo	1880	115	68
44	Toronto	1888	70.2	58.2
45	Vienna	1780	78	51.3
46	Zurich	1868	100	100

Observe that two of the cities are missing data. The data miner might opt to exclude these cities from the dataset, or include them to see if the model can identify them as outliers. This would help spot any bad data that might come through in the future.

Classifying Cities: Model Development

Because the goal in the first phase was to identify groups of cities that have similar characteristics, and those groupings were not predetermined, the data miner decided to use the Microsoft Clustering algorithm. After creating a new Analysis Services project in BI Studio and adding a data source and data source view that included the City dataset, the data miner right-clicked on the Mining Structures folder and selected New Mining Structure. This opened the Data Mining Wizard to create a new mining structure. The wizard asks if the source is relational or OLAP, and then it asks which data mining technique should be used. The data miner chose Microsoft Clustering and specified the city name as the key and the other columns as input, checking the "Allow drill through" box on the final wizard screen. After the wizard was finished, the data miner clicked the Mining Model Viewer tab, which forced the build/deploy/process steps. When this whole process completed, BI Studio presented the cluster diagram shown in Figure 10.7.

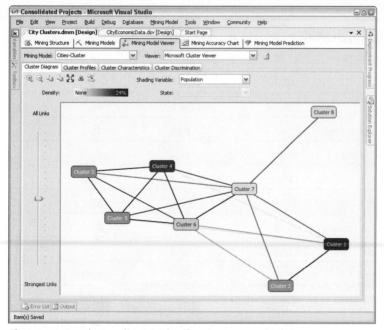

Figure 10.7   Cluster diagram for the city economic data

At first glance, this diagram isn't that helpful. Without knowing anything about the problem, the Microsoft Clustering algorithm is limited to names like Cluster 1 and Cluster 2. At this point, the data miner can explore the model by using the other tabs in the Mining Model Viewer tab, and by using the drill-through feature to see which cities have been assigned to which nodes. The data miner can also use the Microsoft Mining Content Viewer to examine the underlying rules and distributions. The data in Table 10.4 is grouped by cluster and was created by drilling through each cluster and copying the underlying list into a spreadsheet.

Table 10.4   City Economic Data Listed by Cluster

CLUSTER	CITY NAME	AVG WORK HRS	PRICE INDEX	WAGE INDEX
Cluster 1	Bogota	2152	11.5	37.9
	Bombay	2052	5.3	30.3
	Buenos Aires	1971	12.5	56.1
	Caracas	2041	10.9	61.0
	Kuala Lumpur	2167	9.9	43.5
	Lagos	1786	2.7	45.2

(continued)

Table 10.4 *(continued)*

CLUSTER	CITY NAME	AVG WORK HRS	PRICE INDEX	WAGE INDEX
	Mexico City	1944	5.7	49.8
	Nairobi	1958	5.8	45.0
	Panama	2078	13.8	49.2
	Rio de Janeiro	1749	10.5	46.3
	Sao Paulo	1856	11.1	48.9
Cluster 2	Athens	1792	30.4	53.8
	Hong Kong	2375	27.8	63.8
	Johannesburg	1945	24.0	51.1
	Lisbon	1742	18.8	56.2
	Nicosia	1825	28.3	47.9
	Singapore	2042	16.1	64.4
Cluster 7	Seoul	1842	32.7	58.3
	Tel Aviv	2015	27.0	67.3
Cluster 6	Houston	1978	46.3	71.9
	Los Angeles	2068	65.2	79.8
	Taipei	2145	34.5	84.3
Cluster 4	Brussels	1708	50.5	73.8
	Chicago	1924	61.9	73.9
	Dusseldorf	1693	60.2	78.5
	Frankfurt	1650	60.4	74.5
	Luxembourg	1768	71.1	71.1
	Montreal	1827	56.3	72.7
	New York	1942	65.8	83.3
	Sydney	1668	52.1	70.8
	Toronto	1888	58.2	70.2
	Vienna	1780	51.3	78.0
Cluster 5	Amsterdam	1714	49.0	65.6
	Copenhagen	1717	62.9	91.3
	Dublin	1759	41.4	76.0
	London	1737	46.2	84.2

CLUSTER	CITY NAME	AVG WORK HRS	PRICE INDEX	WAGE INDEX
	Madrid	1710	50.0	93.8
	Paris	1744	45.9	81.6
Cluster 3	Geneva	1880	90.3	95.9
	Helsinki	1667	66.6	113.6
	Oslo	1583	63.7	115.5
	Stockholm	1805	39.2	111.3
	Tokyo	1880	68.0	115.0
	Zurich	1868	100.0	100.0
Cluster 8	Cairo			37.1
	Jakarta			43.6

Table 10.4 has a few interesting items. The clusters seem to make general sense given a basic understanding of the world economic situation in 1991. Many of the poorer cities of South and Central America and Africa ended up in Cluster 1. The two cities that had only price data, Cairo and Jakarta, are on their own in Cluster 8, and that cluster was drawn a distance from the other six in Figure 10.7. Cluster 8 seems to be the data anomalies cluster. Beyond this, it's difficult to see what defines a given cluster from the data table. The underlying rules are too complex to reverse engineer by sight. The Microsoft Mining Content Viewer can help by revealing the equations that determined each cluster, but a graphical representation will usually reveal much more than written equations.

Figure 10.8 converts the data from Table 10.4 into a graphical form. Each city is grouped by cluster along the X axis, with work hours plotted on the left Y axis and wage and price indexes on the right Y axis. The order of the clusters was determined by starting with Cluster 1 in Figure 10.7 and following the links. This graph allows the viewer to get a better sense for what makes up the clusters.

Even though Figure 10.8 is a bit busy, it helps clarify the commonalities within each cluster. The cloud-like circles in Figure 10.8 highlight the Price Index data points. The horizontal line in the graph indicates the average Price Index of about 69.2. Clusters 6, 4, and 3 on the upper part of the right side of the graph have a Price Index above average, while Clusters 1, 2, and 7 on the left side are all below average. This graph also makes it easier to identify the characteristics of the individual clusters. For example, Cluster 4 includes cities whose wages are relatively high, with prices that are at the low end of the high price range, and relatively low work hours. These are the cities that make up the day-to-day workforce of their respective countries—we might call this cluster the "Heartland" cities. Cluster 1, on the other hand, has extremely low wages, higher work hours than most, and relatively lower prices. These are the newly developing cities where labor is cheap and people must work long hours to survive. You might call this cluster the "Hard Knock Life" cities. The Bank would likely call it something a bit more politically correct, like the "Developing Cities" cluster. As we mentioned earlier, good names can help crystallize the defining characteristics of each cluster.

Classifying Cities: Model Validation

Some data mining models are easier to test than others. For example, when you're building a prediction model, you can create it based on one historical dataset and test it on another. Having historical data means you already know the right answer, so you can feed the data through the model, see what value it predicts, and compare it to what actually happened.

In the City cluster example, validating the model is not so straightforward. You don't know the classification ahead of time, so you can't compare the assigned cluster with the right cluster—there is no such thing as "right" in this case. Validation of this model came in two stages. First, the data miner went back to the economic analysts and reviewed the model and the results with them. This was a reasonableness test where the domain experts compared the model with their own understanding of the problem. The second test came when the model was applied to the original business problem. In this case the team monitored the classification of new cities to make sure they continued to stand up to the reasonableness test. Ultimately, the question was "Do the classifications seem right, and do they help simplify how the organization works at the city level?" Is it easier and more effective to work with eight clusters rather than 46 (or 4,600) cities?

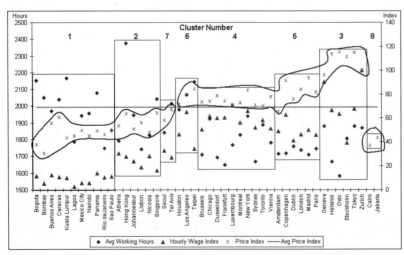

Figure 10.8 A graphical view of the city clusters

Classifying Cities: Implementation

Once the team decided the model would work, or at least that it was worth testing in an operational environment, it was time to move it into production. This can mean a whole range of activities, depending on the nature of the model and the business process to which it's being applied. In this city classification example, new economic data at the city level can arrive at any time. The team decided to have this new data entered into a table in the database and assign clusters to it in a batch process once a night.

The data miner wrote a simple Integration Services package that reads in unassigned cities, submits them to the data mining model for cluster assignment, and writes the full record out to a table called CityMaster with a batch date identifying when the cluster was assigned. Figure 10.9 shows what the data flow for this simple package might look like. This flow has a data viewer inserted right after the Data Mining Query task showing the output of the task. Compare the cluster assignments for Manila (Cluster 2), and Milan (Cluster 7), with the other cities in those clusters in Figure 10.8. Do these assignments pass the reasonableness test?

Implementation would also integrate this package into the rest of the nightly ETL process. The package should include the standard data and process audit functions described in Chapter 6. Ultimately, the process should be part of the package that manages the City dimension.

This nightly data mining batch process is a common one in many DW/BI systems, using a data mining model to populate a calculated field like a Default Risk score across all loan records or a Credit Rating across all customers. These scores can change depending on customer behaviors, like late payments or deposit balances. Every loan and customer may have to be re-scored every night. The same batch process can be used on a one-time basis to address opportunities like identifying customers who are likely to respond to a new product offering.

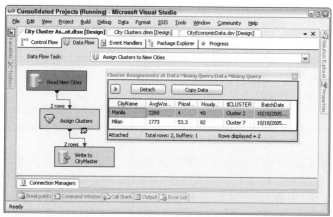

Figure 10.9 An Integration Services package to assign clusters to new cities

Classifying Cities: Maintenance and Assessment

As the data changes, the data mining model will likely change as well. In this case, the data mining model should be re-built as data about additional cities is collected, or data about cities that have already been assigned a cluster is updated. The team would then review the resulting clusters to make sure they make sense from a business perspective. Given the nature of the business process and the changing data, this review should probably happen on a regularly scheduled basis—perhaps monthly to start, then quarterly as the model and data stabilize.

This example shows how classification can be used to improve an organization's business processes. Although this dataset is too small to produce reliable results, it does generate a model that makes sense and shows how that model can be applied to new incoming data.

Case Study: Product Recommendations

The ability to recommend products that might be particularly interesting to a given customer can have a huge impact on how much your customers purchase. This example follows the data mining process from identifying the business requirements through to the implementation of a product recommendation data mining model. It's based on the Adventure Works Cycles dataset provided with SQL Server 2005. Recall from Chapter 1 that Adventure Works Cycles is a manufacturer, wholesaler, and Internet retailer of bicycles and accessories. While Microsoft has taken pains to build some interesting relationships into the data, this data may not be completely real. That is, the purchasing behaviors might not be drawn from the real world, but may in fact be made up. Data mining can help us find only relationships that are in the data.

The SQL Server data mining tutorial steps you through the process of building a model that predicts whether or not someone will be a bike buyer. While this is interesting information, it doesn't help you figure out what to display on the web page. Even if you're pretty certain someone will be a bike buyer, you don't know which bike to show them. Also, what products should you show all those folks who are not bike buyers? Our goal in this example is to create a data mining model that produces a custom list of specific products that you can show to any given web site visitor based on demographic information you might have. To the extent that the custom product list is more appealing than a random list of products, the visitor is more likely to make a purchase.

In this example, we try to give you enough information to work through the model creation process yourself. It's not a complete step-by-step tutorial, but if you've already worked through the SQL Server data mining tutorial, you should be able to follow along and see how it works for yourself.

Product Recommendations: The Business Phase

Recall that the business phase of the data mining process involves identifying business opportunities, and building an understanding of the available data and its ability to support the data mining process. The Adventure Works Cycles data is more complete than many real-world systems we've seen, and it has more than enough customers and purchases to be interesting.

Product Recommendations: Business Opportunities

In many companies, the DW/BI team has to sell the idea of incorporating data mining into the business processes. This is usually either because the business folks don't understand the potential or because the business will have to change the transaction system, which is a big and scary task. Sometimes, the team gets lucky and data mining starts with a request from the business community. This is how it worked in the Adventure Works Cycles example. One of the folks in marketing who is responsible for e-commerce marketing came to the DW/BI team asking for ways to boost web sales. Web sales accounted for about $9,000,000 in the first half of 2004, or about one-third of Adventure Works Cycles total sales. The Marketing group has created a three-part strategy for growing the online business: Bring in more visitors (Attract), turn more visitors into customers (Convert), and develop long-term relationships with customers (Retain). The marketing person who came to the DW/BI team is responsible for the Convert strategy—that is, for converting visitors to customers.

> **TIP** In a case like this, if the Marketing person has a PowerPoint presentation that goes into detail on the marketing strategy, the data miner should review it. We feel sure they have such a presentation.

Because the marketing person is responsible only for conversion, the team will investigate alternatives for increasing the conversion of visitors to customers. They will check to see if the final model also increases the average dollars per sale as a beneficial side effect. After some discussion, the team decided that influencing purchasing behavior (conversion) with relevant recommendations is likely to be the best way to achieve their goals. They translated the idea of recommendations into specifics by deciding to dedicate one section of the left-hand navigation bar on the e-commerce web site to hold a list of six recommended products that will be tailored to the individual visitor. While the marketing person investigated the level of effort required to make this change on the web site, the data miner dug into the availability of relevant data.

Product Recommendations: Data Understanding

After some research, the data miner discovered that when visitors come to the Adventure Works Cycles web site, they are asked to fill out an optional demographics form ("to better serve them"). A few queries revealed that about two-thirds of all visitors actually do fill out the form. Because the form is a required part of the purchase process, the information is also available for all customers. In either case, this demographic information is placed in a database and in cookies in the visitor or customer's browser. The DW/BI system also has all historical purchasing behavior for each customer at the individual product and line item level. Based on this investigation, the data miner felt that sufficient data was available to create a useful mining model for product recommendations.

The data miner knew from experience that behavior-based models (like purchases or page views) are generally more predictive than demographic-based models. However, there were several opportunities to make recommendations where no product-related behavioral data is available but demographic data is available. As a result, the data miner believed that two data mining models might be appropriate: one to provide recommendations on the home page and any non-product pages, and one to provide recommendations on any product-related pages. The first model would be based on demographics and would be used to predict what a visitor might be interested in given their demographic profile. The second model would be based on product interest as indicated by the product associated with each web page they visit or any products added to their cart.

At this point, the data miner wrote up a Data Mining Opportunity document to capture the goals, decisions, and approach. The overall business goal was to increase conversion rates with an ancillary goal of increasing the average dollars per sale. The strategy was to offer products that have a higher probability of being interesting to any given visitor to the web site. This strategy breaks down into two separate data mining models, one based on demographics and one based on product purchases. This decision was considered a starting point with the understanding that it would likely change during the data mining phase. This example goes through the creation of the demographics-based model. The product-based model is left as an exercise for the reader.

The team also agreed on metrics to measure the impact of the program. They would compare before and after data, looking at the change in the ratio of new customer purchases (conversions) to the total unique visitor count in the same time periods. They would also examine the change in the average shopping cart value at the time of checkout. A third impact measure would be to analyze the web logs to see how often customers viewed and clicked on a recommended link.

Product Recommendations: The Data Mining Phase

With the opportunity document as a guide, the data miner decided to begin with the demographics-based model. This section follows the development of the model from data preparation to model development and validation.

Product Recommendations: Data Preparation

The data miner decided the data source should be the AdventureWorksDW relational database. Because no web browsing data was available yet, sales data would be used to link customer demographics to product preferences—if someone actually bought something, they must have had an interest in it. The advantage of sourcing the data from the data warehouse is that it has already been through a rigorous ETL process where it was cleaned and transformed to meet basic business needs. While this is a good starting point, it's often not enough for data mining.

The data miner's first step was to do a little data exploration. This involved running some data profiling reports and creating some queries that examined the contents of the source tables in detail. Because the goal is to relate customer information to product information, there are two levels of granularity to the case sets. The demographic case set is generally made up of one row per observation: in this example, one row per customer. Each row has the customer key and all available demographics and other derived fields that might be useful. The product sales case set is at a lower level of detail, involving customers and the products they bought. Each row in this case set has the customer key and the product model name of the purchased product along with any other information that might be useful. Each customer case set row has a one-to-many relationship with the product sales case set (called a nested case set). You could create a single case set by joining the demographics and sales together up front and creating a denormalized table, but we prefer to rely on the data mining structure to do that for us.

After reviewing the source data in the AdventureWorksDW database, the data miner decided to pull the demographic case data from the DimCustomer table and combine it with other descriptive information from the DimGeography and DimSalesTerritory tables, and to pull the product purchasing case data from the InternetSalesFact table along with some product description fields from DimProduct and related tables. The data exploration also helped the data miner identify several additional transformations that might be useful in creating the data mining model. These are shown in Table 10.5.

Table 10.5   Additional Transformations Used to Create the Example Case Set

TRANSFORMATION	PURPOSE
Convert BirthDate to Age	Reduce the number of distinct values by moving from day to year, and provide a more meaningful value (Age) versus YearOfBirth.
Calculate YearsAsCust	DATEDIFF the DateFirstPurchase from the GetDate() to determine how many years each case has been a customer. This may help as an indicator of customer loyalty.

(continued)

Table 10.5 *(continued)*

TRANSFORMATION	PURPOSE
Create bins for YearlyIncome	Create a discrete variable called IncomeGroup to use as input to algorithms that cannot handle continuous data. Note: This is optional when creating the case set because binning can also be accomplished in the Mining Structure tab, or through the Data Mining Wizard.

As a critical part of data preparation, the data miner recognized the need to split the historical dataset into two subsets: one to train the initial model, and one to test its effectiveness. After a bit of customer count experimentation, the data miner decided to build an Integration Services package to randomly select 18,000 customers from the customer dimension and send 90 percent into the training set and the rest into the test set. The data flow shown in Figure 10.10 is the part of this package that selects the customers, adds the derived columns, splits the set into test and training datasets, and writes them out to separate tables called DMTestSet and DMTrainSet.

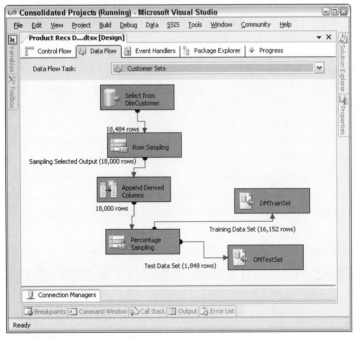

Figure 10.10 An Integration Services data flow to create test and training datasets

TIP This approach works for the Adventure Works Cycles customer dataset because there are only 18,484 customers total. If you have millions of customers, you might look for a more efficient way to extract training and test subsets. One possible approach is to use the last few digits of the customer key (as long as it is truly random). For example, a WHERE clause limiting the last two digits to "42" will return a 1 percent subset.

Another data flow elsewhere in this package uses the two customer sets to extract the product orders for the selected customers and write them out to a table called DMCustPurch. This is the nested product case set. Depending on how rapidly the product list changes, it might make sense to limit the datasets to only those products that have been purchased in the last year and their associated customers.

You can see the tables for the training and test datasets in the Data Source View in Figure 10.11. Figure 10.11 also includes the data model for the nested product case set.

The nested product case set has one or more rows for each customer. Just the fact that someone with a certain set of demographics bought a certain product is all the information you need. Notice from Figure 10.11 that the data miner decided to include some additional fields from the orders fact table that will not play a role in making recommendations but may be helpful in troubleshooting the dataset.

TIP Integration Services makes it easy to create physical tables snapshots of the exact datasets and relationships at a point in time. You can then use these tables to build and test many different mining models over a period of time without tainting the process with changing data. It's common to set up a separate database or even a separate server to support the data mining process and keep the production databases clear of this data mining debris.

The SQL Server 2005 Data Mining Tutorial uses views to define the case sets. This helps keep the proliferation of physical tables in the database to a minimum, but it's not our preferred approach. The views need to be defined carefully; otherwise their contents will change as the data in the underlying database is updated nightly.

At this point, the data miner has enough data in the proper form to move on to the data mining model development process.

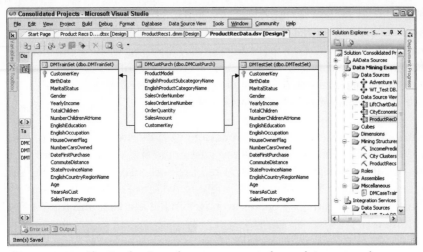

Figure 10.11   The ProductRecs datasets, presented as a data source view

Product Recommendations: Model Development

The data miner began the model development process by creating a new Analysis Services project in the BI Studio called ProductRecs. She added a data source that pointed to the AdventureWorksDW database and created a data source view that included the three tables created in the Integration Services package: DMTrainSet, DMTestSet, and DMCustPurch. After adding the relationships between the tables, the project and data source view looked like the screen capture shown in Figure 10.11. The keys shown in the Train and Test tables are logical primary keys assigned by the data source view.

Next, the data miner used the Data Mining Wizard to create a new mining structure by right-clicking on the Mining Structures folder and selecting New Mining Structure. The data is coming from an existing relational data warehouse, and the data miner chose the Microsoft Decision Trees data mining technique in order to predict the probability of purchasing a given product based on a set of known attributes (the demographics from the registration process). In the Specify Table Types dialog window of the wizard, the data miner checked DMTrainSet as the Case table and DMCustPurch as the Nested table.

The Specify the Training Data window can be a bit tricky because it's unclear what columns should be used in what ways. For this model, all of the demographic variables will be used as input only—you're not trying to predict the Age or Gender of the customer with this model. Also, you need to correctly specify which DMCustPurch columns to include. At a minimum, specify a key for the nested cases.

In this example, ProductModel is the appropriate key, although it's not enforced in the creation of the table. You also need to specify which column or columns to predict. Again, ProductModel is the obvious choice because it contains the description of the products to recommend. The data miner also included EnglishProductCategoryName as a predicted column because it groups the ProductModels and makes it easier to navigate later on in the Model Viewer. Finally, the data miner did not to include the quantity and amount fields because they are not relevant to this model. Remember, these are the nested purchases for each customer case. With a new visitor, you'll know their demographics and can use that as input to the model, but you won't have any purchase information so it makes no sense to include it as available input data. The bottom section of the completed Specify the Training Data window is illustrated in Figure 10.12.

The next step in the Data Mining Wizard is meant to specify the content and data types of the columns in the mining structure. The data miner accepted the defaults at this point and went to the final screen, changing the mining structure name to ProductRecs1, and the mining model name to ProductRecs1-DT (for Decision Trees). After hitting the Finish button, the wizard completed the creation of the mining structure and the definition of the Decision Trees data mining model. The data miner is then able to view and verify the model definitions by viewing the Mining Models tab.

The next step is to deploy and process the model. Typically, a data miner works with one model at a time to avoid the overhead of processing all the models in the project (even though there is only one at this point, there will be more).

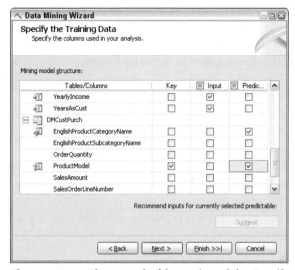

Figure 10.12   The nested table portion of the Specify the Training Data window

TIP To deploy and process the model, select any column in the ProductRecs1-DT model, right-click, and select Process Model. Select Yes to deploy the project, Run at the bottom of the Process Mining Model window, Close in the Process Progress window (when it's finished), and finally Close back in the Process Mining Model window.

The Decision Trees algorithm generates a separate tree for each predicted value (each ProductModel), determining which variables historically have had a relationship with the purchase of that particular product. This means it will build 40 trees, one for each distinct value of the predicted variable, ProductModel, found in the DMCustPurch table.

Once the processing is complete, the data miner is finally able to explore the results. Selecting the Model Viewer tab automatically brings up the currently selected mining model in the appropriate viewer—in this case, the Decision Trees sub-tab of the Microsoft Tree Viewer. The tree shown is for the first item alphabetically in the predicted results set: the tree for the All-Purpose Bike Stand, which seems to have a slight bias toward women. Selecting a more interesting product like the Mountain-200 mountain bike brings up a more interesting tree—or at least one with more nodes.

The first split in the initial Mountain-200 tree is on DateFirstPurchase, and then several other fields come into play at each of the sub-branches. Immediately, the data miner recognized a problem. The DateFirstPurchase field was included in the case set inadvertently because it is an attribute of the customer dimension. However, it's not a good choice for an input field for this model because visitors who have not been converted to customers will not have a DateFirstPurchase by definition. Even worse, after looking at several trees for other bicycle products, it is clear that DateFirstPurchase is also a strong splitter—perhaps because the longer someone has been a customer, the more products they have purchased, and the more likely they are to have purchased a bike. A quick review of all the fields reveals that another field has the same problem: YearsAsCust. This makes sense because the field is a function of DateFirstPurchase, and contains essentially the same information. The data miner decided to remove these fields from the model and reprocess it.

One easy way to do this is to delete the fields from the Mining Structure by right-clicking on the field and selecting Delete. The more cautious way is to remove them from the ProductRecs-DT mining model by changing their type from Input to Ignore in the drop-down menu. This keeps the fields in the Mining Structure, just in case. After changing the type to Ignore on these two fields and reprocessing the model, the decision tree for the Mountain-200 now looks like the one shown in Figure 10.13.

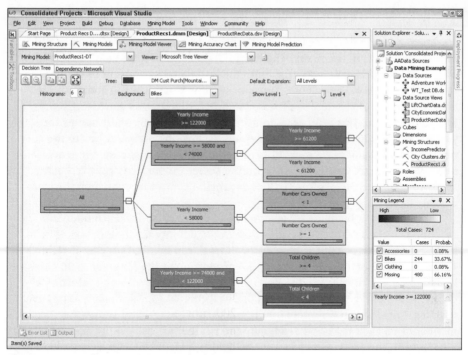

Figure 10.13   The Mountain-200 decision tree

After exploring the model in the Decision Tree tab for a bit, it's useful to switch over to the Dependency Network tab. This tool provides a graphical way to see which demographic variables are predictive of which products (ProductModels). The dependency network shows the relationships between the input variables and the predicted variables. But the meaning of the initial view of the dependency network for this example, shown in Figure 10.14, is not immediately obvious. Each node in the network stands for one of the variables or products in the mining model. Some input variables are predictive of many product models, others only a few. Because we have 15 input variables and 40 individual product models and so many relationships among those variables, we end up with a spider web. In fact, the viewer automatically limits the number of nodes it will display so as not to overwhelm the user.

Fortunately, there's more to the Dependency Network tab than just this view. Zooming in to see the actual names of the variables is a good way to start. Selecting a node highlights the nodes with which it has relationships. The tool uses color and arrow directions to show the nature of those relationships. Finally, the slider on the left of the pane allows the user to limit the number of relationships shown based on the strength of the relationship. The default in this viewer is to show all the relationships. Moving the slider down toward the bottom of the pane removes the weakest relationships in ascending order of strength.

WORKING WITH THE TREE VIEWER

It's worth taking a few minutes to discuss the elements of the tree viewer and how to work with it. The main pane where the picture of the tree is presented holds a lot of information. Starting with the parameter settings at the top of the Decision Tree tab in Figure 10.13, you can see the Mountain-200 is the selected tree. (Okay, you can't really see the whole description unless you select the drop-down menu. This is an argument in favor of using very short names for your case tables and columns.) The Default Expansion parameter box to the right shows that you're viewing All Levels of the tree—in this case, there are four levels but only three are visible on the screen. Some trees have too many levels to display clearly so the Default Expansion control lets you limit the number of levels shown.

The tree itself is made up of several linked boxes or nodes. Each node is essentially a class with certain rules that would determine whether someone belongs in that class. (This is how decision trees can be used for classification.) The background of each node shows the proportion of the Mountain-200 cases in the node. You can change the denominator of the proportion by selecting a choice in the Background drop-down list. In Figure 10.13, this density is relative to Bikes. Because the Mountain-200 is a bike, the background shows the number of bikes in the node divided by the number of cases in the node—in other words, the probability of someone having a Mountain-200 if they are classified in this node. The darker the node, the higher the probability that people in that node own a Mountain-200.

Selecting a node reveals the counts and probabilities for that node along with its classification rules. In Figure 10.13, the node at the top of the second column labeled Yearly Income >= 122000 has been selected. As a result, its values and rules are displayed in the Mining Legend window in the lower right of the screen. We see that 724 cases meet the classification rules for this node. Of these 724 cases, 244 have Mountain-200 bikes, which results in a probability of $244/724 = 33.67\%$. In English, this reads "If you are one of our customers and your income is \$122,000 or greater, the chances are about 1 out of 3 that you'll own a Mountain-200."

When the model is used for predicting, the theory is that probabilities based on existing customers can be applied to the folks who are not yet customers. That is, the chances are about 1 out of 3 that someone with an income of \$122,000 would purchase a Mountain-200. Feed your web visitor's demographic input variables into the model and it will find the nodes that the visitor classifies into and return the trees (ProductModels) that have the nodes with the highest probabilities.

One way to get a better sense of the relationships in the Dependency Network tab is to drag the predictive (input) variables over to one corner of the screen. Figure 10.15 shows the model from Figure 10.14 after the data miner dragged the predictive variables to the upper-right corner.

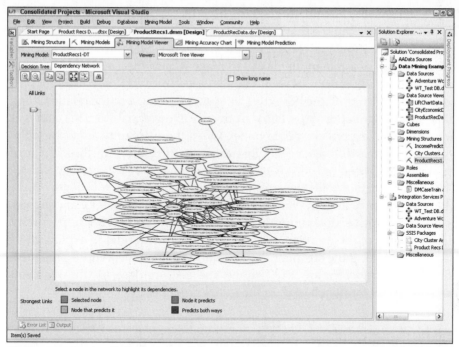

Figure 10.14   The default Dependency Network drawing for the ProductRecs1 Decision Trees model

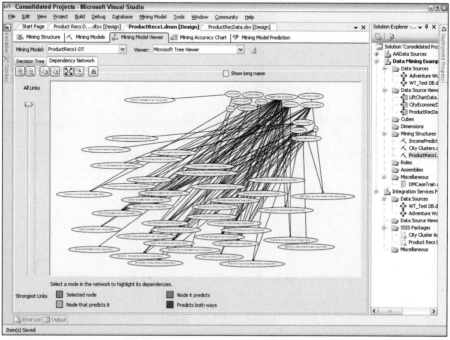

Figure 10.15   The Dependency Network with predictive variables dragged to the upper-right corner

This is still not very helpful. By zooming in on the upper-right corner, as shown in Figure 10.16, you can see that these, in fact, are the input variables. Note that there are only 14 shown in the dependency network. StateProvinceName did not play enough of a role in the model to make it onto the graph. Figure 10.16 has had another adjustment as well: The slider was moved down to about one-third of the way up from the bottom. This shows that most of the relationships, and the strongest relationships, come from only a few variables. This comes as no surprise to an experienced data miner. Often there are only a few variables that really make a difference—it's just difficult to figure out ahead of time which ones they'll be.

The input variables with the strongest relationships shown in Figure 10.16 are English Country Region Name, Yearly Income, and Number Cars Owned. True to the iterative data mining process, this brings up an opportunity. Removing some of the weaker variables will allow the model to explore more relationships among the stronger variables and to generate a more predictive model. For example, Figure 10.17 shows the decision tree for the Women's Mountain Shorts product based on the initial model.

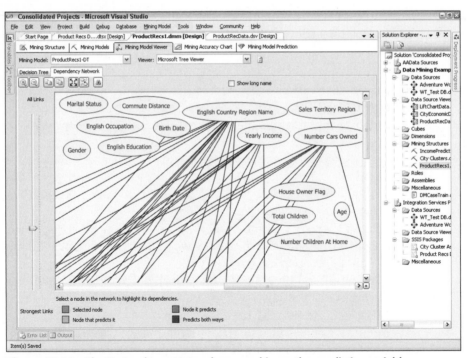

Figure 10.16   The Dependency Network zoomed in on the predictive variables

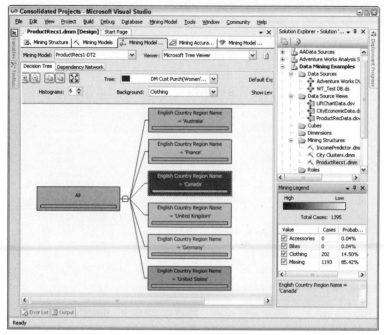

Figure 10.17 The initial decision tree for Women's Mountain Shorts

There is clearly a variation in preference for these shorts by country. About 14.5 percent of the Canadians bought a pair, but less than one-half of one percent of the Germans bought a pair. Given this information, recommending Women's Mountain Shorts to a German web site visitor is probably a waste of time.

Figure 10.18 shows the decision tree for the same product after the model has been narrowed down to five of the strongest input variables shown in Figure 10.16: Age, Yearly Income, English Country Region Name, Number of Children, and House Owner Flag.

The first split is still based on English Country Region Name, but now there is a second split for three of the country nodes. Canada can be split out by income, showing that Canadian customers making >= $74,000 are more likely to own a pair of Women's Mountain Shorts (probability 23.46 percent)—much higher than the 15 percent we saw for Canada based on the English Country Region Name split alone in Figure 10.17.

The process of building a solid data mining model involves exploring as many iterations of the model as possible. This could mean adding variables, taking them out, combining them, adjusting the parameters of the algorithm itself, or trying one of the other algorithms that is appropriate for the problem. This is one of the strengths of the SQL Server Data Mining workbench—it is relatively easy and quick to make these changes and explore the results.

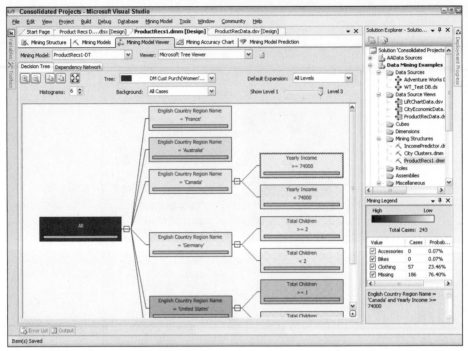

Figure 10.18 The expanded decision tree for Women's Mountain Shorts after reducing the number of input variables

Moving back to the case study, assume that the data miner worked through several iterations and has identified the final candidate. The next step in the process is to validate the model.

Product Recommendations: Model Validation

As we described in the data mining process section, the lift chart and classification matrix in the Mining Accuracy Chart tab are designed to compare and validate models that predict single, discrete variables. The recommendations model is difficult to validate. Rather than one value per customer, the recommendations data mining model generates a probability for each ProductModel for each customer.

Another problem with validating the model is that the data miner doesn't really have historical data to test it with. The test data available, and the data used to build the model, is actually purchasing behavior, not responses to recommendations. For many data mining models, the bottom line is you won't know if it works until you try it.

Meanwhile, the data miner wants to be a bit more comfortable that the model will have a positive impact. One way to see how well the model predicts actual buying behavior is to simulate the lift chart idea in the context of recommendations. At the very least, the data miner could generate a list of the top six recommended products for each customer in the test case set and compare that list to the list of products the person actually bought. Any time a customer has purchased a product on their recommended list, the data miner would count that as a hit. This approach provides a total number of hits for the model, but it doesn't indicate if that number is a good one. You need more information: You need a baseline indication of what sales would be without the recommendations.

In order to create a baseline number for the recommendations model, the data miner also created a list of six random products for each customer in the test case set. Table 10.6 shows the results for these two tests. As it turns out, the random list isn't a realistic baseline. You wouldn't really recommend random products; you would at least use some simple data mining in the form of a query and recommend your six top-selling products to everyone—people are more likely to want popular products. Table 10.6 includes the results for the top six list as well.

Table 10.6   Recommendations Model Validation Data Points

TEST	NUMBER OF HITS	TOTAL POSSIBLE	HIT RATE
Random Baseline	1,508	10,136	14.9%
Top Six Products	3,733	10,136	36.8%
Recommended List	4,181	10,136	41.2%

The data miner and marketing manager learn from Table 10.6 that the model is reasonably effective at predicting what customers bought—it's not great, but it's better than listing the top six products, and a lot better than nothing at all. Note that the hit rate in Table 10.6 has very little to do with the click-through rate you'd expect to see on the web site. The real number will likely be significantly lower. However, based on these results, the data miner and the marketing manager decided to give the model a try and carefully assess its impact on the original goal of the project, increasing the percentage of visitors who become customers, and increasing the average sale amount.

Product Recommendations: The Operations Phase

The decision to go forward moved the project into the Operations phase of the data mining process. The details of the implementation are well beyond the scope of this book, but the high-level steps would involve making the data mining model available to the web server, and writing the ADOMD.NET calls to submit the visitor's demographic information and to receive and post the recommendation list. Figure 10.19 shows an example of the DMX query for the ProductRecs1-DT mining model.

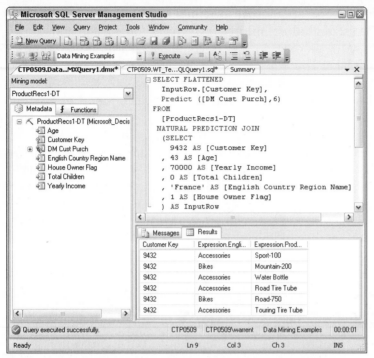

Figure 10.19 Sample DMX for a data mining query to get product recommendations based on an individual's demographics

In this case, for a 43-year-old person from France who makes $70,000 per year, has no children, and owns a house, the model recommendations include a Mountain-200 and a Road-750. This is good—you like seeing those high-revenue bikes in the recommendations list.

Assessing the impact of the model would involve several analyses. First, the team would look at the number of unique visitors over time, and the percentage of visitors that actually become customers before and after the introduction of the recommendation list. Increasing this percentage is one of the goals of providing recommendations in the first place. This analysis would look at the average purchase amount before and after as well. It may be that the conversion rate is not significantly affected, but the average purchase amount goes up because current customers are more interested in the recommendations and end up purchasing more.

The second analysis would look at the web browsing data to see how many people click on one of the recommendation links. The analysis would follow this through to see how many people actually made a purchase. In a large enough organization, it might be worth testing the recommendation list against the top six list.

The model would also have to be maintained on a regular basis because it is built on purchasing behaviors. New product offerings and changes in fashion, preference, and price can have a big impact on the purchasing behaviors—you don't want your recommendations to go stale.

Summary

Congratulations for making it this far. You should have a basic understanding of the data mining concepts and how data mining can have an impact on your organization. Data mining is not just a tool; it's a process of understanding business needs and data issues, working through various alternative models, testing and validating their viability, rolling them out into production, and making sure they address the opportunity and don't get stale.

Early in the chapter we reviewed some basic data mining concepts, describing how data mining is used for several different business tasks: classification, estimation or regression, prediction, association or affinity grouping, clustering or segmentation, anomaly detection, and description and profiling. We then discussed SQL Server 2005's data mining architecture and toolset, reviewing the key components and showing how they fit together. Digging down into the technology, we briefly described the seven algorithms provided with the product and how they applied to the various business tasks.

Next we went into some detail on the process of data mining, outlining a step-by-step approach starting with identifying business opportunities and the associated data, moving through the actual data mining phase with its data preparation, model development, and model validation steps, and ending with the operations phase with the implementation of the model, maintenance, and an assessment of its impact.

Most of the second part of the chapter walked through this process based on two data mining scenarios: a large international lending organization that wants to cluster and classify cities, and an Adventure Works Cycles marketing person who wants to increase the number of web site visitors who become customers by offering targeted product recommendations.

By this point, we hope it's clear that data mining is a powerful set of tools the DW/BI team can use to add significant, measurable business value. And that the SQL Server Data Mining toolset is effective, easy to use, and easy to incorporate into your overall system environment.

We encourage the data miner on the team or in the organization to explore the data mining capabilities of SQL Server 2005. We also encourage everyone who uses the data mining tools to be careful with them. Data mining is a true power tool. As with a chainsaw, you can do amazing things, but you can also hurt yourself. It doesn't help your credibility if you roll out a model based on the clever finding that customers who have been with you longer tend to have purchased more items.

PART

Four

Deploying and Managing the DW/BI System

Working with an Existing Data Warehouse

Doing the best with what you have

Throughout this book, we've been talking as if you're starting from scratch with your data warehouse system. Starting from a blank slate, you gather business requirements, identify priorities, design a business process dimensional model, implement your ETL system, build OLAP databases and data mining models, and develop and deploy BI applications for your user community. Building a data warehouse system is a cyclical process that involves all these steps on each round.

In this chapter we confront the reality that you may have some data warehousing infrastructure in place already. We even let our imaginations run so wild as to consider that your existing DW/BI system might be experiencing some problems. A move to the new Microsoft SQL Server 2005 technology can be a good time to address some existing issues.

After we discuss how to use SQL Server 2005 to improve your existing DW/BI system, we outline the issues that you might encounter as you migrate your infrastructure from SQL Server 2000 to SQL Server 2005. We end the chapter with a discussion of integrating the various BI components of SQL Server 2005 into a heterogeneous environment that includes non-Microsoft components.

The Current State of Affairs

A healthy DW/BI system grows and changes. In our consulting practice we often speak with CIOs who want to know when the data warehouse project will be "done" and resources can be redeployed. Although the initial development phase will eventually end, it's important to understand that the best DW/BI systems will have a permanent level of development activity. As the business changes, especially in a company that engages in mergers and acquisitions, the DW/BI system must evolve in step.

Even the best-designed DW/BI systems can start to experience trouble as they mature. In a recent article titled "Data Warehouse Check-Ups," Margy Ross and Ralph Kimball outlined some common disorders and solutions. We're adapting and extending this list to discuss how to use SQL Server 2005 to revitalize your DW/BI system.

> **REFERENCE** See the article "Data Warehouse Check-Ups" by Margy Ross and Ralph Kimball, *Intelligent Enterprise* (June, 2004). A link to the article is available at www.kimballgroup.com/html/articlesbydate/articles2004.html.

Data Quality

The most serious and common data disorders are poor quality data, incomplete data, and late data. Frequently we find that data quality and delivery problems lead to business users' unwillingness to accept the BI/DW system: The business users simply don't trust the data. Often for good reason.

The good news is that you seldom need to do a lot of research to find out where data quality is suffering. Your users are shouting at you that the numbers are wrong, or they can't get to the data when they need it.

To craft a solution, identify and prioritize the core problems. The business users will help you find the most important starting points, although the DW/BI team needs to temper business needs with a feasibility assessment. For example, customer duplication is a common data quality issue. The business users may be hot to have your team identify unique customers as the first project in your data quality rework. Customer de-duplication is almost always a high value project, but it's also complex and high risk. You may do better to develop your SQL Server 2005 expertise with a project that's a bit less ambitious.

If your existing Extract, Transformation, and Load (ETL) system uses SQL Server 2000 Data Transformation Services (DTS) or is hand coded, it should be easy to find ways to improve quality and speed. If speed is the main issue, turn on DTS logging or evaluate your custom system to identify the main bottlenecks. You may be able to use SQL Server 2005 Integration Services to surgically re-work the problem areas, and leave most of the existing system in place. The more you modularized your existing system, the easier this will be to do. If quality is your main problem, you may be able to rework a relatively small piece of the ETL application by adding data quality screens within an existing transformation process.

You have to prepare for and investigate the possibility that your existing data quality issues are sufficiently severe that the best solution is to start over, one dimension or business process dimensional model at a time. Integration Services is more effective and performs better than DTS or hand coding. However, the greatest improvements are likely to come from a new ETL architecture, rather than by using Integration Services to pave existing cow paths. As politically unattractive as this option is, it could be the best alternative. Major changes that you should consider include:

- Processing daily rather than monthly
- Moving to incremental processing from full refresh
- Standardizing names and addresses in preparation for de-duplication
- Implementing data quality screening

As we describe later in this chapter, when we discuss converting the ETL system from SQL Server 2000 to SQL Server 2005, you may find it useful to create an Integration Services master package that coordinates the ETL system activities. This master package can call DTS packages, SQL scripts, or other processes that may be part of your current environment. With this infrastructure in place, you can be selective about which pieces of your existing ETL system to convert.

Mart Madness

A second kind of data disorder has to do with the way the data is structured for business users' access. We work with many customers who've invested in developing an atomic, non-dimensional, normalized data warehouse that's in good shape. The problem is that business users complain about how hard it is to use the data warehouse. Perhaps you've tried to address this usability issue by spinning out a bunch of departmental data marts, often with dimensional models. We call this "mart madness," and if you're in this situation you already know how hard this structure is to maintain, how much time it takes to bring up a new departmental mart, how much duplication you have between different departments' marts, how seldom a report from one department's mart will foot back to another's, and how difficult or impossible it is to combine data across marts.

There are significant architectural differences between mart madness and the Kimball Method architecture of conformed atomic business process dimensional models. *Conformed* means that business process models use the same dimensions, and snap together to answer enterprise-wide questions and avoid data inconsistencies. *Atomic* means that Kimball Method models are built at the finest grain of data available. Most departmental data marts are built with aggregated data. *Business process dimensional models* means that the design is based on business processes rather than departmental access patterns.

To address mart madness, return to the business requirements and develop the dimensional bus matrix, as we described in Chapter 1. You may be able to use the original business requirements document (if you have one), but you should conduct some new interviews. The bus matrix identifies the link between core business process dimensional models, and also highlights opportunities for improving the ETL system.

The updated business requirements and bus matrix should help clarify where to begin. If you have a well-functioning, non-dimensional data warehouse, use it to populate a Kimball Method dimensional model instead of departmentally focused aggregate data marts. In the short run you may be able to gain significant leverage from your existing infrastructure by building Analysis Services databases directly from the existing data warehouse. In the long run you should tackle the problem of conforming dimensions across the enterprise. Although in theory this conformation might be achievable on the fly, realistically you should plan to save the conformed dimensions and facts as a dimensional data warehouse in the relational database. This is especially true if the existing data warehouse has not been tracking the history of dimension attribute changes.

Business Acceptance Disorder

No matter how correctly your DW/BI system adheres to a methodology, no matter how accurate and timely the data is loaded, no matter how sophisticated the tools you provide to your users, if the business users aren't using the DW/BI system, it's a failure. The underlying problem may be any of those that we discuss in this section: data quality issues or cultural issues. The problem may derive from an insufficient focus on business requirements at the outset. Maybe the problem is something relatively easy to fix, like not enough predefined reports in the BI portal, or not enough user training. The only way to find out what's wrong is to ask the business users.

After you've revisited the business requirements and priorities, you may find a deeper problem—your initial business process dimensional model was of low value to the business users, or it was not delivered properly. Even in the case of a fundamental problem like these, you may be able to get a quick win by loading existing data into Analysis Services. You can build an Analysis Services 2005 cube from a normalized database, although it won't work as well or be as easy to maintain as one that's built from a dimensional model. Combine the new OLAP database with a query and analysis tool and some Reporting

Services reports that are aligned with business requirements, and you may find you've greatly increased business users' valuation of the DW/BI system, at a modest incremental cost.

Infrastructure Disorder

It's common to have a mix of tools and approaches in an enterprise's information infrastructure. As the DW/BI system matures, you bolt on a new ETL product here, a new reporting application there, until you end up with Frankenstein's monster.

SQL Server 2005 in and of itself isn't going to solve this problem. In fact, it's likely to worsen the problem in the short run, as you add new tools and new approaches to the mix. However, if you commit wholly or partially to the Microsoft platform, you can be sensible about which components you migrate to SQL Server, choosing first those parts of your exiting infrastructure that are most problematic and require expensive software licenses.

Infrastructure problems are usually the result of a poorly thought out or non-existent architecture plan, which in turn results from a weak or non-existent business requirements understanding. The best way to address infrastructure disorder is to go back to the business requirements and clarify what the DW/BI system needs to do to meet those requirements. Revisit the architecture design process to create a new high-level architecture model. Next, take this model and overlay the existing product mix and the functions available in SQL Server 2005. Identify the overlaps between the old and new, compare the capabilities and costs, and select the best option for meeting the business requirements. Finally, develop a phased implementation plan to migrate to the new architecture, starting with the capabilities that will support the most important business requirements.

Political and Organizational Problems

The most common reasons for a mature DW/BI system to be in poor health are organizational rather than technical. A healthy DW/BI system is one that supports a lot of use, grows with the addition of new business processes, updates its user interface every few years, and has business users who pepper the DW/BI team with requests for training or new reports.

If your existing DW/BI system is at all successful—or was ever successful in the past—you had a business sponsor. The original business sponsor may have moved on to a new job, or may have lost interest in the project. If you go more than three months without meeting with your business sponsor, or if all new initiatives are driven by IT, you're likely suffering from sponsorship disorder.

The treatment for sponsorship disorder is to recruit a new business sponsor. Even if you plan to upgrade or migrate to SQL Server 2005 for some technical reason (improved features) or other reason (reduced licensing costs), you need to ensure you have an active and engaged business sponsor. Without a business sponsor, you should question your rationale for your proposed project.

Other political and organizational disorders are rooted in the corporate culture. These are difficult to address and again have very little to do with the technology. Examples of problematic corporate cultures are those with an excessive tendency to consensual decision-making—a common characteristic of academic and government organizations—or a culture that does not value *informed* decision-making but instead makes decisions on intuition. The only real solution to these problems lies with corporate management. The best you can realistically do is to bring the issue to management's attention.

> **TIP** This problem is almost insurmountable for us as external consultants. When we encounter such organizations in our consulting practice, we usually walk away. We've battered our heads against this wall too many times to sign up for it again. For you to succeed, you may need patience more than any technology or technique. If you can outlast the old guard and continue to work to find enlightened sponsors, you will eventually succeed.

Perfect Health

We hope that none of the disorders discussed applies to your organization, and your existing DW/BI system is in perfect health. If this is your scenario, you're probably reading this book because you have a new business process that users want you to add to the DW/BI system.

You can and should think critically about which components of the new business process dimensional model to host in SQL Server 2005. To reduce the project's risk, you may want to confine your initial use of SQL Server 2005 to only a few components, like Analysis Services. It would certainly be reasonable to put the relational data for the new dimensional model in the same database as the existing data warehouse, rather than hosting it separately in the SQL Server 2005 relational database. You may have your existing ETL tool make calls to invoke new Integration Services packages, or you may choose to continue using the tools you're comfortable with. Later in this chapter we discuss some integration issues in a heterogeneous environment.

One incentive for migrating part or all of an existing healthy DW/BI system is to minimize license costs. SQL Server is reasonably priced, but be certain you've evaluated the true licensing cost savings. In particular, consider whether the component you're evaluating, like Reporting Services or Analysis

Services, is going to run on a new server. If so, that's an incremental licensing cost unless you have a site license. Also evaluate, as early as possible, whether you'll require SQL Server 2005 Enterprise Edition. This is particularly likely for low latency or high volume systems.

It may very well be true that the licensing cost savings are sufficient to justify a migration project. But it's best to correctly evaluate those savings before all the work is done.

Conversion from SQL Server 2000

In this section we discuss issues around converting an existing SQL Server 2000 DW/BI system to SQL Server 2005. Some components, like the relational database, will convert smoothly. For other components, we recommend a more drastic approach.

Relational Data Warehouse

It should be quite straightforward to upgrade your relational data warehouse database from SQL Server 2000 to SQL Server 2005. Use the Copy Database Wizard to perform the upgrade, as described in Books Online. Note that indexes and constraints are automatically disabled during the upgrade process. You must manually re-enable them.

Although we're certainly not guaranteeing that an upgrade of your relational database to SQL Server 2005 will be trouble-free, we expect a minimum of problems and fuss.

After you've successfully upgraded the existing databases, consider whether to change the database's structure to take advantage of new features in the relational engine. For a relational data warehouse database, the most interesting new feature of the engine is partitioned tables, as we describe in Chapter 4. If you're using UNION ALL views to simulate partitioning in SQL Server 2000, you should convert the structures to partitioned tables. There is no wizard to do this for you, but the conversion should be straightforward. If you used SQL Server 2000 partitioned views you have already tackled the maintenance problem of creating new partitions every new time period. You will need to modify that program to create the new partition and update the partitioning scheme. The logic of the program can probably remain the same, although the exact syntax will differ.

Even if you didn't use partitioned views in SQL Server 2000, you should consider whether to implement partitioning in SQL Server 2005. However, you will need to modify your ETL and database maintenance systems to support your partitioning scheme.

Integration Services

Although Integration Services is descended from SQL Server 2000 DTS, it's substantially different. The fundamental way you approach solving ETL problems is different. Microsoft provides a DTS Migration Wizard to help you upgrade your existing packages.

Don't spend much time migrating packages. Instead, leave most or all of your existing DTS system in production. You can continue to run the DTS packages on a SQL Server 2000 instance. Microsoft includes the DTS runtime executables with the new SQL Server, so you can run DTS packages on SQL Server 2005 if you want to. Let's hope you followed DTS best practices and used variables to set connection properties. If not, you'll need to edit the packages to point to the new server. Your developers will still need access to an instance of SQL Server 2000 in order to edit the old packages.

Whenever you need to perform a substantial edit to a DTS package, strongly consider rewriting it as an Integration Services package. If you used master packages and subpackages in DTS, you'll probably want to rewrite the master package. Recall from Chapter 5 that there's an Integration Services control flow task to execute a DTS package. Of course there is no corresponding DTS task to execute an Integration Services package.

The more expert you are with DTS, the more careful you need to be when upgrading and rewriting your packages. DTS experts rely heavily on the relational database to perform transformations. Integration Services best practice uses the in-memory data flow task. DTS experts wrote strange scripts to modify the flow of data through a package at runtime. These scripts will not upgrade to Integration Services, and this entire technique is supplanted by new constructs like looping containers, conditional flows, error flows, and event handlers.

Analysis Services

Microsoft provides an Analysis Services Migration Wizard, which is available from the Start menu (Start → All Programs → SQL Server 2005 → Analysis Services → Migration Wizard). After the database has been migrated, you can use BI Studio to examine and edit its structure.

It's instructive to explore the structure of the migrated database. Most interesting are the dimension structures, and the MDX script that's generated from Analysis Services 2000 calculated members and cells. However, the best database that you would build from scratch in Analysis Services 2005 is usually different from the migrated structure. The two biggest differences are:

- The dimension structures, discussed at length in Chapter 7
- The database structure, notably the shift to a single cube with multiple measure groups replacing multiple cubes

The most interesting new functionality in Analysis Services isn't available through the migration process. You must explicitly design that functionality, like new hierarchies or many-to-many dimensions, into the cube. And, frankly, it's easier to redesign from scratch than to perform massive edits on a migrated database.

If is perfectly reasonable to migrate old databases as a temporary measure, until your team has time to tackle a fresh design. The migration wizard works pretty well, and a simple migration is straightforward.

Reporting Services

Reporting Services 2000 was released at the end of 2003, and is very closely related to the new 2005 product. As a result, there are no significant upgrade issues to discuss.

The biggest improvements with Reporting Services 2005 are incremental, filling in functionality that was missing from the Reporting Services 2000. The Report Model and Report Builder features provide some functionality for business users to develop ad hoc reports. And, both business users and developers can much more easily develop standard reports using Analysis Services as a source. Not only should query performance improve for dynamic reports, but you will be able to present more complex business measures in a simple report interface.

Data Mining

You can use the same Analysis Services Migration Wizard to help you migrate a data mining model to Analysis Services 2005. After you run the Migration Wizard, use BI Studio to examine and edit the data mining model's structure.

The wizard converts models and their contents to SQL Server 2005, and you can execute a prediction query directly on a converted model. As we describe in Chapter 10, most uses of data mining in production are based on a custom application that issues prediction queries against a trained data mining model. This application, typically written in a Visual Studio language, should continue to function unchanged with the converted data mining model.

Integrating with Non-SQL Server 2005 Components

You can build your entire DW/BI system using Microsoft's technology. Microsoft has added some features to make a Microsoft-only stack work "better together," but these are surprisingly few. If you have good reasons for using a different technology for one or more components, you'll be in good company with a heterogeneous system.

In this section we outline a few of the issues you may encounter with developing and deploying a heterogeneous system.

Replacing the Relational Database

Many customers use Microsoft's business intelligence technology with a non-Microsoft relational database. Among our consulting clients, Oracle is the most common relational database used with SQL Server, although we've seen plenty of IBM's DB2 and a smattering of other technologies.

All of SQL Server's business intelligence components communicate with each other, and the relational database, through a variety of data providers, including OLE DB, ODBC, or .NET providers. The popular databases including those mentioned previously all have OLE DB providers written either by Microsoft, by the relational database vendor, or by a third party—sometimes all three. Any less common database technology is very likely to have an ODBC driver available. All of these options, combined with Microsoft's OLE DB for ODBC and Flat Files providers, enable you to write and read data from a huge variety of sources.

Integration Services with Non-SQL Server RDBMS

Integration Services packages can read data from non-SQL Server sources very efficiently. Integration Services packages can write and update data to non-SQL Server sources. However, because the OLE DB interface does not address bulk loading, Integration Services writes data to the OLE DB destination row by row. This inefficient method of inserting data might be adequate for the daily incremental load process, but it's usually too slow for the historical load. As we describe in Chapter 5, if you need to insert large sets of data into a non-SQL Server database from Integration Services, you should write the data to flat files and then launch your database's bulk loader from Integration Services. As time goes on, we can hope that someone (Microsoft, database companies, or third-party database utility companies) will write high-performance, database-specific Integration Services destination adapters, similar to the one that Microsoft has written for SQL Server.

Analysis Services with Non-SQL Server RDBMS

It's very common to build an Analysis Services OLAP database on top of a non-SQL Server database. Some observers estimate that nearly half of all Analysis Services 2000 implementations were built from non-SQL Server sources. With Analysis Services 2005, you can even build a cube from heterogeneous sources, with some data stored in, say, SQL Server and other data stored in Oracle. (Just how good an idea this is remains an open question!)

The most common stumbling block to populating an Analysis Services database from a non-SQL Server relational source is the performance of the OLE DB provider. As we mentioned previously, Microsoft doesn't write most of these providers. Some providers perform incredibly badly. If you're having performance problems loading your Analysis Services database, investigate alternative providers.

Some DW/BI systems that implemented Analysis Services 2000 on top of non-SQL Server databases found that the SQL issued by Analysis Services performed poorly in the source relational database. A different syntax, or perhaps a query hint, would have made the same SQL operation perform significantly better, but Analysis Services 2000 provided no mechanism for modifying the queries that populate the database. Analysis Services 2005 uses cartridges for different providers, so the SQL can be structured differently from one relational database to another. It would be unusual, but not impossible, for a DW/BI team to modify a cartridge for its own use. Microsoft expects cartridge development to be primarily the province of third-party tool and system developers.

There are a few Analysis Services features that work only with SQL Server source data. The most interesting is proactive caching, which we discuss in Chapter 17. You can use proactive caching with non-SQL source databases, but you'll have fewer options in configuring this feature.

Reporting Services with Non-SQL Server RDBMS

You can use Reporting Services to create and publish reports from non-SQL databases. The same reporting portal can combine reports from multiple sources. In fact, a single report may contain data from multiple sources, although this generally works best as a summary report from one source that drills down (for example on customer key) to detailed data from a second source. The mechanism for this broad connectivity is the same set of OLE DB providers that we have discussed previously.

Reporting Services does require an instance of the SQL Server relational database to hold the report metadata. In many installations the report metadata catalog will require little permanent storage, as metadata catalogs are typically quite small. However, if you use Reporting Services to schedule and archive reports, the cached results are stored in this same report catalog database. These cached reports can be quite large. You may be surprised by how large this SQL Server database is growing.

Data Mining with Non-SQL Server RDBMS

You can use Microsoft's data mining functionality to build models from a non-SQL Server relational database as easily as from SQL Server. There are no known issues.

Replacing Integration Services

As ETL tools have gained a strong foothold in data warehouse infrastructures over the last decade, many customers will be reluctant to migrate from their existing ETL tool to Integration Services. All the major ETL tools work cross-platform, and can populate a SQL Server database. Even if your ETL vendor has not released a version of their product that's specific to SQL Server 2005, your existing version should do a fine job.

There are a few places where Integration Services is extremely useful, even if you're relying on a third-party tool for the bulk of the ETL system. The tasks for processing Analysis Services data mining models and OLAP databases are very convenient. You may set up a small Integration Services package simply to perform these functions. Use your ETL tool's "execute external process" function to launch DTExec and start this package after your load completes. Look to see if your ETL package can pick up status codes returned by DTExec, so you can handle errors gracefully and integrate processing metadata. Of course, you should first look within your existing ETL package to see if it has functionality to process Analysis Services objects. Over time, we expect to see other ETL tool vendors include this capability in their products.

Even if your ETL tool can't process Analysis Services directly, you're not required to use Integration Services. You can set up a script, like VBScript, to control processing.

A second use of Integration Services beyond its role in the ETL system, is for periodic database maintenance activities. This role uses Integration Services database maintenance tasks like "Back up databases" that work only with SQL Server. The classic way to set up database maintenance scripts is to write TSQL scripts, perhaps glued together with some operating system scripting. Alternatively, there are third-party database maintenance utilities. Integration Services is clearly superior to the hand-scripting method of database mainte-nance, and we recommend that you strongly consider using it for this purpose even if you use a third-party ETL tool.

Replacing Analysis Services OLAP, Data Mining, or Reporting Services

The SQL Server 2005 technologies that are closest to the business user—Analy-sis Services OLAP and Data Mining, and Reporting Services—are all easy to swap for non-Microsoft products. There are many third-party alternatives to much of Reporting Services' functionality.

Most major OLAP technologies are cross-platform in terms of their data sources, and can work from a SQL Server relational database. You should be able to implement a non-Microsoft OLAP system like Hyperion or MicroStrat-egy on top of SQL Server 2005 without significant difficulty. These products can read data even from SQL Server partitioned tables without any changes to their code; querying partitioned tables is transparent to the client.

These non-Microsoft products may place different requirements on the underlying relational data model. All prefer or require dimensional structures, which the authors also strongly recommend for supporting Analysis Services. Some non-Microsoft tools are much happier with a snowflake design. Some are significantly less able to hold large data volumes or monster dimensions than Analysis Services, so you may need to implement summary cubes with drillthrough to relational detail. Nonetheless, you can expect no significant problems that are unique to pulling data from SQL Server 2005.

You should expect to find that non-Microsoft data mining tools can readily consume SQL Server data. If those data mining tools include built-in functionality for writing back to the relational database, for example to store results from training the model, you should investigate whether that writeback uses SQL Server's bulk loading API to write efficiently. This may be an important feature for performing data mining on large data volumes.

Using a Non-Microsoft Ad Hoc Query Tool

It's common to use a non-Microsoft ad hoc query tool to construct and execute queries against both the relational database and Analysis Services. Microsoft's ad hoc query tool offerings to date are not best-of-breed, or even close, and many Microsoft-centric DW/BI teams have turned to third-party tools to meet the needs of their power analysts.

If you implement Reporting Services, particularly embedded within a BI portal, you'll significantly reduce the number of business users who truly need ad hoc capabilities. As we discuss in Chapter 9, reports can be parameterized and include fairly sophisticated drill paths. These two features can meet the vast majority of business users' ad hoc needs. Reporting Services' Report Builder provides functionality that meets additional ad hoc requirements, although it's not the very best analytic tool we've ever seen. True ad hoc analysis, where the power user is developing new calculations and exploring the data in new ways, is best performed using tools specifically designed for that kind of interaction. Microsoft currently doesn't offer a good general purpose ad hoc query tool for OLAP, although Microsoft Office Excel Pivot Tables, Web Components, and Data Analyzer offer some functionality. Microsoft is starting to address this glaring hole in its BI product suite. In 2006, the next version of Office is making some progress along the very long road to best-of-breed.

One of the most interesting features of Analysis Services 2005 is the ability to build an OLAP database on any data source, including normalized data. Combined with proactive caching, which may simplify maintenance, Microsoft delivers a lot of the power of the dimensional model without the cost of building a dimensional data warehouse. This is not a great foundation for an enterprise information architecture, but can provide quite significant cost savings in some scenarios. However, in order to reap those savings you need to access the data through the OLAP layer by using a query tool that speaks XML for Analysis. At the time of this writing, that means using either Reporting Services, the Microsoft Office products, or a non-Microsoft query tool designed for OLAP, as we discussed earlier. Any SQL-based query and reporting tool—which includes the vast majority of query and reporting tools on the market—will not work against this architecture.

This area is confusing for readers, in large part because there are so many query and reporting tools on the market, and most of them can access Microsoft data. We'll finish this section by summarizing the two main approaches:

- *Implement Analysis Services as the primary presentation server, with most queries going to Analysis Services.* Set up Reporting Services, preferably within a portal, to serve most queries and reports from Analysis Services. Other Reporting Services reports can source data from the relational databases. Report users can't tell the difference. Provide the power users with an advanced query and analysis client tool designed to work with Analysis Services, probably one sold by a non-Microsoft vendor.

- *Implement a primarily relational data warehouse, with little or no use of Analysis Services OLAP databases.* Build the reporting application with Reporting Services or any other SQL-based reporting toolset. Use your choice of ad hoc query and analysis client tools to access the relational data warehouse and any cubes in your architecture.

The first architecture makes most sense to us in most cases. However, it puts you solidly in the Microsoft camp (and it limits your ad hoc tool choices) unless and until other vendors build query and reporting systems that can take full advantage of Analysis Services databases. Any investment you may have in a SQL-based reporting infrastructure is made obsolete.

If you have recently negotiated a big contract with a SQL-based query and reporting tool vendor, you'll probably choose the second approach. An advantage is that you'll be a bit more in the mainstream and less tied to the somewhat idiosyncratic Microsoft way of implementing business intelligence. If you believe, as we do, that a dimensional database server is a fundamentally better way to access data than direct queries using SQL, then by minimizing or eliminating Analysis Services' role you're not maximizing the advantage from your DW/BI system.

Summary

For a new DW/BI project, or a substantial makeover of an existing system, the Microsoft business intelligence toolset provides a compelling single-vendor platform. Each of the components of the SQL Server BI product set is sufficiently high performance, scalable, easy to use and maintain, and functional enough to meet the majority of business intelligence scenarios.

Microsoft's BI technologies also play well with others, and can be integrated into an existing data warehouse system. There are a relatively small number of features that require you to commit fully to the Microsoft platform. As we described in this chapter, it's easy to combine non-Microsoft data warehousing technologies with SQL Server components. There is no reason to avoid using Microsoft products in a heterogeneous system, if for technical, economic, or political reasons you prefer BI products from a mix of companies.

A heterogeneous DW/BI architecture is particularly compelling in the short to medium term, especially for existing data warehouses that are in less than perfect health. Some of Microsoft's technologies, especially the ability to build OLAP databases from non-dimensional relational sources, can greatly improve the immediate usability and business user acceptance of an existing system.

Security

Balancing safety and opportunity

Security is another one of those black holes of the DW/BI system. It seems straightforward at first glance, but often ends up being more complicated, and using more resources, than originally planned.

As you may recall, Microsoft was hit hard in 2002-2004 by security breaches and gaffes. We don't need to replay those events. But if you're considering using Microsoft technology to manage your DW/BI system—and if you've reached Chapter 12 you probably are—you should understand that these events had a huge impact on Microsoft and SQL Server. We can, and often do, poke fun at Microsoft. But they're more serious than ever about security. If you're also serious about security, and take the necessary steps to educate yourself, keep up-to-date on security bulletins and software updates, and design your system to minimize your attack surface, you'll be in a good position to run a safe system. Microsoft throws so much information and so many security options at you that the greatest risk may be that you'll give up out of frustration and confusion. We hope this chapter helps by highlighting the most important issues for a DW/BI system.

You can minimize the cost and risk of implementing security by—yes!—writing a security plan. That plan should have a section for securing the environment, including the hardware and operating system; a plan for securing the operations and administration of the system; and a plan for securing data. No security plan is complete without a discussion of how to test the security. Designing and implementing tests for whether the right people have access to the right data can be as hard as any other task in developing and operating the DW/BI system.

In this chapter, we talk about the major components of DW/BI system security. These are the components that should be included in your security plan. The easy part is securing the physical environment and operating systems. A serious corporate environment will lock down the physical servers and systems. Turn on only those services and features that are necessary to run your system.

The tasks of defining and implementing security spans the Lifecycle diagram that we've shown in previous chapters. During business requirements gathering, document the real business needs for security. It's important to get senior management's view, but you also need to talk to analysts and other potential users about the kinds of information they need to do their jobs effectively. You may need to push back to senior management, helping them to understand the costs of minimizing access to data. Designing and implementing security occurs in all the boxes of the Architecture, Data, and Applications tracks of the Lifecycle. And the cost of deploying and maintaining security never goes away.

After you've slammed the security doors shut, you need to start re-opening them to allow users into the system. A DW/BI system is valuable only if people can access it. The more information that's broadly available, the more valuable your system will be. Information is an asset. If you keep it in the equivalent of a Swiss bank account with zero interest, or even a savings account at 2 percent, you're doing your organization a disservice. Careful stewardship of data requires that you protect the information that's truly confidential and broadly publish the rest. Some organizations' executive teams and culture are diametrically opposed to open access, but it's worth arguing and pushing. Let's hope your executive sponsor can carry this battle forward.

You need to ensure that only authorized users can access the DW/BI system, and limit everyone's view of data as appropriate. There are as many ways to do this as there are possible configurations for your DW/BI system. This is especially true if you're using non-Microsoft software in your system. The bulk of this chapter is devoted to discussing the most common configurations. The SQL Server documentation in Books Online does a good job of discussing security for Reporting Services, the relational database engine, and Analysis Services. Figuring out how these components work together is harder, so that's where we've focused our attention.

After reading this chapter, you should be able to answer the following questions:

- How do you secure the hardware and operating systems for all the servers in your DW/BI system?
- What kinds of security will you need for different kinds of user access, from running reports to ad hoc query and analysis?

- How should you implement and test security features in the various components of your DW/BI system?

- How can you monitor usage and protect the privacy of your customers?

Identifying the Security Manager

The first thing you must do is to explicitly identify a team member who's responsible for the security of the DW/BI system. If no one owns the problem, it won't be addressed. Define the role in the organizational context: What security is the security manager responsible for? What tasks does the security manager do, and what tasks does he or she direct others to do? The security manager has to be involved in the architecture design and in verifying the actual setup and use of the DW/BI system. Every new component, upgrade, user group, indeed any system change, needs to be examined from a security perspective to make sure it doesn't compromise the system. Many organizations require a mandatory signoff by the security manager as part of the change deployment process.

We recommend that the security manager be part of the DW/BI team. The DW/BI security manager should have a formal relationship with any enterprise security office or Internal Audit. But to be effective, the security manager must be intimately familiar with the DW/BI system. In small organizations, the DW/BI team lead may play the role of the security manager. In any case, it needs to be someone fairly senior, with a broad understanding of the end-to-end system.

Securing the Hardware

The most direct way to access the valuable information in the DW/BI system is to gain physical access to the computers on which the system is running. You absolutely must implement the following simple but essential recommendations for your production system, and should think very seriously about doing so for the development and test servers as well.

- Place the server computers in a locked room with restricted access.

- Disable the option to boot from either the floppy or CD-ROM drive. Consider removing the floppy drive.

- Consider creating a power-on password, and protect the motherboard's settings with a CMOS-access password.

- Consider using a computer case that supports intrusion detection and can be locked. Don't leave the key dangling from the computer.

Securing the Operating System

The second most direct way to access the DW/BI system is by way of the operating system. You should implement the following procedures for all the servers in your development, test, and production systems:

- *Restrict login access.* No business user needs to log on to the servers. Most DW/BI team members don't need to log in, as their tools work remotely. Only system administrators need to log in; others can access services across the network.

  - Ensure the security policy on all servers is set to *not* add Domain Users to the local Users group. By default, Domain Users are usually added to the local Users group, which has login privileges.

  - Ensure the Windows Administrator account on all servers has a strong password.

  - Ensure the Windows Guest account on all servers is disabled.

  - Ensure strong password policies. Strong policies include technical policies, like requiring a mix of letter case and non-alphanumeric characters. Users need to be educated about security as well, to not write down passwords and avoid the many scams that fill our inboxes. This is usually an enterprise-wide concern.

- *Restrict network access.*

  - Ensure the Everyone group does not have access to the server.

  - Disable null sessions to prevent anonymous sessions.

  - Disable unneeded services. For security reasons, consider disabling the Telnet, FTP, SMTP, and NNTP services if they're not needed.

REFERENCE Search Microsoft.com for RestrictAnonymous for a discussion of anonymous sessions.

- *Ensure data folders are secure.* By default, the SQL Server relational database and Analysis Services databases store data in file structures that are appropriately protected. However, you can create Analysis Services partitions in remote locations, which might not be protected. Other sensitive information includes backups and trace logs, and Integration Services packages. Ensure all information is appropriately protected.

- Keep up-to-date with security patches for the operating system. Keep up-to-date with service packs for the SQL Server components.

Securing the Development Environment

It's quite common for development teams to have fairly loose standards—or no standards at all—for management of the development environment. The development environment and servers should be managed professionally, although usually not to the same standards as the test and production systems. The data on the development servers is often sensitive, as it's drawn from the production source systems. You certainly should secure the hardware and operating system as we've just described, within reason. You should have a policy against, or strict procedures for, granting access to development servers to anyone outside the development portion of the organization.

To ease deployment, make the development machines' security environment similar to the production systems. On the other hand, you don't want to lock down the systems so tightly that the developers will have problems getting their work done.

A common approach is to manage shared development resources fairly well, yet allow developers to create private databases. Institute a change control process for the shared resources, like the relational data warehouse data model. Once other team members are depending on a data model, allow changes only weekly, and require 24 hours advance notice.

Once you've instituted change control on the shared resources, you'll see private databases popping up. That's because some team members, in a sensitive part of their development cycle, really need an unchanging database, or they need to change it more frequently. Changes to the shared database can, at times, be incredibly annoying. Because the SQL Server database software is easy to install on a desktop machine, it's hard to prevent private databases from cropping up. If you can't, or don't want to, forbid private databases, make it easy for your team members to secure them. Develop a policy for private databases, including system security procedures—usually the same procedures that you implement for your shared development resources. Better yet, write a lockdown script—probably a combination of a document script and a batch file—to perform basic lockdown.

Developers should use read-only access to the source transaction systems. This is especially true for the DBAs and ETL developers, who may be creating and deleting database objects in the relational data warehouse database. It's not impossible to imagine they could be careless and inadvertently execute a destructive statement against a transaction system.

> **NOTE** If you've ever accidentally created a table in the Master database, you know what we're talking about.

It's safest to use only the minimum privileges necessary to get the job done. In the case of DW/BI system development, that should mean read-only access to the source databases. In a large corporation, this is unlikely to be an issue: Of course the DW/BI team will not have write privileges into a transaction system. In a small company where people wear many hats, it's not uncommon for a DW/BI developer to have high privileges on a production system.

Securing the Data

Now that we've done the basics, we come to the most interesting part of the security plan: securing the data while making it available for users to query.

Providing Open Access for Internal Users

We strongly encourage you to develop a data access policy that is fairly open for corporate users. The best approach is to start from the position that all data should be available to internal users; any exceptions should be justified.

We've worked with organizations that approach the problem from the other direction. Even internally, these folks' natural reaction is to make data available only on a "need to know" basis. They say that the sales manager in one region cannot see sales numbers for other regions. The problem with this mindset should be obvious: A sales manager can't assess her region's performance outside the context of the rest of the company. She may think a 10 percent growth in sales is a great number, until she realizes that all other regions saw 15 percent. The more information you hide, the less valuable your DW/BI system is going to be.

UNEXPECTED VALUE OF OPEN ACCESS

One of our clients had an enlightened data access policy—or perhaps, as a tech startup, they hadn't gotten around to drafting a more restrictive policy. At any rate, they experienced the power of open access. A Customer Care agent—a kid out of high school—was poking around the data and uncovered a trend. A certain kind of trouble ticket was associated with a specific supplier's hardware, hardware which, as it turned out, was not manufactured to specification. Our client wrung several million dollars out of the supplier, and averted unsatisfactory user experiences for many customers. This for a startup, for whom several million dollars and customer satisfaction were tremendously important.

Many organizations would say a Customer Care agent has no business getting a global view of the data. It sounds reasonable to limit an agent's view only to specific tickets. The upside is unknowable in advance, but we've seen it happen often. The doomsday scenarios are easier to see, but many people have a tendency to overstate both the likelihood and potential financial downside of data getting out of the hands of those who "need to know."

DATA ACCESS POLICY

Depending on your organization, the data access policy doesn't have to be a long statement. A reasonable statement would say something like:

Open access to administrative information is provided to employees for the support of corporate functions. Inappropriate use of information is a violation of your employment agreement. Default access is: Open Access to all employees, except for data elements on the Restricted Access list. Restricted Access is a designation applied to certain data elements, and limits access because of legal, ethical, or privacy issues. Access to elements so designated can be obtained with the approval of the designated data trustee. Any request to restrict employee access must be documented to Data Administration by the designated data trustee. Any employee denied access may appeal the denial to Data Administration.

The ideal situation is to have very little truly sensitive information, like employee salaries or social security numbers, in the DW/BI system. Just don't bring it in. It should go without saying that any data around employee compensation is highly sensitive. In a health care environment, details about an individual patient may be equally sensitive, and access is highly regulated as well. We're not saying that you should make such sensitive information widely available. Rather, identify the information that's sensitive and document it as an exception to the general rule of data availability.

In order for an open access policy to work, you must:

- Gain executive sponsorship for the approach. You can't change corporate culture on your own. Many healthcare and law enforcement organizations are hopelessly—and justifiably—paranoid about data security.

- Develop a system use policy statement, which users must sign before gaining access. Set up a mechanism for ensuring users sign this document before accessing the DW/BI system.

- Confirm that executives are willing to carry out any sanctions against security violations implied in the policy statement.

- Gain executive agreement on the list of sensitive data elements.

- Review the security policy at the beginning of every training class.

- Publish (on the BI portal) the detailed security policy, including the list of sensitive data elements.

REFERENCE You can get a good starting draft for a complete data access policy from the Internet. Many universities and government agencies post their policies online. Search for "data access policy."

Itemizing Sensitive Data

Whether you approach the problem from a mindset of "most data is available" or "most data is sensitive," you need to develop a matrix of what data is hidden (or available), and to whom. As you're developing your data sensitivity matrix, remember that the vast majority of system use is at aggregated levels, where sensitivity is usually less.

Our primary concern is read-only access to data. Any writing activities, like developing forecasts and budgets, should be securely managed by an application. Specify the level at which aggregated information becomes available. For example, most people can't see sales by salesperson, but anyone can see aggregated sales at the region or district level, and corporate-wide.

The related sidebar illustrates a sample format of a Data Sensitivity Document highlighting some of the issues that you should be concerned about.

There is a subtlety associated with allowing data access at aggregate levels, but not at the detailed level. Returning to our discussion of sales by salesperson, what if we allow aggregate reporting at the district level, by gender? That could be a really interesting question, but what if a district has only one saleswoman? Anyone in the company could infer her sales figures. There's no easy answer to the inferred data member problem, although we discuss this issue again in the upcoming sections.

Securing Various Types of Data Access

The more restricted data you have, the more difficult it is to provide ad hoc access to the DW/BI system. Look back at the data sensitivity matrix and think about how to implement open access at aggregate levels and restricted access at detailed levels. The easiest way to do that is through an application like a report. Define aggregate-level reports that everyone can see, and limit access to reports that contain sensitive information.

If you allow ad hoc access to the information, you may need to apply complex access rules in the database. This is difficult in the relational database, as we discuss in the section "Relational DW Security." This is a place where Analysis Services really shines: It's possible—and really not that difficult—to meet a wide range of access scenarios by using Analysis Services permissions. In particular, the tool addresses the difficult problem of hiding detailed data but publishing aggregated data for ad hoc access.

SAMPLE DATA SENSITIVITY DOCUMENT

We've never been able to come up with a structured format, like a spreadsheet, that captures all the nuances of what is accessible, at what level, and by whom. Write a document that's as clear and concise as possible. Target this document to the business users because you need to get business agreement about the policies. It's helpful to align the sections by fact table (or set of fact tables), to simplify the process of turning this agreement into a set of database permissions.

SALES

Sales data is captured at the transaction line item level. For each sale, we know the customer, product, salesperson, and channel.

- ◆ *Restricted Access:* None.

- ◆ *Open Access:* Atomic and aggregated sales data, including any base measure and any calculation involving only sales data.

- ◆ *External Access:* None. In the future, we may modify this policy to open access at an aggregate level to reseller partners.

SALES QUOTA

Sales quotas are stored for each salesperson, product category, and quarter.

- ◆ *Restricted Access:* Atomic data at the salesperson level, including any physical and calculated measures based on salesperson. A salesperson's quota information and bonus calculations are available only to:

  - ▪ His or her manager, and up the reporting chain to the VP of Sales.

  - ▪ VP of Sales administrative staff, with permission of VP of Sales.

- ◆ *Open Access:* All physical and calculated measures, at the district level and above.

- ◆ *External Access:* None.

HUMAN RESOURCES

Data warehouse Human Resources information includes employee attributes like name, current manager, home address, and marital status. Currently, there is no HR fact data; the only employee information is descriptive. Note that the descriptive information about employees is largely Restricted. Only a few fields have Open Access:

- ◆ *Open Access:* Employee name, manager name, current department, current job title, office location, office phone.

- ◆ *Restricted Access:* All other attributes of the employee, including home contact info and any personal information. Restricted attribute information is available to an employee's manager, up the reporting chain, and to all HR staff.

- ◆ *External Access:* None

Most client access tools (other than Microsoft Excel) contain some security features. Reporting Services and most third-party tools like Business Objects, Cognos, and Analysis Services-specific tools like Panorama and Proclarity all contain security features. You should carefully examine the security features of any client tool before you decide to rely on those features. If a user has login privileges to the underlying database (Analysis Services or relational), the security must be applied to the database objects. Otherwise, users could simply use Excel or any other client tool to create an ad hoc connection, log on, and browse restricted data.

Many front-end tools, including Reporting Services, can—or even must—be configured to use a shared report execution service account for access to the database server. If your front-end tool manages user security this way, you typically don't even grant database login access to the users. This is very secure, assuming you're exceptionally careful not to compromise the password to the report execution service account.

NOTE If a user is not allowed to see certain data, then he must either be:

- Denied logon privileges to the database containing that data, or

- Denied read privileges to the data table, columns, or rows.

Client-based security is questionable security. Security through obfuscation is not security.

Most implementations have a variety of security requirements. Some reports are available for anyone in the company, some have limited access to the complete report, and some reports return a different result depending on who runs the report. Beyond reporting, you need to support some ad hoc access as well. You need to define some security in Reporting Services as well as the relational database and Analysis Services, to cover all these contingencies. Each component has several kinds of security options, which means you can probably figure out a way to do anything you want. But it also means that it's hard to know where to begin. We try to simplify the problem by first discussing the different types of secure access. Next, we look at how you use SQL Server's components together to deliver the different levels of access.

Unrestricted Reports

An unrestricted report is one that's accessible to everyone in the company, or at least to everyone who can access the reporting portal. In general, the only security on an unrestricted report is whether the person trying to access the report is authenticated. This is handled by the operating system. There's no SQL Server security involved. We like unrestricted reports because organizations benefit from broadly shared information. Unrestricted reports are easy to manage.

The Reporting Services report definition for an unrestricted report should be configured for everyone to use a shared connection. This is the default behavior for Reporting Services—when you define a report, it's normal for everyone who executes the report to use the same database credentials. Windows uses a user's credentials to authorize access to the reporting portal.

Reporting Services reports can query either a relational database or an Analysis Services database (or both, but let's keep it simple). If the report accesses the relational data warehouse, the connection should use a service account that has read-only access. By service account we mean a Windows login (or database account if you're using SQL database security) that is not tied to a person. Instead, the account would be named something like ReportUser. Perhaps the report was designed using a DBA's personal account. Before the report is moved into production, modify it to use a service account with read-only privileges to unrestricted information.

TIP Always use an account with the lowest possible level of permissions. Executing reports on a highly privileged account "should be" safe because the connection is encrypted, but why ask for trouble? Encourage or require your development team to use a shared data source for the report connection when they design a report. Many reports can share a data source, which contains the connection information including server, database, user name, and password. The credential information for a data source definition is encrypted for you.

Users who access the report do not need login privileges into the underlying database. The report's query runs under the service account, not under the user's account.

Restricted Reports

A restricted report, like a public report, is predefined. Not everyone in the organization can access the report, but the report looks the same to everyone who does access it. For example, in a small company anyone in Human Resources can access employees' personal information. Anyone at the executive level can access all corporate financial data.

Restricted reports are a good security model for all but the most sensitive data, other than data found in unrestricted reports. It's easy to implement in the reporting portal, and doesn't require a security layer within the underlying databases.

Restricted reports should use a shared connection, the same way that unrestricted reports do. In fact, it can be the same shared connection. Your security administrator can use Report Manager or Management Studio to define which users and groups have access to which reports and report folders. The security is not at the database level, but instead at the reporting system level.

As with unrestricted reports, business users don't need login privileges into the underlying database to run restricted reports. The report's query is executed by the ReportUser service account. Later in this chapter we describe how to restrict access to reports in Reporting Services.

Filtered Reports

A filtered report is a predefined report that returns a different result set depending on who runs the report. Filtered reports usually are also restricted, and are appropriate for the most sensitive data in your organization. The classic example is salary and job performance information, which is usually available only to an employee's supervisor, or possibly to anyone up the management chain.

In order to implement a filtered report, you need some way to connect the user's name to the list of people, organizations, accounts, and other data elements that they're allowed to see. If the report is run on demand by the user, it must be executed dynamically with the user's credentials; the report can't be cached. In this case, the query underlying the report needs to return the filtered result set. Alternatively, filtered reports can be pushed to users on a daily or weekly basis by emailing individualized reports.

Filtered reports are expensive to develop and maintain. You need to develop a security infrastructure, and maintain the list of what elements each user is privileged to access. You may need to write a simple application to help manage these processes.

Some organizations are dead set against allowing business users to log in to any relational database, including the data warehouse. This feels like superstition to us, as you can secure the database objects to different users. But let's not quibble. If you're committed to barring direct user login to the relational database, but need to deliver filtered reports, you have several options:

- *Define the report to use a stored procedure as its source query.* Pass the user's identification as an input parameter to the stored procedure. The stored procedure must perform the filtering, typically by joining to a table that contains a list of accessible rows for each user ID.

- *Use a data-driven subscription.* This feature of Reporting Services Enterprise Edition is a cost-effective way to distribute individualized reports to many people, for example a monthly budget variance report for each manager's area of responsibility. If the filtered report doesn't need to be run on demand, the data-driven subscription is a neat solution that can use system resources very effectively.

REFERENCE See the Books Online tutorial topic "Creating a Data-Driven Subscription" for detailed instructions on creating a filtered data-driven subscription.

■ If you have only a handful of filtered reports that are limited to only a few people, you can fake filtered reports by creating restricted reports. In other words, create different reports for each department, and grant access only to the appropriate version. This approach has obvious scalability and management problems, and isn't recommended except as a stopgap measure.

If you allow business users to log in to the underlying databases—Analysis Services or the relational data warehouse—you must set up those databases to support ad hoc access. If a user can log in to a database, the database itself must protect access to its objects. Otherwise, users could attach any query tool to the system, and look at any data they want.

Ad Hoc Access

Ad hoc access means the user is allowed to leave the boundaries of predefined reports to create new queries, reports, and analyses. Up to this point, it's been possible to avoid giving database login privileges to users. But a user who needs ad hoc access really needs login privileges.

The best place to perform ad hoc analysis is within Analysis Services. And Analysis Services contains a rich security model that lets you define very fine-grained security profiles, while still delivering reasonable query performance. Analysis Services security has several very nice features. You can:

■ Use dimension-based security to cut down the apparent size of a dimension. In other words, users won't even see dimension members like product names whose data they're not allowed to view. Think of dimension security as hiding full rows and columns of a report.

■ Use cell-based security to limit the data that users see within a report's data grid. Think of cell security as leaving a report's row and column headers in place, but hiding pieces of the report's numeric contents.

■ Mix and match dimension and cell security.

■ Secure detailed data, like sales by salesperson, and still leave broad access to aggregated data, like sales by region.

■ Use dimension attribute security to hide textual data about dimension members, like employees' Social Security numbers.

■ Define a component of a role as starting from empty (access is denied unless specific permission is granted), or from full (access to all elements is granted, then specific permissions revoked).

■ Use role impersonation to easily test security definitions while administering security roles.

We provide more how-to details later in this chapter, in the section on Analysis Services security.

Within the relational database, it's easy to define permissions to tables, views, and columns within a table or view. There's no user interface for defining row-level security. The general approach is to create a separate table that has at least two columns: the business user's ID and a list of keys, like EmployeeKey or SalesPersonKey, that the user is permitted to see. Then you create a view that joins the fact table to the security table on the key column, filtering on the user ID. Each business user who queries this view sees only rows for the keys listed for them in the security table. We provide more details on setting up this view definition later in this chapter, in the section on Relational DW security.

In addition, SQL Server provides column-level encryption. You can encrypt columns with sensitive identifying information, so only users who have the decryption key can ever see the data.

External Reports

An external report is a report from your DW/BI system that's available to people outside your organization. For example, you may let your suppliers see your inventory of their products, or see how well their products are selling.

The easiest way to meet the security requirements for standard external reporting is to use a push model: Email reports to your partners. The data-driven subscription feature of Reporting Services (Enterprise Edition) should meet the majority of external reporting requirements. This is a preferred approach because you don't need to provide any access into your system, and you're completely controlling when the report is run and to whom it's delivered.

Data-driven subscriptions don't meet all external access requirements. You probably don't want to send a daily email to millions of customers about their account status. We're tempted to call this operational reporting, and wash our hands of the problem. Indeed, you should think seriously about whether you want external users accessing the same system that your employees are using to run the business. Most often you'll decide to spin out a data mart, and associated reporting portal, dedicated to this application. You'll need to figure out how to authenticate those external users to allow them into the portal. These users will typically access only filtered reports, using the same techniques we've already discussed.

It's unusual for a company to provide ad hoc access to external people. Those who do are generally in the Information Provider business. You could use SQL Server and other Microsoft technologies to develop a robust Information Provision system, but this topic is beyond the scope of this book.

What Should You Do?

There are so many security features, and combinations of security features, that it seems overwhelming. The first items to knock off the list are unrestricted and restricted predefined reports. Reporting Services handles these very well and easily, whether the report is sourced from the relational database or Analysis Services.

It's harder to decide how to handle filtered predefined reports because there are several options. Your choice is going to be driven by whether you need to also provide ad hoc access to the relational database, or whether the information to be filtered is included in an Analysis Services database.

If you can deliver filtered reports from Analysis Services, that's certainly easiest. Analysis Services' user security model is flexible enough to define any user security plan we've seen.

If the filtered reports must be sourced from the relational database, you still have a bunch of options. Table 12.1 summarizes the main approaches. We've characterized the basic approaches by whether they can support filtering, ad hoc access with and without row filtering, and whether they require user login privileges to the database. We've also specified which approaches we think are easiest to implement.

Next, we turn our attention to describing how to implement security in the various components of the DW/BI system. These components include the operating system, Analysis Services, the relational database, Reporting Services, and even Integration Services.

Windows Integrated Security

Microsoft SQL Server uses Windows Integrated Security as its primary security mechanism. Set up Windows users and groups in the Windows environment—this is usually a task for system administrators rather than someone on the DW team. Then in Management Studio, create a set of roles, like Executives or Marketing, and grant or deny permissions to database objects for each role. Then assign the Windows users and groups to the appropriate roles. In a large enterprise, users will be assigned to several groups and roles.

In a Microsoft-centric enterprise, the users and some or all of the groups will be defined on the domain in Active Directory. In a heterogeneous environment, someone should integrate Active Directory into your environment like LDAP (Lightweight Directory Access Protocol). This is a job for a system administrator rather than a DW/BI expert, so we won't go into any details here. Buy a book or hire a consultant to help you with this project.

Table 12.1 Summary of Approaches for Implementing Data Access Security

APPROACH	AD HOC (NO ROW FILTERED)	AD HOC (NO ROW FILTERING)	AD HOC (WITH FILTERING)	USER LOGIN TO DATABASE NOT REQUIRED	EASY
Predefine Reporting Services (SSRS) reports that execute under service account. Use SSRS security to limit the list of reports to those that each user can access.				✓	✓
Predefine SSRS reports that execute under service account. Maintain a user permissions table in the relational database. Use a stored procedure to execute the source query, or data-driven subscription.	✓			✓	
Predefine SSRS reports that execute under user's account. Maintain a user permissions table in the relational database, and define a row-based security view between it and the fact table.					
Analysis Services Security	✓	✓	✓		
Report Builder Security		✓		✓	✓
User login access to relational, with row-level security	✓	✓	✓		

It's possible to connect to Reporting Services, Analysis Services, and the database engine through mechanisms other than Windows Integrated Security. These options are less secure than truly Integrated Security, so you should consider this approach only if you can't possibly make Integrated Security work in your environment. Even if you use these alternative authentication mechanisms, you'll still need to create Windows users and groups on the database servers, and grant privileges to those groups.

TIP The SQL Server database engine supports database security, where you define users and groups within the SQL Server relational database. Those of us who are older find this security model familiar and comfortable, but it's inherently less secure than Integrated Security and should be avoided.

In this chapter, when we talk about users and groups, we mean Windows Integrated Security users and groups unless we explicitly say otherwise.

Analysis Services Security

When you install Analysis Services 2005, all members of the Administrators local group are granted access to the server and all databases and data. Until you set up roles and explicitly grant access, no other users can even connect to the Analysis Services instance, much less browse data.

Administrative Roles for Analysis Services

First, set up an administrative role for each Analysis Services database. A database administrator has full control over the database, including processing, aggregation design, and security. Analysis Services database administrator is a highly privileged role, but it doesn't require system administrative privileges on the server. If your Analysis Services server contains multiple databases, create a database administrator role for each.

REFERENCE See the Books Online topic "Granting Administrative Access" for details on the database administrator and server administrator roles.

The easiest way to create a role, including an administrative role, is within Management Studio. While you're logged in with server administration privileges, use the Object Browser to navigate down to a database, then to Roles within that database. Right-click to create a new role. You're presented with the Create Role dialog box, illustrated in Figure 12.1. This is a complicated wizard. There are eight pages to work through, which you can see listed on the left-hand side.

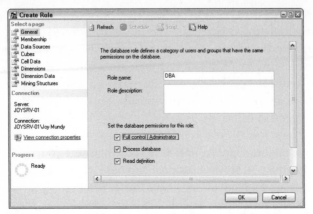

Figure 12.1   Analysis Services database administration role

The person who administers security needs unrestricted access to the cube's data. That's because the security administrator will need to test the roles and permissions. With Analysis Services 2005, the security administrator must have Full Control (Administrator) permissions to the database. This is more permission than a security administrator needs—a security administrator shouldn't be able to process the database or modify aggregations—but it's as fine grained as you can get.

You should take some time to think about how the security administration process will work on the production system. As we describe in the next section of this chapter, the administrator needs to work through three major steps in managing users' access to data:

1. Creating and managing operating system users and groups

2. Creating Analysis Services roles and granting data permissions to those roles

3. Assigning operating system users and groups to Analysis Services roles

Step 1 occurs at the operating system level, using Windows security. It must occur on the production server, an Active Directory server, or both. In most companies, the Windows security issues are handled by your Information Services organization when new employees are hired. You can simply tap into the existing user directory.

Step 2 is more of a development task than an operations task. Role development and testing should take place on the test server, and then be migrated to production using a script, as we describe in Chapter 14. The tools don't prevent you from developing roles on production, but it's unwise.

Step 3 is an operational task that occurs on the production server. The roles, users, and groups are already set up, and the security administrator simply matches them up. The security administrator can use Management Studio to modify the membership in existing roles, as illustrated in Figure 12.2. This screenshot is from the Membership page of the same Create Role Wizard (or the Edit Role Wizard, which looks identical) as in Figure 12.1.

Because the server JOYSRV-01 in this illustration is not on a Windows domain, the only users and groups available are defined locally. Your domain users and groups would also be accessible within this dialog box.

NOTE By default, you can add users and built-in security principles to a role, but not groups. To add a Windows group, select Object Types from the Select Users and Groups dialog box, and add a check to the Groups option.

You may choose to create a second administrative role, for processing cubes and dimensions. This role is useful for operations staff who should not have an account privileged to view data; they can only execute cube processing. A Processing role must have the Process database permission (see Figure 12.1) checked. If you want the operator to be able to use Management Studio instead of simply executing scripts, you'll also need to check the Read definition box. Note that the processing role does not allow the operator to create new partitions, modify aggregations, backup, or restore the database. These operations, like security administration, require Full Control privileges.

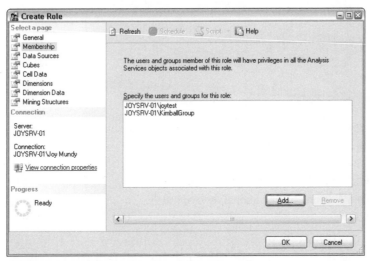

Figure 12.2   Assigning users and groups to roles

User Roles for Analysis Services

Now that you understand how to administer security, it's time for the more interesting topic of how to define users' permissions.

Use the same Create (or Edit) Role Wizard pictured in Figures 12.1 and 12.2 to define user roles. Users, of course, don't need any of the administrative privileges pictured in Figure 12.1; leave those checkboxes unchecked.

Define and test Analysis Services roles on your test server. When you first set up a role, you don't need to assign any users or groups to that role. You can define the role and perform initial tests by impersonating the role while browsing the cube within Management Studio. Figure 12.3 illustrates cube browsing with a different role's credentials. Note that you can switch users (or roles) by clicking on the Change Users icon in the upper left of the browser window, highlighted by the tooltip in Figure 12.3. You can test multiple roles overlaid on top of each other. When you're working on security, you'll quickly get in the habit of looking at the message near the top of the window, informing you of which role or roles you're impersonating.

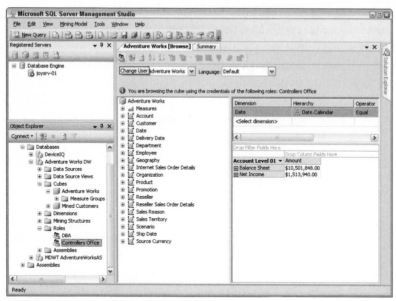

Figure 12.3   Test role definitions by impersonating credentials

Although you might think that the first step in defining a user role is to assign users to the role, that assignment is actually the last step. The next page of the Role Wizard, Data Sources, is also something to skip over most of the time. The Data Source is the source of the Analysis Services database's data, usually a SQL Server relational database. The database and cube definition place a layer between the user and that source; very few users need access to the Data Source. The exception is if the Analysis Services database includes a data mining model, users may need access to a data source in order to perform a predictive query.

REFERENCE See the Books Online topic "Granting Access to Data Sources" for an excellent discussion of the Data Source page of the Roles Wizard

The next page of the Roles Wizard, called Cubes, is where you grant user access to the cubes within the database. You must grant access to a cube; users are not automatically granted cube access. If you simply grant access to a cube and immediately save the role, you've created a role with full access to all the cube's data. If that's not what you want to do, continue through the pages of the wizard to set the appropriate cell and dimension limits for the role.

We'll skip the Cell Data page of the Roles Wizard for a moment, to speak briefly about the Dimensions page. Most implementations won't use the Dimensions page very often. Here, you can specify whether a role can read the metadata for a dimension: exactly how the hierarchies and dimension attributes are set up, and what their properties are. Most users don't need to see this information, but power users and technical folks might be interested. The database administrator will use the Dimensions page to let some users browse the definitions of one or more dimensions, without granting edit or processing privileges.

Finally we come to the interesting part of the Roles Wizard: the Cell Data and Dimension Data pages. Use these pages of the wizard to define cell-level security and dimension-level security in your database role. But before you do that, map out the strategy for this role. Remember that dimension security makes a report grid smaller: It limits the display of dimension attributes. Cell security doesn't change the row or column headers of a report; instead, it replaces some numbers inside the body of the report with #N/A (or a value of your choice). It's easiest to envision dimension versus cell security in the context of a tabular report, but of course the security holds no matter how you're viewing the results of a query.

If you want to hide descriptive information about an employee, like his Social Security number, you use the Dimension Data page. If you want to hide quantitative information, like a salesperson's sales quota, you use the Cell Data page. Think of cell security as security on facts.

Remember that a user or group can have multiple roles: A user can be in both the Marketing role and the Executive role. When Analysis Services combines multiple roles, it does so additively, with a union operation. If a user belongs to two roles, one forbidding access to a data element but the other allowing it, the user will have access to that data element.

There's one quasi-violation of this union rule. If a user has roles with both cell security and dimension security, the dimension security trumps the cell security. In other words, even if a role is permitted to see every fact cell in the cube, that data won't show up if the role can't see the dimension or dimension member. This is just what you'd expect to happen because the dimension security would forbid dimension members from showing up as row and column headers.

When you're testing your role definitions, you will really come to appreciate the role impersonation feature of the cube browser in Management Studio.

Dimension Security

There are two basic approaches to defining dimension security on a dimension attribute: Specify the members that are allowed (all others are excluded), or specify the members that are denied (all others are accessible). In most cases, your choice of whether to specify the allowed set or denied set depends on the relative size of the included and excluded sets of members. There's a second order problem that can be really important: if a new member is added to the dimension, should it be accessible or excluded by default? The safest thing is to specify the members the role is allowed to see. Then when new members are added, they won't be visible to restricted roles until the role definition is explicitly changed.

Figure 12.4 illustrates a simple definition of dimension security on a dimension attribute. In this case, we're using the Deselect all members option to explicitly define the allowed set. Any new members will be excluded.

Figure 12.4 Defining basic dimension security

We've introduced the problem of new dimension members joining the dimension. If this happens rarely, it's not too big a burden to redefine the roles to account for the new member. If the dimension changes rapidly—for example a customer dimension—you'll want to take a different approach.

One of the neatest solutions is to use MDX to define the included (or excluded) set of members. Under the covers you're always using MDX: The pick list illustrated in Figure 12.4 is simply a user interface that generates an MDX expression. In this case, the expression is a list of members. You can see this expression by switching over to the Advanced tab on the Dimension Data page.

A common MDX security expression will include (or exclude) all the children of a parent. For example, imagine you want to create a role that can see all the Product Categories (Bikes, Clothing, Accessories, and Components), cannot see any of the Subcategories under Bikes, but can see all the Subcategories for the other three Categories. Instead of listing the products that are in the brand today, define the MDX expression for the Subcategory attribute of the Product dimension as illustrated in Figure 12.5.

MDX expressions can be a lot more complicated than this, but the Exists function illustrated here, and its close friend the Except function, cover most cases. Books Online has more examples under the topic "Granting Custom Access to Dimension Data." For more complex examples, you should look at a reference book on MDX. Chapter 7 lists several MDX references.

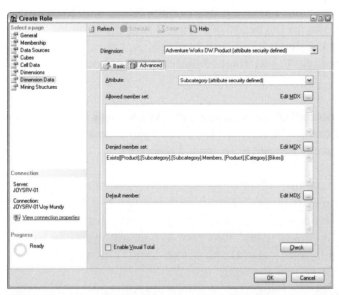

Figure 12.5 Using MDX expressions to define dimension security

There are a few wrinkles associated with dimension security. The first is the behavior of related attributes; the second issue is referred to as Visual Totals.

We introduced related attributes in Chapter 7. One of the common uses of related attributes is to define a natural hierarchy, like Product Category to Subcategory to Brand. Related attributes have an implication for the way dimension security works for denied sets. If you deny access to a specific Product Category, then you're also denying access to its children (Subcategories and Brands). This behavior doesn't come from the definition of a hierarchy between these three attributes. Instead, the behavior is driven by the definition of the relationships between the attributes—which is what makes it a natural hierarchy.

TIP It really feels like the hierarchy definition should be the thing that drives the security relationship, not the related attribute definition that users never see. To help keep it straight, think of the hierarchy merely as a drilldown path for the user interface; it's the underlying related attribute definitions that are really important. A product attribute like Color that has no related attribute to the item you're securing (Product Category in our example), will not be affected by the security definition. Which, after all, makes perfect sense.

The second complexity with dimension security is the notion of Visual Totals, which you can see as an option on the advanced tab of the Dimension Data page in Figure 12.5. Imagine a role that grants permission only to a single product and doesn't restrict the brand level. What should be the subtotal by brand, for the brand containing the one product the role can see? Should the subtotal be the real subtotal for the brand? Or should it be the subtotal for the visible product? The answer depends on your business user requirements. The default behavior is to not use Visual Totals: Subtotals reflect both visible and invisible cells.

TIP This is a difficult concept with a mediocre name. Visual Totals refers to what you would expect the total to be if you were looking at a report, and added all the numbers you're allowed to see on the report.

We usually prefer the default behavior for several reasons. First, the server has to work harder to support Visual Totals. It makes much less use of predefined aggregates. More important, with Visual Totals turned on, you're sowing confusion among your business users. Two people running the same report would come up with different totals at the brand level. This is a situation you've built your DW/BI system to avoid.

A downside of using the default behavior is that users may be able to infer a piece of hidden information. The simplest example is if you're hiding only one product, and showing the true brand total. Any user could calculate the hidden product's sales as the difference between the brand total and the sum of the accessible products' sales.

SOME COMMENTS ON THE SCALABILITY OF DIMENSION SECURITY

Readers who were familiar with Analysis Services 2000 on large scale systems may be wary of dimension security. In the old days, security on large dimensions created memory problems, which could lead to a server crash. The underlying architecture has changed; you no longer need to shy away from dimension security for large dimensions.

Note that for a large dimension—or, more accurately, a dimension attribute with high cardinality—you should define security by creating MDX expressions, rather than explicitly choosing the members from the Basic tab of the Dimension Data page. In fact, that Basic tab will show you only the first 1,000 members. Which is a really good thing, if you think about the user experience of working with an attribute that has cardinality in the millions. If you have more than 1,000 members, the Basic tab displays a Search function.

Cell Security

Cell security affects which numbers or facts are displayed in the grid of a report, and which are blanked out (or replaced with #N/A or some other display element). Cell security, like dimension security, uses MDX expressions to define the cells that are accessible or hidden. Unlike dimension security, the Cell Data page of the Roles Wizard doesn't have any user interface other than entering MDX expressions. Cell security is so flexible that the best UI is the MDX editor window.

Figure 12.6 illustrates the Cube Data page of the Role Wizard. We've started by granting read privileges to one node of data in the Product dimension: those data elements that roll up to the "Bikes" Category. Data for other Categories will display #N/A.

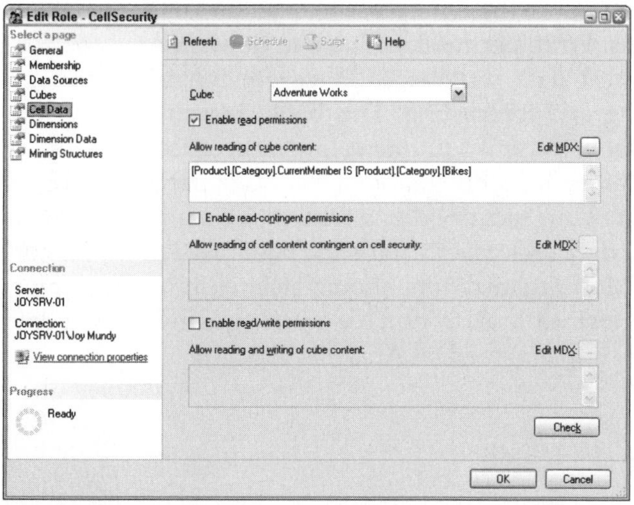

Figure 12.6   Defining cell-level security

NOTE Users in the United States are familiar with the use of #N/A to mean Not Available because that's the convention in Microsoft Excel. Your client application may be able to translate this abbreviation for you. Or, you can specify a different value for the Secured Cell Value property in the user's connection string.

The expression in Figure 12.6 refers to the Product dimension. Data along other dimensions in the cube is currently unrestricted. You can build up an MDX expression that refers to multiple dimensions, with clauses connected by ANDs and ORs. We recommend you start simply and build up the expression piece by piece, testing after each addition.

REFERENCE The Books Online topic "Granting Custom Access to Cell Data" contains a nice set of increasingly complicated cell security definitions.

Look back at Figure 12.6, and notice the option to enable read-contingent permissions. This is an advanced option that most applications will not need. Read contingency is relevant for permissions on derived cells. The definition of read-contingent permissions is the same as for read permissions, but the behavior is different. Read-contingent permission will show a derived cell only if the role has access to all the data that goes into that derived cell. For example, if you have a derived measure for Contribution to Margin, the role could see that measure only if the underlying data to calculate Contribution to Margin is also accessible to that role. The rationale for this feature is similar to the Visual Totals discussion under dimension security: A smart user may be able to infer information that you don't want him to have. We advise caution with implementing read-contingent security. No doubt there are cases where this finesse is important, but it's more likely to leave everyone confused.

Return to Figure 12.6, and notice the third place to enter an MDX expression for read/write permissions. Write permissions have to do with Analysis Services databases that support data writeback. These are typically financial applications like budgeting and forecasting. This book doesn't address this kind of application, but not because it's uninteresting or because it's not part of business intelligence. Rather, it's a huge topic worthy of a paper or book of its own. Within the context of our security discussion, assigning write permission to a portion of the cell data uses exactly the same kind of MDX expression we've already discussed. Most organizations should steer clear of developing write-enabled cubes, and instead look to purchase packaged budgeting and forecasting software that is implemented on Analysis Services.

> **WARNING** Be careful about checking the Read Contingent or Read/Write checkboxes without adding an MDX expression to focus the permission. If you check the Read/Write checkbox but don't add an expression, you're giving the role Read/Write privileges to the entire cube. Similarly for Read Contingent. This is unlikely to be what you intended.

Data Mining Security

The final page of the Roles wizard lets you assign Read, Read/Write, Process, and Browse permissions for data mining structures and the models that use those structures. There's nothing particularly complicated about this page, except the point we noted earlier in this section: If you're enabling data mining predictive queries, the role must also have appropriate permissions to the source database for that drillthrough.

Relational DW Security

If the only access to the relational data warehouse comes through Analysis Services cubes and Reporting Services, then the relational security model is simple. If you'll allow ad hoc access into the relational data warehouse, especially if you have requirements for filtering data (also known as row-level security), the relational security model grows increasingly complex.

No matter how users access the relational data warehouse, begin by thinking about the roles necessary for administering the relational database. After securing the operations, we'll discuss issues around users' security.

Administrative Roles for the Relational Database

The SQL Server database engine has predefined server and database roles. These roles work the same for a DW/BI system as for any other SQL Server database application. Compared to the administrative roles for Analysis Services, the database engine has fine-grained permissions.

Server roles include:

- *bulkadmin:* Has permission to run Bulk Insert. Many experienced database administrators refuse to grant the bulkadmin role to anyone. It's very important that the service account for Integration Services has bulkadmin privileges.
- *dbcreator:* Has permission to create, alter, drop, and restore databases. Only a few members of the DW/BI team or DBA organization should have dbcreator privileges.

- *diskadmin:* Can manage the database's disk files. The ETL service account used to run Integration Services packages may need diskadmin privileges, especially if you automate partition management.

- *processadmin:* Can kill processes, including users' runaway queries. We hope you won't have any runaway queries, but it's indisputably more likely in a data warehousing environment than a transaction system. A relatively small number of people on the DW/BI team (or DBA organization) should have processadmin privileges. But don't hold this privilege too tightly, or you may find the system bogged down because the wrong person is at lunch or out for the day.

- *securityadmin:* Can manage server logins. If you use SQL Server logins (as opposed to the recommended Integrated Security), securityadmin privileges let you reset passwords.

- *serveradmin* and *setupadmin:* Can change system-wide configurations, and are seldom important during the ongoing operations of the DW/BI system.

- *sysadmin:* Can do anything.

Database predefined roles, as you might expect, are database-specific. In other words, a user might be highly privileged in one database, but not even allowed to access a second database. The predefined database roles are:

- *db_accessadmin* and *db_securityadmin:* Used to manage logins and permissions for users and groups, and to assign users to roles.

- *db_datareader* and *db_datawriter:* Can read and insert, update, or delete data from any table in the database. The ETL service account should have db_datareader and db_datawriter privileges.

- *db_denydatareader:* Cannot read any data and *db_denydatawriter* cannot write any data from any table in the database. Unless you have a writeback application, any user login should have db_denydatawriter permissions.

- *db_backupoperator:* Can, you guessed it, back up the database. The ETL service account should have this role, if you're integrating database backup into your ETL system.

- *db_ddladmin:* Can execute any DDL (Data Definition Language) operation, including creating tables and indexes. The ETL service account should have db_ddladmin privileges.

- *db_owner:* Can do anything to the database, including dropping the database.

It's always good practice to grant people, even people on the DW/BI team, as few privileges as they need to get their jobs done. Occasionally people are malicious, but more often they're just careless.

The service account that runs the Integration Services packages needs to have high privileges. You should always run production operations, like the ETL system, under a service account that's not associated with a person's login.

It's common for the DW/BI team members to all have high privileges on the development system. The test system should be set up the same way as production. One of the things you need to test before moving into production is whether the permissions are set correctly. This is a very common task to overlook.

SQL Server 2005 introduces the ANSI-standard concept of a schema. Object names are fully qualified as *server.database.schema.object*. We usually create the data warehouse tables under a single schema, but we've seen people use schemas to segregate dimension, fact, utility, and metadata tables.

TIP Most often, the database is installed as the default instance, and the server name referenced above is the machine name of the server. If you defined the relational database as a named instance, the server name is, unsurprisingly, that name.

User Roles for the Relational Database

There are two main kinds of accounts that issue relational queries in a DW/BI system: service accounts, like those used by Reporting Services, and business user accounts. You're likely to have one or several service accounts. Depending on your business requirements, you may have business user accounts that can log in to the relational database.

Service Account Permissions

Depending on how users access the DW/BI system, you may have only a few user roles to worry about. If you're using Reporting Services, you should expect to create and manage a reporting service account. Like the ETL service account, the reporting service account should not be associated with a person. If you're using Analysis Services, you should create a separate Analysis Services processing account. This account may have the same privileges as the reporting account, but it's foolish to assume they'll always be the same. In some configurations, one account may need more privileges than the other.

We have already said several times that all users should access the relational data warehouse through views, rather than directly querying tables. There are several reasons for this:

- Views let you insulate the user experience from the physical database. It's amazing how much the view layer lets you restructure the database with minimal disruption to the user.

- Views let you hide or rename columns to suit users. You can remove the prefixes (like Dim and Fact, which we use in MDWT_ AdventureWorksDW) from the view names.

- Views let you add row-level security seamlessly.

Create a view on every user-accessible table, even if the view simply selects all columns from the table. Grant user access to the views, not to the tables. This includes the reporting account and the Analysis Services account. Both of these service accounts should use views rather than the underlying tables.

TIP Create all user-oriented views and stored procedures under a single schema, and have that schema own no other objects. This makes it easier for you to find these objects when it comes time to assign permissions.

The reporting service account should have read access to the appropriate views, possibly all the views. As we discuss later in this chapter, Reporting Services secures the reports, so the reporting service account will have greater read privileges than any individual user would. Some reports will use a stored procedure to deliver up the rowset. If so, the reporting account will need execution privileges on those stored procedures. The reporting account should never have write privileges on any table or view. We can't think of a technical way for the encrypted reporting account credentials to be stolen. But the most likely way for those credentials to get out is the obvious one: Someone—presumably on the DW team—tells someone else. There's no point in tempting fate. This is especially true for any custom reporting front-end or non-Microsoft query software that might use a reporting account. Microsoft is very careful about security these days—don't laugh, they really are. You should thoroughly investigate the security mechanisms of any software on your system.

The Analysis Services service account should have read access to the appropriate views, possibly all the views. The Analysis Services users should not need any direct privileges in the relational database.

Business User Roles

Business users will need login privileges into the relational data warehouse database if they need to perform ad hoc analyses and if you have row-level security requirements. In the absence of row-level security requirements, users' ad hoc needs may be able to be met by the Report Builder feature of Reporting Services, which can continue to use the reporting service account. We discuss these issues later in this chapter, in the section "Reporting Services Security."

If business users can log in to the relational data warehouse, you need to grant them only the appropriate permissions. This means read-only permission on the appropriate views, columns, and stored procedures. The easiest way to get started administering security is in Management Studio. In Object Explorer, navigate to the database and select Security → Roles → Database Roles. Create a new role for all information available to anyone with login privileges. We'll call this role BIPublic.

Click Add Objects and add all the views to which everyone has access. As we pointed out earlier, it's much easier to find all the views if you created them under a single schema. For each view object, you should explicitly set the permissions. In general, deny all permissions except Select, as illustrated in Figure 12.7.

You have to work through the object list one view at a time, granting only SELECT privileges This is pretty tedious for a large system, but it's probably faster than scripting it.

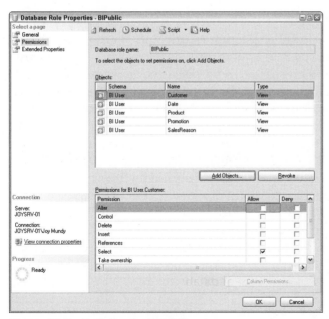

Figure 12.7 Defining the BIPublic role

NOTE What if you want to hide a few columns, like Social Security number, from some users but not others? One approach is to define two views on the table, one with all public information and the other with all public and private information.

The best approach is to encrypt the private information and distribute decryption keys only to the appropriate users.

Create new roles that grant permissions to objects for the subset of people who can access that object. For example, say you protected the Employee dimension from BIPublic, but you want everyone in Human Resources to have access to it. Create a new role for HR, granting access to the appropriate views. Roles are additive, so if you have a user who's a member of both BIPublic and HR, that user can see the Employee view.

The next step is to add users and groups to roles. You can accomplish this on the first page of the Database Role Properties dialog box. Figure 12.7 illustrates the second page of that dialog box. On the first page, you can launch a standard dialog box to add users or other roles to the role you're working on. Continuing our example, you might add all authenticated domain users to the BIPublic role, and all members of the Windows group HRUsers to the HR database role.

Row-Level or Filtering Security

You may need to build row-level or filtering security into your relational data warehouse. What we mean by row-level security is that users' views of sensitive data differ not at the column level, as we discussed in the preceding text, but by rows. One person should see a different set of rows than another person.

There's no row-level security feature of SQL Server, but the classic solution is not difficult to implement. First, create a table that lists users' IDs and the identifiers for the rows they're allowed to see. For example, secure the FactOrders table from MDWT_AdventureWorksDW to limit a user's view of the data only to a specific set of salespeople (identified by SalesRepKey).

Here is some DDL for this permissions table:

```
IF OBJECT_ID ('[dbo].[UserPermissions_SalesRep]', 'U') IS NOT NULL
    DROP TABLE [dbo].[UserPermissions_SalesRep]

CREATE TABLE [dbo].[UserPermissions_SalesRep](
    UserPermissions_SalesRepKey int IDENTITY NOT NULL,
    [UserName] sysname NOT NULL,
    [EmployeeKey] int NOT NULL
CONSTRAINT [PK_UserPermisssions_SalesRep]
    PRIMARY KEY CLUSTERED ([UserPermissions_SalesRepKey] ASC)
)
```

Listing 12.1   Data definition for the UserPermissions_SalesRep table

Next, insert some rows into this table. Let's say that the user Joy is allowed to see only information for employees 272 and 281.

```
INSERT UserPermissions_SalesRep VALUES ('KimballGroup\Joy', 272)
INSERT UserPermissions_SalesRep VALUES ('KimballGroup\Joy', 281)
```

Listing 12.2   INSERT rows that define which employees Joy can see

In the case of Listing 12.2, you're using Windows Integrated Security, and Joy is a user on the KimballGroup domain.

The final step is to create a view definition that joins the fact table to this new permissions table:

```
IF OBJECT_ID ('OrdersSecure', 'V') IS NOT NULL
DROP VIEW OrdersSecure

CREATE VIEW OrdersSecure
AS
SELECT f.* FROM FactOrders f
INNER JOIN UserPermissions_SalesRep u
ON (f.SalesRepKey = u.EmployeeKey)
WHERE u.UserName=SYSTEM_USER
```

Listing 12.3   Define a view to provide row-level security

As you can see by looking at the view definition, the trick is to limit the view to only those rows where the user name in the permissions table is the same user name as the person issuing the query. If you maintain the permissions table, many people can access this OrdersSecure table and see only the appropriate set of rows.

This solution is not as satisfactory as the dimension and cell security that you can define in Analysis Services. You've safely protected the detailed data, but no one can use this view to see company-wide sales. You need to create a second view, simply called Orders, that drops the SalesRepKey. The BIPublic role could consume the Orders table, and use that for most queries about sales volumes. The dual views create a usability problem for ad hoc business users, but it's the best solution the relational database offers.

Note that this view is useful not just for ad hoc querying. You can also set up Reporting Services filtering reports that use the view. When you define that report, you need to pass credentials from the user into the database.

If you need to support filtering reports and row-level security, you should consider building an applet to help maintain the UserPermissions tables. For performance reasons, you want the UserPermissions tables to use the warehouse surrogate keys. But your requirements are probably phrased along the lines of granting permission to all the employees in a department or sales reps in a region. A simple applet could help the security administrator be more effective than writing INSERT statements, and greatly reduce errors.

Testing Relational Security

Even though relational security isn't as complicated as Analysis Services security, it's still plenty complicated. You must thoroughly test all the roles and the combinations of roles.

You can impersonate a user and then run a query. Compare the results of the queries before and after impersonation to evaluate whether the security definitions are correct. The following script shows you how. The script assumes you've created the OrdersSecure view described previously, and also that you created a role BIPublic to which you granted access to OrdersSecure. We further assume that when you run this script, you have sufficiently high privileges that you can create logins and users. Sysadmin would work just fine.

```
USE MDWT_AdventureWorksDW;
GO
--Create a temporary login and user
CREATE LOGIN LoginBIPublic WITH PASSWORD = 'J345#$)thb';
GO
CREATE USER UserBIPublic FOR LOGIN LoginBIPublic;
GO
--Display current execution context. This should come back as you.
SELECT SUSER_NAME(), USER_NAME();
--As a simple, not very accurate test, how many rows can you see?
SELECT COUNT(*) FROM OrdersSecure
--Set the execution context to LoginBIPublic.
EXECUTE AS USER = 'UserBIPublic';
--Verify the execution context is now 'UserBIPublic'.
SELECT SUSER_NAME(), USER_NAME();
--Select from the view. You should get a permissions error
SELECT COUNT(*) FROM OrdersSecure
--Revert back to yourself and add the user to the BIPublic role
REVERT;
EXEC sp_addrolemember @rolename='BIPublic', @membername='UserBIPublic'
GO
--Now select from the view as UserBIPublic. We expect to see zero rows
--because UserBIPublic is not in the UserPermissions table.
EXECUTE AS USER='UserBIPublic';
SELECT COUNT(*) FROM OrdersSecure
--Revert back to yourself
REVERT;

--Remove temporary login and user
DROP LOGIN LoginBIPublic;
DROP USER UserBIPublic;
GO
```

Listing 12.4   Create a temporary user to test security roles

SPECIAL PRIVILEGES FOR POWER USERS

Some of the organizations we've worked with have had a few power users who were not officially part of the DW/BI team, but whose analysis required a sandbox on the database server. These users are probably doing incredibly valuable stuff, and may be working with enough data that they can really benefit from the horsepower of the server. If so, they need specially privileged accounts.

Before we talk about the kind of permissions this power analyst might need, it's worth commenting on an alternative approach: Let the analyst install SQL Server on a local server, and pull down chunks of the database to manipulate as she wishes. This approach has some appeal, but recognize that you will have no idea what this analyst is doing, nor how secure she's keeping her server. Everyone is better off if you provide a managed sandbox, probably on a test server but possibly on production.

If your organization has only a few analysts with these requirements, you could create a separate database for each. Alternatively, create a single sandbox database and set up each user with her own schema to avoid namespace collisions. The power users will need extended privileges in this database. They'll need to be able to create (and drop) tables within their schema. You'll need to monitor the sandbox to ensure these people aren't doing something crazy like copying an entire huge fact table. Set database size limits.

Many database professionals are horrified at the notion of users manipulating large datasets with write privileges. You may consider co-opting these users and making them part of the DW/BI team. But in the ideal world these people are closely tied to the business, and are working on the kinds of projects and analyses the DW/BI system was designed to support. Figure out what they need, and try to give it to them—within reason.

With our security hats on, we recommend that you always run impersonation tests from a script, and bracket the script with CREATE and DROP login and user, as we illustrated here.

Reporting Services Security

Reporting Services can source reports from the relational data warehouse, other relational and even non-relational sources, and from Analysis Services. Reporting Services is a client of the databases, but a special kind of client: one that is also a server, and that contains its own security features.

Administrative Roles for Reporting Services

Reporting Services is installed with a set of predefined roles for administrative and business users. You can modify these roles, or replace them with custom roles. But most organizations will simply assign these predefined roles to various people who are performing administrative tasks.

The relational database and Analysis Services have administrative roles that are clearly the purview of the DW/BI team, and only the DW/BI team. By contrast, your configuration and use of Reporting Services may distribute the administrative workload out to the business units. You may have some business users who need an administrative role.

The predefined roles include:

- *System Administrator:* Set server level features and security, and manage jobs. Clearly this highly privileged role should be granted to only one or two members of the DW/BI team.

- *System User:* View basic information about the report server, including shared scheduling information.

- *Content Manager:* Manage report folders and items within those folders, including security on those items. Content management permissions are not necessarily system-wide. In other words, you could have one person be the content manager for one set of reports like Marketing, and a different person manage Sales reports.

- *Publisher:* Publish content, like a report, to a report server. Some organizations will tightly control publishing rights, linking this role with Content Manager. Others will let anyone publish a report to the enterprise. We recommend being careful about who has publishing rights.

- *My Reports:* Build reports for personal use and store reports in a user-owned folder.

- *Browser:* View the list of reports, and run the reports to which you have access.

Everyone involved with administering the reporting system should understand that securing folders is the most common way to manage user security. Security is inherited through the folder structure, so you can simplify the administrative burden by grouping reports in folders according to how confidential those reports are. When you restrict a folder, you are by default restricting all the items in the folder.

One sensible use of a highly restricted folder is a place to hold reports that are being tested. Testing report definitions and layouts straddles the line between an administrative function and a user function. Often, you want a business person to sign off on the report before it's published more broadly. Using roles and a designated test folder, you can make it easy for the testers to find the reports under development, yet hide those reports from the rest of your organization.

Remember that the security assigned to a folder is the default security setting for any item, like a report, that's created inside that folder. You can change an individual report's settings, but that's a second step that you (or the distributed Content Managers) may forget to take.

You can use either Management Studio or Report Manager to manage permissions. The DW/BI team might use Management Studio; business users who are Content Managers will almost certainly use Report Manager.

User Roles for Reporting Services

When a user connects to Reporting Services, the report list shows only the reports that user is allowed to see. When a report is executed on demand, it's usually executed not with the user's credentials, but instead with a reporting service account used only to execute reports. In this scenario, users do not have login privileges to the underlying database.

Earlier in this chapter we discussed four kinds of security for reports:

- *Unrestricted reports* are available to everyone who can connect to the report server.

- *Restricted reports* are available to a subset of users.

- *Filtered reports* return a different result set depending on who runs the report. Filtered reports use some form of row-level security to filter the results as appropriate for each user, and are usually also restricted.

- *Ad hoc access* is best secured by user permissions in the source database, rather than in Reporting Services. Reporting Services' Report Builder enable some ad hoc querying, enough to meet many users' ad hoc requirements (which are usually quite modest).

REFERENCE You can read about Report Builder's security features in the Books Online topic "Securing Models."

Reporting Services' security model is perfectly targeted for unrestricted and restricted reports. It's very easy to set permissions on folders and reports. You may have a Data Administration team manage this function, or you can distribute some administration out to the departments who design and develop the reports.

Our recommendation for Reporting Services security is to keep it simple. Create a few user groups and assign them different roles and permissions as needed. In the simplest case, you could create two groups and assign permissions as follows:

- *RSStandard:* This group is the default for all users who have access to the DW/BI system. RSStandard does not have access to sensitive information.

- *RSFull:* This group is for those people who need to access sensitive information. In this simple two-level scheme, this group has access to the entire warehouse.

Next, build your sensitive reports in separate projects, which will correspond to directories or folders in Report Manager. Use Management Studio to set the properties for those folders. For example, grant Browse permission on the Home folder to all user groups. Assign Browse permission to the RSFull group for directories that contain sensitive reports. This could even be done at the report level if there are only a few reports that need limited access. Finally, assign the My Reports role to all users so they can load their own reports into the Report Server.

This simple approach can be expanded by adding more groups and assigning them different levels of access. It may make sense to have an RSPowerUser group that has report management permissions. You might even have several of these groups so power users can manage the report directories associated with their departments. For example, the sales power user would be assigned the Content Manager role in the Sales Reports directory.

Earlier in this chapter, in the section "Filtered Reports," we talked about how to deliver filtered report functionality while still prohibiting users from logging into the relational database directly. But maybe you've decided to service filtered reports by using database security, either the relational database or Analysis Services. You'd be most likely to implement filtered reports this way if you've already set up database security to support ad hoc access.

If you want to rely on database security to filter data rows, you need to set up the filtered report so that it doesn't use a shared data source. Instead, you should pass the user's credentials down to the database, whether the relational database or Analysis Services. If you're using Windows Integrated Security, simply set the credentials of the report's data source to Windows NT Integrated Security.

NOTE In an ideal world, you use Windows Integrated Security with trusted domains, and this works great. If you're running Reporting Services on a different computer than the relational database or Analysis Services, and you don't have trusted domains, Windows isn't going to let the credentials hop between the Reporting Services server and the database server. The easiest solution is to enable Kerberos on these servers, but there are other solutions as well.

REFERENCE See the Books Online topic "Best Practices for Authenticating Server and Data Source Connections" and the topic "How to: Configure a Report-Specific Data Source."

Integration Services Security

Integration Services is a back-room operation, so its security story is simple. First, make sure the packages are secure, so no one can mess with package contents. You don't want anyone to replace the package that performs an incremental load of the data warehouse with one that deletes all the data. This is a pretty far-fetched scenario. More likely someone on the team is careless and does something wrong.

Packages can be stored in the file system as XML, or in SQL Server. You should secure the package location. Packages stored in SQL Server are stored in the msdb database, in the table called sysdtspackages90. Simply use the database engine's security to grant limited permissions to msdb and sysdtspackages90, and the package contents are automatically secured. If you store the package on the file system, use Windows security to limit access.

In addition to this basic security, you can sign or encrypt packages. Digitally sign the package and set the package's CheckSignatureOnLoad property to True to prevent anyone from modifying a package's contents. More accurately, what you're doing is telling the package to check for a signature before it runs. If the package has been modified unintentionally, it wouldn't have been signed. If someone maliciously modified the package, they ought not be able to sign it.

Packages contain sensitive information within them, including the connection information to an account that, usually, has very high privileges in the data warehouse database. Integration Services automatically encrypts all connection information for you, but you can go farther and encrypt more of the package contents. There are several encryption options, but they come down to requiring a password before anyone can view the package.

The section of this chapter on Relational Data Warehouse security provides guidance on the kinds of relational database permissions you'll need to provide for the connections from your Integration Services packages to the data warehouse database.

Usage Monitoring

A secure DW/BI system will have usage monitoring in place. In an increasingly regulated world, it's extremely valuable to know who is connected to the system and what they're doing.

In Chapter 15 we talk about how to set up usage monitoring on Analysis Services, Reporting Services, and the relational engine. For some organizations it's sufficient simply to collect logons: who's accessing the database and when? Other organizations need to know exactly who is accessing which information.

Reporting Services monitors usage by default. In addition, Reporting Services provides an option to copy the usage logs from the Reporting Services catalog into a separate database. This option provides a target relational database, Integration Services packages to move the data, and a starter set of reports. This database should suffice for the majority of usage reporting requirements from Reporting Services.

Usage monitoring provides other valuable benefits. It's a valuable tool for performance tuning. Spending a bit of time analyzing how business users are accessing data is very valuable for understanding how to improve your DW/BI system.

If you set up a usage monitoring system—as we strongly recommend—you should inform your business users of what you're doing, why, and how the information will be used.

Protecting Privacy

A DW/BI system with information about consumer behavior has great potential for improving your products, customer service, sales process, and user experience. But it also has great potential for abuse. In many countries, online customers must be able to opt out from providing any personal information or having that information stored permanently. Whether or not it's a regulatory requirement, it's the right thing to do.

Before you go crazy with your new DW/BI system, mining the data to uncover customer patterns and develop targeted customer lists, you should develop a customer privacy policy. Make sure every business user of your system knows the policies for using the data and communicating with customers.

Protect your customers by ensuring that mailing lists can be generated only by a designated List Manager, who keeps track of the lists that have been created, and when each customer has been contacted. This information should be used as input to subsequent list creation to avoid inundating customers with unwelcome offers. CRM and contact management software offers features to track campaigns, promotional offers, and mailings. Set up the DW/BI system to create lists of customer IDs, and then hand that list off to the contact management system.

The safest approach is to leave personally identifying information out of the DW/BI system completely, or stored in an encrypted format.

Summary

The goal of this chapter is to highlight the most important security issues for a DW/BI system, and to help you figure out where and when to secure data. We couldn't possibly cover all the security features of SQL Server, nor all the details of how to implement those features. We hope merely to have provided you with the tools to develop a security plan and security test plan.

One of the most important steps you can take for a secure DW/BI system is to identify which DW/BI team member is in charge of security. That security manager will drive the development and implementation of the security plan.

The easiest pieces of the security plan have to do with physical security and operating system security. There's lots of information available about how to secure servers and the Windows operating system. You just have to commit to doing it.

The harder question, and the one to which we devoted most of this chapter, has to do with securing the data. As we described, securing predefined reports in Reporting Services is easy, painless, and effective. Securing data for ad hoc analysis is a harder problem. You'll definitely find it easier, and the user experience much better, to define security rules in Analysis Services than in the relational database. Analysis Services' security features make this a fairly straightforward task for a wide range of requirements. And because security rules are defined in MDX, even very complicated scenarios are feasible.

Finally, we struggled with how to set up the relational database security to support direct ad hoc access. It's possible—people have been doing it for years—but it's hardly as easy or satisfactory as we'd like.

The SQL Server documentation in Books Online has a strong emphasis on security features. It's as if Microsoft executive management made security a priority. But the security documentation is scattered across the different components, and it isn't always easy to find the information you need. You might be able to cut corners in some aspects of system development, especially if your data volumes are small, but everyone needs to be careful about security.

Metadata Plan

The Bermuda Triangle of data warehousing

Metadata is a vast, relatively uncharted region of the DW/BI system. Some teams sail into it full speed ahead, never to be heard from again. Most teams try to avoid the problem by sailing around it. Unfortunately, the metadata region is smack in the middle of your path to the great new world of business value, and you need to figure out how to navigate it successfully.

One of the first metadata challenges you often face is just trying to figure out what metadata is. To that end, we begin this chapter with a brief definition and description of the three major categories of metadata typically found in a DW/BI system: business, technical, and process metadata. Once you have a sense for what metadata is, your next big challenge is figuring out where to put it. Although SQL Server 2005 has its own ideas on where to keep its metadata, we include a description of the industry standard for storing and exchanging DW/BI metadata: the Common Warehouse Metamodel.

With a common terminology in place, your next challenge will be figuring out exactly what metadata you have and where it comes from. To that end, we explore the various sources and uses of metadata across the SQL Server 2005 toolset. As it turns out, every major component of the toolset is metadata driven. The problem is the metadata is kept in different locations and different formats, so finding and managing the metadata is a bit of a hardship. Finally, we describe a basic, practical approach for dealing with the most important, or at least the most broadly used metadata elements.

Metadata creation and management can be an extremely tangled topic. What we present here is a starting point. Many of you, and certainly those of you in larger organizations, will need to expand on our recommendations and customize them to your environments.

Metadata Basics

One of the most common definitions of metadata we hear is "Metadata is data about data." This is vague to the point of uselessness. It doesn't help you understand what metadata is or why you should care. We think about metadata as *all the information that describes the contents, structures, and operations of the DW/BI system*. Metadata defines the contents of the warehouse, the structures that hold those contents, and the processes that brought those contents into being. In this section, we talk about the purpose of metadata, describe the common types of metadata found in the DW/BI environment, and discuss the concept of the metadata catalog.

The Purpose of Metadata

Metadata serves two main purposes: defining and describing the objects and processes in a system.

Some metadata is used to *define* a process, object, or behavior. When you change the metadata, you change the process. A simple example is the start time of a SQL Server Agent job. Change the value of the start time element and you change the start time of the process. This idea of using metadata to define a process outside the code was an early, practical use of metadata. Separating a program's code from its parameters and definitions allows the developer (and in some cases, the user) to change the parameters and definitions without having to edit and recompile the code. This concept has been around for decades in forms like table-driven programs and configuration files. In a similar fashion, metadata is a core concept of object-oriented programming. The object-oriented concept of properties is essentially metadata, and changing the properties of an object will change how the object behaves or appears, without your having to edit and rebuild the object itself.

Other metadata is used to *describe* an object or process. This kind of descriptive metadata is essentially documentation. If you change the process, but don't change the description, the process itself still works, but your understanding of the process based on its description is now incorrect. Some of the common properties of an object, like its name or description, do not affect its appearance or behavior; they simply describe it in some way. It's this idea of describing that leads to metadata as documentation.

The DW/BI industry often refers to two main categories of metadata: *technical* and *business*. We've added a third category called *process metadata*. As we'll see in the descriptions of these categories that follow, technical metadata is primarily definitional, while business and process metadata are primarily descriptive. Be careful with these categories because there is some overlap. It's best to not get too dogmatic when you are dealing with metadata.

- *Technical metadata* defines the objects and processes that make up the warehouse itself from a technical perspective. This includes the system metadata that defines the data structures themselves, like tables, fields, data types, indexes, and partitions in the relational engine, and databases, dimensions, measures, data mining models, and partitions in Analysis Services. In the ETL process, technical metadata defines the sources and targets for a particular task, the transformations (including business rules and data quality checks), what tasks make up a job, what jobs happen when, and so on.

  This description of technical metadata is cause for some confusion, because some of this technical metadata can also be used as business metadata. Certainly, business users are interested in the tables and columns that are available for query. Security-related metadata also is interesting to both camps. From the technical perspective, the system must be able to identify users, determine what groups they belong to, and assess the validity of their specific request. From the user perspective, knowing what data is available for access can save a lot time and frustration. There are always users who are interested in the ETL transformation rules, especially when the data doesn't make sense to them. On the other hand, some technical metadata elements are of no interest to business users. Few users are interested in the definition of the partition function on a given fact table.

- *Business metadata* describes the contents of the data warehouse in more user-accessible terms. It tells us what data we have, where it comes from, what it means, and what its relationship is to other data in the warehouse. The name and description fields in Analysis Services are good examples of business metadata. Business metadata often serves as documentation for the data warehouse. As such, it may include additional layers of categorization that simplify the user's view by sub-setting tables into business-oriented groups, or omitting certain columns or tables. Data source views and the AttributeHierarchyDisplayFolder properties in Analysis Services serve this purpose. When users browse the metadata to see what's in the warehouse, they are primarily viewing business metadata.

■ *Process metadata* describes the results of various operations in the warehouse. In the ETL process, each task logs key data about its execution, like start time, end time, CPU seconds used, disk reads, disk writes, rows processed, and so on. Similar process metadata is generated when users query the warehouse. This data is initially valuable for troubleshooting the ETL or query process. After people begin using the system, this data is a critical input to the performance monitoring and improvement process. It can also be valuable to monitor user access both as a demonstration of the popularity of the warehouse and for security purposes.

Note that process metadata is really measurement or transaction data for the business processes of building and using the data warehouse. If this is your organization's core business—an information provider that collects sales data for an industry and sells access to that data to many customers, for example—then what we would normally call process metadata becomes the business process data for the fact and dimension tables in the data warehouse. Business folks at this information provider would be most interested in analyzing this process data. It tells them who is using their products, what products they're using, what service level they are receiving, and so on. If you think about it, process metadata is also the business process data for the DW/BI team.

The Metadata Repository

All of these metadata elements need a place to live. Ideally, each tool would keep its metadata in a shared repository where it could be easily reused by other tools and integrated for reporting and analysis purposes. This shared repository would follow standards for how metadata is stored so the repository could be easily accessed by any tool that needs metadata, and new tools could easily replace old tools by simply reading in their metadata.

For example, if you had a shared, centralized repository in your warehouse, you would use your ETL tool to design a package to load your dimensions. The ETL tool would save that package in the repository in a set of structures that at least allow inquiry into the content and structure of the package. If you wanted to know what transforms were applied to the data in a given dimension table, you could query the repository. Some of the metadata that defines the core structures may need to be saved in proprietary XML files, but that metadata could still be retrieved and displayed if it was surrounded by the appropriate descriptive metadata.

Unfortunately, this wonderful, integrated, shared repository is relatively rare in the DW/BI world today, and when it does exist, it must be built and maintained with significant effort. Most DW/BI systems are like the Tower of

Babel, and Microsoft SQL Server 2005 is no exception, with each component in the toolset keeping its own metadata in its own structures and formats.

It may provide some comfort to know that managing metadata is a challenge that is not unique to the Microsoft platform. For decades, people in the software industry have realized that managing metadata is a problem. There have been, and continue to be, major efforts within many companies to build a central metadata repository. At best, these are unstable successes. The amount of effort it takes to build and maintain the central repository ends up being more than most companies are willing to pay. At the same time, several major software companies have tried to address the problem from a product perspective. Most of these products are large-scale, enterprise repositories that are built to handle every kind of system complexity. Implementers have a hard time navigating the product complexity, so most of the functionality remains unused. Again, the cost and effort often brings the project stumbling to its knees. We've often seen initial success at implementation followed by a slow (or rapid) divergence from reality until the repository falls into complete disuse.

Metadata Standards

While projects to build an enterprise repository are often less than successful, the effort continues because there are at least four good reasons to have a standard, shared repository for metadata.

- When tools can exchange metadata, you can reuse existing metadata to help define each new step in the implementation process. Column names and descriptions captured in the data model design step can be used to build the relational tables, reused to populate the OLAP engine, and then used again to help populate the front-end tool's metadata layer, for example.

- If the metadata is in a standard form, your investment in defining objects and processes is protected—you are not locked in to a particular tool. For example, Reporting Services Report Definition Language (RDL) is a language standard that describes a report. If all your reports are stored in RDL, you could potentially switch to a new front-end tool and still be able to use your existing report library. (This benefit is not particularly popular with tool vendors.)

- A central repository gives you a single, common understanding of the contents and structure of the data warehouse—it is the best documentation you could have. And, to the extent that this shared repository holds the official, active metadata for each tool, you know it is the current version and not a copy that may be out of date.

- An integrated metadata repository allows you to more easily assess changes through impact and lineage analysis. The two concepts are essentially like looking down the same pipe from either end. In *impact analysis*, you want to know what downstream elements will be affected as a result of a potential change, like dropping a table. In *lineage analysis*, you want to know how a certain element came into being—what sources and transformations it went through to get to where it is.

You'd like to have a standard repository for metadata—at least in the DW/BI environment. The tools would write their metadata to the repository during the design phase and read it back in during the execution phase. In theory, any tool can write to and read from the standard model.

As it turns out, there is a standard framework for data warehouse-oriented metadata called the Common Warehouse Metamodel (CWM) that was first published by the Object Management Group (OMG) in 2001. The CWM is an object-based attempt to provide a metadata store for the various elements of a data warehouse. As we understand it, the overall standard is composed of three parts:

- *The Common Warehouse Metamodel* (CWM) is a domain model (or metamodel, as OMG calls it) of the data warehouse. It has over a dozen subdomains (or sub-metamodels), including ones to describe relational elements, transformations, OLAP, and front-end components.

- *The Meta Object Facility* (MOF) is essentially the definition language used to define a specific instance of the CWM.

- *XML Metadata Interchange* (XMI) provides the structure to support the interchange of metadata with a standard format based on XML.

We say "as we understand it," because the CWM standards set is long, complex, and difficult to navigate for the average data warehouse professional. The sheer volume of information is daunting with over 1,200 pages of documentation, plus the XML document for XMI, and the interface definition language (IDL) for the MOF. Beyond that, the standard is managed by an object-oriented organization and is based on CORBA and UML. There's a lot to unravel before one can begin to understand it. That said, the metadata manager on your team should spend some time figuring out the CWM and how it plays in your vendors' responses to the metadata problem.

While the CWM was a significant attempt to help solve the problem of metadata proliferation, the current status of the CWM is unclear. Vendor adoption of standards is always slow because each individual tool vendor has a vested interest in keeping its metadata proprietary. In fairness, some vendors believe the CWM is not flexible or comprehensive enough to support their metadata needs. Even so, many ETL and front-end tool vendors claim some level of support for CWM, but what this means is uncertain. For example, it is possible for a tool to write its metadata out to extended, custom structures in the CWM—structures that are essentially unreadable to other tools. This obviously does not help in the exchange or reuse of metadata, even if it does allow the vendor to claim CWM compliance. Further uncertainty comes from the fact that as of the time of this writing, there has been very little recent activity from the OMG on the CWM standard. There are no white papers on the topic on their web site. Version 1.1 of the standard came out in March of 2003, and the most recent press and articles listed on the main CWM page are from the year 2000. While the concept is valuable, it is too soon to celebrate the success of the CWM.

IN THEIR OWN WORDS

Perhaps it's best to let the OMG describe the CWM to help clarify its purpose and contents:

> Since every data management and analysis tool requires different metadata and a different metadata model (known as a metamodel) to solve the data warehouse metadata problem, it is simply not possible to have a single metadata repository that implements a single metamodel for all the metadata in an organization. Instead, what is needed is a standard for interchange of warehouse metadata.
>
> The CWM is a response to these needs. It provides a framework for representing metadata about data sources, data targets, transformations, and analysis, and the processes and operations that create and manage warehouse data and provide lineage information about its use.
>
> > Source: Common Warehouse Metamodel (CWM) Specification Version 1.1, Volume 1, March 2003 http://www.omg.org/docs/formal/03-03-02.pdf
>
> The Common Warehouse Metamodel (CWM) is a specification that describes metadata interchange among data warehousing, business intelligence, knowledge management and portal technologies. The OMG Meta-Object Facility (MOF) bridges the gap between dissimilar meta-models by providing a common basis for meta-models. If two different meta-models are both MOF-conformant, then models based on them can reside in the same repository.
>
> > Source: the Data Warehouse, CWM(tm), And MOF(tm) Resource Page http://www.omg.org/technology/cwm/

METADATA, META DATA, OR META-DATA?

Unfortunately, the state of metadata standards in our industry is reflected in the number of different ways we present the term metadata. The OMG uses a single word, *metadata*; the Data Warehousing Institute uses two words, *meta data*; and some publications have recently started using a hyphenated version, *meta-data*. The fact that we have no standard for the word metadata cannot bode well for the actual standard itself.

In any case, all this talk about standards is definitely a future-oriented discussion for us because SQL Server 2005 does not support the CWM standard.

SQL Server 2005 Metadata

The good news is that the SQL Server toolset is mostly metadata driven. The relational engine has a slew of system tables that define and describe the data structures, activity monitoring, security, and other functions along with a set of stored procedures to manage it. Other components, like Analysis Services and Integration Services are based on similar metadata, but it's kept in an object-oriented structure in XML files. Much, if not all, of the property-based metadata in SQL Server 2005 can be accessed through the various object models.

The bad news is that every major component of SQL Server 2005 keeps its metadata in its own independent structures, from database tables to XML files, which have their own access methods, from SQL Management Objects (SMO) and Analysis Management Objects (AMO) to stored procedures to APIs. Not only do the tools manage their own metadata, but the metadata they use is not integrated across the tools. The flexibility you get from the programmable nature of the tools and the Visual Studio development environment makes it particularly difficult to identify which packages pulled a particular set of data and applied which transformations and loaded it into what relational database, and what cubes and what reports.

As we describe in the next section, the first step in every metadata strategy is to assess the situation. You need to conduct a detailed inventory of what metadata structures are available, which ones are actually being used, what tools you have to view the metadata, and what tools you have to manage it. Table 13.1 provides a convenient summary of the various metadata sources and stores across the SQL Server 2005 BI platform, and identifies various tools for accessing and viewing them. The remainder of this section describes the major components in Table 13.1.

Table 13.1 Metadata Sources and Stores in the SQL Server 2005 BI Platform

TOOL/ COMPONENT	TYPE	CONTENT	ACCESS AND MAINTENANCE METHODS	EXAMPLES	RESOURCE LOCATION
Cross-Tool Components					
SQL Agent	All	Job and schedule definition and execution	SQL Server Studio; stored procedures; SQL Management Objects (SMO).	sp_help_job; dbo .sysjobs_view	BOL search: "automating administrative tasks" or "Programming SMO"
SQL Server Profiler	Process	Relational and Analysis Services engine activity	SQL Server Profiler; SQL Trace.	See Chapter 15.	BOL search: "Introducing SQL Server Profiler"
The SQL Server BI Documentation Center	All	Full range of metadata from relational DB, AS, and SSIS packages	Stand-alone tool creates XML files for web browsing.	Microsoft Developers Network (MSDN) http://msdn. microsoft.com/SQL/ sqlwarehouse/SSIS/ default.aspx	
Microsoft Metadata Whitepaper	All	Microsoft's recommended approach for managing SQL Server 2005 metadata			MSDN: http://msdn .microsoft.com/SQL/ sqlwarehouse/ SSIS/default.aspx
Metadata Reporting Pack for SQL Server Integration Services	Technical ,Process	SSIS package definitions and reports for impact and lineage analysis across the relational DB, AS, SSIS, and Reporting Services	Stand-alone tool to load a metadata database and a viewer, along with SSIS packages and Reporting Services reports.		MSDN: http:// msdn.microsoft.com/ SQL/sqlwarehouse/ SSIS/default.aspx

(continued)

Table 13.1 (continued)

TOOL/ COMPONENT	TYPE	CONTENT	ACCESS AND MAINTENANCE METHODS	EXAMPLES	RESOURCE LOCATION
Relational Engine					
System tables	Technical, Business, Process	Object descriptions, definitions, parameters, security, relationships, and settings	Catalog views (CVs); Information Schema views; SMO.	sys.objects; sys.columns	BOL search: "catalog views"; "information schema views"
System stored procedures	Technical, Business, Process	Integrated system table queries, database management functions	System stored procedures (SPs); SMO.	sp_who (current database processes)	BOL search: "system stored procedures"
Extended properties	Business	Business metadata	Design spreadsheet, SQL Studio, Stored Procedures, Catalog views, and SMO.	See reports in this chapter.	BOL search: "extended properties"
Analysis Services					
AS Object model	Technical, Business, Process	Object descriptions, definitions, parameters, security, relationships, hierarchies, and settings	SQL Server BI - Development Studio; SQL Server Management Studio; Analysis Management Objects (AMO).	See Figure 13.4.	BOL search: "analysis management objects" Default sample location: Program Files\Microsoft SQL Server\90\Samples\ Analysis Services\ - Programmability\ AMO\ AmoBrowser - Administrator\ ActivityViewer

TOOL/COMPONENT	TYPE	CONTENT	ACCESS AND MAINTENANCE METHODS	EXAMPLES	RESOURCE LOCATION
Integration Services					
Integration Services Object model	Technical, Business, Process	Object descriptions, definitions, parameters, security, relationships, hierarchies, and settings	SQL Server Management Studio; Integration Services object model; SQL Server BI Development Studio.		BOL search: "integration services programming" Programming examples: Microsoft SQL Server\90\Samples\Integration Services\Programmin g Samples
Integration Services Package logging, and Integration Services Logging Report Pack	Process	SSIS process metrics	Data written to various log providers. The Logging Report Pack is a set of reports based on SSIS logging data.	See Chapter 15.	BOL search: "Logging Package Execution" Logging Report Pack: Microsoft Developers Network (MSDN) http://msdn.microsoft .com/SQL/ sqlwarehouse/SSIS/ default.aspx
Data Warehouse Audit system	Process	ETL process metrics, data quality flags and metrics	SQL queries; Reports.	See Chapters 6 and 15.	
Reporting Services					
Report Manager	Technical, Business, Process	Report definitions, schedules, folders, security, and so on	SQL Server Management Studio; Report Manager web page; web service (ADO.NET).	See Chapter 9.	

(continued)

Table 13.1 (continued)

TOOL/ COMPONENT	TYPE	CONTENT	ACCESS AND MAINTENANCE METHODS	EXAMPLES	RESOURCE LOCATION
Execution Log	Technical, Business, Process	Server, user and report activity	SQL Script, Report Server reports.	See Chapter 15.	C:\Program Files\ Microsoft SQL Server\ 90\Samples\ Reporting Services\ Report Samples\ Server Management Sample Reports
Report Builder	Technical, Business Models	Semantic layer between user interface and data sources	SQL Server BI Development Studio; Reporting Services object model.	See Figures 13.2 and 13.3.	BOL search: "Reporting Services object model" (yields several topics)
External Components					
System Monitor Performance tool	Process	System level performance (reads, writes, buffers, and so on)	System Monitor, also known as perfmon.	See Chapter 15.	Monitor tool: Administrative Tools/ Performance BOL search: "monitoring performance" (yields several topics)
Active Directory	Technical, Business	Security, organizational info, employee info	System.DirectoryServices namespace in .NET Framework; Query through OLE DB Provider.		BOL search: "Query Active Directory", "OLE DB Directory"

Cross-Tool Components

Several metadata components in SQL Server support more than one tool in the system. We decided to list them once rather than repeating them under each heading:

- *SQL Server Agent* is the job scheduler of the SQL Server world. It contains information about jobs, job steps, and schedules. SQL Server Agent metadata can be accessed through a set of stored procedures, system tables, SQL Management Objects (SMO), and SQL Server Management Studio. From a metadata perspective, it is important to monitor SQL Server Agent's process metadata to make sure jobs are running and completing successfully. Beyond that, even folks in the user community are interested in knowing what jobs are scheduled and when they are supposed to run.

- *SQL Server Profiler* is SQL Server's activity monitoring tool. You define a trace to track the occurrences of specific events, like Audit Logon, and have those occurrences written out to a table or file. SQL Server Profiler can be used interactively from the Profiler tool, or initiated programmatically using stored procedures. Chapter 15 describes using SQL Server Profiler to create an audit log of DW/BI system usage.

- *SQL Server BI Documentation Center (DocCenter)* is a reporting utility designed to create a metadata catalog of sorts. It was developed by the SQL Server Team as an extra to help customers gather and explore metadata from three major sources: the relational engine, Analysis Services, and Integration Services packages. When you run DocCenter, it reads through the system tables or the object models, depending on the subsystem you picked, and creates a set of XML documents along with an XSLT reader. This allows the viewer to navigate the various sets of metadata through a set of standard, linked reports. DocCenter serves a useful role in the survey step of creating a metadata strategy. It can also be used as a basic metadata browser for these major subsystems. DocCenter can be found at the Microsoft Development Network SQL developer center: http://msdn.microsoft.com/SQL/sqlwarehouse/SSIS/default.aspx.

- *Metadata Reporting Pack for SQL Server Integration Services (Metadata Pack)* is another utility designed to create a metadata repository. In this case, a program parses through the Integration Services packages to identify the sources, targets, transformations, and dependencies involved in the data flows. The results of this parsing process are stored in a relational database. Because these sources and targets are often relational, analysis services, and reporting objects, this data can be used to provide impact and lineage analysis from the relational database all the way out to the standard reports. The initial version of the Metadata Pack does not track all the components of an Integration Services package, but the Integration Services team continues to enhance it. The Metadata Pack can also be found at the MSDN SQL developer center.

Relational Engine Metadata

The SQL Server relational engine itself has system tables that can be accessed through a set of system views (called catalog views) or system stored procedures designed to report on the system table contents and, in some cases, to edit the contents. Alternatively, they can be accessed programmatically through SQL Server Management Objects (SMO), which itself supersedes SQL Distributed Management Objects (SQL-DMO).

Business metadata can be stored along with the table and column definitions by using the extended properties function. This allows the developer to append any number of additional descriptive metadata elements onto the database objects. The dimensional model design spreadsheet described in Chapter 2 makes use of extended properties to store several metadata columns like description, comments, example values, and ETL rules. The names of these extended properties must be part of your naming convention so programs and queries can find them.

> **NOTE** "Description" is not a stock extended property name, but Visual Studio will populate an extended property called description through the user interface (see the Books Online topic, "Description Property Dialog Box" for more information).

Process metadata for the relational engine can be captured through the SQL Server Profiler component described earlier in this section. Chapter 15 describes a performance-monitoring log for the relational engine.

Analysis Services

Analysis Services' object model has all the same kinds of metadata that the relational engine has and more. From the definitions of the databases, cubes, dimensions, facts, and attributes to the KPIs, calculated columns, and hierarchy structures, not to mention the data mining models—all are available through the object model. The first and obvious access tools for the developer are the BI Development Studio and the SQL Server Management Studio. Beyond these, you can build custom .NET-based applications that use Analysis Management Objects (AMO) to access the Analysis Services object model.

Analysis Services process metadata can be captured through the SQL Server Profiler component described earlier in this section. Chapter 15 describes a performance-monitoring log for Analysis Services.

The Data Source Views (DSVs) used by Analysis Services, Report Builder, and Integration Services provide an intriguing metadata layer. A DSV is essentially an abstraction layer between the source systems and the processes that reference them. DSVs have a sub-model layer called a diagram that allows the developer to define even simpler sub-views of the DSV, and that supports the idea of role-playing tables. For example, you could create a DSV for the entire data warehouse, with multiple fact tables and all associated dimensions. Then, you could create diagrams in the DSV that include tables for only a given subject area, like Orders. Additional diagrams might cover Shipments, Returns, and Customer Care calls. The entities shown in a DSV don't even have to be tables. You can create a named query in the DSV that looks and acts like a table to any tool that uses the DSV. DSVs also provide an additional descriptive property called FriendlyName. Unfortunately, DSVs are not directly referenced as metadata anywhere outside of the BI Development Studio in the initial release of SQL Server 2005. The Report Builder ad hoc query tool uses a DSV to create its own abstraction layer, called a model. Analysis Services Enterprise Edition offers a capability called Perspectives. Perspectives are similar to diagrams and provide for the logical sub-setting of a cube. These perspectives are used in the creation of Report Builder models based on Analysis Services. Analysis Services also has its own security metadata to provide the ability to limit access to subsets of the data.

Integration Services

As one might expect, SQL Server Integration Services has its own object model. The real difficulty with Integration Services from a metadata perspective is that it's essentially a visual programming environment as opposed to a structured database environment, like the relational engine or Analysis Services. SSIS packages can be incredibly complex and do not follow a common structure. In fact, much of what might be considered Integration Services metadata will actually be the result of defining and using standard naming conventions for packages and tasks. Another difficulty with Integration Services is its time-dependent nature. At any point in time, it is difficult to tell which package was used to execute which load. One day, a certain ETL process could be run from a package saved in the file system. The next day, the ETL developer changes the SQL Agent task to point to another package stored in the database that uses different logic and business rules. While the packages will have distinct GUIDs, the names will be the same. Keeping track of this obviously requires a clear set of development process rules, naming standards, discipline, and monitoring.

Regardless of where a package comes from, it can and should be set up to create its own process metadata. As we describe in Chapter 15, you should turn on logging at the package level, and select from a long list of events to log.

There are several options for determining where the information is logged, including to a database table. Table 13.1 references some example Reporting Services reports on MSDN that demonstrate how to access the log data and use it to track the execution and performance of your SSIS packages.

In addition to this base process-level logging, the data warehouse audit system described in Chapter 6 ties the process metadata back to the actual data that was loaded in a given ETL package. This metadata surfaces in the user interface in the form of an Audit dimension and associated audit tables that allow the user to get a sense for where the data came from and how it was loaded. Chapter 6 also describes an extended version of the audit system that can be used to monitor data quality and flag data quality issues at the row level if necessary.

Reporting Services

Reporting Services is entirely metadata driven. The contents, operation, usage, and security are all described in a set of metadata tables in the ReportServer database. It is possible to query these tables directly to see how Reporting Services works. However, rather than build reports on top of the production database, which could impact performance and potentially break when Microsoft changes the database, it makes sense to extract the process metadata into a separate reporting and analysis schema. Microsoft has included a couple of SQL scripts on the samples that create this schema and update it on a scheduled basis, along with a few example reports written against the schema. Figure 13.1 shows the Reporting Services process metadata schema created by the sample package. Not surprisingly, it is a solid dimensional schema (with the exception of the unnecessary snowflaking of the ReportTypes table from Reports dimension). The Reporting Services database is also surfaced through an object model that itself is accessible through a web service.

Like many front-end tools, Report Builder uses metadata to define the objects, attributes, join paths, and calculations that it needs to formulate a query. This metadata set is called a Report Builder model and is created using the BI Development Studio. The relational version is built on top of its own Data Source View and is kept in the Reporting Services database. Report Builder models used to access Analysis Services are built directly from the Analysis Services cube. We'll show an example of a Report Builder model in the next section.

External Metadata Sources

There are several useful metadata sources that exist in the broader computing environment. Chief among these are the System Monitor tool and Active Directory. If you use a source control tool like Visual Source Safe, you may also consider that tool's data as a metadata source.

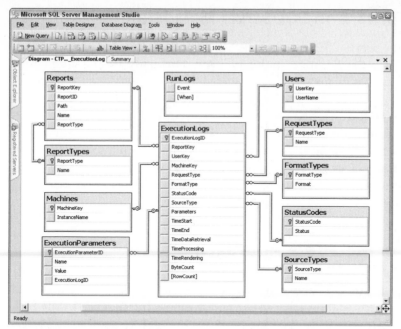

Figure 13.1   Microsoft's Reporting Services process metadata reporting schema

System Monitor

The Windows System Monitor performance tool is familiar to anyone who has done system performance troubleshooting in Windows. It works at the operating system level much like SQL Server Profiler does at the SQL Server level. You can define traces for a whole range of system activities and measures across the BI toolset and in the operating system itself. These traces can be defined to run in the background and to write to log files. If necessary, these logs can be tied back to SQL Profiler logs to help understand the possible causes of any problems. Chapter 15 describes which System Performance indicators are most important to log during regular operations.

Active Directory

Active Directory is Microsoft's network-based user logon management facility. It is a directory structure that can hold user, group, security, and other organizational information. Depending on how your organization is using Active Directory, it can be a source for security-related information. It can also be the system of record for some of the descriptive attributes of the Employee and Organization dimensions. This is another example of where the line between metadata and data can get fuzzy.

Looking Forward on SQL Server Metadata

Clearly the SQL Server 2005 development team understands the importance of metadata from a development point of view. However, even though SQL Server 2005 has lots of metadata, that metadata is not very well integrated. Careful metadata integration and active metadata management did not appear to be Microsoft's top priority for the core SQL Server 2005 product. Fortunately, the development team has been working on a lot of add-on utilities to help fill this gap, many of which are referenced in this chapter. In the past, Microsoft has been a leader on metadata issues, so we would be surprised if upcoming releases of SQL Server did not address the problem of managing and integrating metadata as part of the core product.

A Practical Metadata Approach

This brings us to the question you've all been asking: What do we do about metadata to support data warehousing and business intelligence in the SQL Server 2005 environment? In the long term, we expect Microsoft to tackle the metadata management problem. Meanwhile, you have to figure out what you are going to do about metadata in the short to medium term. It's easy to get trapped in the metadata morass (as the authors can certainly attest). It's a major effort to figure out what metadata to capture, where to capture it, how to integrate it, how it should be used in the warehouse processes, and how to keep it synchronized and maintained. Vendors have been building metadata repositories and maintenance utilities for decades, and companies (some companies) have been trying to use these tools, or tools of their own creation, to tame the metadata beast for just as long. Even so, there are very few examples of large-scale, robust, successful metadata systems. It's a really hard problem.

Again you ask, "So what am I supposed to do?" Well, first, you need to appoint someone on the team to the role of metadata manager. If no one owns the problem, it will not be addressed. The metadata manager is responsible for creating and implementing the metadata strategy. The ideal candidate has to know everything. No joke. If one person has to do the whole thing, he or she will need to have SQL and DBA skills. The metadata manager needs to know how to program in the Visual Studio environment and how to create and publish reports, and needs to understand the business, at a detailed level. Okay, so the metadata manager doesn't need to know everything. If you also have a security manager and a data modeler, they can help, too.

Creating the Metadata Strategy

We believe the following approach is a good compromise between having little or no managed metadata and building an enterprise metadata system. Our main recommendation is to concentrate on business metadata first. Make sure it is correct, complete, and maintained. Also, make sure it is accessible to the business users. Once that's done, provide a way to view the other major metadata stores. We often see a tendency to over-engineer metadata. The key to making this strategy work is to not overdo it. Here's the basic outline:

1. You need to know what's out there. Survey the landscape to identify the various locations, formats, and uses of metadata in SQL Server 2005. The previous section and Table 13.1 give you a starting point. Use the tools described to explore the system for metadata locations. Where there aren't any tools, you will need to create query or programmatic access to the rest of the sources so you can explore and track them. Create a list of the metadata elements you find, including where they are, where they came from, who owns them, how you view and change them, and where and how you might use them.

2. Identify and/or define metadata that needs to be captured and managed. These are the elements you will use more broadly and therefore need to keep updated and distributed throughout the system. What you need to manage depends on a lot of factors: your organizational predisposition to actively manage metadata, the level of support for actively managing metadata on the DW/BI team, and the resources available to address the problem. At the very least, you must manage a basic level of business metadata. We will describe alternative approaches to this later in this section.

3. While you're at it, decide on the definitive location for each metadata element to be managed. This is the location where the element will be stored and edited. It is the source for any copies that are needed by other parts of the system. It might be in the relational database for some elements, in Analysis Services for others, and so on. For some elements, you might decide to keep it in a third-party tool, like ERwin, or Visio, or even your organization's repository tool. In the Adventure Works example, we are using extended properties in the relational database to capture several useful metadata fields. We discussed a rudimentary method for transferring the description, but it would be nice to be able to make all these fields accessible in Analysis Services as well.

4. Create systems to capture any business or process metadata that does not have a home. Try to use all available pre-existing metadata structures, like description fields, before you add your own metadata tables. However, you will likely identify many fields that need a place to live; the comment field in the data model spreadsheet and the Usage History table are good examples of this. If the users are the owners of these elements, they should be responsible for maintaining them. Many of our clients have created a separate metadata database that holds these

metadata tables along with any value-added content tables that are maintained by the business users. It's not too difficult to create a .NET front end to let users manage the contents of these tables.

5. Create programs or tools to share and synchronize metadata as needed. This primarily involves copying the metadata from its master location to whatever subsystem needs it. Fill in the description fields, the source fields, and the business name fields in all the tables, extended properties, and object models from the initial database all the way out to the front-end tools. If these are populated right from the start as part of the design and development process, they will be easier to maintain on an ongoing basis. You will also be able to more easily see what surfaces in the browsers and front-end tools as you move through the process. Note that moving data from one location to another sounds like an ideal task for Integration Services.

6. Educate the DW/BI team and key business users about the importance of metadata and the metadata strategy. Assign metadata creation and updating responsibilities.

7. Design and implement the delivery approach for getting business metadata out to the user community. Typically, this involves creating metadata access tools, like reports and browsers. Often, you need to create a simple metadata repository for business metadata and provide users with a way to browse the repository to find out what's available in the BI system. While you may actually use several reporting tools to provide access to the metadata, this should appear as seamless as possible to the users. The different metadata access tools can all be linked to from a single page in the Navigation Portal. We describe a simple business metadata catalog in detail in the next section.

8. Manage the metadata and monitor usage and compliance. Make sure people know the information is out there and are able to use it. Make sure the metadata is complete and current. Being able to view the metadata is the hardest part of monitoring—especially in the SQL Server 2005 environment—because there are a lot of different metadata sources. A large part of the baseline metadata effort is spent building reports and browsers to provide access to the metadata. Monitoring means you have to actually look at those reports on a regular basis.

Even though this is the balanced strategy between nothing and too much, it is still a fair amount of work. Make sure you include time in your project plan in all development tasks to capture and manage metadata, and that you include separate tasks for the preceding steps.

Business Metadata Reporting

Business metadata is the most important area to address because it supports the largest and most important segment of BI stakeholders—the users—who can't get this information any other way. In other words, the technical folks can usually dig around and find the information they need in order to understand the contents of the data warehouse. The user community, for the most part, doesn't have this skill set (that's why you're here, remember). You must provide them with an easy, accessible way to explore the contents of the DW/BI system if you want them to know what's available. We'll approach the task of providing business metadata to the users from the best case to the worst case.

Analysis Services as Primary Query Platform

If your organization's data and analytical needs are such that Analysis Services can meet them, and you have chosen Analysis Services as your primary user access platform, delivering basic business metadata can be relatively easy. Start with your front-end tool. See what kind of metadata layer it offers. The major front-end tool vendors offer rich metadata layers that can serve as the business metadata catalog. At the very least, this catalog needs a Subject Areas layer that allows individual business process schemas to be viewed separately from the rest of the database and ties related schemas (cubes) together. It helps simplify the data access process for the users if they can see the Orders schema, with its fact table and associated dimensions, without having to wade through all the other tables in the warehouse. The perspectives feature in Analysis Services Enterprise Edition provides this sub-setting capability.

Most of the major front-end tools either provide business metadata fields in their own metadata layer, or pull directly from the metadata fields found in Analysis Services. This would include the descriptions of cubes, dimensions, and attributes, often shown to the user right in the tool's interface. Therefore, filling in the few metadata fields found in Analysis Services is a critical first step to improving users' understanding of the database contents.

If you're using a third-party front-end tool, you need to explore the metadata structures offered by that tool and proceed accordingly. If you're building a complete Microsoft solution, you will need to do a bit more work. The Microsoft tools do provide limited metadata support. For example, a user creating a new report in Report Builder must first select a model—Report Builder's predefined metadata layer. The model selection dialog box in Figure 13.2 shows how Report Builder presents the model along with the metadata description of the model and, if the source is Analysis Services, each cube and perspective in the Analysis Services database from which the model was generated.

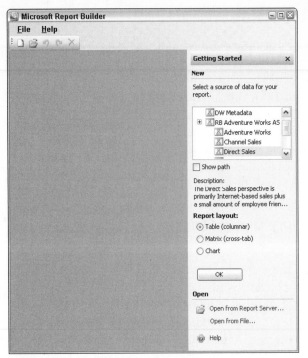

Figure 13.2   Analysis Services metadata in the Report Builder model selection

Figure 13.3 shows another Analysis Services metadata feature called the AttributeHierarchyDisplayFolder property that is used in Report Builder. As we described in Chapter 7, you can use this feature to group related attributes in a hierarchy used for display purposes. In Figure 13.3, a Report Builder user has selected the Customer dimension in the entities pane in the upper left of the window and is presented with three folders that categorize customer attributes into subgroups.

By selecting the Demographic folder, the user sees only those attributes in the Fields: pane in the lower-left portion of the window that are relevant to customer demographics. It is much easier for the user to navigate these display folders to find the attribute they are looking for than it is to search through a single long list of dozens (or hundreds) of attributes.

Beyond this initial display of descriptions and the use of the display folders, Report Builder does a poor job of presenting the limited metadata that's available in the Analysis Services object model. For example, none of the additional dimension, attribute, or measure group descriptions are surfaced in the tool. If Report Builder is your primary end user ad hoc access tool, you will need to provide your users with the ability to explore the contents of the warehouse so they can learn what it contains and how to work with it.

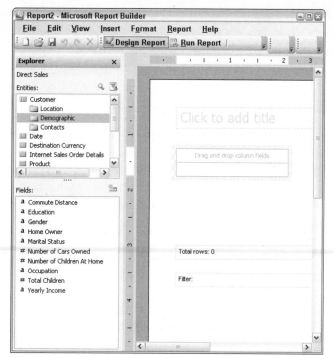

Figure 13.3   Analysis Services display folders in the Report Builder designer

Analysis Services Metadata Browser

Perhaps you've decided your query and reporting tool doesn't do an adequate job of publishing Analysis Services metadata. There are several approaches to bridging this gap; some are more work than others. If Analysis Services is your primary user database, the easiest approach is to build a simple browser that allows the user to navigate the Analysis Services object model. The Samples that ship with SQL Server 2005 include a program called the AMO Browser, shown in Figure 13.4, which allows the user to browse the Analysis Services object model.

Notice that the browser is opened to the same perspective shown in Figure 13.2. The description shown in Report Builder comes from the Description property. This sample program illustrates how to retrieve the properties of various Analysis Services objects. It would be fairly easy for a C# programmer to modify (or a VB programmer to replicate) this program to limit its output to strictly those objects and properties, like name and description, that are interesting to business users. Because this approach is based on the actual Analysis Services database and its contents, it has the advantage of never being out of sync with what users will see in their tools. This makes Analysis Services (and the VS projects that build it) the system of record for these few metadata elements. However, it is limited to the metadata properties provided in Analysis Services: name, friendly-name, and description. Perhaps in the next release, Analysis Services will accommodate the concept of extended properties that can be found in the relational database. This would allow you to add on metadata fields as needed, much like you did when you created your original business process dimensional model in the relational database using the design spreadsheet.

Relational Engine Extended Properties

If your primary user access platform is the relational engine, or if you feel like the Analysis Services properties are too limiting, you can always go back to the relational model and provide a simple set of reports that allows users to explore the metadata in the extended properties that was created from the original business process dimensional modeling spreadsheet back in Chapter 3. Figure 13.5 shows what a simple metadata exploration report for the extended properties of the DimCustomer dimension might look like.

The problem with this approach is it's limited to the relational structures as defined in the relational system tables. There's no intermediate layer that lets you group subsets of tables into business process dimensional models and no display folders to group similar attributes to simplify the user view. And, it doesn't include any other user access platforms like Analysis Services.

Business Metadata Schema

If the extended properties browser still isn't enough, you can create a simple business metadata schema that will support both relational and Analysis Services databases, accommodate multiple subject areas, and allow for additional metadata fields that may not exist elsewhere. Figure 13.6 shows a basic business metadata schema.

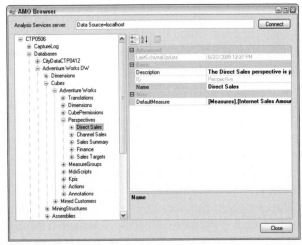

Figure 13.4 The sample Analysis Management Objects browser

Content information for DimCustomer

#	Column Name	Description	Example Values	Source System
1	CustomerKey	Surrogate primary key	1, 2, 3, 4 …	
2	BKAccountNumber	Account Number from the transaction system	AW00000001	AW
3	CustomerType	The type of the customer based on our relationship	Reseller, Individual	Derived in ETL
4	CustomerIDName	Customer full name (Last, First Middle) prepended with CustomerID		Derived in ETL
5	CustomerTitle	Courtesy title	Ms., Mr.	AW
6	FirstName	Customer's first name	Tom, Dick, Harry	AW
7	MiddleName	Customer's middle name (often NULL)		AW
8	LastName	Customer's last name		AW
9	CustomerFullName	Customer's full name as Last, First Middle		Derived in ETL
10	BirthDate	Customer's date of birth		AW
11	MaritalStatus	Customer's marital status	Married, Single, Unknown	AW
12	Gender	Customer's gender	Male, Female, Unknown	AW

Figure 13.5   Exploring the relational database's extended properties

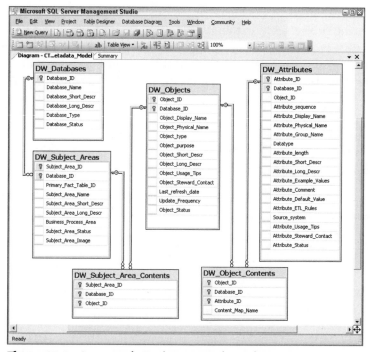

Figure 13.6   An example Business Metadata schema

NOTE The metadata schema is essentially a transaction model meant to keep track of the relationships among the various data elements in the warehouse, and to allow maintaining and updating that data. This is not a dimensional model.

The schema is essentially a hierarchy that starts at the database level in the upper-left corner (with servers and instances collapsed into the database table). Each database can contain zero to many subject areas, each of which contains zero to many objects, each of which contains zero to many attributes. Subject areas are groupings of objects, like business process dimensional models or Analysis Services perspectives or measure groups. The three Contents tables allow you to map the same subject areas into several databases, the same objects into several subject areas, and the same attributes (or columns) into several objects. Your Product dimension will probably participate in several subject areas, like Sales, Customer Care, and Returns.

Figures 13.7 through 13.10 show a series of drill-down reports based on the metadata from the MDWT_AdventureWorksDW data warehouse database. These reports show the Adventure Works metadata as it would appear in the business metadata schema.

Figure 13.7 shows the list of databases on the machine, only a few of which have descriptions in their extended properties. Clicking on one of the databases allows the user to drill down to the next level in the Business Metadata schema.

Figure 13.8 shows the subject areas in the MDWT_AdventureWorksDW database. Note that there are two maintenance subject areas, Audit and Utility, along with the two business process dimensional models, Orders and Exchange Rates. Continuing with the drill-down, Figure 13.9 shows the objects in the Orders subject area.

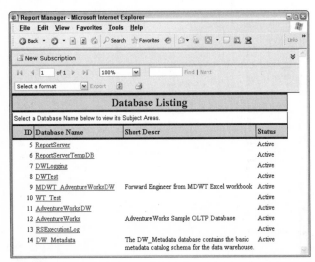

Figure 13.7   Example databases from the Business Metadata schema

Subject Areas in the MDWT_AdventureWorksDW Database

Select a Subject Area Name below to view the Objects it contains.

ID	Subject Area Name	Short Descr	Data Model	Status
1	Audit	Audit tables are used to track the ETL process and to capture specific data quality measures.	Image	Active
2	Utility	Utility tables are used to build the final Fact and Dimension tables.	Image	Active
3	Orders	The Orders Subject Area is about Orders	Image	Active
4	ExchangeRates	The ExchangeRates Subject Area is about ExchangeRates	Image	Active

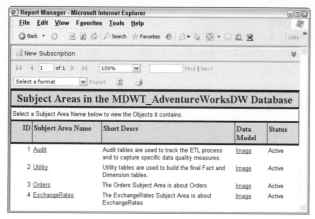

Figure 13.8 Subject areas in the MDWT_AdventureWorksDW database

A subject area essentially corresponds to the dimensions that join to a particular fact table. Finally, Figure 13.10 shows the attributes of the Promotion dimension object.

The metadata properties of the attributes shown in Figure 13.10 are just a few of the potential properties available. These reports constitute an analytical application. Like any analytical application, creating the reports so they flow well and formatting them so they communicate well is a learned skill. Test your efforts on some of the users. Get their feedback on what works and what might be improved. A good metadata browser can help users learn faster and thus accelerate the overall acceptance of the BI system.

Objects in the Orders Subject Area

Select an Object below to view the Attributes it contains.

Object Name	Short Descr	Purpose	Type	Status
DimDate	Date dimension contains one row for every day, beginning at 1/1/2000. There may also be rows for "hasn't happened yet."	Dimension	Table	Active
DimEmployee	Employee info, including sales territory for sales reps	Dimension	Table	Active
DimOrderInfo	OrderInfo is the "junk" dimension that includes miscellaneous information about the Order transaction	Dimension	Table	Active
DimProduct	Information about products	Dimension	Table	Active
DimPromotion	Contains information about marketing promotions	Dimension	Table	Active
AuditDimension	Audit dimension tags each data row with the the process that added or updated it.	Dimension	Table	Active
DimCustomer	The Customer dimension includes all Adventure Works customers	Dimension	Table	Active
DimCurrency	Dimension table that itemizes different currencies	Dimension	Table	Active

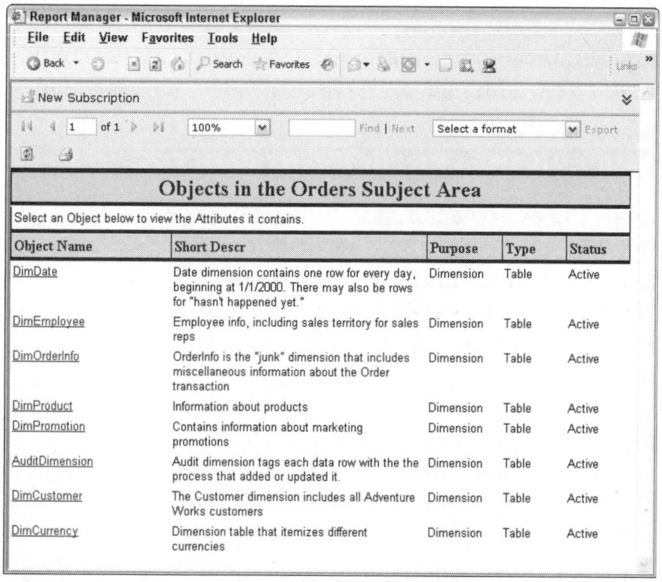

Figure 13.9 Objects in the Orders subject area

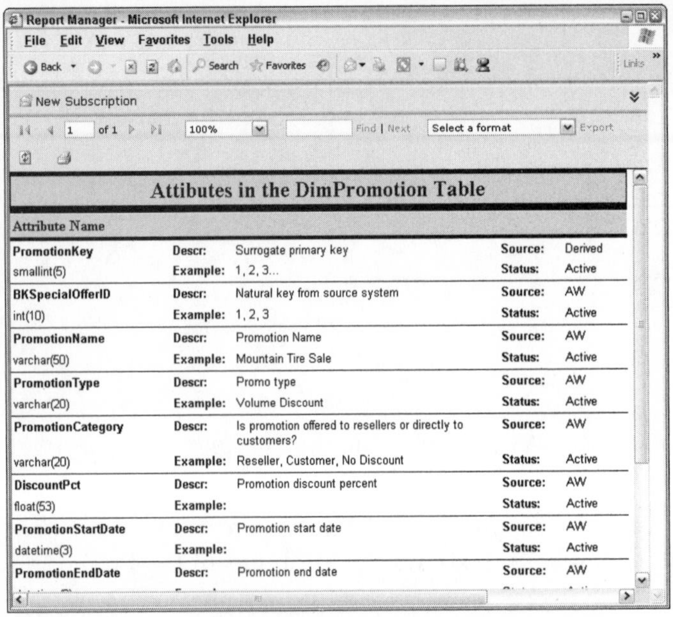

Attibutes in the DimPromotion Table

Attribute Name				
PromotionKey	**Descr:**	Surrogate primary key	**Source:**	Derived
smallint(5)	**Example:**	1, 2, 3...	**Status:**	Active
BKSpecialOfferID	**Descr:**	Natural key from source system	**Source:**	AW
int(10)	**Example:**	1, 2, 3	**Status:**	Active
PromotionName	**Descr:**	Promotion Name	**Source:**	AW
varchar(50)	**Example:**	Mountain Tire Sale	**Status:**	Active
PromotionType	**Descr:**	Promo type	**Source:**	AW
varchar(20)	**Example:**	Volume Discount	**Status:**	Active
PromotionCategory	**Descr:**	Is promotion offered to resellers or directly to customers?	**Source:**	AW
varchar(20)	**Example:**	Reseller, Customer, No Discount	**Status:**	Active
DiscountPct	**Descr:**	Promotion discount percent	**Source:**	AW
float(53)	**Example:**		**Status:**	Active
PromotionStartDate	**Descr:**	Promotion start date	**Source:**	AW
datetime(3)	**Example:**		**Status:**	Active
PromotionEndDate	**Descr:**	Promotion end date	**Source:**	AW

Figure 13.10 Attributes of the Promotion dimension table

The Business Metadata schema is generally as far as we go in terms of creating, managing, and providing access to business metadata and it is meant to be a Pretty Good Practice. We believe the metadata schema is a great example of the 80-20 rule: you get 80 percent of the value of a sophisticated metadata management system with 20 percent of the effort. The four levels in this schema can be used to accommodate a range of designs, platforms, and product editions. There are plenty of enhancements that would make it more detailed and flexible. There are probably a few additional enhancements that will be important for your environment, but beyond that, the return on increased sophistication is pretty low.

THE METADATA SCHEMA AND THE ENHANCEMENT PROCESS

You can find scripts to create the example business metadata schema on the book's web site (www.MsftDWToolkit.com). There are also scripts to do the initial population of the schema based on the relational model. If you used the data model design spreadsheet described in Chapter 3, and if you populated the metadata columns as you were supposed to, this script sweeps all that information into the metadata schema.

If you chose to use the schema and find you need to enhance it, we encourage you to share those enhancements by submitting them as indicated on the book's web site. We'll do our best to make them available to the MDWT community in an open source style, (but without committing to open source standards).

Process Metadata Reporting

There is more metadata work to do beyond business metadata. You will need to create a suite of reports to provide quick, easy insight into what's going on across the BI system right now, and how it is changing over time. These process metadata reports often serve as a starting point for technical folks to assess the status of the system and investigate any problems. Savvy business users want to see if their queries are running and why the system is so slow. We've seen users use these reports to identify the culprit amongst their co-workers and call them up and request that they kill their queries. The data warehouse team and the DBAs will most likely turn to more sophisticated tools, like SQL Server Profiler, to get a better sense of what's really happening and to be able to respond to the situation appropriately.

The process metadata reports include:

- *Reports on active processes in SQL Server:* You can report information on current user activity directly from the SQL Server system views or system stored procedures. You can also set up SQL Profiler trace logs to capture current activity and create a historical log file.

- *Reports on active processes in Analysis Services (provided through object model in the SQL Server 2005 samples directory: Administrator/ ActivityViewer):* You can also set up SQL Profiler trace logs to capture current activity and create a historical log file.

- *Reports on currently running and historical ETL processes:* These can be based on log files and audit tables as described in Table 13.1. You can also view current Integration Services activity in the SQL Server Management Studio.

- *Reports on Reporting Services activity:* You can view history using the Reporting Services execution log schema described in Table 13.1. You can monitor current activity by adding Reporting Services events to the Performance tool.

Publish these reports on the BI web site for all to see. This supports the idea of a single place to go for business information, even for the DW/BI team.

What's interesting in the here-and-now is even more interesting over time. Each of these "real-time" monitoring tools has a historical counterpart. The data warehouse team should set up systems to capture performance and usage data over time, as we describe in Chapter 15. These logs are the input data to warehouse management, performance tuning, long-term capacity planning, and educating management about the use and prevalence of the BI system.

Technical Metadata Reporting

Technical metadata reporting is not the first priority for the warehouse team because most of the development tools are already built with the technical user in mind. That is, they provide the developer or operations person with direct access to the technical metadata. Much of the functionality of SQL Server Management Studio is essentially creating, browsing, and managing technical metadata. The SQL Server team has also created some add-on tools that provide extended metadata browsing capabilities. These are listed in Table 13.1 and were discussed earlier in this chapter.

Ongoing Metadata Management

A metadata system is more than just a set of table or cube definitions—it is also a set of processes that allow you to manage those tables and cubes, obtain and distribute their contents, and keep them current. If you build a separate metadata repository, nightly refreshes of the metadata are typically acceptable. The safest approach would be to trigger a refresh whenever any of the metadata values is changed.

You will also need to build processes, most likely Integration Services packages, to extract key metadata values from the systems of record and copy them to wherever they are needed. These targets could be the business metadata schema, Analysis Services cubes, or even a Report Builder model. You will likely need to create an interface to allow the DW/BI team and business users to edit the business metadata values. This then ties in with assigning maintenance responsibility and monitoring and notification reports. Bottom line, you are building a metadata system, not just filling in a few columns as part of the initial data load.

Summary

Metadata is a fuzzy, complex subject. In this chapter, we defined metadata as information that describes the contents, structures, and operations of the DW/BI system. We described business, technical and process metadata, and briefly discussed the Common Warehouse Metamodel standard for data warehouse metadata. Next, we described the various sources and access methods for SQL Server 2005 metadata. The rest of the chapter was dedicated to our recommended approach for creating and managing metadata in your DW/BI system. Our approach begins with the requirement that the DW/BI team must assign the role of metadata manager to one of the team members. We then provide the metadata manager with eight steps to develop a metadata strategy. These steps are:

1. Do a metadata inventory.
2. Identify key metadata elements that you will actively use and manage.
3. Identify the definitive location (system of record) for each element.
4. Create tools to capture and store any needed elements that do exist in the SQL Server 2005 system.
5. Create tools to synchronize and share metadata as needed.
6. Educate the DW/BI team and key business users about metadata and their metadata roles and responsibilities.
7. Determine and build the metadata delivery approach, especially for business metadata.
8. Manage the metadata system and monitor usage and compliance.

The education step is critical to long-term metadata success. Everyone must view the creation and maintenance of metadata as being of equal importance as any other DW/BI task.

Keep in mind that metadata can evolve into an overwhelming enterprise project that will suck all the energy and enthusiasm out of anyone who gets trapped in its clutches We described our approach as Pretty Good Practice. It requires about 10 percent of the effort involved in a major metadata initiative, but returns a much greater percentage of the value. Use the business value measuring stick to determine how far you need to go down the metadata path.

Deployment

The Great Unveiling

As you see in Figure 14.1, the deployment step in the Business Dimensional Lifecycle is where the three parallel development tracks come back together. This is the great unveiling of the DW/BI system to the business community. The quality of this first impression will strongly influence the acceptance of the system—and you get only one shot at it. Like any big event, there are a lot of details that must fall into place in order for the show to be successful.

Most systems professionals think of deployment as moving code from development to test to production. As far as it goes, they're correct: Deploying code and data to the production servers is a fundamental part of providing end-user access. But the system deployment is only about half of the deployment story. The deployment step in the Lifecycle includes all the pieces needed to give the business users access to the information, and much of this effort starts early in the Lifecycle. While you're creating the architecture and building the data warehouse and the BI applications, you must also be creating documentation, preparing training, and organizing the user support processes. All these operational services need to be in place before the curtain goes up for the first time.

This chapter is split into two parts: The first concentrates on the system deployment process and the second spotlights all the other critical but less technical activities needed to ensure a successful deployment.

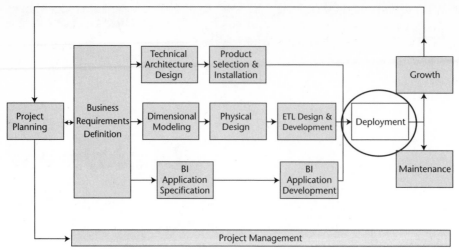

Figure 14.1   The Deployment step in the Business Development Lifecycle

After reading this chapter, you should be able to answer the following questions:

- What needs to be tested in the DW/BI system before deployment?

- How and where should you perform that testing?

- What's the easiest way to deploy the completely new DW/BI system, and how can you safely test and deploy changes to an existing system?

- Why is DW/BI documentation important, and what documentation does your team need to write?

- What kind of support and training will your users need?

System Deployment

Before you actually start deploying your system, you should perform extensive testing. Throughout the development process, you should have been conducting unit tests to confirm that components have been written properly. As we discuss in the next section, you need to perform extensive end-to-end testing, too.

The less time you spend on testing, the harder the deployment process will be. If you don't perform end-to-end testing before you deploy to production, you're guaranteed to find problems on production. If you don't rigorously check data quality, your business users will do it for you, and lose confidence in the DW/BI system at the same time. If you don't check performance and tune the system in advance, you'll have to do it while trying to avoid disrupting business users.

If you test, tune, and adjust the system before you begin deployment, the move to production will be fairly straightforward. This is especially true if this is a new system. Moving incremental changes into production while minimizing end-user impact can be a delicate dance.

Pre-Deployment Testing

To successfully deploy a new DW/BI system, or changes to an existing system, plan ahead and test repeatedly until you've verified:

- *System testing procedures:* Your system testing procedures are sufficiently rigorous that you can prove to users or auditors that the system has been thoroughly tested.
- *Operations process testing:* The databases load and process correctly.
- *Data quality assurance testing:* The data is accurate and complete, both for the historical load and for ongoing incremental loads.
- *Performance testing:* The system performs well both for loads and for queries and reports, with live data rather than a smaller development dataset.
- *Usability testing:* Business users can find what they need and accomplish necessary tasks.
- *Platform and edition testing:* The system runs correctly on the class of hardware and editions of software of the production system.
- *Deployment testing:* Deployment scripts are solid and have been rehearsed.

System Testing Procedures

Your DW/BI system is a software project, in addition to being an exercise in business politics. As part of the deployment process, test that the system works in whole and in part. The testing that we discuss in this section should be formalized to the greatest extent you and your organization can tolerate. The *exact* methodology you use to keep track of tests and results is much less important than having *some* methodology. If your organization already uses a testing methodology, you should be able to make that system work for your DW/BI system. If you don't already use a testing methodology, you should adopt or develop one for this project.

Even though your DW/BI system isn't shrink-wrapped software, it's a complex custom system that requires a professional approach to testing. Too often we see projects devote inadequate time and resources to testing.

Any testing methodology will contain at least four major steps: defining your tests, developing a primary test dataset, developing datasets to test unusual conditions, and running some tests and logging the results.

Define Tests

Make a list of the tests you plan to run, and what the expected outcome is. Figure 14.2 illustrates the kind of information that's useful to collect about each test and serves as a convenient example from which to discuss testing issues. We don't present these spreadsheets as a best practice, although there are worse approaches than using Excel—like the common one of not keeping track at all!

The first thing to notice in Figure 14.2 is that the individual tests are tiny. A test like "Does the ETL process run correctly from start to finish?" is too big to be tested. Keep breaking down tests until you have something simple that's easily verified.

The documentation for each test includes descriptions of how the test should be run and the results verified. Ideally, write scripts to run tests and check results. It's often as easy to automate a test as it is to document the steps you want a person to follow, and it's far easier to run the second or third (or twentieth) time. At the very least, stick the SQL or MDX used to verify a result into the spreadsheet so the tester can find it and copy/paste.

Develop a Primary Test Dataset

Develop a basic test dataset to simulate an incremental load. Later in the deployment process you'll test against live data, but early on it's important to have a known set of test data so you can easily check results. Follow this test dataset all the way through the process, from ETL to the relational and OLAP databases, and into the predefined reports. More than half of the system's tests are usually performed by one normal run through the basic test dataset.

You can include imperfect data in the primary test dataset, as long as your processes have been designed to identify and handle that data during normal operations. For example, perhaps you expect one fact table to have early-arriving facts and you've automated the process of creating a dummy dimension member to ensure referential integrity. Include test data for this normal (but imperfect) data condition within your primary test dataset. The test cases that we described earlier in this chapter should verify that this data is properly handled.

You'll run tests over and over, so automate the process of restoring the test databases to the pre-test state.

Task#	Short name	Description	Procedure	Test Script	Expected Outcome
1.00	**ETL Scheduling and Operations**				
1.01	Job kickoff	Launch the ETL job DWLoadMaster at a specific time	Set the start time in SQL Agent for DWLoadMaster to a specific time (15 min from now)		Log table JobLogs receives a row signalling job kickoff within 10s of launch datetime.
1.02	Peoplesoft dependency (negative)	Verify DWLoadMaster terminates if the Peoplesoft job hasn't finished yet.	Run DWLoadMaster using configuration file test Test01.dtsconfig.	Note: Can we create an auto-restart to try again 3 times before failure?	Log table JobLogs gets a CheckPrereq Failure row. Operator gets an email.
1.03	Peoplesoft dependency (positive)	DWLoadMaster continues if the Peoplesoft job has finished correctly.	Run DWLoadMaster using configuration file test Test02.dtsconfig.	Note: Automate	Log table JobLogs gets a row signalling we're moving past the CheckPrereq step
	etc.				
2.00	**Data Accuracy**				
2.01	Customer dim, incremental row count	Do all new customers from source system end up in the customer dim?	Run DWLoadMaster using configuration file test Test02.dtsconfig.	CheckCustCnt.sql	Result query from scrip counts rows from Ops and new rows from the customer dim. These numbers should be the same (511)
2.02	Customer dim, Type 2 counts	Do customer changes to Type 2 columns result in new row in customer dim?	same	CheckCustType2.sql	Query result set returns same rowcount (7)
	etc.				

Figure 14.2 Example test matrix information

USING INTEGRATION SERVICES CONFIGURATIONS

Integration Services configurations are a powerful tool for modifying the way a package behaves at runtime, without editing the package. This capability is very important for controlling package contents and quality: Once a package's quality has been assured, it should be locked down and not edited again. But some things about a package may have to change. This is particularly true of connectivity information, which almost always changes as you move a package from development to test to production.

You can pull out almost any characteristic of a task or connection into a configuration file. At the time the package is executed, Integration Services reads the configuration files, overwriting the default value of a parameter or variable with its value from the configuration file. You can have many configuration files, and even overwrite the same parameter multiple times. The last configuration file in order will "win."

We've been talking about configuration files, but they're not always files. Configurations are often stored in XML files, but you can also put the value of a parameter into an environment variable, registry entry, or a configuration table in SQL Server.

Some applications, especially those built as shrink-wrapped systems, will make extensive use of configurations. Even the simplest application will probably use them at least twice:

◆ To pass parameter values from a master package to its child packages

◆ To modify package connection information as packages move from development to test and production

The first step is to set up your package to use configurations. Edit the package in BI Studio, and choose Package Configurations from the SSIS menu. Add a new configuration; for now have it go to an XML configuration file.

The Package Configuration Wizard shows you all the Variables, Properties, Connection Managers, and Executables in your package in a tree structure. You can navigate down to select any property from those objects. Within Connection Managers, you might navigate to your target database connection, and choose to put the Server Name in the configuration file. If you're using Windows Integrated Security to execute your packages, and use the same database names on development, test, and production systems, this may be the only property you need to configure.

Note that the Executables whose properties you can configure include any Data Flow tasks in your package, but only at the task (container) level. There aren't any properties available for the steps (transforms) within a Data Flow task. As far as a configuration is concerned, a Data Flow task is a black box.

It's trivial to change the default value of a package variable in the configuration file. For now, just add a variable to the configuration.

As we mentioned, connection information and variable values are by far the most common properties to change in configurations. Another handy trick is to change the Disable property for a task. Perhaps you have a task that you want to run when the property is in test mode (like truncate the target table), but you don't want to run that task in production. Call the Disable property for that task into a configuration, and toggle its value as appropriate when you run the package. Remember, you're trying to avoid editing a tested package, which would be necessary if you simply wanted to delete that task before you rolled the package to production.

You then specify where the configuration file is to be saved. As soon as you exit the Package Configuration Wizard, you can bring up that file in your favorite XML editor (or Notepad). Try modifying one of the values you configured, save the file, and execute the package. The configurations are applied whether you execute the package from within the debug environment in BI Studio, from the command line, or launched as a SQL Agent job. Integration Services will get unhappy, raising errors and warnings, if you've specified a configuration file and it can't find it at runtime.

Develop Multiple Test Datasets

During Operations testing, as we discuss later in this chapter, you're checking that the control flow of the system operates as expected. It's as important to test with bad data as it is to test with good data, especially if you've defined data quality conditions that should cause processing to stop. Plan to create alternative datasets to test error conditions that affect the control flow.

Plan to run tests with at least three sets of data: normal static test data, one or potentially many control flow error datasets, and at least one live source. You could put the test data in whatever data management system suits your fancy, but we find it easiest to put each test dataset in its own SQL Server database on a test server. Name each database to reflect its contents, like RI_Violations. If your real-world ETL process combines data from many sources, you may still want to combine the test datasets into a single SQL Server database for the bulk of your testing. This is very easy to do if all your sources use OLE DB or .NET providers. If you use several types of sources, like flat files and relational sources, develop a system and naming conventions for bundling the different pieces of data that make up one test dataset.

Elsewhere in the testing process, as you get closer to deploying the system, you'll need to test with live data. For now, isolate the control flow error condition testing from the tests of connectivity and integration across multiple systems.

WARNING You absolutely don't want to continually edit Integration Services packages to point to these alternative sources—once a package is open for edit, you have no control over what's being changed. Instead, use the Integration Services configurations feature (see the related sidebar) to change the properties of the source connections. We walk through an example of using configurations in the related sidebar.

Run Tests and Log Results

When you're actually running tests you must keep track of which systems and data you used and what the test results were. There's nothing particularly unusual about this part of testing a DW/BI system. As with any other software and system testing, the important thing is to run the tests and log the results.

Figure 14.3 illustrates the absolute minimum information to collect about each test run. Undoubtedly the most important information is the status of the test and any specific comments about what the tester observed.

Historical Load Data Quality Testing

We've been discussing the system testing process. Now it's time to look at the kinds of tests you need to develop, and the issues to watch out for.

Many DW/BI projects begin by loading a relatively large volume of historical data into the system. You may have built a separate ETL process for loading historical data, different from the incremental processing. This is common if you need to go to heroic efforts to clean and integrate historic data. The historical load must be tested, but it often makes sense to test the data rather than the load process. In other words, perform quality assurance checks on the data before you start with incremental updates, and don't worry about testing the historical load process. It's a lot easier to verify the data than to verify the process. If you verify the starting point and the incremental procedures, and have reliable backup and recovery procedures, you may never run the historical load again. Data quality assurance testing is discussed later in this chapter.

The incremental data loading system, by contrast, requires extensive testing of all the processes, procedures, and control flow paths.

Operations Process Testing

During development, people have been working on one component of the system at a time. Even if your team is very small, you usually isolate subsystems during development. Experienced teams begin small-scale operations and end-to-end testing from the outset. As soon as two components are ready, check how they fit together. Every time you develop another piece of the puzzle, step back and make sure everything still works.

RunDate	5/16/2006				
Who	Tester's Name				
System	Dev (Apollo, Zeus, Minerva)				
Task#	Name	Config	Result	Comment	
1.01	Job kickoff	Test02.dtsconfig	1		
1.02	Peoplesoft dependency (negative)	Test02.dtsconfig	0	Job stopped correctly, but email not sent	
1.03	Peoplesoft dependency (positive)	Test03.dtsconfig	1		
	etc				

Figure 14.3   Example test run log

Now it's time to pull things together and confirm the entire system operates as designed. First, verify end-to-end operations using the primary set of static data that we described earlier in this chapter. The primary testing dataset should run from start (extracting from source systems) to finish (running and delivering reports) without triggering any errors that stop processing.

The operations process testing should verify that ETL jobs start when they should and run correctly under normal operation. Confirm that Analysis Services databases are processed as expected. Verify that standard reports are built on schedule, only after the underlying data has been correctly updated. Use team members' email addresses to confirm that report distribution via email works as expected.

Check all the branches in your incremental ETL processing. Perhaps your scheduling system kicks off the master package at 1:30 a.m., and the first thing the master package does is check to see if the ERP system has finished its nightly processing. Verify that the communication between the ERP and ETL systems works as expected. Does your package run to completion if it starts when the ERP system has finished its work? Does it do the right thing when the ERP process has failed or hasn't yet completed?

As we discuss in Chapter 6, your ETL system should check row counts and checksums. Ideally, you've built processes for handling unusual events, like an unbelievably low or high row count. Test these procedures, using alternative datasets and configurations.

While there are potentially dozens of infrastructure-related problems that surface during operations testing, you'll almost inevitably stumble over security issues. As we described in Chapter 12, system operations should use system accounts that are independent of any individual user ID. The system needs to continue running even if the ETL developer quits and her ID is cancelled.

Depending on your organization, it can take a long time just to get a system account set up, not to mention getting the necessary authorizations into the various source systems, servers, and other resources. In a large organization, you should plan on it taking a few weeks to iron this out (depending on whom you know).

Data Quality Assurance Testing

We can't overemphasize the importance of testing the quality of the data in your DW/BI system. The data needs to be checked very carefully before the system goes live. Develop subsystems and procedures for continuing to check data accuracy after deployment. Delivering bad data is much worse than delivering no data at all.

Data quality testing, at its heart, consists of running a query or report from the source system or systems, running the corresponding query or report from the DW/BI system, and comparing results. The magic comes in knowing the corresponding query or report. You may need significant business knowledge to match up the multiple systems. For this reason and for buy-in from the business community, you must include the business users in the data quality assurance process.

Make sure you can reproduce existing reports to the penny. Sometimes we find during DW/BI system development that existing reports have long been in error. This makes it harder to verify the new reports, but you absolutely must audit them and document any discrepancies. If you have an Internal Audit group, enlist their assistance in this process.

We've often been asked to recommend tools to help test data quality. We don't know of any tools that help with the hard part of testing: determining what data needs to be tested and how to do so. At the very least, the data quality testing reports should include row counts, grand totals and subtotals along major dimensions and hierarchies, and by time.

Your Analysis Services database may include some complex calculations and KPIs. These too are difficult to validate. You should have someone test the calculations externally—usually in Excel—to confirm that the MDX expressions are correct.

Report definitions sometimes include calculations as well. Check everything: in a budget variance report that displays budgets, actuals, and variance. Confirm that the variance is truly the difference between the other columns. Even in this trivial case you may see a penny difference due to rounding. Discuss that rounding with your business users and get a decision from them on how to handle it.

As with other kinds of tests, it's useful to automate data quality tests as much as possible. During testing and deployment, you'll typically run the data quality tests at least three times:

- *Test the historical load:* As we discussed earlier in this chapter, historical load testing is primarily a data quality assurance process.

- *Test the outcome of running the primary test dataset:* This static dataset is usually small, and is easiest to check thoroughly.

- *Test the real data:* Once you start running live data through your test system, you should test the validity of that data, as we describe in the next section.

Any automated data quality tests that you developed for the deployment phase should eventually be folded into the ETL process. Develop processes for logging the results of the ongoing data quality tests, and publish data quality reports to the business community.

Live Testing

Once you're confident that your historical data is accurate and the operational processes are clean, you can begin testing with real data. Before you begin live testing, back up the database after the historical load's data has been tested. Hope for smooth sailing, but plan for rough seas.

Set up the test system so that it points to the same operational sources that you'll use in production. You need to run the live testing for long enough to see real world patterns in the data and operational environment. Nightly loads need at least a week, perhaps several weeks, of exercising with live data before the system launches. If there's an operational cycle that may affect your system, like a monthly closing process, ensure your tests span a complete cycle. If you load data on a monthly cycle, it's not realistic to leave the data in live testing for very many load cycles. Two iterations is a lot better than one, if you can manage it.

There are several reasons to perform live testing:

- *System integration:* No matter how thorough and realistic your test datasets and test systems have been, you probably haven't been connecting to the production systems on a regular basis. All sorts of things can go wrong, beginning with the permissions on the test system's account and server.

- *Data quality testing:* Run your data quality tests against the data after incremental processing.

- *Performance testing:* Performance testing works best against a live load, at least as a final confirmation that performance tuning has been effective.

Performance Testing

The larger and more complex your system is, and the more users—especially ad hoc users—you have, the more important it is for you to conduct rigorous performance testing before you go into production. You want to launch your system with the best performance possible, and you certainly want to be confident that you can perform all processing within the necessary load windows.

You may have several goals for conducting performance tests. The most common are:

- *System tuning:* How can you tweak the system to deliver the best possible performance?

- *System sizing and configuration:* What hardware do you need?

- *Confirmation of service levels:* Will you meet your downtime and query performance requirements?

- *Headroom analysis:* How long will today's system and hardware meet your requirements, as the DW/BI system continues to grow?

As with everything else associated with systems, the performance testing process is best begun with some planning. Specify the goals from your testing process, and develop tests to address those goals.

Rather than thinking about performance testing as associated with each of the components of SQL Server (RDBMS, Analysis Services, and so on), we prefer a more integrated approach. Test processing performance (extract, transformation, load, cube incremental processing, and standard report generation) and query performance (ad hoc queries to Analysis Services and the relational database, on-demand reports to Reporting Services).

System Tuning

Before you run your first test, figure out how you'll evaluate the results of your tests. What will you measure? You need the obvious measure of timing, but if you want any hope of improving performance, you need a lot more information than that. In Chapter 15 we discuss the kinds of information that should be logged during system operation. These counters and event traces are invaluable to diagnose performance problems, both during the testing period and during operations.

Run a baseline test that measures system performance of your best guess of how the system is optimally configured. Imagine that you were going to go into production without doing any performance testing at all. (This thought exercise may strain your imagination, but give it a try.) This baseline test should measure the performance and operating characteristics of that best guess system.

Next, test one change at a time. Change an index. Test. Change a parameter. Test. If you change more than one thing at a time, you'll never know which change was helpful. Use a spreadsheet to track tests and results. If you're trying to wring the last ounce of performance from the system, you may need several iterations. Use the one-change-at-a-time technique to develop an improved optimal configuration. Try a second set of one-at-a-time changes against that new configuration until you're satisfied with the performance.

> **NOTE** We would apologize for providing you with such obvious guidance, except that we've hardly seen anyone conduct performance tests correctly.

It's vital to conduct system tuning performance tests on the nearly completed system as a whole. You can and should unit-test individual components of the system, like cube processing. But unless the production system will run each unit in isolation, this testing is far from conclusive. The biggest problems you'll encounter arise from competition for scarce resources—usually memory—across multiple units of the system.

System Sizing

It's really hard to figure out exactly what system to purchase, and even harder to figure out whether you're better off centralizing your system or distributing processing onto multiple servers. Hardware decisions are often made very early in the project, and hence are typically made for political reasons rather than for technical ones.

In Chapter 4 we provided some very broad guidance on system sizing. To get more specific advice than this, you'll need to turn to one of the following:

- Hardware vendors' sizing tools (if they exist)
- Published performance studies on similar systems (if they exist)
- A knowledgeable consultant who's familiar with both your system and a wide range of similar implementations (if you can find one)
- System sizing performance tests

You can and should request the hardware vendors to provide system sizing tools for your DW/BI system. We hope they'll have such tools, if not at the time of SQL Server 2005's launch, then soon after. But the sad truth is that DW/BI systems tend to be customized, variable, and nearly unique. No tool is going to do a great job of helping you size, much less determine whether you're better off centralizing or distributing. The only way to really figure it out is to perform testing with your system, data, data volumes, and usage patterns. It's seldom feasible to do this long before your initial launch. You'd have to complete the application, then test performance on several alternative hardware configurations, then order and install the chosen system, all before deploying the system in production. Most organizations use a much less exact method of choosing hardware for the initial deployment, then—if performance is poor and tuning doesn't fix it—perform a full-blown system sizing test.

TIP Buy hardware that's bigger than what you think you'll need. Buy expandable systems, especially systems that can hold more memory than you're initially purchasing. 64-bit is very appealing, even if you don't think you need all that memory at the outset. But if you buy a system that lets you upgrade to 8 or 16GB of memory, or more, it'll be much easier for you to adjust to a system that's used more heavily than you initially predicted.

Service Level Confirmation

Increasingly, DW/BI teams are entering into Service Level Agreements with the user community. These agreements cover data latency, user downtime, and often user query performance.

If you have such an agreement in place, then you surely must test that your system is likely to conform to the agreement. This is often a first step that leads to more extensive performance testing for tuning work, or even alternative system sizing and configuration efforts. But if you've cleverly made an agreement with pretty low minimum standards, you may simply need to confirm you're above those standards.

TIP   Service Level Agreements (SLAs) are a valuable tool for focusing management attention on important issues. But don't let your SLA drive you to deliver mediocrity by striving only to meet the stated requirements. Under-promise and over-deliver. Never promise more than your clients are requesting, but always try to deliver more than they've imagined possible.

Be very careful in negotiating Service Level Agreements that include metrics for ad hoc query performance. Don't let yourself agree to an absolute ceiling for ad hoc query times, like all queries complete in 10 seconds. You'd be much better off agreeing that 90 percent of queries would complete in 5 seconds. In a system of any size and complexity, it's always possible to write an ad hoc query that exceeds any reasonable maximum.

Clearly specify in the SLA what you mean by important terms, like query completion. Does this mean on the server side, or does it also include the transport (over a potentially low bandwidth WAN) to the client? The SLA is, basically, a contract between you and your users. You probably don't need to include Legal on this contract, but you should take it seriously. Your management will take it seriously if you don't maintain service levels.

Processing Performance: Getting Data In

Performance testing for the data processing side of the problem is fairly straightforward. The live testing that we described earlier in this chapter is the basis for the processing performance tests.

The simplest approach to building a processing system is to serialize the major components. All ETL work to the RDBMS finishes before you begin cube processing, and that completes before you start generating reports. Such a serialized system is easy to performance test and diagnose, because the units of work are isolated. You can test and tune each unit separately. Unless your load window is very small or your latency requirements approach real time, you'll probably start off with serialized processing.

You may be able to design your processing system so that work is parallelized. You need to process shared dimensions first, but you should be able to start the work on one fact table while a second fact table is still loading. You can make significant improvements in the overall loading time by parallelizing some activities, but this is a much harder system to design and tune. Your performance tests must run on the integrated processing system. All parts of the DW/BI system compete for resources. You can't test each component separately and sum their processing times. This is true even if the different components are distributed across multiple servers because there's always some burden placed on the upstream servers.

Another issue to consider is confirming that changes made to improve the performance of one part of the system don't negatively impact another part of the system. The classic problem is index and aggregation design. You may want lots of indexes and aggregations for queries to run quickly. But these structures must be maintained, which can place an intolerable burden on the processing performance. Every time a change is considered, evaluate the effects on a complete test system before deploying to production.

Query Performance: Getting Data Out

Testing query performance, especially ad hoc query performance, is a much harder problem than testing processing performance. The fundamental problem is that you don't know what your users are going to want to do. You can ask them and get some ideas, but those ideas are going to bear, at best, only a resemblance to reality.

Standard reports are either pre-run and cached, or run on-demand. Typically pre-run reports are executed at the end of the ETL processing, and we consider the work more like a processing workload than a query and reporting workload. You can set up Reporting Services to email the results of a pre-run report to the users; doing so shifts the entire burden of report generation to a scheduled time. Alternatively, users might access the pre-run report from the BI portal, in which case there's a modest on-demand element associated with displaying the report. A solid performance test of pre-run standard reports uses estimated usage patterns for accessing the pre-run reports. For example, 500 people will access the report at random times between 8 a.m. and 9:30 a.m. The relational database where the Reporting Services catalog is stored, the Reporting Services engine, and the web servers are all involved with serving pre-stored reports.

A standard report that's executed on-demand involves more work. The first demand is on the database upon which the report is defined, to serve up the basic data for the report. Then, Reporting Services works on that result set to render the report. Finally, the report is distributed, usually across the web to the user's browser window. On-demand reports are often used for parameterized reports, for infrequently accessed reports that don't warrant pre-executing and storing the results, and for reports with low latency. A good performance test for on-demand reports includes a realistic estimate of who is running the reports, when, and with what parameters. Reports can be cached in memory, which is great for performance. In the absence of real world data about how users are running reports, it's very difficult to accurately estimate the use of the report cache.

Finally, laboratory tests of the performance of ad hoc queries is fiendishly difficult. The first problem is to know what users are going to want to do. You know your predefined reports and other BI applications, but ad hoc is, well, ad hoc. You have to return to your business requirements document to extract information about analyses. Watch (by collecting query text) what the early business users and testers are doing with the system. Of course, if you're testing a system that's already in production, you should collect a broad range of queries from the system logs that we discuss in Chapter 15.

One of the biggest challenges in performance testing ad hoc query loads is how to capture the typical analytic experience. The business user issues a query—either an ad hoc query or a standard report—and then explores around that data by drilling up, drilling down, and launching new related lines of inquiry. The user will look at a screen of information for a while before deciding where next to go. A good ad hoc query performance and scalability test will consist of sets of related queries separated by user think times.

Analysis Services, Reporting Services, and the database engine all have caches from which similar queries can be served. These caches are valuable because they greatly improve performance for the common behavior we just discussed: a chain of queries on a related topic. It's really difficult to design query performance and scale tests that take appropriate advantage of such a cache, without going too far and unrealistically assuming all queries will be resolved from cache.

We have not seen a query-testing tool on the market that adequately addresses this pattern of behavior. This is the main reason you see very few published performance and scalability studies for Analysis Services. To do it well, the authors of a study would need to develop a testing tool. We don't know of anyone who's gone to the considerable trouble of packaging such a home-built tool for you to conduct performance tests at your site.

REFERENCE Check the web site for the internal Microsoft project Project Real, at www.microsoft.com/sql/bi/ProjectReal. It's possible they'll have information, or even a tool, to assist in performance testing. At the time of this writing, no such tool is available.

SQL Server Standard Edition Testing

Your DW/BI team will probably use SQL Server Developer Edition during development. Developer Edition contains all the functionality of Enterprise Edition, which means it has more functionality than is available in Standard Edition.

If you're using Enterprise Edition in production, you may put Developer Edition on your test system (assuming the test system is devoted to testing and isn't used for any production purposes). But if you're using Standard Edition in production, you need to develop a plan to test that the system developed using Developer Edition will actually work on Standard Edition. By far the best way to do this is to run an end-to-end test on a test system with Standard Edition installed.

SQL Server 2005 doesn't throttle Standard Edition's performance. Instead, the difference between Standard and Enterprise Editions is based on features. Thus, you could probably get away with a stand-alone test of Standard Edition functionality on a small test system. A different test system, used for scale and performance testing, may use the much less expensive Developer Edition.

Of all the DW/BI services in SQL Server, Analysis Services has the most features excluded from Standard Edition. The most important differentiating feature is Analysis Services partitioning. You can't define a partitioning strategy for Analysis Services measure groups in Standard Edition. Perspectives are also excluded from Standard Edition.

REFERENCE For a complete list of the SQL Server features that are excluded from Standard Edition, see the Books Online topic "Features Supported by the Editions of SQL Server 2005."

As we describe in Chapter 7, Analysis Services does provide assistance to you during the development cycle, to prevent you from using features that aren't supported in Standard Edition. A wise person would still test.

64-bit Platform Testing

If, as we often recommend, your production hardware is 64-bit, you need to test with 64-bit hardware as well. Serious performance testing must be conducted on 64-bit hardware, as the runtime characteristics between 32-bit and 64-bit platforms will vary widely. But failing that, you do at least need to perform functional testing on a 64-bit box.

So much is the same between the 32-bit and 64-bit platforms that you may be tempted to skip this functional test. Unwise! A particular element to watch out for is an Integration Services Script task, which can be precompiled. A task that was precompiled on Win32 is not going to work on Win64.

Usability Testing

Unless you've developed custom user-oriented software as part of your DW/BI solution, usability testing will not be a huge burden. In large part this is because, with shrink-wrapped front-end tools, there are relatively few things you can change. You can typically change the names of things (columns, tables, and reports), and the way they are organized.

Nonetheless, perform some usability testing with actual business users. As with all usability tests, you need to find fresh minds: people who have not been intimately associated with the project. Walk a few people through the BI portal and the reports, and see what trips them up.

Later in this chapter we discuss user training. If you have a large user community, you may conduct a dry run of the training with a friendly audience. Plan to gather feedback from the users not only about the class itself, but also about the usability of the system. Although this usability feedback is coming late in the process, there's enough time to change the names and organization of the report folders.

Earlier in the system development process, when you start working on the Analysis Services database and defining reports, you should show a draft of the object names to business users. Rely on them to tell you what objects should be called in the interfaces they see. You tried to get object names correct when you were designing the relational database. But often business users change their minds about names when the system gets closer to reality. We let business user names diverge from the physical names, if it helps the business users understand the system. Because there's always at least one layer between the physical relational database and the business user—be it relational views, Analysis Services cubes, Reporting Services Report Models, or all of these layers—you can change names that business users see without messing up your ETL system development. But you do need to get the names right for Analysis Services and the reporting metadata layers.

TIP Another issue to think about early on is the hierarchies within dimensions. Dimension hierarchies often become dropdown lists for ad hoc queries and parameterized reports. During the database design sessions you should think about the user experience associated with large, flat hierarchies. What will the user experience be if they are trying to navigate a dropdown list and you populate a list with 100,000 items? This is a common problem, and not one that's easily fixed at the last minute, just before rollout.

Before your new system goes live, you must have implemented security at the user, role, report, and database levels, as we described in Chapter 12. If users don't have the correct security permissions, the system is—from their point of view—completely unusable.

Deployment

Your deployment process will depend on the system architecture you set up for your DW/BI. In Chapter 4, we described typical small, medium, and large configurations. Each of these will follow the same general deployment process, but will have different specific steps.

If you're implementing a new system, on new hardware, your deployment procedures can be somewhat casual. It's common to use the production system for testing and even user training, before the new system goes live. You can think of the deployment process in this simple case as via email—send a message when the system has passed all tests and is ready to go live.

After that first free deployment, it gets a lot harder. Any modifications to the system—and there are always modifications—should be accomplished with minimal disruption to the business user community. The only way to do this is to:

- Perform testing on a test system that's as identical to the production system as possible.

- Use scripts rather than clicking through a user interface. Any time you need to open a tool and especially to click through a wizard, you open the possibility of doing the wrong thing.

- Develop a deployment process playbook that describes exactly what to do and in what order. This is especially vital if you can't run a script but instead must do something within a tool.

- Test the playbook on the test system before trying it on production.

Relational Database Deployment

There are several ways to deploy a relational database from test to production. The easiest, of course, is to declare the test system to be production (email deployment). But assuming a more realistic world, SQL Server still provides you with several tools for deployment.

If you want to deploy the entire database, for example for a brand new system, you could use backup and restore. You'd need to modify the restore script to move the data files to the correct location on the production server, if your test server is configured differently.

It's more common to script the creation or modification of the target database. The easiest way to do this is to let SQL Server generate the script for you. In Management Studio's Object Explorer window, right-click on an object like a database or table and choose Script (object type) as CREATE. This menu option scripts only the specific object you've chosen. You'll probably need to script several objects.

After you generate the CREATE scripts, you may need to modify the location of data files. Ideally, your test system is configured like your production system, so running the scripts on the test system is an excellent test. If the systems are configured differently, test the scripts as much as possible, and document what is different and what to verify during the production run. Check the scripts into source control.

If you're modifying an existing relational data warehouse by adding a new dimensional model, the process is much the same. Generate CREATE scripts for the new tables and associated objects like indexes and views. If these are truly additions, the impact of creating new empty objects in the production system should be zero (but test it first!).

Over time, you'll surely modify existing tables somewhat. This is a trickier proposition, because if you ALTER a table you run a risk of breaking the existing ETL processes. Certainly you can address this risk by thorough testing.

> **TIP** Recall from Chapter 4 that we recommended you always build a layer of views to abstract access to the relational tables. This view layer can provide valuable flexibility for modifying the production system in steps, keeping the old table and view around until you're confident that you can safely switch over to the new structure.

You may want to bring data from the test system to production, without taking the draconian step of using a full database restore. In this case, you can build simple Integration Services packages—or use Bulk Insert—to copy the data from test to production for the subset of tables.

> **TIP** The Deployment Playbook for deploying a new relational database, or modifications to an existing database, should include the following:
>
> - Any edits to make to SQL scripts (like editing file locations or database names). It's far safer to parameterize these changes, but writing the scripts is a lot more complicated if you do so.
>
> - Any static data in the new database. This data may include configuration data, like a table containing metadata, Integration Services configurations, or global variables. And don't forget to populate any new static dimensions.
>
> - Some mechanism for verifying that the edits were done correctly if edits are made directly in scripts. At the very least, advise the operator to search for specific phrases that should have been changed during the editing process.
>
> - The run command for any scripts, like SQL scripts, including any parameters used in the script execution.

- Integration Services packages to run, which will load data into some or all tables.

- A script or instructions to verify that all completed correctly. There are third-party metadata "differencing" tools that can compare structures between two databases. If you can't get access to such a tool, at the very least you can generate CREATE scripts for the two systems, and use windiff to compare them.

Integration Services Package Deployment

The process of deploying a package from development to test to production is straightforward. The hard part is testing that the package works correctly in its new destination, and there's no magical tool to help with testing.

There are tools to help with package deployment. The first tool is Integration Services configurations, which we discussed earlier in this chapter. Configurations let you change at run-time the characteristics of an Integration Services package, like the connection string to sources, the location of file folders, a parameter or variable value. Changing values at run-time is valuable because it lets you modify the way a package executes without opening and editing the package.

The second feature of Integration Services that simplifies deployment is the aptly named Deployment Utility. The Deployment Utility bundles into a deployment folder all the components associated with a set of packages, including any configuration files, code libraries, or other files that you included in your project. You can copy the deployment folder from one server to another, and then launch the Package Installation Wizard to install the packages.

TIP During the development process, you probably discovered that in most cases you don't need the Deployment Utility and Package Installation Wizard. You can easily copy Integration Services package and configuration files, and they work just fine on the new server. But why rely on a person to remember and document which files to move? The utility and wizard do the right thing for you, reducing the risk of error.

Launch the Deployment Utility from within BI Studio. Open the project that contains the packages you want to deploy. On the Deployment Utility page of the Properties pane, set AllowConfigurationChanges and CreateDeployment Utility to True. Then build the deployment folder by right-clicking the project in Solution Explorer and choosing Build.

During the Build process, BI Studio effectively compiles your DTS packages. It performs error checking and spits out errors and warnings for any problems it sees, like potential data type conversion errors. By default, the deployment folder is created in the bin folder of the solution. If your solution is in c:\ SQLProjects\MDWT Test Project SSIS, then you'd find the build deployment folder along that path in bin\Deployment.

After you copy the deployment folder to the target machine, launch the Package Installation Wizard by double-clicking on the DtsDeploymentManifest .xml file within the deployment folder. You can choose whether to deploy the packages to the file system or the SQL Server relational database.

Some organizations are deeply opposed to using a wizard for deploying to production. Scripts can be fully tested and automated in advance. If you use a wizard like the Package Installation Wizard, you run the risk of someone clicking the wrong box or making a typo during the deployment process. If your organization is adamant about not using wizards, you can write a batch script that calls dtexec. Dtexec is a command line utility, fully documented in Books Online, that will copy, delete, encrypt, or deploy a package into SQL Server or a file folder. If your deployment folder includes multiple packages, you'd need to call dtsexec multiple times to install them one by one. And if your deployment folder contains configuration or other files, your script would also need to move them to the appropriate places.

> **TIP** The Deployment Playbook for deploying a package should include the following:
>
> - **The location of the deployment folder to be copied to the production server.**
> - **Where to copy the deployment folder to.**
> - **Instructions for running the Package Installation Wizard, including all choices to make in the dialog boxes. Alternatively, the command script to run that calls dtexec to install the packages, and which copies other necessary files to the appropriate destinations. Don't forget the configuration files and code libraries.**
> - **Instructions for creating any Windows global variables that the package uses.**
> - **A script or instructions to verify that all completed correctly.**

Analysis Services Database Deployment

As with the other software components of the Microsoft DW/BI solution, there are several ways to deploy a new Analysis Services database, or modifications to an existing database. The best methods for deploying from test to production are to use the Deployment Wizard or the Synchronize Database Wizard. Less appealing is to generate a CREATE database script from Management Studio, just as you would with deploying a relational database. You may think you could simply copy data and metadata files from one system to another, but this final approach is not as simple as it sounds, and is decidedly not recommended.

> **NOTE** Deploying an Analysis Services database into production is very different—and much improved—in Analysis Services 2005.

By the time you're working on plans for deploying the Analysis Services database to production, you've built and deployed it many times, as we describe in Chapter 7. During the development process, you deploy the database onto a development server, and typically process a subset of data. You've been working with the database as a project in BI Studio.

When you deploy the database from development to test, you should use the Deployment Wizard. Make sure you've built, processed, and unit-tested the development database. The basic scripts for deploying to test exist and are ready for you in the project's bin folder. If your project is in c:\SQLProjects\MDWT test Project SSAS, you'd find the deployment scripts along that path in the bin subfolder.

There are four deployment script files in the bin folder. All are in XML format:

- *<ProjectName>.asdatabase:* Contains the main script for all the database objects including dimensions, measure groups, partitions, and so on. Some of the settings in this script are overwritten by the other deployment files. You can launch the Deployment Wizard by double-clicking on this file.

- *<ProjectName>.deploymenttargets:* Contains the target server and database names. By default, these are set from the Deployment page of the Analysis Services project properties in BI Studio at the time the project was built. But you can change these properties at the time you run the Deployment Wizard to actually deploy the database.

- *<ProjectName>.configsettings:* Contains settings about the target environment, like data source connection information and object storage locations. The settings in this file will override the corresponding settings in the asdatabase file.

- *<ProjectName>.deploymentoptions:* Contains settings about the deployment itself, including whether and how to process the database after deployment, and whether to replace any existing partitions.

There are several ways to change the settings in these files. The Deployment Wizard contains a user interface for changing the settings. Alternatively, you can edit the deploymenttargets, configsettings, and deploymentoptions files using any text editor. We recommend that you use the Deployment Wizard UI for the first deployment, from development to test. Later, when you're developing the Playbook for deployment from test to production, edit only the deploymenttargets file directly. The other settings should be fixed and tested so that, for the final deployment, the only thing you're changing is the server name. You shouldn't edit the asdatabase file directly. Any changes should be made in BI Studio, or within the other three deployment files.

In addition to launching the Deployment Wizard by double-clicking on the asdatabase file, you can navigate to the wizard from the Windows Start menu, or from the command line.

REFERENCE See the Books Online topic "Running the Analysis Services Deployment Wizard" for information, including command line options.

If the target database exists already, the Deployment Wizard, by default, will deploy only incremental changes. Over time, you'll modify the structure of your Analysis Services database, adding new calculations and so on. As with the initial database design process, use BI Studio on a development server, deploy the modifications to the test system, develop and test the deployment script, and then deploy changes to production. It would be foolish to skip the testing steps even for relatively minor incremental changes.

The Deployment Wizard deploys a database project from BI Studio onto a database server. It builds the empty database structure. New measure groups and partitions must be populated by processing the partitions. What if you want to copy all or part of a database from one server to another? You could restore from backup, but a better approach is to use the Synchronize Database Wizard, which copies both metadata and data.

The Synchronize Database Wizard can also increase the availability and scalability of your Analysis Services database. One option is to perform all processing on a staging server, and then synchronize the data to the production server. Analysis Services keeps the old database active until all the data is synchronized, at which time users are switched over to the new structure and the old data dropped. As with the Deployment Wizard, Synchronization is smart enough to work on only changed objects. You can choose to exclude security roles from the synchronization. Synchronization is a useful approach if you find cube processing is interfering with query performance, because synchronizing is often less costly to the target server than processing is. Synchronization is also useful for an Analysis Services clustered implementation, as the clustered copies of the database must, obviously, be kept in synch.

BE EXTRA CAREFUL WITH ANALYSIS SERVICES DEPLOYMENTS

You need to be really careful about deploying changes to the Analysis Services database, to make sure you don't inadvertently wipe out important characteristics of your production database. Imagine the following scenario:

◆ You have an Analysis Services database in production.

◆ You've added security roles to that database.

◆ Your ETL system automatically adds new partitions every month.

◆ Now it's time to add a new calculated measure or set.

Because you're being careful, you'll create a new development project by reading the metadata of the production database. This puts your development environment perfectly in synch with production. You develop the new calculated measure.

Maybe you wouldn't mind reprocessing the entire cube, so you figure you'll just build, deploy, and process the cube from development into production (because you've ignored our advice about always testing first!). What happens if someone defined a new role, modified membership in a role, or if a new partition came online in the time span between starting your development project and deploying it? The two systems were in synch at the starting point, but no longer.

Please don't do this. The safest way is to script changes, and very carefully test on your test server, as we recommend.

You can launch the Synchronize Database Wizard from within Management Studio, by right-clicking on a database in the Object Explorer pane and choosing Synchronize. You can execute the synchronization immediately or, more professionally, save the script for execution later.

NOTE The Deployment Wizard deploys an Analysis Services project's metadata, and typically launches data processing from the relational data warehouse. The Synchronize Database Wizard copies a database, including data, from one server to another. A common technique will be to deploy a database from development to test, conduct the appropriate tests, and then synchronize the database from test to production.

REFERENCE For a complete description of the Synchronize Database Wizard, including how to save the resulting script to a file or execute it immediately, see the set of Books Online topics that begin with "Synchronize Database Wizard F1 Help (SSAS)."

An alternative method of deploying a database to production is to generate a CREATE script in Management Studio. This is the same method as we recommend for the relational database. Click on the Analysis Services database in the Object Explorer pane, right-click, and choose to generate the script. This method generates an XML script to create the database, but can't be used to create a piece of the database like a dimension, measure group, or role. This script generation isn't as flexible as the wizards we've already discussed in this chapter, so we recommend you use it primarily to generate documentation.

Reporting Services Report Deployment

Deploying a new report is generally a lot easier and less exciting than deploying or changing a database or package. When you launch a new DW/BI system or add a business process dimensional model, you will probably begin the development of the initial suite of reports on a test server, ideally against a complete set of data. As soon as the production server is populated, migrate any existing reports, and continue report development on the production server. If you use shared data sources for Reporting Services reports, it's a simple task to point the reports to the production databases.

You will modify and create reports far more often than you'll modify the underlying databases. All reports should be tested before they're released to the user community. The most important tests are to ensure the report definitions are accurate. Complex reports that access a lot of data, especially if the reports are run by a lot of people, should be tested for performance. You may find that you need to write a stored procedure to generate the report's dataset as efficiently as possible.

REPORT DEPLOYMENT PROCESS

Complete the following steps to safely deploy a new or changed report on the production system:

◆ Identify the business users who will test and verify the new or changed report.

◆ Create a Reporting Services role ReportTest that includes the DW/BI team and the business users who'll test the report. You may need several report testing roles, if there are a lot of report development projects going on at once.

◆ Set up a TestFolder folder structure in the BI portal that's accessible only to the ReportTest role.

◆ Develop the new report in BI Studio, and deploy it to TestFolder.

◆ Notify the testers that the report's available, and when you expect to hear back from them about it. Your organization may have formal user acceptance procedures for you to rely on here.

◆ When the relevant people have signed off on the report, re-deploy it to its appropriate place in the BI portal, with the appropriate security.

Most companies will develop and test new reports in a private area of the production report server, rather than set up a completely separate test instance of Reporting Services. Standard reports don't change data, so you don't need to worry about damaging the databases. All you need is to insulate most users from the test area, which is easy to do with the Reporting Services security settings discussed in Chapter 12.

WARNING If you develop new reports on the production server, you need to be careful about inexperienced report writers running expensive queries, like joining two fact tables. All right, this warning isn't limited to the inexperienced. Experts can do stupid things, too.

As you may expect, the hardest part of deploying reports isn't technical but political. The greatest challenge is to create policies and procedures that enable your business community to contribute new reports and analyses, while maintaining the appropriate level of control over published reports. You should develop a quality assurance process, and procedures for publishing reports to a broad audience. This is particularly important for highly regulated companies.

NOTE Sometimes, changes to the underlying databases will require that existing reports be modified. Earlier in this chapter we stressed the importance of end-to-end testing for any significant modifications to the DW/BI system. It's really important that the standard report suite be tested before database changes are moved into production. It's usually easy to fix up reports in response to a schema change, but if you forget this step the user experience is the same as if you messed up the underlying data. From their point of view, the DW/BI system is broken. Also, any change that breaks a standard report will likely break user reports as well. If you're implementing these kinds of changes, notify your users early on and discuss what they'll need to do to deal with the changes. You may want to set up a user report migration project to help rewrite some of the key user reports.

Data Warehouse and BI Documentation

We all seem to skimp on documentation in the run up to system deployment. It seems as though the business should be able to use the system without a ton of documentation. After all, we spent a lot of time and trouble organizing and naming things in a sensible way. The bad news here is that the team needs to do a lot of documentation of the system in order to offer a complete solution to the users.

The good news is most of the documentation is really metadata dressed up in presentable clothes. If you've been capturing metadata all along, much of the job now is to create a nice front end for users to access that metadata. If you've been ignoring the metadata issue, you've got a lot of work ahead of you.

As we detail in Chapters 8 and 9, the BI portal is the organization's single source for reporting and analysis and associated information. The main content of the BI portal will be the navigation hierarchy and the standard reports contained therein. Around the edges of the main BI portal page, users should find links to all the documentation and tools described here.

Core Descriptions

The first things to document are the data: the business process subject areas including facts and dimensions, and the tables, columns, calculations, and other rules that make up those subject areas. Standard reports and other BI applications should also be documented, though their documentation is often integrated with the reports themselves.

Business Process Dimensional Model Descriptions

The starting point for most BI documentation is the business process dimensional model. The DW/BI team must write a clear, succinct description of each dimensional model in the warehouse. This document will be the starting point for anyone who wants to understand what's in the DW/BI system. If Orders was the initial row selected on the bus matrix, write a document that describes the Orders dimensional model. This document answers such questions as:

- What's the nature of the business process captured in this data?
- What are the salient business rules?
- What's the grain of the fact table?
- What date range is included in the fact table?
- What data has been left out (and why)?
- What dimensions participate in this business process? Many of the dimensions will need their own descriptive documents that this document can link to.

This document should have a few screen captures that show the target dimensional model in a graphical form (like a data model), some example values, and a few reports to demonstrate the kinds of business questions it can address.

Table and Column Descriptions

Once people have a general understanding of a particular schema, they need to be able to drill down into the details, table by table and column by column. This is where the descriptive metadata you captured when you were building the initial target model comes back into service. Figure 13.10 illustrates this descriptive metadata. The table name, column names, descriptions, comments, and sample values would all be helpful to a user trying to understand the contents of the table in question. Chapter 13 describes a simple data model for pulling this descriptive metadata together in a form that can be the basis for a set of user reports.

If you're using a third-party front-end tool, you'll need to integrate your descriptive metadata into the tool's metadata layer. This typically involves using the tool's administrative client to map the table and column descriptions into the tool's metadata structures. In order to take full advantage of the tool's metadata, plan to create additional entries that define the business process dimensional model, role-playing tables, join paths, and perhaps even calculated fields.

Report Descriptions

Each report must have a base set of descriptive information as part of the standard template described in Chapter 8. Some of this information, like the report title and description, can be written out to the Reporting Services metadata structures when the reports are built or updated. Other information will need to be captured in the metadata repository described in Chapter 13. In particular, the navigation framework described in Chapter 9, and the assignment of individual reports to categories and groups, help people understand what information is available. These category assignments should follow the same organizing framework used to present the reports in the BI portal. In fact, this metadata could be used to dynamically create the portal interface.

Additional Documentation

Data and report documentation are certainly the most commonly used, but other documentation is also important. The most valuable additional documentation comes in the form of online tutorials, support guides, and a list of colleagues who use the system and may be able to help.

As we discuss later in this chapter, you should develop and deliver training to the business users. This training should be mandatory for business users who'll be creating ad hoc queries, but it's useful for everyone. Realistically, not all users will come to a class. Even if you do have 100 percent attendance, users can benefit from online tutorials and class materials. These may be as simple as an annotated version of the classroom materials made available on the web site. Some of the front end tool vendors offer specialized software to develop and deliver online training materials. These systems guide people through the materials, include integrated exercises and self-tests. They also allow you to track who has taken what training, how far they got, and how well they did. While this is more work, it may be worth it in a large, distributed organization.

A support guide will help your business users know whom to call when they have a problem. You should list the escalation hierarchy with contact names, emails, and phone numbers. You may get significant leverage out of publishing a list of frequently asked questions and answers. We discuss user support issues later in this chapter.

Knowing who else is trained can guide users to people close by who may be able to help them. Keep a current list of users available on the BI portal, with an indicator showing which users are designated analytic support people and which users have at least had ad hoc tool training. Include a simple report showing query activity by user in the last month or so, sorted from most to least active.

Additional Functions

The documentation described previously is critical for users to learn about the DW/BI system. Beyond the documentation itself, there are a few tools that make the documentation much more accessible to the users. Primarily, these are a metadata browser, a search function, and warehouse activity monitoring.

- *Metadata browser:* The metadata browser is the reporting and navigation front end for the metadata repository. Microsoft has created standard reports to display and navigate the metadata from several of their main tools, including Integration Services and Reporting Services. Installing these and making them available to your users through a single navigation page is a strong first step in metadata browsing. However, this does not include the basic metadata that describes the contents of the DW/BI system: the business process dimensional models that people will see in the query tools. Create a few Reporting Services reports that allow users to browse this metadata as well. As we describe in Chapter 13, the metadata schema is easy to navigate and can be accessed with a few simple reports.

- *Search function:* The ability to search the contents of the warehouse, and especially the report descriptions, is mandatory in today's "Find" function search-driven world. This presents a bit of a challenge for us architecturally because some of the information users want to search is on the DW/BI web site, some of it is in database tables, and some might even be in XML documents scattered about the system.

- *Warehouse activity monitors:* Power users and the DW/BI team always want to know what's going on in the DW/BI system right now. You might hear this question in slightly different forms, like "Who's on the system?" or "Why is the report so slow?" It's fairly easy to develop a few reports that execute against the SQL Server system tables or Analysis Services database. You can even set up these reports to drill down into the individual user sessions and examine the underlying query. We've been surprised at how well some of our stronger users have been able to understand the issue of query workload by using these reports. Often, they take matters into their own hands when resources are constrained and call the offending user directly. We discuss activity monitoring in greater detail in Chapter 15.

User Training

Back in Chapter 9 we described how one of the main purposes of the BI applications is to provide information for the 90 percent of the organization who'll never learn to access the data directly. Unfortunately, the remaining 10 percent will never learn either, unless you teach them. Offer classes that will help ad hoc users climb the learning curve to master both the ad hoc tool and the underlying data. While you're at it, even though the BI applications should be self-guiding, offer a short class to all folks who will be using the BI applications, even if they never touch the ad hoc tool.

Teaching the advanced users how to directly access the system breaks down into two phases: development and delivery. Development is all of the work it takes to design the curriculum and create the training materials. Delivery is the actual stand-up classroom presentation of the materials and exercises, and the web-based delivery of the materials.

Training Development

It's hard to know when to start developing end user training. You need to start after the database is stable and the front-end ad hoc tool has been selected, but long enough before the actual rollout begins to be able to create and test a solid set of course materials. Development breaks down into two primary tasks: design and development of the course materials. Beyond these, the DW/BI educator might also need to create supporting materials and a training database.

INTRODUCTORY ONE-DAY AD HOC QUERY COURSE OUTLINE

- ◆ **Introduction (gain attention) [30min]**
  - ■ **DW/BI system overview (goals, data, status, and players)**
  - ■ **Goals of the class**
  - ■ **Student expectations for the class**
- ◆ **Tool Overview (Demo) [15]**
  - ■ **Basic elements and user interface**
  - ■ **The query building process**
- ◆ **Exercise 1—Simple query [45]**
- ◆ **Break [15]**
- ◆ **Querying Orders from the Orders Fact table (Demo) [15]**
- ◆ **Exercise 2—Simple multi-table query [45]**
- ◆ **Review and questions [15]**
- ◆ **Lunch [60]**
- ◆ **Working with query templates (Demo) [15]**
- ◆ **Exercise 3—Sales over time [60]**
- ◆ **Exercise 3 review (Demo) [15]**
- ◆ **Break [15]**
- ◆ **Saving, scheduling and sharing reports (Demo) [15]**
- ◆ **Exercise 4—Saving and scheduling reports [30]**
- ◆ **Overall review and next steps [15]**
- ◆ **Exercise 5—Self-paced problem set [75]**

Design and Approach

Before you actually sit down to write the training materials, you need to spend a few minutes thinking at a high level about who your audiences are, what skill levels they have, and how much they'll be using the tools. This will help you determine your overall curriculum. What classes will you offer and how will they relate to each other? The initial rollout of the DW/BI system usually requires two classes: an introductory ad hoc query class that could be one or two days long, and a short BI applications class that may last an hour. After the system has been in use for a few months, you may add an advanced techniques class for ad hoc users. It may also be useful to provide a separate, data-centric class for each new business process dimensional model added to the DW/BI system.

Part of the design process includes outlining each class. The sidebar titled "Introductory One-Day Ad Hoc Query Course Outline" shows a typical outline. The outline will evolve during development, testing, and delivery of the class based on the reality of what it takes to teach people, and how long it takes them to learn.

The outline should include notes about supporting items that will be needed, like:

- Course prerequisites
- Data needed
- Data availability
- Training facilities (desktops, projector, network access, software installed, and so on)
- User IDs
- Printing of materials
- Instructor evaluations

Developing Training Materials

Creating the course materials for hands-on training requires a good sense for computer-based education. Many of the classic communications principles apply. Each module should be short enough to finish within the average adult attention span of 45 minutes to an hour. Each module should follow the same structure, beginning with a summary of the lesson and the key points the student should learn from the module. The body of the module should use a relevant business problem as the motivation for working through the material. Learning how to count the number of customers who responded to a new promotion would be more interesting than learning how to count the number of rows in the TABLES system table, even if the two exercises teach exactly the same concept. The exercises should be well illustrated with screen captures that look exactly like what the students will see on their computers.

REFERENCE Much of the instructional design approach we follow is based on the work of Robert Gagné. His influential books, *The Conditions of Learning and Theory of Instruction* (Harcourt Brace College Publishers; 4th edition, 1985), and his more practical *Principles of Instructional Design* (Gagné, et.al., Wadsworth Publishing; 5th edition, June 15, 2004), take an approach based on cognitive psychology and information-processing theory. These theories posit that there are internal mental processes involved in learning that are influenced by external events.

> **Gagné uses this relationship by viewing instruction as the arrangement of external events to activate and support the internal processes of learning. There is a lot more to creating effective training materials than just writing down a list of "click here" steps.**

The modules should become progressively more complex, with the early ones providing step-by-step instructions and the later ones offering higher-level guidance. This gives the students the opportunity to memorize the basic steps so they can create a report without having to be prompted. Near the end of the class, students should be able to handle an instruction like "Set up the following query:" followed by a screen capture of a completed query. Include bonus exercises at the end of each module to keep the quick learners occupied.

Include time to test the training materials as part of the course development plan. Test each module on a few people from your team, and then test the whole package on a few of your friendly end users. Look for timing, errors, confusing sections, overall understandability, and value. Ask for feedback about what works, what doesn't, and suggestions for improvement. Weave what you learn back into the materials.

Finally, pay careful attention to the design layout of the course materials. Keep it clean, clear, and concise. Use a nice cover page, include reference pages with contact info and phone numbers. At least put it in a 3-ring binder, and consider using spiral or other bindings if you have access to them. (And really, how many of us don't have a 24-hour copy shop close by?) The product quality of these materials reflects directly on the reputation of the DW/BI system. Make it a good reflection.

Developing Supporting Materials

In addition to the course materials, the DW/BI educator is also on the hook to create any needed supporting materials. Examples include online tutorials, cheat sheets, and online help. We discussed online tutorials in the preceding documentation section. Cheat sheets are brief summaries of common commands, processes, terminology, constraint lists, and so on—whatever people use or do on a regular basis that might be hard to remember. A cheat sheet is a single-page document, often meant to be folded into a tri-fold format for easy access and storage. In some ways, these cheat sheets are marketing brochures for the DW/BI system. They will be prominently displayed in your users' offices, so make them look professional. The cheat sheets should also be part of the BI portal content.

The Training Database

If possible, your courses will work directly against the production DW/BI system. However, there are several reasons why this isn't always possible, and you may need to create a training database. Certain kinds of tables, like an accumulating snapshot table, are always changing. The screenshots in exercises that include this table must match what people see when they do the exercise. In a case like this, it may make sense to create a training database with a fixed snapshot of the data. There are other reasons to create a training database. It may be important to mask confidential data, or performance against the production database for certain detailed datasets might be too slow for everyone in the class to execute simultaneously.

In all cases when you need to create a training database, it should be done as early in the course development process as possible. Create a dataset that reflects the world people will be returning to when they leave class.

Level of Effort

Creating a good class takes a lot of work. Count on at least eight hours of work to create an hour of class materials. A one-day class will take about a week and a half to two weeks of hard work for someone with experience developing course materials. If this is your first time, double the estimate to give you more time to research other examples of good materials, and to test the materials you create.

Training Delivery

Training is one of the most important end user activities for the DW/BI team. It is often your first real contact with many of the users. You'll make your first impression and begin building long-term relationships. As this section has shown, creating and delivering quality education is a lot of work, but it's worth spending the time it takes to get it right.

Keep hands-on classes for ad hoc users relatively small—10 to 20 people at a time. The number of workstations in the training facility is usually the limiting factor. Regardless of the class size, have an assistant in the classroom to help answer individual questions during the exercises. Plan to have one assistant for every 10 students.

The BI application one-hour class can be given to much larger groups because the format is presentation and demonstration. Because there's no hands-on content, provide attendees with handouts that include the presentation materials and key screen captures of the demos. People can use these to get started when they get back to their desks.

A day or two before class, send out reminders to all registered students. Verify that you have enough copies of the materials and that the training facility is set up with all needed software installed and working. Provide coffee and snacks for the students, especially for an all-day class.

The day of the class, arrive early and set up the room as you want it. It helps to have a registration area with the registration list, course materials and name tents so people can sign in when they come into the room. Start and end on time. If you're clear about timing and stick to your schedule, people will quickly understand that you're serious.

Although you may have attended many classes, if you haven't taught one before, you're in for a surprise. Teaching a full-day class is exhausting work. If this is your first time teaching, practice with a friendly audience before working with new users. Get feedback on your style and suggestions for improvement.

User Support

A well-designed and well-implemented DW/BI system is much easier to use than any alternative, but it's still not that easy. The DW/BI team will need to provide ongoing support to its user community. We recommend a three-tiered approach to providing user support. The first tier is the web site and self-service support, the second tier is your power users in business groups, and the third tier is the front-end people on DW/BI team (the BI part of the group).

NOTE You can't rely on the existing IT Help Desk to provide much support for the DW/BI system users. At best, we've found that Help Desk personnel can help solve connectivity problems. To provide real help, you need to have business users talk to someone who understands the business problems, data content, and front-end tool. Having your users reinstall the software is not going to cut it.

- *Tier 1, the Web Site:* We've already discussed the support-related contents of the web site in the documentation section. Having great content and the tools to find it (navigation, search, and metadata browser) is fundamental to providing support through the web site. You may need to encourage people to take advantage of the resource. It helps to have a brief demo of the web site in every class to show people where to go for help. This could also be turned into one of the cheat sheets we described earlier. You'll still get calls from people who could have easily found the answer themselves but decided it was easier to call you. In these cases, if the answer is on the web site, walk them through the steps to find it. Once they become aware of the help that's available and comfortable with how to find it, they'll be more likely to try to help themselves first.

- *Tier 2: the Expert Users:* If someone needs help creating an ad hoc query, or needs a specific report that doesn't already exist, they need to talk to someone with the skills to help. Set the expectation that this initial contact should be with someone who is based in the business, preferably in the person's department. We call this support contact the expert user. The expert user will have strong ad hoc query skills, a deep knowledge of the contents of the DW/BI system, and a sense for the business issues that can only come from working in the business. The key to creating this support structure is setting expectations with senior management and the expert users early on. This role should become part of the expert user's job description and performance reviews. They should view themselves as the local pros and should encourage people to ask for help. You need to foster this sense of association with the DW/BI system by treating the expert users well. We've talked about the various points throughout the process where the experts provide input and guidance. All of this involvement serves to emphasize the importance of their role. You must take the task of nurturing these relationships seriously.

- *Tier 3: the DW/BI Team:* When the web site and local experts are unable to solve the problem, the DW/BI team must offer a support resource of last resort. This front-end team actually has responsibilities across all support tiers. They own the BI portal site and must maintain and enhance its content including the BI applications. They own the relationships with and the training of the expert users. And, they provide direct support to the users when needed. This list of responsibilities represents a significant amount of work. Plan to have more people on the DW/BI team dedicated to these front-room tasks than to the back room—in an eight-person DW/BI team, for example, at least four people will be dedicated to front-room responsibilities.

NOTE In some organizations, the BI portion of the DW/BI team gets split off to become its own entity. While there are probably good reasons to do this, we believe the DW/BI system is so closely tied to the business that splitting the two is like what happens when a cartoon character gets cut in half. The bottom half can't see where it's going, and the top half has lost its mobility. It's important to dedicate people to the front-end responsibilities, but separating them into their own organization is generally not productive in the long run.

As we described in Chapter 8, the BI applications should be self-supporting, with pulldown menus, pick lists, and help screens. The DW/BI team will need to monitor its usage, maintain them as the data and data structures change, and extend and enhance them as additional data becomes available. Provide a means for users to give feedback on existing BI applications and request new ones.

Many IT organizations began building their DW/BI systems with the goal of letting users create their own reports. The real goal was a bit more self-serving—the IT folks wanted to get off the report generation treadmill. Unfortunately, while this treadmill may slow down a bit, it never goes away. Even though accessing data is easier, the majority of knowledge workers don't have the time or interest to learn how to meet their own information needs from scratch. Often, these people can be found at senior levels in the organization, so meeting their needs is particularly important. The DW/BI team will need to include creating custom reports in its responsibilities list, and to make sure there are resources available to meet the most important requests. The good news is that these custom reports can almost always be turned into (parameterized) standard reports and integrated into the existing BI application set.

Desktop Readiness and Configuration

The initial deployment must consider issues across the entire information chain, from the source systems to the user's computer screen. Most desktop PCs can handle the rigors of querying, reporting, and analysis. They already support large spreadsheets and Access databases. In some ways, the DW/BI system should reduce the strain on the user's PC by moving most of the data management back to the servers. Don't assume that everything will work fine at the user desktop. Test this assumption well before users attend training.

Before you inspect the situation, decide how much capability a user's desktop machine will need to have. Create a minimum configuration based on the front end tools, the amount of data typically returned, and the complexity of the BI applications. This minimum configuration includes CPU speed, memory, disk space, and monitor size. It should also indicate the base computer type and operating system supported, and browser version requirements. We've been in organizations that insist on supporting multiple operating systems on users' desktops: Windows, Apple, Linux, and UNIX. Obviously, this diversity has a big impact on the architecture and tool selection steps, long before you get to deployment. Let's hope those who are implementing a Microsoft DW/BI system are less interested in supporting multiple types of operating systems, but there are still many flavors of Windows.

When you go out into the user community, consider the following issues.

- *Connectivity:* Connectivity is not usually an issue in today's highly networked organizations, but there could be a problem getting from one part of the organization to another. For example, a remote field office may not have the appropriate network configuration to get to the DW/ BI server. Bandwidth to the desktop is usually not an issue either, but it's worth verifying. You may have some sales reps who work from home and don't have broadband connections. If they're working with large datasets, their user experience may be disappointing. If you know about the problem, you can at least set expectations, even if you can't fix it.

TIP Windows Remote Desktop can be a good, inexpensive solution for bandwidth problems. This feature of WindowsXP Professional and Windows servers works very well across even fairly slow connections. We use it all the time over a virtual private network to shared servers. Many of our clients have reported great success in increasing user satisfaction—especially for salespeople and others who are often on the road.

- *Installation:* Some front-end tools are desktop-based and need to have software installed on the user's machine. Most are now browser-based and don't need local software installed. Be careful, however, as many of the browser-based tools actually download a "plug-in" that runs on the local PC. This can lead to version problems with the client software. Test the installation process from a selection of user machines and document any problems. If the installation process is anything more than clicking a button on the BI portal, make sure you document it clearly and use it to create a set of installation instructions.

Summary

The goal of this chapter is to highlight the most important issues for you to think about when deploying a DW/BI system. Deploying a system safely and successfully requires a lot of work and planning. You need the entire DW/BI team and help from business experts.

The DW/BI team has to focus on developing solid operations and performance tests. Equally important, these back-room folks should concentrate on building and testing a playbook for the actual deployment process. The deployment playbook is vitally important when you're adding new functionality to an existing system, while minimizing end user impact. The goal for the playbook should be to write instructions so clear and simple that anyone could follow them. You shouldn't have to think deep thoughts while you're trying to deploy a system.

The front-room team focuses on queries, reports, and user interactions. During the deployment process, this team concentrates on running quality assurance tests on the data and reports. You have to rely heavily on the business experts for this testing work too. They're the ones who will confirm the data's accuracy. The front-room team also needs to develop system documentation, tools for searching and viewing that documentation, and training for the business users. Unless you've done documentation and training development before, you'll be surprised at how much time it takes to do this "soft" stuff well.

In our experience, problems with deploying a system almost always derive from incomplete testing. Test everything: your procedures, operations, and performance. Test the upgrade scripts. Check the results. Don't approach the actual rollout date with an attitude that says, "This should work." The right attitude is "We've tested this every way we could think of, and it will work."

When you do finally roll out the system, with no wrinkles at all, take a break. You've earned it! Then turn on your usage-monitoring tools, sit back, and watch what the business users are doing with their great new system.

CHAPTER 15

Operations and Maintenance

Trust but verify

We've seen too many DW/BI teams postpone thinking about how to operate their new system until it's nearly in production. When deadlines are looming and users are clamoring for data and reports, it's too late to start designing your operating procedures. You'll be making stuff up as you go along, and Mistakes Will Be Made.

There are two major sets of issues to think about with respect to the ongoing operations of your system. The first set of issues revolves around communicating with, training, and supporting the users. Of course you'll be publishing reports to them about the business, but you also need to communicate with them about the DW/BI system itself. What kind of information or metadata will you share? How will you publish it?

We've already talked about training the user community, but how do you keep that training fresh? What plans do you have for training new users? Will you need to extend the training? In terms of support, how will you answer user questions, both simple questions like how to connect, and very complex analytic questions like how to categorize customers.

The second set of issues focuses on technical systems management. You need to think, long before you go into production, about a host of issues. Your decisions about these operational issues will affect your system configuration and design. These issues include how you're going to monitor resource usage and business usage, and how you're going to report on this same usage. How are you going to automate operations? How will your database administrators kill users' queries?

At launch your system's performance might be great, but with increased data volumes and user load, performance might degrade. How will you identify and solve bottlenecks? How can you be proactive about tuning the system to prevent bottlenecks from forming?

One of your most important tools for improving performance is to implement a partitioning strategy. But partitioning requires a complex data management process during incremental loads. How do you need to modify your ongoing ETL process to accommodate data partitioning?

Finally—but very important—you need to plan for, implement, and test your backup and recovery strategy.

The now-familiar Business Dimensional Lifecycle diagram (see Figure 15.1) places operational issues at the end of the Lifecycle where you loop back around on the next iteration. Operationally that's accurate, but as we discuss throughout this chapter, you need to be planning for safe operations from the outset.

In this chapter you'll find answers to the following questions:

- What do you need to worry about with respect to maintaining and extending the BI portal and BI applications?

- How do you execute Integration Services packages in production?

- How do you monitor the system? What kinds of counters and events should you track? How can you see what users are doing right now, and kill bad queries?

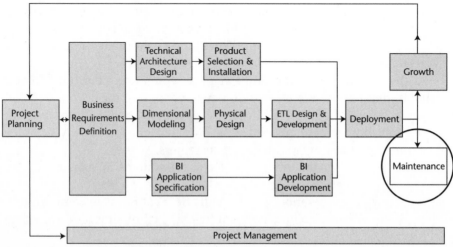

Figure 15.1   The Business Dimensional Lifecycle

- How do you conduct performance tuning of a DW/BI system?
- What data do you need to back up and how often? How should you perform backup and recovery?

Providing User Support

The design and development of your DW/BI system has focused on building a system that's easy to use, intuitive, and performs well. You've built BI applications, be they canned reports, a dashboard portal, a closed loop data mining application, or a combination of all. You've trained the users on the data and applications. What's left to do?

A lot. The business user community will grow and change. Some users will learn the new tools immediately. Others will require some hand-holding and retraining. Even if your system is perfect and the business users catch on immediately, you'll need to bring new employees up-to-speed. On an ongoing basis, it's not unusual to have the same number of people involved with supporting the business users as initially developed the system.

The user-facing part of the DW/BI team engages in the following activities:

- BI portal maintenance and enhancement
- BI application specification and development
- BI Help Desk support and training, discussed in Chapter 14

We've seen the user-facing side of the DW/BI team range in size from dozens of people for large companies with a centralized DW/BI system, to a single person. The smallest organizations often have a single-person shop, but it's really hard for that person to handle the back-room maintenance while communicating effectively with the business users. Ongoing, it's hard to see how you can get by with fewer than two people: one for the back room, and one for the front room.

Maintaining the BI Portal

Even the smallest DW/BI team should maintain an intranet site where users get information about the system. We've talked about this portal already in Chapters 8 and 9, where we discussed how the portal should be organized to find reports; in Chapter 13 where we described the metadata that should be published on the portal; and in Chapter 14 where we talked about documentation and training materials.

Here we briefly present an additional set of information that should go on the portal, having to do with operations and maintenance:

- System status: what is the most recent day of data in each business process dimensional model
- Schedules of planned outages
- Honest and complete status of any unplanned outages
- Clear warnings to users about problems in the system, like data quality issues. Include an honest and complete assessment of when the problems will be fixed.
- The system's current operational status, including:
  - How many queries have been answered in the last hour
  - How many reports generated
  - Current number of active users
  - On-demand report of active queries, how long they've been running, and who's running them
- Proof points about the system's capacity, to foster user confidence in the system:
  - How long the last data load took
  - How big the largest data load was, and how long it took
  - Maximum count of simultaneous users

The DW/BI team must commit to open and complete disclosure to the user community about any problems.

Every 12 to 18 months, you should review the entire DW/BI system. Evaluate what's working well for the users, and what should change. Remember, change is inevitable, and is a sign of a healthy system. As part of this periodic evaluation, consider refreshing the look, layout, and content of the BI portal.

Extending the BI Applications

The initial reports and BI applications for a new business process dimensional model will soon be modified and augmented. Users don't always know what reports and analyses they want until you show them something fairly close. Then they'll tell you what they *don't* want—the report you just created—and, let's hope, give you clearer information about what they now think they need.

The cycle repeats as business imperatives change.

Data mining applications, and other kinds of closed loop systems, are seldom implemented in the first phase of a DW/BI system. First, the basic data is brought online. Then, business users and DW/BI team members build ad hoc models and analyses. This analytic work usually has tremendous value to the business, for example by improving Marketing's understanding of customers, or providing mechanisms for reducing costs. The next step, beyond improving understanding, is to systematize the knowledge gained from ad hoc analysis by building a closed loop system. In our experience, ad hoc analyses are usually valuable enough to provide a positive ROI on the DW/BI investment, and many implementations stop there. Those DW/BI teams that go on to build data mining applications and other kinds of closed loop systems usually reap greatly increased ROI.

The process of developing a closed loop BI system requires close partnership between the business people, who can effectively develop the business rules and analytic models, and the DW/BI team, who will write the system specifications and formalize the models. The majority of the application development effort requires a fairly standard development skill set, which is often met by the same developers who work on the operational systems. The developer needs a relatively small amount of specialized knowledge—for example of the Analysis Services object models—in order to implement the calls into the databases or data mining model.

System Management

Most of this chapter focuses on the back-room requirements for managing your DW/BI system in production. Although we've separated these operational issues into this chapter, you need to think ahead during design and development to ensure you build a maintainable system.

There are several components of the back-room system management:

- Executing and monitoring the ETL system
- Monitoring resources and usage
- Managing data growth and disk space
- Performance tuning
- Managing partitioning
- Backup and recovery
- Generating statistics for the BI portal

The more automated you can make your systems management, the better. At the very least, automate backups and launching the ETL packages. SQL Server provides enough tools that the basics are easy, and there's no excuse for not implementing some system automation.

Unlike many issues where we've talked about how small teams might cut corners, organizations of any size benefit from system automation. Indeed, the smallest organizations are perhaps least equipped to apply human resources to a problem that can be automated. It's hard to imagine how a DW/BI team of one to three people could possibly operate without significant automation.

The ideal management system requires no human intervention except for the occasional troubleshooting. Such a system automatically adds and drops partitions, checks for disk space, reports on performance problems or unusual usage, and corrects the vast majority of data oddities during the ETL process.

No matter how automated your operations are, you must have a plan. Like all plans, your Operations Plan should be written down.

Executing the ETL Packages

During development, you design and execute Integration Services packages within BI Studio. In the development environment, you can set breakpoints, examine variables' values and status, watch the movement of data through a Data Flow task, and explore the data with data viewers. All of these tools are valuable during development, but are of no interest in production. You want the ETL system to execute, upon a schedule, with no human intervention.

Integration Services packages are easy to schedule. SQL Server ships the tools you need: dtexec and SQL Agent. You should already be familiar with dtexec and its friend dtexecui, from the process of testing the Integration Services packages. Dtexec and dtexecui execute a package from the command line. They are basically the same, except that dtexecui brings up a user interface that helps you construct the command by choosing which package to run and picking various options like logging levels and connection information.

TIP Why is this utility called dtexec? It's an artifact of Integration Services' ancestry to SQL Server 2000 DTS. The feature name was changed to Integration Services relatively late in the game, and Microsoft decided not to mess with all the back-end names. The utility will be called dtexec long after DTS fades from our collective memory.

Once you've set up the package execution options, you can create a SQL Agent job to run the package, and then schedule that job. SQL Agent is a standard feature of the SQL Server database.

To schedule an Integration Services job, launch Management Studio and open Object Explorer for the server that you'll use to run SQL Agent. This is often, but not necessarily, the database server on which the Integration Services packages will run. Navigate to the SQL Server Agent folder, and right-click on Jobs to create a new job.

Name the job, and categorize it if you wish. Categorization is extremely useful if you have a lot of jobs. Next, go to the Steps page of the New Job dialog box. When you add a new step, the New Job Step dialog box appears, as illustrated in Figure 15.2.

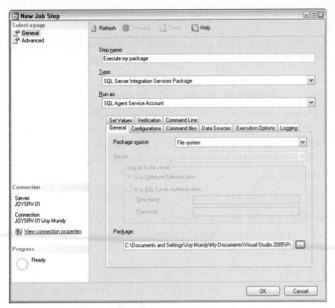

Figure 15.2   SQL Agent New Job Step

Name the step, and set the Type to SQL Server Integration Services package execution. The package execution job step includes a user interface for setting up your Integration Services package. This interface is effectively the same as the one in dtexecui. First identify the package you plan to execute. Packages can be stored remotely but they always execute on the machine that's running SQL Agent. That point is worth repeating: Packages execute within the process of the calling executable, SQL Agent in this case.

Looking back to Figure 15.2, you can see a variety of job configuration options. Most people will never use any of these options, but the most common ones are:

- *Data sources:* Change the database connection information, for example to point to the production servers. Note: We generally prefer to change database connection information in a configuration file, as discussed in the next bullet point.

- *Configurations:* Change the location of a configuration file containing variable values and other object properties. The location of configuration files might be different on your development, test, and production servers (although it's certainly best practice to set up test and production the same way). Of more interest, you can overlay a configuration file to change one or two items, like global variables that contain the date range for which to run the package.

REMOTE PACKAGE EXECUTION

What if you really want to execute a package on a remote server, most likely to isolate the ETL workload from the database servers. You have two options:

◆ Install the relational database and SQL Agent on the remote server, and kick off the job from there. There's no incremental licensing cost to installing the RDBMS on the remote machine, presuming you've already paid to put Integration Services there. If that database instance exists only to run SQL Agent, it's not going to eat up a huge amount of resources. Still, if you're memory constrained, you might not want the RDBMS on that machine at all.

◆ Execute DtExec on the remote server. There are several ways to do this:

■ Create a SQL Agent job on the local server that calls the Operating System (CmdExec). Set up that command to execute dtexec on the remote server.

■ Any package can use the Integration Services Execute Process task to execute dtexec on a remote server. In a distributed ETL scenario, it may make sense to run the Master package on a central server. That Master package in turn executes "child" packages on one or several remote servers.

REFERENCE The dtexec utility is well documented in the Books Online topics "dtexec Utility" and "How to: Run a Package Using the DTExec Utility."

Once you've set up your SQL Agent job step, schedule it to run on the appropriate schedule. In most cases, you'll define one or a small number of SQL Agent jobs for your ETL system. Each job calls a master Integration Services package, which in turn calls subpackages in the correct order. Build logic flow and dependencies into the Integration Services master package, and use SQL Agent only to kick off the main job.

Some organizations have standardized on enterprise-wide job management software like Autosys. SQL Agent is nothing special; if your organization uses such software, by all means conform to the corporate standard. The job management software simply calls dtexec on the computer running Integration Services.

TIP Job management software is designed to handle complex dependencies very well. It can wait until files have arrived in a directory, a table has been loaded, or a flag set, before firing off additional steps. Integration Services can do all these things, too, so we don't expect anyone will buy external job management software to support the ETL system. However, if you have job management software in-house, you should evaluate whether you want to design your Integration Services packages so they leverage this functionality from the external tool.

Monitoring the Business Intelligence System

You need to implement and understand two types of monitoring. First, what's going on in your system? What system resources like memory are being used, when, and by what processes? If you can't monitor system events and resource usage, you'll never be able to troubleshoot and tune your system. The other kind of monitoring focuses on the users: Who's accessing the system, and when? What queries are they running, and how much time are those queries taking? If you don't know what your users are doing, you'll never be able to satisfy them.

Resource Monitoring

Microsoft does a good job of providing tools for you to monitor resource usage for the relational data warehouse, ETL system, Analysis Services database, and BI applications. Consistent and integrated monitoring tools are a significant advantage of the SQL Server toolset. It's not a feature that's sexy or exciting, but it affects your ability to manage your system.

The two most basic tools are familiar to your system administrators: System Monitor and Event Viewer. These Windows monitoring tools are part of the operating system, and the SQL Server components write counters and events that you can view in a standard way. System Monitor counters and events can be written to files or to a SQL Server database. System Monitor is sometimes referred to as Performance Monitor or by the shortened name PerfMon. The Event Viewer is used primarily for logging errors. The Event Viewer is sometimes referred to as the error log.

SQL Server ships with some utilities and functionality that are key to monitoring your DW/BI system. SQL Profiler is a stand-alone utility that you launch from the Start menu. Profiler tracks engine process events, like when a transaction was rolled back or a user logged in. SQL Profiler 2005 is similar to the Profiler familiar from SQL 2000, with several significant improvements. First, you can now profile Analysis Services databases and display events raised by Integration Services. The relational engine and Analysis Services include a flight recorder feature that captures the last sequence of trace events, which can later be placed back using Profiler. The flight recorder is extremely valuable for diagnosing a system crash or other unwelcome event.

The Activity Monitor window in Management Studio shows the current activity on the relational database: who's logged in, what processes are running, and what locks are active. Old hands may prefer the classic system stored procedures like sp_who. Activity Monitor and Profiler present similar information for the relational database. Use Activity Monitor to see what's happening right now. Set up Profiler to capture similar information into a permanent file or database.

The Analysis Services Activity Viewer is a sample utility that ships with SQL Server 2005. The Activity Viewer provides functionality for the Analysis Services database that's analogous to the Activity Monitor window in Management Studio. It's available as a sample utility but isn't integrated into Management Studio.

REFERENCE See the topic "Activity Viewer" in Books Online.

Integration Services and Reporting Services have various mechanisms for logging system information. These features are discussed in the following sections.

System Monitor, SQL Profiler, Integration Services, and Reporting Services can all log their information to SQL Server. You should plan to create databases to hold these log tables.

Baseline Performance

Part of your Operations Plan should be to establish a baseline performance profile for your system. It's orders of magnitude easier to fix a performance problem in the future if you've kept track of how the system performed over time.

The most important measures to track in your performance baseline are pretty obvious: the usage of memory, processors, and disk. Plan to monitor your production servers all the time, perhaps at 15-minute intervals. Store the monitored information, preferably in a SQL Server database. For all the servers in your system, set up System Monitor to track at least the following counters.

For disk usage:

- PhysicalDisk: Avg. Disk sec/Read and Avg. Disk sec/Write.
- PhysicalDisk: Avg. Disk Queue Length. If this counter is consistently too high, it means I/O is being performed so fast that it can't be handled with the physical disk. This is the first place to look if you think your system is I/O bound.

TIP What is a value for PhysicalDisk that's too high? It depends on the configuration of the RAID set for the disk. "Too high" is 2 to 3 times the number of spindles in the RAID set. For a drive that consists of a single disk, then, "too high" is 2 or 3.

For CPU usage:

- Processor: % Processor Time
- System: %Total Processor Time

For memory usage:

- Memory: Available Bytes
- Memory: Pages/sec
- Memory: Page Faults/sec

In addition to the ongoing monitoring, it's really useful to create a fine-grained baseline on a monthly basis. This fine-grained baseline will differ from the ongoing monitoring by sampling performance more frequently, say at 5-second intervals. You may also collect additional counters.

For the monthly detailed logging of the ETL process, ramp up the logging frequency just before kicking off ETL processing, and return to normal levels as soon as the ETL job completes. For the monthly detailed logging of usage, ramp up monitoring for a few hours during a reasonably busy time of day.

Verbose logging can degrade system performance, so you may want to monitor from a remote server. This is especially true if you're writing the logs directly to a SQL Server database rather than to files. For performance reasons, consider writing verbose logs to a file. As the DW/BI team, you should not find it difficult to import the log file into the SQL Server logging database.

Monitoring RDBMS Resources

There are books, classes, and certifications offered on how to monitor a relational database. Much of this information is oriented to transactional databases rather than data warehouse databases, but the concepts are standard. The biggest issue we've seen is educating an experienced transactional DBA on the requirements of a relational data warehouse. Such DBAs inevitably want to improve performance by adding hints to queries, which is impractical for ad hoc use of the relational data warehouse. They like to convert all known queries to stored procedures, which doesn't hurt but doesn't provide much benefit either, as the time to compile the query plan usually pales in comparison to executing the analytic query. They agonize over any denormalizations you've made. And they tend to underestimate the complexity of indexing a dimensional schema, and the cost of maintaining each new index at load time.

It really helps to have the operational DBA involved with the project during the development phase, so they will understand how the system is intended to be used and what the tradeoffs are. If that's not possible, then hand them the system documentation we've been begging you to write. In a large organization, consider hiring and training operational DBAs who focus exclusively on the business intelligence system.

The tools for monitoring and managing the SQL Server relational database are more mature than the other BI components. In addition to the generic System Monitor counters listed previously, the relational database server should also track some counters published by the database engine:

- SQL Server: Buffer Manager Page Reads/sec
- SQL Server: Buffer Manager Page Writes/sec
- Process: Working Set
- SQL Server: Buffer Manager: Buffer Cache Hit Ratio
- SQL Server: Buffer Manager: Total Pages
- SQL Server: Memory Manager: Total Server Memory (KB)

Many DBAs use SQL Server Profiler only in an ad hoc way, to investigate problems. We recommend that you set up a basic trace that runs whenever the database is running. This basic trace should be as lean as possible, so justify every event class that you're logging. Consider tracing the following events:

- *Security Audit: Audit Login and Audit Logout, and Sessions: ExistingConnection*. These event classes are most important for usage monitoring, although user counts affect performance. In some regulated environments, you will be required to capture login/logout information for all users of the system. You may also be required to collect the text of all queries.

- *Database: Log and Data File Autogrow and Autoshrink* (four event classes). These (let's hope infrequent) events can significantly impact system performance.

- *Transactions: SQLTransaction*. In a normal data warehouse database populated by batch processes, there are relatively few (large) transactions. Monitoring transactions is reasonable and not terribly expensive. The closer you move your processing to real time, the more transactions you'll have. The cost of tracing all those transactions may well outweigh the benefits.

- *SQL: BatchCompleted*. Track users' queries and any other SQL being executed. The TextData column shows the SQL being executed. This event class is likely to generate significant data volumes, especially if your trace includes the TextData. You may also want to track SQL: BatchStarting.

REFERENCE The Books Online topics that start with "Monitoring Performance and Tuning Data Stores" contain good information about how to troubleshoot relational database performance.

Monitoring Integration Services

The primary goal for monitoring Integration Services package execution on the production system is to help you evaluate whether and how to improve processing performance. You also want to be able to tie the Audit dimension, discussed in Chapter 6, to information about the package's execution.

The most important tools for monitoring Integration Services are System Monitor (PerfMon) and Integration Services Logging. In addition to the generic System Monitor counters that we listed previously, Integration Services publishes some counters that you can see in PerfMon. These are not as useful as you'd hope because they track information at a high level. What you really want to see is how much memory each step of a data flow is using; instead, you can see how much memory Integration Services is using.

Nonetheless, the following SQLServer:SSIS Pipeline counters are somewhat useful:

- *Buffer Memory*: How much memory is Integration Services using? If this number is larger than the physical memory available to Integration Services, some data is being spooled to disk during processing.
- *Rows Read:* The total number of rows read from source adapters.
- *Rows Written:* The total number of rows written to destination adapters.

The logging that's generated by Integration Services packages is akin to the SQL Server tracing and profiling functionality that we discussed previously. Like Profiler, it tracks events. The kind of events that can be tracked and logged will be familiar to anyone who's run an Integration Services package: It's exactly the same kind of information that you can see in the Execution Results tab every time you execute a package in the BI Studio.

You seldom want to store all those package execution results permanently. Define package logging so that you store information about interesting events only. Most often, you'd set up the packages on your production system so they log to a SQL Server database, though you have several choices.

For every task, and for the overall package, you can track many events, of which the most useful are:

- *OnPreExecute:* Logs a row when execution begins
- *OnPostExecute:* Logs a row when execution ends
- *OnWarning:* Logs a row when the task issues a warning
- *OnError:* Logs a row when the task issues an error

Unfortunately, the Data Flow task is like a black box to the logging system. There are multiple steps and transformations within a Data Flow task, and ideally you'd like to know how long each step takes. This is simply impossible with the logging framework as it exists. Although it's a hard problem, we hope to see Data Flow task logging in a future release.

REFERENCE Check the Microsoft web site www.microsoft.com/sql/bi/
ProjectReal. The Project Real team at SQL BI worries about operational issues
like this one, and may post scripts, workarounds, and other useful information
on this and other problem areas.

If Analysis Services processing is part of your ETL, make sure you gather statistics on it independently and as a component of the overall flow. It's important to establish a baseline for Analysis Services processing as a separate entity because its tuning activities are so different from the other ETL steps. We discuss the Analysis Services counters in the following section, "Monitoring Analysis Services."

Set up logging by editing the package in BI Studio. Choose SSIS → Logging, and specify where the logs will be stored. Note that SQL Profiler is one of the options. Logging to SQL Profiler makes it easier to interleave package events with database events, and is especially useful during testing. However, most people log to a SQL Server table in production. It's best to create a separate database to hold logging information. Integration Services will automatically create its logging table, compellingly named *sysdtslog90*.

You could also store the logs in the file system, or write to a custom log provider. The latter option is interesting if you've purchased a third-party system management product that works with Integration Services.

Specify the events that you want to log on the Details tab of the Configure SSIS Logs Wizard, as illustrated in Figure 15.3.

On a production system, you'll seldom need to capture more events than those listed previously. If a problem should arise, for example if the packages start throwing warnings or errors, you should use your test system to evaluate. Most performance testing and re-work should also occur on test or development systems. That's good because there's no way at run time to change the logging configuration; your only solution is to edit the package.

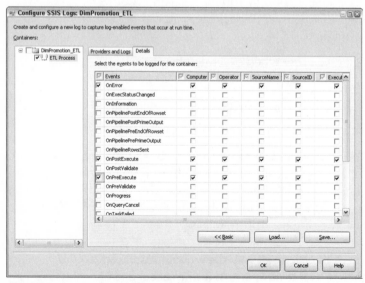

Figure 15.3   Configure Integration Services logging

Once you've executed a package, and logged events to SQL Server, you can report on those logs. A set of basic sample reports is included with SQL Server. These reports are implemented in Reporting Services. You can find them in the Samples folder.

As we described in Chapter 6, you should build your packages to collect information about package execution times, rows inserted into target tables, and possibly other information like the sum of amounts. This metadata is stored in the Audit dimension and, at your discretion, is available to business users for querying. You may choose to pick up additional information from logging, to include with the Audit system.

Finally, you may want to set up package logging to log errors to the application event log, accessible from the Event Viewer. This application event may still be written even if Something Really Bad happens on the database server, which would prevent the standard logging from working properly.

Monitoring Analysis Services

You use the same tools, for the same reasons, to monitor the Analysis Services database as you do for the relational database. The main tools are System Monitor (PerfMon) and SQL Profiler.

In addition to the basic system information we've already discussed, add some Analysis Services counters to your System Monitor configuration. Over 100 counters are available. For the standard monitoring in production, don't over-monitor. We've found the following counters to be useful.

To monitor OLAP query performance, use the MSAS 2005: Storage Engine Query counters:

- Avg time/query
- Total queries requested
- Total queries answered
- Total bytes sent

To monitor connection requests, use the MSAS 2005: Connection counters:

- Total requests or Requests/sec
- Total successes or Successes/sec

If your DW/BI system includes data mining models, you should monitor the performance of both processing and ongoing queries, using the following MSAS 2005: Data Mining Prediction counters:

- Total Predictions or Predictions/sec
- Total Queries or Queries/sec

Analysis Services, like all the BI components of SQL Server, loves memory. Monitor how much Analysis Services is using, and for what purposes, by using the MSAS 2005: Memory counters:

- AggCacheKB
- Memory Usage KB

To evaluate whether you are running short on memory during processing aggregations, use the MSAS 2005: Proc Aggregations counter:

- Temp file bytes written/sec

It's seldom necessary to monitor processing performance as part of the standard monitoring set of counters. SQL Profiler can pick up the important events, like processing starts and stops. Monitor the processing counters (Data Mining Model Processing, Processing, and Proc Aggregations) only during test, or if you need to diagnose a performance or other processing problem.

It's as easy to use SQL Profiler to set up a trace on Analysis Services as it is on the relational database. Create a new trace to Analysis Services, and choose the desired event classes. As with the relational database engine, you can run multiple traces at the same time. We recommend that you set up a basic trace that runs whenever the database is running. This basic trace should be as lean as possible, so justify every event class that you're logging. Consider tracing the following events:

- *Security Audit: Audit Login and Audit Logout.* These event classes are most important for usage monitoring, although user counts affect performance. In some regulated environments, you will be required to capture login/logout information for all users of the system. You may also be required to collect the text of all queries.

- *Security Audit: Audit Backup/Restore Event and Audit Server Starts and Stops.* These two classes should generate few events. The rationale for logging these events should be pretty obvious.

- *Errors and Warnings: Error.* It's always a good idea to log errors.

- *Command Events: Command End.* The types of commands collected by this event class are specified by the event subclass column, and include CREATE, ALTER, PROCESS, and so on. The TextData column contains the text of the command. The Command End event includes the command start and stop times.

- *Query Events: Query End.* Queries can be MDX to a cube, MDX to a data mining model, or SQL, as specified by the event subclass column. The TextData column contains the text of the query. The Query End event includes the query start and stop times.

■ *Progress Reports: Progress Report Begin, End, and Error.* Progress reports occur during dimension and partition processing. You may also want to track Progress Report Current, although this will generate somewhat more information.

Monitoring Reporting Services

The story for monitoring Reporting Services begins in a familiar way, with System Monitor. We'll outline the counters to include in a stripped-down standard monitor. Events are captured for you automatically by Reporting Services, rather than by setting up a trace in Profiler.

As with the other BI components, we recommend that you run System Monitor (PerfMon) all the time with a few counters, storing the results in a SQL Server table. The most important counters to run all the time are listed following.

RS Web Service counters track activity through the web service:

■ *Active Sessions* counts all browser sessions generated from report subscriptions, whether they are still active or not.

■ *Total Requests or Requests/sec* counts all requests made to the report server after the service started.

■ *Total Reports Executed or Reports Executed/sec* counts the number of reports that were executed.

RS Windows Service counters track activity through scheduled activities like snapshots and report subscription and delivery:

■ *Active Sessions* counts all browser sessions generated from report subscriptions, whether they are still active or not.

■ *Report Requests or Requests/sec* counts all requests made to the report server after the service started.

■ *Total Reports Executed or Reports Executed/sec* counts the number of reports that were executed.

If you have implemented Reporting Services on a web farm, these counters track only one server, not the aggregate across the farm. You can easily monitor the multiple servers on a single instance of Systems Monitor, but you'd need to aggregate the web farm servers' counters yourself. You could get fancy and build a data mart for your Reporting Services logging information, or just use a spreadsheet.

The Reporting Services Execution Log is more interesting than the Systems Monitor counters. These logs are captured in the operational database that Reporting Services uses, called the ReportServer database by default. However, you shouldn't report directly from the ReportServer execution logs. These tables are part of the Reporting Services operational system, and reporting directly from them is analogous to reporting directly from any other transaction system.

The Report Server catalog is just like any other transaction system. It will lose history when its transaction logs are truncated. It will lose referential integrity when reports are deleted that have been run in the past, or when users are removed who have used the system in the past. Definitions of the tables and columns may change over time, breaking the existing library of usage reports. It is not easy to query directly because it uses codes instead of descriptions for most of the attributes. Most important, even a simple interactive query could place read locks on the running system, dramatically reducing system performance. For all these reasons, it makes sense to build a simple database that tracks the process of generating reports.

SQL Server has made this easy by providing an Integration Services package that will manage this reporting log database for you. Most people will schedule this package to run nightly, although there's no harm in doing it more or less often. Just make sure that you run it more often than Reporting Services clears execution records. Otherwise execution log entries will be deleted before they're gathered up by the package.

REFERENCE You can read about how to set up and execute that package in the Books Online topic "Querying and Reporting on Report Execution Log Data."

SQL Server also includes some sample reports on the reporting execution log data. The sample reports are oriented to the DW/BI team. Supplement these reports with reports designed for your users and operations environment. As we show in Chapter 16, one of these user-oriented reports should include a time series that shows how overall DW/BI system usage is, one hopes, increasing. Another popular report lists a count of reports run by user or department over the last 30 days. This report has been known to stimulate interest in the DW/BI system by the VPs and directors of those departments.

Usage Monitoring

The usage of your DW/BI system has a huge impact on its performance. Our discussion of resource monitoring suggested that you collect information usage. You should always be collecting counts of queries run and rows returned, by type of application. The System Monitor counters we've outlined previously will collect that information for you.

You also should collect sample queries. Sample queries will help you tune system performance by building new indexes or aggregations. You may be able to identify training opportunities by seeing what strange queries your users are putting together.

Some organizations collect the text of all queries submitted to the system, or at least all ad hoc queries. This is actually a lot of data, and is probably overkill unless you have a compliance mandate for collecting such information. By collecting all queries, all the time, you're placing a non-trivial performance burden on the system. And, your logging database will grow to be quite large.

A reasonable alternative is to turn on query text logging only occasionally, for example from 1 p.m. to 3 p.m. daily or even weekly. For queries into the relational database, this is your best bet. It's simple to create and schedule a profile that captures the appropriate column (TextData) from the SQL:Batch Started event class, and run it for a specific time. The results of this profile would supplement the constant usage monitoring which, presumably, would not include TextData.

The Profiler events that we discussed for Analysis Services will automatically collect query counts by user. You may also choose to collect the MDX and DMX statements that are issued for OLAP and Data Mining queries. Do so by collecting the TextData column of the QueryEvents\Query End event in Profiler. Note, however, that this column collects the query text in a human-readable format. The volume of data collected here is potentially far larger than the query log for usage-based aggregations. As with the relational data warehouse, you may choose to set up Profiler to collect query text for only a few hours a day or week. You should plan to collect query counts at all times.

There's a second query log that's used to support the wizard to design usage-based aggregations. This query log is a server-wide setting, which it's very important to turn on. We describe this second query log later in the chapter, in the section on optimizing aggregation design.

Reporting on Usage

Your BI portal web site should devote a small amount of screen real estate to reporting on system usage. VPs and Directors are often very interested in how much their staff members are using your system. They tend to be competitive people, and simply seeing another department using the DW/BI system has been known to spur a VP to encourage his or her staff to use the system more. So a time series of reporting and ad hoc use by department is a really good report to publish.

The DW/BI team should also know who is doing what with the system, how much, and when. This information is imperative for performance tuning, as well as identifying problem areas and users whose skills may be leveraged more broadly. If you're monitoring the text of ad hoc queries, you should communicate with business users what, how often and why you're monitoring their use, what you plan to do with the information, and who has access to that information. This isn't a big deal; just put a few sentences in the informational document for new users.

Managing Disk Space

One of the most common reasons for ETL job failure is one of the easiest to prevent: running out of disk space.

At the very minimum, set up a System Monitor counter and alert to warn when free space on each disk falls below a certain threshold. The relevant counter is Logical Disk: Free Megabytes. Set up two alerts: one to warn when you're within a month of running out of disk space, and one to blare stridently when you're about a week away.

Figures 15.4 and 15.5 show how to set up System Monitor (PerfMon) to trigger an alert when disk space falls below a threshold, in this case 5,000MB. On the General tab of the dialog box (see Figure 15.4), specify the free space you're looking for, and how often to check. Checking daily is usually fine. On the Action tab you can specify whether to log the alert event to the application event log (always a good idea), send a network message, or launch a program. Figure 15.5 illustrates how to set up the Schedule tab so that the alert will continue running even if the machine reboots or the alert triggers.

How do you know what level of free space to check for? Focus on the big files that you accumulate:

- *Staging files for fact table extracts:* You may keep the fact table extract files online forever, for restartability, recoverability, or regulatory reasons. You may keep 30 days online, and back up the rest. If you keep a set number of extracts on disk, consider the growth in monthly data volumes, especially if your fact table is concerned with a new line of business. Make a conservative guess, and make an entry in your operations plan to re-check this guess periodically.

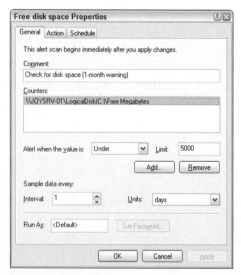

Figure 15.4   Set up a System Monitor alert to warn of low disk space

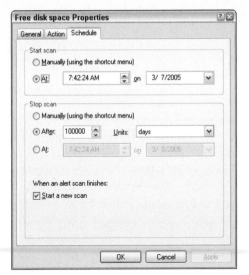

Figure 15.5 Set up alert to continue running after reboot or alert triggers

- *Analysis Services measure group (fact) partitions:* Analysis Services cubes can accumulate data, or you can set them up to keep a rolling window of data, like 37 months.

- *Relational database filegroups (including tempdb):* You should monitor the logical disks on which your database files are located. SQL Server provides additional tools for managing its file space.

It's almost universally true that the incremental disk space you'll be using each month goes to fact data storage, whether in the file system, relational database, or Analysis Services database. Most dimensions are relatively small and static in size, at least compared to fact tables.

When you set up a relational database, you can specify an initial size, an automatic growth factor like 10 percent, and a maximum file size. We recommend that you enable automatic growth as a failsafe, but monitor free space so that you extend database space on your own schedule. This is classic relational database management. There are tons of books available on the subject, and there's nothing particularly unusual for the data warehouse environment—except the overall size of the system and the (usually) batch nature of inserts and updates.

You could get a lot fancier than the simple mechanism we've described here. If your data volumes are accelerating, you should write a little program to look at the sizes of your staging files and Analysis Services databases. Forecast next month's disk requirements based on the recent trend. You could write this program as a Script Task from within Integration Services, and schedule it using SQL Agent. You could go so far as to automatically allocate more disk space for the RDBMS, staging area, or Analysis Services. But do the basics at least: You should be ashamed if you actually run out of disk space on your production system.

Killing Queries

Any DW/BI system that supports ad hoc queries—and we hope that's all of them—needs to be able to kill a query. No matter how hard you try to tune, to educate users, to build front ends that provide a safe environment, it's inevitable that someone will launch a query that's Really Bad. Maybe it will bring back a billion rows. Maybe it's malformed. Maybe it's a good query but expensive enough that you want to run it overnight. The time will come, sooner than you may think, when you need to kill a query.

The system monitoring counters that we described should tell you if there's a monstrous query going on. If you set up an alert, your DBA may receive a message to investigate and possibly intervene.

TIP You could even set up a System Monitor alert to automatically kill any query that's using too many system resources, by having the alert launch a program when it's triggered by a large query. We don't encourage this, as the DW/BI system is designed for users and ad hoc use. Those big queries are often quite valuable. We might consider setting this up for a few hours during high peak time, say 8 to 10 am, when everyone in the company is running their daily reports.

For the relational database, killing a query is a piece of cake. Under the covers, there are two key stored procedures: sp_who and sp_kill. But the best approach is to use SQL Server Management Studio. Within the Object Explorer for the database, navigate to Management → Activity Monitor. Find the offending process and right-click to kill it.

Management Studio, inexplicably, does not include an Activity Monitor for Analysis Services. SQL Server does ship a separate sample application to perform the analogous functions to sp_who and sp_kill.

REFERENCE You can find the Activity Monitor application in the samples folder, at Program Files\Microsoft SQL Server\90\Samples\Analysis Services\ Administrator\ActivityViewer. The source code for this sample application is included. The application includes a small help file, but like the relational database Activity Monitor, the Analysis Services ActivityViewer is straightforward to use.

TIP The samples are not installed by default. During installation (or modification of the existing installation), choose the Advanced button and ensure the samples and sample databases are installed.

Service and Availability Management

The DW/BI team is responsible for ensuring that the system, including data, reports, and other applications, is available to end users. The level of availability required, measured as the amount of acceptable down time, depends on the business impact of the system's unavailability. You should work with the business users to develop a service level agreement (SLA), and build a plan for meeting that specified service level.

When you develop your availability plan, consider the components of the DW/BI system within the context of your entire IT infrastructure. Let's hope your IT team already has plans and procedures for managing hardware, software, software installation media and CD keys, and user names and passwords—all necessary for rebuilding or restoring a system as quickly as possible. Assess the following issues:

- Do any parts of the DW/BI system need continuous, 24-hour-a-day query access? Analysis Services? The relational data warehouse? If so, how do you process new data without compromising availability?

- If continuous query access is not required, how do you ensure that processing fits within the nightly processing window?

- How do you handle situations that require an entire Analysis Services cube to be reprocessed? As discussed in Chapter 7, this can happen if an attribute declared to be unchanging does in fact change, among other reasons.

- How do you recover from a system failure during Integration Services processing? How do you restart a process mid-stream?

- How is the DW/BI system protected against failure of one or more components on the server(s)?

- How is the DW/BI system and data protected against failure within the enterprise, like source system outages, or serious problems with the Active Directory servers?

Develop a plan for addressing these issues to achieve the necessary availability. Test each element of the plan. A well-trained staff that is prepared to handle any contingency is an essential part of any disaster recovery plan.

Your availability plan must explicitly state how you'll detect a problem with a service. Maybe you want to wait for the VP of Marketing to call, but you probably want to be a bit more proactive.

Your Windows system administrators should already have procedures in place for identifying service outages. These procedures probably use System Monitor, Windows Events, or both. Use those same techniques to identify whether the components of your DW/BI system are currently available. If your organization doesn't already use Microsoft Operations Manager (MOM), you should consider purchasing it or a third-party operations manager like Tivoli. Any operations management product will be looking at standard Windows logs like System Monitor and Windows Events, and SQL Server Profiler.

The SLA should be explicit about the availability that's required for each component of the DW/BI system. For Analysis Services, it's particularly important to distinguish between the SLA for unavailability and the SLA for query performance. In many cases, Analysis Services incremental processing can occur in the background, with user access to the cubes undisturbed. During this period, however, query performance may degrade significantly. You need to help your business users understand these tradeoffs, so they can help make the case for a different architecture if needed to meet their availability and performance requirements.

The same issues of availability versus query performance are relevant for the relational data warehouse. Many organizations simply close access to the DW/BI system during ETL processing. Others, with higher availability requirements, will perform the bulk of processing in the background or on a remote server. User query performance on the relational data warehouse usually suffers during ETL processing, perhaps intolerably so. A careful consideration of these issues, and good communication with the users, will help you design a cost-effective architecture that meets your requirements.

Performance Tuning the DW/BI System

The system operations plan should include strategies for periodic performance tuning of all system components. The resource monitoring that we described earlier in the chapter provides the base information you'll need to determine how to improve system performance. If performance is degrading, you need to identify which operations are causing the problem, and whether the primary bottleneck is in memory, disk, or processing power. All the BI components love memory, so it's a good bet to check memory usage first.

The best way to solve resource contention may be to distribute your DW/BI system across multiple servers. A lot of DW/BI teams will try to build an all-in-one system, with the four major BI components (relational database, Integration Services, Analysis Services, and Reporting Services) on a single server. As we discussed in Chapter 4, it's often sensible to distribute across multiple servers. There's no hard and fast rule about which components to group together, although most often we see the relational database and Integration Services on the same box.

Because of the memory requirements of all the components, 64-bit hardware is very appealing. The price of a 64-bit commodity server with 8GB of RAM is astonishingly low. The extra memory can make a huge difference in the performance of your system. It feels intellectually lazy to recommend a hardware upgrade to solve performance problems, but if you've done a good job on your system design it's often the easiest—if not the only—degree of freedom. An exception is in performance tuning for Analysis Services, where it's often fairly easy to extract significant improvement.

No matter what you're doing to improve performance, it's really important to follow good change management and tuning techniques:

- Work on the test system, and script any changes to production.
- Document baseline performance.
- Change one thing at a time.
- Document changes to performance.
- Test all the changes together before moving to production.

Performance Tuning Analysis Services

There are three big things you can do to improve the performance of your Analysis Services database:

- Upgrade your hardware, especially memory, as discussed in the preceding subsection.
- Create an optimal set of aggregations.
- Use partitions to improve query and processing performance.

Optimizing Aggregation Design

We've been saying for decades that the single best way to improve query performance for a DW/BI system is to build aggregations. This is as true for an OLAP system as it's always been for the relational data warehouse. Aggregations are so much better and easier to manage with Analysis Services that we seldom create relational aggregations any more.

When you first design your cube and measure groups, you can use the Aggregation Design Wizard to define aggregations. That wizard highlights the inevitable tradeoff in aggregation design: Query performance increases with the number of aggregations, but processing performance decreases. Optimal aggregation design maximizes query performance while minimizing the processing penalty.

The single best way to optimize aggregation design is to base aggregations on the actual usage of the Analysis Services database: to use the Usage Based Optimization (UBO) Wizard. But before you can design usage-based optimizations, you must capture queries in the query log. The query log is completely separate from the usage monitoring that you capture from Profiler. It's a server-wide set-ting that's used only to gather data for the UBO Wizard. It's not turned on by default.

> **TIP** Set up the query log from within Management Studio by right-clicking on the Analysis Server node in the Object Explorer window and choosing Properties. Store the query log in a SQL Server database that you've created to hold Analysis Services logs. The properties you may need to edit are:
>
> - *Log\Query Log\QueryLogConnectionString:* Set up the connection to the logging database.
> - *Log\Query Log\QueryLogSampling:* The default is 10 (every tenth query is captured).
> - *Log\Query Log\CreateQueryLogTable:* Set to True to automatically create the query log table in SQL Server and start logging.

Launch the UBO Wizard from Management Studio by right-clicking on a measure group's partition and choosing Usage Based Optimization. The UBO Wizard reads the query log and designs aggregations based on your users' queries. These are the aggregations that you really want. The generic aggregations that were created at design time by the Aggregation Design Wizard are inferior to the usage-based aggregations.

As a good practice, use the Aggregation Design Wizard to create a small number of aggregations at design time. An aggregation level of 10 percent is a reasonable maximum; many experts design zero aggregations at the outset. Turn on the query log during the system testing phase, especially testing by business users. As one of the last pre-deployment steps, design usage-based aggregations. During the first few months the new Analysis Services database is in production, redesign aggregations every few weeks. When the database is in a steady state, you can redesign aggregations much less frequently, say on a quarterly basis.

Using Partitions

Partitions are almost as important as usage-based aggregations for improving query performance. Using partitions can also significantly improve processing performance.

> **TIP** You should consider using partitions, or increasing the grain of your existing partitioning, if a partition is larger than 5GB or 20 million rows.

There are two costs to partitioning:

- *Operational complexity:* We discuss this in the next section.

- *Licensing cost:* Partitioning requires SQL Server Enterprise Edition, which is approximately four times as expensive as Standard Edition.

The most obvious partitioning strategy is to partition by date, usually monthly. If your fact table has multiple date roles, like Order Date versus Ship Date, you should consider which role is used most often in users' queries. This is the best choice for query performance, but you might override this choice if another date role provides huge benefits for maintenance operations.

Partitioning improves query performance because the system keeps track of what slice of data is in each partition, and the query optimizer is selective. So if you partition by month, and a query asks for data from only one month, then only one partition is accessed to answer the query.

> **TIP** Analysis Services 2000 required that you manually set the data slice for each partition. Analysis Services 2005 automatically tracks that information for partitions stored in its own MOLAP structure. Partitions that are kept in the relational database still need their slice set by hand.

Partitioning improves processing performance when you process multiple partitions in parallel. This is usually a huge benefit during full processing of the database. Partitioning also improves processing performance if you need to process only the current partition.

> **TIP** Analysis Services 2005 automatically processes multiple partitions in parallel. Parallel processing in Analysis Services 2000 was harder; most people used the parallel processing utility distributed by Microsoft. That utility is no longer necessary.

The more finely you partition, the more you'll improve query and processing performance. You're usually better off by partitioning along multiple dimensions—say Date.Month and Product.Brand—than by partitioning more finely along a single dimension like Date.Day. This makes sense if you think about it: You're more likely to get query selectivity along two dimensions than along one, and you're more likely to be able to process partitions in parallel, especially during incremental processing.

> **TIP** If you create a lot of partitions, you'll find it increasingly awkward to use Management Studio. With a thousand partitions, it may take five minutes to open the database node in order to browse the dimensions and measure groups.

Most implementations will partition evenly along a dimension level like Product.Brand. You don't have to, though. If you have five brands that combined make up 80 percent of sales, and then 500 brands that make up the rest, you might create 6 partitions: one for each large brand, and one for all the rest.

Managing Partitioning

We hope we've convinced you that partitioning your Analysis Services and relational fact tables is a good idea. For Analysis Services, as we just discussed, partitioning can greatly improve query and processing performance. Partitioning can also help you solve some thorny processing problems, particularly with snapshot fact tables.

In the relational data warehouse, partitioned fact tables are easier to manage than non-partitioned tables, particularly for backups. Because you can set partitions to be read-only (more accurately, you set the partition's filegroup to be read-only), incremental backups can be much smaller and faster. Partitioned fact tables can also make the initial load of historical data occur much more quickly and easily. If you're willing to invest in a more complex management system, you can use partitioned fact tables to help you with incremental loads into the relational data warehouse.

Managing Relational Partitions

You'd expect to partition only the fact table in the relational data warehouse. There's no technical reason that you couldn't partition a dimension table, but it's hard to envision a scenario where doing so is helpful.

Almost everyone who partitions the fact table does so by date, and only by date. Unlike Analysis Services, where finer grained partitioning is really helpful, in the relational engine you can partition by a single column only. This section, then, assumes you're partitioning by date, usually by month.

A partitioned table looks and behaves like a single, monolithic table. You can select from, insert into, and update data in the partitioned table using normal SQL. Queries are selective: a query for a single day's data will touch only the partition that contains that day's data. Inserts work correctly: Under the covers SQL Server finds the correct partition and inserts the new row into it. Updates, of course, also work correctly.

Under the covers, you can think of a partitioned table as a set of identically structured tables that are hooked together by metadata. The requirement that the structures be identical is serious: same columns, same column names, same indexes, same constraints, same everything. The only difference is that they can be on different file groups. These details are discussed in greater detail in Chapter 4.

NOTE Partitioned tables are really a single object. The optimizer evaluates a single set of statistics and table-level metadata. Only the underlying storage is partitioned.

In Chapter 4, we talked about how most systems will fast-load identically structured partition tables during the initial historical load, then combine those tables into a single partitioned table. Under normal operations, most people will simply load today's data directly into the partitioned table. As we've already said, SQL Server takes care of sending that data to the correct partition.

With this simple partitioning plan, all you need to do is make sure you have partitions ready before you need them. If you're partitioning monthly, the easiest thing to do is to create the next year's worth of partitions at the end of every year. You should document your operations plan to this effect. It's always dangerous to rely on people to remember to do something once a year—even if it's documented—but in this case no tragedy will ensue if you forget. You can always split a partition later. It takes processing resources, and you should back up your table before you begin, but it's not a big deal.

Fast Loading Daily Partitions

If your incremental fact table loads are huge—10 million or more rows per day—and your load window small, you need to be more creative. It will be really important for you to be able to fast-load even your incremental fact table loads. If you're keeping less than a year of data online you can partition daily, but you shouldn't plan to have more than several hundred partitions online.

To fast-load data into a very large partitioned table, follow these steps:

1. Near the beginning of the Integration Services package that performs the fact table load, clone a table partition. You want an empty table that's structured identically to the target partition table. Name the empty table as MyFactTable_yyyymmdd. You could implement this cloning as an Execute SQL task in Integration Services, using a variable expression to supply the table name. Alternatively, you could use the SQL Server SMO object model and use the Script task. Chapter 4 describes the necessary characteristics of the empty table, including a check constraint.

2. The Data Flow task for the incremental load package is the same as it would be for a non-partitioned table, with one exception. The target is your new empty table rather than the partitioned table. (You could create a view when you create the empty table so that the Data Flow task always has the same target name, or you could parameterize the OLE DB Destination in the Data Flow task.)

3. Load data into your new, empty table, using the fast-load techniques we discussed in Chapter 6.

4. Create the appropriate indexes and foreign key constraints (if any) on the new table. As with the cloning step, you can use an Execute SQL task or a Script task.

5. Switch the newly loaded table with today's data into the partitioned table. Again, you can use an Execute SQL or a Script task. In Chapter 4 we detail what we mean by switching the table into the partition, and show the SQL syntax.

At the end of the month, merge the daily partitions into a monthly partition by bulk inserting the daily data into an empty table, and then switching that new table (now containing a month of data) into the partitioned table. You can implement this as a separate Integration Services package that you'd schedule monthly. Set last month's partition to be read-only.

> **WARNING** Do not merge or split partitions, other than empty partitions. SQL Server will do the right thing, in the sense that it will move the data for you. But it will do it intolerably slowly. Use bulk insert operations into an empty table, and then switch into the partitioned table.

LateArriving Data

Your processing logic has to be a lot more complicated if you'll receive late-arriving data for your daily partitioned fact table. We've worked on very large systems where 70 percent of the data we receive today was from yesterday; 20 percent was from the day before yesterday; and the remaining 10 percent could span back months.

In this scenario, assuming you're still determined to fast-load the daily partition, you need to put a conditional split into the data flow, dividing the clean data stream into yesterday and all other. Fast-load yesterday's data into its own daily partition, and use slow loading techniques for aged data.

> **TIP** In this scenario, you should evaluate the costs and benefits of loading the really old data right away. Does data that's three months old have any value to the DW/BI system? It depends on the business requirements. At the very least, evaluate whether it makes sense to hold onto aged data until the weekend. The data's already late—is it important that the users see it today?

Accumulating Snapshots

An accumulating snapshot is a kind of fact table that keeps track of a process whose state changes over time, like the lifecycle of an order or manufacturing process. The accumulating snapshot fact tends to have lots of date roles (Order

Date, Payment Date, Verification Date, Requested Ship Date, Actual Ship Date) and facts that calculate the amount of time spent between various checkpoints. Each row in the accumulating snapshot tends to receive a lot of updates during its lifecycle.

We hate updates in the DW/BI system. They're slow. They're untidy. They mess up your backup strategies. They really mess up cube processing or any aggregation tables you might be maintaining in the relational data warehouse.

You can lessen the pain of managing an accumulating snapshot if you can ascertain when its life is over: when an order has shipped, a package delivered, or a product manufactured. You can partition the fact table both by the date the process began and by IsCompleted. In this case you have two partitions for each month, one to hold facts that are completed, and one to hold those in process. As we discuss in the next section, Analysis Services will benefit hugely from localizing updates to a subset of the partitions.

Managing Analysis Services Partitions

Managing Analysis Services partitions is almost as easy as managing relational partitions. The main difference, apart from syntax, is that you must process each partition by name—there's no analogous operation for inserting data into the partitioned fact table. The unit of Analysis Services fact processing is the partition.

Partitioning by Month

As with the relational database, most systems will partition their large cubes by month. When you first develop the cube, you'll probably define the partitions by hand and then fully process the cube. Ongoing, you'll need to set up new partitions and incrementally process them. The following steps describe the ongoing process:

1. Near the beginning of the Integration Services package that performs the fact table load, create a new Analysis Services partition. Use the Integration Services task called SQL Server Analysis Services Execute DDL Task, which we'll call the AS-DDL task.

2. Get the basic form of the AS-DDL statement by generating a script for an existing partition in Management Studio (right-click on the partition and choose Script Partition as Create). The AS-DDL statement is in an XML format, and is quite easy to read.

3. You need to make three modifications to the AS-DDL template statement:

   ■ Modify the ID and Name attributes so they're tagged with the current month, for example, MyMeasureGroup_yyyymm.

- Modify the WHERE clause of the source query so it refers to the correct date range. For example, the source query may include a WHERE clause like the following:

```
WHERE DateKey &gt;= 20050300 AND DateKey &lt;= 20050332
```

- Set the SLICE property of the AS-DDL statement to point to the year and month contained within the Analysis Services Partition:

```
<Slice>[Date Dimension].[Calendar Hierarachy].
[Calendar YearMo].&amp;[200503]</Slice>
```

4. Process the new partition.

REFERENCE SQL Server ships an excellent sample that describes how to automate the partition management process. You should modify this sample to fit your own environment. The default location for the sample is C:\Program Files\Microsoft SQL Server\90\Samples\Integration Services\Package Samples\ SyncAdvWorksPartitions Sample.

Partitioning by Two Dimensions

Earlier in this chapter we recommended that you partition very large cubes by a second dimension, say by product family. If you follow this strategy, then each month you'll have multiple partitions, one for each product family.

The script that creates the monthly partition set is obviously more complicated than the single partition case outlined previously. It's a straightforward extension of that logic, with one caveat: Make sure you look for new product families, and add a new partition as necessary. With the Date dimension, you don't need any fancy logic to know when to add a new partition. But with other dimensions, it's perfectly possible for us to receive a new member, like a new product family.

The script that creates the new month's partition set should query the cube to find all possible values for Product Family, and create a partition for each. You should also account for the possibility that a product family is added mid-month, if that event can occur in your environment.

Partitioning and Proactive Caching

Proactive Caching is an important new feature of Analysis Services 2005, which simplifies cube processing. As we describe in Chapter 17, a partition with Proactive Caching turned on isn't processed explicitly by a "Process Partition" command. Instead, Analysis Services monitors the relational database and magically adds new data to the cube as it appears in the source database.

Under normal circumstances turn on Proactive Caching only for the current partition. As soon as a partition ages, turn off Proactive Caching, and do a full process of the partition. It's important to fully process a partition that's been incrementally processed by Proactive Caching. The frequent incremental updates leave the partition in an inefficient state, similar conceptually to a fragmented index in the relational database.

If you're adding data into your relational fact table by switching in partitions, as described earlier in this chapter, you should be aware that Proactive Caching will not pick up this event. In other words, let's say you added a whole month of data to your relational fact table by loading that data into an empty table and then revising the fact table's partitioning strategy. The corresponding Analysis Services partition will remain empty because this event doesn't trigger the Proactive Cache.

The workaround is simple: Create the Analysis Services partition after the fact table partition has been created, populated, and added to the fact table. Fully process the new Analysis Services partition as soon as you create it, to grab this initial set of data. Immediately after processing, turn on Proactive Caching for the new partition. As long as new rows are added to the relational partition through a normal Insert statement, rather than partition switching, the Proactive Caching mechanism will see those rows and add them to the Analysis Services partition.

Snapshot Fact Tables

There are two kinds of snapshot fact tables: the Accumulating Snapshot that we discussed earlier in this chapter, and the Periodic Snapshot fact table. Both of these snapshot fact tables are problematic for the Analysis Services database because both require significant fact row updates.

First, let's discuss the Periodic Snapshot. An example of a Periodic Snapshot fact table is inventory levels. The typical fact table, and associated cube, has inventory levels by warehouse and product for each month end. In the current month, you update inventory levels each day, keeping only current month to date.

Partitions really help you manage the Periodic Snapshot Analysis Services database. On the relational side, you may choose to replace data in the current partition. Or, you may choose to update the existing fact rows. Your decision here is based on what percentage of rows are updated every day. The relational database can accommodate either approach.

In Analysis Services, there is no way to update a fact. You can add new facts, but the only way to process fact updates is to fully reprocess the partition that contains that fact. If you partition your periodic snapshot cube by month, then every day you can fully reprocess the current month's partition.

Accumulating Snapshot cubes track processes with a relatively short life span. They're much harder to manage in Analysis Services because they inevitably require a lot of updates. If you must publish your Accumulating Snapshot schema as an Analysis Services cube, your first hope should be that the data is small enough to completely refresh the cube every load cycle. That would certainly be easiest to maintain, but it's seldom the case.

The solution is to partition both by date and by whether the process has completed. Every month you'll have two partitions: one for processes that have finished, and one for those that have not.

In your Integration Services package, you need to identify which Analysis Services partitions need to be incrementally updated because they've received new rows, and which need to be fully reprocessed because they've received updates.

Incrementally process any IsCompleted=Yes partition that's received a new row. IsCompleted=Yes partitions receive new rows when a transaction that started in that month gets completed today. In other words, let's say today is 5 March 2005. If you opened an order on 28 February, and you finally shipped it today, then you want to incrementally process the February-2005/IsCompleted Analysis Services partition. As far as that partition is concerned, this is a new row so incremental processing will work just fine.

Fully process any IsCompleted=No partition that's received a change. You can assume that the current month's partition always needs to be fully processed. But in the preceding example, you also need to fully process February's NotCompleted partition because the order from February 28 got updated. If the February 28 order had simply been updated—let's say it got shipped but hasn't yet been delivered—you'd still need to fully process the February-2005/NotCompleted partition.

Whew. You can see why people avoid building Accumulating Snapshot cubes.

Within the Integration Services package that manages the relational table, you can set up a loop to identify which cube partitions need to be incrementally and fully processed.

Backup and Recovery

No matter what are the availability requirements on your system, you need a backup and recovery plan. This seems like an intuitively obvious statement, but we've seen any number of DW/BI systems that purported to be in production, but which had no backup plan.

It's as important to have a recovery plan as it is to have a backup plan. And it's equally important to test these procedures. When the inevitable emergency happens, you want to be ready, practiced, and calm. Your test system is an ideal platform for testing these procedures. If you haven't fully tested your recovery procedures, you're lying to yourself and your management that you have a real backup and recovery plan.

In the DW/BI world, you can experience the same kinds of emergencies as transaction systems, from server outages and disk failures to earthquakes and floods. Plan for your daily or monthly load cycle to break down occasionally. Develop your ETL system so that failure is fairly unlikely. But let's face it: The DW/BI system is at the end of a long train of data flows over which you have no control. Only a foolish manager would neglect to plan for backing out a bad load. The auditing system described in Chapter 6 lays the foundation for identifying the rows that were changed during a specific load process.

SQL Server Databases

The relational databases are usually the most vital sets of information to back up regularly. Ideally, back up the following databases after each load:

- Relational data warehouse databases
- Staging databases, if any
- Staging data in the file system, if any
- Metadata databases

You also need to set up a regular schedule to back up the logging databases. Your backup and recovery strategies are intertwined with each database's recovery model. The Simple recovery model lets you restore only to the point of a backup. The transaction log is not backed up. This works fine for many relational data warehouses, where data flows in nightly, weekly, or monthly. The Simple recovery model is appropriately named; it's faster and simpler to manage than the Full recovery model. Nonetheless, as your DW/BI system moves closer to real time, the Full recovery model becomes increasingly appropriate.

REFERENCE See the Books Online topics "Overview of the Recovery Models," "Recovery Models and Supported Restore Operations," and "Selecting a Recovery Model" for more information.

Most systems use the standard SQL Server backup facilities for relational backup and recovery. The relational data warehouse database is usually quite large, and so it's often challenging to run a backup at the end of each (nightly) load cycle. There are several alternatives:

- Store the database on a Storage Area Network (SAN), and use the SAN software to perform the backup. The SAN backup techniques are high performance, and this approach has been a common practice for very large databases with SQL Server 2000.

- Partition the large fact tables, and set aged partitions to be read-only. Perform occasional full backups, but rely primarily on a strategy of filegroup and partial differential backups. Under the simple recovery model, partial backups back up the primary filegroup and all the read-write filegroups. Read-only partitions are backed up when they're filled and converted to read-only status. The innovation of read-only partitions greatly improves your ability to quickly back up the changed portions of the relational data warehouse.

> **REFERENCE** See the Books Online topic "Partial and Partial Differential Backups" for more details.

The logging database is written to constantly. Some DW/BI teams think the logging data is vitally important, and implement a very strong backup strategy. Other teams are sanguine about the notion of losing a week's worth of logging data, and manage the database far more loosely. Obviously, if your logging data contains usage data necessary for regulatory compliance, you need to develop a serious backup and recovery strategy. Use Full recovery mode and a backup strategy appropriate for a transaction database. Books Online, and any number of SQL Server books, are filled with information about backup strategies for transaction databases.

Approaches differ on backup and recovery strategies for the staging databases. Many DW/BI teams think of the data in the staging tables as ephemeral, and back up only the table CREATE scripts. On the other hand, most staging databases contain only data for the most recent loads—for example, the last seven days—so a full database backup is really fast.

You may have built a simple application for business users to manipulate custom hierarchies or other attributes of a dimension. Such an application is a transaction system, however small scale. Typically you want the application to write directly to a different database than the data warehouse, one with Full recovery mode and log backups. Similarly, the metadata database should also be treated more like a transactional database than the large data warehouse database.

The msdb system database may include your Integration Services packages. It will certainly include any SQL Agent job definitions and schedules, and other information used by Management Studio, including information about which databases were backed up. For that reason, the msdb database should always be backed up immediately after any other backup operation. Use Full recovery mode for msdb.

Integration Services

The most important information to back up for Integration Services are the package definitions themselves. Packages can be stored in SQL Server, in the file system, or in a managed mode in the file system called the Package Store.

If the package definitions are stored in SQL Server, they're located in the msdb system database, which as we've already discussed should be backed up religiously.

If the packages are stored in the file system or the Package Store, simply use a file system backup utility like Windows Backup to back up the package definitions, configuration files, and associated information. Of course, package definitions should be under source control, and that source control database backed up too.

As we discussed in Chapters 5 and 6, you may be staging or storing data in the file system. With Integration Services, this is a more common staging area than within the relational database. Use Windows Backup or another copy utility to back up staged data. This is especially vital if you're relying on re-running staged extracts to bring your data warehouse database up-to-date.

Analysis Services

Throughout this book we've encouraged you to think of the Analysis Services database as ephemeral—a database that may need to be fully reprocessed at some point. That's necessary because Analysis Services doesn't support the full level of data manageability, notably updates and deletes, as the relational database. The great benefits provided by Analysis Services in query performance, complex security, a calculation engine, and easy user navigation come at a cost. You need a plan for being able to fully reprocess the dimensional database; never throw away the relational data.

You absolutely must back up the definition of the Analysis Services database: the information that enables you to fully process the database. You might think that, because you have the database definition on your development server and checked into source control, you're safe. You could always re-deploy and re-process the Analysis Services database. That's largely true, but you've probably modified aggregation design and partition strategy on the production database; these changes are not reflected in the version on the development server.

You won't find a formal command or utility for backing up the database's definition. The most straightforward approach is to generate a complete CREATE script for the database, and back up that script.

The recommended method for backing up the Analysis Services database is to use the Analysis Services backup and restore facility in Management Studio. For readers familiar with Analysis Services 2000, the new backup facility overcomes the (severe) limitations of the old archive utility. The greatest drawback of Analysis Services 2005 backup is that it works only at the database level. On the plus side, you can launch the Backup and Restore wizards from Management Studio. From within the wizard, you can script the commands for automated operations. Schedule the backup from SQL Agent or launch it from an Integration Services package. The Analysis Services Samples folder includes source code for a sample application that illustrates how to execute backup and restore programmatically.

The Analysis Services Backup facility backs up all metadata, but only data that's stored in MOLAP format. This includes all data and aggregations for MOLAP partitions, and aggregations only for HOLAP partitions. Data stored in the relational data warehouse should be backed up using relational backup techniques. Plan for your Analysis Services backups to take about as much space as the database itself. Analysis Services databases are stored so efficiently that—unlike relational backups—we see very little additional compression upon backup.

If your Analysis Services database is small, in the tens of gigabytes, the simplest approach is to perform a full backup every load cycle, or whenever you make a metadata change. No matter how efficient the backup utility might be, if your Analysis Services database is multiple terabytes, it's just not practical to perform daily full backups.

TIP If you have a Storage Area Network (SAN), frequent full backups are more practical, with very limited downtime and minimal pressure on server resources. You can circumvent the backup utility and copy the files directly:

- Create a mirror set and wait for it to fully synchronize.

- Stop Analysis Services; break the mirror; restart Analysis Services.

- Mount the mirrored image as a separate drive and perform a file level backup of the entire data folder (Program Files\Microsoft SQL Server\ MSSQL\OLAP\Data).

Our recommended practice is to back up the database whenever the metadata changes. Metadata changes include redesigning aggregations, adding a partition, or changing security groups and permissions. If you just can't do a full backup every time the metadata changes, you should first question why your metadata is changing so often! Assuming you're still in this situation, you *must* capture the database ALTER scripts, always date-time stamped so it's easy to identify which changes have occurred since the last backup.

TIP Always script any metadata change on the production server. Most changes, including security and aggregation design, should be tested on your test server, and then rolled to production using ALTER scripts. Use a script to add new partitions as well, although this routine operation might not have a corresponding action on the test server.

INCREMENTAL BACKUPS

If your Analysis Services database contains multiple terabytes of data, you are probably groaning about this discussion of backup and restore. It actually is possible to perform file system incremental backups—and restores!—of both data and metadata.

Incremental backups can be performed at the system level only—in other words, for all the Analysis Services databases on a server in an integrated way. An incremental backup is machine-wide (restoration is the same). You cannot incrementally back up an individual database, cube, dimension, or partition. The issue is that there are various metadata files that are being updated across the whole system. The only consistent view is at the top.

You must include in the backup both the primary Analysis Services data folder, and any other partition storage locations as a single unit. You should write an Integration Services package that uses AMO to find all such folder locations.

When this backup is running, the system cannot be updating. The safest approach is to stop the Analysis Services service during the incremental backup. You can use RAID and/or SAN technology to minimize system downtime:

1. Form a mirror.

2. Stop Analysis Service (net stop msmdsrv).

3. Break the mirror set.

4. Restart the service (net start msmdsrv).

5. Perform the backup on the mirror.

Some SAN hardware has built-in features that will simplify this process.

As you'll probably agree, incremental backups are sufficiently tricky that you should undertake them only if you must—in other words, only if your database is huge. We hope to see a write-up of this technique, with sample scripts, on www.microsoft.com/sql/bi/ProjectReal.

To restore the Analysis Services database, run the Restore script. Apply any ALTER scripts. Fully process any partition that's gotten new data since the backup—usually just the current partition or partition set. If you have late arriving data, you need to build a more complicated system for identifying which partitions need to be reprocessed.

Reporting Services

All of your Reporting Services report definitions and schedules are in the Report Server database. This database should use Full recovery mode, and be backed up like any transactional database.

Recovery

It is as important to document and test your recovery plan as it is to perform backups. During an emergency is not the time to test out your recovery procedures. We could regale you with sad tales of daily backups to corrupt media that were never tested until too late. Despite the fact that this is kindergarten-level system administration, we are past being astonished at finding people who don't know if their recovery procedures will work.

WARNING We've said it several times already, but once more: Backup without verification is meaningless and a waste of time. You're better off not even doing the backup, and not kidding yourself that you're protected. Good intentions don't count.

Verification doesn't mean checking the checkbox in the utility, which verifies the physical media. That's a good thing to do; it's just not what we're talking about. We're talking about testing the full recovery process, including the BI applications, to make sure everything really works. And it's not just that the scripts work. You need to confirm, by testing, that your staff know what steps to take to successfully restore the system.

Summary

Most of us find it more fun to think about designing and developing, than operating and maintaining. But there's no point in undertaking the design activities if you're not confident your system can operate smoothly, efficiently, and with good performance. And it's important to think about these issues early, during the design and development phases of the system. Good operating procedures are cooked into the system, not tacked on at the end.

This chapter talks about two kinds of operational procedures: front-room operations and back-room operations. Front-room operations, from maintaining the BI portal to extending BI applications and educating users, requires a continuing commitment to meeting the needs of the business. It requires a significant number of ongoing staff, usually as many, if not more, as were involved with the initial development of the front-room systems.

Most of the chapter was devoted to a discussion of back-room operations. We described how to schedule and execute Integration Services packages in a production environment. We introduced some of the issues you will need to consider in order to meet availability and performance SLAs. And we discussed the most important factors to consider when tuning your DW/BI system for excellent performance.

One of the key levers for tuning the Analysis Services database is to partition the data, which improves query performance, processing performance, and manageability. Partitioning of the relational fact table is also valuable, sometimes for performance but most often for manageability. Partitioning doesn't come for free, however. Adding partitioning to your DW/BI system complicates the operating procedures.

The last section of this chapter discusses issues around backing up and restoring your databases and other components of your system. We'll take one last opportunity to remind you to take backup and recovery seriously, or don't do it at all.

PART

Five

Extending the
DW/BI System

Managing Growth

There's no rest for the weary

At this point, unless you plan to include real-time capabilities, you have reached the last step in the Lifecycle. By now, you should have completed the deployment of your first business process dimensional model to great success. The tendency at this point is to feel like you've finished the whole project. We encourage you to celebrate your achievement, and we hate to rain on your parade, but the arrow that goes from the Growth box back to the Project Planning box in Figure 16.1 reminds you that the Lifecycle is an iterative process. You have two major tasks at this point. The first is the obvious extension of the warehouse by adding the next priority business process row in the bus matrix, and by adding new user groups. The second task, now that you've had some success, is to dig in and get the DW/BI system fully woven into the fabric of the organization. This acceptance and integration of the DW/BI system by the business does not happen by accident, and it relies more on political and organizational skills than technical skills.

We start this chapter with a look at how the Lifecycle works as an iterative process and what it means to go back through the Lifecycle for the next implementation round. In particular, we revisit the major sections of the Lifecycle from the perspective of the second and subsequent iterations. Then, we focus on techniques for integrating the DW/BI system into the organization. Most of this effort involves activities that fall under the marketing and communications categories. We offer several strategies for accomplishing business acceptance and integration of the DW/BI system.

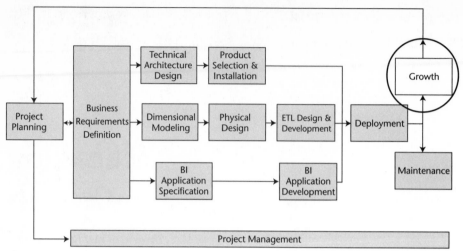

Figure 16.1   The Growth step in the Lifecycle

In addition to business acceptance, you should seek technical acceptance as well. This typically shows itself in the form of downstream information-based systems, like the Customer Relationship Management (CRM) system, turning to the DW/BI system to take advantage of its value-added contents. This downstream usage is an important part of growing the system, but you will need to manage this usage in terms of performance and service level requirements.

Lifecycle Iteration: Growing the DW/BI System

Building a DW/BI system is an iterative process, so adding the next business process dimensional model is just like starting over, only easier. You still need to go through all the boxes on the Lifecycle, but you don't need to reinvent the wheel: you need to consider only the new stuff. For example, you already have your initial data architecture in the form of the bus matrix from your initial requirements gathering process described way back in Chapter 1. You also have the relative business value of each row in the bus matrix from the prioritization process also described in Chapter 1. (Remember the meeting where you worked with senior management to choose the highest value, easiest row on the bus matrix to implement first?) Now, go back and pick up the next business process on the prioritized list and move it through the Lifecycle. It's always a good idea to verify that business priorities haven't changed with your business steering committee.

Business Requirements and Project Management

Business requirements definition is the cornerstone of the Lifecycle, but after the first round, it is usually limited to project-level requirements related to the new business process dimensional model. You will need more detail about this next business process: how do people use this information, what kind of analyses do they create or need, how does it tie in to existing data in the warehouse, what kinds of system or architectural implications do you see, and so on.

The initial part of every iteration will also involve some project planning, but this time it should be easier than the first time around. You now have real-world experience on which you can base your estimates. You already have most of your system infrastructure and development environment in place. You will be able to directly re-use several of the conformed dimensions and much of the ETL modules. In short, project planning should be significantly easier in the second and subsequent iterations.

After gathering project-level business requirements and creating project plans, you'll continue through the Lifecycle by considering the technology, data, and application tracks.

The Technology Track

The second dataset often has significant technical and architectural implications you must deal with in the technology track. For example, the data in this iteration could have problems with data availability, definition, quality, and/or quantity. The technical issues may be something as simple as huge data volumes. Usually, these relate to the reasons you decided to leave this data until later. As a result, you may need to extend your architecture with additional functionality or capacity. In other words, you may need to buy some more software, or buy a new server, or both. For example, this second round may include a second source for customer data. In order to integrate the two sources, you may need additional software to help do the name and address matching. This second set of customer data may be much larger than the first set, driving a need for more disk space, and probably for more CPUs.

The great thing is, you already knew this from your requirements definition and prioritization. And, you set expectations early on that this would happen. In fact, you may have started the purchasing process long before you got to this point.

The Data Track

In the data track, you will develop and implement the dimensional model for this next business process. The modeling process is essentially a repeat of the in-depth dive you did in the first round to do the dimensional design. You will use all the existing conformed dimensions that apply, and typically add a few new dimensions that are specific to this next business process. For example, you may have implemented Orders data in the first round and now you want to bring in Shipments. Shipments will use the same Product and Customer dimensions, but it will also have a new dimension that describes the Shipper.

The ETL process is also essentially the same as in your first pass. Having the standards and examples in place can speed the process significantly, and not having to build all the dimensions saves time as well. However, the second and subsequent business process data models are often more difficult. They may have poor data quality, or large data volumes, or data integration issues, or any number of problems.

The Applications Track

In the Business Intelligence Applications track, you will add a set of standard analyses specifically related to the new business process. Often there are additional, and in many cases more powerful, analyses that incorporate data from both business processes now in the warehouse. For example, a retailer might have loaded sales data in the first iteration of the Lifecycle and is loading external customer demographics data in the second pass. As we described in the data mining chapter, the ability to combine behavioral data, in this case Sales, with descriptive data, in this case demographics, can be extremely powerful. You could use this combination of data to identify certain customer groups and offer them products they are more likely to be interested in. This is where the business intelligence system has a huge opportunity to add business value. Note that this has implications for the technology track—you are not only adding new data, but you will be adding data mining functionality as well.

Deployment, Maintenance, and Growth

As in the first iteration, the three tracks come together in the deployment phase. You will need to train new users, and may want to update the training materials to reflect the new data. You will need to create documentation for the new business process data model and the associated BI applications and make it available on the web site. You will need to complete the full testing cycle before you release the data, and of course, you will need to support both the existing and new users.

Then, once this iteration is complete, you start all over again with the next row on the matrix. Remember that the work of the data warehouse is never done.

Marketing and Expectation Management

At the same time you are project-focused on building the second and subsequent iterations, you need to be outwardly focused on the connections between the data warehouse and the rest of the organization. *Marketing* is probably the wrong term to use for this section because Marketing has a bad reputation with most technical folks—although not as bad as its evil twin, Sales. (Just kidding, some of our best friends are in Sales.) It may be more appealing to view the activities in this section as educational efforts. But call it what you will—in this "what have you done for me lately" world, you must actively and constantly market the BI system.

From an educational perspective, your goal is to make sure everyone knows what they need to know about the BI system. Management needs to know how their investment is going. Specifically, they need to know how it is being used to generate value for the organization. It also helps them to see how it is being used in different parts of the company. Analysts and other knowledge workers need to know how they can use the DW/BI system more effectively and why it's important to them. The IT organization also needs to know what's going on with the DW/BI system. You need close working relationships with the source system managers on the input side of the data warehouse, and with other information-driven systems on the output side of the data warehouse. Fortunately, you have some quantitative and qualitative tools to help educate all these groups. In this section, we start out with an assessment of whom the major stakeholders in the DW/BI system are, and then look at the communication and education tools available to help keep them informed.

The Stakeholders

A map or list of the various stakeholders in the BI system helps ensure you consider the needs of all interested parties. A big challenge for the BI system manager is that everyone is a potential stakeholder, and we mean everyone. In fact, there is no reason the reach of the BI system can't extend beyond the organizational boundaries because there is often significant value to be found in providing information to your customers and suppliers. A good place to start for this list of stakeholders is the communications plan you created as part of the initial project plan. In a way, this section is about creating the ongoing communications plan. Table 16.1 lists the major stakeholders in the DW/BI system along with some of the tools or techniques you can use to keep them informed and engaged.

We have already discussed many of these techniques in earlier chapters. The rest of this chapter concentrates on the engagement techniques that have not been presented before. Because the DW/BI system is all about quantitative measures, we'll start with how to use quantitative techniques as an engagement tool.

Table 16.1 BI System Stakeholders and Engagement Tools

STAKEHOLDERS	TOOLS
Senior management	Usage Reports; Status Notes; User Forums; Senior Staff meetings; BI Steering Committee; BI Web Site
Business community	Usage Reports; Support; Training; Newsletter; User Forums; User surveys; BI Web Site
Senior IT management	Regular briefings; User Forums
Transaction systems	DW/BI knowledge transfer; New product design teams; Master data projects; Scoring feeds
Information-driven systems	Requirements gathering; Data feeds; Support
External data sources	Regular contact; Status reports including failure rates
External users	Requirements gathering; User surveys

Quantitative Techniques

The same systems you use to monitor queries and performance can also give you the data you need to show basic usage across the organization. Use your reporting tools against the usage monitoring system you set up in Chapter 15 to show how usage is changing over time. The example report in Figure 16.2 shows a trend of increasing usage, both in terms of the number of active users and in the average number of queries per user.

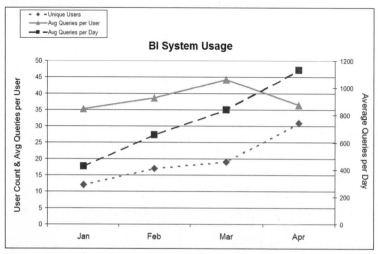

Figure 16.2 An example data warehouse usage report

This is definitely the kind of report you'd like to show to senior management. Obviously, if the usage trends are decreasing, you might not be so eager to share the report, but you'd better figure out why. Other usage reports might include:

- Share of query activity by department (a sorted bar chart)
- Queries by source (automated versus user created)
- Query counts by business process data model (from the fact table)

You should publish reports on the BI portal that show usage at lower levels as well, like the one in Figure 16.3. A department-level BI analyst can view these reports to see who's using the system in their group and who might need help. Publishing these reports is also an indirect way of informing people about the fact that you monitor their usage. After all, the DW/BI system is an organizational asset and you need to manage it responsibly.

An interesting side benefit of publishing usage statistics we've seen in some companies is that it sparks the competitive side of people. Seeing that others are using the system can actually motivate people to begin using it themselves.

Qualitative Techniques

While usage statistics are interesting, they show only activity, not business value. Simple query counts tell you nothing about the content or business impact of those queries. Unfortunately, there's no good way of automatically capturing the value of each analysis in the warehouse. You still have to get this information the old-fashioned way, by talking to people. Essentially, someone on the DW/BI system team has to go out into the user community on a regular basis and ask people to describe what they are doing, assess the business impact it has had, and document it.

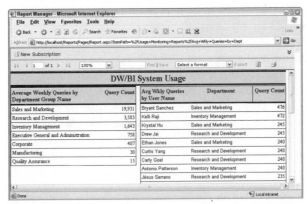

Figure 16.3 An example departmental and user level usage report

THE COMPETITIVE SPIRIT

The manager of a BI system project invited us to attend the quarterly meeting of the regional VPs of a major consumer finance organization. On the way to the meeting we picked up a report of users ranked by their usage that he had just printed for us to see. It was not on the agenda, but it happened to be on top of our stack as we sat down at the table. These were competitive folks in a competitive industry. One of the VPs happened to see the report and pulled it off the stack to examine it. The VP next to him leaned over to see, and within 60 seconds, they were all leaning across the table looking at the report.

One of them observed in a pleased tone that his region was really using the BI system and getting good information from it. At that point, the VP whose region was clearly not using the system turned to the BI system manager and began insisting on getting training scheduled for his region as soon as possible. This was for a region in which the BI system manager had not been able to generate any interest for the prior year. Sometimes a little competition can be a strong motivator.

Most of the time, the impact isn't all that stunning. People do useful things that make a big difference in their lives, but it's not the multi-million dollar hit. For example, you may find a financial analyst who has built several queries to gather baseline data for the annual forecasting process. Gathering this info used to take her several days and now it only takes a few minutes. This is good, but not great.

STEALTH MARKETING

One of our Kimball Group associates experienced the power of simple education at a client where the BI system project manager captured a whole set of high-value stories. Every time someone told her one of these great stories she asked them (and hounded them) to write it up and guesstimate the financial impact on the business in an email memo to her. She then printed the stories, placed them in plastic sleeves and put them in a three-ring binder loudly labeled *DW Success Stories*, and strategically placed it on her desk where everyone could see it. Ultimately, she had well over $100 million of business value documented. People would stop by all the time and page through it. Whenever the BI team went to management for more funding or resources, the binder was strategically placed on the conference room table before the meetings. Ultimately, she parlayed this into several promotions and finally into a senior role in the brand marketing area.

Every so often, you will find someone who has done something that has had a significant impact. They may have done a study that helped them tune marketing promotions in a way that doubled response rates and increased revenue by $700,000. Or, they may have identified a pattern of calls in the customer care data that led to a simple change in the documentation and reduced the call volume by 13 percent (at $6/call, that's over $100,000 per year for a company that takes 500 calls per day). Or they may have analyzed the donor database in a small non-profit organization and identified donors who had dropped out. A special program to reconnect with these people yielded a 63 percent response rate and close to $200,000. You get the idea.

Educating the Business: the User Forum

Finding these high-impact examples is a lot of work. One technique we've used, called the User Forum is an effective way to identify and leverage these qualitative examples of value. The User Forum is a DW/BI event held with the business community. Schedule these on a regular basis: about every six months or so. The meeting is usually 90 minutes and has the same basic agenda every time. Try to schedule the meeting around your main business sponsor, who kicks off the meeting with a short speech about how important the data warehouse is to the organization's success. The first item on the agenda is a brief presentation from the BI team about the current state of the warehouse and your short term plans. The bulk of the meeting is dedicated to two presentations from analysts who used the BI system to generate significant value for the organization. They talk about what they did, how they did it, and what kind of impact it had.

Senior management likes this because they see the impact. Often the head of one department will see what another department has done and realize her group is missing an opportunity. Middle management and analysts like the presentations because they include enough detail so people can see exactly how the analysis was accomplished. They learn new techniques and approaches to the analytical process. Remember the example of the customer care rep who discovered that one particular model of a particular product by a particular manufacturer generated a much higher call rate than average? He worked with the design engineers to pinpoint the problem as a manufacturing defect. This ultimately saved the company several hundred thousand dollars in customer care costs. (It also made the manufacturer a bit unhappy.) This is a great story to present at a User Forum.

In this example, senior management likes the value and other analysts learn from the particular techniques used to solve the problem. Everyone wins! Well, maybe not the manufacturer.

None of this happens by accident. Carefully plan the meeting over the six months leading up to it. Find good presentation candidates with high business value by going around and talking to all your users on a regular basis. Once you find one, work with the user to create a clear, compelling presentation with lots of good screen captures and a summary page that shows the dollar impact of the analysis. Rehearse the presentation with them, especially if they are not experienced presenters. This also helps you get the timing down. You don't want your audience to miss the punch line because you went over your time limit. Contact key attendees to make sure they are going to make it to the meeting. If the CEO or VP of Marketing can't make it, consider rescheduling if she is the sponsor and you want her support or if you think she can learn something by being at the meeting.

Don't be too proud to employ blatant marketing techniques to promote the meeting. The basics almost go without saying: Food and drink are a must. (We found that trays of Krispy Kreme donuts were a big hit.) Consider offering marketing swag as prizes. Since most BI teams are friendly with the marketing group, see if they'll let you raid their goodies closet.

See what we mean when we say you've got to market the BI system actively and constantly?

Educating the Senior Staff

Your top educational priority in the long term should be to continuously and consistently inform senior management about what the DW/BI system is, why it's important, and what it takes to make it happen. The marketing efforts we just described help achieve this priority, but obviously, the greater your access to senior management, the easier this education process will be. This is where the organizational placement of the DW/BI team can have a big influence. Ideally, the head of the team reports to senior management and is considered part of the senior management team. The rationale is that any decisions involving new programs, directions, and initiatives should be made with as much information as possible. Often, senior management will want to explore an idea to see if it is viable before launching any major new initiative. Having a direct line to the DW/BI team can help senior management quickly triage those ideas that should be abandoned and those that should be developed further.

Once an idea begins to gain traction, its development must be accompanied by the appropriate measurement and analytical systems. All too often we've seen a major new initiative taken on by senior management with no means to measure its impact or value. If the data is not collected, you can't analyze it. Unfortunately, having the DW/BI team report to the CEO is a politically difficult structure to create. The CIO and other C-level executives could be threatened by it.

Involving the BI team leader (and potentially the whole BI team) in directly supporting senior management decision making requires a high level of trust and discretion. Suppose, for example, management wants the BI team to assess the impact of potential layoffs as part of a scenario planning process. It would not be good if the BI team lets it slip that "management is planning for layoffs."

Bottom line: however you make it happen, you need to make sure someone on the BI team is involved with senior management and understands where the business is headed so you can be prepared to support it.

Working with Steering Committees

If it's not politically possible for the BI team lead to be part of Senior Staff, another way to get the information you need is to establish an ongoing business steering committee for the BI system. If you used a steering committee as part of the guidance process for the initial phase of the BI system, you have two choices. If the steering committee process and participants worked well, you can simply continue the steering committee in this new advisory role. If it didn't work so well, usually because of specific personalities, you can declare the original steering committee a success and disband it. Then, you can start up the BI system Guidance Council and bring in the people whom you know will be able to work together and give you the information you need. Remember, naming is a big part of the marketing process.

You may also have a different kind of business user steering committee made up of analysts and power users that help prioritize lower level tasks for the BI system. Remembering the importance of naming, you might call this group the BI Working Group.

Business Planning

Few organizations have the foresight to think through the entire lifespan of a new business initiative during the planning stage. Once the decision is made to do something, like launch a new product or line of business, all the focus is on getting it done. Unfortunately, "done" usually means only delivered—it doesn't include the ongoing measurement and assessment efforts. The BI team is typically handed the task of taking whatever useful data is collected from the new system (if any) and somehow integrating it into the rest of the DW/BI system.

Involve the DW/BI team in strategic and tactical planning for new products and systems. The design phase of every new product or system must include considerations for what needs to be measured, how the data will be collected, and how data quality will be maintained. The DW/BI team needs to be involved anywhere new ideas are made real. Often this is in new product planning or business development, but it could be a new sales program or customer service efforts. Your goal is to make sure measurement systems are built into the plan so there are no surprises when it comes time to report on the results.

We've seen this over and over. We worked with a publishing organization that was caught up in their industry's rush to the Internet. In an effort to get there quickly, they developed a whole range of stand-alone marketing and promotion systems, like free trials, invite-a-friend, and email lists to receive the table of contents for a periodical. While the initial value of these efforts was positive, the organization's ability to analyze them and understand their long-term impact was practically zero because the systems had not been built with this in mind. There was no single ID for a customer or prospect, so it was impossible to do a cross-system comparison without first doing complex and costly name and address matching. Even within individual systems, analysis was difficult because the business rules and codes and descriptions were not standardized. Users had to learn the idiosyncrasies of each system before they could successfully query it. It gets worse, but you get the idea.

The main role of the BI team in this product/system planning process is to get the business folks and the developers thinking about what data they will need the system to capture and how they will use the data once the system is in production. You need to encourage them to think about a whole range of issues, including the following:

- Using standard codes and descriptions in the source system.

- Using the existing, single source for production keys for shared entities like customer or product. If there isn't a single source, the BI team should push for the creation of one, as we discuss in the section on master data in this chapter.

- Enforcing data quality during data collection. Avoid free-form entry, make important fields mandatory, and provide appropriate defaults, pick lists, auto-lookups, and in-line validation to improve data quality.

- Capture related information whenever possible—if an account transaction occurs, capture the associated household key if possible.

The DW/BI team can help make it as easy as possible for transaction systems to supply data. In a rapidly evolving systems environment, with lots of custom development, it may make sense to build a general-purpose transaction logging system. This would allow developers to write transaction events out to a standard API. The resulting logs would be in a standard format, potentially XML tagged, that would be easily parsed by the ETL programs. Adding new systems is simply a matter of assigning the appropriate event types and identifying the data that needs to be captured.

System Interconnection

There are three additional areas where the DW/BI system interconnects with other systems in interesting ways. The first is with what we call *downstream systems:* other systems, either transactional or analytical, that pull some of their source data from the data warehouse. The second is a source system that manages what we call master data. *Master data management* is a system designed to be the single source for certain core business objects, like Customer or Product. It's the transaction version of conformed dimensions. The third is *BI web services*, where the DW/BI system offers some of its unique capabilities to other systems via web services. Let's look at downstream systems first.

Downstream Systems

If the DW/BI team does its job well, people will learn to trust the numbers that come out of the data warehouse and it will gradually become the analytical system of record. As a result, other systems will want to use data from the data warehouse rather than try to recreate it themselves. For example, the sales force automation system might want to pull detailed customer data from the warehouse for distribution to remote salespeople. Another example we've seen is the customer care system querying the warehouse to pull customer order history when a service rep needs to respond to a question about an item the customer ordered two years ago. The DW/BI team also needs to make sure it can supply any value-added elements that get created in the warehouse to any other systems that need them. If you calculate a customer lifetime value score, you might want to make sure the customer service people see this on every screen when they answer a call.

Potential interested parties extend beyond the boundaries of the organization. You may need to pull shipment data from your suppliers or provide order history to your customers. You also may need to share data with industry organizations or government agencies. In some companies, an independent subsidiary may need to supply data back up to the parent company to feed their data warehouse or other reporting systems.

The point is, you need to provide tools designed to support system access just like you provide query tools to support business analyst access. These tools could take the form of bulk extracts executed as part of the ETL system, direct queries against the warehouse (either single event or bulk), or even a full-blown metadata-driven data distribution system. Make sure you look around for other systems that could take advantage of the data in the warehouse. And make sure you also recognize the impact this may have on your service level agreements.

Master Data

We realize this may come as a shock, but there are some organizations out there with systems that issue multiple identifiers for the same customer. This usually comes about as a combination of business urgency and lack of communication. One information services provider we worked with just had to get its business on the Internet right away; it built all new customer order systems rather than trying to integrate with its existing systems. While it achieved the goal of getting the company online quickly, it created a nightmare when management tried to understand how many of their existing customers were using the Internet. It was hard to say because there was no way to join the customer data from the two systems together. It also created additional work for the customers because they basically had to re-register as customers if they wanted Internet access. Most often, we see these problems as a result of incomplete and ineffective system integration efforts resulting from acquisitions. One Kimball Group client had 23 customer-facing systems that allowed for 7 or 8 different customer numbers for the same customer as a result of acquisition activities.

Ideally, the transaction systems should all be able to call on a shared source for shared data like customer information, rather than have each system collect and maintain its own version. The goal is to keep the data in one place so when it gets updated, all systems have access to the most current version. We call this shared data *master data* (like the customer master, or the product master). As companies move toward adopting large-scale ERP systems and Customer Relationship Management (CRM) systems, the possibility of true master data is coming closer to reality. It's interesting that many companies still have several major transaction systems rather than having everything in a single ERP system. The big split is between the ERP and CRM vendors, with the biggest battle taking place over who owns the customer master. Vendors on both sides have built APIs and web services to allow for the easy exchange and updating of information based in their systems. The message is, "We have the customer master, but you are welcome to use it." Third-party companies have also sprung up to help solve this problem.

The creation of master data is often at least a five-year process. Typically it begins with the DW/BI team creating a complex ETL process to integrate similar data being created by multiple source systems independently. The DW/BI team often has to do it because the data warehouse needs a conformed customer dimension or product dimension or person dimension, and there is no other way to get it.

At one university we worked with, the DW/BI team had to create a person master table because there were at least five source systems that were collecting person name and address information completely independently of one another. A student would enroll and get an ID number and an entry in the student system. The same student might take a position on a grant project, receiving another ID and another name and address entry in the grants and contracts system. This integration work had to be revisited every day as new people showed up in the source systems, or people changed their addresses in one place, but not another, and so on.

Building a conformed dimension that integrates multiple transaction systems is a big task, and technically not one the data warehouse would be doing if the transaction systems had done the job right in the first place. If you take on this task, you need to aggressively educate the business folks and the transaction systems folks about the cost of fixing a problem that should be handled in the source systems. Do the work you need to in order to meet the business requirements, but continually push to migrate the responsibility for this data integration task back to transaction systems. Ideally, the best way to handle customer attributes is through a centralized master data facility. All changes/updates are handled centrally, real-time as part of the transaction system. Then, all we need to do is extract from the master data.

BI Web Services

Recently we've been seeing DW/BI teams going into the data services business. One BI system director we spoke with had to build a massive customer matching system to integrate and de-duplicate customer data from several source systems. His team took their name and address standardization routines and turned them into a web service, which the transaction system team then decided to use to do in-line lookups in the data capture modules. In this case, the DW/BI team ended up providing the source system developers with the tools they needed to fix the data capture problem.

Customer scoring and data mining present similar opportunities for offering web services developed from the BI system. In fact, many of the queries that come to the data warehouse in support of downstream systems described earlier in this section could easily be supported by web services. Again, like supporting downstream system queries, you have to be careful about the performance and service level implications of offering DW/BI system based web services.

Summary

Once you have successfully rolled out your first iteration of the Lifecycle, you need to make sure you don't become complacent. Managing the growth of the business intelligence and data warehouse system is a complex and subtle process. There is a broad range of interested parties across the organization and beyond its boundaries. Even the obvious growth process that involves adding new data and users can be politically challenging. Beyond that, educating management and analysts about the accomplishments and opportunities associated with the DW/BI system is an ongoing process. As we said, we can call this educating, but you need to make good use of some clever marketing techniques if you hope to be successful.

This chapter also pointed out that managing growth involves managing your relationship with other systems in the organization. In the same way you provide tools for business users to access the warehouse, you need to provide tools for these systems to leverage your work as well.

Ultimately, the BI system will become so tightly integrated into the organization's inner workings that it will become an unquestioned component of how your organization does business. That's when you'll know you've truly been successful.

CHAPTER 17

Real-Time
Business Intelligence

Man waits not for time nor tide—Mark Twain

What does *real time* mean in the context of data warehousing and business intelligence? If you ask your business users what they mean when they ask for real-time data, you'll get such a range of answers that you may decide it simply means faster than they get data today.

Throughout this book we've been assuming the DW/BI system is refreshed periodically, typically daily. All the techniques we've discussed are perfectly appropriate for a daily load cycle, which is the most common cycle for DW/BI systems. In this chapter, we turn our attention to the problem of delivering data to business users throughout the day. This could be every 12 hours, hourly, or possibly even very low latency of seconds.

We'll begin the chapter by confessing that we're not huge fans of the real-time DW/BI system. This isn't to say we don't think real-time data is interesting— just that putting it in the data warehouse database can be very expensive and may be requested impulsively by end users who haven't made a solid case for real-time data. We begin the chapter with a discussion of why, and to whom, real-time data is interesting. We also talk about what makes it challenging to deliver.

Putting aside our doubts, and assuming your business users truly require intraday data, we turn our attention to the hard problem: getting low latency data to the business users. Depending on users' requirements, as well as the technologies you're sourcing data from, there are several ways to deliver real-time data. The easiest approach is to skip the data warehouse database entirely and write reports directly on the source systems or even an Integration Services package.

Next, we talk about several approaches for bringing the real-time data into the DW/BI system. These techniques are most valuable for solving the data transformation and integration problems inherent in complex reporting. There are two approaches:

- Segregate the real-time data in its own database.
- Integrate the real-time data with the rest of the DW/BI system.

As we discuss, neither approach is entirely satisfactory.

If your business users need to perform ad hoc analysis on the real-time data, you should set up Analysis Services to process the incoming data stream. An important set of features of Analysis Services, called *proactive caching*, is the recommended technique for handling real-time data. We describe proactive caching and recommend several alternative configurations for a range of requirements.

Making the Case For (and Against) Real-Time Data

Real-time data sounds so cool. Who would not want to have data that's as fresh and current as possible? And surely we, as professionals, want all enterprise data to be conformed and consistent? What better way than to populate the DW/BI system in real time?

As we discuss in this section, it may sound cool, but it's not so easy.

What Makes Delivering Real-Time Data Hard?

The hardest things about delivering real-time data are, as usual, related to people rather than to technology. Nonetheless, there are some technical challenges, too. Microsoft offers many interesting features to help you with the technical challenges.

First, the people-based challenges. One of the biggest issues for the DW/BI team is to meet both the demands of those who want real-time data, and those who most decidedly do not. You may think that pushing the latency closer to real time would be a win for everyone. Surely, in the absence of any cost of delivering data, we'd all prefer to have real-time data?

Actually, no. Anyone who's trying to develop a non-trivial analysis knows that you need to work on a static dataset, where the numbers aren't changing from moment to moment and query to query. If you try to make these analysts work against a dynamic database, they'll copy a bunch of data to a personal computer: exactly the kind of behavior you're probably hoping to stem with your DW/BI project.

A second person-related problem has to do with the DW/BI team itself. If you add operational duties to this team's charter, you risk having the urgent overwhelm the important. In other words, the real-time operations will co-opt the strategic nature of the DW/BI system. Think about it: This is why strategic groups generally have no operational responsibility.

Now, on to the technical problems.

If you're going to put real-time data in the DW/BI system, you need to use the same conformed dimensions, and surrogate keys, used elsewhere in the DW/BI system. Otherwise, there's really no point. You'll need to process new dimension members, and updates to existing dimension members, in real time. The real-time (and non-real-time) facts that flow in must swap their business keys for the correct surrogate keys.

This is more of a design challenge than it is a computational one. Assuming you receive only those dimension rows that are changing, the ETL for hourly processing should take approximately $\frac{1}{24}$ the time of the ETL for daily processing. The challenge is in the design.

Most DW/BI systems that are updated daily or monthly track dimension changes on a daily basis. In other words, you'll combine potentially many database transactions on a customer account record into a single end-of-day image. And you associate all sales transactions that occurred yesterday with that end-of-day image. This isn't strictly true, but business users almost always prefer this structure. There are some exceptions, especially with online businesses. Daily changes are easier to manage, especially if some of the changing attributes track history as a Type 2 Slowly Changing Dimension.

But if you're consuming and processing dimension change information intraday, you really don't have this option. You need to date and timestamp all Type 2 changes to the dimension member, and you may end up adding several rows for a customer account during the day. This may or may not be what the business users really want.

This Type 2 problem is annoying, but it's not as bad as the Type 1 problem. An update to a Type 1 dimension attribute requires updating the dimension member's row, potentially multiple times during the day. The update itself is mildly problematic. We don't like lots of updates to tables. The worse problem, however, lies with any aggregations—relational aggregate tables, indexed views, or Analysis Services aggregations—that are built on the Type 1 attribute. All of these aggregations need to be adjusted, not just for the data that's flowing in today, but for all time.

WARNING Any precomputed aggregations defined on a Type 1 attribute need to be adjusted (or rebuilt) if the attribute changes. This adjustment affects the entire time series of data. It affects even the fact tables that you're not updating in real time. It affects any fact table that uses that dimension (and has aggregations defined on the Type 1 attribute). The cost of recomputing (or fixing) the aggregations may be bearable for daily processing. It's almost certainly too expensive for data latency of less than a minute—the system constantly would be recomputing aggregations.

With large data volumes, don't define any aggregations on a Type 1 attribute that's updated in real time—neither for the real-time fact table, nor for any other fact table that uses that dimension. This problem is not unique to Microsoft; it's a fundamental issue with real-time data.

In general, we've found that real-time DW/BI systems are harder, more costly, and more time consuming to build. Hence, adding a real-time element to your DW/BI project will greatly increase its risk of failure. We certainly don't recommend including real-time data in a Phase 1 project.

What Makes Real-Time Data Valuable?

Real-time data is valuable if it will help you make an important decision. What type of decision is based on something that happened seconds, minutes, or even hours ago? An operational decision. A CEO might want a whiz-bang real-time monitor on her desktop, but any CEO who's running a company based on what happened five minutes ago should be replaced as soon as possible (unless it's a very small company where the CEO also works the cash register!). Ditto for any VPs and their analytic support staff. Even the VP of Operations focuses on tactics (if not strategy), rather than what's happening right now. That's what line managers are for.

NOTE The exceptions are obvious: major disasters or fundamental changes in the business landscape—like an earthquake, a chemical spill, or a competitor's legal troubles. A CEO is pretty unlikely to learn about such events from a real-time BI dashboard, don't you think?

It's worth repeating this point: Real-time data is intended for operational staff and their direct managers. It's intended for operations. In the vast majority of cases, an operational system—which is, after all, designed to support an operational process—should deliver the real-time data.

We're not saying this operational staff, and the decisions they make, aren't important. Any one decision is small, with a small impact on the business. In aggregate, operational decisions are hugely important. Someone should help these guys out. Maybe that someone is the DW/BI team, which has expertise with business analysis and the query and analysis toolset. Maybe not.

What Should You Do?

The business has a problem: It needs better, more flexible access to real-time data. Business users often look at the DW/BI tools, and ask for that same level of functionality and flexibility on operational systems.

Often, the best solution is to improve the operational systems. If your operational system is purchased—as most are—your company could extend the set of reports that are shipped with the product. If those reports can't be modified, you should think about whether you made a great product selection. But in the meantime, you could certainly replace or extend the packaged reports with a Reporting Services portal. That portal may even be integrated with the DW/BI portal.

The problem is more interesting if the need for real-time data spans several operational data sources. In this case, you must perform significant data transformation and integration steps. For really simple scenarios, where the data is perfectly clean (what alternate universe would that be?), both Analysis Services and Reporting Services can span multiple data sources. But realistically, any integration that's not trivial will require that the data flow through Integration Services. From there it can populate a relational database, or even flow directly into Analysis Services or Reporting Services.

If you attempt to integrate the real-time data directly into the relational data warehouse database, you run into the dimension change issues that we discussed earlier in this chapter. You have two choices:

- Integrate the real-time data into the DW/BI system, using and updating the surrogate keys. This approach can disrupt the user experience for that part of your user community that doesn't use real-time data. It can also be extremely difficult and problematic to manage.

- Keep the real-time data separate, and access it using only business keys. This approach can lead to multiple versions of the truth.

We discuss these approaches later in this chapter. Although the first approach is more intellectually appealing, we don't think it's very practical for most systems. Segregating the real-time data is a more common approach.

We realize we haven't answered the main question: What should you do? Of course, the answer depends on your requirements and environment. Table 17.1 collects some of the approaches we think are most practical and ranks them on key criteria. These criteria are:

- How easy is the approach to implement?

- What kind of latency can the approach deliver? Zero latency (++ in the table) is delivered only by direct queries against the transaction system.

- How well does the approach perform at large scale (data volumes or users)?

- How well does the approach support ad hoc access?

- How well does the approach support access to data that's been transformed and integrated?

- Does the approach meet our standards for consistent reporting across the enterprise (a single version of the truth)? No approach scores better than a zero on this criterion because of the difficulties inherent with real-time data and analysis in a company that also has an integrated DW/BI system.

Table 17.1 Methods for Delivering Real-Time Data

	EASE	LATENCY	PERF /SCALE	AD HOC	INTEGRATE	ENTERPRISE
Source directly from the transaction system						
Create Reporting Services reports directly on the transaction database. By default, reports are executed on demand and contain the most recent data.	+ +	+ +	– –	– –	– –	– –
Create Reporting Services reports directly on the transaction database. Set up the reports either to cache or to snapshot on a schedule of your choice.	+ +	+	–	– –	– –	– –
Create an Analysis Services database directly on the transaction system. Use proactive caching settings.	–	+	+ +	+ +	–	– –
Use Reporting Services Report Builder directly on the transaction database.	+	+ +	– –	+	– –	– –
Populate a relational data warehouse Database in real time						
Use Reporting Services reports on the relational DW.	–	+	+	– –	+ +	0
Use Reporting Services Report Builder on the relational data warehouse.	–	+	+	+	+ +	0
Create an Analysis Services database that you update in real time.	– –	+	+ +	+ +	+ +	0

Perform integration, but skip the relational data warehouse Database

| Write an Integration Services package that integrates and transforms data. Set up a report that sources from that package. | + | + + | – – | – – | + | – |
| Write an Integration Services package that integrates and transforms data. Use that package to populate Analysis Services objects directly. | – – | + | + | + + | + | – |

In Table 17.1, we ranked each criterion on a scale of –2 (noted as – –) to +2 (noted as + +). An "ease" score of + + means the method is the easiest approach for delivering real-time data. No method gets positive marks across the criteria.

The remainder of this chapter describes the technical features in the SQL Server 2005 toolset that enable business users to access data in real time—latency of less than one day.

Executing Reports in Real Time

The most common way to use SQL Server technology to access real-time data is to use Reporting Services. A report written against the transaction system will, by default, be executed on demand using live data. If your system is small, your usage is light, you have few cross-system integration requirements, and no one needs ad hoc access to the real-time data, you can serve real-time data from standard reports.

The main drawback of this approach is that it stresses the transaction system. Many companies decide to build a DW/BI system in part to move reporting off of the transaction systems. A popular report that queries a large section of the relational tables is going to be very expensive to run in real time. You shouldn't abandon Reporting Services immediately, however. It provides several caching features that will help you address this performance problem.

What if your users need to see integrated and cleaned data in real time? Don't abandon Reporting Services yet. It's really easy to source a report directly from an Integration Services package, and depend on Integration Services to perform the transformation and integration.

Later in this chapter we talk about how to populate the relational data warehouse database in real time. The same Reporting Services techniques that we discuss in this section can, of course, be used against a real-time data warehouse database.

Serving Reports from a Cache

To improve the performance of the reporting system, Reporting Services provides some features to reduce latency and use pre-stored reports. The first technique is to cache reports on a schedule. A user can't tell the difference between a cached report and a normal on-demand report, except for the date and time the report ran. The first user to run the report has to wait for the query to execute and the report to render. Subsequent users simply pull the report from the cache. You specify a schedule for each report, detailing how long the report can be cached before it expires. Once the cached report expires, the next query will result in a new, refreshed report being created and cached. Users may be surprised to see uneven query performance from one time the report is run to the next.

Reporting Services caching sounds a lot like Analysis Services proactive caching, which we discuss later in this chapter. The two features address the same problem, but the Analysis Services technique is more complex because it supports ad hoc use of the data.

The second very easy technique for improving performance of reports against live data is to create a snapshot report. A snapshot report is a feature of Reporting Services Enterprise Edition that saves the report's body, including the dataset, in the report catalog database. A snapshot report addresses the problem of cached reports' uneven performance. Someone—we can't predict whom—is going to pay the price of executing a cached report after the old cache has expired. With a snapshot report you could instead schedule the execution of the report to run on a schedule and store its results. You'd probably choose this approach if you're worried that the CEO would be the one who might execute the expired cached report and have to wait for the refresh.

> **REFERENCE** See the Books Online topic "Report Caching in Reporting Services" for more information about cached reports.
>
> See the Books Online topic "Setting Report Execution Properties" for more information about snapshot reports.

Sourcing a Report from an Integration Services Package

As Table 17.1 highlighted, the main problem with connecting Reporting Services directly to the transaction database is that you can't transform or integrate the data. Although a report can be fed from multiple sources, if those sources are misaligned or contain bad data, there's not much you can do. If you can't fix the data in the query SQL used to define the report's data sources, you're out of luck.

Add Integration Services into the picture, and your options expand. The obvious solution is to run an Integration Services package that populates a table or tables, and then run a report on those tables. However, if the transformed data doesn't have permanent value—perhaps because your DW/BI system is updated daily and you plan to leave it that way—you can run a package that generates a report as its output. Or, more accurately, you can create a report that runs an Integration Services package as its input.

This is surprisingly easy to do. Create an Integration Services package with a Data Flow task that generates the rowset that you want as input to the report.

This package can be as simple or complex as you like. In the final step of the Data Flow, where normally you'd write the data to a table, send it to a Data Reader transform. The Data Reader transform doesn't have a nice user interface. You use the advanced properties editor. No worries—all you need to do is to name the transform, as illustrated in Figure 17.1, and also to choose which columns are included. Remember what you named the Data Reader transform because you'll use this name in the report definition in Reporting Services. Save the package—remember where you saved it—and go to a reporting project to define the report.

Create the data source for the report, as illustrated in Figure 17.2. The data source type is SSIS, rather than the normal OLE DB or SQL Server data source type. The connection string is simply the location of the package. In Figure 17.2 we're pointing to a package in the file system.

The report definition is exactly the same as normal, except for the query text. The query text is simply the name of the Data Reader destination transform that you created in Integration Services, as you can see in Figure 17.3.

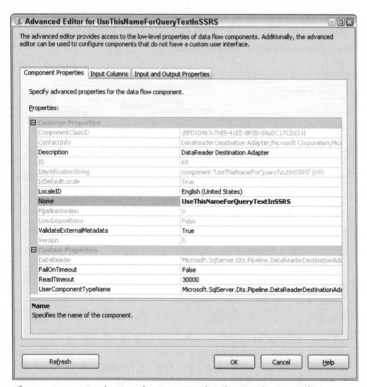

Figure 17.1   Setting up the DataReader destination transform

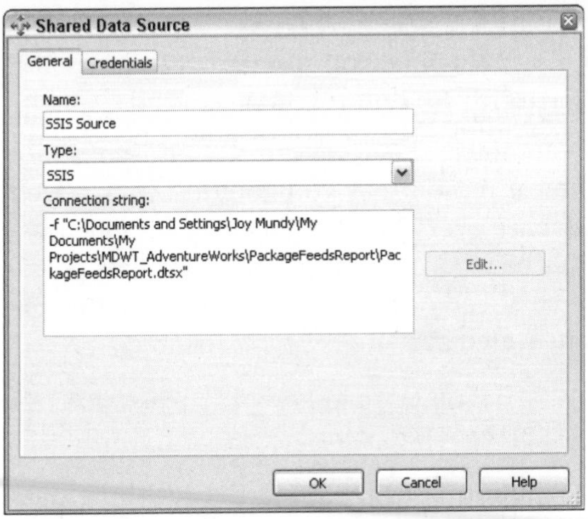

Figure 17.2 Setting up the report's data source

This is a very simple technique for serving up a predefined report on a constructed dataset. The biggest drawback is that there's no built-in way to parameterize the report. With a modest development effort you could use environment variables to communicate between a custom reporting portal and Integration Services, but that's hardly an out-of-the-box experience.

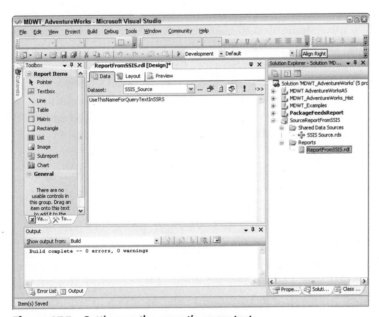

Figure 17.3 Setting up the report's query text

Loading the DW/BI System in Real Time

It's time to discuss how to load the DW/BI system in real time. The problems with loading the relational data warehouse database are design issues, not technology issues. There's no technical reason that you couldn't trickle-feed your relational data warehouse database every hour, even every minute, possibly even faster. Integration Services has lots of features that make this possible, even easy. The problem, as we've already discussed, is meeting a diverse set of requirements with a single integrated system.

The Integrated Approach

The most intellectually appealing solution is to integrate the real-time data into the DW/BI system. This means processing dimension changes in real time: updating Type 1 attributes in place for all conformed dimensions, and correctly handling all Type 2 attribute changes for all conformed dimensions.

In this approach, the Integration Services packages are very similar to what you may already have designed for daily processing. In the simplest case, you'd simply run those packages more often. This assertion is over-simplifying the situation, but the main point is that the real-time packages are not wildly different from the packages for daily processing. Here are some differences, and issues to watch out for:

- The source data must be limited to changed rows. Sometimes, with daily processing, you may pull all dimension rows—and occasionally all fact rows—and use Integration Services to identify changes. You would implement this approach only if you have a poorly designed source system that can't deliver a set of changed rows. This technique, obviously, doesn't scale well in real time. If you can't get a feed of only changed rows for medium-sized dimensions and facts, real-time processing is infeasible.

- With real-time feeds, you're far more likely to encounter referential integrity violations—facts that refer to dimension members that don't exist in your dimension table—than during daily processing. You should design the fact table surrogate key lookup process to handle this event gracefully, as discussed in Chapter 6.

- Partitioned tables aren't as useful as you might think for improving processing performance. Unless you're loading into an empty partition, you can't use fast bulk loading. You might use partitions to support hourly micro-batch processing with fast loading. But creating a new partition for loading every minute seems unworkable. We discussed partitioned tables in Chapter 4.

LOCATION OF THE REAL-TIME LAYER

It's usually best to put the current database on the same server as the historical data warehouse database. Presumably, your users will need to combine current and historical data. Although distributed queries are feasible, it's easier and works better if all the data is on the same server.

- For micro-batch intraday processing, use DTExec or SQL Agent to launch the master package on a schedule (like hourly or every 15 minutes).

- You can't set up Integration Services to feed the DW/BI system continuously. But you can effectively simulate a continuous feed by embedding the Data Flow task in a WHILE loop that never ends (for example, WHILE 1=1). You should monitor the package execution so it can be restarted automatically, should the package actually terminate for any reason.

- Evaluate whether it makes sense to source from BizTalk or the SQL Server Service Broker queue, or Microsoft Management Queue (MSMQ).

- Educate your business users about how and why the results of their queries might change from one minute to the next. Be prepared for power users to grab a chunk of data and download it to their PCs, where they can Excel it to death.

The Real-Time Layer

If you need to integrate and transform data in real time, you should use Integration Services. We recommend that you set up a separate database to hold the real-time layer. Use Integration Services to populate this real-time database intraday. The database should store data for the current day only.

You can call this real-time database whatever you want—except please, don't call it a data warehouse! *Operational data store* may be the best term, although this term (like *data mart*) has been used and misused so often that it triggers a violent reaction in some people. We'll stick with the less controversial term *real-time layer*.

Even if you don't have a compelling need to query integrated data in real time, you may still develop a real-time layer. The database we describe in this section is very similar to the relational data warehouse database. By populating it in real time, you can spread much of the ETL burden over 24 hours, and reduce the time required to perform the DW/BI system's daily update.

WHY USE BUSINESS KEYS IN THE REAL-TIME LAYER?

The reason we recommend that the real-time layer use business keys instead of surrogate keys is to avoid updating the enterprise conformed dimensions throughout the day. As we described previously, there are two reasons you would want to avoid updating the conformed dimensions:

- ◆ Many business users don't want to see intraday changes to dimension attributes.

- ◆ Any Type-1 (update in place) to a dimension attribute invalidates all pre-computed aggregations that involve that attribute, for all fact tables, for all history.

Data Model for the Real-Time Layer

The real-time layer should contain tables that are structured similarly to the relational data warehouse database, except that these tables do not contain surrogate keys. Start with the fact tables that you plan to track in real time. These fact tables should look just like the corresponding fact table in the data warehouse database, with the same columns in the same order. The exceptions are vital:

- The real-time fact table contains dimension business keys instead of surrogate keys. In other words, it's the fact table just before the key substitution step.

- The real-time fact table contains the date and time of the transaction, and any other information necessary to identify the transaction, like a transaction number. We generally recommend that you include such information in the main fact table, too, but certainly be sure to include it here.

Use a similar approach for the design of the dimension tables in the real-time database. First, you may want to include only those dimensions that are used by the facts you're tracking in real time. Create those dimension tables so they look just like the main dimension tables, but without the surrogate primary key or SCD-2 tracking columns like RowStartDate. Make sure you keep a datetime stamp for when the dimension member was added or changed.

TIP Almost all real-time fact tables are transaction-grain facts. Snapshot facts, and particularly accumulating snapshot fact tables, are nearly impossible to maintain in real time. Stick to the underlying transaction grain.

Processing the Real-Time Data

In this section we briefly describe how to process the real-time data. There are four steps:

1. Start the day right. Start each day by moving the real-time data you collected yesterday into the data warehouse database and emptying out the tables in the real-time database. The easiest way to do this is to have two copies of the real-time database structure, and flip-flop between them at midnight.

2. Collect new rows and updates. As transactions occur in the source system, you need to collect them, run them through Integration Services packages, and write them to the real-time database. Use the techniques we described earlier in this chapter for running a package frequently or continuously. Collect all new facts, new dimension members, and changes to dimension members. For dimensions, continuously update all attributes during the day in the real-time database, without worrying about whether those attributes are Type1 or Type2.

TIP If business users are querying the real-time database, you need to maintain referential integrity between facts and dimensions. This means you'd need to institute complex logic for grabbing a dimension member from the data warehouse database, if you haven't seen a change for that dimension member yet today. You would do better to copy the entire start-of-day dimension to the real-time database before you begin working on today's transactions. Make sure the real-time copy of the dimension has enough information that you can easily find any rows you've touched today.

3. Perform end-of-day processing. At the end of the day, the real-time database contains all the new dimension members that were added today, as well as the current end-of-day state of any dimension member that experienced an update to an attribute. All new facts are stored in the fact table. All these tables have their business keys, but other than that they're clean and happy. In most cases, end-of-day processing means processing the dimensions to integrate the changes into the data warehouse dimension table. The end-of-day processing package for a dimension consists of little more than the slowly changing dimension transform that we described in Chapter 6. Similarly, the end-of-day processing package for a fact table consists of the surrogate key lookup pipeline from Chapter 6. This processing should be fast.

4. Clean up. It's a good idea to back up all these transactions. The easiest way to do this is to back up the entire database, which after all contains only today's data. Then clear out all the data, because you'll be using this database tomorrow.

Querying the Real-Time Layer

You've populated your real-time database with today's data. As the day goes on, the database is updated—perhaps hourly, perhaps more often. How will users query that data?

The vast majority of use of real-time data is through reports and applications rather than ad hoc queries. Most analysts aren't very interested in real-time data. Most people who are excited about real-time data are in operational roles, which means they are report consumers.

A report on only today's data is straightforward. The problem comes when you need to combine today's data with some historical data. The reason this is a little challenging is that the real-time database has business keys, and the data warehouse database uses surrogate keys.

Your team needs to define reports and predefined queries that stitch together the real-time database and the data warehouse database. This may be as simple as a query that UNIONs today with history, or you may need to join the result sets. Today's data is always queried with the current set of attributes. Depending on the report's business requirements, the historical data will include either the current attributes from the real-time partition or the historical attributes from the data warehouse. Given the nature of operational information needs, it's more likely that you'll use the current image of the dimension for the entire report.

If the real-time database is on the same server as the data warehouse database, a SQL expert can usually write a SQL statement to perform this integration. If the databases are on different servers, you could use a SQL Server distributed query. Or, try sourcing the report from an Integration Services package, as we discussed previously in this chapter.

Using Analysis Services to Deliver Real-Time Data

In this book, we've encouraged an architecture that uses Analysis Services as the primary query engine for your DW/BI system. The advantages of user-oriented metadata, support for complex analytic expressions, and generally excellent query performance are appealing to consumers of real-time data, too. Many DW/BI users also need to access purely operational data and would like the same rich tools in the real-time environment.

Microsoft provides some interesting functionality that you can use to deliver real-time data in Analysis Services. The two most important features are:

- The ability to build an Analysis Services database directly from a transactional (normalized) data structure, without first putting that data in the data warehouse database. You may have seen this functionality described as the Unified Dimensional Model, or UDM. The UDM simply refers to the Analysis Services database definition metadata.

- The ability to populate an Analysis Services database automatically, as data flows into the relational source.

Building Cubes from Normalized Data

Just for kicks, start up BI Studio and run the Analysis Services cube designer wizard against the AdventureWorks database, rather than the AdventureWorksDW or MDWT_AdventureWorksDW databases. As you will see, you can build a cube against a normalized database, and the design works surprisingly well.

You could create an Analysis Services layer atop each of your normalized transaction databases and always use Analysis Services for your query engine. The most obvious objection to this approach—that the transaction database has data quality issues that will gum up your cube—is partially addressed by a number of features in Analysis Services that will help fix up those data quality issues. We've not talked about these features in this book because we want you to build a clean, conformed, dimensional relational data warehouse database, and define simpler cubes on top of that structure.

The reason we advocate what may seem a more complex architecture is that the cube-on-transaction-database approach works only when the underlying transaction database is really clean, already integrated, and contains all the data you need. In other words, when the underlying database is like AdventureWorks.

The ability to create an Analysis Services database against a normalized source database will appeal to small organizations and departments who don't have technical resources. Perhaps the most valuable use of this feature is in packaged transaction systems. The software development companies that write operational systems could do their customers a real service by shipping an Analysis Services database with their software. In this case, we'd have to hope that the product development team could (and would) address the worst data quality issues revealed by allowing ad hoc access in a rich environment like Analysis Services.

> **NOTE** To date, most existing ERP software companies haven't done a good job of addressing data quality and enterprise data integration issues. But hope is cheap.

Proactive Caching

One of the biggest challenges of processing cubes in real time is knowing when the system has received new data. The proactive caching feature of Analysis Services 2005 Enterprise Edition addresses this problem. Proactive caching consists of two components:

REVIEW OF STORAGE MODE (MOLAP, HOLAP, ROLAP)

In Chapter 7 we described the three storage modes of Analysis Services: MOLAP, HOLAP, and ROLAP. At that time, we recommended that you use MOLAP almost always, and we've not discussed the issue since then. Now we finally get to a subject where the different storage modes are more important. Let's quickly review:

♦ **MOLAP** copies the atomic data from the relational source and stores it in Analysis Services MOLAP format. Pre-computed aggregations are also stored in MOLAP format. MOLAP storage has the best performance at query time because the MOLAP storage mode is highly optimized and indexed for dimensional access.

♦ **HOLAP** queries the atomic data from the relational source and uses it to generate pre-computed aggregations. Only the aggregations are stored in MOLAP format. Queries to the atomic data are pushed back to the relational database. HOLAP is our least favorite storage mode because you pay almost the same cost at processing time as MOLAP, but you don't reap anywhere near the benefits at query time.

♦ **ROLAP** keeps all the data in the relational database, both atomic data and aggregations. Analysis Services manages the creation of the aggregations for you. ROLAP performs significantly worse at query time than the other two options, and it's surprisingly slow at processing time as well. Processing the summary tables is much slower because you have to accept the burden of the relational engine's overhead. ROLAP is an excellent choice for a small, real-time partition with few or zero aggregations (summaries). It's a terrible choice for all partitions of a terabyte-sized database.

Storage mode is a decision that you make for each Analysis Services partition. Different partitions of the same measure group can have different storage modes and aggregation designs.

- A mechanism for watching the relational database from which the cube is sourced, to identify new data.

- Sophisticated caching that enables uninterrupted high-performance querying while the new data is being processed and added to the cube.

Proactive caching itself does not provide real-time capability; it is a feature that helps you manage your real-time business needs. You can use Management Studio to set proactive caching settings for dimensions, and also for facts on a partition-by-partition basis. A key setting is the data latency—the time spent inactive—between the time when source data can be changed and when it must be available to end users.

RECOMMENDED STORAGE MODE

The best choice for very low-latency real-time systems is to use MOLAP storage for the vast majority of the cube. Define one small Analysis Services partition—most often just for the current day or even the current hour—as ROLAP with few or zero aggregations.

If your business users' definition of real time is longer (for example hourly), you may be able to use MOLAP for the real-time partition. Each of these choices requires very different settings for the proactive cache, discussed in the text that follows.

When a business user issues a query of a database partition that has proactive caching enabled, Analysis Services first checks the data latency settings that you defined. If you said latency was one hour, and the partition was last refreshed 20 minutes ago, the query will resolve from the partition's MOLAP cache. If the partition is out of date, Analysis Services will direct the query to the underlying relational source. This all happens automatically, as illustrated in Figure 17.4.

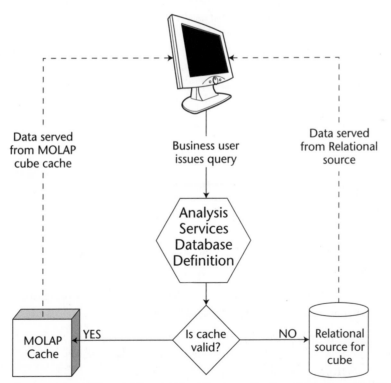

Figure 17.4   With proactive caching, the query is directed to the appropriate data store.

WARNING If the relational source system is the transaction system, you need to be very careful. Queries that you might think would be handled entirely by Analysis Services can be pushed through to the relational database and can affect system performance. You must test the proactive caching settings carefully, with a realistic workload, before you go live. Otherwise you run the risk of making the transaction system DBAs justifiably irate.

Proactive cache settings are defined for each partition and dimension. Most often you'll define proactive caching only for a very small partition, perhaps for the current day. The occasional querying into the relational source occurs only for this partition and only when the cache is out of date. The part of the query that asks for older data would simply access those static partitions. Analysis Services breaks apart the query for you, and sends it to the appropriate places. Then it stitches the result set back together for you, and performs any necessary calculations and aggregations.

Let's talk more about what happens when the cache is out of date. We've already said the query goes off to the relational data source, but what's going on with the cache? Analysis Services—more precisely, the Proactive Caching Management Thread—is listening to the relational database for activity. It also knows the settings you've defined for the partition, notably the latency setting. If data has been added to the database, and the latency level has been reached, this thread starts processing that new data. It's during this processing period that queries are redirected to the relational database.

The query performance during the cache refresh process will degrade somewhat. There's a lot of stuff going on during this period, even if data volumes are small:

- Analysis Services is grabbing new data from the relational database and processing it.
- The partition's cache is being updated from that data.
- Analysis Services is figuring out which part of users' queries to send to the relational engine.
- The relational engine is serving up these users' queries.
- Analysis Services is stitching the result sets back together again.
- Analysis Services performs any computations, like calculated measures, that would normally be performed on a result set.

This is impressively complex functionality that really will deliver data, with all the advantages of Analysis Services databases, within the latency specified. In other words, users do get real-time data.

Fortunately for the user, the cache building is done as a background thread and assigned a low priority. This means users' queries are given higher priority than the background proactive caching thread. If at any time during this rebuild process someone initiates a process that will change the data in the cube, for example by re-processing the cube or doing a writeback to the cube, the background proactive caching thread to rebuild the MOLAP cache will be cancelled. Similarly, if Analysis Services receives another notification of a data change, the MOLAP cache rebuilding process will be cancelled. It's important to be aware of this behavior so you can ensure the correct properties are set for the proactive caching feature based on your business requirements. We talk more about these settings in the next section.

After we discuss the proactive caching settings, we'll talk about how to set up the notification mechanism. There are several methods for communicating between the relational source and Analysis Services, each—naturally—with advantages and disadvantages.

Setting Up Proactive Caching Policies on a Partition

You can set up proactive caching in either BI Studio or Management Studio. Both approaches use the same user interface. We consider dealing with partitions and storage modes to be primarily a management, rather than a development, activity, so we prefer to use Management Studio. If you're working with a development database—as you should do at the outset—it doesn't matter. For test and certainly for production systems, of course, you must carefully script these configuration changes, as we described in Chapter 14.

You'll find the user interface for setting proactive caching properties in the Partition Properties dialog box, illustrated in Figure 17.5.

WHAT'S ALL THIS ABOUT CACHING?

The proactive cache is just a partition, whose processing is managed automatically by Analysis Services. Microsoft calls it a cache because it sounds better. We understand their desire to send this message because we've spent a lot of time arguing with people who hate that the Analysis Services MOLAP storage copies the atomic data. Computers copy data all the time:

- ◆ All data gets copied into memory as it's accessed.
- ◆ Web browsers cache copies of web pages locally.
- ◆ Relational databases copy data for index structures.

Nobody objects to these forms of data copying because the systems manage them for you automatically. The same is true of Analysis Services, particularly with proactive caching.

So, yes, we agree this thing we're talking about qualifies as a cache.

But, for the purposes of building and managing the system, you need to understand what's going on. The proactive cache is simply a partition like any other. The only difference is that its processing is managed automatically by Analysis Services, using the proactive caching settings that you define.

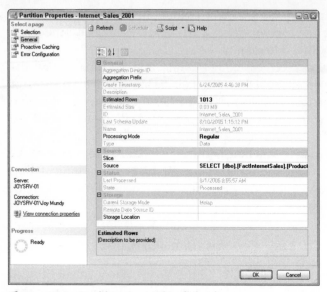

Figure 17.5   Partition Properties dialog box

The dialog box has four pages listed in the upper left, including the Proactive Caching page, illustrated in Figure 17.6. You can choose between seven standard configurations on the Proactive Caching page, ranging from real-time ROLAP on the left, to MOLAP on the right. These are standard sets of settings to simplify your task; you can set customized configurations if you wish.

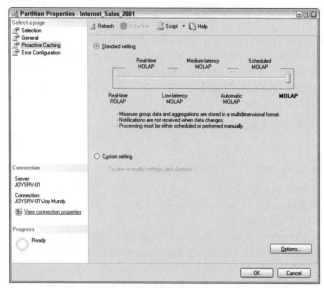

Figure 17.6   The Proactive Caching page of the Partition Properties dialog box

You can set all the properties for proactive caching by clicking the Options button on the Proactive Caching page. You're presented with the Storage Options dialog box illustrated in Figure 17.7.

If proactive caching is turned off, as it is by default for the MOLAP and Scheduled MOLAP configurations, most of the settings are unavailable. Turn them on by checking the Enable proactive caching checkbox at the top of the Storage Options dialog box.

These settings are a bit confusing at first glance. You need to understand all the settings, and how they work together, to correctly set up proactive caching for your technical environment and business requirements.

- *Silence interval* is the amount of time that must elapse from the time Analysis Services detects change in the relational data before it starts rebuilding the MOLAP cache. As soon as a data change is detected, a time counter starts to count down to the specified silence interval time. If a new data change is detected, the silence interval time is reset once again. The purpose of the silence interval is to let some kind of batch process—like the ETL process that loads your data warehouse database—finish before you kick off proactive cache processing. Otherwise, every little change in the relational database might launch proactive cache processing.

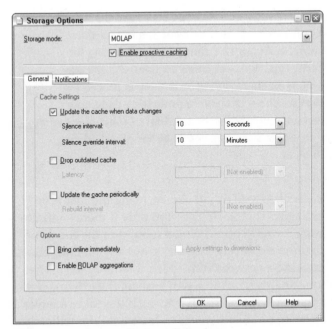

Figure 17.7   Storage Options dialog box

- *Silence override interval* does what it sounds like: It lets you override the Silence interval. If your relational source is, for example, a transaction system, you may never get a quiet moment in which to start processing. The Silence override interval lets you say, basically, "Wait for 10 seconds of silence before you start processing, but if it's been more than 10 minutes just go ahead."

- *Latency* defines how long users are allowed to query an old image of the data. Even if the underlying database is changing constantly, you may want users to query a consistent dataset for up to an hour (or five minutes, or whatever latency suits your business requirements). The real-time partition (cache) is dropped when the latency limit is reached. In order to set Latency, you must check the Drop outdated cache checkbox. During the interval between when the real-time cache is dropped and rebuilt, Analysis Services will direct the queries to the underlying relational database.

- *Rebuild interval* will rebuild the real-time partition on a specific interval, regardless of whether Analysis Services has received notification from the relational database that new data have arrived. In order to set the Rebuild Interval, you must check the Update cache periodically checkbox.

WARNING The alert reader will recognize that you could use the Rebuild interval setting to automatically refresh your cube even in non-real-time situations, like daily processing. In Figure 17.6, the predefined setting for Scheduled MOLAP does exactly this. However, there's a flaw with the way this feature works. It kicks off at an elapsed time after the last processing completes. If processing takes one hour and you're processing daily, your partition processing will start an hour later every day. That's probably not what you want. If you're not in a real-time situation, you're better off scheduling processing in Integration Services.

- *Bring online immediately* will, as you might expect, bring the real-time partition online immediately. This setting applies only if there's infinite latency—in other words, if you're not forcing a rebuild of the real-time partition after a certain amount of time. As we've already mentioned, most people will be creating a new real-time partition every day. When you create the partition, Analysis Services will grab all the existing data for today and process the real-time partition (cache). If this takes a while, you may want your users to be able to query today's data immediately. By selecting this option, you're telling Analysis Services to send users to the relational database until the first processing of the day has completed. In most cases this isn't going to have a huge impact, as you'll create a new daily partition right around midnight, when there's very little data to process or user queries to redirect.

■ *Enable ROLAP aggregations* sets up indexed or materialized views in the relational database. These indexed views will be used during those periods when a MOLAP real-time partition is being processed, and queries are redirected to the relational database.

WARNING Indexed views can be expensive for the relational database to maintain, especially if the underlying table receives updates in addition to inserts. We'd be reluctant to use this setting ever, and certainly not if the relational database is a transaction system.

■ *Apply settings to dimensions* is an option that's available only if you're setting up an entire cube for proactive caching. It will propagate the proactive caching settings to all the cube's dimensions.

WARNING Only if your entire cube is very small, several gigabytes in size or less, should you consider using proactive caching on the entire cube and all its dimensions. Maybe a software developer who's integrating Analysis Services into a packaged ERP system would use this feature. We'd never consider using this option for an enterprise DW/BI system.

Receiving Notifications of Data Changes

In the preceding discussion, we talked about what Analysis Services does when it receives a notification that the data in the source relational database has changed. But we didn't describe what that notification looks like and how you set it up. You have several options, summarized in Table 17.2.

Obviously, we have a preference for the polling mechanism, although the trace events approach is so easy that it's really appealing. On the other hand, if you're implementing a real-time Analysis Services database, you've already crossed the line on ease-of-use, so setting up polling shouldn't be too much additional burden. It's hard for us to understand why you'd implement the client-initiated approach. It seems way too difficult in comparison to the other methods.

Figure 17.8 illustrates the Notifications tab of the Storage Options (proactive caching) dialog box, in which we're defining polling for incremental processing.

Table 17.2 Methods for Receiving Notification of Data Changes

OPTION	DESCRIPTION	PROS	CONS
Trace Events	You identify the table to track. Analysis Services sets up and monitors a trace in the relational database.	Easiest to use	Available only if the source database is SQL Server Requires full reprocessing of the real-time partition Requires that the Analysis Services service account have administrator privileges on the relational database server Delivery of the events is not 100 percent guaranteed
Client-initiated	You write an application that figures out when the underlying table has changed. Communicate that change to Analysis Services via a Web Service call.	Ooh, a Web Service call Can be used with non-SQL Server sources Flexible	Requires full reprocessing of the real-time partition Sketchy documentation; difficult to set up Requires actual coding
Polling	You specify a query for Analysis Services to execute against the source database server. A change in the query results from one poll to the next means the data has changed.	Supports incremental processing of the partition Can be used with non-SQL Server sources Flexible Moderately easy	Somewhat more complex than Trace Events

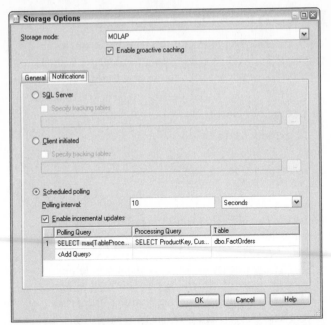

Figure 17.8   Defining polling parameters for incremental processing

Set up the following parameters:

- *Polling interval* is the frequency at which to poll the source database.

- *Enable incremental updates* is a checkbox that, yes, enables incremental updates. If you check this box, you'll need to specify a processing query and a table. If you don't check this box, the entire real-time partition will be fully processed every time the data changes.

- *Polling query* is the text of the SQL query to determine whether new data has been added. What this query looks like depends on your source system. The polling query should return a scalar: one row and one column.

- *Processing query* is the text of the SQL query to determine which new data to add. This query, and the associated partition incremental processing, is launched only if the polling query indicates that data has changed. As we describe in the associated sidebar ("Sample Polling and Processing Queries"), Analysis Services makes available to you the old and new values of the polling query, for you to parameterize the processing query. You don't need to use these parameters, but it's usually the best way to implement the processing query.

- *Table* specifies the relational table from which the partition is sourced.

SAMPLE POLLING AND PROCESSING QUERIES

We will walk through a simple example of polling and processing queries. Perhaps your real-time partition is sourced directly from a transaction system. Hopefully you have a transaction ID, or a transaction date and time. Your polling query could be

```
SELECT max(TrxnDateTime) FROM MyTrxnTable
```

The corresponding processing query could be

```
SELECT <list of columns>
FROM MyTrxnTable
WHERE TrxnDateTime > ISNULL(?, -1)
AND TrxnDateTime <= ?
```

The first question mark refers to the old value from the polling query, and the second refers to the current value. The `ISNULL` logic is there for the first time the partition is processed.

The `<list of columns>` is a little tricky. You need to return them in the correct order. To do so, exit from this part of the dialog box (click OK to save your work!), and go back out to the General page of the Partition Properties dialog box. (You may have forgotten, but all the proactive caching settings are managed in a subpage of the Partition Properties dialog.) From the General page, grab the Source property of the partition, copy it, and then go back to where you were to paste it as the processing query. Whew! Don't forget to add the `WHERE` clause we described previously.

Incremental processing is a great technique for delivering data with medium latency of, say, hourly. If your data volumes are quite large, this technique will let you deliver MOLAP query performance with reasonably quick and efficient processing.

If you need very low latency, you're probably best off using a relational real-time partition with no aggregations. In this case, you don't need any processing at all. With extremely large data volumes, you may want to create hourly real-time partitions.

WARNING Don't set up frequent incremental processing on a partition that lives for a long time. Incremental processing of a partition increases its size (and hence reduces its query performance). It's best practice to occasionally fully process a partition that undergoes frequent incremental processing. A day-old partition that's been updated hourly is a good candidate for full processing. This would be a good time to merge that daily partition into a monthly or weekly partition.

Setting Up Proactive Caching Policies on a Dimension

The process, and options, for setting up proactive caching on a dimension are the same as for a partition. For the most part, just re-read the two sections immediately preceding this one, and replace "partition" with "dimension."

There are a few points for us to highlight. First, we assume you're not using the (terrifying, to us) option of setting up a whole cube with the same proactive caching settings. Set up settings for a single dimension by right-clicking on the dimension in Management Studio and choosing Properties. You'll see the same proactive caching page and options as for a partition—as far as we can tell, they're exactly the same dialog boxes.

It's important for you to remember that these proactive cache settings are for the entire dimension, and all uses of that dimension. You really need to think through the implications of setting up a dimension to use proactive caching. Non-real-time cubes, measure groups, even partitions will be affected by changes to the dimension. On the one hand, this is a good thing, because you certainly want a single view of an entity like Customer. But realistically, as we discussed at the beginning of this chapter, you may be burdening non-real-time users with a lot of confusing changes—and burdening your system with a lot of reprocessing—if you haven't thoroughly considered the big picture.

> **WARNING** Type 1 dimension attributes, which are updated in place, are problematic for real-time systems. For dimensions that are updated in real time, we recommend that you avoid building stored aggregations on a Type 1 attribute that's frequently updated. This is particularly important if your database is large. And remember, a Type 1 update affects all partitions that use that dimension, not just the real-time partition.
>
> Although we discussed this issue at the beginning of this chapter, it's worth repeating. Any aggregation that's built on a Type 1 attribute is invalidated any time a member is updated. Now, these aggregations will rebuild in the background, so for daily updating this usually isn't a huge problem. But if you're in real-time mode and updating hourly (or more frequently), this constant rebuilding of aggregations could be never-ending.
>
> To set up an Analysis Services dimension attribute so it doesn't participate in aggregations, go to the Cube Editor in BI Studio. Set the AggregationUsage property of the dimension attribute in the cube to None. Note: AggregationUsage is a property of the dimension attribute within the cube, so you'll need to set it in all the cubes that use this dimension.

Unless you set up a fairly complex polling mechanism, you run a risk of having proactive caching kick off for a partition before its corresponding dimension is processed. In this case, you may attempt to process a fact row that doesn't have a corresponding member in the Analysis Services dimension.

In Chapter 7 we briefly mentioned Analysis Services functionality that handles referential integrity violations for you. We said your DW/BI system should forbid RI violations so we recommended that you not use these features.

In a real-time environment, especially for a cube that's sourced directly from a transaction system, you *do* need these features. Even for a cube that's sourced from a data warehouse database, you still run a greater risk of handling fact rows before their dimension rows have been processed.

The default error processing, which you can change from the Error Configuration page of the Partition Properties dialog box, is probably what you want for a real-time partition. This configuration will report errors, and convert RI violations to an unknown member, but is relatively unlikely to halt processing because of errors. We really hate that you might need the ability to move ahead with junky data, but in some real-time scenarios, that's what you'll need to do.

Using Integration Services with Analysis Services in Real Time

Proactive caching allows you to configure processing of Analysis Services objects based upon changes in the relational database or at periodic time intervals. If you're delivering data to business users with a latency of less than a day, you should see first if proactive caching meets your requirements.

If you can't or don't want to use proactive caching, you can still update cubes with a latency of less than a day. Integration Services provides several mechanisms for working with Analysis Services databases:

- Use the Analysis Services Execute DDL task to automate the definition of new partitions, like a new real-time daily partition. You can also use this task to automate Analysis Services backups.

- Use the Analysis Services Processing task to process an OLAP database or data mining model, as we described in Chapter 15.

- Within a Data Flow task, use the Dimension Processing transform to populate an Analysis Services dimension directly from the Integration Services pipeline. In normal usage, the last step of a data flow task is usually to write the transformed data into a relational table. A later step would use the Analysis Services Processing task to process the dimension. Instead, you could use the Dimension Processing transform to write the data directly into an Analysis Services partition. We don't recommend this approach for most applications because you generally want a permanent record in the relational database. Nonetheless, this transform can be useful in a low-latency system, especially if you write the data to the relational database at the same time it goes into Analysis Services.

■ Similarly, the Partition Processing transform will write the data flow directly into an Analysis Services partition.

We expect most systems to use the Analysis Services Execute DDL and Analysis Services Processing tasks. Of course, non-real-time systems will use these tasks for all of their Analysis Services processing. Even a real-time system that's using proactive caching will use these tasks to set up new partitions, merge the daily partition into a larger partition, and perform periodic full processing of partitions that have been incrementally updated with proactive caching.

The Dimension Processing and Partition Processing transforms within the Data Flow are interesting features. If you're in the business of providing information, you may use these features to deliver cubes to your customers. As we've said throughout this book, however, most systems should store the clean, integrated data in a relational database.

If, for whatever reason, you have performance problems in writing the data to your relational database, you may save substantial time by multicasting the data flow and populating an Analysis Services partition directly from the flow. This processing would occur at the same time you're writing a copy of the data to the relational database, and could reduce the time it takes for processing to complete.

Summary

We've spent a lot of time in this chapter talking about the challenges of real-time DW/BI systems. These challenges are even greater if you're trying to deliver real-time data that's consistent across the enterprise with the well-managed data warehouse database.

Our goal in this chapter is to present you with a realistic description of the challenges, the alternatives and their pros and cons, and practical advice for implementing each significant alternative.

These alternatives start with encouraging you to keep the real-time data out of the data warehouse database, and away from the DW/BI team. We've seen strategic-thinking DW/BI teams get sucked into delivering real-time data, never to be heard from again. A lot of the business requirements for real-time data can be met by the transaction system owners using the very nice functionality in SQL Server, especially Reporting Services but also Analysis Services, directly against the transaction systems.

If you need to present data in real time that integrates information from multiple sources, you will need to use Integration Services. Some problems can be solved by building reports (or cubes) that are populated directly from the Integration Services pipeline. Most often, however, you will want the results of these expensive integration and transformation operations in the relational database. We described several designs and techniques for populating the DW/BI system in real time.

We believe that the greatest benefit to the real-time functionality offered in SQL Server 2005 will be to software vendors who are building and improving operational systems, and the future customers of those systems. Ideally, the operational systems will present information in a useful, timely, flexible way. We hope software developers will use these features to deliver products that delight rather than frustrate their users.

CHAPTER 18

Present Imperatives and Future Outlook

The endless loop

Our goal with this book was to teach you how to build a *successful* business intelligence system and its underlying data warehouse using the Microsoft SQL Server 2005 product set. In this chapter we provide a brief review of the overall approach we described and highlight the elements that are critical to success. We conclude with a brief wish list of how we hope to see the Microsoft BI toolset evolve over the next few years.

The Big Risks in a DW/BI Project

We can't resist showing you the Business Dimensional Lifecycle drawing one last time. This time, we've grouped the Lifecycle task boxes into phases that align more closely with the actual order of occurrence than with the major sections of the book. These phases are:

- Requirements, realities, plans, and designs
- Developing the databases and applications
- Deploying and managing the DW/BI system
- Extending the DW/BI system

These phases are essentially linear with each phase building on the previous one.

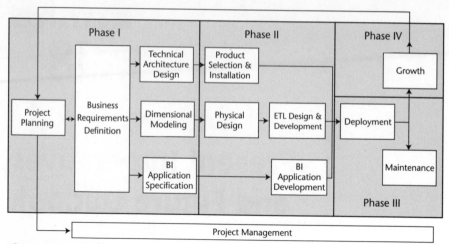

Figure 18.1   The four phases of the Business Dimensional Lifecycle

Phase I—Requirements, Realities, Plans, and Designs

Phase I involves understanding and prioritizing the business requirements, and creating the system architecture, business process dimensional model, and applications specification needed to meet the top-priority requirements.

The biggest problem we see in the projects we get called into is that the DW/BI team essentially skipped Phase I. Other than doing some project planning around system development tasks, they dove right into developing the databases. This haste leads to unnecessary pain and suffering and is often fatal to the project. A good way to tell if you're headed in the wrong direction is that the technology involved in Phase I should be limited to a project management tool, a word processor, a presentation tool, a modeling tool, and a spreadsheet. If you're installing server machines or SQL Server at this point, you're getting ahead of yourself.

After skipping the requirements step, the next most common problems in Phase I are failing to secure business sponsorship, and failing to take on full responsibility for the BI applications.

Phase II—Developing the Databases and Applications

Phase II is the hard, systems-oriented work of designing and developing the ETL systems, the DW/BI databases, and the BI applications. This is the comfort zone for most DW/BI teams. It's where you wrestle with the tough technical issues, like how to handle changes in various attributes, or how to recreate historical facts. Every decision, every design tradeoff in Phase II, must weigh the development effort against the business requirements identified in Phase I.

Without those requirements, the design decisions are based on technical expediency. Statements like "The eight-character Product description is fine—it's always worked in the source system and it will save a lot of space," and "We'll save a lot of time if we include only the base numbers; the users can create any calculations they like on the fly" are warning flags that your developers are making decisions that will undermine the ultimate acceptance and success of the system. These statements are much harder to make when the primary goal of the DW/BI team is to meet a set of clearly defined user requirements.

Building the BI applications is the fun part of Phase II (well, for some of us, it's all fun). You get to play with the data, building reports and other applications that you can show to the business users and get immediate feedback on. The technology is pretty easy and straightforward—although not without its frustrations—and the development process usually goes quite swiftly. Even if you need to develop complex analytic applications, perhaps including data mining technology, this is generally easier and more fun than slogging through the mountains of bad data that you uncover when building the ETL system.

The biggest risk in Phase II is that some teams think of this phase as the complete project. These teams are doomed to fail because they don't do the upfront planning and design work in Phase I. Although Phase II is where the hard technical challenges are met and overcome, these technical challenges are seldom the point of failure. Missing the underlying business requirements is the root cause of almost every collapse.

Beyond that egregious error, the most common risk we see in Phase II involves underestimating the effort required to extract, cleanse, transform, and load the required data. It's always worse than it initially appeared.

It's also common for a team to omit the BI applications from its project. This is a bad idea. First of all, why cut out the fun and rewarding piece of the project? Second and most important, if you don't pave the path to the door of the data warehouse, only a few hardy souls will make the trek. The other risk is to start designing the BI applications too late, or without involving the business users. Getting user input on the BI applications early will help you validate your design and allow you to make relatively minor adjustments to the DW/BI system that can really please the business users.

Phase III—Deploying and Managing the DW/BI System

The effort in Phase III revolves around the testing, training, and support needed to reach an all-systems-are-go state. This involves making sure the system works as promised, the data is correct, the users are properly trained and prepared, the system is documented, the standard reports are working and are correct, support is available, and deployment and maintenance plans are in place and tested.

The biggest problem in Phase III comes when the team views its primary goal as delivering technology rather than a solution. In this case, most of the user-oriented work in Phase III is seen as "not our job" or unnecessary. The team defines success as making the database available. But if the goal is to meet the business requirements, all of the pieces in Phase III are crucial links in the chain. Omit any piece and the chain will break. The team must view success as delivering real, measurable, substantial business value.

Another common problem in Phase III is associated with underestimating the effort required to fully test and maintain the DW/BI system, and to start the planning for ongoing operations too late in the development cycle. For example, your strategy for backing up each day's extract is inextricably linked to the ETL system. If you don't think about this issue until the system is developed and ready for deployment, your maintenance plan may be awkward or weak.

Quality-assuring the data in the DW/BI system takes a lot of time to do right. You should get the business users involved with this process. They need to have full confidence in the data, and what better way than to have helped with the testing? Besides, sometimes deep business knowledge is needed to determine whether the data truly is accurate.

Phase IV—Extending the DW/BI System

Extending the DW/BI system is about adding new business process dimensional models to the databases, adding new users, and adding new BI applications. In short, it's about going back through the Lifecycle again and again, incrementally filling in the bus matrix to build a solid, robust enterprise information infrastructure. One or more of these new business process dimensional models may require data that's near real-time. As we discussed in Chapter 17, including real-time data in the DW/BI system presents some interesting technical and design challenges.

The two main challenges in this phase are an interesting paradox. Often, the success of the first round leads to too much demand and the DW/BI team must carefully balance these demands and maintain an achievable scope based on prioritized business requirements. This may also involve securing additional resources and revisiting priorities with senior management.

At the same time, the DW/BI team must begin an ongoing education program to make sure the organization understands and takes advantage of the incredible asset that is the DW/BI system. In the age of what have you done for me lately, the DW/BI team needs to have a detailed, compelling answer.

What We Like in the Microsoft BI Toolset

The appeal of a single source technology provider, like Microsoft and SQL Server 2005, is that it makes the process of building a DW/BI system easier in several ways. First, many elements of the architecture are predefined. The major technology issues you need to tackle involve data sizing, server configurations, and performance, rather than which products to buy and whether they work well together. Some organizations may need to develop or buy functionality to meet specific business requirements, like large-scale consumer name and address matching. Many organizations will also want to add one or more third-party, user-oriented query tools to the mix.

The Microsoft toolset includes credible versions of all the tools you need to build and deliver a solid, viable data warehouse and business intelligence system. Some components of the SQL Server 2005 architecture are more than credible: Analysis Services, for example, is one of the top OLAP engines available.

Many of the tools are designed specifically to support dimensional data warehouses. For example, Integration Services has the Slowly Changing Dimension transformation, and Analysis Services is built with dimensional constructs from the ground up.

The tools are open and programmable. If you want to build a heterogeneous DW/BI solution, you can swap out any component. If you want to build a fully automated DW/BI management system, you can script any operation in practically any programming language you wish.

The toolset includes software beyond SQL Server. This book has focused almost exclusively on SQL Server 2005 because DW/BI at Microsoft begins in SQL Server. But it doesn't end there. Even the version of Office that's available at the time of this writing, and as SQL Server 2005 ships, is functional and extremely popular for accessing and manipulating data. Business users love Excel, and that's where they want their data to end up. The Office suite can access the DW/BI system directly (albeit awkwardly), and Reporting Services makes it easy for a business user to save a report to Excel.

Future Directions: Room for Improvement

There are organizations dedicated to trying to figure out what Microsoft is going to do next. We have no interest in playing that game, so rather than trying to predict the future, we'll highlight a few of the areas we'd like to see Microsoft improve on.

Query Tools

Excel, despite being the most popular data tool on the market, is not the ideal query and reporting tool. There are several problems, the most troubling of which is that Excel is fundamentally a two-dimensional grid. It's hard for us to imagine how the Excel team will address this issue without creating a whole new product, or breaking the existing (hugely valuable) product. Lucky for us, this isn't our problem.

The existing query interfaces for Excel are imperfect, too. Queries from Excel into the Analysis Services database are limited. The mechanism for specifying a relational query is archaic. We detested it 12 years ago when we first saw it, and it hasn't improved since then.

CIOs hate Excel for the same reason business users love it: Where's the control? Because Excel pulls data to the local PC, it's really hard for an organization to control what happens to it after that. Users can create all sorts of crazy calculations. They can email data to their friends. They can attempt to download a billion-row result set.

We've seen pre-release demos of the next version of Office that address some of these issues. In addition, the Report Builder functionality in Reporting Services is a promising start for an ad hoc query tool. It's a bit raw as SQL Server 2005 releases, but we expect it to evolve and, we hope, integrate seamlessly with Office.

Metadata

The Microsoft toolset is full of metadata, as we discussed in Chapter 13. But the metadata doesn't talk to each other: It's a bunch of metadata islands with a few tenuous bridges thrown across between them. At the time of this writing, it's your job to build or buy a coherent metadata bridge.

The lack of integrated metadata hasn't prevented Microsoft's past customers from successfully implementing a DW/BI system—or else they'd have demanded a solution in this version of the toolset. Indeed, through the years we've seen very few good metadata implementations on any platform. But because Microsoft owns the entire toolset, they should find it easier to provide an innovative, interesting, and valuable metadata solution than is possible with a heterogeneous architecture. We hope they decide to leverage this opportunity soon.

Relational Database Engine

The relational database engine is primarily designed to support a transaction load. We can't comment on its advantages and disadvantages in that role. From a DW/BI point of view, we find several things puzzling or frustrating.

Ad hoc query optimization is inconsistent. Mostly, the query optimizer does a good job with ad hoc queries against a dimensional model, and the relational database engine performs extremely well. But its performance is variable. For some queries, the optimizer takes a path that is clearly suboptimal. And the nature of ad hoc queries makes adding optimizer hints a nonviable solution. The Analysis Services query optimizer does a much more consistent job of resolving dimensional queries, even if you strip away its advantage of precomputed aggregations. Why can't the relational database engine perform at the same level?

We're thrilled to finally have true partitioning in the relational engine, so we don't want to seem like complainers, but managing relational partitions is a headache, especially when you have a rolling set of partitions to maintain over time. In Chapter 4 we walked through the periodic process of managing partitions. All the tools are there, but it should be an order of magnitude easier to manage partitions than it is.

Other relational database engines support an "upsert" syntax that in a single statement will update and insert data into a table. Granted, Integration Services greatly reduces the need for an upsert statement, but an upsert that allows fast loading would be extremely valuable.

Analysis Services

Analysis Services is a bit overwhelming in the SQL Server 2005 release. The wizards are helpful, but they still leave you with a lot of hand work to do in an environment that's necessarily complex. We certainly wouldn't expect any but the most intrepid power users to succeed at developing their own cubes from scratch. Granted, Analysis Services is targeted not at this market but at the enterprise DW/BI system. Still, we know many analysts who'd like to throw together a cube in order to explore a specific analytic problem.

The other big flaw we see in Analysis Services is its inability to respond to SQL queries. It can handle only the very simplest SQL—syntax too simple to be useful. Although MDX is superior to SQL for analytics, people with expertise and investment in SQL and SQL-based tools are reluctant to move to Analysis Services. It seems unrealistic to expect the world to move to MDX-based tools in order to take advantage of even the most basic Analysis Services functionality.

Analytic Applications

Microsoft develops transaction systems, including the Great Plains tools and Commerce Server, among others. We certainly hope to see the next versions of these packaged applications include embedded analytics in a graceful, well-designed way. As we discussed in Chapter 17, the delivery of real-time business information is (or should be) primarily a responsibility of the transaction systems. These packaged applications have a great toolset and a single, integrated platform. Their analytics ought to be great as well.

Integration

The greatest problem with the Microsoft BI toolset, underlying the criticisms we've already discussed, is *integration*—or, more accurately, the lack of integration. The various components of even the SQL Server BI tools—the relational database, Analysis Services, Integration Services, and Reporting Services—sometimes appear to be built by different groups. And other Microsoft technologies outside that core set, like Office and BizTalk, appear to be developed by different companies.

While we understand why this situation occurs, it's time for a more holistic view of business intelligence at Microsoft.

Conclusion

As fun as it is to criticize Microsoft, its DW/BI toolset—notably SQL Server 2005—contains the features necessary to build a complete DW/BI system. The tools are relatively easy to use, and will scale from small operations like the hypothetical Adventure Works Cycles to large enterprises with significant data volumes. The smaller implementations can rely heavily on wizards, and not worry too much about all the technical details. Large systems will use the wizards to get started, but will need to dig far deeper into the products.

Microsoft is delivering the technology you need, but you are the ones who will put that technology to use. If you can maintain your focus on the needs of the business users and on adding business value, you should be able to build a great DW/BI system.

Good luck!

Index

Also available from Ralph Kimball